Hub van Wersch came to India for the first time in 1972. He married an Indian hailing from Maharashtra and has been visiting and studying the country since then. Van Wersch qualified as a social anthropologist at the University of Amsterdam in the Netherlands. His study of the greatest industrial cataclysm of our time, *Bombay Textile Strike 1982–83*, was widely acclaimed as a substantial contribution to the understanding of the disastrous developments during that period.

Later Van Wersch moved to different fields of activity (communication and politics). Apart from scientific contributions, he presently writes novels and short stories.

PRAISE

'The book continues to be the foundational academic study of this key moment in the contemporary history of South Asian labour.'

– Professor Ravi Ahuja,
Georg-August-Universität, Göttingen, Germany

'A most important contribution to the study of labour relations and Government legislations which has such a pervading influence.'

– A. Thyagarajan, *The Hindu*

'The strike was the story not only of employers and workers, but of the government, the police, the press, the unions, the peasants who donated food and the relatives who maintained the striking workers. The most impressive contribution of the book is narrating how each of them related to the strike. The outcome is a grimmer picture than was portrayed in the press.'

– Tirthankar Roy, *The Indian Economic and Social History Review*

'One may disagree with some of van Wersch's views and formulations. One can hardly disagree, however, about the immense value of the results of his research into the Bombay textile strike. It undoubtedly fills, and fills very competently, a glaring gap in the chronicle of the trade union movement and labour struggles in India.'

– Bagaram Tulpule, *Economic and Political Weekly*

'The massive tome of more than 200,000 words is the result of a year of study in Bombay, including residence in a workers' chawl in Prabhadevi, extensive interviews and careful analysis of secondary materials. The thesis dispels many popular myths put out by the mass media, and lends substance to what the intelligentisa has believed all along. A close look at this description of a strike which might get into the Guinness Book is eminently worthwhile.'

– E.A. Ramaswamy, *Business India*

THE 1982–83 BOMBAY TEXTILE STRIKE
AND
THE UNMAKING OF A LABOURERS' CITY

Hub van Wersch

SPEAKING TIGER PUBLISHING PVT. LTD
4381/4, Ansari Road, Daryaganj
New Delhi 110002

This edition published in paperback by Speaking Tiger 2019

Published in India by Speaking Tiger in paperback in 2019

ISBN: 978-93-88874-15-1
eISBN: 978-93-88874-16-18

10 9 8 7 6 5 4 3 2 1

Typeset in Times New Roman by Jojy Philip, New Delhi
Printed at R.S. Paper, Greater Noida

For

Jairam, Anil, Shamrao, Haricharan and Baluram

CONTENTS

LIST OF TABLES

Key to numeration: 1 lakh = 1,00,000
1 crore = 10 million

ABBREVIATIONS

AICC	All India Congress Committee
AITUC	All India Trade Union Congress
ATIRA	Ahmedabad Textile Industry's Research Association
BIR Act	Bombay Industrial Relations Act, 1946
BMOA	Bombay Millowners' Association (also: MOA)
BMS	Bharatiya Mazdoor Sabha
BTRA	Bombay Textile Research Association
CITU	Centre of Indian Trade Unions
CM	chief minister
COD	Charter of Demands
CPI	Communist Party of India
CPI (M)	Communist Party of India (Marxist)
DA	Dearness Allowance
ESIS	Employees State Insurance Act, 1948
ESMA	Essential Service Maintenance Act
FE	*Financial Express*
GKS	Girni Kamgar Sabha (Janata Party) Girni Kamgar Sena (Shiv Sena)
GKU	Girni Kamgar Union (later: MGKU)
GOI	Government of India
GOM	Government of Maharashtra
HMS	Hind Mazdoor Sabha
HOSOCTI	*Handbook of Statistics on Cotton-Textile Industry*
HPC	High Power Committee
HRA	House Rent Allowance
ICMF	Indian Cotton Mills' Federation
IE	*Indian Express*

ILO	International Labour Organization
INTUC	Indian National Trade Union Congress
KKS	Kapad Kamgar Sanghatana
LBGKU	Lal Bawta Girni Kamgar Union
LNP	Lal Nishan Party
MGKU	Maharashtra General Kamgar Union (Datta Samant)
	Maharashtra Girni Kamgar Union (Datta Samant)
	Mumbai Girni Kamgar Union (before: GKU)
MLA	Member of the Legislative Assembly
MMS	Mill Mazdoor Sabha
MOA	Millowners' Association (Bombay)
MP	Member of Parliament.
NSA	National Security Act
NTC	National Textile Corporation
RMMS	Rashtriya Mill Mazdoor Sangh
SSS	Sarva Shramik Sangh
SV	Shramik Vichar
SC	Scheduled Castes
TLA	Textile Labour Association (Ahmedabad)
TOI	*Times of India*
TUJAC	Trade Unions Joint Action Committee

PREFACE

> During that time [1982–83], a strike had begun in my father's [textile] mill, which never ended. And by trusting upon the union leader's assurances, my father eventually passed away … Father passed away, and the mill has closed down too. And now, on the same textile mill lands stands a huge and posh [shopping] mall. Whenever I see a poor and helpless person in that mall, I feel that in their mind the strike still goes on.
>
> – *Mumbai Meri Jaan*, 2008

The above text that evokes the historic 1982–83 Mumbai textile strike is from a Hindi film *Mumbai Meri Jaan*. The film, released in 2008, revolves around the serial bomb blasts that took place in 2006 in the Mumbai local trains. The reference to the mill workers and the 1982–83 strike appears very briefly and only towards the end of the film when Tukaram Patil, a policeman performed by actor Paresh Rawal, is giving a farewell speech on the eve of his retirement. While talking about Mumbai's transformations, Patil talks about his mill worker father and how the trade union leader's misjudgement resulted in the eventual closure of the textile mills which subsequently jeopardised the lives of mill workers and their families. Over the past two decades, the 1982–83 strike conducted by the Mumbai mill workers has appeared in popular Marathi and Hindi feature films but mostly in the background.[1] Typically, the movies depict the 1982–83 strike whereby an honest but stubborn trade union leader is shown accountable for the demise of the textile industry and the subsequent joblessness among mill workers and the indebtedness that their families had to undergo. While the films tend to reinforce the views of the state and the mill owners, they nonetheless inform us about the condition of labour, their position in the city and the social and economic transformations of Girangaon,[2] the city's working-class district. Firstly, the films tell us that the 1982–83 strike was a crucial moment for the city's mill workers and its failure led to the rapid downward mobility of tens of thousands of families. Secondly, it suggests that the roots of the present day gentrification of spaces once occupied by the textile mill and working-class neighbourhood lay in the failure of the 1982–83 strike. Thirdly, the renewal of the said spaces into shopping malls, fancy residential complexes and the high-end entertainment spaces *de facto* excludes the city's working classes and the labouring poor.[3] The feeling of exclusion has indeed caused massive resentment amongst the city's former working classes and the labouring poor, which results in the continuation of the strike in the 'minds' of the excluded. Lastly, unlike the films from the 1950s until the late 1980s,[4] labour and their conditions do not offer the core story or characters for the films, but it merely provides context or a passing reference.[5] In a way, this is not surprising but a reflection of the developments since the 1980s which, as Ahuja argues, saw a severe depreciation of "labour'" as a political category (Ahuja, 2013: ix).

Since the late 1980s protests by the working classes in Mumbai became increasingly weaker in staking their claims. As industrial actions from the late 1980s and 1990s reveal that while workers protest did attract solidarity from the artists, writers and leaders of opposition parties (in some cases ruling party too), it did not translate into the working classes occupying the centre stage in politics (Iswalkar, 2009). It then clearly suggests that 1982–83 strike heralded, as Van Wersch suggests, *the end of an era* as it was the last unified industrial action organised by the city's mill workers. The failure of this strike paved the way for the spatial-economic transformations of Girangaon which subsequently had broader social and political implications for the city's working classes and labouring poor. The catastrophic outcome of the strike also had national level implications, as Mumbai's mill workers held the vanguard position of the country's labour movement. Today the situation is such that the history of the significance of the textile industry and the contribution of the workers for the development of Mumbai city is on the verge of being wiped out from the public memory.

Despite the unique position of the 1982–83 strike in the history of Mumbai and for the country's labour movement, very little has been written about the event[6] and much less about its aftereffects. In this regard, even today Hub van Wersch's *The 1982–83 Bombay Textile Strike and the Unmaking of a Labourers City* is the only scholarly account that presents a rigorous analysis of the event. It is in Van Wersch's work that one finds a thorough multi-method investigation of the 1982–83 strike. It navigates us through the complexities revolving around the event, the numerous factors that led to the decline of the textile mills, the organisation of the strike, its appeal among the workers, and the role played by the state, the mill owners, the trade unions, the political class and the print media.

The 1982–83 strike was the last attempt by the Mumbai mill workers to display a unified militant resistance against the Indian state and the capital. However, the millowners were able to put down the strike by colluding with the state and the Rashtriya Mill Mazdoor Sangh (RMMS), the officially recognised trade union and the sole bargaining agent for the workers. During the strike, itself majority of the private mill owners had sub-contracted the cloth production to Bhiwandi, the power loom centre on the outskirts of Mumbai. Therefore, the mill owners were less keen on running the mills after the strike was over. Citing the 'losses' their business incurred during the strike, the mill owners sought state's permission to sell 'surplus' portion of the mill lands in the real estate market to generate interest-free capital. Despite workers' opposition, the state eventually introduced the Development Control Regulations (DCR) 58 in 1991 which for the first time gave the mill owners the permission to sell parts of mill lands for the revival of the textile mills and payment of workers' dues. DCR 58 was further amended in 2001, paving the way for the eventual closure of the textile mills. The pressures of the real estate market, an ever-growing service sector economy and to cater to the necessities of the city's elites, the upper middle classes and the 'new' middle class (Fernandes, 2006) also hastened the factory closures. These processes have radically transformed the working class district, spatially and economically, which in turn has led to the dissolution of the twin character of the city whereby the city's elite occupied the southern part, and the working classes held the central part of the city with its distinct character. Thus, the transformation of Girangaon, as a part of remodelling Mumbai into a 'world-class city,' has resulted in the shrinking of the already limited space for the working classes and labouring poor. Moreover, it has pushed the already fragile working classes to the faraway suburbs of the city and in some cases to their places of origin in the countryside.

The disastrous outcome of the 1982–83 strike, thus, not only resulted in working classes losing their rights and privileges earned through various decades of struggles but it heralded the unmaking of *kaamgarachi* or *shramikanchi* (labourers) Mumbai. This journey of Mumbai as a labourers' city began during the sustained industrial actions carried out by the mill workers during 1928–29. These strikes brought together various strands with the mill workers and strengthened the social and cultural institutions that had its roots in the late 19th century social and economic development of Mumbai. It is this idea of a labourers' city that was rapidly dismantled following the failure of the 1982–83 strike. The unmaking of the organised workforce is now complete, and the claims of the working classes over cityscapes are no longer recognised; a clear indication of a near complete unmaking of Mumbai as a labourers city.

STRIKES, LABOURERS AND THE CITY

Large-scale industrial manufacturing centres around the world have been sites for organised industrial and political action by the working classes (Silver, 2003). Industrial action or calls for a strike, in general, refers to the withdrawal of labour or a breach of contract of the service or any deviation from regular work such as the slow-down by the workforce. The ability of the working classes to collectively withdraw their labour in industrial cities produced anxieties for the capital and the state alike. On some occasions, workers were successful in obtaining their demands; in others, the employers, in connivance with the state, and at times by using extra-legal elements, were able to put down the strike. While strikes became a weapon for the working classes to obtain their 'economic' demands, workers mobilisation were not restricted to the confines of the factory. As Chandavarkar (1994: 173) has demonstrated, strikes in Bombay spilled into the working class neighbourhoods, 'where millowners recruited blacklegs and strikers mobilised pickets, money-lenders extended or withdrew credits and landlords demanded or waived their rents, [and] the momentum of industrial action continuously forged and reconstituted the political traditions of Girangaon'. As the working classes became politicised, their lives got increasingly entangled into issues that brought the politics of workplace and neighbourhoods in contact with the national politics and internationally too.

The differences amongst the Indian working classes along caste, religious and regional lines and economic backwardness led scholars from the 'western' perspective to assume that 'class' was not a useful category of analysis for examining the Indian labour scenario. The underlying assumption here was that a particular stage of industrialisation was a pre-condition for 'class consciousness'. Historians have challenged these assumptions, especially the understanding of unilinear process industrialisation that would inevitably shape societies in a single direction. Empirical evidence from India challenges the Orientalist view of the Indian society and economy which had assigned it unique and exceptional status. For instance, a comparative analysis of the industrial actions by Susan Wolcott suggests, that 'strikes [in Bombay presidency] were much more frequent than their English or American' counterparts (Wolcott, 2008: 463). Furthermore, 'in the turbulent interwar period, the days lost to strikes per year per worker in cotton textiles rose only to 1.8 in England and to 2.36 in the United States, compared to 23 in the Bombay Presidency' (Wolcott 2008: 463). Once western scholars began engaging with 'the competing confiscating identities of ethnicity and religion, kinship and gender, neighbourhood and nation' (Chandavarkar 1998: 10), there has been rethinking about the issues that made the India case a unique and exceptional. The parallel developments of industrial actions in the Global South and North continued in the later part of the twentieth century too. In the early 1980s as the miners in England went on a strike, so did the textile mill workers of Mumbai enforcing a total strike for the first six months and then went on for eighteen months involving 247, 189 workers.

Indian working classes have displayed moments of solidarity during various strikes like their counterparts elsewhere. However, scholars have also noted how during the strikes, and even in its aftermath, differences among the workers resulted in caste and communal violence (Basu 2004, Chandavarkar 1994, Fernandes 1997, Joshi 2003). As the working classes got roped into the questions of colonialism and nationalism, political representation and partition, caste and communalism, it brought to the fore fissures within them. Therefore, it is necessary to re-examine the categories such as the 'striker' and 'strike-breakers' by exploring its linkages with the social institutions of gender, caste, religion, region and language. Such an approach will ascertain which social groups bore the brunt of rationalisation, and why certain groups were able to sustain industrial action for a longer period, while others were recruited as strike breakers. Besides, the said investigation can be done fruitfully done by separately looking at working-class localities inhabited by the upper caste and OBC Hindus, Muslims and Dalits. Essentially, this will enable us to apprehend how caste and religious specific neighbourhoods, while displaying a strong sense of unity during several strikes, also became *warring camps*, to use Ambedkar's phrase, during caste and communal riots, as well as on various questions of social, political and national importance.

Strikes and the Making of Labourers Mumbai

For a large part of the twentieth century, Girangaon remained a centre for iconic political mobilisations on questions of caste, gender, religion, language, nation and class. Strikes worked as a catalyst for not only defining the workers' movement, but it enabled workers' claim to a stake in the city's social framework (Chandavarkar, 2009). This remained true for all industrial centres in India such as Mumbai, Ahmedabad, Kolkata and Kanpur. However, Mumbai became the centre for nationalist struggles as well as against the capitalists and the colonial state. In these mobilisations, the city's workers played a crucial role and eventually assumed the role of the vanguard of the workers' movement in the country. Since the late 19th century onwards Mumbai mill workers struck down the work on questions of wages and working conditions but also on social and political questions. At times these factors came together, such as the mill workers' strike of 1908. It is widely known that the 1908 strike by Mumbai mill workers was in response to the arrest of B.G. Tilak, the conservative Brahmin nationalist, who was charged with sedition by the colonial state. However, it has been argued that the arrest merely provided a pretext and that the strike was essentially against the 'unbearable conditions of work and life to which labour has been subjected since the beginning of the industrial era' (Karnik 1967 cited in Cashman 1975: 184). While the state used its coercive apparatus to silence workers protests, it did not deter the latter from organising industrial and political action. Once the working classes acquired the centre stage in the political arena it boosted their moral capacity to not only fight for their rights as workers but as stakeholders in the political and social processes. The general strike of 1928 that took place between April and October and the subsequent strikes that occurred between November 1928 till September 1929 firmly laid the grounds for workers claim in the city's civic life; and more significantly for the making of Mumbai as *shramikanchi* or *kaamgarachi* (labourers) city.

During the 1928–29 strikes Girangaon 'came to be represented as a distinct locality of mill workers' because of its 'unique ability' at various points, 'to form a community despite the differences' and tensions along the lines of caste, class, religion and region (Shaikh 2011: 71). Between April 1928 and September 1929, two general strikes took place in the Bombay city involving 150,000 workers in eighty textile mills (Chandavarkar 1999: 205). Altogether the strikes that took place in 1928 and 1929 resulted in the loss of 32 million working days and had a complete paralysing effect on the textile industry (Ambedkar, 2014b: 203). The general strike of 1928 began in April and lasted for six months ending in October in favour of the mill workers (Chandavarkar 1999: 214). The industry-wide strike by the textile mill workers received support from other workers in the city such as the 'tramwaymen, railway workers, municipal workers, printers, oil mill workers and some dock workers' (Ibid: 217). Following the general strike of 1928, nearly eighty strikes took place October 1928 and March 1929 (Ibid: 214). The unity displayed by the mill workers during the general strike of 1928 and the solidarity it received from the city's working classes 'impressed many observers and participants' (Ibid: 219). It was probably these developments that prompted Vitthal Varerkar, novelist, playwright and Communist sympathiser at the time, to name the region surrounded by textile mills and working-class neighbourhoods as Girangaon in his classic novel *Dhavta Dhota*[7] (Ibid: 219). Girangaon does not have any defined boundaries but 'stretches over a thousand acres, from Byculla to Dadar and from Mahalaxmi to Elphinstone Road, the central part of the island of Bombay' (Adarkar and Menon 2004: 4).

It was during the 1928–29 strikes that Communists gained control over the labour movement 'through their skilful organisation of mill and neighbourhood committees' (Chandavarkar 1999: 211). As a result, Chandavarkar argues, Girangaon 'appeared to be a communist stronghold, at times even an insurrectionary centre' (Chandavarkar, 2009: 150). While it is generally accepted that communists acquired an important position during the strikes of 1928–29, they were by no means the only force (Omvedt, 1976: 248-267; Pol, 2015: chapter 4; Lieten 1982). Wide-Ranging non-communist unions were involved in the strikes and argued during the Meerut Trial that the Communist role in the labour unrest was 'grossly inflated' (Azhar, Forthcoming). The late 1920s saw the radicalisation of anti-caste politics in India under Ambedkar's leadership that vehemently challenged mainstream nationalists, moderates and the communists on the questions of caste. The Dalit working-class neighbourhoods[8] in Mumbai that played a crucial role in the anti-caste mass mobilisations (Pol, 2015: 15-66) challenged the Communist politics too. Likewise, the Communist politics faced stiff opposition in the Muslim working class areas from leaders of Khilafat committee leaders such as Shaukat Ali and Mohammad Ali. Both of them allied with Ambedkar during the 1930s over the question of communal representation (Pol 2015). It is, therefore, important to take into account the divergent and competing forces in Mumbai to understand the fissures within the working classes that came to the fore '[t]owards the end of 1928' strike in the form of 'Brahmin-non-Brahmin; caste Hindu-outcaste and Hindu-Muslim' (Lieten, 1982: 699).

During the 1928 strike, Ambedkar highlighted the exclusion of Dalits from the high-paid weaving department jobs,[9] which was not merely 'a scramble for jobs' as Chandavarkar (1994: 226-227) has rightly argued, but it was 'an expression of caste consciousness which extended beyond the workplace.' Ambedkar threatened the Communist unions that he 'will dissuade the depressed classes [Dalits] from taking part in the strike' if their right to work in all mill departments was not recognised (Ambedkar, 2014a: 474). The Communists leadership very reluctantly accepted Dalit workers right to work in the weaving department and placed it among the seventeen demands presented to the mill owners. However, the millowners snubbed the Communists by arguing that if the exclusion of Dalits from the weaving department 'was an injustice, they certainly were not responsible for it' (Ambedkar 2014: 474).

While Ambedkar supported the 1928 general strike after his demands were accepted, he objected to the one in 1929. The 1929 strike, Ambedkar argued, was called in response to a minor issue, which was the dismissal of Girni Kamgar Union's members from the Wadia Group of Mills (Pol 2015: 101). Moreover, Ambedkar opined that the industrial actions of 1928 had pushed Dalit workers towards extreme indigence and indebtedness (Ambedkar, 2005: 19), and, as such, they were not in a position to participate in yet another strike. Moreover, Dalits could not rely upon farmlands during the long drawn industrial actions, which was the case with their non-Dalit counterparts It is for these reasons, when the 1929 general strike was going on, Ambedkar facilitated the supply of Dalit workers' to various mills (Lieten, 1982: 699; Mehta, 1954: 121). Dalits also confronted the Communists on the practices of untouchability in the Girni Kamgar Union office.[10] Even though Communists and Ambedkar led Dalit working classes remained at loggerheads, in 1938 Ambedkar's Independent Labour Party successfully organised a one-day strike in co-operation with the Communists and Socialists against the Bombay Industrial Disputes Act which sought to make 'strikes under certain circumstances illegal' (Ambedkar 2014: 203).

Like the Dalit working-class neighbourhoods, the Communist also faced opposition in the Muslims neighbourhoods.[11] During the 1928 strike, the Khilafat committee led by Shaukat Ali offered financial support to the Girni Kamgar Union 'ear-marked for [the relief] of Muslim mill workers only', which the GKU rejected arguing that it would 'bring communalism into the strike' (Dange 1932: 128). Later, Shaukat Ali, together with the members of the Khilafat committee urged Muslim workers to resume the work in the mill owned by the Muslim entrepreneur, the Fazalbhoy. The Khilafat leaders too faced a challenge from the Shaukat Usmani who was organising the Muslims workers in the Madanpura region. Also, the *julaha-ansari* weavers came under the influence of the All India Momin conference in the 1920s that sought to highlight the plight of *julaha* weavers. The Momin conference was opposed to the Muslim league and stood in opposition to the idea of partition. As for the upper caste Hindu areas, the Hindu Mahasabha made their presence felt and contributed to the instigation of communal violence (Ganneri 2014). Despite the diverse political strands and responses on wide-ranging issues, the strikes that took place between 1928 and 1929 laid the foundation for making Mumbai a labourers city.

The 1928–29 strikes provided the opportunity for the articulation of social and political issues around the labour question. While various groups confronted each other, at times in a violent manner, they also came together on several occasions. The introduction of electoral politics led major political parties to woo the labour constituency. In the post-independence period, the mill workers played a central role in the formation of Maharashtra state, especially in retaining Mumbai as the capital of the state. During this struggle, more than 100 activists lost their lives, a vast majority of whom were mill workers. It is then not surprising that the Maharashtra state was formed on 1st May 1960, coinciding with the International Labour Day. It is workers' participation in such mobilisations that boosted their moral capacity for staking claim over the city's social fabric.

The Unmaking of the Labourers Mumbai

If the 1928–29 general strikes laid the foundation for the making of Mumbai as a labourers city, the historic eighteen-month long strike of 1982–83 heralded its unmaking. As Van Wersch puts it, the 1982–83 strike that lasted for about 18.5 months, was a result of 'the outcome of pent up frustrations over a number of years'. The strike involving 247, 189 workers exemplified their unified resistance against the capital-state nexus. The 1982–83 strike was the last industrial action by the Mumbai mill workers when the city witnessed industry-wide strike bringing the workforce to the centre of politics. The failure of the 1982–83 strike crucially led to the reversal of the entitlements that the mill workers had obtained through various struggles and fundamentally altered workers' claim over the city's social fabric. Following the strike, as Van Wersch states, the workers lost the 'fighting spirit' which they have demonstrated historically. Most importantly, the failure of the strike resulted in the gradual dismantling of the various social, political and cultural institutions that contributed to the rhythms of Girangaon. These factors suggest that the industrial action of 1982–83 is indeed a key moment in the history of Mumbai as well as for the country's labour movement.

Towards Involuntary Servitude

The failure of the 1982–83 strike was not merely a loss of that particular industrial action, but it had ramifications for the future strikes of the working classes. Throughout the strike, the state used its police machinery to threaten and inflict violence on the workers to break the industrial action. The judiciary took long in deciding on the case that challenged the RMMS status as the representative union and the bureaucracy too assisted in delaying the process. Once the strike was put down by the mill owners in connivance with the state and the officially recognised trade union, the RMMS, about 91,251 workers were retrenched. The ones who were taken back to work had to return on deeply unfavourable terms. As Van Wersch notes, first, a large number of workers who returned to work 'did not receive the payments they were entitled to.' Secondly, workers had to confront an entirely hostile environment inside the factory. They 'were fined for the slightest mistakes…and often abused and very easily charge-sheeted.' Thus, the mill management gave a strong message to the workers that 'henceforth no resistance against its policy would be brooked.' Thirdly, before accepting the jobs workers 'had to sign a statement in which they declared that they had participated in an illegal strike and they would henceforth refrain from agitation' and 'not cause trouble in future'. Left with little choice workers were compelled to sign the statement without even having the opportunity to read it. The penalising of the mill workers for participating in the 1982–83 strike was 'nothing short of making the worker a slave' as Ambedkar argued in the Bombay Legislative Assembly in 1938[12] (Ambedkar, 2014b: 207). And slavery is, Ambedkar stated further, was 'nothing else but involuntary servitude' (Ibid: 207). It is in the state of *involuntary servitude* that the Mumbai mill workers found themselves.

The attempts by the state to term strike illegal under some conditions goes back to the introduction of Bombay Industrial Disputes (BID) Act by the provincial government in 1938. The BID Act was opposed by various labour organisers which culminated in the successful organisation of one-day strike by Ambedkar's Independent Labour Party. The Socialists, Communists and other unions supported the strike. As a result, the state did not pursue the legislation. However, as Van Wersch notes, the Congress-ruled state later introduced the Bombay Industrial Relations (BIR) Act in 1947 whereby it did 'not forbid strikes *de jure* but the conditions which have to be fulfilled before a lawful strike can take place amount to a virtual ban on strikes. The cumulative effect of the whole structure of conciliation, adjudication and arbitration amounts to a *de facto* ban on strike.' Moreover, the Congress appointed its trade union the RMMS as a representative union as the sole bargaining agent for the textile industry and made it difficult for other unions to get rid of it. During the 1982–83 strike, as Van Wersch documents, the Samant led union was in a position to dislodge the representative union but the state agencies, both the bureaucracy and the judiciary, ensured that the RMMS retained its position. As a result, after the strike was put down by the state and mill owners, the RMMS became aggressive towards the strikers and penalised them for participating in the industrial action. It is probably this reason that a section of mill workers constantly evokes that the 1982-83 strike was never called off. For the workers 'the strike symbolised their whole struggle for emancipation' and given the fact they were pushed into *involuntary servitude* it continues for them even today.

Survival Strategy: The Rural Connection

In examining the urban industrial strikes, workers' maintenance of their rural ties has been a subject of debate. The rural ties maintained by the workers were interpreted as a sign of rural mentality, backwardness, being villagers at heart; and was seen as an obstacle for the formation of trade unions. Scholars have challenged these assumptions by arguing the uncertain working and living conditions in the cities resulted in workers relying on their rural connections. Furthermore, it has been argued that rural bases strengthened workers' collective bargaining power and they were able to prolong their industrial actions in the urban areas (Basu 2004, Chandavarkar 1994). However, not much is known as to how the workers responded to their prolonged stay in the villages when the strikes went on for a longer period. Van Wersch provides us with a glimpse of workers experiences of staying in the countryside during the 1982–83 strike period. He also demonstrates that while farmers' solidarity for the

1982–83 striking workers gave them a much needed moral strength but the material support was not sufficient enough to sustain their livelihood.

Similar to the previous industrial actions in Mumbai, during the 1982–83 strikes too, a section of mill workers left for their villages as survival and coping strategy. From the evidence presented by Van Wersch, it becomes clear that even though the mill workers tried their hands on the farm work, they soon found out that they are not put their 'heart into cultivating the land.' They also realised that farming was a tedious, boring and straining job. More importantly, to work under the scorching sun was extremely physically demanding and for these reasons they hated it. Besides work-related challenges, at the family level workers experienced being treated with disrespect and were confronted with regular quarrels. It is precisely for this reason; they looked forward to the restarting of the mills. This is not to suggest the workers romanticised the millwork as they were aware of the fact that '[w]orking in the mill was madness'. The working conditions were rotten, and it severely affected their health to the point of collapse. These findings suggest that workers had immersed entirely into the urbanised social fabric even as some of them may have left their families in the villages.

During the 1982–83 strike, one of the most celebrated aspects was the solidarity expressed by the farmers in providing food grains and financial to the striking workers. Van Wersch goes deeper into testing such claims. While symbolically the solidarity offered moral support to the striking workers, in practical terms it turned out to be of limited help to a tiny minority. Van Wersch shows that 87 per cent of the workers who received financial aid, 'did not get more than Rs.100.' Regarding food grain, 42 workers received 'a total quantity of 5-15 kgs of food-grain, 8 [workers] received 16-30 kgs and only 2 [workers] received more.' Thus, Van Wersch concludes that the material 'support was far from substantial and meant only a minor contribution to their means of surviving this trying period.' Van Wersch's research findings concur with David Washbrook's contention that in the long historical context it was the income earned by the workers in the factory that subsidised the countryside and not the other way round (Washbrook 1981: 704).

Politics and Fissures

The 1982–83 strike is considered as a necessary political act. Is it the case, or was it merely an economic struggle? From Van Wersch's account, it is clear that the 1982–83 strike 'cannot be dubbed a political struggle' mainly because demands were predominantly economic such as permanency of *badlis*, improvement of labour conditions, changes in workloads and wage hike. In my view, the strike led by Datta Samant did not disturb the electoral allegiances of their activists and those participating in the strike. For instance, Shiv Sena activists participated 'in Samant's new textile union' but back in their neighbourhoods they supported Shiv Sena during elections (Adarkar and Menon, 2004: 356-357). In a way, this is not surprising given the fact that the mill workers invited Samant to lead their struggle not because of his political ideology but his ability to negotiate workers' demands.

In the history of Mumbai mill workers, the strikes were usually followed by caste and communal violence. However, Van Wersch notes that in his study, there was 'no trace of communal fissures in the strike' and even when the 'ranks of the workers started breaking [down]' there was no communal dimension to it. Unlike the previous strikes, there were no immediate riots after the strike was over in 1983. However, anti-Muslim riots did take place in 1984 in Bhiwandi, where the private mill owners had sub-contracted the production of cloth. Parts of Mumbai that had a substantial Muslim population were also affected by the 1984 riots. During the 1992–93 anti-Muslim pogroms, Shiv Sena activists became physically aggressive, and on occasionally violent, towards the Muslim workers in the textile mills, other factories and in the Mazgaon Docks. The aggravating circumstances in the city meant that often Muslim workers were unable to report to work for an extended period and therefore faced dismissal.

One possible explanation why riots did not take place after the strike was over in 1983, could be derived from Thomas Hansen's (2001) study on Mumbai. Hansen (2001: 163) noted that Muslims were victims of the rationalisation process since the 1960s.[13] Muslim workers' expulsion was nearly complete during and immediately after the 1982–83 strike. My doctoral research fieldwork in the Muslim dominated areas of Madanpura and Mominpura in 2008–09 also concur with these findings (Mhaskar, 2013). I had great difficulty in locating Muslim mill workers in these areas who worked in the mills till the late 1990s and early 2000s. Most of the Muslim mill workers I met had lost their jobs during or before the 1982–83 strike and diverted to other occupations such as taxi driving, selling perishables commodities and engaging in wide-ranging repair work.[14]

Similarly, women too faced the brunt of rationalisation already from the 1940s onwards (Mhaskar, 2012: 63-64). In the 1940s women mill workers constituted 16 percent of the total workforce. By the early 1980s, women proportion came down to merely 2 percent. So, at the time of 1982–83 strike, itself women workers had already become a minor force. As for the Dalits, their proportion too had come down from 12 percent in 1940 to 8 percent in the late 1970s. Moreover, Dalits, especially the Mahars who converted to Buddhism, diverted to non-textile jobs such as the 'Railways, BEST (Brihanmumbai Electric Supply and Transport) and the Municipalities' which provided housing facilities, 'which was an important consideration' (Mhaskar, 2014: 116-117). Therefore, it appears that the numbers of various socially vulnerable groups were already on the decline and they had diverted to non-textile occupations. Unlike the previous strikes, the mill owners after the 1982–83 strike were also less keen on running the factories and were hostile towards those who had returned to work. These changes might explain why riots did not take place after the 1982–83 strike in Mumbai.

THE 1982–83 STRIKE AS THE ANCHOR FOR THE PRESENT

During my fieldwork for doctoral research (Mhaskar 2012) in 2008–09, there were umpteen times when I wanted to talk about the state of affairs of the textile workers from the late 1990s onwards, but the discussion would swiftly move to the 1982–83 strike. Observers, activists, school teachers, the older residents of Girangaon and not least the ones who worked in various professions in the vicinity had a story to share about 1982–83 strike. It signalled the importance of the historic strike and that without taking that event into account it will not be possible to understand the contemporary condition of the mill workers and the transformations that are underway in Girangaon.

The failure of strike resulted in the breaking of the morale of the striking workers as more than 90,000 workers were not taken back to work. Furthermore, the mill owners cited the 'losses' they incurred during the strike and demanded the state's permission to sell the 'surplus' portion of the mill land in the real estate market. The mill owners argued that this would enable them to generate interest-free capital for the revival and modernisation of textile mills and clear workers' dues (Singh, 1987: 539). However, the Kotwal committee appointed by the government rejected this appeal and suggested that the government 'take over the lands to house textile workers' (Ibid: 539). The opposition to the mill land sale resulted in nine mill owners closing down their units citing their inability to handle the financial losses. The closures of nine textile mills between 1987 and 1989 affected nearly 25,000 workers. Interestingly, none of the established labour unions took up this issue.

After the failure of the 1982–83 strike, there was a void in Mumbai's labour movement. At this juncture, workers belonging to different political formations such as the Communists, the Socialists, the centrist Congress and the Shiv Sena (Hindu militant and nativist political party) gathered under the leadership of Datta Iswalkar. They formed a new platform called Bandh Girni Kamgar Sangharsh Samiti (BGKSS) [Closed Mill Workers' Struggle Committee] on 2nd October 1989 (Iswalkar, 2009: 4). This rainbow coalition received infrastructural support from the Socialist Party to which Iswalkar belonged. However, the scale and intensity of the later strikes were much lower, and it was never an industry-wide strike. Moreover, the unions struggled initially to re-open the mills, then focused on obtaining better dues to the workers. It suggested that the unions were prepared for the eventual closure of the mills and were organising for better compensation. Eventually, the mills reopened, but the mill owners too got the permission to sell parts of mill lands in the real estate market. In what may seem surprising, for the first time the recognised union RMMS organised demonstrations supporting mill land sale. Across Mumbai, RMMS painted walls with the slogan in the Marathi language that read *nako amhala jaminicha tukada, amhala hava aahe bhakaricha tukada* (we do not want a share of land; we want a piece of bread).[15] With the recognised union on their side, the mill owners colluded with the ruling Congress (I) party in obtaining the permission to sell the surplus land under 1991 Development Control Regulations 58 (DCR 1991).

DCR 1991 is a breakthrough in the land use regulations, as for the first time, mill lands could be used for commercial/residential purpose with the 'condition that they use the resultant funds for revival of the mills' (Adarkar, 2006: 99). However, this provision was misused by the mill owners as none of them revived the textile mills. Further amendments were made in DCR in 2001 which allowed for the sale of entire mill lands in the real estate market. As a result, by 2006 nearly all textile mills closed down, including the most modernised and profit making such as the Century and Bombay Dyeing mills. The closure of mills resulted in large-scale layoffs of the workers and their movement towards the suburbs of Mumbai. However, the ex-millworkers' reorganisation on the housing brought them back to the centre of Mumbai city and Maharashtra politics. As the number of ex-millworkers gathered in large numbers, it pressurised all political parties to pay attention to their demands. All trade unions are organising the ex-millworkers on the housing question invariably evoked the 1982–83 strike. Leaders of mainstream political parties who came to speak on ex-millworkers forums also referred to the event.

Ex-Millworkers Mobilisation and the 1982–83 Strike

The gentrification of Girangaon following the closure of textile mills resulted in a gradual expulsion of the residents to city's far-away suburbs and to the villages where workers have returned after the shutdown. The re-organisation of the ex-millworkers took the form of petitioning and appealing to the political class. The mobilisation of ex-millworkers was not militant but petition oriented whereby Member of Parliaments and Legislative Assemblies, and Municipal Councillors were requested to look into their demands. One of the striking aspects of the post-closure mobilisation was that the mill workers who lost their jobs during the 1982–83 strike also became beneficiaries of the new housing demanded by the ex-millworkers. Given the fact that a significant number of Girangaon residents were Marathi speakers from Konkan and Westerns Maharashtra, it became imperative for the mainstream political parties (Shiv Sena, BJP, Congress and Nationalist Congress Party), to address the current plight of the mill workers. It was not uncommon that the discussion on the current state of textile mill closures and the fate of workers in Mumbai would invariably bring us to a conversation about the 1982–83 strike. The mainstream political parties too evoked the 1982–83 strike but by targeting Datta Samant's misjudgement during the industrial action which according to them resulted in the current socio-economic marginalisation of the mill workers.

In February 2018, Raj Thackeray,[16] the leader of Maharashtra Navanirman Sena (MNS),[17] conducted a public interview of the Maratha leader Sharad Pawar from the Nationalist Congress Party (NCP). The conversation titled as *Shodh Marathi Manacha* (In Search of Marathi Mind) discussed various challenges before contemporary Maharashtra. The 1982–83 textile strike figured prominently during the dialogue. Pawar told the audience that he along with the Shiv Sena chief Bal Thackeray and the Socialist trade union leader George Fernandes organised a meeting amidst the 1982–83 strike to oppose striking leader Datta Samant. Pawar stated that they were concerned that if the mills did not re-start, the owners would eventually close down the mills and construct high-rise towers. This narrative too held Datta Samant accountable for the closure of textile mills and the dispersal of the Marathi speaking workers from the city's working-class district. This narrative conveniently ignores the fact that it was under Pawar's Chief Ministership that introduced Development Control (DC) regulations in 1991, which for the first time permitted the mill owners to sell parts of the mill lands in the real estate market. The DC regulations were further amended in 2001 allowing mill owners to use the entire mill lands for non-industrial (read real estate) development. These developments hastened the closure of the textile mills, including the ones that were most modernised and profit making such as the Bombay Dyeing and Century Mills. Secondly, during the mid-1990s it was Raj Thackeray who bought the Kohinoor Mill lands in Dadar when Shiv Sena BJP was ruling the Maharashtra state. On the Kohinoor mill, land stands a high rise tower which is named as Kohinoor Heights. It is precisely for these reasons that both political leaders narrate the source of mill workers' plight in the misjudgement of the striking leader.

Industrial Closures and Maratha Mobilisation for Reservation

The closure of textile mills and other large-scale manufacturing industries in Mumbai and the subsequent transformation of the city has led to the emergence of politics for the reservation of the Marathas in employment and education (Mhaskar, 2016). Several studies have documented that the Marathas as a caste, not only dominated the industrial workforce but also they had a significant share in the well-paid occupations. For instance, according to a survey conducted by the Bombay Mill Owners Association in 1940, the percentage of Maratha male workers in the textile workforce was 51% (Gokhale, 1957: 116). My research on the aftermath of the textile mill closures shows that even during the decline and dwindling of job opportunities the Marathas continued their dominant position. Of the total 924 ex-millworkers surveyed in 2009 and who continue to live in the city, the Maratha male workers constituted about 36% of the total workforce. This dominance also meant that as a caste group the Marathas were the most affected by the closure of large-scale manufacturing industries in Mumbai.

Maratha workers in the manufacturing industries had little option but to migrate back to their villages or find alternative employment in the informal sector. A large section of the Marathas opted for reverse migration, and this process has been most prominent in western Maharashtra and Konkan region. Of the two, however, the former has a more significant concentration of Marathas. Not surprisingly it is western Maharashtra that has been a major centre for Maratha mobilisation around the reservation question. These developments severely affected Maratha youth from the *wadivarcha* (small and marginal farmers) strata who had historically migrated to Mumbai to take up well-paid jobs despite having little or no education. They had a guaranteed job in the organised manufacturing industries where their parents or relatives had worked and were as such, handed down through generations. Now, however, both the *wadivarcha*, as well as urban lower middle-class Maratha youth have little choice but to work as security guards, courier boys, or engage in the kind of odd jobs clubbed under the nomenclature 'house-keeping'. None of these jobs provides working conditions which previous generations had access to in the organised manufacturing sector.

The problems for the Maratha youths further got complicated with Mumbai's transformation into a service sector economy, which demanded a workforce with altogether different skills and knowledge than what was needed in the manufacturing industries.

In the service sector economy, knowledge of English became a necessity, not just for mobility but also to obtain better-paid jobs at the lower level. As a result, even those individuals who would have received slightly better education but in the vernacular medium found it challenging to get well-paid jobs. These developments signalled the disappearance of better-paid job opportunities for individuals with little education or vernacular training. As a result, there was no option before the rural labour migrants but to work in the informal sector. Such jobs, as is widely known, are marked by low wages, long and unpredictable working hours, lack of clear-cut conditions of work and a total absence of social security provisions. While these changes in the political economy affected individuals across castes and religions, it had a significant impact on the Marathas from the urban lower middle class and *wadivarcha* strata who had earlier dominated well-paid blue-collar occupations (Mhaskar, 2016).

In such a context, the only possibility of securing well-paid employment for individuals with little, or vernacular education, is in the government sector. The government sector follows the constitutional provisions of reserving jobs for the Scheduled Castes, Scheduled Tribes and Other Backward Castes. Marathas being part of the general category face competition from the other privileged caste groups. Therefore, for the Marathas, reservation seems like the only way to obtain a larger share of government jobs. Hence, the demand for reservation has a notably stronger appeal among the urban lower-middle class and *wadivarcha* Maratha youth. Marathas are not alone in seeing reservation as a panacea for their problems. The Patels in Gujarat and Jats in Haryana too have demanded reservation. However, one can say with certainty that in the case of Marathas the roots of the demand for reservation lies in the changing political economy of Mumbai.

DISSOLUTION OF GIRANGAON INTO 'WORLD CLASS' MUMBAI

> [A]s the mill areas of Lower Parel change inexorably, altering the skyline of Mumbai and signalling a new phase in the life of this great metropolis, all the big [advertising] agencies ... and the

> lot have moved into Lower Parel as well. True to "positioning" though, they prefer to call it Upper Worli (Narayan, 2004).

The above observation by a journalist informs us that the gentrification process in Girangaon is not only transforming the working class district spatially and economically, but space itself is assigned new names. This process is resulting in the dissolution of the dual character of the city into a world-class Mumbai. Describing the dual character of the city, Klein (1986: 728-29) argued that there are two Bombays, 'one inhabited by a cosmopolitan elite nestled in the fashionable western enclaves of the city, the other full of chawls crowded, insanitary, ill-ventilated slums, and filthy lanes, stables and godowns, a city in which proletariat was penned together and savaged together by disease.' The transformations of Mumbai into a world-class city has whittled down the proletarian Mumbai (read Girangaon) that was dominated by the textile industry, working-class neighbourhoods, popular theatres, smaller restaurants and local tea shops. 'World class' Mumbai is marked by huge shopping malls, multiplexes, upscale bars, restaurants and nightclubs that cater to the needs of the newly emerging middle and affluent classes.

The dissolution of Girangaon into 'world class Mumbai' has its roots in the failure of the 1982–83 strike. Mumbai workers had earlier confronted with unsuccessful strikes too. Even the 1928 strike, which laid the foundation for the making of Mumbai as a labourers city, concluded with more or less maintaining the status quo. However, 'it was a great moral victory' noted Lieten (1982: 697) as workers compelled the mill owners to negotiate with 'their accredited representatives and discuss with them the terms and conditions of their service' (Ibid: 697). In contrast, the 1982–83 strike resulted in a large section of workers losing their jobs, and those who returned had to enter into *involuntary servitude* as they were robbed workers of their moral capacity to confront the state and the capital militantly. It is this crucial moment in the history of Mumbai city and the organised working classes that Van Wersch's has labouriously documented in this book. It provides us with a rich and detailed account of the significance of the textile industry, the conditions which resulted in the historic strike, various strategies deployed by the workers and the counter-strategies employed by the mill owners in collusion with the state and the recognised union, the RMMS. This study opens up many important ways of looking at the trajectory of Mumbai city, where the rights of the working classes and labouring poor that was always fragile, have been considerably shrunk, and their claims over cityscapes are no longer recognised, thus depriving them of their right to a meaningful livelihood. A near complete unmaking of the working class district and by extension *labourers Mumbai* is taking place.

– **Sumeet Mhaskar**
Associate Professor, O.P. Jindal Global University and
Junior Research Partner, Max Planck Institute for
the Study of Religious and Ethnic Diversity

February 2019

NOTES

1. The other films which has a passing reference to the strike or when the event appears in backgrounds are Vaastav: The Reality (1999), Aga Bai Arechya (2004) and Dagdi Chawl (2015). The 2010 bilingual film City of Gold, Mumbai 1982: Ek Ankahee Kahani (Hindi) and Lalbaug Parel (Marathi) is an exception. Although, the film supposedly deals with the 1982–83 strike but mixes events from the early 1980s with that of the 1990s.
2. Village [Gaon] of Textile Mills [Giran].
3. India's first ever full-fledged shopping mall *Crossroads* was built in the working class district in 1999 by the Piramal Holdings Limited—India's first shopping mall management company. When it was built, Crossroads acquired the status of a 'monument' and was therefore visited by city's residents in large numbers. It was around this time the owners made an explicit policy to only allow entry to individuals carrying mobile phones, credit cards, and charged an entry ticket. Back then in 1999 mobile phones had just entered the market and very few individuals could afford it. Mobile phones with the most basic functions costed around Rs. 50,000, and the outgoing call charges were Rs.16 per minute and incoming calls Rs.8 per minute.
4. The films include Boot Polish (1954), Naya Daur (1957), Paigham (1959), Namak Haram (1973), Deewar (1975), Gaman (1978), Kaala Patthar (1979), Albert Pinto Ko Gussa Kyoon Aata Hai (1980), Mazdoor (1983), Coolie (1983), Aghaat (1984), and Koyla (1987),

Disha (1990). These post-independence Hindi films until the late 1980s depicted the lives of the working classes and labouring poor with empathy and sincerity. This was mainly because of the association of prominent writers, poets and artists with the working classes through Indian People Theatre Association.

5. The exception here is the 2010 bilingual film City of Gold, Mumbai 1982: Ek Ankahee Kahani (Hindi) and Lalbaug Parel (Marathi).
6. The notable exception is the journalistic account of the strike by (Bakshi, 1986)
7. Flying Shuttle, (Varerkar, 1972).
8. Dalits lived in the Bombay Improvement Trust (BIT) *chawls* located in Byculla and Agripada region, and in the Bombay Development Department (BDD) *chawls* of Naigaum, Worli and Delisle Road, and in Parel, Nagpada, Kamathipura and Dharavi (Shaikh 2011: 57). However, Dalits often faced discrimination in the housing market and were forced to live in gimcrack sheds (Chandavarkar 1994: 181).
9. The caste Hindus, particularly the Marathas, objected to the employment of the Dalits as weavers because they 'risked defilement and pollution' as 'each time a weft bobbin required replacement, the yarn had to be sucked on to the shuttle' (Chandavarkar 1994: 226-227).
10. Until the early 1930s, untouchability was practised in the Girni Kamgar Union's office whereby two separate water pots were maintained, one for the Dalit workers and another for the non-Dalits workers. It was only after R. B. More, one of the first generation Dalits to join in the Communist Party, objected. After his intervention only one water pot was kept in the office (More, 2003: 173).
11. Muslims were concentrated in the neighbourhoods of Madanpura, Mominpura, Nagpada and Zakeria Bandar.
12. Ambedkar's comment on the strike in 1938 was in response to the introduction of Bombay Industrial Disputes Act which sought to curb workers right to organise industrial actions.
13. Since the 1960s as jobs became scarcer in the textile mills, some workers were successful in deploying their identities to hold to their jobs but others could not. This situation resulted in conflicts. As Hansen (2001: 163) notes: 'One of these conflicts [between Hindus and Muslims] had to do with the threading of the large looms in the weaving shed, an operation that was often done by *ansaris* and required that they wet the cotton thread with their mouths. Non-Muslim workers would then regard the cloth as polluted and would refuse to touch'. Interestingly, high-caste Hindus, especially the Marathas, have historically expressed similar prejudice against Dalits to prevent them from working in the weaving shed (Chandavarkar 1994, 226–7).

14. On Muslim mill workers' occupational choices after the textile mill closures, see (Mhaskar, 2018).
15. Interview with Narayan Ghagre, Secretary of the Communist Party of India Office in Kalachowki, January 2012.
16. Army for the Reconstruction of Maharashtra
17. Raj Thackeray is nephew of late Shiv Sena chief Bal Thackeray and the founder of the Bharatiya Vidyarthi Sena, a student wing of Shiv Sena. He left the Shiv Sena over the issue of leadership in 2006 and formed his own political outfit, Maharashtra Navanirman Sena.

PART I

The Story of the Strike

INTRODUCTION

BACKGROUND

The widespread and long enduring Bombay textile strike that erupted on 18 January 1982, has, in spite of its unprecedented duration, not received the attention one would expect of an event of such magnitude. This is surprising as the Bombay strike cut deeply into the lives of lakhs of textile workers and their families who depend on the textile industry for their livelihood. The strike itself was not unexpected although the support for it and the tenacity of the workers involved surprised everyone. The lack of scholarly interest in this subject contrasts sharply with the interest in another recent historic struggle, the miners' strike in England (1984–85), which has already produced a vast body of literature.

The Bombay strike has to be understood in the context of the vexing problems which had been plaguing the industry for many years. These were of an economic and technological nature but they had also a strong labour component. The chronic nature of the labour problems in the Bombay textile industry is visible in its post-war history of strikes and in the dissatisfaction of the workers with the representative union, the Rashtriya Mill Mazdoor Sangh (RMMS). The past two decades saw the erosion of the position of the Bombay textile workers as the vanguard of the urban labour force. New, capital-intensive industries with fewer workers came rapidly to the forefront; industries which could afford to pay higher wages to their workers, adding fuel to the rising discontent of their counterparts in the textile industry.

Till the adoption of the textile policy of 1985, the Indian textile industry was divided in three sectors (handlooms, powerlooms and mills), each catering to a particular segment of the market and distinguished by its employed technology, products and labour conditions. Prior to the strike the mill sector had been suffering in the internal market from the unchecked growth of production in the powerloom sector which claimed an ever-larger share of the total textile production. As a result, the contribution of the mill sector to the production of cotton cloth (its most important product), declined rapidly whereas the production of blended cloth was stagnant.

The performance of the mills was also hampered by poor capacity utilization and obsolete machinery, a situation arising from subsequent government policies and disinclination of millowners to reinvest profits in the mills. Internationally, the production of textiles experienced a recession at the time of the strike and in the case of India, export was threatened by the production of other developing countries like Pakistan and China which proved more successful in their efforts to gain a larger market share of total textile production. It was in this climate of both national and international recession that the Bombay textile strike occurred.

As far as the strike is concerned, only certain aspects of the struggle have been highlighted in the literature, such as the workers' rejection of all existing unions in the textile industry and their choice of an outsider (Dr Datta Samant) as the strike leader. Further, the break with the system of referring labour disputes to courts has been noted as has the chronic nature of labour problems in the textile industry. With regard to the latter, the strike provoked severe criticism of the prevailing industrial legislation, the BIR Act in particular. The literature also focused on the economic conditions in the textile industry, the technology (obsolete machinery) employed by the mills and the internal and external markets.

However, several other important aspects went largely unnoticed. For instance, the views and attitudes of the striking workers have remained underexposed. The same goes for changes in the views of the participants in this prolonged battle between labour and capital. Again, far too little is known about the various strategies resorted to by the workers in order to survive. The pressures to which all the actors in this drama were subjected have not received systematic attention either. Similarly, the role of the government during the strike, both at the state and national levels, has hardly drawn serious attention. Employers and the government commonly harped upon the use of violence by the strike leader and his men to explain the success of the strike in terms of strike participation. Yet most of what has been said about the application of muscle-power was based on assumptions or purposely given disinformation and may have served ulterior purposes. In any case it ought to have been examined as unsubstantiated accusations about the use of such means created an image of the strike as an essentially violent encounter between those who wanted to resume work and those who did not. The press contributed to presenting a one-sided and sometimes distorted picture of the strike but the role of the press in the struggle has not been analysed.

So far no study has appeared in which a coherent effort has been made to co-relate all these aspects. The present study attempts to fill this gap and intends to provide data allowing for a comprehensive view of the dramatic events that took place prior to and in the course of the strike. In doing so the main focus has been on the workers as their position has largely been ignored by the media and scant attention has been paid to it in the literature. This is borne out by the fact that there are no studies available based on penetrating and systematic interviews with the textile workers themselves. More energy has been devoted to analysing the objectives and strategies of workers' representatives, that is, the trade unions active in the textile industry.

Surveying the field of literature and the many lacunae in our knowledge about the strike and its context, it was decided to try to find an answer to basically three broad questions: 1. What possibilities did the textile workers have of surviving a long period without any regular income? 2. Did the textile strike affect various categories of workers (permanent workers and *badli*s in particular) equally or is it possible to discern differences between workers from prosperous and from backward textile mills? 3. Does the shift in union loyalty which became manifest during the strike signify the end of the workers' confidence in the opportunities of improving their situation while remaining within the boundaries of the law and utilizing the assistance of the existing unions and the political parties to which these unions are affiliated?

AVAILABLE SOURCES

In order to place the answers to these questions in a proper perspective, it was found necessary to unravel the developments leading to the strike and during the strike. For this the following written sources were at my disposal: articles in professional journals and other periodicals, the annual reports of the Mill Owners' Association (MOA) and the Indian Cotton Mills Federation (ICMF) memoranda, government reports, files of trade unions, the archives of various research centres in Bombay, a few books presenting a journalistic account of the struggle, private correspondence, countless press reports and pamphlets. For a study of the wider political context it appeared to be useful to examine the minutes of the debates pertaining to the strike in the Lok Sabha, Rajya Sabha, Legislative Assembly and Legislative Council. However, all this material did not provide sufficient insight into the complexities of the subject and the evidence had to be supplemented by interviews with the principal actors in the textile drama. In the course of fieldwork, scores of exhaustive interviews were, therefore, conducted with managers, millowners, government officials and trade unionists.

As indicated before, the press played a prominent role in informing the public about the causes of the strike and the various developments during the confrontation. Yet, so far no critical and systematic appraisal of press reports has been made which made it desirable to include a study of at least some newspapers in the research in order to arrive at a tentative assessment of the role of the press during the strike. To this end the archives of two English newspapers (those with the largest circulation) and two Marathi dailies have been scrutinized for strike coverage for the entire duration of the strike.

PHASES IN FIELDWORK

As the research questions focused on the workers' views and strategies it was decided to select a stratified sample of 150 textile workers (belonging to two mills) for exhaustive and searching interviews. Some of the main findings emerging from these interviews would be cross-checked with the aid of a sample of 100 workers selected at random from other mills. Naturally, this second set of interviews would be less weighty as only a limited number of questions would be asked.

In order to gain a first-hand knowledge about the working and living conditions of the workers and to be able to ask them the right type of questions during the interviews, I had hoped to spend at least four months in a chawl, sharing a crowded room with workers. Due to unforeseen difficulties and the scope and exigencies of other aspects of the research, this period ultimately had to be cut down to six weeks. Yet even this brief period provided valuable information and a deeper insight into the lives of the workers than would have been possible in the absence of such a direct and penetrating confrontation with their way of life. The warm and friendly relations built up with my roommates in that short spell of time turned out to be important at a later stage too, at a time when I needed their help to dispel the suspicion of other workers about the motives of my research. My former roomcompanions were able to introduce me to some of their colleagues staying in different chawls.

The fieldwork was done in two phases of six months each and was interrupted by a period of equal duration during which I returned to the Netherlands to assess the data collected and prepare for the second phase. During the first period of fieldwork (January 1986–June 1986), I concentrated on collecting documents and studying the available sources. The time was also utilized for discussions with employers and government officials and establishing contacts with several trade unions active in the textile industry. A very important element in the first phase was the stay in a chawl in Prabhadevi. To complement the picture and to obtain an impression of the labour conditions of the workers I also visited several textile mills.

The second phase (December 1986–June 1987) was largely devoted to interviewing the workers in the samples. At the same time the discussions I was having with trade union leaders were intensified. Studying the files of a number of newspapers proved to be another time-consuming task in this phase. In order to understand the changes in the position of the workers during the strike, 150 workers were to be selected for interviews. The guiding principle here was the idea that possible differences between various categories of workers would surface more easily if there was a conspicuous contrast in the labour conditions of the various categories of workers. For that reason it was decided to select seventy-five workers from a prosperous mill utilizing modern machinery, and seventy-five from a backward mill facing a bleak future using obsolete machinery. But other criteria had to be matched as well. The subdivision of the sample provided for proportionate numbers of permanent workers and *badli*s. Originally, I also intended to select workers from several departments in the two mills in proportion to the number of people employed in these departments. Unfortunately, this idea had soon to be abandoned as neither departmental division nor the requisite number of workers were available. Besides, it was triumph enough to be able to interview the requisite number of workers matching some basic criteria.

As next to nothing was known about the fate of the tens of thousands of workers who, voluntarily or not, left the textile industry following the strike, it was decided to include a proportionate number of them in the sample. Apart from obvious and expected difficulties in tracing these workers, there was also the problem of evaluating the magnitude of this group. This made fixing a percentage for the number of workers matching this criterion hazardous. In the end I decided to allocate one-third of the sample to workers who lost their jobs after the strike. This decision proved to be a happy one because later it was possible to establish that probably 30 to 35 per cent of the striking workers had lost their jobs as a result of struggle. Table 1 gives a category-wise division of the sample. In the case of the 150 workers from the big sample, the problems involved in finding sufficient workers were immense. The difficulties in finding workers for the small sample were comparatively minor. A detailed account of these difficulties and of the context of the interviews is given in Appendix A.

TABLE I

Division of Sample

	Finlay	*Spring*	*Total*
Employed	35 Permanent	35 Permanent	70
	15 *Badli*	15 *Badli*	30
Unemployed	25 Permanent	18 Permanent	43
	7 *Badli*		7
Total	75	75	150

For the sake of clarity the book has been divided in two parts. Part I explores the historic, the socio-economic and the political context of the struggle. This gives a description of the strike as a social process of which the outcome is determined by a number of factors which are not necessarily or directly related to the strike and its causes. Part II contains data exclusively dealing with the position, the views and the strategies of textile workers. Many statements made in the first part are based on the findings presented in the second part of the book. By relegating the supporting evidence pertaining to the workers' views and strategies to the second part, it is possible to obtain an overview of the entire struggle by reading only Part I.

Note: Wherever it was found necessary, the names and other particulars of textile workers and employees of organizations have been changed in order to protect their identity. This does not pertain to official spokesman of government, millowners and trade unions.

Chapter One

SIGNIFICANCE OF THE TEXTILE INDUSTRY

BOMBAY AND TEXTILES: EVOLUTION

The rise of Bombay as the most important Indian centre of industry and trade cannot be separated from the emergence and development of the textile industry in the city. The historical and material conditions enabling the textile industry to take root in the peninsula reach back to the seventeenth century. At that time Bombay was just a cluster of small islands near the coast inhabited predominantly by a population of fishermen (Kolis).[1] The coastal area, known as the Konkan, was separated from the hinterland by a range of mountains (Ghats) stretching from the north to the south. The Ghats, which were difficult to surmount, effectively acted as a barrier between the people living on the Maharashtrian plain (the Deccan plateau) and those in the coastal region. As a result communication between these regions remained minimal, although they were similar in terms of religion and language. The most important groups populating the land were the Brahmins (with Deshasta Brahmins and Chitpavans being the most numerous) and Marathas (with Marathas proper and Maratha Kunbis as the most important sections).[2]

Although any bird's-eye view of the history of Bombay is likely to be arbitrary, it would be reasonable to start at the time that Bombay came into the possession of the Portuguese as the cluster of islands were not of much interest or importance, political or economic, prior to that time. By the end of the sixteenth century, the Portuguese power and presence on the Indian west coast began shrinking as Mughal interest in expanding their territory to the south grew and with the appearance of the Dutch at sea. In order to survive these threats the Portuguese entered into an alliance with Malik Ambar, ruler of the Nizamsahi dynasty. After the death of Ambar, the Mughal advance became so threatening that the Portuguese entered into an agreement with the Mughal emperor (1634).[3]

Thirty years later, in November 1664, the island of Bombay passed into the hands of the British crown when the king of Portugal, on the occasion of his sister's marriage to the king of England, ceded this territory as part of the dowry. The English king thereupon offered Bombay to the British East India Company (EIC) at an annual rent of ten pound sterling. The EIC had been looking for another harbour than Surat as the conditions under which the Company had to operate there (trade controls, custom duties, no fortifications) were not conducive to the expansion of trade (M. Kosambi, 1985).

Shortly afterwards Shivaji, who had been gradually expanding his power from the heartland of the Deccan, started making his presence felt. In due time Shivaji would conquer a territory covering large parts of present-day Gujarat and Maharashtra, thereby presenting a formidable threat to the survival of the Mughal empire. By the end of his reign Shivaji controlled the entire Konkan region barring some Portuguese possessions and the English settlement on the island of Bombay. Maratha power, not long after the death of Shivaji, embodied by the Poona-based Peshwa rule, politically insulated the coastal region from the inland for most of the eighteenth century as did the Ghats physically.[4]

Under the aegis of the British EIC, attempts were made to set up a textile industry in Bombay but the initiative failed as it was impossible to induce a sufficient number of weavers to settle in Bombay which had not much to offer beyond swamps and stretches of marshy land connecting the seven islands (Kosambi, 1985). The one thing that Bombay did possess was an excellent natural harbour.

Utilizing the harbour facilities, the Company was more successful in promoting Bombay as a centre of trade than of industry and in 1687 the Company shifted its headquarters in western India to this new acquisition. For a long time most of the goods shipped from Bombay to Europe did come from Surat or, more generally, Gujarat. At first cotton textiles marked the trade but by the end of the eighteenth century, raw cotton would take its place. In 1759 the rulers of Bombay, with the connivance of the Marathas, launched an attack on Surat as a result of which this port too, was brought under their control. In due time Surat lost its importance with a corresponding rise in the significance of Bombay.

In the course of the nineteenth century, the British managed to greatly enhance their power over the Indian subcontinent and the conclusion of the Treaty of Bassein (December 1802) with Baji Rao II, the titular ruler of the Maratha kingdom, proved to be of great significance in that. When the Peshwa, struggling to maintain control over the crumbling Maratha empire, sought British military assistance to solve internal problems, the British secured the right to station an army at Poona (Cantonment). This gave them a great military advantage. A few years later the British army defeated the Peshwa and took possession of his dominions which were clubbed together to constitute the Bombay Presidency.

In an administrative sense the unification of the Deccan and the Konkan had been achieved. Some time later Gujarat and Sindh were added to this administrative entity. Important for the further development of Bombay was the decision to make Bombay instead of Poona the capital of the presidency. This decision made the construction of road and railway connections between the two cities for military and administrative purposes unavoidable and this implied the end of the Ghats as a physical barrier between Bombay and the hinterland.

The increase in trade in the Bombay harbour during the second half of the nineteenth century was greatly helped by factors like the Industrial Revolution in England, requiring ever-larger supplies of raw material (cotton), the related construction of railways in India and the opening of the Suez Canal in 1869 which greatly reduced the time needed to cross the seas between Britain and India. An adequate supply of cotton to Britain necessitated an easy access to the cotton-growing areas and this gave a boost to road and railway construction and, when the cotton started coming in, to the development of Bombay as a harbour.

The opening up of the Deccan, the road and railway connections with Gujarat and Bombay's excellent location on the coast made it possible for this city to become the most important harbour in India. Bombay started attracting bankers and merchants in ever-growing numbers. Very few of these were from Maharashtra, the composition of castes in this state (with a small but dominant Brahmin component) had made this unlikely. In the eighteenth century, Maharashtra had seen the emergence of a business class ('*savakar*s') that could have provided the necessary money and talent but this group of predominantly Brahmin origin was only interested in providing loans to the military rulers of the time and its fate was sealed with the end of Peshwa rule.[5] Of the people who flocked to Bombay, the Parsis, Jains, Hindu trading castes such as the Banias and Bhatias (often denoted as Gujaratis on the strength of their origin), and several Muslim groups from Gujarat were most noticeable. They started shaping the commercial life of the rising metropolis which numbered about 180,000 inhabitants by 1814.

Bombay became a melting pot of religions, languages and cultures. It was a city of immigrants, accounting for 69 per cent at the census of 1872 and not less than 84 per cent in 1921. The growth of the population of the city was equally remarkable, from 644,405 in 1872 to over a million in 1921 (Kooiman, 1978: 6). The diversity of its inhabitants greatly added to the metropolitan character of the city. Apart from a Hindu majority of approximately 70 per cent, there was a strong Muslim minority of 18 per cent, a comparatively large Christian and Jewish community and a dense concentration of Jains and Parsis.[6] The living together of so many groups of different ethnic and religious origin could have dissolved itself into a faceless hybrid culture but this did not happen as the various communities managed to preserve their distinct characteristics. They were helped in this by the fact that each group came to dominate a specific area (Brahmins in Girgaon, Muslims in Madanpura and Byculla, Parsis in Khetwadi, Maratha workers in the areas surrounding the mills, Europeans in the Fort area, and so on). Numerically these groups varied greatly but they also differed in their economic and political clout. In economic terms there appeared to be next to no relation (if at all, a reversed one) between the size of a group and the power it wielded. This is particularly true if one compares the performance of the numerous Muslims to that of the Parsis, a community numbering in all not more than a 100,000 persons in the period 1872–1972.

The Parsis exercised a great influence over economic life in the city and over the textile industry.[7] Many of the first millowners belonged to this versatile community. Not less than nine out of thirteen cotton mills established in Bombay prior to 1870 were started by Parsis and forty-nine out of the 175 directors in the Bombay textile industry in 1925 were Parsis (Kulke, 1978: 56–57). Given their city orientation, high level of education and strong financial position, Parsis were likely to seek employment in trading, banking or book-keeping and not so much in factory labour or agriculture. But they were also to be found in technical professions in the mills where they were employed as mechanical engineers or masters in the carding, spinning or weaving departments.

This has been so right from the beginning as the British technicians who had been brought to Bombay by the millowners at the inception of the industry, did not know the local language and had to be assisted by interpreters who were familiar with English as well as local languages and could understand technical problems. These assistants, who made a career with the mills after the British technicians left, were quite often Parsis (Kooiman, 1978: 19).

Something similar is true for Jains, albeit to a much smaller degree as is borne out by a study by Jain who found that members of this community, too, are disproportionately and strongly represented among Indian managers (Jain, 1971: 68–87). Jain also found that Muslims are hardly represented at all in this category. Christians on the other hand occupy a place of prominence, most conspicuously so in the foreign sector. Part of this phenomenon may be accounted for by nepotism and the tendency to appoint persons of the same region and/or denomination.[8]

It was not before the middle of the nineteenth century that someone took advantage of the many facilities Bombay had to offer to produce textiles. It was the Parsi Nanabhoy Davar who unified a number of rich merchants in what became the first textile mill, the Bombay Spinning and Weaving Company, located at Tardeo and becoming operative in 1856. The results must have been encouraging as a second mill was started a couple of years later. Nearly at the same time other Bombay businessmen planned to start textile mills leading to the foundation of the Oriental Spinning and Weaving Company which became operative in 1858 (Morris, 1965: 25). These examples were followed by other entrepreneurs, and in 1875 Bombay counted twenty-seven textile mills, a number that would surpass eighty at the end of the century.[9]

The capital required for all enterprises was usually indigenous but whereas the first mills seem to have been planned with care (an effort being made to instal adequate machinery), speculative capital took the stage later on.[10] Those who furnished the capital to start a mill became 'managing agents'. However, their interference with the textile industry did not stop at furnishing the required capital for setting up a production unit. They were also deeply involved in running the industry (Kooiman, 1978: 16). Often they were solely bent on making money and they seemed willing to use any money-saving device to maximize profits. From the ranks of their relatives and friends they appointed directors or managers to look after the day-to-day running of the mills. These executives were given limited powers only. One of the powers denied to them was the right to appoint or dismiss heads of departments, a privilege the managing agent kept to himself. As a result, the middle-level cadre felt more obliged to the managing agent than to the manager and, consequently, lower-level personnel could be used to spy on the managers.

Under these circumstances it is not surprising that there was considerable job mobility among the managers. But in spite of their limited powers, the lot of managers was not an unhappy one and they were in a favourable position to enrich themselves at the expense of the mills.[11] The tendency to look for a quick profit did not allow for long-term planning. As a result the short-term perspective of many managing agents has been seen to explain the slow innovation of the industry. However, it is questionable whether this attitude really serves to explain technological backwardness because adhering to labour-intensive procedures (without, of course, caring much for labour conditions) could, in the Indian context, well have proved to be more profitable than innovation as labour was very cheap.[12] In spite of the fast-expanding Indian textile industry, the import of cotton goods into India in terms of rupees as well as metres kept on growing in the last quarter of the nineteenth century. In this period the quantity of imported cotton goods doubled (M. Desai, 1971).

As far as the production of textiles was concerned, the Indian textile mills concentrated on spinning, that is, the production of cotton yarn, and most of this was exported. At the turn of the century, however, India's export of textiles became more vulnerable to international competition, particularly from Japan and China. The exports of yarn to China, that till then had imported nearly half of the Indian yarn production, were substantially reduced. Bombay was hit hardest by this development. One of the effects of this setback in exports was an increased attention to weaving (Mehta, 1954: 170). When Lokamanya Tilak launched the Swadeshi movement in 1905, the millowners welcomed the campaign even if they objected to the political objectives of the movement (Swaraj).[13] Predominantly concerned with money-making, the leading financial circles in the city were naturally not of a radical bent and on the whole favoured British rule but this did not prevent traders and industrialists from utilizing the freedom movement in their attempts to achieve fiscal autonomy (Kooiman, 1978: 8).

The Indian textile industry benefited from the outbreak of the First World War as the imports of cloth and yarn from Britain were cut down while at the same time the profit margin in the textile industry reached unprecedented levels (Morris, 1965: 25). This boom period extended till 1922 after which the competition from Japan on the international scene became fiercer, while on the domestic front labour would become ever more restive, culminating in the impressive textile strikes of the 1920s and subsequent labour unrest in the 1930s.

Meanwhile the textile industry had rapidly become the most important employer in the city, giving employment to lakhs of people in the mills and related industries. The average daily employment in the mills more than doubled between 1900 and 1925 when 153,000 workers were employed. It is safe to assume that a great many more were economically dependent on the mills if the effect on trade, transport, energy, food and clothing is taken into account. On the basis of this consideration Kooiman estimates that in 1931 half of the population in the city must have been economically dependent on the textile industry (Kooiman, 1978: 6).

Internationally important changes took place in the decades preceding the Second World War. The British textile industry declined and Japan emerged as a very competitive producer and exporter of textiles. These developments are reflected in figures relating to spindleage and loomage. Table 1.1 gives these figures for the period 1913–39. They will become even more telling when they are supplemented by figures indicating the type of technology used. In 1927 Japan used practically only modern ring spindles (99 per cent), particularly suited for the medium and lower counts for spinning. Only 24 per cent of the spindles in the UK at that time were of the same type, the other spindles being selfactors. Even India at that stage possessed 89 per cent ring spindles (Nijhuis, 1950: 30–33).[14] From the employers' point of view the installation of modern machinery had the additional advantage that, apart from higher production, the ring spindles and automatic looms required less skill from the worker. In adopting more modern machinery the UK was lagging behind, as may also be deduced from the figures pertaining to looms. The percentage share of automatic looms in the total number of looms for the countries mentioned above in 1930 was 81 per cent for the USA, 28 per cent for Japan, 2.4 per cent for the UK and 1 per cent for India (ibid).[15]

TABLE 1.1

Looms and Spindles as Percentage of World Total

	Looms			*Spindles*		
	1913	*1928*	*1936*	*1913*	*1928*	*1936*
UK	28.7	23.7	16.4	38.8	34.1	24.8
USA	24.8	23.6	18.7	22.0	21.2	17.7
Japan	0.7	2.6	10.8	1.6	4.0	7.9
British India	3.4	5.3	6.6	4.2	5.3	6.9

Source: Nijhuis, 1950: 19–23

Japan's success as a producer of cheap cloth was felt in India after the First World War and grew to become a serious threat to the imports from Britain in the 1930s, 'necessitating' preferential treatment for the British as well as tariff barriers (Modi–Lees Pact), However, this agreement with the British was followed shortly afterwards by the

Indo-Japanese Agreement (1934) in which Japan was accorded the 'most favoured nation' treatment. This pact had been forced on India as the Japanese had retaliated to the increased rate of import duties on Japanese goods earlier by boycotting the purchase of Indian cotton (Mehta, 1954: 182).

As indicated before, the problems besetting the textile industry on the domestic front, particularly with regard to labour, became ever more manifest after the First World War.[16] A series of price rises during and after the First World War triggered off at first unrelated strikes in several mills, culminating in the general strikes of 1919 and 1920 during which important wage concessions were made by the Millowners' Association on behalf of the owners. But a few years later, the millowners struck back after the workers had downed their tools during a strike lasting six weeks. Taking advantage of the general depression, the millowners reduced the earnings of the workers in 1925 by 11.5 per cent. However, the wage reduction did not stop here, with individual millowners showing a tendency to reduce wages further whenever the circumstances permitted. This, in combination with retrenchments, prepared the ground for the great strike of 1928 which was to last six months and which saw the rise into prominence of the communist Girni Kamgar Union.

There had been earlier forms of organization of mill workers but the structure of those founded by social reformers, was rather loose. The first of such organizations, the Bombay Mill-hands Association (BMA) established in 1890, is a case in point. The BMA was founded by N.M. Lokhanday, a social reformer belonging to the Satyashodhak Samaj (a progressive Brahmin reform movement in Maharashtra). Lokhanday organized public meetings, agitated for a weekly holiday and, more generally, drew attention to the plight of the textile workers. The association, however, did not have rules, statutes or formal membership but represented workers' grievances to the government and the public (Punekar, 1981: 208; Michael, 1979: 93). It was not before the communists came to dominate the labour scene that trade unions proper started taking root in Bombay.[17]

When communist activists were victimized after the 1928 strike the stage was set for another struggle the following year. The atmosphere did not ease after that and large-scale wage cuts in 1933–34 were a prelude to the 1934 strike when workers downed their tools for two months. The role played by the communists in this strike was less significant than before. Success was hampered by the lack of cooperation from the jobbers who by then had lost interest in the trade unions. The phenomenon of trade unions as a new form of organization of workers has nevertheless come to stay with the textile industry since the eruption of the strikes in the 1920s.

Prior to the emergence of the unions the workers did not possess a high degree of formal organization but their resilience in times of conflict had nevertheless become quite clear and surprised the millowners and government alike. The rural origin of the labour force was an essential element in that. Throughout the labour history of the textile workers in Bombay it proved to be of crucial importance that most workers had strong connections with their places of origin. Whenever a strike tended to last weeks or even months, workers would leave the city to return to their villages where chances of survival were thought to be better than in the city. The strike under investigation is no exception to that rule.

Central in the organization of workers in the early stages of the industry was the jobber, a man who controlled a specific group of workers (usually coming from the same region) who owed him obeisance. This control was not limited to the factory (indicated by the power to employ a worker and assign a duty to him), but was also visible in the living quarters of the workers. Based on personal contact there existed a clientele relationship between the jobber and workers. Inside the mill he was the link between workers and the management but even outside it is hard to exaggerate his importance. He was the centre of a social network regulating the lives of scores of workers. The workers he controlled had to render personal services to him but on the other hand, workers could also turn to him in times of distress. The jobber was willing to lend them money which, of course, increased their dependence on him.

Yet, the power of the jobber, although great, was by no means, unlimited as there was always a chance that workers might shift their loyalty to another jobber. At times his power was curbed by the presence of a 'dada' in the locality and at a later stage the unions would effectively undermine his position. A dada was a strong-man (at times a worker) who, because of his physical prowess, was often employed for the collection of rent. With his following a dada could exercise very real physical power and could, like the jobber, be an instrument in making or breaking a strike. The roles of the jobber and dada could also merge (Chandavarkar, 1981).

It was not before the trade unions had found a way of dealing with the power wielded by jobbers that workers could be absorbed in the unions to any significant degree. Several methods were tried simultaneously. Sometimes jobbers were coaxed into joining the union by offering them prominent positions. At other times the unions launched direct attacks on the jobbers. The relation between the jobber and union has always been uneasy although it was often a symbiotic relationship. By joining a union a jobber could retain his following or enhance his status (for example as president of a union). For the union his entry had the great advantage that the transition from the personal, particularistic group to the impersonal, administrative machinery was facilitated by his presence, as pointed out by Kooiman (Kooiman, 1977). The transfer of power from the jobbers to the unions has been a lengthy but irrevocable process and today the jobber holds no power beyond the gates of the mill whereas inside his power depends on the specific task assigned to him (assistant jobber, jobber, head jobber).[18] In no case does his authority surpass that of a supervisor, as will be shown later.

The foregoing raises the question of who decides today and on what grounds on the employment of textile workers. Although the jobbers tried to defend themselves against a gradual erosion of their position (including their right to recruit workers), they could not prevent it. Changes in the technology employed by the mills also contributed to the loss of status of the jobber.[19] But the shift in the balance of power did not mean an end to all malpractices attaching the system of labour recruitment. The post-war history of the textile industry bears witness to that. In fact, some of the evil practices attributed to the jobber in the past seem to have been inherited by the unions.

With a view to eliminating injustice and corruption in the recruitment of labour and in order to ensure an adequate supply of labour the then government of Bombay introduced the Decasualization Scheme in January 1950. This scheme had been prepared in consultation with the MOA and intended to create a pool from which the mill management would draw the required substitute labour. Recruiting workers directly was forbidden. Every person who had ever worked in the textile industry and who was unemployed could register as a *badli*. Seniority was decided on the basis of service (total time worked) and literacy. Three groups were created with illiterates in the lowest category, literates with less than one year service in the second category and literates who could claim more service as well as illiterates with service of three years or more in the first category.[20]

One of the weakest points of the scheme was that it applied only to the mills that decided to accept it. There were other shortcomings too. In case of a vacancy the employer was to contact one of four sectional offices which would recommend and send a worker.[21] After reporting at the gate of the mill such a worker would meet the labour officer and the departmental head. Next he would be referred to a jobber or supervisor who would report whether the employee was suitable or not. This procedure still leaves considerable power in the hands of supervisors and jobbers. If the worker was judged to be unsuitable he would be rejected and if he was fortunate he might afterwards be sent to another mill. The administration of the scheme was first under the commissioner of labour but was in 1962 transferred to the director of employment.

The Badli Labour Inquiry Committee noted in 1968 that the scheme had many drawbacks. It failed to regulate employment of *badli* labour, it was not administered efficiently and during the months of April, May and June, the scheme used to break down completely. The mills often felt the need for workers trained in a particular occupation and as the supply via the Decasualization Scheme was said to be inadequate, they started recruiting directly. Apart from that, certain workers appeared capable of interfering with the process of recruiting workers. The director of employment testified before the Committee that workers had an incentive to go directly to the mill gates instead of to the sectional offices and that some of them had influence with the mills and got employment. The report contains a list of complaints with regard to the operation of the scheme, including the use of false certificates and threats.[22] Although we are unaware of research that may have been undertaken recently to study the progress in the proper application of the Decasualization Scheme, there seems to be no reason to be optimistic.[23]

Comparison with Other Industries

In the foregoing narration, the historical development of the Indian textile industry has been sketched. It is time to see what importance the industry enjoys in the wider context of the Indian economy. Even a cursory glance at the cotton textile industry makes it clear that it is of vital importance to the Indian economy not just in terms of value added but even more as a source of employment. The textile industry, inclusive of the organized and decentralized sector, provides employment to at least ten million people. If one adds to this the people employed in related industries like textile machinery, manufacture of dyes and chemicals, marketing, transport (not to mention the millions of cotton growers), and so on, then it becomes clear that the textile industry as a whole can be considered to be the single most important industry in India.[24] This situation is not new and dates back to days far before Independence as has been shown earlier.

Although employment in the textile industry in the organized sector is fairly limited in comparison with the overall generation of employment in the textile industry, the employment potential of the mills is by no means negligible. The Indian textile mills in 1982 provided employment to approximately one million people. In terms of employment the textile mills in the organized sector occupied the second place at the end of the 1970s (15.1 per cent), the first place being taken by food products (16.8 per cent). Next to textiles came power generation (8.8 per cent).[25] Other indicators of the importance of an industry are related to the contribution it makes to gross output and the total value added. The picture of the financial impact of the textile industry in this respect is somewhat different. Although the significance of the textile mills is considerable, this appears to be less than one might expect going by the number of people employed in the industry. The reasons for this will be discussed later. In terms of value added the cotton textile industry occupied the second place (shared with the group 'generation of electricity') contributing 10.9 per cent after 'chemicals and chemical products' with 12.5 per cent (ibid).

The importance of the textile industry at the national level is in Maharashtra also reflected at the state level. In the organized sector the industry emerges even here as the most important source of employment, providing work to some three lakhs of workers (including those working in the silk industry and synthetics in 1977.[26] In the aftermath of the strike the situation changed drastically although the textile industry remained the single largest employer for some more time. Other substantial sources of employment in Maharashtra are transport, food and beverages, chemicals, (electrical) machinery. Due to its high degree of industrialization, Maharashtra occupied the first place in 1978 for the generation of value added by manufacture in the factory sector, namely 25 per cent of the all-India total, followed by West Bengal (11.6 per cent), Gujarat (10.2 per cent) and Tamil Nadu (9.9 per cent).[27]

The industrialization of Maharashtra has been particularly noticeable in the past two decades as may be gauged from the increase in the number of factories (from 8,233 in 1961 to 16,594 in 1981). This was accompanied by a rise in employment in the organized sector from nearly eight lakhs to nearly twelve lakhs in the same period, which means an increase of some 50 per cent (Sakhalkar, 1985). The productive capital, however, saw a rise which surpassed that of the increase in employment manifold (from Rs 619 crore to Rs 7,096 crore), and the same is true for the industrial output.

This indicates a shift in favour of capital-intensive industries, a shift which had a strong bearing on the outbreak of the textile strike in that the workers' wages in the new industries proved to be consistently higher than those in the textile industry. Chemicals, for example, contributed in the beginning of the 1980s nearly 25 per cent of the total value added in the state whereas the share of this industry in employment was merely 9 per cent (as compared with 24 per cent for cotton textiles). Similarly, the output per worker in the chemical industry was Rs 3,08,000 while this was only Rs 46,600 in the cotton textile industry. Not surprisingly, the annual average emoluments per worker were the highest in the chemical industry (Rs 14,367), whereas this figure was Rs 7,120 for textile workers. This last figure was even below the average for all industries which came to Rs 8,463 (ibid.).

The importance of the great disparity in wages in Maharashtra is hard to exaggerate. Textile workers compare their wage package with that of workers in other industries who quite often live in the same compounds. As the textile workers had once been the vanguard of all industrial workers in terms of labour conditions and pay, there was ample cause for dissatisfaction in the new situation. The employers, of course, seized on figures displaying poor productivity in textiles and capital intensity in new industries to argue their incapacity to pay more. In the memorandum submitted by the MOA to the Deshpande Committee in 1982 the millowners went into great detail to establish this point.[28] Time and again the employers stressed that the real comparison should not be with wages in other industries but rather with wages in the unorganized sector.[29] In a supplementary Memorandum to the aforesaid committee the typical MOA reasoning is to be found. After observing that out of a total workforce in India of 281 million not less than 253 million are absorbed in the unorganized sector, the text reads:

> Those engaged in the organized sector are only 28 million of which 18.8 million are working in the public sector and 9.2 million are working in the, private sector. In the organized sector, those engaged in manufacturing industries are just 6 million. These are among the fortunate few in the country who get fairest possible treatment by way of basic wages, dearness allowance (which takes care of rise in the prices of even pan, supari, tobacco and intoxicants), bonus, paid casual leave, paid privilege leave, paid festival holidays, health insurance, provident fund, gratuity, family pension and deposit-linked insurance.[30]

The MOA did not forget to point out subsequently that the costs of a wage increase would have to be recovered from the consumer and that the buyers of cloth are substantially those in the unorganized sector 'who do not have any such income benefits as are enjoyed by 6 million people employed in manufacturing industries'.

Depicting the workers in the organized sector as a spoiled and pampered lot comes in for questioning if one looks at the depressing working and living conditions of the workers in the textile industry, but the argument also suffers from the fallacy that the inadequate earnings of people working in the unorganized sector should be the standard for deciding the wage level in the organized sector, unless one wants to reduce the whole population to abject poverty. Apart from that, the millowners seem to be oblivious to the fact that those textile workers who migrated from their village of origin, leaving their families behind, substantially contribute to the income of their dependents in the villages. Without this contribution sheer survival would become a major problem for them (see Chapter 6).

It may be concluded that the textile industry, both inside and outside the mill sector, plays a pivotal role in the Indian economy. The industry generates income and employment for millions of people and changes within the industry are bound to have a crucial impact on all those who depend on it for their livelihood.

International Market

In spite of a gigantic domestic market, India has never restricted itself to producing solely for its own market. Because of that India has always had a share of the world trade in textiles, the importance of which varied according to national and international circumstances. In the 1950s, India abandoned export limitations but this did not result in a major export drive as the profitability of export as compared with production for the domestic market was not particularly attractive. More recently the significance of the export of textile products for the Indian economy has been considerable, as is indicated by its percentage share in all exports.[31] At present there is virtually a boom in textile exports. According to the latest figures, textiles emerged as the most important foreign exchange earner, accounting for 24 per cent of the total earnings in 1987–88.[32] At the same time, however, other developing countries started becoming more and more competitive.

There are many factors influencing India's export performance, such as the cotton crops and the availability of high-quality yarn. Others are related to the ever-growing importance of synthetic fibres and fabrics in the textile industry and the protective stance of developed countries, restricting imports by means of quotas and tariff barriers. A few years ago these quotas were not much of a problem for India because the country was not in a position to fulfil the quotas allotted to it. The possibilities offered by these neglected opportunities thereafter dawned on the millowners' associations and the millowners, and they decided to act.[33] Efforts to improve the situation soon followed and with a large measure of success. The poor quota utilization, as exemplified by the export to the EEC, one of the major export markets for India, has been fully rectified. In 1982, for example, India could not fulfil more than 15 per cent of its EEC fabrics quota. A year later India fulfilled 42 per cent of this quota, in 1984, 76 per cent. After falling back to approximately 50 per cent in 1985 and 1986, the quota utilization for fabrics reached a peak level of 101 per cent in 1987.[34]

Even more important than the EEC is the Soviet market, the USSR being the single largest consumer of Indian textiles. By value the USSR bought 46.6 per cent of the total cotton textile export in 1983 (as against 52.3 per cent in 1982) and the EEC 27.7 per cent (as against 17.9 per cent the year earlier).[35] Figures for 1982 and subsequent years given by the ICMF are somewhat confusing. Sometimes they relate to the combined mill-made and powerloom cotton textile export, at other times only to mill-made export. In the *Report for the Year 1982–83* it is not stated whether the given percentages refer to the volume of export or to its value. A drastic change in the position of the Soviet Union as the most important buyer of Indian textiles was to be noted in 1987 when the quantity of cloth ordered by the USSR fell by more than 50 per cent. This development is just an indication of the dynamic developments in the textile industry.

As for the export of yarn, Czechoslovakia, Bulgaria and Bangladesh are the most important buyers but on the whole this export was very limited in scope as compared with the export of yarn by Pakistan that accounted for 20 per cent of the world trade in yarn in 1984.[36] However, the situation with regard to the export of yarn changed almost overnight as may be deduced from Table 1.3 showing an impressive expansion of yarn exports in 1987 in terms of value. The increase of these exports in terms of quantity corresponds with this picture, namely from less than ten million kgs in 1985 to over 86 million kgs in 1987 which means a nearly tenfold expansion in less than two years, Even so, in that last year the exported yarn was not more than 6 per cent of the total Indian yarn production. Being convinced that there is an immense potential for export of cotton and blended yarns, the ICMF and Texprocil have requested the government to exempt certain types of yarn from the ceilings fixed by the Indian government.

The persistent growth in preference of synthetic products by consumers world-wide is one more problem the textile industry has to face. This preference is related to so-called wash and wear qualities of synthetic products (durability factor/easy care) and is not restricted to wealthy countries and affluent sections of society. Changes in consumer preferences are also becoming more manifest in the USSR as was reported by an Indian delegation visiting the USSR in 1988. The Indians were given to understand that a radical change in demand was in the offing in favour of high-value items like polyester-blended fabrics, velvets, flannel, denims and the like.[37]

Between 1950 and 1970 the share of synthetic fibres in the use of all fibres in the world rose from less than 1 per cent to more than 20 per cent, and in 1978 this figure had already reached 36 per cent (Kapoor and Jain, 1982). India's share in the world market, based as it was on cotton, declined from 1950 to 1972 after which it rose again. The better performance since 1972 was in essence related to stagnation of domestic demand and a simultaneous encouragement of exports by the government by removing export limitations and by means of subsidies. It has to be borne in mind that the term 'textile export' refers to the whole range of textile products like yarn, cloth, made-ups (for example, bed-linen, pillow cases, towels), garments, hosiery and other cotton manufactures (for example, ropes, tapes, shoelaces, and so on). Till 1972 only the export of cloth and yarn was of some consequence for India but after that the situation changed drastically as may be deduced from Table 1.2 and Table 1.3.

TABLE 1.2

Exports of Apparel and Hosiery and Contribution to Textile Foreign Exchange Earnings (in Crore Rs)

Year	*Cotton Apparel*	*Cotton Hosiery*	*Other Cotton Mfrs.*	*Total*	*% of total textile earnings*
1966	2.6	0.2	10.1	12.9	16.3
1969	4.4	0.3	13.7	18.4	15.7
1972	24.8	0.9	20.6	46.3	26.6
1975	111.9	7.6	37.5	157.0	50.7
1978	286.9	14.2	53.1	354.2	59.8
1981	483.8	56.5	94.4	634.7	66.2
1984	638.2	89.2	56.6	784.0	58.9
1985	768.1	104.9	71.6	944.6	62.1
1986	839.3	158.5	51.1	1052.9	63.7
1987	1255.8	277.9	65.1	1598.8	59.3

Source: Computed from HOSOCTI, ICMF, 1988a: 81.

It appears that apparel and hosiery quickly became the most important foreign exchange earners in the textile industry in the 1970s and this remained so in the 1980s. In this context it is important to note that apparel and hosiery arc produced outside the mill sector.

Indian cotton cloth export since Independence offers a rather erratic picture. Not accounting for yearly fluctuations, it is clear that after a rise in the export of cloth in the mid-1950s (with a peak year in 1957) a steady decline set in till the early 1970s. After that strong fluctuations were observed, the nadir being reached in 1982 with an export of 200 million sq. metres only, for which the strike is held responsible.[38] But the exports of cloth have picked up since then. As observed before, the decline in the quantity of exported cotton cloth till the textile strike was more than counterbalanced by the booming export of cotton apparel and hosiery, particularly since the mid-1970s.

At the time of the textile strike an international recession had become visible in the production of textiles and clothing by the industrially developed countries. In 1983, production in this group started improving but this was wholly attributable to a recovery in the USA where this development was greatly helped by a remarkable expansion of consumer demand.[39] Exchanges of textiles and clothing between industrial countries, however, stagnated in 1983 while exports to developing countries declined considerably. Exceptions to the general slackness in trade were offered by Italy and Japan.[40] Developing countries offering a more direct and serious threat to India's efforts at textile exports are Pakistan and China who offer better quality goods at cheaper prices. The Cotton Textiles Export Promotion Council (Texprocil) has been for a long time well aware of the poor performance of the industry. The problem was summed up neatly in a letter to the commerce ministry in which it said: 'The only way for us to increase exports is either to give Chinese quality or Pakistani prices' (ICMF 1983: 44) .

The uncompetitive prices, and generally poorer quality of Indian products, which have been held largely responsible for the decline in exports in the past, led a couple of years ago to criticism from the Soviet side, obliging the mills to rapidly improve their output as the country could not afford to lose such a significant customer. In 1985 the ICMF reported bright prospects again in the trade with the USSR. In the field of clothing the dominant Asian suppliers to the western markets are Hong Kong, Taiwan and South Korea.[41] The conspicuous performance of these nations triggered off promotion of self-interest amounting to disunity among the developing nations while negotiating with the EEC.[42]

Looking at the value of the Indian exported goods over the years there is, of course, a steep rise in terms of rupees (see Table 1.3). To arrive at a more realistic picture of the developments in the field of exports, the figures provided in this Table would have to be corrected for inflation but the fast-rising importance of exports for the textile industry as a whole after 1972 is nevertheless unmistakable. In combination with Table 1.2, Table 1.3 stresses the significant contribution of apparel and hosiery to the foreign exchange earnings in the textile industry. During the last decade the share of apparel and hosiery hovered around 60 per cent of the total export earnings whereas the increase was tenfold in terms of value.

TABLE 1.3
Export of Cotton Textiles (in Crore Rs)

	Mills		*Handlooms*		*Powerlooms*		*Total*
Year	*Cloth*	*Yarn*	*Cloth*	*Mfrs**	*Cloth*	*Mfrs.**	*Value***
1966	49.2	8.7	6.7	1.7	0.1	0.1	79.2
1969	63.1	23.7	7.2	4.2	0.4	0.5	117.5
1972	81.1	22.7	14.7	6.9	1.3	0.6	173.7
1975	100.3	6.3	31.8	11.1	1.8	1.3	309.6
1978	115.7	14.0	62.2	29.2	14.9	1.9	592.1
1981	156.1	22.5	83.0	40.2	16.7	5.5	958.5
1984	276.6	36.5	96.4	59.8	55.4	23.1	1331.7
1985	275.3	44.1	94.4	74.5	62.3	26.5	1521.6
1986	269.1	61.8	81.4	77.9	84.6	29.9	1653.8
1987	338.9	327.9	96.5	119.0	166.0	46.9	2693.9

* Other cotton manufactures.
** Total value of export earnings in textiles.

Source: Compiled from HOSOCTI, ICMF, 1986: 73.

As has been pointed out elsewhere, the separate figures for handlooms and powerlooms (the former decentralized sector) are not reliable and caution is necessary. Combining the figures for these sectors, however, it appears that the share of handlooms and powerlooms in the total export earnings gradually increased at the expense of the mill sector. It is fairly certain that till 1978 this increase was due to enhanced export performance of handlooms after which a decline set in. From 1976 onwards powerlooms rapidly emerged as the new competitor for exports, first in the field of production of cloth and a few years later also with regard to other manufactures.

The officially acknowledged share of powerlooms in the export earnings grew from 1 per cent in 1975 to almost 6 per cent some eight years later. During the strike period powerlooms apparently leapt forward. Table 1.3 shows that the value of export of handloom products increased rapidly, almost tripling in the course of the past seven years. But in terms of the percentage share of handloom products to the total value of cotton textile export, the contribution of handlooms decreased. By looking at the export of handloom cloth in terms of metres the picture is not quite as clear. It appears then that the export figures fluctuate wildly-making it hard to discern a pattern in these movements.

As regards the sort of products that are being exported by the mills, it should be noted that grey cloth is the most important item constituting 46.7 per cent of the cloth export in 1984, the second place being taken by printed cloth (34 per cent). However, a better idea of the variety of exported cloth and, eventually, of the need to start full-scale modernization, will be gained by looking at the count-wise categories of cloth.[43] Coarse and lower varieties of cloth have always taken the lion's share and the same is true for cotton yarn where counts below 20s were dominant (HOSOCTI, ICMF, 1986: 76). As far as yarn is concerned, this will remain so for some more time as the world demand for cotton yarn is confined to coarse and lower medium counts, a point acknowledged by the ICMF.[44] In terms of volume the export of cloth and yarn (including finer varieties) kept declining till 1982. Lumping together the various categories of coarse and medium cloth it appears that apart from an interruption in 1975, the export share of fine and superfine cloth steadily declined from 18 per cent in 1970 to less than 6 per cent in 1983. A similar picture is by yarn exports till 1981 after which the export share of the higher counts increased considerably, particularly for counts between 40s and 60s (HOSOCTI, ICMF, 1988a: 84).

Expansion of loomage and import of modern machinery for the organized sector has been asked for in the past on the plea that automatic looms will produce for export. Whenever such import of machinery at concessional rates was allowed it was noticed that after some time the machinery was only partially used for export (Mohota, 1976: 121–4). Recently, too, the millowners succeeded in bending the conditions for modernization laid down by the government to suit their needs. When the ICMF in 1983 (in the wake of the strike) applied for import at concessional duty of air-jet looms, water-jet looms and rotor spinning machines, the ministry of finance stipulated that 75 per cent of the goods produced by such looms and spinning machines should for a period of eight years be exported. The ICMF and Texprocil successfully objected to this obligation and saw in 1984 the period reduced to five years. After this they intended to get the export obligation further reduced to 50 per cent.[45]

In his analysis of the Indian textile industry since the 1950s, Mohota concluded that modernization of the industry would be of no use if its sole object was export promotion (Mohota, 1976). In the light of the data presented so far, this broad conclusion must be modified as it does not allow for the differences between mills (some better suited to cater to the needs of the export market than others) nor for the growing importance of textile exports as an earner of foreign exchange. Given the turn of events since 1982 and the rise in the importance of textile exports for the Indian economy, full-scale modernization may be crucial for a limited number of mills but not so vital for a great many others. The extent to which this is necessary will largely depend on their products and the market for which they wish to produce.

This is not to say that modernization can be dispensed with in the case of those mills that solely produce for the domestic market. It is likely that the government will have to come to the rescue of the financially weaker mills for such modernization schemes. Because of that there is room to question the need for supporting the export-oriented units with public funds. They are usually financially stronger and better capable of attracting loans from commercial banks. Besides, due to the nature of their more sophisticated products they are in a better position to pass on the costs to the consumer. This problem will be discussed in greater detail below.

Home Market

The irresistible growth in the production share of the decentralized sector is in essence due to the increase in the number of powerlooms. The mills lost a great deal of their market share to the mushrooming powerlooms which might not have been the case with a liberal import policy for fibre, a different duty structure and, most importantly, permission to expand their production capacity. In order to trace the changes in cloth production it is necessary to know the figures for the production of cotton, blended and synthetic products separately. Table 1.4 provides these figures for the period 1970–87 for cotton and blended fabrics. A separate Table presenting the figures for synthetic fabrics has been omitted as almost all the production comes from the decentralized sector.

Table 1.4 shows the rapid decline of the mills in the production of cotton cloth with a corresponding increase in output by the decentralized sector. Actually, the picture has been completely reversed in the course of merely thirty-five years. In 1951 the mills still produced 79 per cent of all cotton cloth, in 1955 it had become 74 per cent, another five years later the mills share had been reduced to 70 per cent and in 1965 the figure had fallen to 60 per cent (Mohota, 1976: 28–9). The rest of the story is told by Table 1.4.

Not counting a slight increase in the 1980s, it appears that the overall production of cotton cloth was stagnant in the period 1970–87 whereas this production had seen a regular expansion between 1950 and 1964 after which the growth stopped. But the picture is worse if one allows for population growth because then it is clear that the per capita availability of cotton cloth has declined ever since the 1960s (Table 1.5). It must be noted here that taking 1964 as a starting point is misleading as the per capita availability of cloth in the preceding seven years had never reached the high 1964 level. In 1959, for example, the per capita figure was at a low ebb with 14.99 metres.

The production of blended cloth, in contrast, kept growing from the 1970s, albeit irregularly. This holds true even after correcting for population growth. The years 1980, 1982 and 1983 show a distinct decrease which might be partly attributed to the Bombay textile strike although this does not explain why the production recovered so slowly afterwards.

TABLE 1.4

Production of Woven Fabrics from Cotton and Blends in Mills and Decentralized Sector (by percentage)

Year	*Cotton*			*Blended*		
	Mills %	*D.S.* %	*Total (in m.m.)**	*Mills* %	*D.S.* %	*Total (in m.m.)**
1970	53.0	47.0	7849	58.4	41.6	149
1971	53.8	46.2	7356	59.7	40.3	248
1972	52.9	47.1	8022	49.0	51.0	199
1973	53.6	46.4	7771	51.6	48.4	250
1974	52.1	47.9	8284	58.7	41.3	211
1975	50.2	49.8	8034	63.7	36.3	367
1976	48.8	51.2	7945	57.6	42.4	597
1977	46.7	53.3	6902	61.1	38.9	1458
1978	44.4	55.6	7325	56.2	43.8	1748
1979	42.5	57.5	7540	56.3	43.7	1673
1980	41.8	58.2	8314	56.4	43.6	1231
1981	38.7	61.3	8120	58.9	41.1	1560
1982**	29.9	70.1	7837	53.8	46.2	1265
1983	31.4	68.6	8615	61.5	38.5	1332
1984 (P)	29.1	70.9	8830	62.7	37.3	1253
1985 (P)	28.7	71.3	9301	58.8	41.2	1249
1986 (P)	26.5	73.5	9272	60.6	39.4	1433
1987 (P)	23.9	76.1	9617	59.5	40.5	1347

* m.m. = million metres

** Includes provisional figures for Bombay mills.

Source: Computed from HOSOCTI, ICMF, 1988, a: 33

The production of synthetics has so far been solely the preserve of powerlooms, with only a very minor role reserved for the composite mills, as a result of government policy. However, the recent changes in the textile policy (as embodied by the National Textile Policy [NTP] announced in 1985) might reverse this picture in due course. The production of purely man-made fabrics doubled in the last decade, namely from 1,009 million metres in 1976 to 2,070 million metres in 1986. But the per capita availability of synthetic fabrics since 1964 increased by only 57 per cent and showed conspicuous fluctuation not corresponding to the movements of the production of blended cloth (see Table 1.5). That the production of synthetics did not suffer during the strike period is largely explained by the fact that this cloth is essentially produced (that is, more than 99 per cent) by the decentralized sector which remained unaffected by the strike.

TABLE 1.5

Per Capita Availability of Woven Cloth (in metres)*

Year	*Cotton Cloth*	*Blended/ Mixed*	*Man-made Fibres*	*Total*
1964	15.21	N.A.	1.62	16.83
1966	13.94	N.A.	1.65	15.59
1968	14.36	N.A.	1.89	16.25
1970	13.55	0.28	1.71	15.54
1972	13.14	0.35	1.59	15.08
1974	12.80	0.36	1.35	14.51
1976	11.22	0.96	1.56	13.74
1978	10.09	2.69	2.25	15.03
1980	11.05	1.82	1.94	14.81
1981	10.53	2.25	2.05	14.83
1982	10.05	1.79	1.90	13.74
1983	10.83	1.85	2.12	14.80
1984	10.53	1.70	2.31	14.54
1985	10.98	1.65	2.40	15.03
1986	10.70	1.86	2.54	15.10
1987	10.49	1.70	2.54	14.73

* Figures based on total cloth production in India plus actual imports minus actual exports of cloth

Source: Compiled from ICMF Submissions 1985b: 20 & HOSOCTI, ICMF, 1988a: 42

If the per capita availability of cloth in the three categories is put together it seems on the face of it that there is a steady decline till the mid-1970s followed by a stagnation in the 1980s (Table 1.5). This, of course, gives a distorted picture as one has to account for the durability factor because blended and synthetic materials are more durable than cotton fabrics. The weight which should be given to this factor is uncertain, however. The durability of non-cotton products is usually placed between 2.1 and four times the durability of cotton. After a steep rise and a peak at the end of the 1970s, the availability of blended cloth appears to be stable in the 1980s. The availability of synthetic fabrics, on the other hand, shows a gradual but persistent increase.

It goes without saying that the per capita availability of cloth since the 1970s will show quite a different picture if one allows for a fourth factor in terms of the durability of synthetic fabrics. Chandrasekhar worked out the differences in per capita availability of cloth based on the factors 2.1 and four for the period 1971–77 and concluded that there had been a decrease in consumption in both cases. If one doesn't pay heed to the durability factor at all, it appears that the decrease is 13.7 per cent. On the basis of factor 2.1 this would be 10.5 per cent and with a fourth factor it would come to a decrease of 5.2 per cent (Chandrasekhar, 1984).[46]

As the purchase of cloth is strongly income-dependent, one is tempted to believe that the rural areas, given the generally low level of income, would not benefit much, if at all, by an increase in the availability of more durable but also more expensive cloth. A survey conducted by the government in 1974–75 supports this contention. According to data supplied by the National Sample Survey there are tremendous differences in cloth consumption and these are related to the level of income, as is borne out by Table 1.6. The Table also shows how utterly misleading the figures for per capita availability of cloth can be if they are not related to income. From the Table it appears that the bottom 40 per cent of the income groups in India consumed on an average not more than two metres per capita a year. The finding is all the more disconcerting if one takes into account that the share of this group in the total population might be of the same magnitude. This would indicate that much of the debate on the beneficial effects of the substitution of cotton by synthetics is irrelevant.

Analysing the demand and supply of textile products in the period 1970–84, Goswami concluded that considerations of durability play a major role in the purchase of synthetics even in the poorer households and are actually of less importance for middle and higher

TABLE 1.6
Expenditure on and Consumption of Cloth by Different Income Groups in Rural Areas (1974–75)

Income Groups (% households)	*Annual per capita expenditure in Rs*	*Expenditure on cloth in %*	*Average cloth per head (mtrs)*
5	216	1.4	0.8
5–10	295	1.4	1.1
10–20	367	1.5	1.5
20–30	443	2.0	2.4
30–40	514	2.4	3.3
40–50	586	4.2	6.5
50–60	667	5.0	8.9
60–70	784	5.9	11.9
70–80	878	7.3	17.2
80–90	1052	9.3	26.1
90–95	1260	10.7	35.9
95–100	1370	14.1	51.3
Overall	685	6.5	11.9

Source: MOA, 1983b: 332

income groups (Goswami, 1985). Goswami found that except for the lowest incomes (that is, below Rs 3,000 per household per annum) there is a distinct move towards blended and synthetic products. But the group with an income lower than Rs 3,000 per year is quite substantial in India, representing approximately 25 per cent of the population in 1981.

The figures supplied in Table 1.7 seem to support Goswami's findings but on the basis of consumption of cloth in metres alone it is not possible to distinguish between coarser and finer varieties of cotton cloth whereas this distinction is essential in discussing the importance of the durability and consumption of cloth. Goswami's conclusions seem to be corroborated by a similar study by ATIRA which revealed that the expenditure for cotton dropped even for very low income groups (both rural and urban) with a corresponding increase in the budget shares of synthetic and polyester cotton textiles (Iyer and Narasimham, 1985). Unfortunately, the figures of

TABLE 1.7

Per Capita Household Consumption of Textiles at Different Income Levels: All India

Annual Income in Rupees	*Year*	*Cotton (mtrs)*	*Non-cotton (mtrs)*	*Blended (mtrs)*	*Total (mtrs)*
0–3,000	1981	7.86	0.37	0.63	8.86
	1982	7.42	0.36	0.68	8.46
	1983	7.67	0.52	0.68	8.87
	1984	7.47	0.67	0.66	8.80
	1985	8.41	0.70	0.75	9.86
3,000–5,999	1981	8.77	0.54	1.05	10.36
	1982	8.79	0.60	1.32	10.71
	1983	8.56	0.86	1.18	10.60
	1984	9.30	1.14	1.12	11.56
	1985	9.92	1.24	1.33	12.49
6,000–9,999	1981	9.39	0.96	1.80	12.15
	1982	10.67	1.13	2.21	14.00
	1983	9.97	1.18	1.89	13.04
	1984	10.18	1.48	1.93	13.59
	1985	10.98	1.67	2.14	14.79
10,000–19,999	1981	11.54	1.39	2.81	15.74
	1982	11.69	1.62	3.48	16.79
	1983	12.42	2.06	3.28	17.76
	1984	10.81	2.22	2.98	16.01
	1985	11.77	2.72	3.39	17.88
20,000–39,999	1981*	11.89	2.67	3.47	18.03
	1982	12.86	2.21	4.71	19.78
	1983	11.13	2.64	3.41	17.18
	1984	10.37	3.37	3.28	17.02
	1985	10.80	3.26	3.96	18.02
40,000–.....	1981*	*	*	*	*
	1982	10.43	3.85	3.95	18.23
	1983	13.18	3.30	4.65	21.13
	1984	11.45	4.64	3.74	19.83
	1985	12.76	6.76	4.55	24.07

* Included in the income group Rs 20,000–Rs 39,999

Source: HOSOCTI, ICMF, 1984b, 1986 and 1988a.

Goswami and those of the ATIRA study cannot really be compared as the latter study analysed the purchasing behaviour of only two income groups, that is, below and above Rs 1,000 per capita per year in both rural and urban areas. Iyer and Narasimham found that the total per capita expenditure on textiles (corrected for price rise) in the period 1974–83 rose and as the consumption of textiles was found to be constant these findings seem to indicate that the trend towards more expensive and durable cloth is less income dependent than one might expect. The conclusions of both these studies, however, are in part contradicted by Chandrasekhar who holds that considerations of durability are particularly important to the middle and higher income groups who are also the most important consumers of durable cloth (Chandrasekhar, 1984).

Although on the demand side, changes in the pattern of consumption of cloth are still a moot question, the picture on the supply side is less uncertain. As far as the mills are concerned it is clear that their contribution to the production of cotton cloth rapidly declined whereas their share in the production of blended cloth fluctuated between 50 and 60 per cent in the past fifteen years. In terms of metres, the increase in blended cloth production has shown no improvement since 1977 and this stagnant production has not been able to make up for the loss in cotton production. The mills' share in the production of pure synthetic fabrics has been negligible. These developments have not affected all mills to the same degree nor have they responded to it in the same manner, as will be shown below.

Technological Constraints

The technological backwardness of the Indian textile industry as a whole has been observed in numerous articles and reports. The employers have used this state of affairs to highlight the constraints under which the industry has to operate, to explain the poor performance in exports and to obtain government support for modernization. Labour representatives, on the other hand, cited the technological backwardness to explain the often inhuman labour conditions in the mills. The obsolescence of the machinery being used in spinning, weaving and processing has been identified as being one of the main causes of the sickness in the industry, but cause and effect may well have changed places in this presentation of facts as there is not much evidence to substantiate this view.

The technological backwardness is not new (India has been at the rear-end for decades) and it is to be found in all stages of the production process. As far as the mills are concerned this is largely explained by the integrated character of this process, all stages being closely interlinked not just within the processes of spinning and weaving but also between spinning and weaving. It is not very meaningful to switch to high-speed looms if there is no corresponding modernization of the preceding spinning process enabling increased production. Modernization at one end will have to lead to modernization all along the line, at all the intermediate stages. Such a complete overhaul of the production process requires enormous capital investment and the representatives of the mill owners have always been quick to point out the necessity of government support.

The employers feel entitled to soft loans (thereby utilizing public funds) and successfully harp upon the theme of imminent unemployment if they do not get this as the mill would have to close down for lack of finances. Modernization of the textile industry also implies large-scale displacement of workers and for that reason such proposals were met with great suspicion by labour. Exploitation of labour on the one hand and of the public on the other, gained the millowners in the course of time a bloodsucking image and hindered their efforts at modernization. From the millowners' point of view, the Bombay textile strike came as a blessing in disguise because it offered them a golden opportunity to get rid of labour without having to pay retrenchment benefits. It was the cheapest but also the most painful way (that is, for the workers) to carry out this operation.

Given the fact that India has the largest cotton producing area in the world it is only natural that cotton occupies the most important place in production for the domestic and the international market. However, cotton cultivation is very extensive, the yield per acre being one of the lowest in the world (see Table 1.8). In fact, there has hardly been any improvement in the cotton yield in India over the past thirty years. Between 1981 and 1984 the world average cotton yield per acre was 414 lbs whereas India produced only 141 lbs per acre which compares very poorly with Egypt's 890 lbs, USSR's 762 lbs, China's 580 lbs or even Pakistan's 273 lbs (HOSOCTI, ICMF, 1986: 102).[47]

TABLE 1.8

Area and Production of Cotton, 1983–84: Select Countries

	Area in 1,000 acres	*% world acreage*	*Production in million bales**	*% world total*
India	19,187	24.5	5.9	8.7
China	15,085	19.2	21.3	31.5
USSR	7,900	10.1	12.3	18.2
US	7,348	9.4	7.8	11.5
Pakistan	5,487	7.0	2.1	3.2
Brazil	4,880	6.2	2.6	3.8
Turkey	1,499	1.9	2.4	3.5
Uganda	1,304	1.7	0.1	0.1
Argentina	1,214	1.5	0.8	1.2
Egypt	1,036	1.3	1.8	2.7

* 1 bale = 478 lbs or 217 kg.

Source: Computed from HOSOCTI, ICMF, 1986: 102

It is not just that there is ample scope for improvement of yields in India but also that the quality of the cotton leaves much to be desired. At the time of Independence, India possessed valuable cotton areas but in consequence of the partition possibly the best part of this acreage fell to Pakistan.[48] The generally poor quality of Indian cotton is related to appearance and strength. The cotton is usually dirty, has variable staple length and contains much immature fibre leading to a high rate of breakage. This strongly influences the processes of spinning, weaving and finishing. Yarn defects ultimately result in cloth defects which again determine the scope for sales, particularly in the field of exports. The World Bank in its study of the Indian textile industry in 1975 classified the raw cotton available as belonging to the lowest quality and because of that providing one of the most serious handicaps for the industry.[49]

Low productivity in cotton cultivation is also the hallmark of the Indian situation with regard to use of spindles and looms. Prior to the Second World War, the Indian situation with regard to spinning machines compared favourably with other countries but due to overutilization during the war and neglect of modernization afterwards the Indian position deteriorated. In 1983 India possessed an impressive twenty-four million spindles (15.7 per cent of the world total) but there were only 5,500 open-end rotors (0.1 per cent of the world total) that are capable of a much higher production than the conventional ring spindles. According to the ICMF the productivity of a rotor equals that of two and a half to five spindles, depending on the count produced and the speed of the rotor (ICMF, 1985b: 10). As said before, the output per spindle is greatly affected by the input, that is, the quality of the cotton. According to the MOA the growing of cotton, particularly long and extra long staple varieties, has in recent years improved considerably. This again has a favourable effect on the output per spindle because of fewer machine stoppages and a lower twist requirement. Proper maintenance is another way to improve the output per spindle.[50]

The productivity of the looms is not very different from that of the spindles (see Table 1.9). The mill sector had in 1983 some 209,690 looms (7.3 per cent of the world total) but whereas 81.5 per cent of all the looms in the world are automatic India has only 25.1 per cent automatic looms. And even this figure is inflated as it is necessary to distinguish between automatic looms with and without shuttles, the last type being far superior in terms of productivity.[51] The ICMF estimates the production capacity of a shuttleless loom to be three to five times that of a shuttle loom (ibid.). Table 1.9 compares the Indian situation with that of some other textile-producing countries. It appears that India utilizes ordinary looms to a far greater extent (75 per cent) than any of the major cloth-producing countries.[52]

The Indian backwardness in terms of yield per hectare is striking and the same goes for the productivity of looms and spindles. This low productivity is related to inefficient use of available resources, specific market conditions (at home and abroad) but also to the sheer age of the machinery. Numerous reports and studies in the near and distant past concluded that the applied technology and machinery in the textile industry was and still is hopelessly obsolete. To be sure, the age of machinery in itself is not a sufficient criterion to judge the performance of the industry. Good maintenance and periodic upgrading might ensure a better output than the age factor alone would suggest. However, after visiting a number of mills in Bombay one is led to believe that proper maintenance and upgrading of machinery rank low on the priority list of the management of the textile mills.[53]

TABLE 1.9

Loomage in Select Countries at the End of 1983

	Automatic looms		*Total looms including ordinary*	*% autom. looms to tot. looms*
	Shuttle	*Shuttleless*		
India*	51,850	720	209,690	25.1
China	574,000	1,000	625,000	92.0
USSR	180,000	80,000	270,000	96.3
USA	146,610	52,030	198,640	100.0
Pakistan*	24,400	470	30,870	80.6
Egypt	37,440	1,660	61,900	63.1
Taiwan	58,650	4,750	70,400	90.1
Hong Kong	18,100	4,000	22,100	100.0
Japan	108,610	22,500	277,700	47.2
South Korea	46,700	2,000	48,700	100.0
Thailand	64,130	570	69,700	92.8
Brazil	130,000	5,500	140,500	96.4
Indonesia	53,950	3,650	92,600	62.2
Italy	21,220	12,230	34,080	98.2
Turkey	33,230	2,870	42,500	84.9

* Relates to organized sector only

Source: HOSOCTI, ICMF, 1986: 98–9

Chandrasekhar collected data regarding the age of the machinery utilized in the mill sector and found that in 1951 more than 43 per cent of the machinery (spread over all departments) was more than forty years old and another 27 per cent older than twenty-five years. A quarter of a century later the situation seemed not to have altered materially. In a sample covering forty-seven mills in 1976 it was found that the percentages for machinery older than forty years appeared to be 39.2 per cent for the blow room, 45.3 per cent for carding, 38.9 per cent for drawing, 30.2 per cent for spinning, 24.8 per cent for weaving preparatory and 36.1 per cent for weaving (Chandrasekhar, 1984). The list could easily be completed with data from the World Bank in which it is also observed that the machinery is operated in conditions of almost abominable squalor. With the exception of Century Mills, the mills visited during the fieldwork corroborated this state of affairs, the labour conditions in many departments ranging from the depressing to dismal. Again, in a study seeking to explode the 'myth' that there is no innovation in Indian manufacturing firms, Sinha made a notable exception for the Indian textile industry (Sinha, 1983). One is forced to accept the truth of the following observation: 'Most Indian cotton textile mills are thus museums, or worse, graveyards of machinery' (Bidwai, 1983).

Although it is plain that innovation and modernization of the industry cannot be postponed, the extent to which this should take place is less certain. Generalizing about modernization obscures the fact that there may be considerable differences between individual mills catering to different needs and groups. Without spelling out the needs for each mill separately, modernization is often held out as a panacea for all the problems besieging the industry. Such a view starts from the assumption that modernization in itself is a blessing and even a must if the industry wishes to survive, although the relation between modernization and survival is a complicated one in the Indian context, as is borne out by the introduction of various schemes to modernize the industry.

The government has been running several financial institutions like the Industrial Finance Corporation of' India (IFCI), Industrial Credit and Investment Corporation of India (ICICI) and the Industrial Development Bank of India (IDBI) with the view to promoting industries of key significance to the Indian economy and to supply resources to facilitate the process of modernization. More than 56 per cent of the soft loans disbursed by these institutions till 1982 had been given to the textile industry, the second place being taken by the engineering industry (19 per cent). What is more revealing is that the units that benefited most from the various schemes appear to be those that are classified as the strongest units (who also stand much better chances of obtaining loans from commercial banks as their capacity to repay is unquestioned). By the end of 1981, 50 per cent of the soft loans given to the textile industry were granted to the strongest applicants, 11 per cent to the weaker applicants and 39 per cent to the weakest applicants.[54]

Changes in the applied technology in the textile industry are fast and far-reaching. In a modern mill, one worker can handle thousands of spindles or a great number of fully automated looms. The looms increased their speed from 190 picks per minute to 2,000 picks per minute, a speed, however, which cannot be used for handling cotton fibres.[55] All these changes were triggered off in the developed countries as they were facing problems of labour costs, labour shortage and stiff international competition. The innovations sought to reduce the share of wage costs in the total costs of production, thereby making the products more competitive.

Table 1.10 shows the costs of labour and the number of hours/days worked in mills in some Western and Asian countries. These labour costs include social charges, if any, paid by the employer. The differences are enormous, the highest paid workers not only working the least number of hours per day but also the least number of days per year and vice versa. While studying these figures it has to be borne in mind that the fairly low ranking of the USA in terms of labour costs is the result of the recent devaluation of the dollar. The impact of this development is mainly on the textile trade between

TABLE 1.10

Costs and Hours of Labour in Textile Industry in 1987 (select countries)

Country	*Cost per hour per operator in US $*	*Number of operator hours per year*	*Number of operator days per year*	*Number of operating days per mill per year*
Switzerland	15.70	2092	245	235
Holland	13.75	1727	216	217
Italy	12.67	1709	224	268
Japan	11.99	2023	253	251
USA	9.24	2204	245	241
Taiwan	2.09	2496	312	354
Hong Kong	1.93	2381	298	340
S. Korea	1.77	2388	286	308
India	0.65	2454	311	339
Pakistan	0.37	2328	291	304
China	0.23	2464	308	N.A.

Source: Werner International, 1987

the USA and Europe because the Western European textile products became less competitive in the US market and vice versa. Another effect has been that the cost competitiveness of Asian countries as compared with West European producers of textiles has improved.

Of course, the competitiveness of an industry is not solely dependent on labour costs. Another crucial factor is, for example, productivity. Apart from that there are factors like the availability and quality of raw material, energy, services and so on. The Table also shows that mills in Asia (Japan excluded) are working practically every day of the year. The situation in India is in many respects (comparatively low wages, abundance of labour, production of raw material) quite different from that of Western countries and new techniques are therefore at best only in part suitable for adoption. In the past, export remained dormant but, as shown earlier, this picture has changed dramatically in recent years.

What has not changed, however, is the abundance of cheap labour and the overriding importance of cotton as raw material. Unlike the case in Western countries, in India therefore, no strong case can be made for a full-scale concentration on synthetics. For export purposes India is in a better position to concentrate on cotton or blended products than competing with the industrialized countries in the field of synthetic products which will require ever larger investments in sophisticated machinery with a corresponding shrinkage of employment.

This is not to say, of course, that innovations are not called for and even less that obnoxious labour conditions should not be altered. But it does mean that changes should be in accordance with priorities arising from the specific needs of the country and not from those of a group of export-oriented enterprises like Century Mills or Reliance. It was with this objective in mind that the World Bank in the study mentioned above refrained from advocating wholesale modernization, realizing that nothing much could be gained by adjusting employment in the industry to world standards while simultaneously contributing substantially to unemployment.[56]

In his analysis of the textile industry up to 1973, Mohota discussed the need for modernization as the representatives of the millowners had been clamouring that all the problems of the industry were attributable to it. He found that in 1972 all the problems suddenly seemed to have vanished and explains this phenomenon by the bumper cotton crop that year allowing for a better capacity utilization, lower overheads and higher productivity (Mohota, 1976: 113).[57] As far as the costs of modernization arc concerned, Mohota concluded that the advantages of higher production would be outweighed by the required outlay of capital. He advocated a shift from handlooms to powerlooms as being a more sensible step towards augmentation of production (Mohota, 1976: 157). If he had included the substantial costs of retrenchment of labour in his calculations he would have come to even more discomforting conclusions. Mohota's observations are corroborated by the findings of the National Productivity Council which show that there is a persistent decline in capital productivity in the textile industry in the period 1956–79 in spite of modernization. The output per spindle and loom appeared to have decreased, the replacement of obsolete spindles and looms by modern ones notwithstanding.[58]

Part of this amazing finding can be explained by the underutilization of machinery which has come to stay with the industry. The capacity utilization in the Indian textile industry has been poor and stagnant for decades. The average utilization of spindles in the mill sector, that is, in three shifts, rose from 1950 to 1964 when a peak was reached of 82 per cent. After that a decline set in (Mohota 1976: 35–38). Not counting a sudden drop to 65 per cent in 1982, the average spindle utilization in the past fifteen years hovered around 75 per cent. The average utilization of looms till the 1970s has been lower still and fluctuated around 65 per cent (ibid.). Due to an intensification of loom activity, in the third shift in particular, the average loom utilization hovered around 76 per cent in the 1970s but came down drastically in the 1980s and has been no more than 61 per cent on an average in the period 1982–87.[59] The secretary-general of the ICMF, C.V. Radhakrishnan, ascribes this to the obsolescence of the machinery resulting in uneconomic performance and to the redundancy of looms (interview, 21 February 1986). The surplus capacity poses in a way a threat to the viability of healthy units in that it eats into the profit margin of these units in times of favourable market conditions whereas such spindles and looms remain idle at other times.

Idle capacity explains some of the low capital productivity and so does poor maintenance but a more satisfactory explanation is probably stagnation of demand in the domestic market which does not allow for full utilization of machinery, be it obsolete or modern. Analysing technical change in the Indian textile industry, Chandrasekhar concludes that the rate of technical change is constrained by the rate of growth of the market. Rapid introduction of new techniques 'necessitates an expansion of production beyond that warranted by the output augmenting character of technical change itself' (Chandrasekhar, 1984). If the modern machinery had been utilized for the purpose for which it was meant (that is, export) then the problem might have been less acute but the few firms that took to large-scale modernization have been falling back on the domestic market whenever they faced serious problems with export, thereby adding to the problems of the other mills (Mohota 1976: 120–24).

It could be argued that a clear division between the mills in terms of export orientation could solve this problem but it remains to be seen whether such a scheme is feasible. In tune with a recommendation of the World Bank to allow a segment of the industry to produce textiles of international quality in order to boost exports and to combat a deficit in the balance of trade, the government decided in December 1980 to set up 100 per cent export-oriented units. These units would be given concessions relating to exemption from duties for import of capital goods and raw material and other facilities (no excise duties on finished products, no ceilings on export quota). In addition they were allowed to sell rejects in the domestic market up to 5 per cent. In February 1982, the ICMF expressed doubts regarding the workability of such units and suggested that the level of rejects be raised to 25 per cent (MOA, 1983b: 47). When this was granted the chairman of Texprocil pleaded in December 1983 that even this did not suffice and that further support was required (MOA, 1984: 70). This indicates that the domestic market is used by the stronger mills (the same that are largely shaping the policy of the ICMF and MOA) as a buffer and that there is a great deal of opportunism in the demands made by the millowners.[60]

Chandrasekhar predicts the emergence of an oligopolistic structure in the textile industry, that is, a small number of mills (for example, Reliance, Bombay Dyeing, Century, Khatau Makanji) producing high-quality goods that are price inelastic. Their products are such that they do not compete with the products of the other mills or even the decentralized sector (Chandrasekhar, 1984). As these products allow for a higher profit margin, the necessarily high level of investments in modern equipment, processing and sales would pay back in due time. Helped by the price inelasticity, the higher costs of production of costly fabrics and cloth will be passed on to the consumer which is not feasible in the case of the cheaper textiles. In other words, their 'oligopolistic position permits firms in the luxury sector to both meet the costs of such strategy and even earn high profit margins' (ibid.).[61] Whether one agrees with this prediction or not it is obvious that the demand side should be given more attention when discussing the need for modernization. Embarking on a scheme of full-scale modernization with disregard of constraints dictated by changes in demand, consumer preference and the required technology will only serve the aims of a small but vocal section of the textile industry. It will at the same time be detrimental to its employment potential.

IMPORTANCE OF POWERLOOMS

Competition

From the data supplied above it is clear that powerlooms play a vital role in the Indian textile industry.[62] They also played a significant role at the time of the strike. First of all, the powerlooms allowed mills to continue production of cloth through subcontracting, a practice which helped them to tide over the crisis. Secondly, the output of the powerlooms helped to avert the danger of a shortage of cloth in the domestic market. Thirdly, for the striking workers the existence of the powerloom sector was important as an avenue of alternative employment, particularly for the weavers. But it has to be noted that inasmuch as the powerloom sector contributed to the chances of survival for certain categories of textile workers, this sector also contributed to undermining the chances of success of the strike.

Unfortunately, as will be shown later, it is not possible to measure the importance of the powerlooms for the strike in quantitative terms. The significance of the powerlooms rose rapidly right from the start but became most conspicuous in the two decades preceding the formulation of the New Textile Policy (NTP) in 1985. Table 1.11 shows the growth of cotton cloth production in the decentralized sector whereas Table 1.12 indicates the growth in the number of powerlooms in recent years.

TABLE 1.11
Output of Cotton Cloth in the Decentralized Sector

Year	*Handloom and powerloom (m.m.)**	*% of total cotton cloth production*
1951	1,013	21.4
1956	1,663	25.5
1961	2,372	33.6
1965	3,056	40.0
1970	3,692	47.0
1975	4,002	49.8
1980	4,838	58.2
1985 (P)	6,634	71.3
1987 (P)	7,309	76.0

P = Provisional
m.m. = million metres

Source: HOSOCTI, ICMF (various issues)

TABLE 1.12
Growth of Powerlooms

Year	*Number of powerlooms (in lakhs)*
1977	3.48
1980	4.52
1981	4.99
1982	5.73
1983	6.65
1984	7.00

Source: ICMF, 1985b: 6

It is worth noting that the figures in Table 1.12 only refer to the number of authorized looms whereas everyone in the textile industry agrees that the real number in 1984, for example, surpassed eight lakhs. This means that at that time there were approximately four times as many looms in the powerloom sector as in the organized sector. The share the powerlooms have in the total output of cloth in the decentralized sector is less certain. Even the powerloom associations themselves do not agree on a figure.[63] But although the powerlooms outnumber the looms in the mills several times, they have not been able to reach the same level of productivity. This points to low capacity utilization. Doraiswami and Iyer put the effective loom utilization at 50 per cent and the production per loom per day at twenty-two metres (Doraiswamy and Iyer, 1985).

In order to stem the swelling tide of the unauthorized powerlooms in the 1950s, the central government decided to treat the bigger powerloom units in the same way as mills in the organized sector in terms of taxation and the applicability of labour laws. One of the unintended consequences of the new policy was that owners of large units started splitting up their factories into units not exceeding four looms. In doing so they evaded paying taxes (the excise duty on powerlooms is dependent upon the number of looms under single ownership), applying labour laws and continued to benefit from the measures promoting the decentralized sector. According to a survey in 1956 by the Powerloom Enquiry Committee in the then state of Bombay, only 23 per cent of the powerlooms working on cotton were installed in units operating with four looms or less, 42 per cent in units with five to twenty-five looms and 35 per cent in units with more than twenty-five looms. In 1974 not less than 90 per cent appeared to belong to small units.[64] This development contributed considerably to the already obscure state of affairs in the powerloom sector. The phenomenon of fragmentation is also to be found in the art silk industry and for the same reasons. This has led some authors to believe that this practice will become the chief mode of exploitation of workers.[65]

Central to the discussion on the inherent strengths and weaknesses of the powerlooms as compared with the mills are the differences in costs of production. It is no surprise that the representatives of the organized and the decentralized sectors hold conflicting views on this. Powerloom associations keep referring to the findings of the Ashoka Mehta Committee (1964), a committee appointed by the government to look into the problems of the powerloom sector. This committee observed that the powerlooms suffered a cost handicap of 8 per cent during production as compared with the mills. This percentage was calculated after accounting for differences in costs of yarn, manufacturing charges and wages (it is noteworthy that the committee concluded that this handicap existed in spite of attributing to the powerlooms a 'wage advantage' over the mills of some 50 per cent). Besides, the committee allowed for a marketing disability suffered by the powerlooms at about 10 to 12 per cent, thus fixing the overall handicap at 18 to 20 per cent vis-à-vis the mills.[66]

While referring to the findings of the Mehta Committee the powerloom associations hold that in the years between 1964 and 1985, the scale of the balance went down even more in favour of the mills as the prices of yarn and manufacturing charges (overheads and sundries in particular) went up whereas the wage difference came down, thereby creating an additional handicap for the powerlooms of 11.5 per cent, bringing the total handicap to some 32 per cent now.[67]

The millowners, on the other hand, stick to studies published by textile research institutes like ATIRA showing that the powerlooms have a lower cost of production due to the wage factor and fiscal benefits.[68] In the ICMF submissions mentioned before, examples are given of certain types of cloth (cotton 20s × 20s and cotton 40s × 40s) in the production of which powerlooms would have a clear advantage over the mills as far as manufacturing costs and wages are concerned (ICMF 1985b: 6). In the variety 20s/20s the powerlooms would have an advantage of some 17 per cent. In the variety 40s/40s the advantage would even be 21 per cent.

The powerloom associations, on their part, claim that the chosen examples give a wholly false picture as those particular counts are hardly produced by the powerlooms and that the figures would change considerably if other varieties had been selected. Besides, the figures for wages are termed obsolete and would refer to a situation prevailing in the early 1970s. The examples were nevertheless the backbone of the ICMF plea to withdraw preferential treatment for the powerlooms in the decentralized sector. How successful the ICMF has been in convincing the government of its point of view may be deduced from the text of the NTP which was to follow and which showed a striking resemblance to the ICMF submissions.

The complaint of the powerloom associations that the examples are not representative has some substance. If the findings of a recent ATIRA study, taking a more balanced view of the production of cloth, had been available at that time, the textile policy might well have been different. In this study it was found that, as far as the costs of cotton cloth is concerned, the production of grey fabrics in the powerloom sector would on an average be lower by about 5 per cent as compared with the mills (ATIRA, 1985b: 104–11). But with regard to polyester blends, however, it was found that the powerlooms would have a disadvantage of some 5 per cent. This phenomenon is explained by the high cost of polyester yarn for the powerlooms. Besides, in the ICMF examples no allowance was made for the marketing disabilities of the powerloom sector as the Ashoka Mehta Committee had done.

Subcontracting

An important aspect of the complex relationship between mills and powerlooms relates to the phenomenon of subcontracting which is supposed to have taken place on a large scale and is thought to have reached a peak during the textile strike.[69] Although there is undeniably a tremendous impact of the powerlooms on the production of cloth (this sector eating into the market shares of both mills and handlooms), it is very hard to obtain accurate data regarding this sector as powerlooms have traditionally operated in an atmosphere of illegality. Figures for the production of cloth in the decentralized sector are notoriously deceptive as part of the powerloom production is counted as handloom production and because of subcontracting (Chandrasekhar, 1982; Jain, 1983, Eapen, 1984). This last aspect is of particular interest here as it is likely that the powerlooms contributed substantially to the failure of the strike. The various powerloom associations in Bhiwandi pride themselves on having been able to provide enough cloth to the mills throughout the strike period to enable them to live up to their commitments.

Subcontracting in this context relates to the situation in which a mill utilizes the advantages of the powerloom sector for (part of) the manufacture of cloth. The similarity in the process of production in mills and powerlooms made it easy to do so and the absence of labour laws, strong unions and the low wages made it attractive. The assistance of the powerlooms might be sought for the production of cloth (be it cotton, blended or synthetic) which could afterwards be processed by the mill, but also for processing cloth (dyeing, finishing, printing). Opportunism is the hallmark of the relations between mills (or any other outside financier for that matter) and powerlooms. The scale on which subcontracting actually takes and took place remains totally obscure. In times of recession the mill, agent or trader simply withdraws and leaves the producer in the powerloom sector to his own devices.

A positive aspect of this otherwise exploitative relationship can be that the producer (instructed by the principal) gets acquainted with techniques and processes which might enable him in due time to start producing independently. This, in fact, did happen in a number of cases as was claimed by representatives of several powerloom organizations. This independence must not be exaggerated, of course, as the producer will require capital and will remain dependent on raw material and marketing facilities (cf. Breman, 1980; Papola, 1981). Although subcontracting has a considerable impact on employment and income, the terms are usually such that the individual who accepts the terms offered by the trader finds himself at the losing end because the trader or employer transfers his problems and risks to the people he employs.

Women are particularly vulnerable in that respect as their dependence on (additional) income promotes a tendency to accept ever weaker positions (Bienefeld, 1981; Banerjee 1985). In her study of the position of women in the textile industry in Coimbatore, Baud concludes that subcontracting contributes to the emancipation of women and she views the growth of the powerloom sector as a positive development as one-third of the workers in this sector are women (Baud, 1984, 1985). Leaving the labour conditions aside, it is questionable whether the high participation of women in Coimbatore in employment created by way of subcontracting is indicative of the situation in the rest of India.[70]

The position of women in the mills is different and somewhat better than of women outside the organized sector although a gradual decrease in their numbers in this sector has become manifest (Kumar, 1983). Again, in the south of India they are present in larger numbers in the mills than in Bombay or Ahmedabad. They are usually employed in the reeling and cone-winding departments but they may also be employed for checking cloth or as sweepers. Nevertheless, the percentage share of women inside the mills in Tamil Nadu came down gradually from 15.4 per cent in 1960 to 7.7 per cent in 1981.[71]

According to information collected by the textile commissioner pertaining to the period 1974–81 in Bombay, women constituted 4 to 4.5 per cent of the total workforce but the real figure may be lower as an investigation carried out by the MOA in several mills showed that employment of women was only slightly over 2.1 per cent.[72]

Meanwhile, it seems next to impossible to arrive at a reasonably accurate estimate of the production of powerlooms on behalf of the mills during the strike. Reliable figures regarding the number of workers seeking employment in the powerlooms during the strike cannot be obtained either. In newspaper articles of the time one is usually informed, about thousands of workers seeking employment in the powerloom sector.[73] It must be noted here that at no point during the strike was there an acute shortage of cloth in the market which might have been followed by a subsequent rise in prices. This is only partially explained by the marketing of the stocks the mills had prior to the strike even though it is true that the stocks in the Bombay mills had been increasing in the four months preceding the strike and had reached the same level as in February 1981 (Report for the Year, 1982, MOA: 474). Other factors explaining the availability of cloth in the Bombay market throughout the strike are the gradual resumption of the production by the mills in the course of the strike and cloth coming in from elsewhere.

The importance of this last factor is difficult to judge. Although it was widely believed that the textile strike in Bombay greatly benefited the textile industry elsewhere in the country (cf. Moses 1982), there is only scanty evidence to support this contention. As far as the mill sector is concerned, the output of all types of cloth suffered a substantial setback in 1982 which would not have been so had the other mills been able to compensate for the shortfall in the Bombay production.[74] The importance of production by the powerlooms for the availability of cloth in the market is a fourth element in the explanation.

The various powerloom associations in Bhiwandi agree that the strike period was a boom period for them but they differ in the importance they attach to subcontracting. D.K. Karve, director of the Bhiwandi Textile Manufacturers' Association (BTMA), maintains that the stronger mills in particular, such as Bombay Dyeing and Khatau, were able to retain their market position due to the production of cloth in Bhiwandi and that subcontracting was restricted to synthetics (interview, 25 February 1986). The chairman of the same organization, P.W. Karwa, attributes a much greater role to subcontracting and believes that the growth of the powerlooms in Bhiwandi over the years is solely due to the system of subcontracting. He thinks that 40 per cent of the mills availed themselves of this during the strike and he adds that the other mills might have done the same but on a *benami* basis.[75] N.S. Ansari, president of the Powerloom Weavers' Association, claims that with the exception of NTC mills all mills took to subcontracting.[76]

The representatives of the millowners are more consistent in their story about subcontracting. ICMF Secretary-General Radhakrishnan claims that there was hardly any use of the powerlooms during the strike and that if mills resorted to such practices this was done essentially by persons who were only marginally interested in the textile industry, apparently referring to those millowners who either divert funds from the mills to other more profitable industries or to those who merely treat the mill as an enterprise to be drained of its profits. MOA chairman M.C. Shah too insists that only very few mills took to subcontracting but he adds the interesting detail that the MOA encouraged subcontracting during the strike to reduce losses in the mills (interview, 28 February 1986). Shah and MOA Secretary-General Vijayanagar make it a point to explain that a distinction should be made between mill *companies* giving contracts and individual mill *managers* investing money in the powerloom sector as a profitable business.[77] In this respect Vijayanagar has no difficulty in admitting that the role of the outside financier (attracted by the possibilities of tax evasion and exploitation of labour) was essential in the growth of the powerloom sector (interview, 30 January 1986).[78]

Role of the Unions

Despite its importance in terms of employment, the powerloom sector never attracted the serious attention of the trade unions. This is essentially because of the difficulties in organizing the powerloom workers although these workers are concentrated in a few centres only. The absence of strong unions plays into the hands of the employers, leaving the workers defenceless. A visit to Bhiwandi reminds one of scenes usually associated with the beginning of the Industrial

Revolution: thousands of persons sleeping in or next to numberless ramshackle sheds in which the deafening sound of the looms is heard twenty-four hours of the day, no ventilation, no proper light; children doing tedious work for long hours, dust and dirt everywhere. The situation is such that employers do not even make a pretence at hiding the total lack of proper working conditions.

In fact, the entire organization of the powerloom industry in Bhiwandi (the single largest powerloom centre in Maharashtra and even India) resembles a state of anarchy.[79] The exact number of powerlooms is unknown as is the specification of their production, the ownership of looms, the quantity of work done on behalf of the mills, the number of workers employed, the extent to which minimum wages are paid and so on. All figures relating to these aspects are based on estimates, thereby making proper planning difficult, not to speak of the problems of policy implementation. The Ashoka Mehta Committee had commented upon the intransparency of the situation in Bhiwandi way back in 1964. The committee pointed to the complex structure of ownership of looms, the differences in techniques and machinery used and the variety in products. The committee had also observed the tendency among the weavers to reduce the number of picks in order to increase the yardage production even though this meant deterioration of quality (GOI, 1964: 71).[80]

It is no surprise then that under these circumstances the trade unions active in the textile industry have never felt a strong urge to address themselves to the welfare of the powerloom workers, among whom there is hardly any degree of unionization. With few exceptions the unions prefer the easy access to the workers offered by the mills to the tiresome and unrewarding labour of organizing the workers in the powerlooms although everyone agrees that the fate of the latter is far worse and that unionization is badly needed.[81]

Datta Samant, for example, feels that it is impossible to organize the workers in powerloom centres as the workers are defenceless against the exploitative strategies of the employers (interview, 18 March 1986). One wonders what a trade union is meant for. Haribhau Naik, president of the RMMS agrees that workers in these centres ought to be organized but complains of lack of people willing to undertake this arduous task: 'You must stay with them and live with them if you want to gain their confidence' (interview,

28 May 1986). Similar views are expressed in other quarters of the trade union field, explaining the absence of trade union activity in this very important area. This neglect has serious consequences for the organization of textile labour in the long run. It enables employers to use subcontracting as an integral part of the growth strategy of their enterprises. It may become possible to pay higher wages to mill workers against an increase in productivity which in turn will lead to an ever widening gap between these workers and those in the smaller unorganized units (see Nagaraj, 1984).

Even if it is true that the living and working conditions in powerloom centres are more often than not inhuman and that the rise of this sector coincided with the strangling of the much more labour-intensive handlooms, unions did not conclude that the powerloom sector, providing employment to lakhs of workers, should be wiped out. For instance, Y. Chavan, president of the SSS (which has active unions in Bhiwandi and Ichalkaranji) feels that the unemployment resulting from the elimination of the powerlooms is unacceptable and that attention should therefore be focused on improving the living and working conditions in the powerloom centres (interview, 18 March 1986), G.V. Chitnis, secretary-general of the Mumbai Girni Kamgar Union, also prefers upgrading the looms and improvement in the labour conditions in the powerloom sector with or without the assistance of the government. Other unions suggested measures like product reservation in order to save the employment in all the sectors of the textile industry. But judging from the textile policy it appears that the government has given up trying to satisfy everyone and promoting the welfare of all sectors simultaneously. The powerlooms are going to be hurt first. The extent to which handlooms will be affected depends largely on how serious the government is in protecting the interests of the handloom weavers. If experience is anything to go by, the prospects for this category too are gloomy.

HANDLOOMS

Of all the sectors of the textile industry the handlooms have by far the greatest employment potential but just as in the case of the powerlooms much basic data are uncertain. The exact number of handlooms in India, for example, is unknown and placed anywhere between thirty and fifty lakhs.[82] A great number of them are not utilized or only utilized in certain periods. The level of productivity is very low. Almost one-third of the handlooms arc permanently idle and an estimated 50 per cent of the remaining looms are under-utilized (Doraiswami and Iyer, 1985: 93).[83] Starting from the assumption that a fully utilized loom provides work to 2.4 persons on a full-time basis or to four persons not on a full-time basis (as calculated by the ministry of commerce), it seems reasonably safe to state that some ten million people and possibly fifteen million find employment in the handloom sector.[84]

However, an analysis of the available statistical evidence by the World Bank in 1975 based on the output of handlooms and powerlooms questions this estimate. Given the all too shabby performance of the handlooms, the study concluded: 'The grave implication of these figures is that the handloom industry, described by the Task Force on Textile Industries as being second in importance to agriculture, is nothing more than a facade maintained to permit large scale evasion of excise duties on powerloom fabrics' (MOA, 1983b: 311). Whether one agrees with this conclusion or not, the threat being posed by the powerlooms to the employment potential of the handlooms is very real and explosive. Jain quotes the report of the Sivaraman Committee (1974) stating that every new powerloom renders six handlooms idle. On the basis of data collected from several sources, Jain estimates that between 1974 and 1981 some 231,000 new powerlooms were started, thereby eliminating 1,386,000 handlooms and by implication 3,326,400 jobs in the handloom sector on full-time basis or 5,544,000 job opportunities on a part-time basis (Jain, 1983). Even if one questions the findings of the Sivaraman Committee it is hard to deny that the very existence of millions of handloom weavers is threatened, particularly when one appreciates that the introduction of new powerlooms did not stop in 1981.

Under the circumstances it would have been a natural course for the government to protect the interests of the handloom weavers by strong measures and subsequent strict implementation but the government did not go far beyond paying lip-service to the handlooms in successive Five Year Plans and textile policies. This, of course, could not prevent the progressive deterioration of the position of the handlooms over the years. This process may well have received an impetus now with the NTP in which the employment potential of the handloom sector and its income generating aspects were made subservient to the production of cloth at affordable prices. In this regard the handlooms suffer from the serious handicap of a very low productivity level which largely explains why this sector could not provide sufficient cloth for the home market.

As far as the costs of production in the handloom sector are concerned, a recent ATIRA study pointed out that these are consistently higher as compared with those of mills and powerlooms for the production of yarn and fabrics most commonly produced in the mills. This was found to be true in spite of great differences in wages (the rate for handlooms put at 25 per cent of that in the mills), lower overheads and much longer working hours.[85] Over the years various measures have been suggested to improve the performance of the handlooms, such as upgradation of looms, conversion of handlooms to powerlooms, product reservation and setting up of cooperative societies.[86] On the face of it this did have some impact. Official figures do show a growth in output in the handloom sector (Table 1.13).

TABLE 1.13

Fabric Production in Various Sectors (in million metres)

Year	*Mills*	*Handlooms*	*Powerlooms*	*Total*
1978–79	4,328	2,432	3,948	10,708
1979–80	4,085	2,462	3,835	10,382
1980–81	4,168	2,680	4,140	10,998
1981–82	3,808	2,626	4,547	10,981
1982–83	3,132	2,788	4,684	10,614
1983–84*	3,515	2,994	5,255	11,764

* Estimates

Source: Doraiswamy and Iyer, 1985: 94

But in studying the figures supplied in Table 1.13 the observations which have been made in the preceding paragraph should be borne in mind. The data suggest that the handlooms increased their production by 23.1 per cent in a time span of only six years but if it were possible to correct it for the influence of the powerlooms the picture would look quite different. The output of powerlooms and handlooms has been based on the delivery of yarn to the decentralized sector by spinning and composite mills. The assumption here has always been that cone yarn is used by the powerlooms whereas hank yarn is exclusively utilized by handlooms.

However, the powerlooms increasingly started converting hank yarn into cone yarn, a point which has been acknowledged by members of the Planning Commission who estimated that as a result in 1978–79 handloom production was overstated by 500 million metres and powerloom production understated by the same quantity (Jain, 1983).[87] In fact, the output of powerlooms finds its way to the market under the names not only of mills but also as handloom production. Unfortunately, to what extent powerlooms have been selling their output as handloom production cannot be established.

The absence of reliable data regarding the size and output of the handloom sector, differences in applied technology, product specification and types of ownership seriously hampered the framing of a proper policy in the event of the government wanting to come to terms with the problems besetting the handlooms. Of late the government has realized this and decided to conduct a census of the handlooms, the results of which will be useful in answering a great number of questions. With the aid of the census data it may be possible, for example, to accurately estimate the success of product-reservation, one of the keystones in the protection of handlooms, a reservation which seems to have been observed by the other sectors (most particularly by the powerlooms) mainly in the breach. The census can also provide useful information on the number of women involved in handloom production, the importance of this activity for the family budget and the effect this has on the position of women in the family.

The census might also throw light on the importance of the controlled cloth scheme for the handloom sector, the usefulness of which has been questioned by many (Jain, 1985, Goswami, 1985). In order to help the handlooms and to ensure sufficient production of cheap cloth, the government subsidized the production of such cloth (called 'Janata cloth') by handlooms in cooperative societies. At the same time, the mills were *obliged* to produce a certain quantity of similar cloth (called 'controlled cloth') at prices determined by the government. The millowners objected to this obligation as the production of controlled cloth proved to be unprofitable.

The negative effect of controlled cloth production by the mills was already clear to the government in 1978. George Fernandes, the then minister of industry, declared that the scheme had not been successful and was actually one of the important causes of sickness of the weaker mills. This forced the government to exempt a large number of mills from producing controlled cloth with the result that the availability of this cloth dropped sharply and became 'totally inadequate to meet the requirements of the weaker sections of the population' (*Report for the Year, 1982*, MOA: 370). The government thereupon reviewed this policy. The mills were no longer forced to produce controlled cloth but were asked to pay part of the expenses of production of this cloth by the handlooms in the form of an excise duty.[88] So far the production of controlled cloth (which has now been completely shifted to the handlooms) has on the one hand not generated much income in the handloom sector and on the other relieved the mills of a burden.[89]

The attempt to organize the weavers in cooperative societies where they would benefit from marketing facilities and government subsidies for the production of Janata cloth hasn't met with success either. The management of the cooperative societies itself has run into great problems and the modernization of looms seems to bypass the ordinary weaver.[90] Whatever measures have been tried so far do not seem to have worked. The gradual hollowing out of the position of the weavers was not stopped by them but might, at best, have been slowed down.

GOVERNMENT POLICY ON MILLS, POWERLOOMS, HANDLOOMS

Two years after the textile strike, and partly in response to it, the government announced a new textile policy (henceforth: NTP) on 6 June 1985. This policy provides in several ways a clear break with the past and is bound to affect the various sectors of the textile industry considerably while chiefly promoting the interests of the mill sector. The concern for the mills is undoubtedly its most remarkable aspect and it is no wonder that the millowners hailed the NTP as the only way out of the problems. But even though the new policy benefits the mill sector as a whole, textile workers have much less reason to be happy as the NTP paves the way for full-scale modernization with accompanying loss of employment.

The timing of this change in policy particularly suited the Bombay millowners because it came soon after the disastrous textile strike which made it possible for them to rid themselves of surplus labour without having to pay the customary costs of retrenchment. The memorandum of the Indian Cotton Mills Federation (ICMF), which was written and submitted shortly before the announcement of the NTP, reads, in fact, as a blueprint for this much debated policy.[91] It is curious to see that barely three months passed between the submissions by the ICMF to the Expert Committee framing the new policy and its announcement.[92] Government offices rarely show such speed and efficiency in working on matters of such far-reaching consequences and it is understandable that this caused suspicion.

The associations of owners of powerlooms in Bhiwandi, the most important centre of powerlooms in India, are convinced that the policy was largely directed against them.[93] According to M.Y. Momin, president of the Bhiwandi Powerloom Weavers' Federation (BPWF), the federation was not even asked to offer its views on the needs of the textile industry. It must be stated here that there is no front in the powerloom sector comparable to that of the millowners in the organized sector and the government may have found it inconvenient to get in touch with the numerous interest groups operating in the powerloom sector.[94]

The effects on the powerlooms meanwhile seemed nothing short of dramatic. The powerloom associations claimed that in the months following the announcement of the NTP some 40 per cent of the looms in Bhiwandi had to close down and that further closures lay ahead.[95] To support this contention the findings of an inspection team of the office of the textile commissioner were quoted.[96] This inspection seemed to confirm the ominous predictions by the BPWF and BTMA but in November 1985 another inspection was carried out during which it was found that the situation had improved considerably. A third inspection followed in February 1986 and according to the office of the textile commissioner the situation in Bhiwandi at that time was nearing normalcy (the percentage of looms lying idle not surpassing 15 per cent).

In order to understand the changes in the policy of the government regarding the various sectors (mills, powerlooms and handlooms) of the textile industry and the importance attached to the development of cotton, essential aspects of recent policy statements highlighting the differences before and after the strike have been listed below. To be sure, this survey is not intended to suggest that the strike *caused* the changes in policy because many more factors (the chronic sickness of the textile industry in particular) influenced the birth of the NTP.

Changes in Policy Statements Regarding the Textile Industry

Powerlooms

1978	Existing unauthorized powerlooms would be officially registered but legislation would follow to stop the growth of powerlooms. Support to decentralized sector to fulfil the role assigned to it while providing maximization of employment.
1981	Growth of powerlooms would be curbed. Existing unauthorized looms would be registered. Expansion only permissible in respect of handloom co-operative societies.
1985	All powerlooms (including the unauthorized ones) to be compulsorily registered. The powerloom and organized sectors would henceforth be treated at par and compete on basis of their inherent strengths. Effective steps would be taken to stop powerlooms from encroaching upon territory reserved for handlooms.

Handlooms

1978	The promise of effective implementation of the policy of reserving certain items for production by handlooms only. Controlled cloth would ultimately be shifted to the handlooms. Mills would not be allowed to produce more than 400 million metres a year and the responsibility for this would be with the NTC.
1981	Revival of dormant looms in the handloom sector, modernization of handlooms. Maximum possible growth of handlooms to generate more employment. Reservation exclusively for handlooms to be continued. Increased share in production of controlled cloth. Efforts to improve export performance of handlooms.
1985	At end of Seventh Five Year Plan (1990) only handlooms will produce controlled cloth of which the quantum will be more than 650 million metres. Reservation of articles not only maintained but now protected by law under the Handloom Act, 1985.

	Production of blended and mixed products shall be encouraged, availability of yarn shall be ensured. More emphasis on encouragement of cooperatives and modernization of looms. Census of handlooms to follow.
Mills	
1978	No expansion permitted in the weaving capacity of mills. Balance to be maintained between the use of cotton and synthetic fibres ensuring maximum income and employment for cotton growers. No mention of closures.
1981	Restricted promotion of man-made fibres. Marginal expansion of looms in mill sector will only be permitted for purposes of export. Steps to augment production of Indian textile machinery industry in order to support modernization programme (protection of indigenous industry). Steps to ensure availability of synthetic fibres and yarn (augmented as necessary by imports). No talk of closures.
1985	Non-viable units (including those of the NTC) will be allowed to close down. Funds for rehabilitation of workers affected by retrenchment or closure will have to be created. Liberal import of machinery not manufactured in India will be permitted. Full fibre flexibility between cotton and man-made fibres or yarn. Capacity expansion of mills allowed to realize economies of scale and reduction of costs. Adequate funds to be provided for modernization of mills.
Cotton	
1978	Production of cotton would be enhanced through better yields with the aid of irrigation. Cotton growers would get a minimum price. Use of synthetics would never be allowed to be detrimental to cotton growers.
1981	Adequate availability of cotton is the *sine qua non* for the growth of the industry. Assurance of reasonable prices. Support to improvement of yields.
1985	Assured offtake of the produce of cotton growers at remunerative prices. Industry to receive adequate quantity of cotton at reasonable prices. The industry would be given full fibre flexibility as between cotton and man-made fibres/yarn.

Source: Statements on Textile Policy: August 1978, March 1981, June 1985.

From the above it appears that as compared with earlier plans the swing of advantages in the last policy went predominantly to the mill sector. Millowners had for a long time been clamouring for greater flexibility in the import and use of fibres and machinery, the possibility of closing down units, the removal of protective measures benefiting the powerloom sector but in vain. Although in 1981 the government had felt it necessary to change the 1978 policy 'in view of several drawbacks' impeding the speedy growth of the industry, the proposed changes were still miles away from what the millowners wanted.[97] A few years later the government seems to have capitulated to the demands of the millowners, acknowledging that the industry had been subjected to 'a number of controls and regulations, many of which have become irrelevant or unnecessary with the passage of time'. Sterner measures were needed as 'the present crisis of the industry is neither cyclical nor temporary, but suggests deeper structural weaknesses' (Statement on Textile Policy, June 1985).

What did these weaknesses look like? In 1981 the government aimed at six objectives. The first three related to a balanced growth of all sectors of the textile industry, increase in production of cloth of acceptable quality and maximum possible growth of handlooms. The 1978 policy had been more or less the same but in 1985 it was observed that the multiplicity of objectives had inhibited the achievement of the main task of the textile industry, described as 'the need to increase the production of cloth of acceptable quality at reasonable prices to meet the clothing requirements of a growing population'. This main objective would determine the future textile policy.

Another weakness, according to the government, related to looking at the industry in terms of sectors (such as organized mills, powerlooms, handlooms) or fibre use (cotton, man-made, woollen, silk) rather than 'in terms of the stages of its manufacturing process, namely, spinning, weaving and processing'.[98] The earlier approach was held to be unfruitful as it led to the emergence of special interests on the one hand and fossilization on the other. Hence the justification for treating the powerlooms at par with the mills.

Certain things did not change, like the pious verbal support for the handloom sector because of its employment potential and the possibility of enhancing the income of handloom weavers. The very same arguments were used to promote sericulture in successive plans. Similarly, spinning in the khadi sector had been receiving 'encouragement' in the various plans because of the employment and income-generating potential in rural areas. Cotton growers were time and again assured that remunerative prices would be paid.

The powerloom associations rejected the NTP as vigorously as the millowners embraced it, but the reaction of the representatives of the handlooms was somewhat more complex as it is hard to refuse tempting promises. The Handloom (Reservation of Articles for Production) Act, 1985, an outgrowth of the new policy, was welcomed as the keystone for the success of the NTP as a whole. However, the president of the All-India Handloom Fabrics Marketing Cooperative Society, R. Ansari, warned that if the protection of handlooms was not taken seriously (as had been the case in the past) the NTP would 'ring the bell for death of this cottage industry, as by that time the mechanized sector shall completely swallow the handlooms'.[99] The society also warned that the production of controlled cloth by the handlooms would not provide relief because the wage-earning capacity in that type of production was and is far too low.

The concern of the handloom sector for the proper implementation of the NTP is understandable as for decades the real threat to the handlooms had come from the mushrooming powerlooms, a threat which had already been noticed in the 1940s (Eapen, 1984). Report after report had pointed to this development but precious little was done to curb the trend. Differences of opinion between state governments and the central government and among state governments (Maharashtra versus Tamil Nadu) surfaced in the process (ibid.). Looking at the truly explosive growth of the powerloom sector, most particularly in Maharashtra, it requires a great deal of imagination to believe that the state government seriously wanted to thwart the emerging powerloom threat. In fact, the Textile Enquiry Committee under the chairmanship of N. Kanungo noted as far back as 1952 the great problems in dismantling unauthorized looms: 'Besides this, the detection and punishment. of unauthorized weavers could not succeed because of non-cooperation of some state governments.'[100]

For its justification of the removal of capacity and fibre constraints in what was formerly called the mill sector, the NTP relied on a 'large unsatisfied demand for durable synthetic and blended fabrics at cheaper prices'. However, this hardly explains the preferential treatment given to the mills for this aspect is not central to the main objective of the policy, described as the need 'to increase the production of cloth of acceptable quality at reasonable prices to meet the clothing requirements of a growing population'. It is the people at the bottom rung of society, that is, with the lowest income, who are still predominantly dependent on cotton fabrics.

Maybe more important than this, is that the decision seems to contradict the avowed concern with the employment factor. More sophisticated cloth requires more sophisticated (usually automatic) machinery rendering numerous workers redundant. Besides, scope, direction as well as causes and effects of the changes in demand are a moot question. Goswami, for instance, feels that durability of cloth is not an important consideration for the middle and higher income groups but it is one for the lower groups. He concludes that demand for textiles is stimulated by price reductions of synthetic and blended fabrics and that this will become visible in the purchasing behaviour of even the lowest income groups (Goswami, 1985). Jain, however, believes that the NTP will ultimately speed up the production of durable cloth for the rich, adversely affecting the availability of cloth for the poor (Jain, 1985). Other authors focused on the relation between demand and technological change in the textile industry. In this context Chandrasekhar observed that the rate of change is dependent on the income distribution which at present favours a few well-placed mills. In this manner the development of an oligopolistic section within the industry is promoted but this section does not necessarily compete with the more backward mills (Chandrasekhar, 1984).

It is likely that in obliging the millowners, the government also sought to curb the smuggling of cloth. This element should not be underrated although the scale on which the smuggling is done remains unknown.[101] Cloth originating from Singapore, China and Dubai reaches the Indian market as do synthetic yarns from Korea and Taiwan. The extent to which this occurs would, according to some, largely explain why the powerlooms can produce at sharply competitive prices.[102] The bulk of the textile products finding their way into India are synthetics and blended products because import duties and taxation on such products at various stages have made it profitable to smuggle them into the country. The costs of production abroad appear to be low enough to make illegal import attractive.

One way to combat this evil consists in removing certain financial barriers for the production of yarn and cloth. In that way price differentials can be reduced, thereby effectively undermining the rationale for smuggling. The NTP holds out a promise of this: 'fiscal levies on man-made fibres/yarn, and on the intermediates used as inputs for the production of such fibres/yarn, shall be progressively reduced in such a manner as to facilitate absorption of increased domestic production'. Another aspect of smuggling relates to the practice of procuring cloth in an Indian powerloom centre, taking it to a printing house where it is provided with a well-known brand name and selling it in the market. Hundreds of such malafide printing houses are supposed to have been established in recent years.[103]

Based on experience with the powerless product reservation scheme, the limited scope of the controlled cloth scheme (affecting only 10 per cent of the handloom weavers, namely those working for cooperatives) and the poor earnings in this scheme for the weavers concerned, Jain predicts the end of the handloom industry altogether (Jain 1983; 1985). According to him, the facilities given to the mills in 1985 will lead to rapid modernization and increased production of cloth by the mills which in turn will lead to a greater market share, thereby eliminating the already battered handlooms. Jain fears that the transfer of production of controlled cloth to the handlooms will only accelerate their end given its poor remuneration. The future for the handlooms is certainly bleak but serious implementation of protection of handlooms might delay the process of withering away and maintain an important source of employment.

NOTES

1. The names of these islands have been preserved in the names of the corresponding quarters of the city: Matunga, Mahim, Worli, Parel, Mazagaon, Colaba (Colaba and Smaller Colaba). Reclamation of land connected the islands in the form of a peninsula, a process that was completed by 1838.
2. See R.E. Enthoven, *The Tribes and Castes of Bombay*, vols 1 and 111 (Enthoven, 1975); I. Karve (1975: 9–40).

3. GOM, 1972, 157–60.
4. For a history of life and times of Shivaji, see S. Sen, 1928; G.S. Sardesai, 1949; J. Sarkar, 1973; S.M. Pagadi, 1974; M.G. Ranade, 1974; James Grant Duff, 1986.
5. V.D. Divekar, 1982: 427–43.
6. In the last century, but possibly even long before that, Bombay was the main centre of activity for the Parsis as appears from subsequent census data showing that a majority of all Indian Parsis settled down in the city. Of all Indian Parsis in 1961, more than 77 per cent lived in Maharashtra and practically all of them in Bombay (Kulke, 1978: 39). Looking at a division of the population according to religion in the same year, Parsis appeared to be by far the most urbanized community (94 per cent), followed by Jains (54 per cent), Muslims (27 per cent) and Christians (23 per cent). Kulke points to a remarkable decrease in the number of Parsis living outside Bombay after 1951, which he attributes to 'their uncertainty and apprehensions about the future, which arose after the withdrawal of British rule that had been so favourable for them' (ibid.). He also draws attention to the unprecedented decline in the Parsi population from the beginning of this century.
7. There is a similarity here in the development of Bombay as a centre of industry and Ahmedabad, where a small group of families controlled banks and trade. This group quickly grasped the opportunities offered by the cotton trade and industry and established the first textile mills (R.K. Ray, 1982).
8. As far as Hindu employers are concerned, Jain found that they did not just prefer to appoint Hindus but, more specifically, they tended to favour members of their own caste (Jain, 1971: 98). Nepotism was found to be much more rampant in the private sector than in the public sector where appropriate education and work experience are far more important. Jain concludes that the type of management available in a country is dependent not just on the stage of the economy but also on factors like 'the extent of widespread education, the prevalent communal climate in the larger society, and the general maturity in the economic thinking of the entrepreneurial groups' (Jain, 1971: 180).
9. For a description of the early millowners, see also the publication of the MOA on the occasion of the centenary of the organization: MOA, *Hundred Years of Dedicated Service 1875–1975* (Bombay, 1975).
10. Morris distinguishes three phases in the development of the industry. In the first period (1855–90) there was a rapid growth in the number of textile mills and a concentration on yarn production. In the second phase (1890–1922), the entry of new units slowed down and the

emphasis shifted to weaving as well as to production of finer counts. In the third period (1923–47) followed a reduction in the number of mills, retrenchment but also an improvement in applied technology and organization (Morris, 1965: 27).

11. That this is not merely something from the past was pointed out by a middle-level executive from Bombay Dyeing who had been fired in 1983 after refusing to comply any longer with malpractices indulged in by the management (interview, 23 May 1986).
12. The system of managing agents has drawn a lot of attention and these agents are usually associated with short-sighted selfish behaviour (Cf. Morris, 1965: 34–8; Kooiman, 1978: 16–9; Newman, 1981: 33–4; D'Cunha, 1983: 94–5). In most cases the agents held a majority share at the time a mill was established and if they sold shares they took care that they didn't lose control over the mill. In the beginning they were even paid a commission on production, sometimes leading to a situation in which the mill produced stock irrespective of demand.
13. The Swadeshi movement intended to stimulate the Indian economy and industry by promoting the consumption of indigenous products and simultaneous boycott of foreign products. See 'Lokamanya Tilak' by Dhananjay Keer for an account of Tilak's life and influence on the nationalist movement (Keer, 1969). A critical assessment of the game is given by Cashman (Cashman, 1968).
14. Nijhuis points out that the use of the selfactor had certain advantages in spinning yarn of higher counts which might partly explain the British backlog. Similarly, the ordinary looms at that time could compete with automatic looms for certain varieties of cloth. This appeared to be true even recently (Kimoth and Garde, 1977).
15. After the Second World War the loomage in the UK was further reduced to 11.5 per cent of the world total in 1948 and Japan's spindleage came down drastically to 2.8 per cent of the world total. The reduction in the UK was largely the result of eliminating obsolete and idle capacity. Japan's capacity reduction in both loomage and spindleage had become necessary as Japan had faced serious marketing problems in the years preceding the war and as the Allied forces were bent on curbing Japan's export potential.
16. The following account is chiefly based on descriptions given by M.D. Morris (1965), D. Kooiman (1977, 1978, 1980), R. Newman (1981), G.K. Lieten (1982, 1984).
17. The establishment of the first Indian trade union is usually credited to B.P. Wadia who established the Madras (Textile) Labour Union on 27 April 1918. However, R.C. Saxena and S.R. Saxena mention the formation of a union among weavers in Ahmedabad in 1917 and

the Aluminium Labour Union in Madras in the same year (Saxena, 1984, 127).

18. In spite of it many negative connotations, the term 'jobber' has taken deep root in the industry and is used in all official agreements. Cf. *Handbook of Service Conditions of Operatives and Clerks in the Bombay Cotton Textile Industry* (MOA, 1980).
19. The strong impact of technological changes on the status of the *mistri* or jobber has been ably argued by Sheth. He described attempts by the management of a mill (presumably in Ahmedabad) to improve the status of jobbers, efforts which failed to produce results. Sheth states three basic causes for failure: (a) the tendency of *mistri*s to get unionized, (b) the appointment of formally trained technicians above the rank of *mistri* and, c) the language of modern management becoming increasingly incomprehensible to the *mistri*s (Sheth, 1972).
20. The principal objects of the scheme were: '(1) To regulate recruitment of labour with a view to avoiding wastage of manpower; (2) to increase efficiency and production by reducing labour turnover; (3) to reduce the waiting period of unemployed textile workers; (4) to eliminate bribery, corruption and favouritism in the recruitment of textile workers; (5) to encourage the systematic training of textile workers with a view to ensuring a steady supply of efficient workers' (*Report of the Badli Labour Inquiry Committee, Cotton Textile Industry–1967* (GOM, 1968: 15).
21. The sectional offices are at Naigaum, Worli, Kalachowki and Delisle Road.
22. The report observes: 'The Director pointed out that at times threats were given by the workers to the staff of the Decasualization Offices to recommend certain persons and in the event such persons were not recommended their life would be in danger and if they recommended the persons suggested, the staff would get gratification in terms of money. But such instances were few' (GOM, 1968: 18).
23. During the research, a labour officer of Raghuvanshi Mills mentioned pressure to make a worker permanent, irrespective of his achievements and of seniority, as one of the causes for the strike (interview, 8 February 1986).
24. The Government of India has repeatedly acknowledged this fact in subsequent statements on textile policy, pointing at its employment potential, the fact that the industry caters to one of the basic needs of the people and—more recently—its contribution to exports (Cf. *Statement on Textile Policy*, 1978 (reprinted in MOA, 1983b: 369–74), *Statement on Textile Policy*, 1981, 1985 (GOI, 1985).
25. GOI, 1981: 289.

26. *Directory and Yearbook 1982* (*Times of India*), 178.
27. GOI, 1981: 289.
28. Having observed that in the cotton textile industry 54 per cent of net value is distributed as wages against 14.5 per cent in chemicals, the memorandum states: 'If, therefore, the wages of textile workmen are to be equated to those of the workmen of chemicals and engineering units, which would mean almost the doubling of present wages, then the wage burden on the industry will go beyond the entire availability of net value added' (MOA, 1983b, 219).
29. See for example, the MOA publication on the eve of the strike: 'Textile strike in seven mills for higher bonus and threatened general strike for higher wages and fringe benefits—Is there any justification?', *Financial Express*, 15 January 1982. The point was reiterated in a discussion with the secretary-general of the MOA (interview, 28 January 1986).
30. Supplementary Memorandum submitted by the MOA on 24 January 1983.
31. Of the total value of all commodities exported, the cotton textile contribution was 13 per cent in 1981, 11.3 per cent in 1982, 10.8 per cent in 1983, 11.5 per cent in 1984 and 13 per cent in 1985 (see ICMF Reports for the years 1981–85).
32. Figure obtained from Draft Annual Report 1987–88 kindly made available by the ICMF.
33. The relevant ICMF view states: 'We are no longer in a position to clutch to the pretext that India's exports are suffering on account of the restraint-levels. If we fail now to perform, we shall have to blame ourselves' (ICMF, 1983: 51).
34. ICMF, 1988b.
35. MOA, 1984: 75.
36. ICMF, 1985a: 56.
37. ICMF, 1988b.
38. In his speech to the Annual General Meeting of the Texprocil in December 1983, the chairman, R.S. Mehra, held the strike responsible for problems in exporting textiles to the USSR, the most important buyer of mill-made and powerloom-made cotton textiles. He added that the situation would have been worse if the exporters hadn't switched to mills outside Bombay (MOA, 1984: 70). See also yearly reports by MOA and ICMF.
39. In the years 1982, 1983 and 1984, the USA imported clothing worth 8.2 billion dollars, 10.4 billion dollars and 14.6 billion dollars respectively. The imports of the EEC in the same period declined.
40. The Italian net trade in textiles and clothing kept growing from the early 1980s, reaching a value of 6.3 billion dollars in 1984 (International

Trade 1984/85, GATT). After a setback in 1982, the exports of Japan for both clothing and textiles grew significantly (most of the clothing exports going to the USA). The average net trade in textiles and clothing for Japan hovered around 2.6 billion dollars in the period 1981–84.

41. Hong Kong too benefited greatly from a remarkable improvement in clothing exports to the USA as did the Republic of Korea. However, the strong export performance in clothing shown by Hong Kong since the beginning of the 1980s has to be weighed against its enormous imports of textiles in the same period, bringing its net trade to 1.44 billion dollars on an average in the period 1981–84 as against 5.84 billion for Korea and 4.43 billion for Taiwan (see International Trade 1984/85, GATT, Geneva 1985: Table A 18).
42. See 'Coming Apart at the Seams', *Far Eastern Economic Review*, 19 March 1982; 'Tough Talking Ahead', *Far Eastern Economic Review*, 28 May 1982.
43. Categories of cloth prior to 1976: Coarse (average count below 17s), Medium B (average count between 17s and 26s), Medium A (average count between 26s and 35s), Fine (average count between 35s and 48s), Superfine (average above 48s). From 1976 onwards, Medium A has been extended to 4 IS, Fine ranges between 41s and 61s and Superfine is above 61s.
44. ICMF, 1985a: 56.
45. ICMF, 1984a: 78.
46. Chandrasekhar started from the assumption that within the decentralized sector only viscose fibres were used for pure and blended products whereas the mills used synthetic fibres for all man-made fabrics.
47. The average cotton yield per hectare in India was 144 kg in 1984. Within the country the same widely differing levels of productivity are found as in the comparison between countries. The three states with the largest area under cotton in 1983–84 in per centages of the total area under cotton were Maharashtra (34 per cent), Gujarat (18 per cent) and Karnataka (11.5 per cent). The highest yield per hectare, however, was found in Andhra Pradesh (346 kg), Tamil Nadu (255 kg) and Haryana (238 kg). Due to the differences in cotton acreage and yield per hectare the three states producing most of the Indian cotton were Gujarat (22 per cent), Maharashtra (18 per cent) and AP (15 per cent). From an analysis of the irrigated area under cotton it appears that usually the best producers are far ahead of Maharashtra in terms of irrigation (cf. ICMF, 1986: 56).
48. According to figures supplied by the Indian Central Cotton Committee, the predecessor of the Indian Council of Agricultural Research, two-fifths of the cotton crop (which included 45 per cent of the long and

medium staple component) was lost to Pakistan at the time of partition (Quoted by V.B. Kulkarni, 'Textile Industry: Are Cotton Exports Desirable?' *Economic Times*, 7 August 1980).

49. This handicap has not stopped the spinners from adding to the problems as appears from the following observation in the report of the World Bank: 'In addition the nominal staple lengths produced are always too short for the end uses for which they are intended. As a result gross overspinning, i.e. spinning a yarn finer than that for which a cotton is, by international standards, suitable, is the norm in India' (Quoted in MOA, 1983b: 377).

50. As far as the operation of machinery is concerned, it is amazing to see how little attention is paid to removal of short fibres accumulating in and on machinery, thereby posing serious health hazards to the workers and also affecting the quality of yarn and cloth by causing yarn breakages in spinning and loom stoppages in weaving.

51. In his study of technical change in the Indian cotton mills, Chandrasekhar sums up the characteristics of the loom at present utilized in the mill sector. It has to be understood that the shuttleless loom in this scheme would rank under automatic looms:

	Ordinary	*Semi-Automatic*	*Automatic*
Pirn change	No automatic pirn change.	No automatic pirn change.	Automatic pirn change.
Weft breakage	Automatically stops—worker mends it.	Automatically stops—worker mends it.	Automatically stops—worker mends it.
Warp breakage	Does not stop automatically. Worker stops and mends it.	Automatically stops—worker mends it	Automatically stops—worker mends it.
Number of looms per weaver	2–4	Mostly 4	12–24

Source: Chandrasekhar, 1984.

52. Goswami is of the opinion that the output of automatic looms is not very different from that of the ordinary looms but makes an exception for the very high speed looms. Quoting a study by ATIRA, Goswami also states that although a weaver should be able to handle sixteen automatic looms (against four ordinary looms), in practice this figure is just 4.3 automatic looms (against 2.6 non-automatic looms).

53. In the course of 1987 the author visited the following mills in Bombay: Century Mills, Bombay Dyeing, Shree Ram Mills, Mumbai Textile

Mills, New City of Bombay. In the carding department of Mumbai Textile Mills machines dating back to 1922 and 1924 were being used and even one machine from 1914. In the loom sheds of various mills sixty-year-old looms were being utilized. The labour conditions (space, ventilation, light, temperature) matched the obsolete machinery. Despite its reputation as a financially healthy and modern mill the labour conditions in Bombay Dyeing were not very different from those in the other mills. It must be observed, however, that even in a sophisticated textile mill like Nijverdal Ten Cate in the Netherlands troublesome aspects of the production process like the deafening noise in the loom sheds and lack of sufficient space between the machines could be noted during a visit in 1985.

54. 'The Textile Crisis', *Business India*, 15–28 February 1982.
55. See 'A Crisis of Modernisation', *Business India*, 15–28 February 1982.
56. The World Bank concluded that as far as spinning is concerned it would be sensible to instal high productivity modern machinery in large mills with a corresponding reduction of the work force but the same was not true for the other phases of the production process: 'In weaving, however, there is some scope for the use of very labour intensive handlooms and the main channel of production should continue to be based on relatively labour intensive use of non-automatic powerlooms. Labour-saving automatic looms are needed only to meet quality requirements for higher grade fabrics. In finishing, too, continued use of labour intensive methods can be justified for most processes and fabrics' (quoted in MOA, 1983b: 380).
57. In fact, Mohota reduces the whole question of sickness of the industry to a problem of adequate cotton supply and he finds ample evidence for this contention in the period 1950–72. The events related to the 1972 bumper crop neatly confirmed his idea about cotton supply as the crux of the matter but he totally neglects the marketing problems following a steep rise in production (stagnation of demand). It is the most serious shortcoming of this otherwise interesting study.
58. See 'A Crisis of Modernisation', *Business India*, 15–28 February 1982.
59. Computed from HOSOCTI, ICMF, 1988a: 24–26.
60. Even a mill with a record of poor performance in the past like the New City of Bombay is at present predominantly producing for export. According to General Manager R.S. Chankum, not less than 65 per cent of the present production was meant for export (interview, 26 May 1987).
61. See also A.V. Desai, 'Technology and Market Structure, under Government Regulation: A Case Study of Indian Textile Industry' (Desai, 1983).

62. The term 'powerloom' refers to a mechanical loom used for weaving cloth and similar to the looms used by the mills. In fact, the looms often originate from there. If a mill wanted to modernize the old machinery was discarded and this equipment found a new destination in the so-called 'powerloom sector'. The difference between the mills and the powerlooms in regard to the production of cloth is more one of scale than of kind.
63. The Bhiwandi Textile Manufacturers' Association (BTMA) stated in a letter to the minister of textiles (deploring the effect of the NTP on the powerlooms) that of the total cloth production in the country, 40 per cent has to be attributed to the mills, 30 per cent to the powerlooms and 30 per cent to the handlooms (Letter d. 18 June 1985). However, the Bhiwandi Powerloom Weavers' Federation (BPWF) to which the BTMA affiliates, stated in a Memorandum addressed to the PM that the figure for the mills is 30 per cent, for the powerlooms 45 per cent and for the handlooms 25 per cent.
64. Chandrasekhar, 'Growth of Decentralised Sector', *Economic Times*, 9 and 10 August 1982.
65. See, for example, Radha Iyer, 'Where Small Is Not Beautiful', *Business Standard*, 8 August 1982.
66. GOI, 1964: 77–79.
67. What the powerloom association conveniently forgot to mention is that the Mehta Committee also stressed that the structure within the powerloom sector was quite complicated, pushing up or reducing the costs from unit to unit: 'This makes it difficult to determine a centralized pattern which could be applied uniformly to the powerloom establishments according to the different size groups' (*Powerloom Enquiry Committee Report* (1964), 78).
68. ATIRA works in close cooperation with other textile research centres like the Bombay Textile Research Association (BTRA), its southern counterpart, SITRA and its northern counterpart, NITRA. The first three institutes together submitted a confidential report to the ministry of textiles, Government of India, called 'The Textile Industry in India: A Review of Policy', prior to the announcement of the NTP in 1985. Afterwards they also reviewed this policy.
69. In his analysis of subcontracting in Indian manufacturing industries Nagaraj distinguishes four types of subcontracting but all of these share the characteristic of an unequal economic bargaining strength between the parent firm and the subcontractor. For the variant of shifting of complete segments of the production process to a contractor (as in the relation between mills and powerlooms) he reserves the term 'activity subcontracting' (Nagaraj, 1984).

70. M.Y. Momin, president of the Bhiwandi Powerloom Weavers' Federation, estimated that not more than 5 per cent of the workers in Bhiwandi are women (interview, 24 February 1986). His impression was confirmed by P.W. Karwa, chairman of the Bhiwandi Textile Manufacturers' Association, who added that there is only work for women at the preparatory stage, that is, in making the weft and the warp.
71. Letter of Southern India Millowners' Association to ICMF, d. 20 June 1983.
72. Figures obtained from ICMF files. In 1968 the Badli Labour Inquiry Committee published data obtained from the millowners from which it appears that the number of women employed in the Bombay textile industry declined gradually over the years: 13,438 women in 1956, 12,356 in 1957, 11,686 in 1958, 10,689 in 1959 and 9,806 in 1960 (GOM, 1968: 35). In 1967 the number had dwindled further to 8,165 women (: 4).

    In a letter to the ICMF the Madhya Pradesh Millowners' Association reported in 1983 that the number of women in the mills in the five preceding years hovered around 2.3 per cent. In a letter from the Ahmedabad Millowners' Association to the ICMF (d. 21 June 1983) it is stated that the number of women employed in the mills in Ahmedabad had been around 2,500 over the past five years.
73. D.K. Karve, director of the BTMA in Bhiwandi believes that this number never exceeded 6,000 whereas Hardikar, in the *Indian Express*, speaks of 15,000 workers going to Bhiwandi ('Powerlooms Defy Mill Strike', *Indian Express*, 23 January 1983). In the same newspaper the figure of 20,000 workers was mentioned a day earlier but nobody is able to provide convincing evidence. A surprisingly large number of workers from the research sample appeared to have worked in powerlooms in Bombay itself.
74. K. Kanoria, president of the Eastern India Textile Mills' Association declared that his region did not benefit at all from the strike (*Business Standard*, 31 August 1982). The case for powerlooms is different. From all the powerloom centres in the country, Bhiwandi is certain to have benefited most from the strike due to its proximity to Bombay. Even so it is hard to establish a causal relation as the uninterrupted growth of the powerloom sector for decades would have manifested itself also in the absence of the strike. The emergence of many new powerlooms in Gujarat in the same period has also been noted (Eapen and Nagaraj, 1983).
75. The *benami* system is very common and implies that traders (master weavers) or mill agents (this could be relatives or friends of millowners) supply the yarn from which the cloth is then woven. The weaver or

loom owner is paid a price per metre for the woven cloth. This price has been fixed in advance. If need be these agents or traders provide the capital required for expansion of looms. For a critical assessment of the position of the master weaver, see A.R. Momin, 'Tensions in an Industrial Slum', *EPW*, Feb. 1974.

76. The scope of subcontracting seems anybody's guess. Besides, figures relating to the number of mills involved in subcontracting have nothing to tell about the extent to which those mills utilized this method. Ansari admitted that it is impossible to give useful estimates as there are no records.

77. The official view of the millowners' representatives is substantially weakened if one talks to individual millowners and managers. G. Mantri, personnel manager of Standard Mills, speaks of 60 per cent of the mills indulging in subcontracting (interview, 7 February 1986). His colleague of Mafatlal, G. Joshi, agrees that many mills took to subcontracting and afterwards stamped and sold the powerloom cloth under their own brand name (interview, 19 February 1986).

78. One of the most striking examples of a textile group utilizing the advantages offered by the powerloom sector is probably that of Reliance Industries, the textile empire under the chairmanship of Dhirubhai Ambani who claims that not less than 25,000 powerloom units produce cloth for his company ('Everyone Can't Win', *Update*, 28 June 1985). Other examples are Orkay Silk Mills and Gwalior Rayon.

79. The situation in Bhiwandi is not unique although nowhere else in India is it found on such a scale. Vaidya studied the situation of powerloom workers in Ichalkaranji and came to similar findings. Due to the prevailing chaos (authorized looms co-existing with unauthorized looms in the same shed and belonging to various owners) it was not even possible for her to draw a proper sample. It turned out that 10 per cent of those employed on the looms were children below the age of fourteen (Vaidya, 1981: 23). Radha Iyer reported on the situation in the art silk industry in Bombay (*Business Standard*, 31 August 1982). More recently the South Gujarat University explored the situation in Surat at the request of the High Court and the findings are very similar to the situation in Bhiwandi ('The Sweatshops of Surat', *Business Standard*, 6 March 1985).

80. Chairman of the BTMA, P.W. Karwa, throws light on the operations within the powerlooms sector when he states that it is beyond anybody's control to supervise the production in the powerloom sector. He adds: 'Within this sector it is practice never to give the required specifications. When you say that this or that quality of controlled cloth has to be produced you will get less' (interview, 24 February 1986).

81. Momin states that in 1974 there were not more than three unions in Bhiwandi: Textile Mazdoor Sabha (the representative union recognized by the government and affiliated to the Socialist Party), Lal Bawta Powerloom Kamgar Union (CITU) and Bhiwandi Powerloom and Sizing Workers' Congress (INTUC) (Momin, 1974).
82. The dy. minister of commerce stated in the Lok Sabha on 13 August 1982 that there were 30.2 lakh handlooms in the country not counting domestic looms. The ministry of information had put the figure in 1981 at thirty-eight lakh looms out of which 12.7 lakhs were in the cooperative sector (GOI, 1981: 329). The ICMF felt in 1985 that there were thirty-five lakh handlooms (ICMF 1985b: 5) whereas R. Ansari, president of the All-India Handloom Fabrics Marketing Cooperative Society, put the figure for the same year at fifty lakhs.
83. Out of the 30.2 lakh handlooms in India claimed by the minister of commerce in 1982 more than 50 per cent were situated in three states only: Andhra Pradesh 17.5 per cent, Uttar Pradesh 16.8 per cent and Tamil Nadu 18.4 per cent. The ministry estimated that there were another eight lakh domestic looms in addition to the 30.2 lakh (MOA, 1983b: 37).
84. The ministry of commerce concluded after a comparative study in 1980 that the introduction of one powerloom implied the end of six handlooms (Jain 1983). According to the same source a handloom provides work to 2.4 persons on a full time basis whereas this figure is 2.5 for a powerloom. The powerloom associations in Bhiwandi predict that the NTP will displace twenty-five lakh powerloom workers (see Bhiwandi Powerloom Weavers' Federation 1985: Memorandum submitted to PM Rajiv Gandhi, 14 October 1985). This is certainly a gross overstatement as it would imply the total destruction of the whole powerloom sector.
85. For the study, sixteen varieties of fabrics were selected (ten cotton and six blended) evenly spread over low, medium and high counts (ATIRA, 1985: 100–19).
86. In the second Five Year Plan, the government envisaged the introduction of 35,000 powerlooms in the handloom sector, thereby promoting the emergence of a new class of entrepreneurs in this sector. Chandrasekhar claims that the major change within the handloom sector has been the growth of the number of weavers working under a master weaver at the expense of independent weavers ('Growth of Decentralized Sector', *Economic Times*, 9 August 1982). The effort to organize the weavers in cooperatives has met with partial success only, 33 per cent of the handlooms coming under the aegis of these cooperatives.

87. The conversion of hank yarn to cones in Bhiwandi was flatly denied by the chairman of the BTMA, P.W. Karwa, with the argument that this would be a lengthy process and far too cumbersome to be profitable (interview, 24 February 1986).
88. According to ICMF Secretary-General Radhakrishnan, the government annually collects in this manner about Rs 180 crores from the industry (interview, 21 February 1986).
89. Soon after the announcement of the NTP, the president of the All-India Fabrics Marketing Cooperative Society, R. Ansari, warned: 'The fact is that production of controlled cloth scheme [*sic*] with its existing wage capacity today will hardly be able to provide any relief handloom sector mainly because the wage earning capacity in this variety of production will be so low that it will be almost impossible for a weaver's family to have two meals a day,' (quoted from undated newspaper cutting found at the BUILD Documentation Centre in Bombay). As for the millowners, ICMF Secretary-General Radhakrishnan gives two reasons for their satisfaction. Firstly, it liberated them from the obligation to manufacture cloth against unremunerative prices and, secondly, the controlled cloth competed with their other output while marketing their products (interview, 21 February 1986).
90. Ansari reports on the sorry state of affairs in many State Apex Weaver Cooperative Societies where no elections have been held for years, where proper administration is completely lacking and where the weavers have no chance to voice their grievances. Ansari complains that in practically all cases the state governments have taken over these societies and made them into a political playground.
91. The groundwork for the new policy had been laid by an Expert Committee on the Textile Industry constituted with the purpose of suggesting measures for improving the production of the three sectors in the textile industry. To this committee the ICMF submitted its suggestions after having been asked to do so. In the final text there is not a place to be found where the objectives of the policy are different from those of the millowners.
92. The ICMF had earlier also conveyed its ideas to the committee (see Letter of the ICMF to the Expert Committee, 27 February 1987).
93. On 14 October 1985 the Bhiwandi Powerloom Weavers' Federation (BPWF) addressed itself through a memorandum to PM Rajiv Gandhi highlighting the problems of the industry as a result of the NTP. The BPWF is a body to which eight associations are affiliated: (1) Bhiwandi Textile Manufacturers' Association, (2) Silk and Art Silk Manufacturers' Association, (3) Thane District Industrial Cooperative Association, (4) Small Powerloom Owners' Association, (5) Bhiwandi

Weavers' Cooperative Society, (6) Sarvodaya Small Powerloom Owners' Association, (7) Powerloom Weavers Association, (8) Bhiwandi Nizampur Powerloom Owners' Association.

94. The lack of cohesion among employers in the powerloom sector was acknowledged by the director of the BTMA, D.K. Karve: 'There is no unity among the owners but when they are faced with similar problems they might come together. Now they only unite when there is calamity but afterwards everyone goes his own way' (interview, 25 February 1986).

95. The most devastating effect was supposed to have taken place in the category of the art silk looms where 75 per cent of the looms were said to have stopped production (Letter of the BTMA to Sharad Pawar, then one of Maharashtra's leading politicians, then CM, d. 23 September 1985). A few days earlier the Art Silk Weaving Industry submitted a memorandum to Minister V.P. Singh (d. 13 September 1985), impressing on him the problems of the industry.

96. A team of officials belonging to the office of the commissioner of textiles visited Bhiwandi on 16 October 1985 without giving prior notice. The team inspected at random 153 powerloom units in which in total 4,754 looms were installed. In a number of cases the doors had to be opened forcibly as the owners were absent. It appeared that 38 per cent of the looms were lying idle. It was found that this was more so in the case of cotton looms (40 per cent of all cotton looms) than for art silk (30 per cent of all art silk looms). It is interesting to note that the team also found many unlicensed looms and that the owners of a great number of looms were virtually unknown. Source: Information obtained from the office of the commissioner of textiles.

97. The government dismissed the earlier policy stating that: 'The policy did not take a longer-term view of the need of the industry as also the changing pattern of demand in domestic as well as international markets' (Statement on Textile Policy by the minister of commerce, 9 March 1981).

98. This theme had earlier been raised by the former MOA chairman Kantikumar Podar in 1980: 'We should start thinking not in terms of sectors but of the entire industry' (*Financial Express*, 22 and 23 May 1980). Podar suggested that the organized sector should be given the task of reorganizing production and marketing in the decentralized sector.

99. A study in May 1985 by Arti Kaul revealed that not a single handloom or powerloom weaver was aware of the existence of the scheme of product reservation (Quoted in 'Textile Policy: At Millowners' Interest?', *Background Papers,* no. 3, 1985, BUILD). A study group

of the ministry of commerce reported in 1981 a total apathy to enforcement of the reservation scheme (ibid.).

100. Quoted by R.D. Mohota (Mohota, 1976: 163).
101. R.N. Joshi, general manager of Shree Ram Mills, estimated that cloth worth about Rs 3,000 crores is annually smuggled into the country (interview, 24 January 1987). L.C. Jain gives a figure of Rs 2,000 crores per annum ('Textile Policy, 1985', *Economic Times*, 26 and 27 September 1985). Praful Bidwai believes that 600 to 800 million metres of synthetic fabrics are annually smuggled into the country ('From Riches To Rags', *TOI,* 19 and 20 March 1984). Iyer and Narasimham mentioned the possibility of 1,000 million metres coming into the country every year (Iyer and Narasimham, 1985).
102. 'From Riches To Rags', P. Bidwai, *Times of India*, 19 and 20 March 1984.
103. *Indian Express*, 28 July 1984.

Chapter Two

THE STRIKE

PRELUDE TO THE STRIKE

Post-war History of Unions in the Textile Industry

Performance of the RMMS: The textile strike that rocked the trade union world in the 1980s was for the workers the outcome of pent-up frustrations over a number of years. Although it is easy to pinpoint the date on which the strike began and to cite its immediate cause, it is impossible to give the date of origin of the many frustrations underlying it. Labour struggles are usually the result of conditions prevailing long before the actual stoppage of work, outbreak of a strike or any other demonstration of dissatisfaction of workers with the circumstances under which they have to toil, and the textile strike is an excellent example of that.

The performance of the RMMS has been mentioned time and again as one of the root causes of the strike. The RMMS is the sole representative of the textile workers under the Bombay Industrial

Relations Act (BIR Act), an Act dating back to 1946 and replacing the Bombay Industrial Disputes Act, 1938 for the textile industry.[1] The object of this piece of hotly debated legislation was the regulation of the relations of employers and employees and the provision of rules for the settlement of industrial disputes. Immediately after the Second World War the Congress was politically all-powerful. The popularity enjoyed by the Congress crossed barriers of caste and class and emanated from its continued struggle for freedom during the war (the Quit India Movement, 1942). The communists, on the other hand, had lost their hold over labour because of their vacillating stand during the war.

The picture of the trade union scene during and shortly after the war is confused.[2] Due to mergers in the years prior to the outbreak of the Second World War, the AITUC was the most important trade union federation in 1940. The Red Trade Union Congress, a break-away group of the AITUC, had returned to the parent organization in 1935 and the National Trade Union Federation (founded after the reformists walked out of the AITUC in 1929) returned to its fold in 1940. However, the war itself put the AITUC in a quandary.[3] Broadly speaking, there were three groups at that time in the AITUC whose ideas could not be reconciled. One group, the nationalists, opposed war efforts on the ground that it would be meaningless to fight for freedom in Europe without a guarantee that India would become independent after the war was over. Another group, under the leadership of M.N. Roy, wished to support the war against fascist Germany, walked out of the AITUC and founded the Indian Federation of Labour (IFL) in 1941. This organization rapidly got government recognition as the representative of Indian workers. The third current consisted of communists who were averse to the war efforts as they saw no point in weakening the Indian position by strengthening the hands of the imperialists. Their attitude changed, however, the day Soviet Russia and the Allied Forces joined hands in their fight against the Axis Powers.[4]

Although the AITUC and IFL were practically of equal strength in 1941, the British-favoured IFL had moved far ahead by 1943. The AITUC remained a house divided. The communists' opposition to Great Britain resulted in many communists being jailed. But the picture began to change when Soviet Russia became involved in the war and Mahatma Gandhi started the Quit India Movement, because then the British thought it wiser to release the communists and arrest the nationalists instead. With the nationalist leaders in jail the communists now got ample opportunity to capture the AITUC. Their power increased when the recognition of the IFL was withdrawn after the war and given to the AITUC. The Congress naturally didn't feel happy about the communist takeover of the AITUC and soon felt the need to have its own trade union wing, resulting in the establishment of the Indian National Trade Union Congress (INTUC) in May 1947.

The problems did not come to an end here as disgruntled socialists in the AITUC left the organization to launch the Hind Mazdoor Panchayat in December 1948, which later merged with the remnants of the IFL to form the Hind Mazdoor Sabha (HMS). This merger had hardly taken place when radicals in the new organization resented its moderate philosophy and decided to quit. This again led to the establishment of the United Trade Union Congress (UTUC) in April 1949. Divisions within the trade union movement continued in the 1950s whereas trade unionism as a whole experienced a boom period.[5]

As this is not the place to write a history of the various branches of the trade union movement it may suffice to say that the post-war fissures in the trade union movement became permanent in the 1950s and cooperation between rival unions and federations was only possible temporarily and on local issues. To this it may be added that splits in any major political party since that time found expression in a corresponding split within the trade union movement which speaks volumes about the way political parties and trade unions are interlinked. Having said this, it is time to return to the events shaping the history of the RMMS.[6]

As stated before, the stand taken by the communists during the war cost them dearly. They lost the confidence of those workers who were disturbed by their attitude to the war, many of whom were more attracted by promises held out by the Congress. Soon after the war, Congress activists constituted the RMMS which claimed a membership of 32,000 in 1947 against 39,500 claimed by the communists (Morris, 1955). In the same year the communists, backed by the socialist Mill Mazdoor Sabha (MMS) conducted a nearly total one-day strike but the government was bent on giving the RMMS the status of representative union under the BIR Act. Morris observes that no election was held to determine the representative union and he concludes that the representative status of the Sangh is a 'legal fiction' (ibid.). Having achieved this status, the RMMS became nevertheless, the sole bargaining agent for the workers, a position the Sangh has held till today despite several attempts to topple it.

The RMMS had been preceded by the Rastriya Girni Kamgar Sangh, which was founded in 1939 by Congress workers who had received training in the Textile Labour Association (Ahmedabad) and was wholly based on Gandhian principles. G.D. Ambekar, one of these early activists, chose the textile industry in Bombay as his field of work and became the main architect of the RMMS. Although Ambekar himself came to be regarded as a respected trade unionist, the Sangh soon lost credibility as it developed into the type of union employers call 'responsible'. The docility of the Sangh became all too clear in subsequent labour struggles which were all led by unrecognized unions whereas the Sangh confined itself to signing agreements and wage settlements. In doing so the Sangh often managed to harvest where it had not sown and to reap fruits of the pressure caused by its own disappointing performance.

Dissatisfaction with the ideology adhered to by the RMMS led at an early stage to a split in the Sangh. This had caused the foundation of the socialist-oriented MMS in the wake of a rally of textile workers in June 1947. Shortly afterwards, the MMS would be instrumental in giving birth to the Hind Mazdoor Sabha (HMS) which came under the leadership of Asoka Mehta (December 1948). The MMS has remained a strong pillar of the HMS ever since. At the time of bonus in 1950 tension built up, culminating in a massive strike under the general leadership of Asoka Mehta. This strike was called by the MMS and it lasted a full two months. It was triggered off by the demand for bonus as a matter of right for all mill workers instead of the prevailing system which made payment of bonus dependent on the profits of a mill.[7]

Prior to this strike the Industrial Court had awarded two months basic wages as bonus for 1949 but it had excluded four mills from this payment. The MMS insisted on three months' bonus for all mills. The strike, which began on 14 August 1950, faced severe state repression and had to be called off on 16 October without a new settlement. In the course of this struggle the president of the MMS, D.G. Mahajani, and the general secretary, Raja Kulkarni, were sentenced to six months of rigorous imprisonment for calling an illegal strike. There were several violent clashes during which twelve workers are said to have died and in the end the resistance was broken (Desai, 1982; Bakshi, 1987: 10).

Even though the government had clamped a ban on public meetings in the mill areas, large meetings were held in the suburbs of Bombay and addressed by people like Jayaprakash Narayan and Ram Manohar Lohia. The strong support for the strike and the MMS was in part evoked by the workers' growing conviction that Independence might have brought freedom to the country but this did not mean liberation from oppression for them. James feels that bread and butter issues were more important to the workers and that the strike had failed because it was basically intended as a show of strength for the Socialist Party rather than as an avenue for economic gain for the workers (James, 1958). The Girni Kamgar Union (GKU), the union that had played such an important role in the great strikes of the 1920s and in subsequent years, had meanwhile receded to the background. Although the GKU tried to move forward in 1950 it did not make much headway.

During this struggle the possibility was discussed of applying for the status of representative union under the BIR Act, which implied the need for derecognition of the Sangh. But after initial success this matter was not pursued tenaciously and soon the effort was abandoned. Morris states that the membership of the Sangh at that time had declined so much under the influence of the socialist and communist agitation that the registrar cancelled the representative status of the RMMS but this decision was reversed by the Industrial Court (Morris, 1955). This development shows a striking resemblance to the events during the strike in the 1980s. Several members of the Executive Committee of the MMS had opposed the idea of gaining the status of representative union on the ground that the union would lose its right to strike once it succeeded in becoming the representative union. However, since this strike the MMS and HMS insisted that a secret ballot should be adopted to decide which union has the support of the majority of the workers in an industry or enterprise.

In the years following this struggle the MMS confined itself to organizing the workers in the silk textile industry, textile processing industry and hosiery industry in which it did become the representative union under the BIR Act. In retrospect Asoka Mehta attributed the failure of this strike to his and the workers' lack of experience in dealing with such immense struggles and to the determination of the government not to give in to avoid affording the socialists' political advantage in the upcoming general elections. Not having clamoured persistently for the ouster of the Sangh he thought had been another grave mistake (Bakshi, 1987: 11).

Subsequent years showed agitation in several mills and the management of China Mills was even confronted with a strike lasting two months but none of this unrest culminated in a general strike. The issue of forming a stale on linguistic principles (that is, Maharashtra with Marathi as the binding agent), provided an opportunity for all the forces opposing the Congress to unite in the Samyukta Maharashtra Samiti. On this platform the idea was launched to try to unite the working class and this resulted in the foundation of the Mumbai Girni Kamgar Union (MGKU) in 1960.* The textile workers readily responded to this initiative and Y. Chavan, who was at the time secretary of the newly formed union, claims that within a single day one lakh workers joined the union. The MGKU conducted a fifty-day strike in support of the agitation for the formation of Maharashtra State, a confrontation during which 105 workers are thought to have died (Bakshi, 1987: 13).

In the course of this struggle a more persistent attempt was made to dislodge the RMMS and to take over the status of the representative union. The effort was backed by all leftist-oriented parties. The response was impressive but although the ouster of the RMMS as the representative union seemed imminent in the beginning (the registrar of trade unions acknowledging that the MGKU had sufficient members for the purpose), the RMMS won the battle in the end by successfully appealing in the Industrial Court against derecognition. Y. Chavan recalls that the president of the court discovered a technical flaw in the application for recognition by the MGKU (namely that the secretary-general of the new union had not been duly elected) and dismissed the case (interview, 18 March 1986).

---

* This union should not be confused with Samant's Maharashtra Girni Kamgar Union which bears the same initials.

On 1 May 1960, Maharashtra State was born and with the achievement of that goal the Samyukta Maharashtra Samiti (and the MGKU along with it) withered away. Most of the participants in this platform of the opposition withdrew and they also left the MGKU but the communists and the activists of the Lal Nishan Party remained in the union. Although the influence of the MGKU was clearly on the wane, the union was still considered to be a force to reckon with in 1962, as may be deduced from the fact that employers found it necessary to discuss labour problems with the MGKU irrespective of its lack of legal status.[8] The point is noteworthy as the employers refused to talk with Samant's unrecognized Maharashtra Girni Kamgar Union in 1982 although it was undeniable that a vast majority of the workers had rallied behind him.

Internal bickering and dissension meanwhile further damaged the image of the Sangh. In 1966 the communist leader S.A. Dange, who shot into prominence in the course of the strikes in the 1920s, once again gave a strike call only to withdraw the ensuing strike after twelve days when the chief minister assured him that the workers would be given 'fair treatment' by the millowners. Nothing much came out of this. Basic issues concerning wages, permanency of *badli*s and recognition remained unresolved. New eruptions of general labour unrest were to follow in 1971, 1974 and 1979. The earlier observed post-war disintegration of the communists in the political field was also to be noted in the textile industry where the CITU (which sprang from a rift in the ranks of the AITUC in 1970) launched a new radical union styled the Lal Bawta Girni Kamgar Union (LBGKU). Although this new union claimed a membership of about 11,000 workers in 1981, the union never commanded much influence and was reduced to insignificance in the course of the strike of 1982. Thereafter it could lay claim to a following of no more than 1,000 workers.[9] Over the years the number of workers' unions in the textile industry multiplied (see also Table 2.1) but in spite of that—and to some extent because of that—effective power remained in the hands of the Sangh, much to the chagrin of the workers.[10]

In 1970 the Sangh signed an agreement in which a moderate rise in wages was linked with increased productivity and rationalization. Shortly afterwards a Bonus Bill was introduced in Parliament making 8.33 per cent the statutory minimum bonus. The mills were then not faring badly and by the end of the year some declared an even higher bonus than that proposed in the Bill but in spite of that the Sangh seemed willing to sign a bonus agreement with the employers allowing for a mere 4 per cent bonus.[11] This naturally provoked a strong reaction, leading to spontaneous but organized action in 1971. In each mill a committee was formed comprising persons of different political affiliations but united in their opposition to the Sangh.

TABLE 2.1

Unions Active in the Bombay Textile Industry

Girni Kamgar Sabha (GKS): Founded by the Janata Party during the Emergency (June 1975–January 1977). The union is affiliated to the Bharatiya Mazdoor Sabha.
Girni Kamgar Sena (GKS): Affiliated to the Shiv Sena, a regionally based communal party active in the years before the strike of 1982/3.
Kapad Kamgar Sanghatana (KKS): Affiliate of the Sarva Shramik Sangh, the trade union wing of the regionally based communist Lal Nishan Party (LNP).
Lal Bawta Girni Kamgar Union (LBGKU): Communist union affiliated to the CITU, the trade union wing of the Communist Party of India (Marxist).
Maharashtra Girni Kamgar Union (MGKU): Founded on the eve of the strike by Datta Samant who launched in 1982 the independent Kamgar Aghadi Party. The MGKU and Kamgar Aghadi have the same leader and therefore, there is strong mutual support.
Mumbai Girni Kamgar Union (MGKU): Affiliates to the AITUC, the trade union wing of the Communist Party of India (CPI). The union was preceded by the Girni Karngar Union which was registered in May 1928.
Mill Mazdoor Sabha (MMS): Socialist union (founded in June 1947 and affiliated to the Hind Mazdoor Sabha. The MMS is today the representative union in the silk, hosiery and processing industries.
Rashtriya Mill Mazdoor Sangh: Representative union in the cotton-textile industry founded in 1947. The union affiliates to the INTUC, the trade union wing of the Congress Party. The union was preceded by the Rashtriya Girni Kamgar Sangh founded in 1939.

However, the resistance met with strong repression and soon collapsed, partly due to the fact that an important section of the workers found a compulsory bonus of 8.33 per cent sufficient.[12] Apart from that, the strike was undermined by a rapprochement between the Sangh and a splinter section under the leadership of Vasantrao Hoshing (later president of the RMMS) who had quit the post of secretary-general of the Sangh in 1966 after a disagreement with the leadership. The remaining groups supporting the strike did not succeed in utilizing the strong anti-Sangh sentiments (in many mills RMMS activists had been chased away and more than 400 were reported to have been injured) and ended up fighting each other.[13]

The next battle was fought in 1974 when the textile industry was paralysed for a period of forty-two days (from December 1973 till February 1974). In July 1973, the RMMS and MOA agreed on the introduction of a seven-days-a-week working system which robbed the workers of their common weekly holiday and gave them a weekly holiday by rotation instead. The reason for this change had been the millowners' wish to increase production.[14] The workers felt let down by the Sangh and showed their displeasure by token strikes on two Sundays, a call for which had been given by the MGKU, but in the end the seven-day working system was introduced.[15] The workers also had serious grievances of long standing regarding workloads, wages and Dearness Allowance. Encouraged by the success of the token strikes, the MGKU gave a call for a general strike during a huge meeting on 15 August 1973. In this way the MGKU wanted, inter alia, to press for higher wages, a weekly holiday and job reservation for women.[16]

Dissatisfaction surfaced once again in December when a strike call was given for the 30th of that month but on 28 December the RMMS reached an agreement with the MOA providing for a complicated settlement resulting in a wage increase for the workers of Rs 17 to Rs 53, depending on their income. This could not stop the agitation and under the leadership of the communist leader S.A. Dange the strike started on 30 December. The struggle was continued in January 1974 with morchas* and a gherao† of the Vidhan Sabha

---

* Marathi term for demonstrations or protest marches commonly used instead of the English terms.

† Derived from the Hindi verb 'gherna' (in Marathi 'gherne') which means to encircle, to besiege, to blockade. 'Gherao' is the imperative and denotes the encircling of a person or an object to increase pressure. The strategy is often resorted to by workers and by political activists during labour disputes.

(Legislative Assembly) in the city. The determination of the workers was kept alive by the high rate of inflation at that time which called for a substantial wage increase. Finally, a second agreement was hammered out providing for a moderate additional DA and annual increments of Rs 4 for a period of three years. With this poor result (which greatly disappointed many workers) Dange called off the strike. The seven-day week was left untouched and, as during the earlier agitation, scores of activists were dismissed, their places being taken by RMMS sympathizers.[17]

The last big confrontation between the workers and the millowners prior to the strike in the 1980s was in 1979, two years after the Janata Party had come to power and the Emergency had been lifted. During the Emergency, the Janata Party supported the launching of the Girni Kamgar Sabha (GKS), an affiliate to the HMS, which attempted to replace the Sangh as the representative union. Sensing the dissatisfaction among the workers, the GKS and the MGKU joined hands and gave a strike call for 30 November. Meanwhile, negotiations between the Sangh and the MOA were in progress and when a confrontation seemed inevitable government intervention was sought. The agitation ended the day before the strike was supposed to start when CM Sharad Pawar and the then Union minister for industries, George Fernandes, at the request of the Sangh and the MOA settled the strike with an offer of an ad hoc wage increase of Rs 45 per month and an increment of Rs 6 per month for a period of five years from January 1980 onwards (Fernandes–Pawar Pact).[18]

Counting on important changes in the labour laws which seemed in the offing, the GKS failed to devote its energy to organizing the workers on a mill-to-mill basis and omitted to take advantage of the political climate of the time. The other unions did not do so either. This settlement too, left a large section of the workers dissatisfied and increased the feeling that nothing was to be gained by involving politicians. With the disintegration of the Janata, following the return to power of Indira Gandhi, the GKS too was reduced to insignificance and although the union was still in existence at the end of 1981 it was not in a position to play an important role in the strike that was to follow.

It has been shown that workers were far from happy with the presence and performance of the RMMS in the textile industry but was the opposite true for the millowners? Going by the statements of their official representatives, the secretaries-general of the MOA and ICMF, they had nothing to complain about. The Sangh behaved 'responsibly', was well aware of the problems and exigencies of the industry and was prepared to fight it out in court (and abide by its decision) in case of differences of opinion. However, while acknowledging the advantages of an agreeable Sangh to the textile industry, managers and millowners were aware of the shortcomings of the union and some are prepared to state them.[19]

While talking about the causes of the strike G. Mantri, personnel manager of Standard Mills, says, for example: 'What gave Samant the weapon? The weapon was generally prevailing discontent amongst the working class about the activists of the RMMS' (interview, 7 February 1986). His colleague from Shree Ram mills, S.T. Puntambekar, points at the elections within the Sangh: 'Instead of having regular elections for the office bearers, the same office bearers continued to be in office for three, four years without elections. So naturally the workers were frustrated. That is partly due to the fact that the government was always backing the RMMS. The government didn't point out to the RMMS leaders that they should have regular elections' (interview, 5 February 1986).

Labour Officer K.S. Dave from Raghuvanshi Mills mentions favouritism practised by the Sangh at times of recruitment as one of the causes of dissatisfaction: 'If I am pressurized by the union to make a worker permanent irrespective of his achievements and seniority then others will suffer and be dissatisfied' (interview, 8 February 1986). This aspect of Sangh behaviour is confirmed by MOA-chairman M.C. Shah: 'Certain workers had problems because those that helped them to get the job were taking money from them.' According to him, representatives of the Sangh, the official Union, were collecting a percentage from the bonus on the adjustment of *badli*s and on provision of employment. That was the main cause of dissatisfaction and this combined well with Samant's reputation for delivering substantial wage hikes (interview, 28 February 1986).

Another scathing comment is made by General Manager R.N. Joshi (Shree Ram Mills): 'They [RMMS representatives] went to the worker who wanted his gratuity and told him that they were able to settle his problem fast provided they were given a cut. Similarly, they put pressure on the management saying that if this man is thrown out then he should be paid compensation and if the money came then the RMMS representative would have his share of it' (interview, 24 January 1987). As administrators of the cooperative credit societies of the mills and as members of the boards of the provident funds, Sangh representatives were no saints either: 'The RMMS was also controlling the cooperative society and used to grant loans to their own supporters for an interest of say 7 or 8 per cent. Other needy workers went to the society and had to pay fantastic rates of interest, sometimes more than 100 per cent' (ibid). Joshi states that he gathered this information from the workers when they resumed duty after the strike: 'This was my own initiative because I was very curious to know as to what made them go on such a long strike' (ibid.). He also confirms that the Sangh leaders were very close to the management, particularly to the labour officers of the mills.

This state of affairs was not restricted to the private sector; it was prevalent also in the National Textile Corporation as has been acknowledged by M.S. Divekar, director of the NTC (South Maharashtra). Divekar admits that many leaders of the Sangh were corrupt but attributes this to the inability of the top leaders to control the second rank leadership within the Sangh (interview, 9 April 1987).

The Sangh leaders themselves have little to say about this long list of accusations. RMMS president Hoshing, who was ousted during the strike, offers the following lame excuse: 'If you are in power for a long time there will always be some dissatisfaction. I had led the RMMS for a long time so naturally they blamed the leader' (interview, 20 May 1987). The secretary-general at that time, Bhai Bhosale, is more straightforward when he says: 'I don't want to say that there was nothing wrong and that we were very clean and very perfect. I also don't blame you for thinking that there was something wrong with the RMMS or with me and that the workers left the RMMS for that reason but the same person is now going to their rescue [refers to his come-back after the strike]' (interview, 30 May 1987).

The statements of managers and labour officers certainly feed the impression that the Sangh did little to make itself popular. As will be shown later, most of the complaints were also heard from workers of Finlay Mills and Bombay Dyeing. It may be concluded that the dissatisfaction among the workers was of long standing and that little wind was needed to fan the flames.

Significance of the Union Structure: It goes without saying that the achievements of the Sangh were not the same everywhere and that serious acts of corruption and abuse of power were not to be found in just any mill but the complaints are too numerous and too widespread to be discarded easily. There is no guarantee, of course, that another union in power in the textile industry would not have succumbed to the temptations and possibilities offered by the way the industry is organized. But this observation does not absolve the Sangh of responsibility. The frequent misuse of power raises the question of whether such abuse is inherent in the way the RMMS is structured and whether more democratic functioning of the union can be ensured by overhauling the system of representation. In this context it may be useful to juxtapose the union structure of the RMMS and MGKU.

It has been observed that the inner democracy of the Sangh did not and does not function properly and that this is a perennial source of discontent. It is remarkable that the unsatisfactory performance of the Sangh could continue in spite of an elaborate system of representation designed to ensure the members' voice in union matters. However, rules and regulations as laid down in the Constitution of the union are not strictly adhered to, resulting in manipulation, fraud or nepotism. Although the Constitution is certainly no model of clarity (the terms used being poorly defined and overlapping in content), it does offer a framework within which democracy could be realized.[20]

The organizational structure of the Sangh is pyramidal with the Joint Board of Representatives (JBR) as the apex body. The JBR elects office bearers like the president, vice president and secretary-general. This body also appoints members of the Advisory Committee and gives advice to the Executive Committee which manages the day-to-day affairs of the union. The JBR is composed of all the members of the various Boards of Representatives, each representing an industry (the Sangh is represented in several branches of the textile industry such as cotton, woollen, silk, hosiery, dyeing, printing and bleaching). Lastly, the Board of Representatives is composed of all the members of the Representatives' Committees consisting of persons elected by the ordinary members from each department in the mills.

The Board of Representatives is thus at the level of each separate industry (and/or mill) what the JBR is for the textile industry as a whole, and these boards have to be considered the backbone of the structure as they ultimately decide on the course of action. The size of a Representatives' Committee (whose members are also members of the Board of Representatives) is determined by the number of members in an industry (and/or mill), with the understanding that there will be one representative for every hundred members. This last condition is necessary because otherwise workers in non-cotton industries might easily be over-represented on the JBR as there are many different branches within the textile industry whereas the power of the RMMS is essentially dependent on its position in the cotton textile industry.

In order to facilitate the smooth day-to-day working of the union, an Executive Committee is formed consisting of the office bearers, honorary members and seventy-five to hundred members elected by the JBR. There is a parallel for the Executive Committee at the mill level, namely a Mill Committee constituted by all members of the Board of Representatives from a specific mill/unit. These Mill Committees function under the aegis of the Executive Committee. From the above it appears that the election of members of the Representatives Committee is crucial and also that the power one wields within the RMMS depends on the number of representatives on whom one can count. The structure itself, although unwieldy, reflects democratic thinking and offers (at least in theory) opportunities to the ordinary member to influence trade union affairs.

Compared with this elaborate system, the structure of Samant's union empire offers a study in contrast as there is a minimum of formal relationships. In all there are six main branches in which thousands of unions (Datta Samant is incapable of giving a precise figure) are incorporated. The three main branches at the time of the strike were the Maharashtra General Kamgar Union (MGKU) founded in 1975, the Maharashtra Girni Kamgar Union (MGKU) founded on the eve of the strike and the vital BEST Kamgar Union. The Maharashtra General Kamgar Union caters to capital-intensive industries like chemicals, rubber, pharmaceuticals, textile processing, food processing and so on. The Constitution of the subsequently formed Maharashtra Girni Kamgar Union is modelled after this and is the same for all practical purposes.

The most important body within Samant's trade union empire is the Managing Committee, usually presided over by Datta Samant. The powers and duties of this committee seem to combine those of the JBR and the Executive Committee of the Sangh.[21] At the shop-floor level, a worker has the opportunity of expressing his views to representatives of Samant's unions. If a problem exceeds the personal level and is of general interest and/or if demands have to be backed up with a strike, a deputation of a unit approaches Samant who is in the habit of dealing summarily with all the problems brought to his notice.[22]

It appears that the ultimate decisions are the prerogative of the leadership, that is, Datta Samant. This, of course, raises the question of what is to be done if members do not agree with the policy of the union. Here, too, there are noteworthy differences between the RMMS and the MGKU. Important in this respect is the existence or absence of the provision to remove office bearers. The Constitution of the Sangh gives the power to remove members of the Executive Committee, or any other representative, to the JBR but, unfortunately, the Constitution does not specify whether such a decision can be taken by a simple majority or not.

In the case of the MGKU we find that a member of the Managing Committee can only be removed at the annual general meeting and after three-fourths of the members so decide. This is virtually a dead right as it would usually be impossible to mobilize more than 75 per cent of the members to unseat an office bearer. The only option left to a dissatisfied member then is to quit the union, a crude notion of take it or leave it. Under these circumstances it may be very difficult for members who want to have a say in union matters to develop any lasting commitment to the union. They will remain with the union only as long as the leaders' views are not too different from their own.

On the face of it, one is obliged to believe that the chances of realizing union democracy within Samant's MGKU are no better than those within the RMMS, a fact which is also borne out by the number of meetings of the various committees deciding on the policies of the union. Samant's Managing Committee is supposed to meet only four times a year as against twelve times a year in case of the Sangh's Executive Committee and four times for the JBR. It may even seem that the Sangh offers far better prospects for running the union democratically than does the MGKU, but theory and practice do not coincide. Within the Sangh, leaders have on several occasions tried to remain in power by using means of a very dubious nature. In fact, the behaviour of Sangh representatives at all levels so undermined the image of the RMMS that the government decided to forcibly replace its leadership during the strike with the help of the INTUC. But even with a completely new leadership the difficulties continued unabated.

On the other hand, although Datta Samant has a highly personal style of operating his unions, charges of bribing worker representatives and manipulation of votes have not been raised against him. It seems that disgruntled union members in the case of Samant's unions vote with their feet. Many activists, for example, who joined the MGKU at an early stage and grew disenchanted with the possibilities of influencing Samant's ideas and policies have meanwhile dropped out. Within a different framework they might have remained within the MGKU but, of course, in that case Samant would also not have been Samant. On the strength of Samant's popularity it may be said that workers do not bother much about the formal structure of the union. This is not so surprising as the personality of the leader in Indian trade unionism has always been far more important than, for example, in the West.

However, it would be premature and unwarranted to conclude that this shows that workers are apparently not interested in union democracy. It would be more just to say that workers are only prepared to forego principles of democratic functioning as long as the man at the helm of the union embodies their aspirations and/or anger and seems capable of realizing their demands. If the union fails in that respect, the worker has no qualms in breaking his allegiance, as was demonstrated before, during and after the strike under investigation.

Inviting Data Samant

When textile workers struck work for a day in September 1981 there was no indication that this event, bearing the characteristics of a ritual, would in due time turn into the biggest strike the Indian subcontinent has ever witnessed. The term 'biggest strike' is somewhat ambiguous as criteria of scale and duration are being mixed up.[23] Although it is not too difficult to find examples of strikes lasting longer than the officially acknowledged eighteen and a half months that the textile strike lasted, or involving more people than the roughly 2.5 lakh textile workers, it will be very difficult to find examples matching both these figures simultaneously. There may not even be another parallel in world history.[24]

Just as in any other year the agitation was for a proper bonus settlement and as before the prevailing expectation was that the unrest would subside after some positive result had been achieved. The amount of bonus to be paid differed from mill to mill, changed over the years and depended, inter alia, on the formula being used to arrive at the allocable surplus. The concept of bonus too changed considerably, as is clear from the many amendments to the Bonus Act of 1965. The Payment of Bonus Ordinance, 1980 provided for a minimum of 8.33 per cent and a maximum of 20 per cent, and its special feature was that from 1980 onwards bonus could be linked with productivity instead of being based on profits.[25] Payment of bonus is a form of profit-sharing and a reward for the contribution of labour to capital. Some employers, however, have still not understood the nature of this payment.[26]

Although the Trade Union Joint Action Committee (TUJAC), a platform for unions belonging to the opposition, threatened an indefinite strike in the event of the demands not being met, no one took this very seriously. The one-day strike in September was nevertheless a great success and a noteworthy aspect was the participation of workers belonging to the Girni Kamgar Sena in spite of instructions of its leaders to the contrary (Patankar, 1983). A few weeks later the RMMS and the MOA thought that they had sorted out the problems and on 22 October they presented an agreement which would cost the private mills Rs 20.6 crores. The thirteen mills under the National Textile Corporation (NTC) declared that a bonus would be paid amounting to Rs 2.4 crores. The differences in the paying capacity of the mills had been taken into account and because of that the bonus varied between 8.33 per cent (the minimum required by law) and 17.33 per cent. Nine mills (including Standard Mills) were to pay the highest amount whereas thirty-four mills were to pay less than 12.5 per cent.

However, unlike earlier years the matter did not end here. The next day workers from fifteen mills staged a sit-down strike to protest the outcome of the negotiations. Sensing the mood of the workers, the Mumbai Girni Kamgar Union threatened an indefinite strike.[27]

This time too, the cry failed to evoke a strong response as the union no longer had a large following among the workers.* On 22 October everything at first seemed to follow the usual pattern when workers of seven mills resumed duty. Something appeared to be wrong, however, when the workers of the other mills remained on strike. The percentage of bonus to be given in these mills was as follows: Prakash Cotton Mills 8.33, Hindoostan Spinning and Weaving (four mills) 11, Shree Niwas 12 and Standard Mills 17.33.[28]

Apart from the strike for a higher bonus in these seven mills another strike was on in Madhusudan Mills, but here the agitation was for a wage hike. All in all some 34,000 workers had struck work which represented roughly 14 per cent of the workforce. Still there seemed no reason for the millowners to panic, accustomed as they were to acts of defiance on the part of the workers at bonus time. There had been resistance against the quantum of bonus before and usually such agitation subsided within days. There seemed no reason to think it would be any different this time. Yet, dramatic events lay ahead.

The very next day, 23 October, proved to be decisive for much of what was to follow. On that day striking workers, totally ignoring the presence of all established trade unions in the textile industry, decided to seek the intervention of an outsider who had fired their imagination and whose stature had risen over the years in spite of the countless attacks on his person and on the way he dealt with labour problems. In fact, what was mostly ridiculed or despised as adventurism or irresponsible trade unionism by employers and trade unionists alike, was precisely what seemed to draw workers towards him (see also Chapter 7). Hundreds of workers from Standard Mills, one of the mills that would have to pay the highest bonus, walked that day from the gates of the mill to the residence of the both famous and infamous Datta Samant (the adjective generally depending on political preferences and/or economic interests) in Ghatkopar with the demand that he should lead them in the strike.[29]

* G.V. Chitnis, secretary-general of the Mumbai Girni Kamgar Union, claimed a membership of 35,000 in 1986 (interview, 11 April 1986). But this could be a gross overstatement as practically no worker in the research sample mentioned membership of his union in 1987.

If they had thought that they would be received with open arms they were in for a rude shock. Dr Samant declined the honour and informed them that he didn't want to lead them as their industry was regulated by the BIR Act. Because of this fact it would be too difficult. Apart from that he had no wish to add to the burden of the many responsibilities he already shouldered. However, the workers, not to be easily denied, staged a dharna* at his home, staying there throughout the night in an effort to compel him to accept leadership. When Samant found that the workers were determined to face the problems ahead squarely and that the prospect of prolonged suffering in the course of a struggle would not deter them he decided to give in.

The news spread like wildfire, and when Datta Samant addressed a gate meeting at Standard Mills in the morning of 26 October, thousands of workers of the mills on strike gathered near the gate, turning the meeting into a massive rally. Interrupted by thunderous cheers of approval, Samant declared that the fight would not just be for higher bonus but also for wage increase and permanency of *badli*s. It was the first of a series of meetings and rallies which would draw ever larger audiences, of sometimes over a lakh. In the days to follow Samant's office was flooded by workers from mills where no strike was taking place and who repeated the wish of the Standard Mill workers, which was that 'Doctor' should lead them in the struggle. Datta Samant grew convinced that the request made by the Standard workers was no accident but the expression of deeply felt anger shared by all workers.

The massive support from the workers for Samant took the other unions operating in the textile industry by surprise and left them with the question of what attitude to adopt. There was only one red flag union that wasted no time in waiting for the cat to jump and this was the communist-oriented Sarva Shramik Sangh (SSS) led by the independent Lal Nishan Party, which had a union in the textile industry called the Kapad Kamgar Sanghatana. Their support to the workers' cause was immediate and unconditional, and it was the SSS again that would share the dais with Datta Samant on the eve of the strike.

---

* A dharna is a sit-down protest, resorted to for the achievement of a specific purpose, lasting hours or days as the case may be.

Hoping to recover ground that they had lost a few years earlier, the Shiv Sena-affiliated Girni Kamgar Sena (GKS) also acted with speed. Sena leader Bal Thackeray at once called for a one-day strike on the first of November, putting up a charter of demands in which a wage increase of not less than Rs 200 per month was claimed. To this was added the threat that an indefinite strike would follow if this demand was not met by mid-November. Practically all the workers participated in this strike but Thackeray's threat stood exposed as empty when the militant action ended there. The formidable response to the one-day strike was a sure indication of the workers' mood and their readiness for battle but in the process it also showed that the workers at that point had not yet developed a strong commitment to Datta Samant. This would change in the weeks ahead. There would be one more outburst of Shiv Sena militancy after about a year but the impact of that would be negligible as the party and its affiliated union had meanwhile lost all credibility among the textile workers.*

Pressurized by the textile workers of both the striking mills and those that were not on strike, Samant announced during a huge meeting on 30 October the founding of a new textile union, the Maharashtra Girni Kamgar Union (MGKU). He too threatened to start an indefinite strike from mid-November onwards if the demands he had put up were not met. These demands included a wage hike of unheard proportions (Rs 200 to Rs 400 per month, depending on occupation), permanency for *badli* workers and improvement of leave facilities, but it is particularly the first demand that is remembered by the public at large. The boldness of the demand was likely to send shivers down the spines of employers in the city and it was on this demand that the millowners would concentrate when they attacked and ridiculed Samant for his irresponsible behaviour.

Yet there was reason for the workers to believe that the demands stood a chance of being accepted. Had not the same Samant forced the management of Empire Dyeing, a processing unit, to give a wage increase of Rs 150 to Rs 200 just a few months earlier? In that mill, as in so many others in which Samant had no locus standi, the doctor had represented the workers' case even though his was not

* For a chronology of the most important events during the strike refer to Appendix B.

the representative union. In Empire Dyeing the MMS had the legal right to represent the workers.[30] Leaving aside the case of Empire Dyeing, there was no gainsaying the fact that Samant's militancy had gained workers in many industries in the Bombay–Thane belt wage hikes that were unknown to the industrial world before he appeared on the scene. These achievements had been widely publicized and discussed. In the course of the years workers in new industries, such as chemicals and electronics, had rapidly taken a lead over the textile workers with regard to wages. The RMMS was aware of the fact that textile workers compared their income with that of workers in capital-intensive industries but this did not lead to remedial action.[31]

What was true for wages was also true for bonus, and percentages of 25 or even 30 per cent bonus in these new industries were not unheard of.[32] For the mill workers there seemed to be a tempting opportunity now to make up for the backlog in one blow by combining demands for higher bonus and wage increases. Day by day tension increased and the voices demanding the immediate start of an indefinite strike became more vociferous and widespread. Comrade Dange, a prominent leader of the undisputedly greatest textile strike till that day (that is, in 1928), told the workers to prepare for a long struggle. Clouds were gathering rapidly over Bombay as the signal for the march towards the battlefield had been given and this was reflected in the newspaper articles of the time.[33]

Last Minute Attempts at Conciliation

The then CM A.R. Antulay, whose position had been under attack for several months already due to his high-handed style of governing and who was tried in court because of alleged misuse of power, tried to ease the situation. It is possible that Antulay, with this initiative, hoped to divert attention from his person to what was rapidly becoming a major labour problem. But whatever his motivation, on 10 November the state government issued a Press Note in which it announced the formation of a High Power Committee (HPC) under the chairmanship of the CM himself. This committee would consider the demands of the textile workers and try to reach an equitable solution after an impartial inquiry. The MOA welcomed the constitution of the HPC and promised its full cooperation.

The proceedings of the HPC have never been discussed although they represent a curious episode in the ensuing strike. On 2 December 1981 the names of the other members of the committee were made public. It appeared that Antulay would be assisted by two Congress MLAs, Dr S.R. Jichkar (the later minister of state for general administration and known to be sympathetic to Samant) and Bhaurao Raghoji Patil (who eventually came to oppose the Congress' inertia with regard to the strike). The government stated that the recommendations of the HPC would be made within two months.

Immediately after Antulay issued the press statement of 10 November regarding the HPC, he pleaded with Samant to postpone the indefinite strike in order to give the HPC a chance to find a solution. Samant eventually did so after learning that the centre would come to the rescue of the workers. Antulay also asked him to call off the current bonus strike in the seven mills but this Samant was not prepared to do, claiming that the workers involved were in no mood to accept that. Samant was not exaggerating for the fervour at that time was such that witnesses were inclined to believe that a revolutionary situation was rapidly building up.

There is clear evidence that the workers resented Samant's postponement of the indefinite strike and it took him a great deal of persuasion to convince them of the desirability of this strategy. Although there is no proof that Samant at that stage was bent on continuing the bonus strike in order to increase the pressure on the HPC, it is understandable that he had no objections to its continuation either and he is not known to have made sincere efforts to end it. As for the millowners, there is some evidence that already in November they had decided that whatever happened they would not give in and that they would ensure that Datta Samant found his Waterloo in the textile industry.[34]

Bhaurao Patil, one of the three members of the HPC, claims that the idea of establishing the committee had come from Rajiv Gandhi who sent an emissary to Bombay in October 1981 to ward off the imminent strike. Patil himself arranged for a meeting at the Taj Mahal Hotel where Gandhi's emissary and Datta Samant had a secret meeting. Having obtained an assurance that a substantial wage increase would follow soon, Samant, according to Patil, was ready to postpone the strike by two and a half months (interview,

11 May 1986). Datta Samant recalls having met a person from Delhi at that time and having promised to prevent the strike if interim relief was given (interview, 17 May 1986). However, Samant did not reveal this willingness to compromise to the striking workers who, instead, were told to prepare for a fight to the finish.

As soon as the millowners heard about Rajiv Gandhi's initiative to set up a committee to look into the complaints of the workers, they approached the then minister of finance, Pranab Mukherjee, with the request not to interfere in the bonus issue and to leave this to the discretion of the government of Maharashtra. However, the attitude of the millowners turned a somersault when they learnt that the recommendations of the HPC would provide for an ad hoc wage increase of Rs 150. Bhaurao Patil states that the millowners were informally briefed about this possibility and that Antulay made it very clear to them that he was determined to force such a decision on them (interview, 11 May 1986). Confronted with this unexpected danger the MOA now pleaded with Delhi to interfere, pointing out to the centre that such a wage increase would adversely affect the already weak position of the private mills and even more that of the public mills in the National Textile Corporation (NTC). The MOA thereupon wanted to disengage itself from the HPC but needed an excuse to withdraw from the proceedings of the committee. This excuse was provided by the ongoing bonus strike (ibid.).

Discussions with Datta Samant and M.C. Shah (chairman of the MOA after the strike) corroborate Patil's reading of the developments. Asked whether the MOA had anticipated Antulay's resignation and therefore, wanted to withdraw from the proceedings of the HPC, Shah replied that the MOA felt that the association might face a major problem by accepting the HPC recommendations. Asked for an explanation he added: 'Because we thought that the committee might decide to give Rs 150 to the workers and the industry couldn't afford that. You see, we were also receiving some reports of what was going on in that committee and that is why we took that decision' (interview, 28 February 1986).

According to Patil, most of the work in the HPC was done by Jichkar who collected a lot of incriminating evidence exposing the various methods by which mills in the city manipulated their accounts and administration in order to give a distorted picture of the profit and loss.[35] Unfortunately, the material collected by the HPC was never made public as the proceedings of the committee were hampered first by lack of cooperation from the parties concerned and later by the exit of CM Antulay who was forced to resign on 12 January 1982, barely a week before the commencement of the indefinite strike. The work of the HPC, therefore, ended before a report could be published. Antulay's resignation followed a verdict by the High Court which found him guilty of using cement permits in return for gifts to the Indira Gandhi Pratibha Prathisthan, a trust managed by him. The verdict triggered off a seemingly unending war in the courtroom.[36]

Immediately after its inception the HPC had approached the MOA, RMMS and MGKU for information, views or demands relating to the problem at hand but the response seems to have been discouraging. The relevant circular was issued on 6 December but Patil claims that no one took the trouble to react which, if true, effectively curbed the progress of the HPCs work. However, in an affidavit to the High Court in August 1982, Datta Samant declared that he had never obstructed the proceedings of the HPC and had also replied to the committee's questionnaire. Given the fact that the HPC seemed inclined to grant an extraordinary wage increase (something which was not hidden from Samant) there is no reason why Samant should not have cooperated. His idea of cooperation certainly differed from Patil's and although Samant had agreed to postpone the general strike, he plainly refused to call off the bonus strike. Samant's image as a militant leader left him with no choice. He was not in a position to go beyond token cooperation as he had to avoid being associated with the spineless behaviour of unions in the past (the performance of the Shiv Sena was still fresh in mind); unions that had compromised the demands of the workers for a few rupees.

Patil found that although he had warned Datta Samant several times that the MOA would dissociate itself from the HPC if the bonus strike was not withdrawn, Datta Samant refused to oblige. The MOA, indeed, lost no time and on 20 December (less than three weeks after the formal constitution of the HPC) the MOA declared that there was no point in extending cooperation to the committee as the government had not succeeded in restoring industrial peace. This step was followed a few days later by the publication of an apology of half a page in the *Times of India* under the headline 'Textile Strike: Let the Public

Know the Facts' (*Times of India*, 24 December 1981). Along with this the MOA published a letter written by Hareshchandra Maganlal (chairman of the MOA) on behalf of the association to CM Antulay. In this Maganlal draws attention to the stand adopted by the RMMS as expressed in a letter from the Sangh (d. 19 November 1981) to the CM. In that letter the RMMS underlined the necessity for the MGKU to withdraw the bonus strike as well as other agitations in order to enable the HPC to function properly. The agitations mentioned by the Sangh referred to so-called 'terrorist activities' which, according to the Sangh, were being perpetrated by the adherents of Datta Samant in order to ensure the success of the strike, an accusation which was proved to be utterly hollow in the following months. The Sangh also strongly objected to the idea that unions other than the representative union under the BIR Act would be consulted by the committee (ibid.).

The way the HPC went about its business did not please the Sangh but the union had no objection to the state government stepping in as the government, unlike the Sangh, could force the millowners to accept the terms once a decision was reached. Reflecting on the outcome of the strike Vasantrao Hoshing, president of the RMMS during the strike, says: 'The Antulay Committee was forced on them (the millowners) and they disliked it, Unfortunately, Dr Samant did not take the advantage offered by the High-power Committee otherwise the workers would have got immediate relief. We were ready to abide by the decisions of the committee. The employers said that they could not give anything but we couldn't accept that. We felt that it would be right if a third party would decide in the matter … but Dr Samant spoiled it' (interview, 20 May 1986).

It is surprising to note how positively the former president of the Sangh judges the work of the HPC. The Sangh always claims to operate within the framework of the BIR Act and had the HPC been successful this would have implied bypassing this act for the representative union is not allowed to question the terms of an agreement once they have been accepted. Secondly, a modification would clearly have been the result of the pressure put up by the MGKU which had no business under the BIR Act to represent the workers' grievances. However, the fact that no agreement would be possible without the approval of the Sangh may partly explain the appreciation for the work of the HPC. In the event of the negotiations resulting in a substantial revision of wages, the Sangh could have claimed credit for that and their continuation of power would have been assured.

Whatever the motivation of the Sangh leaders may have been, the conditions under which Samant accepted the leadership of the textile workers were such that it is fairly certain that it was beyond his power to call off the bonus strike even had he wanted to. In doing so he would have lost his hold over the workers who had flocked to him because of his reputation for militancy. Besides, even if he had been able to do so it is highly unlikely that the millowners would have accepted any substantial wage hike and this time the workers were not to be sent home with a few rupees. It should be remembered that the millowners unilaterally ended cooperation with the HPC as soon as they discovered that the recommendations, if anything, provided for a considerable wage increase. However, less than that would not have been acceptable to the workers and so it may be concluded that having come to this stage, escalation of the conflict could not be averted. The time for a settlement had obviously not arrived.

While Antulay and the ill-fated HPC were heading for an inglorious end, the atmosphere in the mill areas became ever more tense. In the first week of December PM Indira Gandhi visited Bombay and Samant tried to meet her in order to brief her on the position of the workers but he was curtly informed that he would not be received but that he was free to leave a memorandum with her secretary (*Times of India*, 4 December 1981). On 8 December Samant repeated his threat of a general strike if the intervention by the HPC did not produce any results. For this he was publicly criticized by the RMMS president, Hoshing who, anticipating the events to come, warned him that not just Samant but the millowners too were eagerly awaiting the strike (*Times of India*, 9 December 1981). At the end of the month Samant nevertheless announced a one-day warning strike on 6 January 1982. This strike, as the one on 1 November, was a complete success and once more it appeared that the Sangh had no control whatsoever over the workers as the plea to ignore the strike call was heeded by none except some staunch RMMS supporters.

On 10 January 1982, pay day, the determination of the workers to start a decisive battle on the issues of wages and bonus (and by implication against the Sangh) received a fillip when the RMMS activists started collecting membership fees. The presence of the Sangh led to skirmishes in several mills and to a violent clash in Kohinoor Mills where the Sangh representatives called in the police but were eventually forced to withdraw from the premises. This event immensely angered the workers and during a hastily called meeting by the newly formed MGKU in Bhoiwada, workers demanded the immediate start of the strike (Patankar, 1983; Javed, 1983).

The pressure on Samant to announce the date of the strike did not diminish in the days following and with the collapse of the proceedings of the HPC and the fall of Antulay, Samant seemed to be left with no argument to postpone the strike. During a meeting of activists on 13 January it was decided that the strike would start on the 18th. Meanwhile the centre, alarmed by press reports, seems to have felt uneasy about the imminent strike and made a last minute effort to avert it. Once again the device of a secret meeting was utilized and as before the result seemed promising. Datta Samant gives the following account: 'It was Buta Singh … now minister … he came two days prior to the strike. I was at Nasik. He called me and we had a meeting at twelve o'clock at night at the residence of minister Hire of the Maharashtra government. He felt that the strike should not take place and I said that I didn't want it either but that he should give some money to the workers. What is the amount you want, he asked. So I said: Rs 150 to Rs 200. He asked: With such a small amount you would be satisfied? I said: yes, this is an interim relief and subsequently we can have the committee' (interview, 17 May 1986).

Singh appeared to be pleasantly surprised and promised Samant that a decision would be taken on these lines. After having asked Samant to wait for his phone call, Singh returned to Delhi to contact PM Indira Gandhi and Rajiv Gandhi but the phone call never came and two days after the commencement of the strike Singh feebly informed Samant that he had not been able to achieve anything. According to Samant, Singh's words were: 'I don't know, they sent me to you to avoid the strike and reach a settlement but now they are talking so negatively that nothing can be done. I am sorry' (ibid.). On several later occasions Samant would refer to this meeting without, however, disclosing the name of the emissary or any other details.[37] With the failure of this attempt at conciliation the last opportunity of averting the strike was lost and during a mammoth rally near Nardulla Tank on 17 January 1982, Samant announced that the indefinite strikes fiercely sought by so many workers and dreaded only by a few, was to start the following day. The die had been cast, irrevocably.

The Stand of the Government and the Millowners

From the forgoing it may be deduced that the millowners and the central government were rapidly finding each other in the last days before the strike. For the government it was important to curb the menace posed by Samant, who by his rashness not only threatened to create serious problems for the NTC and the private mills but also in general showed a disregard for all established practices of conflict resolution. It was certainly no remote possibility that one day he would shift his attention to other vital industries, tearing up in the process the fabric of the recently adopted Essential Services Maintenance Act (ESMA), condemned by the opposition parties and unions as a Black Act. Even without major labour problems, the central government was having a trying time with growing dissension within the Congress Party, scheduled elections in several states and the ever-imminent threat of the genie of communalism trying to escape the bottle, particularly in Punjab.

The government had no need of a new working class of Datta Samant's mould. Samant's empire had been growing far too fast and if he gained a foothold in the textile industry it was likely that other industries too would succumb to the brash doctor's tactics. The textile industry would serve as an excellent stepping stone for Samant to conquer other industries and in due time it might be Samant who, with intolerable demands and militant action, would determine the economic course in the country instead of the government or the industrialists. This, of course, was the blackest scenario possible but even so there was ample reason to be concerned about the Samant factor and the millowners' complaints, therefore, did not fall on deaf ears.

The millowners had largely similar reasons to oppose Samant's entry in the textile industry. If Samant's attempts proved successful they stood to lose the cooperation of the 'responsible' RMMS and this would have unpredictable but in any case severe consequences for the industry. The wage bill would rise immeasurably, work stoppages and strikes might become a regular feature and settlements decided by an Industrial Court years after a demand had been raised might prove to be a matter of the past. Depending on his hold over the labour force, Samant might also have been able to extort much better awards after government interference than the Sangh had ever been capable of. For a combination of these reasons it was better to cut him down to size at the outset.

The fear of the millowners was adequately expressed in a memorandum submitted in the course of the strike to the Tripartite Committee:

> However, having gained ascendancy in some of the chemical and engineering industries, the militant leadership universalized its approach of wresting demands by force and spread its tentacles over the Bombay cotton textile industry in the hope that, as the workmen employed in it represented the hard core of hired labour in Bombay, any success in textiles would be a passport to gain suzerainty over the entire hired labour in Bombay.[38]

As for the present danger, there seemed to be a chance of averting the strike by way of a wage increase although the agreement in force was to last till December 1984. If such an amended agreement could be concluded with the Sangh the dual purpose of enhancing the image of the Sangh and diminishing the influence of Samant's MGKU might be served. According to at least one author, the MOA worked out two strategies when the bonus strike showed no signs of collapsing. If Samant behaved 'reasonably' and called off the strike the government might announce a wage increase of Rs 100 which would then be accepted by the millowners. This would be an increase without parallel in the history of the MOA and would suffice to undermine the morale of the workers should Samant still want to go ahead with his indefinite strike (Javed Anand, 1983). Alternatively, should Samant decide not to call off the bonus strike nor accept the terms to be decided by the government, the blame for the failure of the HPC could be attributed to him and the consequences would have to be faced by the workers. As the millowners believed that the strike would last a few weeks or two months at the most, the mills would have an opportunity of disposing of unsold stocks (ibid.).

Unfortunately, Anand does not indicate on what evidence this scenario is based. Against it pleads the speed with which the MOA withdrew itself from the proceedings of the HPC and its blank refusal afterwards (in the course of the strike) to come to any accommodation that might be acceptable to a large section of workers, as will be shown. The employers evidently opted for the hard line; strikers refusing to budge would have to be broken. This is not to say that a strategy such as that suggested by Javed Anand might not have been in the mind of some millowners but there is no evidence that this view ever became the unofficial line adopted by the MOA. Within such a vast industry as the Bombay textile industry, mills differ a great deal in their economic performance and prosperity and for that reason there were bound to be various positions adopted by individual millowners. These positions at times clashed and the managers of the stronger mills in particular suggested greater flexibility and a provision for substantial wage increases on several occasions before and during the strike. But these were views of a minority not being able to bring about a noticeable change in the MOA policy towards the strike or to cause a rupture in the association as has sometimes been suggested but never convincingly demonstrated.[39]

As appears from press reports, some millowners would in the course of the strike air views (usually anonymous) which seemed to point at a split in the ranks of the MOA on the issue of the strike but at no point did a rupture really occur.[40] The former Labour Commissioner P.J. Ovid recalls that the owner of Bombay Dyeing was one of those who wanted to give in: 'Some of them wanted to buckle, like Nusli Wadia of Bombay Dyeing. He felt that he could afford to settle the issue with his workers' (interview, 3 January 1987). But such millowners were advised not to break the ranks of the employers and in the end the dissidents among the millowners too always toed the line adopted by the MOA. There were compelling reasons for them to do so as the government fully supported the stand taken by the MOA. The affluent mills were no less dependent on the goodwill of the government than were the poorer mills because of their stake in the export of textiles, import of fibres or machinery, funds for modernization and reduction of levies and duties. A millowner could ill afford to risk the wrath of the government even if willing to risk the anger of the majority of his colleagues.[41]

General Manager R.N. Joshi of Shree Ram Mills acknowledges that the central government wanted the millowners to put up a tough fight, promising help once the struggle was over (interview, 24 January 1987). For that reason the millowners were united from the outset but as the strike progressed some felt that the losses incurred were far too high. They strove to find an amicable solution but to no avail. Joshi: 'Samant was sticking to his guns and would rather fight to death than accept a moderation of demands. When these millowners saw that a rapprochement was not possible they joined the common front again' (ibid.).

Datta Samant, in turn, is convinced that the real fault lay with the government and with the PM in particular: 'She told the millowners not to talk with me. Indira Gandhi wanted to teach me a lesson. At the same time the interests of the employers would be protected and the working class would be quiet in future. The PM is mainly responsible for breaking the strike' (interview, 17 May 1986). Samant's indiction of PM Indira Gandhi is not wholly baseless and his claim that the centre wanted to cut him down to size (and the working class in the process) is corroborated by the labour laws that had been enacted in preceding years.

On 27 July 1981 the President of India promulgated the Essential Services Maintenance Ordinance which was later ratified by Parliament as the Essential Services Maintenance Act (ESMA). This Act (passed after a marathon debate of seventeen hours) met with fierce resistance from all opposition parties in the Lok Sabha and provoked strong condemnation from the trade unions. But the commotion did not go beyond verbal resistance which is somewhat surprising as the ordinance was reminiscent of the days of the Emergency.[42] The press too, with few exceptions, was highly critical of the ESMA which gave sweeping powers to the government; powers unnecessary in the prevailing industrial climate. The ESMA, as well as later laws, curbed the right to strike to such an extent that it has become ever more difficult to reconcile Indian labour legislation with the objectives of the ILO to which the Indian government claims to subscribe (Ben-Israel, 1988: 105–12).

The ESMA banned strikes of a large number of industries considered 'essential', as in the case of those falling under the purview of the Industries (Development and Regulations) Act, 1951. This Act applied to industries as diverse as electrical equipment, energy-generating plants, machinery production, telecommunications, food processing, leather goods, pottery, among others. The ESMA, apart from prohibiting strikes, gave the right to the police to arrest without warrant 'any person who is reasonably suspected of having committed any offence and the right to confiscate properties of a trade union'. Abetting a strike was made punishable with imprisonment of up to one year.[43]

J.B. Kripalani described the Act in the *Indian Express* as 'draconian' in nature and stated that such an Act ought not to be contemplated even when a nation is at war.[44] Other papers refrained from such extreme statements but questioned the raison d'être of the Act and suggested that the government mainly aimed at wooing big business and/or prepared an all-out attack on the workers' earnings.[45] During a rally on 23 November the National Campaign Committee of Trade Unions (comprising all central trade union organizations in the country with the exception of INTUC) decided on a country-wide general strike on 19 January 1982 to oppose the ESMA and focus attention on the unemployed agricultural workers and the rising cost of living.[46] The textile strike was going to be the first major confrontation between the government and labour since the enactment of the ESMA. The strike would demonstrate what use the government would make of the ESMA.

Datta Samant, with his INTUC past, had his own problems with the general strike announced for 19 January. Samant had not yet reached the stage when he wanted to declare war on the ruling party and neither did he want to lose the confidence of the workers. He may have thought that he had found a way out of the dilemma by starting the indefinite textile strike one day before the all-India strike. He probably hoped to appease the central trade union organizations by doing so and avoid being accused of strike breaking and at the same time show the government that the textile strike and the general strike were two entirely different agitations.[47] As another gesture of goodwill towards the Congress and government, Samant ordered his workers in the Bombay Electric Supply and Transport Company (BEST) to keep the buses on the road on 19 January. Samant's behaviour then would prove a hindrance to trade union unity in Bombay during the strike.

The BEST incident deserves attention as it graphically illustrates what hurdles have to be overcome before unions can put aside their differences in the overriding interest of the working class they claim to fight for. The representative union in BEST was George Fernandes' BEST Workers' Union but whether this union rightfully claimed the support of the majority of the employees, as Fernandes repeatedly averred, was doubtful. Samant, in any case, vigorously contested the claim and was ready to prove on any occasion that the BEST workers were really with him. Samant's BEST Kamgar Union claimed a following of no less than 85 per cent of the workers. The ensuing battles for a hold over BEST Company strained the relations between the two leaders.[48]

When the opposition trade union leaders called for a Bombay bandh* in April 1982 it was Fernandes' turn for lukewarm support which hampered the success of the strike. In October 1982 a new conflict surfaced when Samant announced a Maharashtra bandh lasting three days and starting on 11 October. Probably fearing that the BEST employees might favourably respond to the call, Fernandes supported the bandh but changed its objective (stated as support to the textile strike) as well as its duration. Fernandes declared that the strike in BEST would be indefinite and for the purpose of increases in DA, House Rent Allowance and Leave Travel Allowance, leaving the public to decide what the BEST employees would actually be on strike for (*TOI*, 11 October 1982).

The Fernandes–Samant tussle was on the front pages of newspapers for several days thereafter. On 13 October Samant declared that he wanted the BEST workers to resume duty the next day whereas Fernandes appeared determined to continue the strike while calling on Samant not to test his strength, adding that in any case 90 per cent of the buses would not ply. The next day, however, 65 per cent of the buses appeared on the roads and two days later Fernandes called off the strike 'at the request of the CM' (*TOI*, 18 October 1982). The battle caused great ill will and it would take several years before the two leaders could come together in a common front against the government (*TOI*, 16 January 1987).

---

* The term bandh is derived from the Hindi verb bandh karna which means to close. The purpose of a 'bandh' is to call a halt to all or a particular category of economic activity.

Stocks and Their Disposal

From what has been said before it appears that the millowners had no wish to see Samant emerge as the new trade union leader in the textile industry. But that does not exclude the possibility that they welcomed the strike for a variety of reasons. A point which has been often mentioned was the presence of overstocks in the mills. If the stocks were piling up then a strike would enable the millowners to dispose of them. This is important as it shows, if this really was true, how poorly the strike was timed. Leaving aside the difficulties arising out of the varying stocks from mill to mill (and hence the importance of the argument in different cases), it ought to be possible to establish the importance of this aspect for the mill sector as a whole. A few relevant figures are available.

In the *Financial Express*, a paper sympathetic to the plight of the millowners, an article appeared in May 1982 stating that the Bombay mills had meanwhile cleared 'the entire. inventory of stocks, valued at a little less than Rs 100 crores, lying with them on the eve of the strike'.[49] Unfortunately no details are given. The only figures published so far by the MOA relate to stocks of cloth in the Bombay mills in 1981 and the first two months of 1982 but figures for the strike period have been omitted without explanation (*Report for the Year 1982*, MOA 1983b: 474). The available figures show that the total stocks of cotton cloth in the Bombay mills on the eve of the strike were 64,000 bales, the equivalent of 96 million metres or 25.7 per cent of all stocks in the country. What has to be decided is whether these stocks had reached such a level that they could have acted as an incentive for the millowners to welcome or even provoke the strike.

It would have been useful if detailed figures for Bombay stocks over a long period had been available. In the absence of such data some idea may be gained by looking at the scope and fluctuations of stocks on a national level (inclusive of Bombay stocks) and to see what pattern these show over the years. There is a strong correlation, of course, between consumer demand, production and stocks (movements in consumer demand being reflected in the stocks). If these figures are anything to go by then it would seem that the other cloth-producing centres in the country did not benefit much from the paralysis to which the Bombay mills were subjected.[50] But even so, this still doesn't tell us whether the Bombay mills disposed of their stocks. The all-India figures show a fairly regular pattern of ups and downs, with the lowest point in the period 1975–85 being reached in January 1983. However, it is not possible to conclude that this is significantly below what one might expect (and in that case an indication that non-Bombay mills took advantage of the strike) before one has adjusted for the Bombay stocks as these account for roughly 25 per cent of all stocks in India. In December 1983 the all-India stocks (Bombay stocks were by then included again) reached 259,000 bales, a level which had not been reached since 1976 but was not much above the level prevalent in February 1982 (at the beginning of the strike).

If the Bombay mills had been able to empty their storehouses during the strike (as suggested by the *Financial Times*) then this sudden increase in the marketing of their stock is a sure sign that the already sluggish demand stagnated overnight and that would leave us to explain why the Bombay mills under these circumstances had no difficulty in marketing their products. The obvious explanation would be that because the Bombay mills did not produce much in the course of 1982, the opportunities to market their stocks increased with this sharply reduced production. What points at a successful disposal of the Bombay stocks is that these reached the highest level for 1981 in December, namely 72,600 bales (109 million metres) but had come down to 64,000 bales a month later, after which our information stops.

An interesting account of the manner in which the millowners tried to protect themselves against damage (which might be) caused by the strike is given by Bhovalekar, a former employee of Bombay Dyeing. He was given the task of removing stocks and papers from the premises:

> I handled two operations, one before and one during the strike. The first time I arranged for the removal of documents which were needed for administration. Management was sure that Datta Samant would not allow anyone to enter the mill. To keep up production, documents and bills were required for book-keeping and I had to take them out of the mill. This was done at night time because the striking workers were watching the movements

> of the management. At daytime we had arranged for 'tempos' [trucks] and they were brought in on the 16th of January 1982. In the evening the executives of the company came separately, each using his own vehicle. At night we broke open the locks from the backside of the mill and loaded the tempos. We did not put on the lights, everything was done in the dark. In the early morning the trucks drove to the 'beach house flats' owned by Bombay Dyeing and situated in Prabhadevi. So the very day that the strike started, management started working from its new offices.
>
> In a similar fashion I arranged the removal of chemicals required for finishing certain cloth. Others shifted certain types of fabrics, even unfinished cloth was removed. The responsibility for that rested with the department concerned. From the office in Prabhadevi instructions were issued to the sectional heads and through them to the heads of the various departments. Some people of the staff and many technicians were instructed to go to Bhiwandi. These persons were conversant with spinning and weaving and could give the know-how and explain the technique of manufacturing cloth of the quality required by Bombay Dyeing. Other materials like chemicals and dye stuff were sent to Ichalkaranji where they were needed in the printing process. After some time I was instructed by the management to give certain types of stamps to companies in Bhiwandi and Ichalkaranji. From this I understood that the cloth was being produced in those places and that later on a stamp of Bombay Dyeing was put on it. In that way the mill managed to fulfil its obligations. [interview, 23 May 1986]

Another indication of the measure of success achieved by the mills in clearing their stocks can be gauged from several articles in the press but, unfortunately, these reports are rarely based on the eyewitness accounts.

Although the importance of the stocks should not be exaggerated (even in peak periods the stocks are only slightly more than an entire month's production) there is good reason to believe that they did play a role in the stand taken by millowners. The monthly average of cloth stocks in Bombay was 92.8 million metres in 1979, 97 million in 1980 and 92.1 million in 1981. This shows a considerable decrease in the period 1980-81 but in the latter part of 1981 the picture started changing. More important is that at the same time the monthly cloth production decreased. This production was 83 million metres in January 1981 but came down to 65 million in October (when the bonus strike started). It came still further down to 50 million in December as a result of this agitation.[51]

The fact that the stocks increased by the end of the year in spite of decreasing production may certainly have contributed to the uncompromising stand taken by the millowners and illustrates that the timing of the strike, from an employers' point of view, could hardly have been better. In discussions with millowners and their representatives, the point of the piling up of stocks is usually brushed aside with the remark that standing charges like depreciation, maintenance, interest on loans were so high that it would be silly to invite a strike to merely dispose of overstocks. On the face of it this seems fairly reasonable but if one adds to overstocks the general slack in demand then the picture changes altogether.[52]

One has to guess why there were still no month-wise figures available in 1986 for Bombay stocks during and after the strike. A reason for this delay could be that it would not serve the millowners' request for modernization funds and loans if it could be established that they successfully marketed all their stocks during the strike. It would also be detrimental to the aspired image of the MOA as benevolent employers if it could be proved that the millowners wilfully provoked the strike in order to clear these stocks. However, on the strength of the available data this cannot be established.

What can be said is that the stocks by the end of 1981 were unusually large and that the existence of these stocks in combination with the general sluggishness of demand may have acted as a strong stimulus to the employers to put up a grim face, even to the extent of welcoming the strike. As time passed, other advantages such as the possibility of rationalization and large-scale retrenchment free of cost became apparent. But these aspects were not foremost in the mind of the employers on the eve of the strike as nobody foresaw the duration of the struggle nor the subsequent, nearly unlimited possibilities of disposing of labour once the strike had been declared illegal. The weight of these last factors would increase week by week and all mills, private and nationalized, prosperous and backward, would in the end avail themselves of this 'golden' opportunity.

STRIKE DYNAMICS

Profile of the Leader

It has been pointed out by many analysts that the emergence of Datta Samant on the labour scene in Bombay signified the beginning of a new phase in trade unionism (M. Kadam, 1982; Patankar, 1982, Kurian and Chhachhi, 1982; Bhattacherjee, 1987). 'Novelties' introduced by Samant include strong militancy (expressed by long-drawn battles and the supposed use of violent means), bypassing legal procedures and plant-level, production-oriented negotiations. It has already been indicated in the preceding paragraphs why the Bombay textile workers wanted Datta Samant, a complete outsider in the textile industry, to lead them in the struggle against the millowners and the RMMS but this must be explored in greater detail. A related question is whether the workers could also have chosen someone else or another union to guide them in the struggle ahead. The answer to this question is essential if only because the choice of this particular leader largely determined the rigid stand taken by employers and government, with all its disastrous consequences.

In establishing his union in a factory or an industry Samant usually challenged the existing balance of power, causing a lot of inter-union rivalry. In combination with the elements mentioned above, this raised the question of whether his modus operandi indicated a break with the past and whether his popularity among the workers meant that the workers' views and expectations of trade unionism were changing. It must be remembered that within the textile industry the influence of the red flag unions (most notably that of the Mumbai Girni Kamgar Union) had dwindled to such an extent that they were incapable of adequately expressing and spearheading the frustrated mood of the workers. It was not only a matter of the ability to do so but also of willingness. In the past decades the red flag unions had not been overly successful in leading struggles in the textile industry and this had undermined their position. Opposing the Sangh proved an arduous task and the times for a strike in 1982 were far from favourable with the stagnating demand and a large section of the mill sector craving for modernization which would necessarily lead to retrenchment.

Apart from the communist unions not much leadership was available at the time of the strike in the Bombay labour field.

Excluding the leaders of the Sangh, Bombay knew only a few trade unionists of sufficient stature to have been in a position to attract and capture the attention of the textile workers at large. Union leaders, of course, there were many but few with enough clout to make them a force to reckon with and fewer still were connected with the textile industry. Prominent leaders of the time were the renowned Dange, George Fernandes, R.J. Mehta and Datta Samant.

Following the impressive strikes of 1928–29 Dange wielded tremendous influence in the Bombay textile industry for decades but his importance gradually ebbed away after Independence. Whenever there was trouble in the textile industry Dange would be involved (instigating and even leading strikes) and he was sure to be consulted even in those struggles in which he did not take an active part. But his command over the workers faded, reaching perhaps its nadir after the 1974 settlement during which he secured a minimal wage increase after a forty-two days' strike. His loss of control over the workers and his age (he was past eighty at the time) made it impossible for him to play the role in the 1980s which he had so successfully played in the 1920s.

The steady development of the industrial scene after the Second World War and the growing opportunities for profitable business accompanying it, enabled the rise of trade-unionship often denoted as 'responsible', based as it was on collaboration between labour and capital, finding expression in productivity deals and the willingness to follow legal procedures and abide by the decisions of the courts. In Bombay R.J. Mehta became the exponent of this brand of trade unionism (Pendse, 1981). Mehta, whose Free Trade Unions Movement has two unions in the textile industry (Mumbai Textile Mazdoor Sabha and Mumbai Textile Technicians' and Officers' Association), dealt roughly with the employers and at times demanded substantial concessions from them. In return he promised considerable increases in production and he was known to live up to these promises.[53] He also fought long battles in court, up to the Supreme Court, and was often successful in the end.

However, in the mid-1960s, at a time that the growth of modern industries slowed down and the Congress' hold over the workers declined, George Fernandes' star rose, showing a type of militancy that was absent in Mehta's approach. This does not mean that

Mehta's influence or the era of 'responsible trade unionism' abruptly came to an end. It may be more precise to say that several different trends were noticeable simultaneously. It was also a period in which (particularly in the new industries) more and more company-based unions emerged that were not affiliated to any of the existing general bodies of the trade unions (ibid.).

At the end of the 1960s and the beginning of the 1970s Bombay witnessed a Shiv Sena wave that seemed directed to strike at the roots of communist strongholds among industrial workers. Sena activists did not eschew violent methods to break strikes and for a short time they seemed to be successful but soon the Sena was to give way to the Samant wave. Samant's fame as a trade union leader started spreading after he clashed with the Shiv Sena over control of the workers of the Godrej factories in 1972. Samant's entry in the trade union field is strongly associated with this incident although he had actually been in the field since the 1960s but it was not before the Godrej incident that his name began figuring on the front pages of newspapers all over the country. In his attempt to take over the lead from the Sena in Godrej there followed a violent flash, leaving two people dead and resulting in Samant's arrest.[54]

Datta Samant, who had become a member of the Congress a year earlier, was sent to jail for about a year but this stood him in good stead as it gained him martyrdom and established his reputation for militancy. A great number of workers of various industries rallied behind the doctor who till then had been addressing himself mainly to the plight of the stone quarry workers in Ghatkopar. It was on their behalf that Datta Samant had established his first union in the 1960s, the Maharashtra Khan Kamgar Union. He had also founded a tenants' organization for them, to protect them against exploitation by landlords and to secure reasonable rents. It had been with the support of these grateful workers that he was elected to the State Assembly as an independent candidate, defeating a Congress opponent. A few years later he was approached by the Congress to join that party and in 1972 he was elected on a Congress ticket. But it was with the Godrej incident that he shot into prominence. He now became a working class hero almost overnight. Datta Samant was well aware of the advantages of the Godrej case: 'The press and the MOA painted me as a Naxalite, as anti-labour, as corrupt, as violent. All over the country this picture was spread but it also helped me in solving the problems, so it was not all that bad' (interview, 17 May 1986).

Right from the start of his career in trade unionism Samant showed no great desire to cooperate with other unions. He held the view that trade unions all over the country had become politicized and subjected the workers' interests to their political aims. Samant was not much interested in ideological problems and confined himself to agitating for financial demands which naturally gained him the reputation of being economistic. He also felt that unions usually watered down their demands in the course of a struggle, which did not agree with his uncompromising nature. Although striving to achieve a non-political image, Samant had enough political acumen to remain a member of the Congress which, at least in the beginning, offered some protection. The Congress may have felt that the party could benefit from the presence of a trade union leader in its ranks whose style of leadership gained the trust of ever more workers and who thereby camouflaged the absence of militancy in the Congress' trade union wing, the INTUC.

However, the honeymoon would be short-lived, Samant was too strong a man to be fettered by the rules and regulations of the docile INTUC and before long the Congress was faced with the problem of how to control this young firebrand. Samant resisted efforts to enlist him in the INTUC but his relation with that organization has remained somewhat obscure.[55] It is likely that both Samant and the INTUC saw advantages in a vague relationship and decided not to press the matter. Samant's membership of the Congress meanwhile created confusion in the minds of those who wished to look at him as a radical trade unionist and many years after he had left the party he would still meet with suspicion because of his Congress background.[56]

In the years prior to the Emergency, Datta Samant consolidated and expanded his base among industrial workers, particularly in the new industries. That his image as a fiery trade union leader did not suffer during the Emergency (June 1975–January 1977) in spite of his affiliation to the Congress Party, is probably because he, like many other trade unionists, was detained by the very same Congress during those years. Once again he could reap the fruits of being jailed. The post-Emergency years witnessed a restless, militant labour force in Bombay asserting itself in many struggles in which the initiative was often taken by the workers, bypassing the leadership of established unions. Fernandes was at that time out of the picture as he had temporarily exchanged the cloak of a trade unionist for the suit of a minister. Samant now emerged undisputedly as the most prominent leader and authentic spokesman for the workers' grievances, being involved in more than half of the strikes in the Bombay–Thane–Belapur industrial belt in 1977 (Pendse, 1981). Fernandes acknowledged the loss of many workers to Samant in those years but attributed this to the 'migratory character' of the working class, meaning thereby that workers keep 'migrating' from one union to another.[57]

In the historic elections of March 1977, the Congress was replaced at the centre by the Janata and this gave the INTUC the opportunity to adjust its policies and to tune in with the belligerent mood of the workers, no longer hampered by the consideration that militant trade unionism might jeopardize the interests of the Congress. The possibility of destabilizing the Janata government may have acted as an incentive for a more militant stand while it assured the INTUC at the same time a hold over the workers.[58] After the Congress returned to power the INTUC once again retreated to 'responsible trade unionism'.

From this brief overview it appears that several of the characteristics ascribed to Samant's style of trade unionism were already present in Bombay before he took the stage. One of these elements relates to the emergence of plant-based independent unions, a phenomenon preceding Samant's arrival on the scene. These unions usually refrained from ideological warfare and restricted themselves to fighting for financial gains, and in this they appeared to be successful. Another characteristic relates to militancy. It may be necessary here to distinguish between militant mass action (as expressed in strikes) and violent tactics directed against individuals. There is a similarity here between the methods adopted by R.J. Mehta and Datta Samant.

Mehta had provided several examples of strikes of long duration but it may be true that Samant resorted to this strategy more quickly. Apart from that, to Samant's trade unionism was attributed the use of violence against individuals (workers and employers alike), but such violence was not new either. Mehta, who possibly attempted to neutralize the effect of his waning influence, has often been accused of having introduced such methods in the Bombay trade union world at the end of the 1960s and this earned him the name of 'father of the labour mafia'.[59] This may be an exaggeration but evidence that it was Samant who introduced strong-arm tactics in trade unionism is lacking. Of late Mehta seems to have shunned the use of violent means for purely practical reasons.[60] Mehta's style of dealing with labour problems was nevertheless followed by others like his former associate Vijay Kamble (president of the Shramik Utkarsh Sabha) and Gulab Joshi who shunned being termed labour leaders, the latter taking pride in being labelled a mafia boss.[61] That relations between trade unions in the textile industry and the underworld can be touchingly hearty is also borne out by a statement of the former secretary-general of the RMMS, Bhai Bhosale, who claims that he could prevent murders through his connections with the underworld.[62]

Refusing to take balance sheets as the basis for his demands and not being willing to refer disputes for arbitration (thereby cutting short legal procedures), is said to be another characteristic of Samant's style of operating and it is probably the most distinctive. Even if Samant can hardly be called the inventor of this way of dealing with wage problems it is true that he became its most notable exponent. In bypassing the law Samant expressed the anger and frustrations of a large section of the working class, a section that had grown tired of the poor results produced by the legalistic approach. This method was even aped by the red flag unions, the supposed vanguard of the industrial workers.

Summing up, it can be said that what put Datta Samant apart from other trade unionists and what made him attractive to lakhs of work was not any one single characteristic of his brand of trade unionism but the blending of these elements and the success he seemed to achieve with it. As important for his triumphal march into the Bombay labour field was his ability to represent the workers' mood at a time when no one else seemed capable of doing so. He was uncompromising and he fought on issues (essentially financial) that were of direct concern to the workers who preferred bread to ideology. Samant's rise reflects the political state of mind of the workers and explains the disappointment felt in left circles. He broke with 'bourgeois legalism' without, however, denouncing 'bourgeois values'.

Besides, Samant's success was at the cost of all other unions, left and right, and it is understandable that the left-wing parties did not rush forward to support the strike once it had been declared. They too stood to gain by a 'Waterloo' for Samant in the textile industry. Because of this there were no unions available in the textile industry at the time of the strike who could effectively guide the textile workers. The few trade unionists who dominated the Bombay labour scene did not have a large following among the textile workers, if at all, and even if they had been interested in the textile industry they were hardly equipped to express the mood of the workers. In the words of Pendse: 'The limitations of the red flag trade unions created a vacuum of leadership and representation among the Bombay working class. The Datta Samant wave could only be conceivable in such a vacuum' (Pendse, 1981).

Main Issues

Demands by the MGKU: On several occasions prior to and during the strike the employers and the government accused Samant of changing his demands and/or of not having submitted a properly framed Charter Of Demands (COD) before embarking on a general strike.[63] An obvious problem here was that the MGKU was not the representative union and as such lacked the right to negotiate on behalf of the workers or to present a COD. It is therefore scarcely logical for employers to make so much out of the absence of such a document. However, it is true that the demands put up by the MGKU showed flexibility (or lack of stability, for that matter) in the course of the strike. On the other hand, there is evidence to show that Samant did more than make mere press statements about the objectives of the strike (as claimed by the MOA) and that he did communicate his demands formally to the millowners.[64] Whether the millowners rightly complained about the absence of a COD or not, it is clear that the mere handing over of a list of demands by the MGKU would not have positively influenced their attitude towards Samant's union for they persistently refused to negotiate with a union lacking the status of a representative union.

As the conflict started with the bonus issue, an increase in the amount of bonus was naturally the first demand made by Samant. But within days other demands were added as it was obvious that bonus was too narrow an issue to launch an all-out attack on the millowners for the improvement of the position of the textile workers.

In order to broaden the struggle, wage demands were formulated and permanency of *badli*s started figuring on the list of demands. In a COD which, according to Datta Samant, dates back to January 1982 (the precise date of which he was unable to give), the first demand mentioned is a revision of wages providing for an ad hoc increase per month of Rs 120 to Rs 195 (depending on years of service).

The second demand referred to the payment of House Rent Allowance (Rs 52 per month) and the third to Leave Travel Allowance (Rs 42 per month). There was also a demand for Educational Allowance (Rs 30 per month). Put together these demands meant a flat wage increase of Rs 244 to Rs 319. Other demands referred to a substantial improvement in leave facilities such as privilege leave, casual leave, sick leave and paid holidays. Next there was a demand for yearly increments in wages and the last demand related to the *badli* problem and stated that all the *badli* workmen who had worked for an aggregate period of 240 days should be made permanent. The rationale for all the demands was, according to this document, to ensure benefits 'commensurate with the hard work put in by the workmen under strenuous and hazardous conditions' and comparing reasonably with those earned by workers in other industries in the area while ensuring a 'satisfactory' standard of living. In an annexure to this COD the union suggested that the Bombay mills be divided into three broad groups on the basis of their capacity to pay. The idea of a division of the mills on the strength of their financial position would later on be taken up by the centre but not for the sake of a wage increase but for the provision of loans.

It is quite understandable that the demands sent a shock wave through the ranks of the employers but that is not the same as saying that the demands were unjustified, for the financial basis of industrial workers, including those in the textile industry, had been eroded over the years. With the exception of workers in capital-intensive industries, real wages either had stagnated or deteriorated, and the lowest paid workers had been the worst sufferers. The Annual Survey of Industries, for example, showed that only in fourteen subgroups out of 195 subgroups in the manufacturing industries had the real wages increased in the period 1973–78.[65] Apart from this, one has to take into account that in some of these fourteen groups the wages were so distressingly low (for example, bidi, coal tar) that even after a very substantial improvement in real wages the concerned workers would still not be provided with more than a bare minimum.

What was the situation in the textile industry? Figures presented by the MGKU tended to overlook various elements of wages such as benefits. Because of this the wages seemed lower than they were (at least on paper). The lowest paid worker in the textile industry earned Rs 705.50 per month in November 1982. This amount included a basic of Rs 282.52, DA of Rs 377.50 and an ad hoc increase of Rs 45 (Fernandes–Pawar Award of 1979).[66] In addition the worker received Rs 264.40 fringe benefits such as provident fund, gratuity insurance, bonus, leave with wages, paid festival holidays and casual leave. The total wage packet came to Rs 969 per month. These wages were certainly below the wages paid in capital-intensive industries but a comparison with, for example, the petrochemical, pharmaceutical or engineering industry suffers from several drawbacks.

Whether one likes it or not, it is undeniable that such industries are in a better position to offer higher wages than the textile mills. In their case the wage factor in the total cost of production is much lower, the profitability in terms of value added is usually higher and the burden of higher wages can be more easily passed on to the consumer. It must be realized that the output of some of the capital-intensive industries like chemicals, dye stuff, power, fuel, machinery and other equipment serves as the input of the textile industry. In other words, the finished products of many capital-intensive industries is raw material for the labour-intensive textile industry. It is, therefore, easier for the first group of industries to pass on rises in prices to their customers than it is for the latter. There is another difference. The chemical and engineering industries are factory-based as regards their inputs while the textile industry is agro-based and subject to the vagaries of the seasons. For all these reasons a comparison of wages between capital-intensive industries with a small labour component and wages in the textile industry is fraught with risks.[67]

This is not to say that the textile workers had no axe to grind. The need for virtual wage jumps in order to cope with rising prices and inflation, particularly in case of an agreement lasting five years (as in the case of the Bombay textile industry), can be deduced from figures supplied by the ICMF. The Consumer Price Index (1960 x 100) for industrial workers in Bombay was 124 in 1965, 180 in 1970, 303 in 1975, 390 in 1980 and 599 in 1984.[68]

In a Hind Mazdoor Sabha-sponsored study, analysing post-war developments in wages and prices, it was found that the real wages of the industrial workers declined in the years preceding the strike. Other studies corroborate this finding (cf. R. Chatterji, 1980). The predictable result of stagnation of real income, and most certainly of decline, in the face of increased productivity is labour unrest. The study observed that the character of subsequent struggles cannot be described as offensive: 'However, as the average real wage level had suffered a decline, these struggles will have to be conceptualized as defensive struggles of the Indian working class in the face of galloping inflation. When the wages are at or below subsistence level and the rate of neutralization for rise in the cost of living is scarcely adequate, the workers' struggles for protecting their real wages become inevitable.'[69]

Although the wages within the composite textile mills are above subsistence level, the pinch of rising prices was felt acutely and the agreement concluded between the Sangh and millowners, which was to last till December 1984, stood in the way. Besides, the virtual wage freeze was having repercussions on the families of the textile workers in the rural areas which enhanced the need for speedy and substantial wage increases.

Datta Samant has been blamed alternately for being vague and rigid about his demands but there is ample evidence that he was neither. In so far as his financial demands were known they were indeed unheard of in the history of the textile industry. He refused to even look at balance sheets and there was a great risk in this. He alleged that the whole industry was fraudulent and that it was capable of meeting his demands. The success of the strike depended on large-scale participation and such unsubstantiated allegations served that purpose but he knew that the paying capacity of the mills varied greatly, as did their practices of book-keeping one might add. In putting up such high-pitched demands, he stimulated the workers to be adamant but he also prompted them to make sacrifices for possibly unrealizable gains.

Because of this he has been accused of waging a war at the expense of the workers. In his defence it may be said that in framing the demands he merely expressed the wishes of the workers and also that he was far from rigid about them. In letters to the PM, the mayor of Bombay, in articles in newspapers, in private talks and in statements during mass rallies which were reported in the press, Samant showed his willingness to negotiate.[70] The events relating to the proceedings in the High Power Committee are a case in point. He was prepared to accept that the paying capacity of all mills was not the same (which made him suggest three broad categories). He was ready to deal with millowners on an individual basis and he accepted that a final settlement could show a substantial difference between what he demanded and what he got.

There are a few more points to be discussed regarding the demands of the MGKU. One relates to the absence of any demand pointing to the need to do something about the often terrible conditions of labour in the mills or to the presence of the RMMS in the textile industry. To start with the latter. Throughout the strike a battle was fought for derecognition of the RMMS and a cry was raised for scrapping of the BIR Act. These two 'demands' are usually clubbed together although they are quite distinct. Within trade union circles these demands are held to be crucial for understanding the problems in the textile industry as also for finding a solution to them.

First, it must be pointed out that the idea that Samant applied for recognition of his own union as the representative union, but that this recognition was withheld in spite of his massive support, is a common misunderstanding. This view was not just widely propagated by the press but at times even by Samant. However, Samant never applied for recognition of his union under the BIR Act as he knew that he would not succeed. What he did try to achieve was terminating the recognition of the Sangh as the representative union under the BIR Act. If he would succeed in that it would only be a matter of time before his union replaced the Sangh. The simple reason for not applying for the status of a representative union was that he had declared a strike. That was illegal under the Act. Because of that the MGKU stood disqualified for registration as the representative union. The most he could hope for was to establish that the RMMS did not qualify for that status either, and if he could do that he would be in an excellent position to muster enough support to qualify in due time.[71]

The tremendous difficulties he had in proving that the Sangh did indeed have fewer members than 25 per cent of the workers in the industry (the minimum required by the BIR Act), speaks volumes about the way the law protects the representative union and is the subject of chapter 3. It explains why he wanted the Act to be repealed which he stressed incessantly in speeches during gate meetings and rallies. Samant never tired of claiming that he wanted a 'secret ballot' instead of 'verification of membership' to decide the strength of a union. This wish could, of course, never figure on a list of demands to be submitted to the employers but neither is it to be found in the letter to the PM and other documents.

The reason for this may be that there is an uneasy relation between his desire to do away with the BIR Act altogether and his wish to achieve derecognition of the Sangh. Samant certainly wanted for his MGKU the position enjoyed by the Sangh as this offered many advantages, but this would also mean operating within the framework of the BIR Act. This Act made it quite difficult to dislodge the Sangh and therefore, he despised it. To repeal or even amend the Act a parliamentary majority was required which seemed impossible, given the hold of the Congress in Maharashtra. If he was obliged to conclude that there was no chance of doing away with the Act, the second best course would be to strive to take over the position of the Sangh as the representative union. But, naturally, this would work against the first aim, namely scrapping the Act. He, therefore, was pursuing two actually mutually excluding goals simultaneously: a. to scrap the BIR Act and b. to become the representative union (some time after the Sangh had lost that status) under that very Act.

Working conditions: The last problem to be discussed are the working conditions in the mills. These have been criticized by many and the attention is generally focused on aspects like heat, noise, illnesses (caused by constant inhalation of cotton particles and fibres ultimately leading to byssinosis), and unsafe machinery leading to accidents.[72] The conditions vary from department to department and mill to mill, making it difficult to generalize them but they do deserve more attention than they were given by Samant and the MGKU. The tremendous noise to which particularly the weavers in the loom sheds are exposed does create hearing loss and eventually even incurable deafness. The threshold limit values (TLV) indicate sound pressure levels that represent conditions to which workers may be exposed without adverse effects on their ability to hear and understand normal speech. The criteria utilized by the American Conference of Governmental Industrial Hygienists (ACGIH) are as follows:

Duration per day (hours)	*Sound level (dBA)*
8	85
4	90
2	95
1	100
½	105
¼	110

Source: Quoted by Purushothama (1978)

The noisiest departments in the mills are the large weaving shed (100–105 dBA), shuttleless weaving shed (90–96 dBA) and the draw frames and spinning frames (89–96 dBA).[73] Entering a loom shed, be it big or small, makes for an unforgettable experience which is better forgotten. It is obvious that workers in these departments (who have to remain there throughout their shift) are exposed far too long to high noise levels that are detrimental to their hearing capacity. The Indian Factories Act does not contain provisions to protect workers from excessive noise and no research has been done to measure the damage already done.[74]

Heat and humidity are other factors affecting the health of textile workers, particularly in departments where steam is being used such as in bleaching, boiling, finishing, dyeing and drying. Open flames are used in the process of singeing cloth and the machinery too contributes to the heat problem as do the bodies of the workers, necessitating proper air conditioning. This, of course, is practically non-existent. It must be admitted that due to climatic circumstances the problems of maintaining a reasonable temperature within the departments of the mills are far greater in India than in the West. A system, for example, of circulating air through the shed to ensure adequate supply of fresh air may, in fact, add to the cooling problems.

Prolonged exposure to high temperature causes thermal stress and expresses itself in heat syncope (sudden collapse after lowering of blood pressure), heat stroke (loss of consciousness or convulsions when the body temperature rises above 40.5°C), hyperpyrexia (cessation of sweating, hot and dry skin), and heat exhaustion (caused by shortage of water and salt in the body).[75] Accidents resulting from an excess of heat are usually restricted to cases of single workers but Kumar states that in a period of sixteen years in at least four mills in Maharashtra the workers were en masse affected by thermal stress.[76]

As far as byssinosis is concerned, Harwant Singh describes several stages: Grade half—occasional chest tightness on the first day of the work week; Grade 1—consistent chest tightness and/or breathlessness on the first day of the week; Grade 2—chest tightness and/or breathlessness on Mondays and other days; Grade 3—breathlessness on all days because of reduced breathing capacity leading to permanent incapacity.[77] As the symptoms (cough and phlegm) usually become manifest on the first day of the working week, the disease is also known as 'Monday fever'. In the course of the week the body apparently adjusts itself to the exposure to cotton dust contaminated with dirt like leaves, stems and insects. Workers in the blow room are most vulnerable to the disease because of the very high level of dust. Other departments like carding, winding and drawing also have high dust levels.[78]

The scale on which byssinosis is prevalent is not exactly known. One of the problems is that once the final stage has been reached it is very difficult to prove that this condition resulted from exposure to cotton dust and not from smoking, atmospheric pollution in the city or chronic bronchitis (which again may be stimulated by exposure to cotton dust).[79] Singh estimates that one in five cotton operatives has the disease in some stage of development, a finding which seems to be corroborated by Khogali's study in Sudan (Khogali, 1976; Singh, 1978). According to a study undertaken in the Bombay textile mills by KEM Hospital, MGM Hospital and the Central Labour Institute in the period 1970–75, the incidence of byssinosis was 12 per cent in the group of workers exposed to cotton dust.[80] An incidence of 12 per cent (at the low side) and 20 per cent (at the high side) should be alarming but G. Davay, medical inspector of Factories (Maharashtra), held the view that this figure is inflated as many health problems are attributed to byssinosis although they have nothing to do with it.[81]

Lastly, workers in the textile industry are exposed to risks because of the many chemicals that are being used at several stages of the production process. Contact with acids, alkalies, oxidizing agents, reducing agents, detergents, solvents and the like may cause burns or, in the long run, dermatitis, eczema and other skin diseases (the risks are particularly high in the finishing department).[82] For the bleaching of cloth, sodium hypochlorite is widely used (which is chlorine gas bubbled into caustic soda solution) which may affect the eyes, nose and throat. Other products being used are formaldehyde (for the finishing of cotton or rayon) pentachlorophenol (to prevent the growth of micro-organisms in fabrics), caustic soda (for bleaching, mercerizing and dyeing), sulphuric acid and hydrochloric acid (utilized in dyeing). All these substances require great care in handling but due to the workload, inadequate safety measures or lack of proper control they pose great health hazards to the workers concerned. It is to be considered a flaw in Samant's approach and that of the MGKU that the conditions of labour in the textile industry, even though they figured prominently in speeches, have not been given the attention they deserve by including them in a COD.

From what has been said so far, it nevertheless appears that Samant cannot be accused of having been rigid about the demands. At a very early stage he didn't even mind an honourable settlement being signed by the Sangh (*Sunday Observer*, 1 November 1981) bus as time progressed this idea was no longer palatable. Samant's willingness to negotiate did not extend to sacrificing what he considered to be the just demands of the workers for a quick solution and a handful of rupees. Leaving the workers apart, Samant's reputation as a militant and uncorrupt leader (at least among workers) would not have allowed him to do so either. Naturally, his views developed and underwent change in the course of the strike as he had to reckon with changing circumstances. The right question to be asked, therefore, is not why he did not stick to his demands but whether he changed them sufficiently to allow for a solution. Did he listen carefully to the workers whose interests he sought to protect and whose expectations did not remain the same throughout the strike either? As will be shown in Chapter 7 there is room for doubting his wisdom in continuing a struggle in the face of a certain defeat, risking thereby the complete demoralization of the striking workers. The suggestion, however, that he was never really prepared to come to terms with employees and /or the government cannot be sustained.

Response by the Sangh: Prior to the bonus strike, on 12 October 1981, the Girni Kamgar Sena (GKS) submitted demands to the MOA by gate-crashing into the office of the association and leaving a COD. According to the millowners, these demands implied a wage increase of some Rs 400 to Rs 650 per month.[83] Shortly afterwards, however, the Sena backed out and their claims therefore, became irrelevant. The action taken by the Sena and the imminent threat of Samant entering the textile industry meanwhile forced the RMMS too, to submit demands. The millowners knew very well that the Sangh would not have raised its voice had there been no pressure from rival unions, that is, the demands made first by the GKS and later by the MGKU.[84] The Notice of Change of the Sangh was served on the MOA on 19 November 1981, and pressed for revision of minimum wages and DA, House Rent Allowance (at a rate of 10 per cent of total wages), improvement of leave facilities and even for leave travel concessions and commutation allowance.

The workers, of course, were not to be beguiled by this late show of concern. Sensing the mood of the workers the Sangh could ill afford to appear wholly insensitive and delivered a COD merely in order not to be outdone. Acknowledging this, MOA Secretary-General Vijayanagar oversimplifies matters greatly, however, when he tries to reduce the whole conflict to a case of inter-union rivalry. According to Vijayanagar, Sena chief Bal Thackeray wanted to prove that he was more powerful than Datta Samant while the RMMS felt that the union could reign supreme because of the support of the ruling party (interview, 30 January 1986).

Under the circumstances, the demands by the RMMS were simply brushed aside by the MOA on the plea that there was still an agreement in force till December 1984 and that the Sangh had no business to change its terms before the expiry date. Against this the Sangh stated in an apology, distributed as a brochure several months after the beginning of the strike, that it had reserved the right to review its demand for better pay scales if the situation changed and, obviously, the RMMS felt that this situation had come to pass.[85] It is interesting to see that the Sangh at that stage (mid-1982) flatly rejected the MOA plea of incapacity to pay, yet this argument would be hurled at the MGKU every time its demands were discussed. Seven months later the Sangh would submit a memorandum demanding a wage rise that by implication would even outdo the demands made by Samant.

The afore-mentioned brochure is also interesting for another reason. The text claimed that the Sangh had been able to make not less than 40,000 *badli*s permanent in the period 1978–81 and that in the face of these figures 'the MGKU argument of exploitation of 40 per cent of the total complement of textile workers [the supposed per centage of *badli*s in the total workforce] must fall to the ground'. More important than the Sangh reference to the confused arithmetic of the MGKU regarding the percentage of *badli*s in the industry is the fact that the Sangh seemed to suggest that there was no need for *badli*s to feel dissatisfied.[86]

This sharply contrasts with a statement submitted by the RMMS to the Tripartite Committee in January 1983 in which the same figure of 40,000 *badli*s being made permanent in recent years is to be found. The committee, appointed by the Government of India in August 1982 to study the problems of the Indian textile industry, was one of the few and feeble attempts by the central government to come to terms with the problems expressed by and partially also caused by the ongoing strike. The idea for such a committee took shape after the RMMS had put pressure on the centre to constitute a committee to look into the working conditions within the textile industry throughout the country.

In the said statement the Sangh not only boldly claimed that the *badli* system as an institution had outlived its utility but even declared it to be the root cause of the labour trouble: 'The present system of ad hoc recruitment of *badli*s has been the main source of dissatisfaction among workers; it unnecessarily inflates the *badli* registers and thus curtails the opportunities for employment to the existing *badli* workers.'[87] After acknowledging that production in the mills should not suffer because of absenteeism, the Sangh felt that it should be possible for each mill to arrive at estimates of hardcore absenteeism while taking the seasonal variations into account and concluded that the number of *badli*s required for the purpose of maintaining production could be reduced to a bare minimum. If the committee did not agree with this, the Sangh offered the alternative of giving all *badli*s a subsistence wage of 50 per cent of their daily wages on all the days when they were not employed.

Although the emphasis laid in this text on the malpractices accompanying the *badli* system, is a gross overstatement of the importance attached to it by the workers, the argument merits discussion. It is astonishing and disturbing to find that decades after the weaknesses of the *badli* system had been pointed out by a committee appointed by the government of Maharashtra, nothing much had changed. Right from its inception the *badli* system has been justified on the ground that 'production should not suffer on account of absenteeism among permanent workers'.[88] It was, therefore, logical that the size of the *badli* component in the workforce should be in consonance with the actual rate of absenteeism in the textile industry but the committee found it hard to obtain reliable figures. It appeared that various definitions of absenteeism were used by the mills: 'Some mills supplied figures only of unauthorized absence while others included absenteeism on account of authorized leave in their compilation.'[89]

The committee recommended that the labour force in any unit should be equivalent to the monthly absenteeism increased by 25 per cent but given the uncertainty regarding the magnitude of absenteeism this suggestion hung in mid-air and left the millowners free to do as they pleased. The committee observed, inter alia, that many permanent posts were kept vacant and that *badli*s continued to be appointed in those places for a long time. It was also noted that the average number of days worked by *badli*s varied greatly per mill. In some of the Bombay mills 70 per cent of the total number of *badli*s got work almost every day. Other *badli*s, however, barely managed to get work for four days a month. The MOA reported to the committee that on an average *badli*s got work for eighteen days per month.

In the textile industry, absenteeism is usually greatest in May and June whereas August shows the highest attendance figures. The committee did not go into the causes of absenteeism, a problem which has received a lot of attention over the years.[90] These causes are manifold and relate to (often interrelated) factors like commitment, job satisfaction, rural connections, maladjustment, sickness, domestic duties, social obligations, housing conditions and indebtedness. This last factor proved to be significant because workers tend to be absent after pay day in order to avoid payment of debts. This aspect was also borne out by a study carried out by the Ambekar Institute for Labour Studies in Bombay. It is noteworthy that this study concluded that absenteeism and loss of production are much less interlinked than one might expect, which greatly undermines the rationale for having a substantial *badli* force. The study observed that the lack of correspondence between the absenteeism pattern and that of 'spindles and looms shut down due to absent workers', seems to indicate that the stoppage of machinery is due to reasons other than that of absenteeism alone.[91]

In the memorandum submitted by the Sangh to the Tripartite Committee, few demands were made specific but even so the Sangh demanded a House Rent Allowance of 15 per cent of the wages, a conveyance allowance of Rs 2 per day, a revision of the wage structure and, most importantly, full neutralization of the rise in cost the of living since 1976.[92] In that year the consumer price index was 300 (1960 x 100) whereas this figure had grown to 490 by 1982.[93] The Sangh stated in the memorandum that the lowest paid worker in the industry should have got Rs 800 in 1976 whereas the MOA had stated that the same worker received about Rs 940 by the end of 1981. In the memorandum, the Sangh refrained from working out the implications of the demand for full neutralization but going by this demand the wages of the lowest paid workers would have to be increased by some Rs 350 above the prevailing wages to a total of Rs 1300. Never before had the Sangh come with such breathtaking demands; demands that on the whole were kept purposely vague but in which the impact of the strike is clearly visible.

The statement of the RMMS was submitted as an appendix to the memorandum submitted by the Indian National Textile Workers Federation (INTWF), which claims to represent 5.5 lakhs of textile workers in the country and also affiliates to the INTUC: In the text of the memorandum it is stressed that the views expressed should be treated as the views of both the RMMS and INTWF. The INTWF, too, flayed the millowners for not being willing to seriously consider wage demands: 'Whether it is workers' demands for better remuneration, provision of welfare facilities, or even improvement of working conditions, the one patent argument from the employer has been his incapacity to pay.[94]

The INTWF points to the fact that whenever the employers were faced in the past with cases in which the costs of production would rise (for example, due to rises in costs of raw material), they would always find ways to absorb the resultant costs in spite of having pleaded an incapacity to do so. The memorandum sourly observes: 'Thus, where the "capacity to pay" argument becomes unacceptable, the employer always falls back on his other capacity: the capacity to absorb. It is only when it comes to demands for the most important element in the production process, the human element, that he has succeeded thus far with his usual ploy of incapacity to pay.'[95] That the employers managed to get away with this argument is, of course, something for which the RMMS and INTWF bear responsibility. Whatever the merits of the argument, the tone is surprisingly critical and would not have been unbecoming of the MGKU. The fact that the strike had been dragging on for a full year at that time will have been more than coincidental.

The Tripartite Committee would ultimately agree on suggesting a House Rent Allowance to the central government but the claim for additional wages would be rejected as this would jeopardize the chances of survival of the industry. Taking the balance sheets provided by the MOA as its basis, the committee divided the mills into several categories and judged that twenty-nine mills out of fifty-four (owned by thirty-six mill companies) were in a very bad and twenty-five in good shape. Even so there was no question of going into the demands made by the MGKU, Shiv Sena or RMMS as these appeared to be exorbitant. The committee concluded that these demands had to be treated as 'unrealistic, far-fetched and far too disproportionate to the financial position of the industry as a whole as disclosed by the balance sheets of the companies concerned'.[96]

After the strike was over and when the expiry date of the last agreement between Sangh and MOA had finally arrived, the Sangh served another COD on the millowners but in this one the demands were toned down although still considerable. In the memorandum of January 1985, a wage rise of Rs 125 was asked for, a leave travel allowance of Rs 33 per month, a conveyance allowance of Rs 30 and a revision of the wage system. Put together these demands would amount to a wage hike of nearly Rs 190 which is, in fact, not much below what Datta Samant had asked for a few years earlier and for which he had been ridiculed by the Sangh. However, it may be possible to argue that the need for such demands had rapidly increased in the intermediate years due to price rises. The demands on behalf of the *badli*s had been reframed: 15 per cent of the *badli* force should get all the benefits of the permanent workers and 15 to 25 per cent should get a minimum guaranteed work of thirteen days per month.[97] As the millowners refused to give in, the dispute was as usual referred to the CM who on 29 September 1985 declared an interim wage relief of Rs 70. The demands were subsequently referred for arbitration to the Industrial Court where the matter was still pending in February 1987.

Manipulation of Balance Sheets

One argument consistently used by the millowners when they had to explain why nothing was done to settle the strike, was that the financial position of the mills did not allow for wage increases of the kind demanded by Samant. This argument was put up for the whole industry although there was great diversity in the paying capacity of the mills as indicated earlier (see also Appendix D). The situation, for example, for Bombay Dyeing was not comparable with that of Finlay Mills or a mill in the NTC. A problem in deciding the paying capacity of a mill is that the only document a union can go by is the balance sheet which is notoriously unreliable and for that reason discarded by Datta Samant. Even the judiciary is ready to admit that balance sheets should not be taken at face value and accepts that wage demands need not necessarily be based on the figures produced by the mills in their balance sheets.

There are two rulings of the Supreme Court in which this problem has been dealt with. In the first case the Supreme Court observed:

> It has to be borne in mind that in many cases the directors of the companies may feel inclined to make incorrect statements in these balance sheets for ulterior purposes. While that is no reason to suspect every statement made in these balance sheets, the position is clear that we cannot presume the statements made therein to be always correct. The burden is on the party who

> asserts a statement to be correct to prove the same by relevant and acceptable evidence.[98]

In the second case the Supreme Court noted:

> The accounts of a company are prepared by the management. The balance sheet and the profit and loss account are also prepared by the company's officers. The labour have no concern in it. When so much depends on this item, the principles of equity and justice demand that an Industrial Court should insist upon a clear proof of the same and also give a real and adequate opportunity to the labour to canvass the correctness of the particulars furnished by the employer.[99]

A more recent (and for the demands raised during the strike very relevant) verdict in which the same reasoning is to be found was given by the Industrial Court of Gujarat with reference to House Rent Allowance (HRA). On the eve of the strike, the Court ruled that the Ahmedabad Millowners' Association was obliged to pay HRA to the textile workers even though there was no precedent for that within the Indian textile industry. The Court observed that there were several ways of assessing the financial position of the industry and did not attach much value to ratios like current assets to current liabilities or capital versus debt as such ratios were computed for special purposes. The Court did not want to look either at the paying capacity of some of the weaker mills but, instead, upheld that only the broad picture of the industry had to be taken into account.[100]

The one tangible and positive result of the strike (at least from the workers' point of view) was the recommendation by the Tripartite Committee to grant HRA to the Bombay textile workers in accordance with their income.[101] It was the only recommendation decided upon unanimously and it was essentially based on the same considerations which guided the Industrial Court in Gujarat. But, contrary to the caution recommended by the said Court in dealing with the financial statistics given by the mills, the committee took the balance sheets provided by the MOA as the sole basis for deciding the justification of the demands. The committee touched upon the theme of possible malversations but discarded such suspicions as ill-founded: 'In the absence of any identity of the holders of any black or unaccounted money, their mere supposed existence cannot be but an illusion for all practical purposes.'[102] The report continues: 'Limited companies cannot be assumed to have earned or held any money or assets beyond what their audited accounts disclose. It would indeed be sheer fantacy [sic] to assume to the contrary in disregard of the plain and hard realities.'[103] Even the representatives of the RMMS on the committee could not endorse such a view and Haribhau Naik (the new president of the Sangh) submitted an extensive note of dissent in which it was argued that there was room for granting additional wages.

To prove that a balance sheet is not manipulated is an arduous as well as hazardous task as all the evidence marshalled by the management might be questioned and raise new doubts. But if the balance sheet cannot be taken as the basis for deciding the paying capacity of a mill, this should pose a problem to the unions too. On what ground should one argue that a demand is reasonable, that management can afford to pay? It appears that demands and agreements are settled in a shadowy world in which evidence (balance sheets) does not play a prominent role. An experienced trade unionist like R.J. Mehta boasts that whenever management wants to repudiate demands on the strength of a balance sheet, he challenges the correctness of the same and usually successfully:

> Demands in this country are not made on the basis of the balance sheet but they are made on the basis of the strength you can muster. Even if the balance sheet shows losses you might still gain a wage hike of Rs 500. There is no risk of demanding too much. How many companies have closed down after giving in to the demands of Dr Samant? Where has that capacity to pay come from? It means that the balance sheets are false [interview, 4 April 1986].

Kisan Tulpule, president of the Mill Mazdoor Sabha, declares that he too, never refers to balance sheets while making demands: 'I am required to refer to the balance sheet when I take the case to the court but I ignore the balance sheets. We never say: your balance is wrong. We just neglect it. This procedure is accepted by the employers. Meanwhile I put up pressure by the workers, demonstrations and such things' (interview, 17 March 1986). He explains: 'All balance sheets are prepared by the company's auditors for the sake of income tax and shareholders and these will never give you the correct picture. If I have to base my bonus demand on those balance sheets, I will always get the minimum bonus whereas I usually settle for 18 to 20 per cent bonus. Now, how is that possible? From where does the money come?' (ibid.).[104] That balance sheets are irrelevant for putting up a demand is also acknowledged by M.G. Kotwal, leader of the Transport and Dock Workers Union (TDWU) in Bombay and chairman of the Kotwal Committee nominated in 1986 to study the effects of the textile strike on employment.

However, former president of the RMMS, V. Hoshing, states that he used to base his demands 'on the balance sheets as well as the potential of the industry as can be derived from the market conditions, international competition and on information supplied by workers' (interview, 20 May 1986). To take all these factors into account and attribute the correct weight to each of them seems to be an enormous task, far beyond the capacity of an ordinary union and it is likely that in the end the whole problem is reduced to mere guesswork. Hoshing's successor at the helm of the Sangh, Haribhau Naik, seems to have adjusted himself to the new responsibilities for he, too, attaches great value to balance sheets and seems to believe that the burden to prove them wrong is on the shoulders of the union: 'If a union distrusts a balance sheet, it must prove that the same is wrong. It is not enough to say that the sheets are wrong' (interview, 28 May 1986).

But even Datta Samant, who had a reputation for summarily rejecting all figures produced by management, must nevertheless have some yardstick to measure the paying capacity of a company. Even more than Hoshing, he appeared to have confidence in the capacity of workers to gauge the financial position of a plant:

> They [the workers] know how much raw material has been brought. They know how the working was as compared with last year. Theirs is a good judgement although it is not 100 per cent. Secondly, I don't believe that a company will close down if the wages are 10 to 15 per cent of the costs of production. Finally, we also take the overall position of the company in the industry into consideration [interview, 19 May 1986].

The element of information given by workers seems vital in the reduction of the complexity of reality to manageable proportions as is confirmed by other trade unionists.

In discussing the relevance of balance sheets for negotiations between employers and unions it must be taken into account that these documents serve different purposes at different times. In the private sector, the management may feel that it is important to underrate the real results in order to avoid taxes, duties or for the purpose of getting loans from the government and subsidies. On the other hand, in the public sector there is the reverse tendency as management has a stake in giving a rosy picture in order to boast of its performance or to camouflage weaknesses. Whatever the reason may be for the management to hide the real financial position of a company, it is widely believed that their figures cannot be taken at face value; a point acknowledged by former Labour Commissioner P.J. Ovid.[105]

Numerous are the stories about the various ways in which mills practise fraud. What complicates matters is that fraud is practised by mills in different ways, to varying degrees and at different levels. V.S. Deshpande, chairman of the Tripartite Committee appointed to study the problems in the textile industry, distinguishes fraud with the purpose of benefiting the company from fraud for the sake of filling one's own pocket. In the latter case the company is as much the loser as is the government (tax evasion) and the workers (less scope for wage hikes) whereas in the first case owners and shareholders benefit from the malpractices. But for the trade unions such distinctions are irrelevant. Deshpande does not believe that it is easy to cheat as fraud implies cooperation from many persons: 'People inside the company can know what is going on. Fraud can be known to many persons and are you going to involve all of them? The general feeling that managers are committing frauds and raising parallel economies is neither here nor there' (interview, 6 June 1987).

The extent to which people at all levels are involved in malpractices could be far greater than Deshpande expects but that this presupposes that many will know of what is going on cannot be denied. However, those involved have obvious reasons not to speak. History seems to support the idea that even ordinary workers may have a fairly accurate idea of what is going on.[106]

Although no generalization about the textile industry in Bombay will stand the test of falsification there is certainly a lot that justifies the general distrust of the modus operandi of the mills. It would be naïve to believe that mills refrain from window-dressing tricks such as writing off excessive depreciation, making unwarranted provisions for various expenses, recording fictitious sales which are cancelled the following year as 'sales returns' and so on. It is not without reason that under the aegis of the Ambekar Institute for Labour Studies, a textbook was prepared for middle-level trade union leaders in which several of these techniques are explained.[107]

Frauds in book-keeping is bound to create black money and the millowners are widely believed to practise it. Generally speaking, the black money economy in India has taken on gigantic proportions although the very nature of this economy does not allow for precise figures. Ram Chugh and Uppal attribute the growing incidence of black money in India to an extremely low risk of being caught:

> Many a time, governmental officials in law enforcement agencies join hands with tax-evaders for mutual benefits rather than restraining the latter. This collusion between the tax evading businessmen, landowners, smugglers and the bureaucracy sets in a chain reaction for the generation of black income in different sections of the economy without much check [1986: 51].

If there is no collusion between law-enforcing agencies and tax-evaders then there might be an understanding between the latter and the police, as was recently shown in Gujarat.[108]

Double book-keeping is unavoidable if mills generate black money by way of tax evasion and a general feeling prevails that most mills utilize this device to hide profits, enabling them to pay lower taxes and wages, but Deshpande's remark is true that allegations are rarely substantiated by facts.[109] The scale of tax evasion by mills might nevertheless be substantial, as became clear during a tax raid in Ahmedabad.[110] To say that accusations about malpractices are all too often of a general kind is not the same as denying their correctness but it is a sure indication of the many problems connected with establishing such practices. In the case of the mills the accounts have to be audited by a statutory auditor who is no employee of the company and therefore independent, but even if such a person is determined to bring out the truth, his or her chances of doing so are slim.

Two major points where fraud occurs are the point of purchasing (raw) material and the point of sale of products. It is the task of the statutory chartered accountant to check whether fraud was committed here but if he goes by the available documents he will not get far. The renowned trade unionist Bagaram Tulpule (HMS), once appointed general manager of the Durgapur Steel Plant to sort out the problems in the steel industry, opines:

> It is practically undetectable for a chartered accountant to know at what price material has been purchased. The buyer and the seller might have secret agreements. The same is true at the time when the products are sold with the help of a sales agent who might be a friend or a relative. The mill might sell its products at a low price and the agent might sell it at a high price and they might share the benefit [interview, 17 February 1986].

For mills concentrating on export there is the possibility of generating black money through underinvoicing of exports and overinvoicing of imports. Another way of diverting money is the appointment of 'marketing consultants' who might be friends or relatives of the millowners and to whom large sums might be paid for their services.

That millowners and management may pursue conflicting goals is illustrated by the example of Bombay Dyeing. A. Bhovalekar, a former employee working in the department of dyes and chemicals and charged with the task of purchasing materials, had to buy chemicals of inferior quality. For several years he complied with the wishes of his superiors but according to him he was fired when he refused to do that any longer. Bhovalekar explains the procedure:

> I'll give you the example of caustic soda liquid. When I was working this soda was available for Rs 5,050 a tonne but our management was offered the same caustic soda for Rs 4,850 so I expected something fishy about it and informed my boss. Yet the order was placed and the goods delivered but after ten days we found that the degrees dwindled day by day. I tested the strength and found it to be only 50 per cent of what it should have been.

So in the long run this would practically double the price for the required amount of soda' (interview, 23 May 1986).

There seems to be no gain for the management in purchasing material of an inferior quality, but he explains:

> That is not true. You see, if you give someone a certain volume of business you will get a certain commission. So if the quality is bad you will require greater quantities and thereby secure a higher commission. A person who offers a product of inferior quality is prepared to give a high commission. The millowner is not getting anything out of this … but the persons in between, those of the ranks of management and those in the departments, they have interests in this' [ibid.].

Bhovalekar has a similar story to tell about the manipulation of stocks, something which might occur along the whole line of production. He admits that he was used to classifying certain material as unfit for production. This was particularly attractive in the case of chemicals for which an import licence was required. Such licences were only given for the production of particular commodities. Only part of the dyes thus received would then be utilized and the rest would be sold in the open market as 'non-serviceable dyes' where they would fetch a handsome price.

What Bhovalekar did with chemicals could also be done in other departments with spare parts, cotton, and other materials. A comparison between the amount of cloth produced from the same quantity and quality of cotton by mills in the NTC and in the private sector might be revealing.[111] Bhovalekar, who at one time had the confidence of the management, is still in the possession of a lot of incriminating evidence (bills, registers and cash-books) relating to the years 1974 and 1975, which according to him proves double book-keeping by Bombay Dyeing. However, he is not prepared to part with the evidence as he himself made the entries in the cash-books and his name figures on many of the invoices.[112]

Since the early days of the industry the millowners have been accused of siphoning off money from the mills to other, more profitable enterprises. Here, too, evidence is usually lacking as has rightly been pointed out by MOA Secretary-General Vijayanagar in an apology written a few years before the strike.[113] He asserts that diversification by itself does not reduce the availability of funds for the replacement of existing machinery as long as it takes place within the same corporate framework. Higher profits generated in that way will go to the common pool of its own internal resources: 'In fact, in all those cases where cotton textile companies have been able to diversify their activities in this manner it has proved highly beneficial to their textile production—a field generally known for its low profitability.' Unfortunately, Vijayanagar does not substantiate this claim any more than his opponents do theirs.

The case of Mukesh Mills could be quoted to illustrate that Vijayanagar's picture of reality is as rosy as that of his critics is black. Mukesh Mills was one of the first mills in the city during the strike to apply for permission to close down, a request which was at first turned down by the government (*TOI*, 26 August 1982). A few months later there followed an unexplained fire in the mill but although even the Sangh suspected foul play the Government refused to investigate the case (*TOI*, 18 December 1982). Not long before this event the owner had received a loan to modernize the mill, modernization which according to workers of the mill never took place. Following the fire and pointing at the ongoing strike the millowner once again applied for closure and this time he was given permission.[114]

Examples will not suffice to discredit a whole industry as the reverse is equally true. It may be taken for granted that in a number of mills management eschew the techniques described here. But although there is no way of estimating the extent to which millowners drain money from the mills or managers enrich themselves at the expense of everybody else or supervisors and heads of departments increase their income by cooperating with malpractices, the examples given explain why it is justifiable to follow the dealings of millowners and managers Argus-eyed.[115]

The Political Scene

Behind the Battle Lines: Having discussed the leadership of the strike and the issues involved in the struggle, it is time to take a look at the political context in which the strike was taking place as this to a large extent determined the outcome of the strike. For instance, the willingness of the millowners to negotiate with Samant was in no small measure shaped by the stance of the government. The tremendous support of the workers for Samant appeared to be a less important factor in bringing the millowners to the negotiation table than the hard line adopted by the government which forbade such negotiations.

The support Datta Samant enjoyed among the textile workers became abundantly clear on 18 January 1982 when not a single worker of the entire labour force reported for duty and all mills remained closed. This demonstration of support for a man who had been abused by both employers and the Sangh, and who had been accused of having secured benefits for workers only after the use of violence, did not fail to impress the press. All newspapers reported that the strike was total and peaceful. Nowhere was a picket-line to be seen near the gates of the mills and nowhere else did incidents occur justifying Samant's reputation for militant means. This picture of desolate mills, desolate even in the absence of striking workers guarding the gates, would continue for days, weeks and in the end, even months.

The various unions active in the textile industry were well aware of Samant's popularity among the workers as they had witnessed the huge rallies preceding the strike and sensed the fervour of the workers. In great numbers, workers had shifted their loyalty to Samant whose image had assumed Messianic proportions. Those unions who had not done so already lost no time in expressing their support for the strike. These included the Mumbai Girni Kamgar Union which had threatened a general strike earlier in August 1981. Within days Datta Samant's MGKU received verbal support from other textile unions like the Lal Bawta Mill Mazdoor Union, Kapad Kamgar Sanghatana and the Girni Kamgar Sena. Most unions did not want to go beyond token support and kept a low profile as they preferred to wait and see; trying to prepare themselves for the task of leading the workers back into their fold once the strike collapsed. But the strike did not collapse—there was no sign of it—and the unions were forced to show more involvement and appreciation as they ran the risk of being swept away by the MGKU, losing the tiny patch of ground they could still stand on.

On the political scene CM Antulay who, probably for sheer political exigencies, was taken to be favourably inclined towards the textile workers, was replaced on 20 January 1982 by Anandrao (Babasaheb) Bhosale. The political unrest in Maharashtra had its parallel at the centre where PM Indira Gandhi sought to master the problems with continuous reshuffles of her cabinet and with the introduction of a new twenty-point programme to replace an earlier version. A dominant characteristic of the new programme was its emphasis on the need to work harder. The textile strike, coming in the Year of Productivity, seemed a flagrant contradiction of this philosophy. The problems in the Congress induced a reshuffle of the cabinet in February 1982 and another one, the seventh in a time span of about two and a half years, in September the same year.[116]

Apart from growing tensions within her own party, Indira Gandhi had to cope with other serious problems in 1982 like the rebellion of her daughter-in-law Maneka. This young widow refused to obey the wishes of her mother-in-law any longer and started a political campaign, capitalizing on the sentiments following the death of her husband Sanjay Gandhi, and undermining the position of the PM. In Punjab grew the menace of communalism and separatism, accompanied by rapidly rising violence. Ever more militant Sikhs flocked to the banner of the extremist leader Jamail Singh Bhindranwale and clamoured for autonomy. By the end of the year, the protests in Punjab seemed to spell doom for the country. Other regions demanded Indira Gandhi's attention as well. In June 1982 the voters in Kerala, West Bengal, Haryana and Himachal Pradesh cast their votes and the results were indicative of a decline in the strength of the Congress Party. Andhra Pradesh witnessed the rising star of the former film actor N.T. Rama Rao who challenged the position of the Congress Party in that state.

As a gesture of goodwill the new CM in Maharashtra invited Datta Samant for talks on the strike three days after he had assumed office. If Samant ever believed that CM Bhosale would take a sympathetic view of the strike and would bring the employers to the negotiating table in order to ensure industrial peace, he would soon be proved wrong. Before the end of the month Bhosale had talked already to the millowners and a few days after that the CM would appeal to the workers to resume duty prior to any consideration of their demands, a theme on which he would be harping throughout his short tenure. In the first week of February he publicly stated that the strike was illegal (*TOI*, 7 February 1982).

Bhosale's time in office as CM was beset with problems. Confidence in the Congress had been shaken by fierce in-group fighting and Antulay's ignominious exit. Within fourteen days of his nomination as CM, Bhosale appointed the same Antulay as chairman of the Irrigation Development Corporation of Maharashtra which did not help to soothe the feelings of the anti-Antulay camp. As a result of the problems within the ruling Congress Party, Maharashtra would see a train of eight CMs holding office in less than ten years and, if one includes Antulay, not less than four CMs held office during the strike period alone.[117] But whatever the fluctuations in the balance of power within the Congress and in spite of some voices of dissent, at no time did there appear to be a group strong enough to effectively influence the line adopted by the party at an early stage; namely, that no discussions should be held with Datta Samant and that the workers should resume duty before their problems could be sorted out.

This stand was fully in line with the employers' point of view. The millowners had lost no time in briefing the PM and had sent a strong delegation to meet her on 3 February.[118] These representatives pointed at the illegality of the strike and at the possible consequences of the textile stir if the government was going to put a premium on the strike by negotiating with Samant. The central government needed no persuasion, and in order to back Bhosale, the Union minister for labour, Bhagwat Jha Azad, publicly declared in the first week of February that the centre fully endorsed the stand taken by the government of Maharashtra with regard, to the strike (*TOI*, 5 February 1982). This was reiterated by Commerce Minister Shivaraj Patil ten days later (*Nava Kal*, 16 February 1982).

The visit of the delegation of the millowners to the capital to meet the PM was, for no apparent reason, reported in the press only a week after it took place. The employers took the opportunity to 'desperately' plead for greater credit facilities, to ask for funds to enable the textile industry to carry out the much wanted modernization and to plead for measures curbing the multiplication of unions.[119] They also stressed that the present problem was the result of inter-union rivalry and this point was not lost on the PM. The political climate was favourable to the millowners as the PM was bent on muzzling militant trade unionism, as had recently been illustrated by the ESMA but had been visible long before that. Six months later a new labour law, the

Industrial Disputes (Amendment) Bill, would be passed in Parliament with new restrictions fettering the trade union movement.[120]

Having declared the strike illegal, it should have been clear to the public that there was no point in government discussions with the strike leader. To maintain a semblance of real concern for the genuine demands of the workers, however, it was decided to revive the High-power Committee which had become defunct after the fall of Antulay. However, minister of state for the labour, B.M. Gaekwad, added that reconstitution would only take place if the representatives of employers and employees asked for it (*TOI*, 9 February 1982). As this was not the case, the findings of the committee (which according to at least one press report contained unnerving evidence of fraud and malpractices perpetrated by the mills) would never be published.[121] A few days later, the fate of the HPC was effectively sealed when CM Bhosale declared: 'There is no need for such a committee as one of its members, Dr. Jichkar, has become a minister' (*The Daily*, 11 February 1982). With the promotion of Jichkar to the ranks of the top administrators of the state, the government and millowners could rest assured that the findings would never see the light of day. Samant would ask in vain for these findings during a tumultuous meeting in March 1982 in the State Legislature.

Throughout the strike, CM Bhosale adopted a tough stand but he appeared incapable of finding an imaginative answer to the problems at hand. A question to be decided here is whether he wanted to find a solution but was prevented from doing so or whether he willingly carried out policies decided in Delhi between millowners and the Union government. In any case it is certain that whatever he did (or rather, did not do) had the blessings of Delhi as he is not known to have been rebuked by the centre at any time for not finding a solution to the strike. It is remarkable that a government incapable of working out a solution to an urgent problem of this magnitude could remain in power for so long.

When Bhosale finally had to stand aside for Vasantdada Patil nothing changed in government policy towards the strike, which is a sure sign that Bhosale's lack of initiative in that regard was not the reason why he had to quit. One may, therefore, safely conclude that his approach was always in consonance with the views prevailing in Delhi. But his views did not just accidentally coincide with those at the centre. Circumstantial evidence supports the contention that in all likelihood the plans were worked out in the capital and that Bhosale depended completely on instructions from Delhi for any step regarding the strike.

Firstly, there is the astonishing lack of initiative shown by the state government under Bhosale to bring about a solution. Even when the government—in the face of the fact that the strike had lasted more than eleven months—was publicly chided by a judge of the Bombay High Court for refusing to refer the conflict to the Industrial Court, nothing happened.[122] Virtually all the clauses of the relevant section in the BIR Act were applicable to the textile strike. However, the state government merely declared that no one had asked the government to refer the case to the Industrial Court, thereby simply ignoring the fact that it could have taken the initiative itself (*TOI*, 22 December 1982). Besides, although the millowners had not explicitly asked for arbitration, they were certainly not against it. During the annual meeting of the MOA in 1982, Chairman Maganlal had voiced the view that the state government should refer the case to the Industrial Court (*Economic Times*, 23 June 1982). Justice S.C. Pratap condemned the failure of the government to do so later as a 'breach of statutory duty' but to no avail.[123]

Secondly, on several occasions the centre sent emissaries and ministers to Bombay 'to solve the problem', as the customary phrase in the press was. That they arrived in Bombay to perform what should have been the task of the state government clearly shows where the decisions were taken. Discussions with the secretary-generals of the ICMF and the MOA confirm this reading of events.

Thirdly, there are the visits Bhosale paid to Delhi to meet the PM. Though some of these visits were meant to be top secret they were noticed and subsequently reported by the press. The first was in the third week of February, a few weeks after he had become CM (*TOI*, 16 February 1982). The next time he went to see the PM to apprise her of the developments in the textile stir was in June (*TOI*, 9 June 1982). The third time Bhosale is known to have been in Delhi, accompanied by MOA-Chairman Maganlal, was in July (*TOI*, 9 July 1982). The very next day the Union government announced that a tripartite panel would be appointed to study the problems in the Indian textile industry, including the labour conflict in Bombay. There is little that can explain the need for a newly appointed CM in Maharashtra to visit Delhi that often, except the urge to discuss the strike, which may be termed the most important issue for Maharashtra at that time.

Mere discussion of the strike with the PM and/or the central ministers is no conclusive evidence of the contention that Delhi determined what policy should be followed by the state government but discussions with representatives of the employers confirm the impression that the CM was only a figurehead as far as the strike was concerned. On the strength of Bhosale's visits to Delhi one could also argue, of course, that he did make an effort to end the strike and that he merely went to Delhi to seek approval of the steps he wished to take. If that really was the case then Delhi must have turned down all his proposals as no serious steps were ever taken. One might also wish to see Bhosale as a helpless prisoner of Delhi who nolens volens had to do what he was told to do. But then Bhosale on no occasion showed so much as sympathy for the plight of the workers or gave the slightest hint that he disagreed with Delhi, and it follows that even if he was not given the room to pursue his own policies he must have been in full agreement with the instructions he received.

In the Indian context it is not unusual for the centre to interfere with problems at the state level, most particularly not when the position of the Congress is at stake. In this case, too, evidence shows that the centre deemed it fit to control the developments. Bhosale, who was not considered to be a political heavyweight, had right from the start the impossible tasks of reconciling warring factions within the party and ending the textile strike without alienating the workers from the Congress. It proved to be more than he could chew.

When on 18 August even the police started rioting in Bombay, leaving five people dead and necessitating curfew in the city, his end seemed near. The various problems, in addition to an unfortunate family affair in which his daughter-in-law filed a suit against him, caused the *Times of India* to predict his imminent exit on the front page: 'Bhosale Will Be Replaced Soon' (*TOI*, 28 August 1982). Contrary to this prediction, the CM survived the crisis only to face a new one in December which ultimately led to his downfall. In February 1983 Maharashtra was presented with a new CM, Vasantrao Patil, once president of the RMMS.

A few days before this event, the centre seems to have made up its mind to drop the leaders of the Sangh, President Hoshing and Secretary-General A.T. Bhosale. Both gentlemen were given the opportunity to offer their resignations. Their position had gradually become untenable and even within Congress circles they had been severely criticized. Already in April 1982 their position had come under attack and within the Congress some had suggested that their removal might be necessary to restore the confidence in the RMMS (*Economic Times*, 14 April 1982). Maybe because of the fact that sacrificing the Sangh leaders at that stage might be interpreted as an acknowledgement of the bankruptcy of Sangh policy and a moral victory for Datta Samant, this idea did not materialize then.

In October their ousting seemed once more imminent but the Sangh leaders stalled this move, stating that any attempt to solve the problem without them would imply 'virtual elimination of their union, paving the way for permanent control of the Samant union on the textile industry (*Indian Express*, 26 October 1982). It could be that the centre succumbed to this reasoning as they survived this crisis too but in January the following year their leadership was at last terminated and they had to abandon the field as did CM Bhosale.

Hoshing and Bhosale were an easy target for those who wished to put the blame for the strike solely on the Sangh as they represented the fact of the Sangh. The anger of frustrated workers towards them surfaced during the police riots in August in the course of which their houses were ransacked, presumably by irate workers. The centre may have believed that in sacrificing them tensions within the party might be eased and that by the same token the textile workers could be convinced of the sincerity of the government. If that really was the case then the government totally underrated the extent of the resentment felt by the workers, an anger from which the government was not excluded. In February 1983 the two Sangh leaders were replaced by the former INTWF President Haribhau Naik (minister of state for labour under Antulay) and Manohar Phalke (brother-in-law of the then reigning CM Vasantdada Patil who had barely assumed office). Problems continued, however.

Bhai Bhosale, so unceremoniously dropped as secretary-general, prepared a comeback and within two years of the strike the new leadership was faced with a no confidence motion which was supported by 428 of the 1008 representatives present. Without bothering to figure out how many of the remaining 580 representatives abstained from voting (as prescribed by the rules) the president, Haribhau Naik, took it that everyone else was in favour of a continuation of his presidency and left the meeting.[124] Those who moved the motion vehemently opposed this procedure and took the case to court where it still rested in May 1987. Bhosale accuses the present secretary-general, Manohar Phalke, not just of incompetence but also of bribing 300 representatives and of giving nomination papers to workers who did not even belong to the Sangh: 'According to the rules no one who is a member of a rival union can be a candidate but even members of the Shiv Sena and Datta Samant's union were asked to become representatives for the RMMS' (interview, 30 May 1987).

Dissent and Mediation: The lack of initiative by the Congress did not have the approval of everyone within the ranks of the party. Party workers were concerned about the negative impact of this approach on the working class and they feared that the already battered image of the party would suffer on account of it. In March, a meeting of the Maharashtra Pradesh Congress Committee (MPCC) was largely devoted to the ongoing strike but although the meeting lasted more than four hours the only comment given afterwards was that the party adhered to the principle of not negotiating with a union lacking representative status (*TOI*, 21 March 1982). Not satisfied with that, party activists some time later sought to approach the PM in the hope that she would intervene and end the strike. But given Indira Gandhi's aversion to militant trade unionism, this attempt, predictably, did not meet with success either.

In May, there followed a meeting of office bearers of the Congress during which it was declared that the strike represented a spontaneous outburst of feelings of frustrated workers. The office bearers also disapproved of the stand taken by the government of Maharashtra (resumption of work prior to any talks) and rebuked the government for failing to take constructive steps which could bring about a solution (*TOI*, 10 May 1982). Once again the hope was expressed that the PM would come to the rescue of the workers. Gajanan Loke, former secretary-general of the MPCC, went to the extent of condemning the pro-millowners stand adopted by the RMMS. As before, however, the call of the office bearers would fall on deaf ears and an initiative by Ramrao Adik to start a discussion within the party on alternatives to end the strike met with the same fate (*The Daily*, 28 May 1982).

In October, dissidents within the Congress announced a rally of MPs and MLAs who were critical of the RMMS as well as of the government. This meeting, organized by B. Patil, erstwhile member of the HPC and a Congress MLA himself, would be presided by J. Dhote, a Congress MP. Patil was one of the very few who knew the findings of the HPC and maybe as a result of that he was no friend of the millowners. Staying in the heart of the textile area in the city, he was painfully aware of the feelings of the workers (during the police riots in August his house too had been ransacked along with those of the RMMS leaders). The attitude of Patil and that of most other dissidents to the strike was probably determined by a mixture of genuine concern for the fate of the workers and a realization that something drastic had to be done if the affiliation of Congress voters among the workers was to be retained. Whatever their motivation may have been, the Congress dissidents adopted a resolution during their rally asking the PM to resolve the strike and to scrap the BIR Act (*TOI*, 1 November 1982). This last point had gained importance over time and it is worth noting that even within the Congress not everyone hailed this piece of labour legislation. But this time, too, the criticism failed to draw any response and it seems that those Congress members who for one reason or the other wanted to change the party line lost heart as not much was heard of them afterwards.

It was inevitable that with the passage of time many persons, each for his own reasons, would try their hands at finding a solution to the strike (women were conspicuously absent). A list of such people would naturally include the names of politicians and trade unionists (the stand adopted by the trade unions is dealt with in the next chapter), but also the names of religious leaders, judges, workers and journalists would figure on it. Many of these efforts were not sincere and merely served the purpose of gaining publicity, others were expressions of pious hopes and good intentions but empty of content. None were to be successful. Some of the more remarkable initiatives will be briefly discussed here.

One of the first to make an attempt at conciliation was Comrade Dange who called on CM Bhosale to arrange for a meeting of all the unions in the textile industry to discuss the strike (*TOI*, 5 February 1982) but this call would go unheeded. On several occasions during the strike Dange would offer comments on the developments but this would have little or no impact. Towards the end of the strike (May 1983) Dange would once again call for fresh talks on the textile stir but this too remained ineffective as the struggle was practically over by then (*Indian Express*, 3 May 1983). To the inconsequential efforts to solve the strike must be counted the attempt made by a Jain leader who started discussions with Samant and the millowners, declaring that he would use religious powers to end the strike. These were apparently insufficient as the attempt failed (*TOI*, 26 February 1982). Equally ineffective was the plea by the Catholic Bishops' Conference of India, a year later (*TOI*, 13 January 1983).

More serious were the efforts by the new mayor of Bombay, P.S. Pai, who belonged to the Bharatiya Janata Party and who was elected in the first week of April 1982. Barely a week after he assumed office, Pai chided the government of Maharashtra for not finding a solution to the strike (*TOI*, 14 April 1982). Pai followed this up by staging an eight hour dharna near Hutatma Chowk in an effort to draw public attention to the workers' plight. In the first week of May, Pai would give his blessing to the idea of sending a delegation of the Bombay Municipal Corporation to see the PM in order to force a breakthrough in the strike. This indicates that Pai had come to realize that the decisions were not taken in Bombay but in Delhi. In October, Pai would nevertheless make one more attempt to hammer out a solution to the strike within Maharashtra by heading a panel to which he invited the state government, millowners and all the trade unions, including the Sangh. The state government and the MOA, however, informed him that they saw no point in attending the discussions now that the Tripartite Committee had started its work. They preferred to wait for the outcome of the deliberations of this committee. The RMMS, too, refused to come and so this effort also came to naught (*TOI*, 7 October 1982).

When the strike was more than five months old, a group of forty workers, representing twelve mills in the city, and claiming to be independent, presented itself to the press. These workers, under the leadership of one Madhu Mehta, gave a press conference declaring that they wanted the strike to end and that everything was negotiable except the position of the Sangh. (*The Daily*, 29 June 1982). It is curious to note that the millowners, who had stubbornly refused to meet Datta Samant, had no objection to meeting this group of self-styled representatives. These so-called 'unaffiliated workers' were received for discussions and a few days later, the two parties agreed that the millowners would pay an advance of Rs 650 to workers who resumed duty. The 'agreement' was duly reported by the press (*TOI*, 8 July 1982). This strange sequence of events raises the suspicion that the millowners hatched the whole plot with the dual purpose of luring workers back to the mills while at the same time creating an image of willingness to negotiate. The 'concession' to which they obligated themselves did not cost them anything special as this was exactly within the limits agreed upon with the centre. This became clear the very next day when the Union government announced in Parliament that the millowners would pay an advance of Rs 650 in addition to which an interim relief of Rs 30 would be paid.[125]

Vasantrao Patil, a man who was sounded in April 1982 for the post of president of the RMMS and who did not seem to be averse to the idea, was one of the many politicians trying his luck with the strike.[126] At that time Patil was secretary-general of the All-India Congress Committee (AICC). In May he announced his intention to end the stalemate, an effort in which he would be assisted a few days later by Y.B. Chavan, former deputy PM. Their effort must have stranded rapidly as nothing further was heard of it. The next month it was the turn of Ramrao Adik, former minister of finance, to try to bring Samant and the millowners together. Adik claimed to have the blessing of PM Indira Gandhi but this was flatly denied by CM Bhosale after the latter returned from a visit to Delhi (*TOI*, 10 June 1982). In July the renowned Gulzarilal Nanda (officiating PM after the death of Jawaharlal Nehru and again after the death of Lal Bahadur Shastri) tackled the textile problem but he found Samant uncompromising and left it there (*Nava Kal*, 30 August 1982; *Textile India*, August 1982).

The efforts of the various Congress leaders were futile and consequently proved to be abortive but they were given wide publicity. The failure of their attempts was as much the result of rivalries within the Congress as of the simple fact that these mediators had nothing to offer. They seemed primarily propelled by a desire for personal glory. Ending the stalemate and resolving the strike would naturally be a feat of major political importance. It is striking that although the state government adopted an inactive and rigid stand towards the strike, the efforts at mediation by persons who were no emissaries and had no bargaining authority whatsoever would be quoted by the same government when its policy of wait and watch was questioned in the Legislative Assembly.

Grilled about the failure of the state government to find a solution to the strike, Labour Minister Gaekwad referred to attempts made by Dange, Joshi, Adik and Nanda (*TOI*, 11 September 1982). Half a year earlier the same minister had justified the immobility of the government by referring to the appointment of a Tripartite Committee which was then in the offing (*TOI*, 16 March 1982). It is sad to see, and ill bespeaks the concern of the government both at state and at national levels, that nearly four months had to pass between the proposal to establish such a committee and the announcement of a decision to do so. Neither the state government nor the Union government appeared to be in a hurry and when the terms of reference of the committee were finally known, it turned out that a study of the labour problems in Bombay was just one of the tasks assigned to it.

From the foregoing it appears that the relations between the millowners and the government, both at state and at national levels, were cordial. In fact, these may never have been better. Judging from the harmonious relations between employers and the government, the stocks and the prevalent market conditions, the timing of the strike was very poor. But there was at least one factor which seemed to enhance its chances of success. On 21 January 1982, the newspapers brought the news that the Soviet Union wanted to place an order for 200 million square metres of cotton cloth to be delivered in the course of the year. The millowners were certainly eager to get this order and some of them believed that the news strengthened the hands of the MGKU but as the 'letters of credit' accompanying such an order still had to arrive, there was no pressing need to give in (*TOI*, 10 February 1982). When these letters did arrive the news was not given wide publicity by the MOA (probably for tactical reasons). In the first week of July the newspapers reported that the Soviet Union had made it known that it would not accept the strike as an excuse for failing to deliver the goods (*TOI*, 4 July 1982).

Whether the USSR was at any stage willing to use the order of cloth to put pressure on millowners and the government is a matter of speculation.[127] It is more likely that the Soviet Union needed the cloth badly to clothe its citizens. Given the ties between the two countries, it seems unlikely that Moscow wanted to jeopardize its relations with India by supporting a strike in which labour was not only facing the employers but also the government. In August, the newspapers would report that the obligation to deliver cloth to the Soviet Union posed serious problems to the mills in Bombay even though many of them had started working again. In what way this problem was solved is unknown but it is likely that the powerlooms and the mills outside Bombay had been able to compensate for the poor performance of the Bombay mills, for in November the Soviet Union would once again order 200 square million metres of cotton cloth to be delivered in 1983 (*TOI*, 16 November 1982).

Even if the delivery of sufficient cloth was not a serious problem, the maintenance of proper quality did place the industry in difficulties. V.P. Singh, at that time Union minister of commerce, stated in the Rajya Sabha that the government had not received any complaints from the Soviet trade authorities about the quality of cotton fabrics exported to the USSR. However, Singh had to admit that the government was aware of the suggestion made by a representative of the USSR during a meeting of the Textiles Export Promotion Council (Texprocil) on 16 November 1982. The representative had warned that 'immediate steps should be taken to improve the quality of cotton fabrics exported to the USSR from India in the interest of the expansion of Indo-USSR trade in this sector'.[128]

It is astonishing, and an illustration of the influence of the millowners on textile policy, that in spite of this warning, the Textile Committee shortly afterwards issued an order (dated 24 December 1982) cancelling pre-shipment inspection of the cloth to be exported to the USSR. The Textile Committee, a platform for regular meetings between millowners and representatives of the government, did so in violation of the existing regulations on the plea that such inspection had become superfluous as Russian officials had inspected the cloth already.[129] This arbitrary behaviour immensely irritated Singh, who, as soon as he learnt of it, issued an order (20 February 1983) overruling the instructions of the Textile Committee and restoring the inspections. However, it was not within his competence to dissolve the Textile Committee, which he regretted.[130] Apart from this incident no other instance is known of a collision between government and millowners in the course of the strike.

Prophesying the End: If the government cannot be accused of having been overzealous in trying to find a way out of the problem, the workers did not come to the rescue of the government either by rushing back to the mills. In fact, they showed astonishing staying power. Just how successful they were in that was never revealed as the government concealed the attendance figures from the public and put up a smoke-screen by pointing to the number of mills that had reopened.

Against the MOA's and Bhosale's repeated claims of the imminent collapse of the strike, Samant placed his challenge of calling off the strike provided the workers wanted it. This challenge was thrown in various ways. Sometimes Samant said that he agreed to call off the strike provided a majority of the workers wanted it (*TOI*, 12 February 1982) and at other times he boasted that he would do so if only one per cent of the workers were willing to resume. In both cases he proposed to take a secret ballot but neither the government nor the millowners were prepared to agree to this. Instead, they proceeded to inform the press that the end of the strike was near.

Whether it was after the defeat of Samant in elections or at times of festivals like Holi and Diwali, the millowners and the government always piped the same tune, the song of the collapsing strike. The fact that they were proved wrong time and again seemed to make no difference. Just how phoney such claims were, may be deduced from statistics obtained from the ICMF (see Table 2.2). It has to be borne in mind that the average production of cloth in the Bombay mills prior to the strike hovered around 96 million metres per month in 1981 and the average production of yarn then was 14.3 million kg per month. These figures refer to the production of cotton, blended and 100 per cent of non-cotton products.[131]

The Table shows how utterly deceptive the government claims were that week after week more mills were reopening. For example, on 19 March 1982 Labour Minister Gaekwad stated that twenty-nine mills had resumed production but he refrained from giving

TABLE 2.2

Attendance and Production Figures of the Bombay Mills during the Strike

Month	*I**	*Labour com-plem. (000s)*	*Machine activity all shifts*		*Production during month*	
			Looms (000s)	*Spindles (000s)*	*Yarn (000s Kgs)*	*Cloth (000s Mtrs)*
Jan '82	2	0.1	–	–	–	–
Feb	7	3.3	13	68	N.A.	N.A.
March	29	8.0	28	165	188	784
April	37	15.8	80	392	366	1914
May	41	16.3	90	393	707	3974
June	41	25.0	169	645	959	5914
July	45	27.3	184	866	1456	9766
Aug	47	37.0	244	1108	1615	11120
Sept	49	41.5	306	1383	2259	14154
Oct	50	39.9	292	1348	3164	21129
Nov	51	59.7	445	2002	3492	23080
Dec	51	76.1	638	3011	5006	31455
Jan '83	51	78.1	615	3259	6078	38411
Feb	52	87.2	718	4070	6966	42692
March	52	110.9	979	5477	8884	57073
April	51	110.5	1033	6109	9622	61359
May	51	116.0	1042	6078	10644	68079
June	51	122.6	1090	6465	10755	70106
July	51	122.9	1096	6603	10742	71555
Aug	51	126.7	1099	6730	11723	77176
Sept	51	117.6	1015	6206	10864	68906
Oct	48	113.6	986	5903	11452	71802
Nov	45	111.7	1001	5859	10935	67885

* Number of mills reopened at the end of the month

Source: ICMF Statements, Monthly Statistical Abstract, March 1984

figures about the numbers of workers who had rejoined or about the quantity of cloth produced. Had he done so it would have been clear to everyone that the strike was still holding strongly.

It has to be realized that the attendance figures also include watch and ward personnel who prior to the strike accounted for approximately 6,000 persons and technical and supervisory staff, normally rated at 21,000 persons. In total these two categories make up for about 11 per cent of all employees in the textile industry. Neither the staff nor watch and ward personnel were on strike and they were, therefore, the first to man the empty mills after the gates were opened. If one corrects this it will be seen that the attendance was even poorer than the Table seems to indicate. In the face of the attendance figures given above, Bhosale's announcement in May 1982 that the strike would be resolved before mid-June as the workers had come to realize the futility of their struggle, stands exposed as wholly baseless (*TOI*, 23 May 1982).

How the real situation was in the middle of the strike for each mill in the private sector separately may be deduced from the percentage of spindles and looms that were actually working (see Table 2.3). While studying these figures it must be taken into account that whatever machine activity is shown, includes work done by new recruits who helped to boost production. Secondly, the percentages do not indicate whether the machinery was used in one, two or three shifts. From a statistical survey of the MOA in January 1983 the following figures are derived: twenty mills were working three shifts, twelve mills were working two shifts, eighteen mills were working one shift, seven mills did not produce, three mills had not yet even reopened (Mukesh, Sitaram, New City). This means that, going by the MOA figures, ten mills were producing nothing at all one year after the commencement of the strike whereas the others were producing only partially. There is a difference to be noted here between private and nationalized mills. The latter, with the exception of the India United group (NTC North), reopened on the whole about half a year later than the private mills, namely in December 1982 as against June for most private mills.

Table 2.3 also shows that the two mills where working assumed normal proportions at a relatively early stage were Century and Bombay Dyeing (Spring Mills). In the case of Century there is probably a connection with the harsh policy pursued by the management of the mill in the course of the strike and the liberal use of fresh recruits to keep production going. According to the Kotwal Committee, not more than 47 per cent of the old labour force of Century was employed after the strike. For Spring Mills the figure was 60 per cent.[132] Another important factor, and one which is commonly overlooked, may have been the housing facilities provided by both these mills to sizeable sections of their workforce. In the case of Century some 40 per cent of the workers are housed in rooms and buildings belonging to the company.[133] Bombay Dyeing too houses its employees in chawls* and these provide inexpensive and comparatively good accommodation which many workers must have found hard to give up, particularly in the context of Bombay's housing famine. In the course of the interviews with the workers it appeared that the risk of losing these housing facilities, whatever their worth, was for many workers a major deterrent in prolonging the strike.

TABLE 2.3

Percentage of Looms and Spindles Working in Private Bombay Mills in August 1982

Name Unit	*Owner/Chairman*	*Working %*	
		Looms	*Spindles*
Spring (Bombay Dyeing)	Nusli Wadia	94.7	70.1
Textile (Bombay Dyeing)	Nusli Wadia	51.7	29.7
Bradbury	Kumar Karnani	–	–
Century	B.K. Birla	100.0	88.3
Dawn	Bansi S. Mehta	–	29.4
Elphinstone	K.L. Jalan	27.6	8.4
Finlay	Ratanji Mulji	–	–
Gold Mohur	,,	33.0	36.0
Hindoostan	S. Thackersey	55.0	47.2
Crown	,,	73.0	59.0
Jam	R. Sethi	3.3	3.8
Kamala	Board of Directors	–	–
Khatau	Makanji /Khatau	55.8	76.4
Kohinoor (1 & 2)	Nanjundiah	–	–
Kohinoor (3)	,,	–	–

* A Marathi word for rows of single room tenements with shared toilet facilities.

Name Unit	*Owner/Chairman*	*Working %*	
		Looms	*Spindles*
Mafatlal (2)	A.N. Mafatlal	75.5	62.3
Mafatlal (3)	,,	37.2	14.7
Matulya Mills	Y.N. Mafatlal	91.9	40.0
Modern Mills	Jatia	–	–
Morarjee (1)	Piramal	70.9	44.0
Morarjee (2)	,,	35.5	21.6
Mukesh Textile Mills	Agarwal	–	–
New City of Bombay	Gautam Kanoria	–	–
New Great Eastern	Tulsidas Kanoria	–	–
Phoenix Mills	R. Ruia	–	46.1
Piramal Spg & Wvg	Piramal	45.6	38.1
Podar	Podar	15.1	19.6
Prakash Cotton Mills	Jalan	–	–
Raguvanshi	H. Maganlal	77.3	12.7
Ruby Mills	M.C. Shah	70.6	48.7
Shree Madhusudan	R.N. Bangur	–	–
Shree Niwas Cotton	B. Somani	16.6	9.7
Shree Ram Mills	A.S. Kasliwal	17.7	2.4
Shree Sitaram	Board of Directors	–	–
Simplex	S.R. Damani	31.9	27.0
Standard	R.N. Mafatlal	25.3	49.7
New China	"	59.3	41.6
Svadeshi	Naval H. Tata	–	–
Swan	J.P. Goenka	28.7	47.3
Coorla	"	35.3	27.4
Tata	Naval H. Tata	–	–
Victoria	M. Mangaldas	36.1	19.3

Source: Compiled from Mill Statement 1983 and letter MOA to Finance Minister P.K. Mukherjee d. 22 August 1982.

Political Turn: It is possible to divide the strike period into three phases. The first is the period prior to the strike when tensions rapidly built up and the stage was set for the outbreak of the strike. The second phase is marked by the commencement of the strike and activities such as the formation of workers' committees, morchas* and rallies in the city, food drives in the hinterland and Samant's rural tour. The third phase started in August 1982 with the campaigns to fill the jails. No clear pattern of strike-related activities is to be discerned after the several jail bharo† campaigns which distinguish yet another phase and the strike gradually tapered off.

In April 1983 an attempt was made to revive the strike by launching a campaign to put pressure on the workers to leave the mills (mill chodo)‡ but the very fact that such a campaign was believed necessary, displays the imminent collapse of the strike. In this last phase there have also been some long marches in rural districts (Kolhapur, Sangli, Satara, Pune) and huge morchas in the city even as late as 1 August and 2 September. But the mill chodo, the long marches and the morchas signified the agony of a strike that failed rather than a distinct phase in the struggle.

However, amidst all the turmoil connected with organizing the strike, Datta Samant found time to pursue another line of activity. During his rural tour in March 1982 he had ventured the view that a political party championing the cause of the industrial and agricultural labourers would be desirable, a statement that had been welcomed by the LNP. Already in April that year Samant decided that the time had come to test this idea and he registered with his Kamgar Aghadi (Workers' Party) as an independent candidate to contest the elections in Thane for a seat in the Lok Sabha. Samant, at that time, did not have a clear-cut political programme, for which he was blamed by the left parties that were very suspicious of his moves. Even as late as 1987 it appeared that the programme of the Kamgar Aghadi was far from exhaustive and displayed many lacunae. This is not surprising given the superhuman tasks Samant wished to shoulder all by himself: like running thousands of unions and being politically active at the same time.

Samant sought to win the favour of the voters by claiming that he would consistently defend the position of the workers in Parliament. Fearing the political impact of a victory of Datta Samant in Thane

---

* Hindi word denoting a procession organized as a protest.

† To fill

‡ To leave

the RMMS tried to thwart his efforts by supporting other candidates (*TOI*, 16 May 1982). At the same time CM Bhosale accused Samant of being unmindful of the fate of the textile workers and subordinating their interests to his political aims. Whether the results were influenced by this propaganda or not, Samant lost the elections by a wide margin. J. Patil, candidate for the Bharatiya Janata Party, won with 144,458 votes as against 71,885 for Datta Samant. Even the Congress candidate, Prabhakar Hegde, fared better than him with nearly 100,000 votes (*TOI*, 21 May 1982).

Datta Samant attributed his defeat to the great number of workers who stayed at that time in the villages. Subsequent elections in which Samant participated could not establish the truth of this argument but the continuation of the strike did not suffer in the least from Samant's defeat in Thane, which may be an indication that the two were simply not related or at least to a much smaller degree than is generally believed. During and after the elections in Thane, Samant became more outspoken in his criticism of the Congress Party which resulted in a cautious rapprochement between Samant and the communists who had so far considered him a lackey of the bourgeois state. The events in this election provided, nevertheless, a basis for future cooperation.

In July 1983, at the rear end of the strike, there would follow elections in Sangli, a stronghold of the Congress and the centre of power of the former CM Vasantdada Patil. All the opposition parties united behind Shantaram Patil, a leading activist of the LNP and an active supporter of the strike. During the election campaigns Samant visited Kolhapur, Satara and Pune, often in the company of the SSS president, Y. Chavan. Many textile workers who had returned to the villages took part in the campaigning and many others donated money. Due to the vigorous efforts of the LNP/MGKU camp, Vasantdada Patil was forced to devote much more time to this election than in the past. But in spite of all the canvassing Vasantdada Patil was elected with 53,000 votes as against 14,000 for S. Patil.

This time Samant's supporters tried to soften the defeat by pointing at the sizeable number of votes comrade Shantaram Patil collected in the teeth of overwhelming support for Vasantdada Patil.[134] But subsequent elections, too, did not show overwhelming support for Datta Samant's moves in the political field. His success there, in any case, is not to be compared with his impressive performance in the field of trade unionism which raises the question of why he should have started a political party in the first place. Till the beginning of the textile strike Samant monotonously accused all political parties of being merely interested in the votes of the workers. Did the foundation of the Kamgar Aghadi indicate a somersault in Samant's thinking or was it but a logical step following the conclusion that no one could defend the workers' cause in the political arena better than he could?

Datta Samant himself said that his political activities were the necessary sequel to his trade unionism: 'I learnt from the strike and from my experience as a trade unionist that the Indian working class must get involved in politics. They can't do without politics because only in that manner can they pressurize their demands' (interview, 17 May 1986). One would expect that someone who is convinced that it is unavoidable to extend the activities from the field of trade unionism to politics, would at least believe in the possibility of converting workers to his point of view. As it is, no purpose is served by merely enlarging the range of political alternatives with yet another powerless party. The only justification for such a step would be the deep-felt need by a person or a group of persons to represent certain principles or to protect certain interests which no one else would care to do. Samant's foremost concern, however related to labour politics, a field which he could equally well serve as a trade unionist. By attempting to float a party which did not catch on, Samant ran the risk of reducing his influence, instead of enhancing his clout.

Samant seemed to be aware that the prospects were gloomy. He did not entertain high hopes of establishing a real labour alternative and felt that it was very difficult to organize workers politically on labour issues: 'In my experience the labour class is totally ignorant when they decide about their votes. In India voting is not mature. The voting is always for the Congress whatever view you offer. The workers are not even interested in voting for labour problems. Besides, whatever the programme, the government is not going to accept any of my programmes' (interview, 19 May 1986).

In spite of this negative view, Samant believed that his influence in Parliament benefited from his trade union activities and vice versa. But the major gain seems to be that the status of an MP provided him with a more respectable image which was at times helpful when negotiating with employers. He was not ready to admit that both the fields, politics and trade unionism, might suffer from his divided attention. 'Whatever I am saying at gate meetings, I am also saying in the Parliament. There is no such division, on the contrary. In the Parliament too they accept me as a real representative of the workmen' (ibid.). Taking account of the moderate gains Samant expected to achieve by being politically active, the answer to the question of what purpose was served by entering the political field with his own party remained obscure. At best one might say that Samant was continuing the struggle with other means and was leading the (textile) workers in a new direction, but the question of efficacy cannot be overlooked in that. Lastly, there was the possibility that others might take political advantage of his popularity but given Samant's limited success so far and his very personal style of handling problems there seemed little prospect of that.

Role of the Press

The role of the press during the long-drawn-out battle has been widely criticized. In essence the criticism is twofold and relates to a quantitative and a qualitative aspect of the reports on the strike. The quantitative aspect simply means that the press, the English newspapers in particular, devoted far too little attention to an event of such magnitude as the ongoing strike. As far as the qualitative aspect is concerned there is near unanimity among writers of a leftist persuasion that the newspapers in general took an anti-labour stand and based their reports predominantly on the information provided by the government of Maharashtra and MOA. However, so far no systematic investigation has been made to prove the correctness of these assumptions.[135]

In order to be able to be more specific a limited number of newspapers were scrutinized for the entire strike period (that is, from 18 January 1982 till 2 August 1983) with regard to press reports relating to the strike in the widest sense. Both quantitative as well as qualitative aspects were taken into consideration. It is clear that as far as quantitative aspects are concerned there is the problem of defining a 'strike-related event'. For clarity's sake it must be stated that only reports in which the strike was mentioned explicitly were taken into account. This means, for example, that articles dealing with problems of cotton growers or the need for modernization in the textile industry, in which the strike was not mentioned, were not counted although there may have been a connection with the Bombay textile strike.

The most important English newspapers in Maharashtra at that time were the *Times of India (TOI)* and *Indian Express (IE)*, both with a Bombay edition and wide circulation. The English-speaking and reading section of Maharashtrian society was to a large extent influenced by these two newspapers. Of course, this readership also obtained news from the radio and television, but the scope of the research programme didn't permit the inclusion of audio-visual media. Naturally, there were and are many more English newspapers available in Maharashtra but as far as circulation is concerned they lag way behind.[136]

To obtain an idea of the way the strike was reported in the Marathi press it could be argued that here, too, the newspapers with the widest circulation (that is, *Loksatta* and *Maharashtra Times*) would have to be selected. However, it seemed more important to have a look at the newspapers read by the textile workers themselves. An obvious choice here would be *Nava Kal* (with a claimed 70,000 readers) and *Mumbai Sakal* (with approximately 30,000 readers). It was decided to focus on *Nava Kal* as 76 per cent of the workers in the sample who were asked which newspaper they read during the strike, reported that it had been *Nava Kal*.

Shramik Vichar, another Marathi daily, was selected for a different reason. It had only a very limited circulation (about 3,000 subscribers) but its influence was far greater than the circulation leads one to believe. *Shramik Vichar* was widely read in trade union circles because of its dedication to the workers' cause. The newspaper was the mouthpiece of the LNP (the party that stood with the MGKU and Datta Samant throughout the strike), and advocated a rather independent brand of communist ideology. This daily reached the cadres of the unions but was also read out to workers in rural areas during the strike.

In Tables 2.4 and 2.5 the findings regarding the quantitative aspect are presented. While studying these figures a few things have to be borne in mind. It goes without saying that the attention an article attracts is largely decided by the place it finds in the columns of the newspaper. A place on the front page is far more important than one of similar size on one of the inner pages. Because of this a distinction has been made between the display on the front page and the display on other pages. The Table shows that *Shramik Vichar* and (to a lesser extent) *Nava Kal* published an overwhelming proportion of their articles on the front page as opposed to *IE* and *TOI* (the differences between *TOI* and *IE* are less striking). This is somewhat misleading as both *Shramik Vichar* and *Nava Kal* consisted of a few pages only and this, in combination with the difference in value attached to the strike, explains why the majority of articles on the strike in *Shramik Vichar* and *Nava Kal* reached the front page.

TABLE 2.4

Number of Articles in the Period 18 January 1982 till 2 August 1983

*Space articles column-wise**	*Newspaper*					
	Indian Express		*Times of India*		*Nava Kal*	
1	255	(41)	98	(18)	14	(11)
2	91	(18)	106	(41)	81	(70)
3	28	(14)	29	(18)	74	(71)
4	18	(6)	5	(5)	132	(132)
5 or more	8	(4)	2		8	(5)
Total	400	(83)	240	(82)	309	(289)

* The figures in brackets indicate the display on the front page.

TABLE 2.5

Number of Articles in the Period January 1982 to May 1982

*Space articles column-wise**	*Newspaper*			
	Nava Kal		*Shramik Vichar*	
1	3	(3)	23	(19)
2	21	(20)	53	(30)
3	22	(21)	57	(38)
4	47	(47)	50	(35)
5 or more	7	(7)	24	(3)
Total	100	(98)	207	(125)

* The figures in brackets indicate the display on the front page.

Another problem relates to the availability of the selected newspapers. The figures for the *IE* would have been higher if the newspaper had appeared in the period from 18 January 1982 to 21 February 1982 (a span of time covered by the quantitative analysis).[137] Even during the two months directly preceding the strike, the *IE* was not sold. As explained elsewhere, the textile strike developed from the struggle for a higher bonus in seven mills and for a wage hike in one mill, a struggle commencing on 20 October 1981. Because the *IE* did not appear for two months in the period prior to the strike it was decided not to include the period from 21 October 1981 to 18 January 1982. In the case of *Shramik Vichar,* table-wise counting was done only for a period of four months, it being obvious that this paper surpassed all the others in its attention to the strike due to its partisan stand. For comparison this period has been juxtaposed with the findings for *Nava Kal* in the same period.

From the Table it appears that all newspapers devoted considerable space to the strike. As might be expected, the lead is taken by *Nava Kal* and *Shramik Vichar (SV)*. But in all newspapers hundreds of short and longer articles supplied a steady stream of news enabling readers to keep abreast of strike-related developments. Within the time span of a year and a half there have been, of course, peak periods coinciding with developments on the political front promising a breakthrough. However, as we shall shortly see, all this news was of a very fragmentary nature in the case of the English newspapers and did not allow for a comprehensive view of the events taking place. It was also biased as far as the sources were concerned.

From a comparison of the number of articles in *Shramik Vichar* and *Nava Kal*, it transpires that there is a lot of difference between the two. *Shramik Vichar,* as a dedicated daily, devoted considerably more attention to the strike than *Nava Kal.* It is also clear that the *IE,* although never near *Nava Kal,* is far ahead of the *TOI* in terms of space devoted to the strike. This is definitely so with regard to single-column articles. The total of printed articles is 400 in the case of *IE* as against 240 for the *TOI.* The total number of articles in *IE* even surpasses the number of articles in *Nava Kal* (309). But this numeric approach easily creates a wrong impression for although *Nava Kal* printed a smaller number of articles than *IE,* the space devoted to the strike in the former was definitely greater as is clear from the number of long articles (four-column articles in particular). Whatever the limitations of the numeric approach, it cannot be maintained that the newspapers under investigation neglected the strike as a subject. The often repeated but rarely substantiated complaint voiced by leftist-oriented trade unionists and activists that the English press paid no attention to the strike falls flat. Much more important, however, is the qualitative aspect of the news.

CONTENTS

On the whole the selected English newspapers restricted themselves to reports on the numerous attempts at conciliation, the proceedings of various committees, predictions of the imminent collapse of the strike, attendance in the mills, violent incidents and ample presentation of the views of the government, millowners and the RMMS. The constantly repeated predictions of the end of the strike were, wishful thinking apart, based on production and attendance figures supplied by the MOA and unquestioningly reproduced by government officials and newspapers.

It is possible to discern a difference between the *TOI* and *IE* with regard to the tendency of the reports. In spite of what has been observed before, the *TOI* cannot be considered to be anti-strike or even anti-Samant as far as the textile strike is concerned. The way the newspaper dealt with the strike simply reveals a lack of interest in the fate of the striking workers. The daily did not go beyond printing what prominent actors in the strike had to say. The one article in which the fate of the striking workers is highlighted *(TOI,* 1 August 1982), shows a condemnation of the RMMS and support for the strike. Criticism of the government by politicians and trade union leaders as well as denials by Datta Samant of the correctness of figures were duly printed.

The case of the *IE* is different but not better. The picture here is more complicated and less consistent. What has been said before about the absence of analytical articles remains true and, with a rare exception, the same goes for concern with the strikers' plight. This is somewhat surprising as the daily deemed it fit to publish a seven-column article during the strike by Moin Qazi on the plight of a small group of weavers in the Deccan who were threatened in their existence by competition from the powerlooms (*IE,* May 1982). On the whole the paper seemed to seize every opportunity to discredit the strike and its leader.

On 25 June 1982, the *IE* opened with a seven-column article under the headline 'Attempt on Bhosale', in which it was alleged that a striking worker from Century Mills tried to kill CM Bhosale. The article suggested that the worker belonged to Samant's union and the fact that the man claimed that he did not belong to any union—as was subsequently established and printed by other newspapers—was never published.[138] *Nava Kal*, too, prominently reported the incident but stated correctly that the assailant did not belong to a union. *Shramik Vichar* on the other hand tried to put the blame on the Shiv Sena (26 June 1982).

It is typical of the *IE* that a few months later when Datta Samant was attacked with a khukri (dagger) by a worker belonging to the Shiv Sena, it failed to report the matter altogether although the *TOI* brought out the news on its front page (*TOI,* 2 October 1982). Predictably, *Shramik Vichar* made it the lead article of the paper (2 October 1982). The police confirmed this incident which might easily have turned into a tragedy.[139] That the *IE* brought the news about the attack on the CM but not the one on the strike leader was consistent with the attempt to paint Samant in the darkest possible colours. It did not fit in this approach to provide Samant with a cloak of martyrdom. By repeatedly reporting on a 'fear psychosis among millmen', the *IE* tried to create an image of the strike as one dominated by extreme violence and it sought to put the blame for that on Samant's MGKU. After a year the daily reported that eleven persons had been killed during the strike (seven workers and four officers) which was a totally incorrect statement. Furthermore, the newspaper refrained from naming the source of this essential information (*IE,* 30 December 1982).

Again, when irate striking workers in Bombay damaged furniture in the courtroom and some cars outside the court premises after hearing that the case regarding derecognition of the RMMS had been adjourned, the *IE* opened the front page the following day with this news under the headline: 'Millmen Run Amuck in Court' (*IE,* 19 November 1982). The *TOI* did not even carry the news. *Shramik Vichar* did publish an account of the incident along with an apology from Datta Samant for the behaviour of the workers (20 November 1982).

If the *IE* presented the plight of the striking workers at all it was with the intention of pointing out the senselessness of the strike as in the case of a worker who committed suicide by setting fire to himself. In this there was little regard for cause and effect. Under a two-column headline ('Textile Worker Immolates Himself'), the reader is informed that an employee of Jupiter Mills put an end to his life 'unable to withstand the financial burden thrust upon him by the prolonged textile strike' (*IE,* 15 October 1982). At the end of the article, however, the reader learns that the worker had resumed his duty six months earlier.

In spite of its negative attitude towards the strike and towards Datta Samant, the paper supported one of the vital claims of the workers, that is, secret ballot to decide the representative union. In an editorial on the strike the paper observed that the strike demonstrated that the prevailing verification system can result in a total alienation between workers and the recognized union. The paper concludes: 'A Secret Ballot Would Rectify Matters' (*IE,* 13 January 1983).

As far as the contents are concerned it is all too obvious that there was an almost total lack of intelligent journalism on the part of both the *TOI* and the *IE.* Except for a few articles by Praful Bidwai in the *TOI* during the first ten months of the strike and Vinay Hardikar in the *IE* after one year, well-researched analytical articles seeking to expose the root causes of the strike are glaringly lacking in both these dailies. This is particularly surprising given the fact that the strike was taking place in the heart of the city (a Pune-based paper like *Shramik Vichar* did not share the advantage of proximate location).

If there is much to say against the way the *IE* reported on strike-related events, the picture is not altogether positive for *Shramik Vichar* either. During the police riots in Bombay on 18 August 1982 the residences of RMMS leaders Hoshing and Bhai Bhosale were ransacked but *Shramik Vichar* failed to note that striking textile workers participated in this well-directed attack.[140] The news about the defeat of Datta Samant in the by-elections in Thane (May 1982) was introduced in a veiled manner. Again, when the Registrar of Trade Unions in Bombay on 5 November decided that there was no case for derecognition of the RMMS (a point clamoured for by the MGKU and Datta Samant), the paper failed to report this vital decision.

It is likely that strategic reasons prevailed in these cases but it betrays the partisan character of the daily. With the exception of analytical articles written by leaders like Y.B.Chavan and D.S. Kulkarni, the quality of the day-to-day news was on the whole poor because of the way the information was dealt with and its lack of precision. The fact that many readers of *Shramik Vichar* are simple workers does not justify shabby treatment of the news. However, it must also be stated that the paper, more than any other, devoted a great deal of space to articles attempting to expose the root causes of the strike.

It is not possible to present a similar analysis for the other dailies and periodicals. There is, however, not much evidence to support the contention that a consistently hostile attitude towards the strike was taken by them. Even a paper like the *Financial Express* (*FE*), which endorses employers' views, published at times articles critical of the MOA, Government and RMMS.[141] To be sure, the *FE* had no sympathy for the strike and did its best to create a violent image of the strikers. To this end the paper used at times vicious devices, like the accusation in an editorial that a reign of terror prevailed in the mill areas leading to hundreds of violent encounters 'causing injury and even death to nearly 500 textile workers and supervisory personnel' (*FE*, 19 April 1982). Such a phrase suggests a number of killings running into scores or even hundreds of workers. It is worth noting that the daily wrote this only three months after the beginning of the strike at a time when the striking workers were still determined not to resume work before they had won the battle and even the need for picketing was not felt.

The *Economic Times* devoted considerable space to the views of the main actors in the textile drama and to discussing intricate problems and solutions relating to the strike. It seems that the extent to which this was done in a newspaper depended largely on the presence or availability of a dedicated labour correspondent (for example, Javed Anand writing for *The Daily,* Radha Iyer for *Business Standard* or Rajni Bakshi for *The Telegraph* and *Sunday Observer).* On the whole, however, the strike did not draw much serious attention. What is true for dailies is also true for weeklies and other periodicals. *India Today,* for example, at that time the most renowned Indian fortnightly, published just five articles on the strike in a time span of twenty months.

Considering the poor attention given to the strike in India itself it is hardly surprising that this immense struggle did not attract much attention abroad either. This sharply contrasts with the space devoted in the press to other remarkable struggles like the miners' strike in England (March 1984–March 1985) or the still more recent miners' strike in South Africa which lasted only three weeks. In the latter case the racial overtones of the strike may explain the worldwide attention it received but this element was absent in the English strike which nevertheless evoked widespread international interest.

ADVERTISEMENTS

A completely different aspect of the role of the press in the textile strike relates to the way the columns were used by the millowners to carry out propaganda or threaten or entice, as the case may be, the workers to resume duty. This was done on a large scale and may well have influenced the views of readers. The millowners had an advantage here as the workers under the leadership of Samant could not use this device for lack of funds.

At a very early stage the MOA decided to make use of this propaganda weapon. In an advertisement covering half a page on the eve of the strike (*TOI*, 24 December 1981) the MOA explains in detail what, according to this organization, caused the present labour trouble in the industry.[142] The MOA took the opportunity of publishing along with this text, the letter it wrote to CM Antulay announcing its withdrawal from the proceedings of the High Power Committee (HPC). In this letter the MOA justified its withdrawal by referring to the ongoing bonus strike in seven mills, the doubts of Samant regarding the bona fides of the HPC and the lack of cooperation from other actors (RMMS, NTC) in the industry. The text also expressed 'dismay' at the decision of the government to consider the demands of the workers and make recommendations within two months.

In the days to follow, the mills in which the bonus strike was in progress would one after the other give notices through the columns of *Nava Kal* threatening striking workers with dismissal or cancellation of *badli* passes (December 1982, passim). The day before the strike started the MOA published a full page text in *Nava Kal* asking the reader whether the strike was really necessary (17 January 1982). In the weeks to follow requests to resume work and threats were to follow. The MOA and individual mills chiefly used the papers to give notices and warn the workers of the consequences of their behaviour.

After the Labour Court declared the strike illegal on 10 February 1982 the management of, for example, Bombay Dyeing published this decision in *Nava Kal* and advised the workers to resume duty (18 February 1982). In *Mid-day* the MOA refuted a number of Samant's statements by calling them lies (23 February 1982). Another spate of advertisements was to follow in March. By the end of the month the secretary-general of the MOA launched a frontal attack on Samant, questioning his capabilities as a labour leader (*The Daily,* 31 March 1982).

The next wave of notices given by the mills was in September 1982. In this the millowners referred to an appeal by the Union labour minister given three months earlier to resume work. Notices of this kind appeared in *Mumbai Sakal* and *Kesari* (14 September 1982); *Loksatta* and *Navbharat Times* (15 September 1982). The workers were once again given a 'last chance' to resume duty. In the orders of dismissal that followed upon these public notices the managers refer specifically to the publications in the aforesaid newspapers.

All these efforts, however, did not bear the fruit the millowners hoped for and before long another campaign began to win over the striking workers instead of bullying them. In this the millowners paid special attention to the families of the workers as they (rightly) believed that these families were of vital importance in the decision to resume duty. In flagrant contradiction to the theme they had been harping upon so far, that is, the so-called extreme violence during the strike without which the struggle would have collapsed long ago, they now stressed the peaceful environment of the mills. According to an article in the *TOI* on this subject, the text of one advertisement read: 'Bring your wife and children and family members to see how peaceful the atmosphere in the mill area is' (*TOI,* 8 November 1982).

From the above it appears that the millowners utilized the press in many different ways. In those papers in which they could not hope for space on the news pages to expound their views regarding the strike and the problems of the textile industry (as in the *FE*), they simply bought space. They chose the Marathi dailies but not solely Marathi papers for issuing notices to the workers and they used the English newspapers to try to convince the upper strata of the society of the fairness of their stand and their views. The workers, however, could only *hope* for sympathetic treatment by journalists in newspapers in which they would never be able to raise their voice.

The press in turn failed in its task of criticism. The figures regarding production of cloth and mill attendance supplied by the MOA and the government (not based on independent investigations but simply taken from the employers) were indiscriminately accepted and printed. The same goes for the continuous predictions of the end of the strike. In this the press showed a docile attitude, thereby contributing to a distorted picture of the real situation and by implication undermined the position of the striking workers. Although, all in all, considerable space was given to strike-related events, little of this had substance and although (with a few exceptions) the press did not take a hostile view of the strike it is sad to note that there was hardly any real concern for the fate of the workers either.

NOTES

1. The BIR Act applies to the several textile industries in Maharashtra such as cotton, silk, woollen, hosiery and processing, and to sugar, cooperative banks, electricity generation, electricity supply and BEST. The Act operates on an industry-cum-region basis. The industries were selected because of their homogeneity within the industry (production units mainly differing in size but not so much in applied technology), enabling standardization of wages, occupation and service conditions.
2. The following account is mainly based on V.B. Karnik (1966), C.K. Johri (1967), S.C. Jha (1970), V.P. Michael (1979), Punekar e.a. (1981), E.A. and U. Ramaswamy (1981), S. Jawaid (1982).
3. The dilemma faced by the AITUC is neatly summed up by a resolution passed in 1940: 'As the present war between Great Britain on the one side and the Fascist Powers on the other is claimed by Britain to be waged for the vindication of the principles of freedom and democracy and not for any imperialistic purpose, India without having any sympathy for either imperialism or fascism, naturally claims for herself freedom and a democratic Government before she can be expected to take part in the war' (Quoted by Punekar e. a., 1981: 212).
4. The dramatic change by the communists is exemplified by the resolution adopted at a CPI congress in May 1943 in Bombay: 'It is the patriotic duty of the workers to strengthen defence by taking the initiative for organizing more production and better transport and against stoppage

of work, irrespective of what the boss or the bureaucrat does … Communists take a bold and open stand against strikes as they injure the defence of the country by holding up production.' (Quoted by Jha, 1970: 166).

5. Source: Punekar e.a., 1981, 213; Johri, 1967: 30–31.
6. Trying to outline the post-war developments within the RMMS is far from easy as this history has not been well documented. To the best of my knowledge no books or other studies are available analysing the post-war history of the Sangh. For the first decade after the war the studies by Ralph James and M.D. Morris provide useful data. Judging from experience during fieldwork, the Sangh is not keen on persons who appear to be inquisitive. A lot of what is to follow about the period between 1945 and 1980, therefore, had to be based on articles in newspapers and recollections of witnesses.
7. Valuable information regarding the position of the MMS in 1950 was made available by Dr Shanta Vaidya, head of the Research Section of the Maniben Kara Institute which is sponsored by the Hind Mazdoor Sabha.
8. Kumar Ketkar, 'RMMS: Historical Perspective', *The Economic Times*, 26 April 1982.
9. S.Y. Kolhatkar, president of the CITU in Maharashtra (interview, 17 April 1986).
10. There have been many more unions in the Bombay textile industry than those listed in Table 2.1 but the registration of most of these unions has meanwhile been cancelled. See Thakker for a comprehensive overview of the labour organizations in the period 1924–59 (Thakker, 1962: 89–90).
11. Radha Iyer, 'Samant's Textile Trap', *Business Standard*, 30 December 1981.
12. This point was stressed by G.V. Chitnis, secretary-general of the MGKU (interview, 11 April 1986).
13. Ibid.
14. *Handbook of Service Conditions 1980*, MOA, 1980: 334 (Agreement dated 5 July 1973 regarding the introduction of a seven-days-a-week working system).
15. *See* 'Millowners to the Rescue', *Economic and Political Weekly*, 28 July 1973.
16. Information regarding the position of the MGKU in this strike is based on data collected by Dr Shanta Vaidya.
17. Desai states that many workers were left with the feeling that they had been used by Dange in order to secure the election of his daughter Rosa Deshpande to the Lok Sabha against Ramrao Adik (Desai, 1982). These elections took place at the same time and the strike was called

off the day after the elections. Strong resentment against the Dange-settlement was still noticeable during my fieldwork in 1987. The wage increase secured by Dange is often mocked as the 'Dange allowance'.

18. Award dated 29 November 1979 regarding ad hoc increase of wages and annual increments (MOA, 1980: 278–87).
19. In an article on the occasion of the 500th day of the strike the journal *Indian Management* (21 June 1983) observed that the representative union never had the support of the majority of the workers at any time during its existence.
20. See *Constitution and Rules of the RMMS (Bombay, 1983).*
21. The powers are very briefly stated in Article 12 of the *Constitution and Rules of the Maharashtra General Kamgar Union*: 'The Managing Committee, subject to the provision of Section 21 of the Trade Union Act, 1926, the affairs of the Union, financial and otherwise, shall be conducted by a Managing Committee consisting of the office bearers and not more than twenty other members elected at the annual General Meeting' (sic).
22. It is a special experience to observe Datta Samant dealing with routine union matters. Within the shortest possible time (rarely spending more than ten minutes on a case), he listens to the scores of delegations that daily visit his home office and gives advice, passes a judgement or determines a strategy. There is no time left for formalities. Given the fact that he wants to run thousands of unions there is no alternative to this modus operandi.
23. A related problem is that in strikes of long duration employees tend to look for other jobs which makes it difficult to decide on the date of the end of a strike, particularly when such a strike is never called off. *India Today* offers the example of a strike in National Boilers where 200 employees had been on a strike for more than four years but in the meantime Datta Samant found them new jobs without, however, ending the strike ('The Striking Terror', *India Today*, 28 February 1982). Another trade union leader famous for his prolonged battles is R.J. Mehta who claims to have conducted a strike lasting twenty months involving the staff of the head office of Bombay Dyeing and another one of twenty-eight months with the workers of Bush Radio ('Whither Trade Union Movement?', *Industrial Times*, 13–26 April 1987).
24. The scope and duration of the textile strike was recently matched by the historic miners' strike in England which lasted from March 1984 to March 1985. The strike, under the leadership of the National Union of Mineworkers (NUM) presided over by Arthur Scargill, involved 220,000 workers. The strike was triggered off by plans to restructure the industry at the cost of 20,000 job opportunities and the closure

of twenty mines. It escalated when truck drivers, sailors and dock workers extended their support but in the end the strike fizzled out. Facing defeat a small majority of the workers voted against Scargill's proposal to continue the struggle and decided to resume duty exactly one year after miners in Cortonwood (Yorkshire) had downed their tools. At least four people died in the course of several incidents during the strike. The police arrested nearly 10,000 people and in economic terms the strike meant a loss of some Rs 10,000 crores. A noteworthy aspect of the strike is the support the miners got from many sides (including substantial financial help from workers in the Soviet Union). The strike ended without an agreement with the employers but also without breaking the influence of Scargill who was appointed president of the NUM till the year 2003. The strike also bared the tensions among the workers themselves. A dissident section founded a new miners' union (UDM) in December 1985 (*Keesings Historisch Archief*, 9 July 1987, 439–43).

Another impressive strike drawing worldwide attention was the strike in August 1987 of the National Union of Mineworkers (NUM) in South Africa (9–30 August). The secretary-general of the NUM, Cyril Ramaphosa, declared that 3.5 lakhs of miners in forty-four mines participated in the strike whereas the employers said that about 2.5 lakhs of workers in thirty-one mines (thirteen coal mines and eighteen gold mines) were involved. Wage demands, caused by the lack of parity in wages (white workers earning five times as much as their black colleagues), triggered it off. The costs of this brief strike in terms of human lives were immense. Not less than eleven workers died in confrontations with security officers of the mines and in clashes between strikers and strike breakers. The strike ended after concessions from the employers (wage increases of between 17 and 24 per cent, improvement in fringe benefits) which were not very different from earlier proposals made by them. No agreement was reached on the fate of some 40,000 workers who had been dismissed in the course of the strike nor on the closure of certain mines (*Keesings Historisch Archief*, 3 September 1987, 561–3).

25. See L.C. Dhingra, 'The Concept, Evolution and Nature of Bonus', *Indian Labour Journal*, 1983, vol. 24, no. 3.
26. Speaking about bonus the then secretary-general of the MOA, M.S. Sanikop, remarked: 'Every year round Diwali we pay bonus ... some baksheesh ... baksheesh in the sense of appreciation of the work done by the worker' (interview, 13 January 1986). In an analysis of the evolution of bonus Dhingra concluded that it came to be judicially recognized very soon that bonus was neither a gratuitous payment

made by the employer to his workmen nor a deferred wage and that a claim for bonus could be legitimately made by workers because of the contribution of labour to capital (Dhingra, 1983).

27. Javed Anand, 'A Chronology of Events', *The 10th Month: Bombay's Historic Textile Strike* (Bombay, 1983).

28. See apology published by MOA: 'Textile strike in seven mills for higher bonus and threatened general strike for higher wages and fringe benefits – Is there any justification?', *FE*, 15 January 1982.

29. A vivid description of the situation in Standard Mills and the stand taken by activists of other unions with regard to Samant's leadership is to be found in Bakshi's '*The Long Haul*' (Bakshi, 1987: 19–24). For an account of the tempering of the workers' zeal by the Lal Bawta Union in Prakash Cotton, see *The Red Flag*, March 1983.

30. Referring to the case, Kisan Tulpule, president of the MMS, states that the management had approached him with a proposal of retrenchment which he turned down. When the workers shifted their loyalty to Samant a fantastic wage hike was realized with the understanding that the workforce would shrink by some 45 per cent as proposed earlier. Tulpule accuses Datta Samant of being ready to sacrifice employment for the sake of short-term gains (interview, 17 March 1986). This complaint is quite common in trade union circles.

31. In a memorandum jointly presented by RMMS and INTWF to the Tripartite Committee (established during the strike in order to study the problems of the textile industry), the hypothetical example is given of two brothers, one working in a textile mill with outmoded machinery requiring great human effort for its operation and one in a modern factory with sophisticated machinery requiring less effort. The text states: 'Basically their educational standards are the same. The wage earned by the textile worker is much less as compared to that of his brother though in terms of labour input the position may be just the reverse. No worker can be expected to suffer this anomaly of more work for less wages and more wages for less work' (Memorandum by INTWF and RMMS, January 1983).

32. See Javed Anand, 'Textile Mills: RMMS Crumbling?', *Sunday Observer*, 1 November 1981.

33. Cf. 'Textile Mills: RMMS Crumbling?', *Sunday Observer*, 1 November 1981; 'Samant Tentacles Spreading', *Times of India*, 5 November 1981; 'Dr Samant Postpones Indefinite Strike', *Nava Kal*, 13 November 1981; 'The Coming Showdown in the Textiles Industry', *Business Standard*, 22 December 1981.

34. P. Bidwai quotes an anonymous textile magnate stating that the management of the seven mills in which the bonus strike was taking

place had already conveyed to Antulay that under no circumstances were they going to pay higher bonus ('Shift in Balance of Forces', *Times of India*, 2 December 1981.)

35. When contacted, Dr Jichkar confirmed that he collected a lot of evidence throwing light on the dubious practices of many mills and readily offered to show this to me (interview, 16 February 1987). However, this promise was never kept for in spite of many persistent attempts later on he failed to produce the records. Shortly after the dissolution of the HPC, Jichkar was appointed as a minister in the new cabinet.
36. *See* 'Courtroom Clashes', *India Today*, 15 May 1984; 'Timely Retreat', *India Today*, 15 July 1984; 'Awaiting Judgement Day', *India Today*, 15 March 1985.
37. To this Samant's brother, P.N. Samant, adds that Singh later told him that the situation had changed so drastically that he did not even dare to propose the solution of the problem by means of a substantial wage hike (interview, 29 May 1987).
38. As quoted in *Report for the Year 1982*, (MOA, 1983b: 203).
39. Bhattacherjee, for instance, in his study on the evolution of unionism in the Bombay textile industry, concluded that the strike resulted in the 'virtual disintegration of the once powerful and internally homogenous BMOA' (Bhattacherjee, 1988: 24).
40. Cf. 'Bid to End Mill Strike by Monday', *TOI*, 17 April 1982; 'Millowners' Ranks Split', *Daily*, 13 July 1982.
41. R.N. Joshi, general manager of Shree Ram Mills, had this to say about the internal tensions at the time of the beginning of the strike: 'You could divide the MOA members in two groups. A group of three or four owners of affluent mills and the other millowners. Within the MOA the demands of the striking workers were discussed and the general feeling prevailed that if these were to be conceded this would mean the death-knell to the industry. The majority felt that we must stop this and that we should thrash out this once and forever. The weaker mills pointed out that accepting the demands would mean handing over the mill to the NTC because they were not capable of meeting such high-pitched demands. After a long discussion it was decided to make a united front and not to give in' (interview, 24 January 1987).
42. Radha Iyer pointed out that it was not the first time since Independence that the power of labour had been curbed, but this does not adequately explain the absence of stern actions and labour agitation ('No Right to Strike', *Business Standard*, 13 August 1981).
43. Ibid.
44. 'A Pious Lady and Her Acts', *IE*, 1 August 1981.

45. See editorials in *TOI* (28 July), *The Economic Times* (29 July), *Patriot* (29 July) in 1981 as quoted by *New Age* (2 August 1981).
46. 'Why This Strike?', *New Age*, 27 December 1981.
47. Cf. 'Bombay Textile Strike has Political Overtones', *Economic Times*, 14 January 1982; 'Is Datta Samant Finished?', *Sunday*, 29 May 1983.
48. Javed Anand has drawn attention to the prominent role played by BEST for the success of any bandh in Bombay as a complete strike of the buses will paralyse the city ('Year of the Textile Strike', *Daily*, 15 January 1982).
49. 'Strike-bound Mills Exhaust Inventory', *Financial Express*, 31 May 1982.
50. There is an inexplicable difference of some 95 million metres in the figure for the highest stock of cloth in February 1982 as presented by the ICMF (373 million metres) and that given by the MOA (278 million metres). See *Report for the Year 1982* (MOA 1983b: XVIII).
51. 'Balance Sheet of Textile Strike', *Commerce*, 22 May 1982.
52. Bombay mills provide for a large part of the total cloth production in textile mills in the country. In the decade prior to the strike, Bombay's share in Indian cloth production hovered between 25 per cent and 29 per cent with the notable exception of 1977 when Bombay's share was 40 per cent (Computed from: *Report for the Year 1982* (MOA 1983b: 473).
53. Mehta states that his philosophy of trade unionism rests on two pillars, namely the economic interest of the workmen and the viability of the industrial unit. 'If workmen get a rise of 20 per cent in their wages I assure a rise of 7 to 10 per cent in the productivity. This means an increase of the workload. Before we decide on that we have studied the process of production. The increase of workload should be reasonable. All of this presupposes discipline. We don't take the cases of workers who are absent without a good reason or who are assaulting other workers. On the contrary, we suggest the management to remove such people. Therefore we are the most unpopular union in this country' (interview, 26 April 1986).
54. Although he did not manage to replace the established union in Godrej, Samant claims that 90 per cent of the workers are really on his side and that ever since then Godrej workers secure substantial benefits from mere token resistance: 'The workers call me at the gate meetings but if you ask management they will tell you that they broke my union and that they always sign with the internal union. Sometimes the management gives even more than I have demanded to the puppet union just to keep me out' (interview, 17 May 1986).
55. During the Emergency Datta Samant was arrested under the Maintenance of Internal Security Act (MISA). According to Dada

Samant, his brother, Datta was then prompted to join the INTUC if he wanted to be released but he did not oblige. However, several authors state that Samant was a member of the INTUC. Jagannath Sharma informs us that Samant finally broke with the INTUC as he could not reconcile himself to the clause pertaining to the means to be adopted for resolving conflicts. In the Gandhian tradition, the INTUC clause stresses peaceful means consistent with truth and non-violence (*Indian Management*, 21 July 1983). Pendse has it that Samant remained in the INTUC till 1980, after which he was 'disaffiliated' but not expelled, on the flimsy ground of non-payment of dues (Pendse, 1981).

56. About his brother's membership of the Congress, Dada says: 'Personally I feel that he was a misnomer in the Congress and I told him so at the time he joined the Congress but he came to realize his mistake and he now opposes the Congress with vigour' (interview, 15 April 1986).
57. *Sunday*, 29 May 1983.
58. It has been frequently observed that the INTUC adopts a much more militant stand in states with a non-Congress government, as appears to be the case from the situation in Kerala and West Bengal.
59. Mehta's contamination with the bacilli of violence surfaces in his comments on the textile strike: 'That strike was not violent at all. In a major strike of more than two lakhs of workers eight or nine incidents of murder is nothing!' (interview, 26 April 1986).
60. Pointing to the need to support a worker who indulged in violence inside as well as outside court Mehta now holds: 'This violence is costly, both in terms of money and time. It costs nothing less than Rs 1,00,000 to fight a murder case. There are chances that the worker might lose his case. This has been my experience and that is why I rely more on law and negotiations than on '*mara mari*' [violent actions] though there was a time when violence could apparently deliver the goods' (*Industrial Times*, 13–26 April 1987).
61. Gulab Joshi, president of the Kamgar Utkarsh Sabha, explained his position as follows: 'I do not deny that I am a mafia boss. I have studied, although I have no formal education, all the books on labour mafia and their style of functioning. And some of their strategies that I have adopted are proving to be very successful' (*Industrial Times*, 13–26 April 1987).
62. Speaking about the problems in recent years in the Sangh, Bhosale asserted : 'I know the underworld in Bombay very well. If I had not known them so well there might have been four or five murders. Phalke approached so many goondas, gangsters and offered them Rs 25,000 or Rs 50,000 to kill my supporters but fortunately all these

hired mafiosi were knowing me, you see. It is not my business to know them but we are having good relations and they know that I am a gentleman' (interview, 30 May 1987).

63. Labour Minister B.M. Gaekwad stated in March 1982 in the Legislative Assembly that the state government had not yet received the demands of the MGKU (*Legislative Assembly Debates*, GOM, 1982a: 15 March). Union Commerce Minister Shivraj Patil declared in the Rajya Sabha as late as October 1982: 'Those who have been responsible for the strike did not spell out the demands of the workers in clear terms. However, as time passed they made their demands in a piecemeal manner' (*Rajya Sabha Debates*, GOI, 1982b: 14 October). The same complaint is to be found in a speech of Naval Tata, president of the Employers' Federation of India, at the annual general meeting of the Federation in May 1982. The point was reiterated by R.L.N. Vijayanagar, secretary-general of the MOA (interview, 28 January 1986).
64. In December 1981 Samant made a vain attempt to see the PM when she came to Bombay and left a memorandum for her stating the demands of the workers, as has been reported by the press. In an affidavit before the Bombay High Court in August 1982, Samant claimed to have prepared a COD on behalf of the textile workmen and having sent copies to the government and the MOA. R.N. Joshi, general manager of Shree Ram Mills, confirms that Samant submitted a COD to the MOA: 'There is no question about it. He did. But we cannot consider such a COD as his was not the recognized union' (interview, 24 January 1987).
65. Figures quoted in *Labour in Free India* (HMS, 1983: 18).
66. *Report of the Tripartite Committee on Cotton Textile Industry* (GOI, 1983d: 103).
67. In a memorandum submitted to the Tripartite Committee, the MOA has drawn attention to these differences. The employers observed that modern manufacturing industries succumbed to coercive tactics of militant labour leaders 'because, in spite of high wages, they were found to be distributing only a small portion of their value added being only 14.5 per cent in the case of chemicals and chemical products industries, and 21 to 25 per cent in the case of rubber, plastics, petroleum, coal products and engineering industries in contrast to a big slice of 54 per cent in the case of the cotton textile industry' (MOA, 1983:b 203).
68. ICMF, 1986: 114.
69. *Labour in Free India* (HMS, 1983: 6).
70. Cf. Letter to PM d. 1 October 1982; letter to Mayor Pai d. 6 October 1982; 'Let Us Negotiate', *Economic Times*, 17 October 1982, an article written by Datta Samant.

71. The relevant sections in the Act are 13 (dealing with the requirements for application for registration, and 14 (dealing with registration itself). This last section specifies six conditions which have to be satisfied prior to registration. The fifth provision reads: '... that the Registrar shall not register any union if at any time, within six months immediately preceding the date of the application for registration or thereafter the union has instigated, aided or assisted the commencement or continuation of a strike or stoppage which has been held or declared to be illegal' (BIR Act, Sec. 14 [5]).
72. A lively account of the working conditions inside the mills is to be found in *Girni Kamgar: Vedana ani Vidroha* (= Mill Workers: Agony and Hatred), by Gulab Gajarmal, a former mill worker of Shree Ram Mills.
73. 'Health Hazards in Textile Industry: The Noise Nuisance', S. Purushothama, *Science Today*, February 1978.
74. Ibid.
75. 'The Horror of Heat and Humidity', S. Kumar, *Science Today*, February 1978.
76. Ibid.
77. 'Byssinosis', Harwant Singh, *Science Today*, February 1978.
78. 'The Scourge of the Cotton Dust', V.A. Shenai, *Science Today*, February 1978.
79. 'Byssinosis: A Follow-up Study of Cotton Ginnery Workers in the Sudan', M. Khogali in *British Journal of Industrial Medicine*, No. 33 (166–74), 1976.
80. 'The Scourge of the Cotton Dust', V.A. Shenai, *Science Today*, February 1978.
81. 'The State's Point of View', *Science Today*, February 1978. Davay, however, also admitted that byssinosis often goes unnoticed: 'Waste-handlers in textile mills are the most exposed to cotton dust. Also, those who clean the machinery on holidays inhale a lot of dust. They are mostly contract labourers and usually are not covered by any study group. This way, quite a large group of textile workers prone to byssinosis may go undetected' (ibid). For more information on byssinosis see 'Byssinosis in Card-room Workers in Swedish Cotton Mills', L. Belin (Belin, 1965); 'Relationships Between Dust Level and Byssinosis and Bronchitis in Lancashire Cotton Mills', G. Berry (Berry, 1974).
82. 'Chemical Hazards in Textile Mills', V.A. Shenai, *Science Today*, February 1978.
83. See 'Statement by MOA', *FE*, 15 January 1982. A specification of these demands working out to a total of Rs 696 per month per worker is to be found in the memorandum submitted by the MOA to the Tripartite Committee (MOA, 1983b: 211).

84. MOA, 1983b: 212.
85. See leaflet by RMMS: *Strike in the Bombay Textile Mills: The Position of the RMMS* (Bombay, 1982).
86. As will be shown in the next chapter, it is far from easy to arrive at the correct figures for *badli*s and permanent workers in the textile industry either before or after the strike. Samant's confusion is therefore understandable. In a letter to the PM, dated 1 October 1982, he speaks of a total of 2.3 lakhs of textile workers in Bombay with a component of one lakh *badli*s (this would come to 43.4 per cent) whereas a couple of days later he repeats that figure and takes it to be 30 per cent of the total labour force (letter to the mayor of Bombay d. 6 October 1982) which implies that the total labour force be put at more than 3.3 lakhs.
87. See Appendix (Statement by the RMMS) INTWF memorandum submitted to the Tripartite Committee, January 1983: 30.
88. *Report of the Badli Labour Inquiry Committee Cotton Textile Industry: 1967* (GOM, 1968: 7).
89. GOM, 1968: 8.
90. Cf. D. Sinha, 'Personal Factors and Absenteeism', *The Indian Journal of Social Work*, no. 4, 1961; K.G. Desai, 'Absenteeism in Industry', *The Indian Journal of Social Work* no. 1, 1966; *Absenteeism: A Case Study in Textile Industry* (Ambekar Institute for Labour Studies, Bombay, 1977).
91. AILS, 1977: 8.
92. Appendix to the INTWF memorandum 1983, pp. 28–36.
93. Consumer price index numbers for industrial workers in Bombay in *HOSOCTI*, ICMF, 1986: 114.
94. INTWF memorandum, 1983: 24.
95. Ibid., pp. 24–25.
96. *Report of the Tripartite Committee on Cotton Textile Industry* (Seoptember 1983), p. 132. The Report did not get the approval of the RMMS, which was a party to the committee, and was never, placed before Parliament. It is interesting that apart from a note of dissent by the RMMS there was another one by former Labour Commissioner D.G. Kale who felt that an increase of Rs 50 would not be unreasonable.
97. Note captioned 'Extension of agreement reached between the MOA and RMMS regarding demands of the Bombay Cotton Textile Workers in Mofussil areas', Office of the Commissioner of Labour, Bombay (undated).
98. Petlad T.R. 'Dye Works vs Dyes and Chemical Workers' Union', Supreme Court, Pt-I, L.L.J., 1960.
99. Khandesh Spinning and Weaving Mills Co. vs R.G. Kamgar Sangha, Supreme Court, Pt-I, L.L.J., 1960.

100. Textile Labour Association vs Ahmedabad Millowners' Association, Industrial Court, 28 November 1981.
101. The committee suggested that all the employees in the industry should be divided in three groups on the basis of their wages (exclusive of bonus and fringe benefits). Employees earning wages up to Rs 750 should receive Rs 32 HRA, those earning up to Rs 1250 should get Rs 45 and those above should receive Rs 65.
102. GOI, 1983d: p. 133.
103. Ibid.
104. Tulpule states that the employers accept his way of handling demands as they lost an earlier battle when he had challenged them in court: 'At that time there were about sixty mills. Of these forty submitted balance sheets, maybe the others didn't because their financial administration was not quite in order. I analysed the figures and could prove that mills made huge profits and that there was no problem to agree to our demands' (interview, 17 March 1986). His position was, according to him, upheld by the High Court and later the Supreme Court.
105. The labour commissioner cautioned the management of the mills to avoid a show of affluence as it would be more difficult to argue afterwards that there was no money for wage increases: 'Dr Samant certainly had a point in distrusting balance sheets. I myself have seen the way the inventories are inflated. It is one of the easiest ways to make money. Suppose you have stocks, spare parts. The valuation of that is left to you, so you can easily underrate it. The allegation of manipulation is correct but it can't be established without tremendous effort' (interview, 3 January 1987).
106. There seems nothing new in this: The purchase of cotton, for example, seems to have been a source of malpractice for a long time. In an article on corruption in the textile industry in the last century we read that it was the task of a *mukaddam* (headman) to take delivery of the cotton, weigh it and transport it to the mill. He was bribed to take less cotton and of inferior quality than was bargained for. His servant would weigh the cotton upon arrival in the mill. The clerk of the mill, who had to certify for receipt of the cotton, would sit at a distance of hundreds of yards from the weighing machine and supervise the weighing. A number of people would receive their cut of the illegal profits but the servant of the *mukaddam* would see the least of it (C. Deshmukh, 'Textile Industry: Era of Labour Awakening', *Indian Express*, 13 September 1982).
107. Ravi Gangal, *Understanding Financial Statements: A Guide for Trade Unions* (Popular Prakashan, Bombay, 1986).

108. In the course of a massive raid in Surat, eighty out of a total of 435 tax inspectors were attacked and seven wounded seriously when owners of mills and shops hastily recruited gangs to stop the tax officials from doing their duty. Goondas entered workshops, destroyed documents and identity papers and beat up inspectors while the police refused to act (*The Telegraph*, 30 May 1985).
109. Cf. 'Fiddling With Figures: An Honest Accountant's Nightmare', in *The 10th Month: Bombay's Historic Textile Strike* (Bombay, 1983); Ranjan Chitta, 'Bombay Textile Strike', *Mainstream*, 26 February 1983.
110. The *Indian Express* reported on a raid by income-tax officials on a textile mill group in Ahmedabad in the course of which it was found that not less than Rs 6 crores of tax had been evaded. The evasion was revealed from a set of secret diaries seized from the desk of one of the directors (*IE*, 3 February 1983).
111. According to a newspaper report, the HPC compared the amount of cloth produced by mills in the NTC and in the private sector on the basis of the same quantity of cotton and found that the private mills produced much less cloth than might have been expected. This was attributed to 'glaring irregularities' in the booking of wastage, which might have gained a mill crores of rupees in the course of the years (*The Daily*, 6 February 1982).
112. Aided by documents, Bhovalekar explained that Bombay Dyeing illegally earned Rs 10 lakhs on chemicals and dyes alone in 1974. For the presence of the papers in his house he offers the following explanation: 'You see, the papers that are in my custody now were first at the mill but I was asked to remove them for certain reasons. Everybody at that time had faith in me. They said: "Bhovalekar, you keep that with you" and now it still is with me. They may have forgotten about it.'
113. R.L.N Vijayanagar, *Diversion of Funds: Myth or Reality?* (Bombay, 1978).
114. For a detailed account of the curious events that occurred in Mukesh Mills see 'How to Kill a Mill and Make a Profit', *Sunday Observer*, 4 March 1984.
115. The RMMS, too, did not refrain from exposing the mismanagement as is shown by an elaborate memorandum submitted to the PM after the strike. In this document the Sangh accused Finlay and Gold Mohur of having misused six crores of rupees which belonged to the workers as this money was part of Provident Fund, unpaid wages, and so on. The two mills were also said to have 8,000 workers on the roll whereas they employed only 850 workers (*The Indian Textile Monitor*, September–October 1983: 14).

116. 'The Cabinet Carousel', *India Today*, 30 September 1982.
117. When V.P. Naik left office in 1975 he had been CM for more than ten years. Naik was followed by S.B. Chavan who was replaced by Vasantdada Patil in 1977. Shortly afterwards (when the Janata government took over) Patil had to abandon the field to Sharad Pawar who in his turn had to leave when Indira Gandhi returned to power and decided to nominate Antulay as CM (1980). Antulay's tenure ended in a scandal and Babasaheb Bhosale was given the task of sorting out the problems. Failing to do so he was replaced by Vasantdada Patil (1983) who returned for a very brief period after which he was appointed governor in Rajasthan. His successor was Shivajirao Nilangekar who had to quit ingloriously in March 1986 after a scandal over the examination papers of his daughter and was succeeded by S.B. Chavan again who in turn was succeeded in office by Sharad Pawar in 1988.
118. The delegation included inter alia the secretary-general of the MOA, the secretary-general of the ICMF and the chairman of the ICMF (*TOI*, 9 February 1982).
119. MOA, 1983b: 33–34.
120. Cf. 'Labour Bill Passed Amid Uproar', *TOI* 10 August 1982. As a protest against this Bill, introduced by Labour Minister Bhagwat Jha Azad, the entire opposition walked out of the House.
121. Cf. 'Mill workers get raw deal', *The Daily*, 6 February 1982.
122. The relevant section of the BIR Act is Section 7.3: 'Notwithstanding anything contained in this Act, the [State] Government may, at any time, refer an Industrial dispute to the arbitration of the Industrial Court, if on a report made by the Labour Officer or otherwise it satisfied that: (1) by reason of the continuance of the dispute, (a) a serious outbreak of disorder or a breach of the public peace is likely to occur; or (b) serious or prolonged hardship to a large section of the community is likely to be caused; or (c) the industry concerned is likely to be seriously affected or the prospects and scope for employment therein curtailed; or (2) the dispute is not likely to be settled by other means; or (3) it is necessary in the public interest to do so.
123. Pratap sourly observed that although the judiciary did everything it could to find a speedy solution, this process was frustrated by 'the most unexpected quarter, the state government'. He added, 'In the life history of these workers and in their struggle for justice, the strike here, irrespective of political opportunism of rival unions and the hypnotic powers of their respective leaders, reflects a classic resistance movement based on the hallowed twin principles of non-cooperation and by and large, non-violence' (*TOI*, 24 December 1982). Pratap also

feared that confidence in the judiciary would be seriously undermined as a result of the stand taken by the government.

124. This reading of the events was given by the treasurer of the RMMS, Mrs E. D'Souza (interview, 30 May 1986).
125. This proposition was rejected by Samant and in September, Madhu Mehta would address himself in an open letter to Samant, accusing him of not being ready to make any concession at the expense of the suffering workers. Mehta also claimed that the proposition made by the centre was, in fact, his idea (*Mid-day*, 12 September 1982).
126. See *Economic Times*, 14 April 1982 and subsequent days.
127. One is reminded of the miners' strike in England (March 1984–March 1985), during which workers in the USSR were allowed to donate 500,000 pounds sterling to the striking miners.
128. *Rajya Sabha Debates* (GOI, 1983b: 22 March).
129. In the Rajya Sabha, Singh explained that the Textile Committee is a statutory body constituted by the Indian government under the Textile Committee Act, 1963. The committee consists of ex-officio members of the office of the Textile Commissioner, Commerce Ministry and representatives of the MOA and ICMF. Members are, inter alia, the textile commissioner, the chairman of TEXPROCIL, the Chairman of the MOA and the joint secretary of the commerce ministry.
130. As he explained to the House, Singh felt disturbed because for a period of twenty days, the Textile Committee flatly denied the existence of an instruction to do away with the pre-shipment inspections ('... they were lying for twenty days') (*Rajya Sabha Debates*, GOI 1983b: 22 March).
131. Cf. *Report for the Year 1982* (MOA, 1983b: xvii). For cotton yarn production in Bombay in 1981, the report gives a total of 235.4 million kgs but this should probably have been 135.4 as the figure for all remaining yarn is given as 35.8 million kgs and the total yarn production is put at 171.2 million kgs.
132. *Kotwal Committee Report* (GOM 1987: 38).
133. The labour officer of Century Mills acknowledged the importance of this aspect while giving an incredible description of the housing facilities given to the workers: 'These are spacious rooms with kitchen and bathroom and a surface for which you would have to pay a high rent anywhere else in Bombay. In return we expect some loyalty from the workers (interview, 14 January 1987). One need not take these exaggerations at face value and yet realize that even a room shared by many is precious accommodation to needy workers, given Bombay's housing famine.
134. Cf. *Shramik Vichar*, 6 and 8 July 1983; *Garjana*, vol. 41, no. 7/8, July 1983.

135. One of the rare attempts to support the impression that at least the English press took a consistently negative view of the striking workers is a report by the Bombay Union of Journalists. One cannot, however, decide whether the examples given are representative for the quoted newspapers ('Bombay Textile Strike and the Press', *Mainstream*, 26 February 1983).
136. In fact, there is astonishingly extensive press activity in India and in the state of Maharashtra in particular. In recent years the tree of newspapers and periodicals has been growing fast and it is still to be seen whether it has reached a peak. In Maharashtra in 1983, there were 177 dailies (of which 127 were in Marathi), 664 weeklies (of which 370 were in Marathi), 1215 fortnightlies and monthlies together (of which 455 in Marathi). As far as Bombay is concerned, there were twelve English, three Hindi and twelve Marathi daily newspapers in the city in 1983. Source: *Mass Media in India*, 1985, 1986 (GOI, 1986), pp. 178–84.
137. At that time the newspaper did not appear due to a lock-out following a sit-in which occurred on 31 October 1981 (see *Economic Scene*, May 1982). The strike was sparked off after an attempt by dissatisfied employees of the *IE* to start a union which would come under the leadership of Datta Samant. In the ensuing conflict the owner, Ramnath Goenka, announced a closure of the Bombay office, a decision that had to be revoked. Datta Samant's inimical view of the *IE* may have its roots here. The clash certainly caused ill will (see *India Today*, 28 February 1982).
138. Information to be found in an undated police report kindly made available by the commissioner of police in Bombay.
139. Ibid.
140. It is interesting to note that RMMS president, Hoshing, tried to belittle the part of the striking workers in the assault on his house: 'There may have been workers amongst them but in the end it was just mass frenzy' (interview, 20 May 1986). Hoshing, of course, had his own good reasons for making the attack appear to be a coincidence during the riots and not an assault expressing the anger of the textile workers on strike.
141. See, for exaple, *FE*, 28 July 1982; *FE*, 30 September 1982; *FE*, 12 October 1982; *FE*, 9 July 1983.
142. Although this way of addressing the public is certainly unusual in a labour conflict it is by no means a unique phenomenon in the Indian context. The pharmaceutical industry Pfizer Ltd used this device in 1977 to explain why the management decided on a lock-out (*TOI*, July 1977). Hotel Bombay International placed its labour problems before

the public when a strike was imminent (*Evening News*, 7 February 1980) and again placed an advertisement when union leaders were suspended (*Mid-day*, 11 February 1980). More recently Dr Beck & Co. Ltd warned its employees to resume duty after an Industrial Court had declared their strike illegal (*Maharashtra Herald*, 8 January 1987; *Indian Express*, 15 January 1987).

Chapter Three

STRIKE STRATEGIES

WORKERS' STRATEGIES

Position of the Unions

Cooperation in the TUJAC: The idea of a general strike in the textile industry emanated first from the left-oriented unions united in the Trade Unions' Joint Action Committee (Kamgar Sanghatana Samyukti Kruti Samiti). Their sympathy for such action is clear from their contribution to the heating up of the atmosphere prior to the strike and their participation in warning strikes, such as those on 27 September 1981 and 6 January 1982. During the strike their support became visible in the collections of money and grain, organization of independent meetings as well as in their participation in rallies in which they shared the dais with Datta Samant and the MGKU. However, their position was very ambivalent and their participation in strike-related activities remained moderate with the notable exception of the Sarva Shramik Sangh which threw in its lot with Samant's MGKU. The hesitation of the other socialist and communist unions is understandable. Many leaders among them had right from the outset serious misgivings about the feasibility of an indefinite strike. On the other hand, they saw and sensed the mood of the workers and realized that if they wanted to avoid being swept away completely they were left with no other option than to jump onto the MGKU bandwagon.

Under the circumstances, moderate support promised the highest returns enabling them to sustain their (battered) position in the industry as some of the credit could be claimed in the event of success and most of the failure could be attributed to Samant in the event of failure. Datta Samant became increasingly aware of this and that realization in combination with insurmountable ideological differences largely explains why he was averse to negotiations with the government and/or the millowners in the company of the red flag unions. However, his reluctance to involve them in negotiations, in attempts at conciliation or in the development of strike strategies would also militate against the success of the strike, apart from providing the left unions with a ready excuse to drop out. Not being tied to success as strongly as the MGKU/SSS combine, the red flag unions were in a better position to gauge much earlier and more accurately changes in the mood of the workers, but their motives being suspect, their warnings were too easily explained away as subtle attempts to undermine the workers' morale.

The lack of dynamism displayed by the red flag unions is reflected in press reports of the time in which they figured only marginally. In September 1981, the SSS-affiliated Kapad Kamgar Sanghatana, the Mumbai Girni Kamgar Union (AITUC), the Lal Bawta Mill Mazdoor Union (CITU) and the Girni Kamgar Sabha (BMS), all members of the TTUJAC, called for a one-day strike which was successful. Of all these unions only the SSS would cross the floor to Datta Samant, for better or for worse. It would be the SSS again which would function as a channel of communication between Datta Samant and the TUJAC, and which would repeatedly appeal to the other TUJAC partners to shed their reservations and join the struggle.

Examples of concerted action after the initial declaration of support for Samant's indefinite strike by all non-INTUC unions are not many and the peak period seems to have been July and August 1982. One such action was a state-wide strike of all industrial workers planned for 19 April, in which lakhs of workers participated, according to *Shramik Vichar*, mouthpiece of the LNP to which the SSS is affiliated. But according to several English newspapers this general strike proved only partially successful. Both the accounts may have been right and only betray a difference in the respective attitudes towards the strike. INTUC-affiliated unions took no part in the bandh. A month later the TUJAC leaders decided to see the CM to discuss the strike, the outcome of which was predictable (*Nava Kal*, 19 May 1982).

Possibly in response to a call by Datta Samant on 1 June to join hands, the TUJAC organized selective strike actions such as blocking roads on 4 June. This resulted in lathi charges by the police and the arrest of 430 persons (*TOI*, 5 June 1982). Another solidarity strike was planned for 8 July after which preparations would be made for a strike paralysing the textile industry throughout Maharashtra. But this last strike did not materialize (*TOI*, 20 June 1982). The strike on 8 July was claimed to have been a success by Samant but the MOA dubbed it a flop. On 12 July the TUJAC announced that demonstrations would be held and gheraos staged at the residences of all Congress MLAs in Maharashtra. The success of this action was only partial as many MLAs took care to be absent and others got away by paying mere lip service to the cause (*Shramik Vichar*, 20 July 1982).

Probably the most impressive display of solidarity was a huge meeting near Nardulla Tank (Prabhadevi) in Bombay in the third week of July 1982 during which a resolution was adopted, to be sent to PM Indira Gandhi, setting out the demands of the workers. Datta Samant then shared the dais with the TUJAC and declared that much was negotiable but not the demand that the right of the RMMS to represent the workers should come to an end and the BIR Act be scrapped (*TOI*, 19 July 1982). The meeting may be considered the pinnacle of the cooperation between the TUJAC and Samant, and the text of the resolution bears this out.

Having observed that the PM had made it known through the Janata Party leader S.M. Joshi that her government was not averse to talks with the strike leaders, the TUJAC suggested that such talks should commence immediately between the strike leaders, the TUJAC, MOA and the government. The text begins by drawing attention to the labour conditions in the mills and proceeds to clamour for derecognition of the Sangh and the repeal of the BIR Act. After having pointed to the plight of the *badli*s, the text concludes by demanding 'substantial' wage increases to be determined at once and appeals for payment of adequate monetary relief ('but not in the form of advance') to the textile workers who had been without wages for six to nine months.[1] What is striking is the value attached to derecognition of the RMMS and scrapping of the BIR Act, which were not issues foremost in the mind of Datta Samant when he launched the indefinite strike.

Following this event, the leaders of the TUJAC announced that they had decided to participate in a jail bharo campaign (*Nava Kal*, 21 July 1982). After this show of unity the TUJAC got in touch with the government and in the first week of August S. Dhube, representing the TUJAC, would meet Labour Minister Azad to discuss the strike. Later in August, the leadership of unions affiliating to the CITU, AITUC and HMS participated in demonstrations during which thousands of persons courted arrest but thereafter the activities of the TUJAC dwindled (*TOI,* 17 August 1982). The morchas and jail bharos were the last significant demonstrations of solidarity. Even so, the TUJAC unions afterwards consistently refused to cooperate with the Tripartite Committee appointed by the government, considering such discussions superfluous and an example of dilatory tactics. In this there is little room for heroism, for as the TUJAC was well aware, no agreement which was not concluded by Datta Samant or at least approved of by him would be acceptable to the mass of the textile workers.

In September *Nava Kal* brought the news that the TUJAC leaders were unhappy about developments, feeling side-tracked by Datta Samant in the formulation of plans. The union leaders complained about Samant's solitary style of handling the strike and dropped out (*Nava Kal*, 13 September 1982). Following this report the paper announced that the Mumbai Girni Kamgar Union would start its own satyagraha (that is, jail bharo) from 17 September onwards. In the course of this campaign 399 workers are reported to have been arrested (*Nava Kal*, 24 September 1982). In the latter part of the strike the tone of the TUJAC would become ever more critical and they would lend mere token support. Some time after the first anniversary of the strike Indrajit Gupta, general secretary of the AITUC, issued a statement in which the government was rebuked for its anti-labour stance but also Datta Samant for his lack of initiative. Samant's manner of handling the strike single-handed to the exclusion of the other trade unions in the field is also criticized (*Flashes from Trade Unions*, 10 February 1983).

These two observations did not go down well with Y. Chavan, president of the SSS, who replied in a letter to Gupta that there was no dearth of initiatives by Samant to enlist the cooperation of other trade unions but that the responsibility for the failure of concerted action rested with unions indulging in strike-breaking activities. Chavan specifically mentioned the Bharatiya Mazdoor Sangh and the Hind Mazdoor Panchayat (both members of the National Campaign Committee), but he also accused the state bodies of the AITUC and CITU of having long since given up all hope of victory. Besides, many activists of these last two organizations had returned to the mills 'to the great consternation and indignation of their class brothers' (Letter to Indrajit Gupta d. 30 March 1983).

The vigour with which Chavan even at that stage defended the prospects of success, taking heart from the meeting between Commerce Minister V.P. Singh and Datta Samant earlier that month, is astonishing. Against his better judgement, while admitting that 'several thousand workers' had resumed duty, he avers that 'the major section of the 250 thousand permanent and *badli* workers' were still valiantly fighting in Bombay and in the villages (ibid.) Those in the villages were credited with the mobilization of agricultural labourers and small peasants as also with collecting 'as much as four thousand quintals of grain' which had been sent to Bombay.[2] In the face of defeat Chavan still clings to the illusion that the chances of getting the BIR Act repealed are 'the best today provided all honest pro-working class forces' unite behind the heroic textile workers in Bombay (ibid.) The utterances of Singh at that juncture were the last straw the strike leaders could clutch at but very soon even that would disappear.

The reluctant support of the CPI in Maharashtra for Datta Samant, abundantly clear at the end of the strike, was already visible in the beginning in a booklet written by B.S. Dhume, vice president of the AITUC, who criticized Samant's obstinacy some forty days after the strike had begun. Dhume wondered how Samant could put up wage demands of Rs 300 in just any industry without paying heed to the paying capacity of a company. After having extolled the role played by the communists in the textile industry in the past, he expressed regret that Samant did not mention the ousting of the Sangh, the scrapping of the BIR Act and the stand taken by the government.[3] The tendency to credit the TUJAC (and the AITUC along with it) with substantial contribution to the success of the strike was still visible in August 1982 when Dhume denied that the strike was led by Datta Samant and insisted: '… the fact is that it is led by the strike action committee consisting of the unions traditionally working in the textile industry and Samant'.[4] It was a clear case of wishful thinking, not borne out by the facts.

Differences in approach: In spite of all the criticism, it is clearly acknowledged by all red flag unions that Datta Samant alone had caught the imagination if not the heart of the workers. Analysing Samant's success with the workers, G.V. Chitnis, secretary-general of the Mumbai Girni Kamgar Union (AITUC), granted that Samant had a reputation for being capable of delivering the goods while none of the other unions was strong enough to fight the workers' cause:

> Why could we not organize all the workers in the field? The reason is that Datta Samant and his leadership were of a non-political nature and therefore all workers could follow him whether they owned allegiance to Congress, Shiv Sena, Janata or any other party. He said that he was only interested in the demands of the workers. This stand made him acceptable to all. We could not do that because as soon as it would become clear that a particular red flag union was conducting the strike some groups of workers would drop out due to inter-union rivalry [interview, 11 April 1986].

Chitnis draws a comparison between the 1974 strike, during which the Mumbai Girni Kamgar Union received good support, and the last strike and concludes that this time there was unprecedented unity. He is not however willing to admit that the contribution of his union to the strike on this occasion was far less than on the earlier occasion. He emphasizes that the demands in 1982 were the same as those his union had been fighting for since 1966, which is why he feels that his union stood wholeheartedly behind the strike. 'Secondly, we saw the desire among the workers to fight for the demands. Thirdly, unless there was a mass struggle the demands could not be pressed' (ibid.). The second motive seems to have been the propelling force behind the activities of his union, leaving it with no choice.

Surveying the outcome of the struggle, Chitnis feels that Samant failed in several respects, such as consistency in his demands and in realizing the magnitude of the opposition:

> Samant conquered the textile industry without firing a single shot: he came, he saw, he conquered. The workers fell before him. If Samant would win in textile industry he would be entering other industries also. Here the battle was not with one single millowner but with the entire millowners' association, the core of Indian capitalism. Not only that, he was also facing the government, the biggest employer in textile industry. This explains the determination of the government and the employers [ibid.]

Chitnis condemns Samant for not settling the strike when there was an opportunity and a need for doing so after nine or ten months: 'At that time a review of the policy and strategy should have taken place. We suggested this to Samant but he did not agree with it. We said that a dialogue had to be opened with the government, that a committee of all trade unions should meet the PM to try to break the ice' (ibid.)

Samant, however, would not listen to warnings and refused to discuss the strike with others. Chitnis argues that this was because Samant was too greatly influenced by the younger workers who demanded the full pound of flesh. These workers had fewer responsibilities, were more radical but also less experienced and failed to grasp the possibilities of the situation. He touches a commonly sensitive point when he says:

> This section is very vocal but there is another section, usually larger, which is less active and more silent. You should strike a balance between the wishes of both these sections and keep them united. So Samant should not have given in to the pressure put on him by these younger workers because many workers wanted the strike to end and started going back to the mills. Samant did not grasp the real mood of the workers [ibid.]

Y. Chavan, president of the SSS with a claimed membership of 15,000, cannot agree with this, being convinced that workers by and large stood behind Samant throughout the strike. Had he felt differently he would not have been in a position to defend the view that—whatever the ideas and strategies of the leadership—the decision on the course of action ultimately has to be made by the rank and file. Taking for granted that sympathy for Samant implied agreement with the policies he pursued, the SSS had no difficulty in backing Datta Samant when it was obvious that Samant had the confidence of the mass of workers. Speaking about the necessity of abiding by the wishes of the rank and file, Chavan says:

> We believe that people learn by experience and this implies that we feel that a decision supported by a majority should get a chance to be implemented. Even if it doesn't work out well people will learn, the leadership will learn and better policy will be decided upon in the future. The basis of trade unionism is not party ideology. The day-to-day grievances of the masses of working people are the basis [interview, 18 March 1986].

The SSS has no union of its own any longer in the textile industry but its influence today is by no means less than before the strike, and may be regarded as being inversely proportionate to its size. The power of the SSS grew as a result of its impressive strike-related activities and close association with Samant and the MGKU. Prior to the strike the SSS had one affiliated union in the textile industry, the Kapad, Kamgar Sanghatana with a claimed 4,000 members, which merged with Samant's MGKU as soon as the latter was founded. According to Chavan, 'When we found that the masses had unanimously chosen Samant's leadership, we felt that if we would still try to enhance the influence of our organization that would cause a disruption of the working class unity and we dissolved our own organization' (ibid.)

The SSS has no regrets about this drastic step as the union now successfully works in the organization 'that has the support of the masses'. Their entrenchment is such that some observers feel that it is the SSS which is riding the MGKU horse. This seems, however, a gross overstatement, ignoring the symbolic significance of Datta Samant (not easily replaced by the SSS), as well as his habit of taking unilateral decisions. The cooperation between the MGKU and SSS is nevertheless striking and if the spirit of unity and resistance among the textile workers in Bombay is not yet completely lost, this is in essence due to the strenuous efforts of the SSS to support the workers wherever possible.

The SSS president, for obvious reasons, is not prepared to find fault with Samant although he acknowledges that many active workers grew frustrated when they found that they had no say in the strategy chalked out by Samant during the strike and turned away disappointedly from the MGKU.[5] Guardedly, Chavan admits that 'formally speaking' these activists may have been right but in the same breath feels that they were traditional in approach and did not take into consideration how the masses were thinking and being goaded to think. Yet, even he is obliged to note that Samant's empire lacked proper structure and that this might have been a cause for dissatisfaction.

If the Mumbai Girni Kamgar Union did not fare well during the strike, the Lal Bawta Girni Kamgar Union (CITU) fared worse. Prior to the strike it claimed a membership of 10,000 workers spread over seven mills. This number dwindled to a mere 1,000 workers spread over three mills after the strike. The slide in numbers in this union (an offshoot of the Mumbai Girni Kamgar Union) is due to its lack of concern with the developments in the textile industry. S.Y. Kolhatkar, president of the CITU (Maharashtra), believes that the initiatives of his union stopped after the support of a one-day strike in 1979 (interview, 17 April 1986). As a consequence, its support for the indefinite strike was moderate and the union lost all hold over the workers in spite of a number of meetings (ibid.). Curiously, Kolhatkar attributes the lack of response from the workers to the disappointing performance over the years of the Mumbai Girni Kamgar Union. In many of the struggles initiated by the latter the CITU participated too and in consequence 'the workers could not distinguish between us and the Mumbai Girni Kamgar Union'.

The limited support of the CITU (collecting grain and money) came to an end after a year when the union informed Datta Samant that there was no point in carrying on the strike and that he should concentrate on finding a way out: 'We persuaded him to write to the central government in response to an offer that had been made. The government was ready to negotiate with the TUJAC of which Samant was a member. We discussed the draft of a letter but finally, after everyone agreed, Samant refused to sign. His view was that if any negotiations were to be started these negotiations would have to be with him only' (ibid.)

Ignoring Samant's difficulty in accepting the cooperation of the red flag unions, Kolhatkar prefers to believe that a solution to the strike was blocked by Samant's vanity which did not permit him to share with others the credit for ending the stalemate. Kolhatkar opines that there had been several occasions for ending the strike.

Even at a late stage there appeared to be an opportunity when he himself met B.G. Deshmukh (Secretary of the labour ministry) in Delhi. The Secretary seemed willing to offer a wage increase of Rs 70 provided it was accepted. Returning from Delhi, Kolhatkar discovered that nobody was interested in the proposition, and it was at this stage that the CITU, and the Lal Bawta Mill Mazdoor Union along with it, dropped out.

Datta Samant explains his reluctance to accept help by saying that initially nobody came to his rescue as everybody expected the strike to fizzle out in a couple of weeks. In the face of the massive support of the workers for him, the red flag unions changed their policy but even so Samant was certain that no left union was happy with the type of trade unionism he represented. After a year the left parties told their workers to resume work. Samant:

> There are two explanations for this. They didn't like the idea of my union becoming the dominant union in the industry and, secondly, the strategy of the left unions is more politically oriented. They are not interested in getting economic gains for the workers...they want some kind of permanent agitation, some kind of workers' involvement throughout their lives [interview, 17 May 1986].

As for his refusal to accept the presence of other trade unions at the negotiating table, Samant's view was that if the bargaining is conducted by unions other than the one leading the strike, this tends to adversely affect the outcome of the negotiations.

In discussing the strategy adopted by the trade unions active in the textile industry during the strike, no mention has been made of the need to paralyse the production of cloth in centres outside Bombay, although it was certain that many mills utilized the facilities offered by powerloom centres to keep the production going. The absence of references to this aspect of the strike is conspicuous. But although the established unions failed to pay attention to this element, purposely or not, some groups were aware of the need to involve the powerloom workers in the struggle.

In a pamphlet published by a group called Revolutionary Workers Coordinating Committee (RWCC) dated 17 July 1982, serious doubts were raised about the possibility of success of the strike if this aspect was neglected The pamphlet hinted at the reason for this omission by stating that the old red flag parties, the CPI, CPI(M) and LNP, were in favour of the government policy of production in the small-scale sector, which is why they do not want to expose the conditions under which it was taking place. The text explains that in this sector workers have to toil for a pittance under utterly oppressive labour conditions. The RWCC derides the strike leaders who boast that so many workers returned to the villages as 'this is precisely what the owners want so that they can have a clear road to close down unprofitable mills, induct automatic machinery, shift mills to the rural areas, sell their valuable land in the heart of Bombay, in other words do exactly what they please'.[6]

The pamphlet pointed out that the strike leaders had so far refused to take steps to explain this issue to the powerloom workers or to initiate steps that might lead to a halt of production in the powerloom and other mill centres, first of all in the 40,000 powerlooms in the city. Next the text raises the disturbing question of how a strike in which production is ongoing can be successful. Powerloom workers should be brought out in support of the textile workers by demanding the same facilities as mill workers. The pamphlet ends with an appeal to unite the struggle of powerloom workers and mill workers against the millowners.

Although a halt of production in powerlooms would have aggravated the problems for a number of mills in the city, the pamphlet facilely bypasses the tremendous organizational problems involved in trying to realize a strike in powerloom centres like Bhiwandi, though the same cannot be said for the powerlooms in Bombay itself. Outside Bombay the powerloom workers were aware that the strike in the city meant more business for them and it would have proved to be an uphill task to convince them of the desirability of joining a strike for better wages in Bombay when their own lagged far behind. Besides, thousands of striking workers managed to survive only because this sector provided them a living. This was corroborated by interviews. Not less than twenty workers (or 13 per cent of the sample) appeared to have worked on powerlooms during the strike for periods varying from a few weeks to several months. Some worked in Bombay as well as in Bhiwandi. It appeared to be very difficult to make these workers understand that in doing so they had contributed to the failure of the strike. Given the state of near anarchy in the powerloom sector (most particularly in Bhiwandi), it is quite understandable that the unions were disinclined to concentrate their efforts on this aspect of the strike.

Workers' Committees

Possibly the most striking characteristic of the strike was its spontaneity, finding expression in the sudden shift of loyalty towards a complete outsider in the industry. This characteristic was also borne out by the formation of workers' committees, repeatedly declared to be the backbone of the strike, without which the strike would have collapsed much sooner (cf. Dhume, 1982; G. Singh, 1983; R. Bakshi, 1987). These committees have also been credited with a leading role in the decision-making process during the strike. True, mill committees had already been formed before the strike began and they were instrumental in seeking Samant's leadership. Zone and area committees, too, operated at an early stage, a couple of months after the beginning of the struggle. But, unless one wishes to credit the various types of workers' committees with the bullying of strike-breakers and the beating up of Sangh activists, there is little to support the contention that they were as crucial for the success of the strike as has been suggested.[7]

In some cases it was only a matter of reviving committees which had been active in earlier struggles and had been lying dormant. In other cases, young workers without former committee experience decided to establish a committee. As the police made the proper functioning of all these committees increasingly difficult (Section 144, arbitrary arrests), many active workers went underground and some resurfaced in zone and area committees.[8] In every zone about six mill committees operated which were entrusted with the tasks of canvassing for the strike and providing a channel of communication between the workers and the strike leadership. The area committees were based in the suburbs and had to perform the same functions as the mill and zone committees in the city.[9] About a year after the strike, zone and area committees were to be integrated in a Central Committee but at that stage disintegration, as a result of frictions with Samant, was already clearly visible.

What tasks were assigned to these workers' committees? They played a role in the organization of meetings and rallies, the collection and distribution of food and money, the organization of morchas and gheraos and, most importantly, in staying in touch with the workers on strike. If the committees had been successful in performing all these tasks then one could rightly attribute a crucial role to them in the continuation of the struggle. But in spite of the unquestioned relevance of all these activities, only a small section of the workers in the sample appeared to be aware of even the existence of any workers' committees and a still smaller group attached much value to them.

This came as a surprise because much had been made of these committees in many accounts of the strike. In the *Marxist Bulletin,* for example, it was declared in May 1982 that the factory mill committees were the, 'central unit of organization and that the lack of organization in Samant's approach allowed them enormous freedom of initiative at the local level'.[10] Speaking about the area committees, Bakshi informs us that they played a key role in keeping the strike alive, cutting across trade union and party affiliations 'to create solidarity among a diverse variety of industrial workers' (Bakshi, 1987, 123).[11]

Great care was, therefore, taken that the workers in the sample understood the questions relating to the existence and the activities of mill, zone and area committees (various names and descriptions were tried) but it was all too obvious that apart from the food distribution, very few had come into contact with members of such committees. This was as much the case for workers in Bombay Dyeing (usually living in the heart of the textile area) as for the Finlay workers (often staying far away and spread over the city). If these committees had been the link between the strike leadership and the rank and file of the workers, as various authors have claimed, then a great many more workers should at least have known about them. In some cases workers who themselves had been very active at the beginning of the strike and participated in the work of the committees appeared to have lost interest after a couple of months (see case study no. 3). That the committees did not fare well may also be deduced from repeated appeals to join such committees.

A very active worker from Shree Ram Mills, Gulab Gajarmal, wrote several pamphlets inviting workers to join the committees, stating that there was a great need for volunteers in many mill committees. One of these leaflets, published in December 1982, was captioned: 'Why is it necessary to strengthen the mill committees?' In this Gulab Gajarmal warned against the spinelessness of many committee members who were satisfied with repeating what the strike leadership said. Gloom prevailed:

> The zone representatives have not made any preparations for future decisions because they did not unite the good and dedicated activists who appeared in the course of this long struggle. Also, the union officials have not been made aware of what really goes on at the mill gates so no activist has any idea of the direction in which this battle will progress. Therefore even though a mill activist may be motivated he is powerless because he has no authority to take any decision in this strike.

One is led to believe that workers who had returned to their villages during the strike had fewer opportunities of getting in touch with the workers' committees which would explain the general ignorance. But it was found that most of the workers who did not know about the activities of the committees appeared to have stayed in the city. In all, more than 62 per cent of the workers in the sample appeared to have no knowledge of the existence and activities of the workers' committees.

This raises the question of what created the impression that the various committees were vital for the prolongation of the strike. Part of the answer is provided by looking at the many tasks these committees were expected to perform and, undoubtedly, did perform in a number of cases. These tasks were vital and had the committees really been able to shoulder them, it would certainly have had a great impact on the outcome of the strike. But assigning a task or attributing a function to a committee is not the same as living up to it. If we take into account the individuals by whom the committees were manned we find that usually the most active workers found a place in them as they were seeking ways of expressing their involvement in the strike and to influence its course. These workers would not have been satisfied with merely attending meetings and joining marches. It is to be expected that they, the vanguard of the rank and file of Samant's MGKU, would soon feel the need for greater action. Such workers would find each other at the mill gates or at the office of the MGKU and soon realize the need to get organized, first at the mill level but later also at a higher (zone) level and would act accordingly. It appears, however, that there were far too few active workers to establish a force capable of reaching all levels of the textile labour field.

Other unions active in the textile industry too have and/or had a system of shop-level presentation. Keeping such an elaborate system alive is, of course, much easier for the representative union than for contesting unions but even so mill committees, linked to opposing unions, existed in the past and were active in times of labour unrest.[12] The formation of such committees in the present strike, therefore, was a continuation of a trend with a long history. But their rapid development may have been hampered by the exodus to the villages. In other words: what was beneficial for the survival of the strikers may well have been detrimental to the success of their organization. Apart from handling organizational tasks, the main purpose of these committees, whether attached to a union or not, has always been to convey the views of the workers to the strike leaders and to explain the strike strategy to the workers. In doing so the committees could exercise influence on both the leadership and the workers and in that way they could contribute to shaping the events.

This strike was different in the sense that its leadership was tied down essentially to one man—Datta Samant. Unfortunately, Samant was not the type of person who cared much for consultation. The tremendous support he received was enough proof to him that he represented the workers' feelings, their hopes and anger. Every meeting convinced him that the workers were with him. Therefore, he did not feel the need for deliberations on the course of action, consultation that ran the risk of his strategy of militancy (supported by endurance) being watered down. Discussions with him were a one way traffic and those who entertained conflicting views hardly had an opportunity to air them and even less to influence his decisions.

As the strike progressed, many active workers and many labour activists became increasingly dissatisfied with this and dropped out. Samant could afford such an attitude as he knew that there was no one else to whom the workers would turn and it was easy to create the impression that those who were not for him should be taken to be against him. The sheer presence of mill committees and a few zone and area committees cannot hide the fact that their influence on the decisions taken by Samant was by no means great. It would not be unjust to say that Samant's very popularity blocked the way for massive and active participation of lakhs of workers in specific strike-related action. The mill and zone committees simply did not get a chance to work out different approaches to the strike even if they had wanted to. The leader was too powerful for that.

Things might have been different had Samant felt the need for a well-thought-out strategy for conducting the strike. For the development of such a plan and its execution he would have required detailed information and cooperation from the activists among the workers, from a network of committees. But no such strategy providing for massive, coercive and sustained action existed. The rural tour he made, a move displaying an awareness of the need to broaden the ambit of the struggle, was an idea suggested to him by the activists of the LNP and one of the rare instances of the application of unconventional means. Typically, this campaign necessitated close cooperation from the LNP without which the whole operation might not have taken place.

On the whole Samant's tactics were simple, if not minimal. He did not go much beyond delivering speeches near mill gates and at mass rallies, and heading morchas and jail bharos. For the initiation and organization of these activities he did not require an elaborate system of workers' committees although the success, particularly of the jail bharo campaigns might have been far greater had such a network existed. With the assistance of a substantial cadre of worker activists, together establishing an effective network, providing leadership at the lower level and sustaining the action in Samant's absence, the outcome of the strike might well have been different. The strike now seemed largely a one man show for the performance of which Samant relied on the endurance of the workers and the assistance of a handful of trusted lieutenants like T.S. Borade, Vidhyadhar Budbadkar, D.P. Mungekar, B.S. Talekar and, of course, his experienced brother P.N. (Dada) Samant. Datta Samant knew that the struggle would be long and fearing that the workers might be tempted to give in, he preferred not to have them around, which is why he sent them back to the villages.

This is not to say that Samant was insincere in his efforts to find a solution or that he was basically motivated by personal aggrandizement but proper infrastructure in his union empire was and still is painfully lacking. Such an infrastructure is indispensable in a struggle on the scale of the textile strike. Prior to the strike Samant had always dealt with labour struggles on a small scale and he was used to dealing with them single-handed.[13] Now he adopted the same methods in the textile strike, but what had worked in single factories would not work for a whole industry. As long as only a few unions in his union empire conducted strikes, it was always possible to sustain a prolonged struggle with the assistance of the main body (solidarity strikes, collection of funds, food grains and the like) but now that a whole industry was paralysed the policy of remaining on strike for better or for worse proved self-defeating.

A strong network of mill and zone committees would also have been able to detect changes in the mood of the workers at an early stage and might have been able to modify policies accordingly. This leads to another point illustrating that the mill and zone committees were ineffective. The fact that a majority of the workers in the sample acknowledged that they had wanted to resume work after a period of about six months but refrained from doing so for fear of violence (see Chapter 7), proves that the committees were either insufficiently aware of this change or chose to ignore it. In the first case they would clearly prove to have been out of touch with the workers and in the second they would rapidly become so.

Lastly, the question of how the impression prevailed that workers' committees played such a dominant role in the strike should also be considered from the point of view of who reported on the strike. It must then be noted that the strike was followed closely by only a handful of labour correspondents, many of whom had little sympathy for Datta Samant's arbitrary behaviour. They attempted to discover the voice of the common worker and were inclined to believe that the mill and zonal committees were the platforms where the genuine feelings of the workers could be detected in their purest form.[14] It is fairly certain that the misconception about the importance of the workers' committees originated here.

The Rural Connection

Exodus to the Villages: The connections of Bombay textile workers with their places of origin have been important throughout their history. These connections have greatly influenced the lives of their families in the rural hinterland as well as their own lives in the city. Some key elements in this relation between the rural hinterland and Bombay are, (1) the employment offered by the city mills, (2) the flow of money from the city to the hinterland in the form of wages and, (3) an unusually high incidence of absenteeism. The first two aspects will be dealt with in detail in chapter 6. Other less obvious aspects are, (1) the possibilities of surviving a strike by returning to the village, (2) the chances of extending support to workers on strike in Bombay by means of collections of grain and money and, (3) the revitalization of struggles for emancipation in the rural areas with the assistance of mill workers who temporarily or permanently return to the village (for example, jail bharo campaigns). We shall discuss the last three elements here.

It has been stated by advocates and adversaries of the strike alike that its incredibly long duration was essentially due to the rural connections of the workers who returned to their home villages. There is no denying that tens of thousands of textile workers boarded buses in the days following the commencement of the strike. In doing so they responded to appeals made by Datta Samant but they also acted in accordance with past behaviour and their realization that the village offered better chances of survival. In the history of the Bombay textile workers, the village always acted as a refuge for workers on strike. In the present exceptionally long strike, the importance of the rural hinterland could only be greater still. There is, therefore, no denying the significance of the rural connection for the strike at this general level but this changes as soon as one tries to be more specific.

In order to gauge the importance of this connection one would need figures establishing the extent to which workers took recourse to the various opportunities offered by the hinterland, preferably category-wise. No such figures are available. In their absence the significance of the rural connections could also be established (at least tentatively) by finding out exactly how many workers left the city. Understandably such data were never collected either which means that one has to rely on estimates of knowledgeable people, each of whom may have his/her own reason for a certain figure. It was found that the estimates of the number of textile workers leaving the city during the strike vary greatly and are anywhere between 33 and 80 per cent of the entire labour force. It is tempting to fix the figure arbitrarily at 55 per cent but there would be no justification for that. It might very well be that some of the estimates are more realistic than others but, unfortunately, there is no way of finding out whose estimates deserve more credit.

L.K. Deshpande, who conducted a survey among textile workers in the course of the strike, believes that one-third of the labour force left the city and he bases this on a pilot study.[15] Former Labour Commissioner P.J. Ovid believes that 40 per cent of the workers returned to the villages but he has no hard evidence to support this contention (interview, 1 February 1987). In a report written in the middle of the strike Gurbir Singh put the figure at about 45 per cent but here too, there is no substantiation of this impression.[16] In the *Marxist Bulletin* of May 1982 it is recorded that 70 per cent of the strikers had gone back to their villages.[17] Datta Samant asserted several times that as many as 80 per cent of the workers left the city. Questioned about this he toned down the figure, explaining that he based this percentage on the attendance of meetings and enquiries by MGKU activists: 'I say that the majority had gone. It may be 60 per cent, 70 per cent or 80 per cent, that we don't know' (interview, 19 May 1986). His brother Dada mentioned a figure of 50 per cent, a percentage also given by former RMMS president, V. Hoshing. Hoshing, like Datta Samant, claims to base this figure on information collected by the union.[18]

From this brief survey it appears that the real figure of the number of workers who left for their villages is just anybody's guess. The surprisingly great differences call, nevertheless, for an explanation. It may be that Datta Samant's upper limit has been inspired by the need to explain away the disappointing participation in jail bharos, morchas and meetings as the strike progressed. Also, if his meetings were heavily attended it would be all the more impressive if it could be said that this was so even though 80 per cent of the workers had left for their villages. The reverse might be true for the bottom line adhered to by the labour commissioner. The government, millowners and Sangh had a common interest in reducing the significance of Samant's actions. If his meetings and campaigns did not show overwhelming participation, this would prove that he was losing ground. The importance of all Samant's activities could be reduced further still if it could be claimed that a majority of the workers were in Bombay during the campaigns.

Another point has to be taken into consideration. No one seems to have paid attention to the fact that it would have been very difficult to arrive at a reliable estimate even if it *had* been possible to count the number of workers leaving the city. The picture remains blurred. Thousands of workers returned after three, six or nine months to see what was going on. Many of them might even at that time have hoped or even tried to resume work but finding the atmosphere uncongenial or even downright hostile, they may have decided to return to their villages once more. This is not as far-fetched as it may seem for a substantial majority of the workers in the sample who left for their villages mentioned having visited Bombay once, twice or more times during the strike. Some stayed just a couple of days, other lingered for weeks or months together. Many of those who returned to Bombay prior to finally resuming work (or finding that they had been dismissed), stated that they made an attempt to get their job back during their visit(s) to Bombay.

To add all these workers to the group who voluntarily stayed in the village throughout the strike would be incorrect. Neither would it be justifiable to add them to the group of Sangh supporters who remained in the city or to those that were opposed to the strike for different reasons, groups of unknown magnitude. There is also the problem of families who got separated during the strike (wife returning to the village, children remaining in Bombay for their schooling). It is pointless to fix a figure arbitrarily as the lack of evidence and the complexity of the situation does not allow for that. What may be said is that even if only 40 per cent of the workers returned to their villages, this group still comprised some 1,00,000 workers and that returning to the village, therefore, has to be considered an important avenue for survival. In Chapter 5 the various employment opportunities offered by the village are discussed in detail.

While living in the village the workers were often without proper information about the situation in Bombay. They ran the risk of losing heart as a result. A visit by the strike leader to their places of origin would certainly do a lot to keep them united. If their active support could be enlisted to collect food and money this might even ease the problems of their fellow workers in the city. There was also the opportunity of pointing out the need for cooperation between industrial and agricultural labourers, which might create a bond between these different groups of workers. It was, therefore, decided that Datta Samant would undertake a rural tour in the second half of February and March. His visit to the rural areas, suggested and largely organized by LNP activists, did not go unnoticed. Also, the English newspapers flashed the news briefly. This initiative deserves attention as it was an acknowledgement by the strike leadership of the importance of some of the less obvious aspects of the rural connection.

At the same time Datta Samant sought the cooperation of the peasant leader Sharad Joshi whose following among the farmers and middle peasants was considerable and whose assistance would increase the pressure on the government. The attempt proved to be abortive. Subsequent efforts at mediation by Joshi would not produce results either.[19] In the wake of this tour extensive grain collections followed. With the exception of the Konkan, Samant visited the most important regions from where the textile workers originate: Kolhapur, Satara, Sangli and Pune. The news of his arrival was spread through pamphlets and posters. During the tour Samant was accompanied by prominent activists of the MGKU such as T.S. Borade, a man with exceptional oratorical abilities, SSS leaders like Y. Chavan and D.S. Kulkarni and a host of other platform speakers who, on various occasions, would address the crowds.

Workers and peasants, from far and near, flocked to the places where the famous doctor was to stop to deliver a speech appealing to the assembled workers to intensify their strike efforts, and to accept gifts. They came walking, cycling or in vans. Bags of grain and rice were also brought there, often on bullock carts. People waited patiently for long hours to catch a glimpse of the strike leader. The time schedules were never precise and on one occasion (a meeting in Rahimatpur) some 25,000 persons waited till 11.30 p.m. before Samant finally showed up.[20] The enthusiasm shown during these meetings by textile workers and agricultural labourers alike was apparently not shared by the local administration which usually took a negative view of such events and tried to prevent them by refusing permission for meetings. In spite of that thousands of persons thronged Samant's meeting places. Other groups and parties too tried to mobilize the rural folk with rallies but usually with much less success.[21]

The presence of striking textile workers in the villages was bound to have an impact on village life, the scope of which naturally depended on the number of strikers in the village and their proportional share in the population but it also varied in accordance with the support from parties and groups that helped them to get organized. The Lal Nishan Party (with the assistance of activists of the SSS and its affiliate the KKS) appeared to be the most active political party. It vehemently tried to lay the foundations for a lasting bond between industrial and agricultural workers. For that reason the LNP suggested to Datta Samant that he undertake a tour of the rural areas with the dual purpose of encouraging the workers staying in the villages and enlisting the support of agricultural labourers and peasants. In these attempts the LNP tried to cover all regions in which there were substantial clusters of textile workers. In Sangli its efforts were complemented by a like-minded organization, the Shakti Mukti Dal.

Food Drives: The support extended by the people living in the rural areas to the workers in Bombay in terms of food and money is indicative (though not the only indicator) of the significance of the rural connection. In assessing its scope it appears to be very difficult to arrive at a comprehensive view of the total support, be it in the form of food and financial collections or any other strike-related activities. The situation for Bombay, where workers of many factories donated money for the success of the strike, is not much better.[22] Unfortunately, the majority of the newspapers hardly reported on activities to support the strike which might be taken to mean that they were limited in scope but it could equally well point at journalistic indifference. As far as reporting on strike-related activities in the rural hinterland is concerned it is likely, indeed, that the city-based newspapers were simply not interested in them. There were very few exceptions to this general lack of interest. *Nava Kal* did report such news, usually restricting itself to information on the collection and distribution of food and money. But the news was of a very incidental nature, scattered over the months of April–August 1982. It also reported on the jail bharo campaign in the Konkan region in November.[23]

Probably the only paper that closely followed the developments in the hinterland and the many activities largely initiated there by the LNP, was *Shramik Vichar*. The quality of this news, however, in terms of precise information was poor, apart from the additional problem that *Shramik Vichar* took a partisan stand in the strike. Successes of Datta Samant in other industries were enlarged on to boost the morale of the striking workers and his failures concealed.[24] There were scores of articles highlighting the support from agricultural labourers, peasants and small farmers but the usefulness of this material for judging the scope of support from the hinterland, not to mention the degree to which a unity between agricultural and industrial labourers was realized, is questionable. The reports merely inform the reader that workers of such and such factory donated a day's wages or that so many kilograms of grain were promised or collected in a particular village at a certain time and sent to Bombay. However, all this news taken together does not give an accurate picture of the scale on which the rural areas materially contributed to the success of the strike and thereby of the significance of this aspect of the rural connection.

In the first few months of the strike, the activities of the LNP concentrated on Samant's rural tour and the collection of rice, grain, jowar, money and on the organization of demonstrations but later on jail bharos in many talukas were organized. These shifts in activities, probably induced by a dwindling response to the food drives, are faithfully reflected in the columns of *Shramik Vichar*, the organ of the LNP. Other unions and groupings also collected money and food and organized meetings but their contribution to the cause of the striking workers is by their own acknowledgement much less, besides being equally poorly documented. In the heat of the struggle no one bothered to carefully register donations in cash and kind. Whatever administration existed appears to have been haphazard. There was no central point in Bombay where all donations were first collected before being distributed to the needy workers. Apart from that, some donors organized their own distribution of money and food.[25] What ultimately remains are inadequate reports (predominantly in *Shramik Vichar*) about factories, rural organizations or peasants announcing support or giving it. As a result the precise scope of the support given will remain unknown.

On the strength of the newspaper reports alone it is not even possible to say whether these contributions and donations were substantial. Leaders from the MGKU and the LNP have tried to make much of this support. Their statements were, however, generally based on impressions. According to Dada Samant:

> The support was tremendous. We brought 3,000 bags of wheat and jowar from all over Maharashtra to Bombay, given by the farmers who were related to the textile workers. The harvest had just been and they sent the bags by truck loads. We collected Rs three crores cash from other industrial workers and all this was distributed. I think this was very exceptional [interview, 15 April 1986].

In an open letter, in which the claim is refuted that Samant's MGKU did nothing to activate other sections of society, Y. Chavan, president of the SSS, spoke about 4,000 quintals of grain being collected in the countryside on behalf of the workers.[26]

There is, however, no way of checking the accuracy of these statements although this should not be taken to mean that the claims themselves are improbable. But, as in the case of the number of people leaving for the villages, the figures might have been inflated with ulterior motives. As far as donations are concerned, there is also the problem that one has to reckon with differences between what people say they will offer and what they actually donate. But that does not seem to be the problem here as the statements restrict themselves to what was really collected. What induces caution, however, is that not all grain collected in the rural areas seems to have reached Bombay. One of the workers in the sample, who took part in collecting rice and food grains, stated that he stopped doing so when trucks carrying the food were intercepted by the police, emptied and sent back. What happened to the grain thus confiscated is unknown. It will not have reached the needy workers.

Apart from that one has to conclude that even if the amounts of money and food that the strike leaders speak of were collected, this would still be a drop in the ocean. Rs three crores for at a minimum one lakh workers in the city would mean Rs 300 per person and 4,000 quintals of grain would come to four kgs per worker. Although this support was very welcome it will not have reached far in alleviating the suffering of the workers. True, not all workers availed themselves of the support and with the passage of time ever more would resume work thereby leaving a greater share for those who continued the strike, but even so the donations could do little to relieve the distress.

In order to get some idea of the extent to which workers benefited from the donations in the course of the strike, relevant questions were included in the interviews. Judging the answers it was taken for granted that the food and financial support that did reach Bombay was distributed fairly by the MGKU. This was done with the aid of the various workers' committees. It is also understood that in doing so the personal circumstances of the worker and his family were taken into account, some receiving thrice as much as others. From all the workers in the sample some 40 per cent appeared to have received help in cash or in kind. These donations rarely exceeded ten kg of wheat (portions of five kgs appeared to be the rule) or Rs 50 in cash. Besides, these workers received help only once or twice. It is clear from these figures that in the best of cases the donated food and money only marginally helped them to stay alive—ten kgs of wheat and Rs 50 will not last long in a strike lasting a year and a half. If the sample results do provide an indication of the support received by workers from other mills then it must be concluded that in spite of statements to the contrary the total material support was very limited in scope.

The collection and distribution of food and money were not just limited in scope but also in time and took place mainly in the months following Datta Samant's rural tour in February 1982. After July nothing much is to be found in the newspapers or in other documents on material support of any kind and it seems fair to assume that this support ebbed away. It could not be otherwise as there are tremendous problems involved in trying to sustain the attention and sympathy of the public in such long-drawn-out strikes.

This, of course, does not deny the possibility of the scale of support being unprecedented. In fact, this is likely to have been the case. To the best of my knowledge there have been no comparable food drives and money collections in earlier struggles. One is tempted to believe that this points to a growing awareness among agricultural labourers and small peasants in the rural hinterland that the struggles for better wages in the city and for higher income in the rural areas ought to be combined. This, however, is a matter of speculation.

The leadership of the LNP insists that those who responded to the food drive were essentially agricultural labourers and small and middle peasants. It has also been said that the workers who participated in the grain collections first (as is natural) approached their relatives and friends. This leaves plenty of room for the possibility that the contributors were chiefly emotionally moved by the plight of the workers rather than by any political consideration. There is nothing wrong with that but it cannot be used as evidence for the desired growth of political awareness among agricultural labourers or of the realization among all workers that the struggles of industrial and agricultural labourers need to be combined.

Jail Bharo Campaigns: The grain collections being over, another eruption of strike-related activities in the rural areas was to follow in August and September when jail bharo campaigns were launched (the first on 16 August) throughout Maharashtra, including Bombay. The news of the jail bharo campaigns was spread with the aid of pamphlets, posters and newspaper reports. Outside Bombay the jail bharo campaigns would be conducted in Sindhu Durg, Kolhapur and Sangli but the newspapers would usually focus on the developments in the metropolis.

In the various reports on these campaigns, it is often impossible to distinguish between the number of arrests being made inside and outside Bombay. Samant claimed that some 50,000 workers courted arrest on 16 August but spokesmen of the police reduced that figure to 5,000 who were practically all released the same day (*TOI,* 17 August 1982). The difference in figures is, apart from the customary overestimation and underrating, understandable as most workers who offered themselves for arrest were simply not arrested but dispersed. By refusing to arrest all those who offered themselves, the campaign was robbed of much of its glory and its badly needed martyrs. From the point of view of the state this was an effective answer to a campaign which might otherwise have unnerved the public and might have disrupted the entire jail system.

The second jail bharo andolan* started on 17 September, a day on which 1,500 workers were arrested in Bombay. But the zeal of the workers tapered off quickly. In the course of a week less than 5,000 workers courted arrest as against Samant's hope that this figure could

---

* The term 'jail bharo andolan', a mixture of English and Hindi, signifies an agitation in the course of which the participants offer themselves for arrest. The reason for such a 'fill the jail campaign' is to call public attention to the need to redress a wrong experienced by a particular group. The method is derived from strategies propagated by Mahatma Gandhi in the course of India's struggle for freedom.

be reached daily (*TOI,* 23 September 1982). The figures given by *Shramik Vichar* confirm the general picture that the campaign did not catch on. Even Datta Samant admitted that the participation was disappointing and ascribed this to the return of the textile workers to the villages (*TOI,* 26 September 1982). But if this was really an explanation for the low response at that time then it might rightly be asked why greater success was not achieved in the countryside.

A new vigorous attempt to draw public attention to the ongoing strike was made in October when yet another jail bharo campaign was planned in combination with a three days' strike in Samant-ruled industrial enterprises in Maharashtra starting on 11 October. Workers ignored the ban order regarding unlawful gatherings which resulted in violent clashes with the police on the first day of the strike and the arrest of 5,300 persons, including the brothers Dada and Datta Samant. Datta Samant would be in jail for fourteen days. This campaign led to the unfortunate tussle with George Fernandes regarding the participation of the BEST workers. The success of the jail bharo campaign outside Bombay seems to have been moderate although a noteworthy aspect of it was the conspicuous participation of women in it.[27] *Shramik Vichar* reported that in all over 11,000 persons had been arrested in Bombay and in the districts of Thane, Nasik and Aurangabad in the course of the three days that the agitation lasted (*Shramik Vichar,* 13 October 1982). With this last campaign the activities in the rural areas were practically over. In February and March 1983 there would follow a few long marches but these came too late to influence the outcome of the strike in any way.

In the course of the strike, the LNP stressed consistently that the stay of textile workers in the villages was a potential source of organizational strength, a source that could be tapped to bring about a unity between agricultural and industrial labourers. The often better-educated textile worker could use his organizational experience (obtained in trade union activity) to organize labour in the rural hinterland. However, there is little evidence that this was done to any appreciable degree in spite of some cheerful articles in the press.[28] One of the more successful attempts in this regard seems to be the work undertaken by the SSKKMS: Shoshit Shetkari, Kashtakari, Kamgar Mukti Sangarsh (Exploited Peasants, Toilers, Workers' Liberation Struggles). This organization was founded in the wake of the strike with the help of textile workers who had returned to their villages. Today the SSKKMS operates in the Khanapur taluka in Sangli district, a taluka to which approximately 5,000 textile workers belonged. During their long stay in the village these workers were forced to seek employment under the Employment Guarantee Scheme (see also Chapter 5) which brought them into close contact with the village poor and resulted in the establishment of the SSKKMS, an organization formed to improve the lot of agricultural labourers and without any political affiliation.[29]

Summarizing, it may be concluded that the rural connection had an important bearing on the chances for the survival of the workers. In this the present strike did not differ from similar struggles in the past. This connection (sometimes dubbed 'rural nexus') provided also the basis for collections of food and money as well as for participation in jail bharo campaigns, but the success of both these activities was limited even though it may have surpassed whatever was achieved in earlier struggles. Barring a few examples, there is no evidence that the strike had a significant impact on the unification of the struggles of agricultural and industrial labourers (the so-called worker—peasant alliance) and statements to that effect must be treated with caution.[30] The situation might have been different if the communist parties had shown a sincere interest in developing such ties but that was not the case. The few examples that do exist now are insufficient to declare that the strike was instrumental in forging a new link between the city and the rural hinterland as has been done by several authors (Patankar, 1982, 1983; Omvedt, 1983).[31]

The Use of Violence

Impact of an Image: Millowners and the government have consistently attributed the unexpected success of the strike to the violent means supposedly adopted by Datta Samant and his MGKU. The MOA used to speak of 'a fear psychosis' created in the minds of the workers as a result of beatings, stabbings and murders. Many newspapers uncritically aped this phrase without stopping to check the extent to which Samant's MGKU could really be blamed for the use of means so easily attributed to it. The press reports about murders meanwhile did much to increase the tension and instilled fear in the hearts of countless textile workers. They also provided the millowners with an excuse to seek police protection for the workers who resumed duty. This contributed considerably to a negative view of the strike by the public at large.

It is surprising that with all the talk about violence nobody bothered to systematically collect data on this aspect of the strike. No one knew for certain, for example, how many murders were committed during the strike but everyone volunteered estimates which would be anywhere between a 'few' and 'many'. The confusion prevailed unabated even after the strike.[32] In the atmosphere prevailing at the time the estimates took at times vicious forms but even if no condemnation of the strike was intended, the estimates would easily be twice or thrice as high as the facts warranted.[33]

Everyone may have had his own reasons for making statements about the murders taking place but if the police had taken stock of the incidents carefully and if the circumstances of an act of violence had been studied properly such confusion could have been avoided. There are also those (particularly among supporters of Samant) who seek to create the impression that the strike was essentially a non-violent affair. They (wish to) believe that there was no violence worth the name during the strike and that the workers stayed away from the mills voluntarily. This view cannot be sustained either as will be shown. It may be stated at the outset that in a strike of such duration, involving so many people and with the stakes being so high, violence was bound to occur. Here an attempt will be made to assess the scope of this violence.

In order to establish the real proportion of violence the newspapers are of little use. They were predominantly dependent for their information on the police which had been instructed to maintain law and order in the city and tended to see a striking worker behind every tree. In order to obtain an overview of the situation during the strike, the office of the commissioner of police in Bombay collected information from the various police stations in the city in April/May 1987 and provided the statistics given below from Table 3.1. These data are the only available on the subject. It appears that in all 248 cases of hurt/violence were registered during the entire strike. As the murder cases fired the imagination of the public at large and received wide publicity, it is justifiable to start the discussion with these.

TABLE 3.1

Cases of Violence Registered during the Textile Workers' Strike from 18 January 1982 to 1 August 1983

Offences/ Criminal Acts	*Total Cases*	*Total Accused Arrested*	*'A' Cases**	*Cases Pending Trial*	*No. Cases Convicted*	*No. Cases Acquitted*
I	178	237	49	29	3	97
II	59	72	18	9	–	32
III	3	3	2	–	–	1
IV	4	42	–	2	–	2
V	4	12	1	3	–	–
TOTAL	248	366	70	43	3	132

* 'A' Cases: true but undetected
I = Common assaults (beatings with or without weapons, stabbings)
II = Criminal intimidation (threats)
III = Violent acts (for example, brickbatting, throwing soda water bottles)
IV = Rioting
V = Murder cases

Source: Office of Commissioner of Police, Bombay, May 1987.

The first thing to be observed is that not eight or twelve or 'many' strike-related murders took place in the period under investigation but 'only' four (all of them in 1982). The first case of murder took place on 18 March and took the life of a worker from Bombay Dyeing (Spring Mills) who was attacked by four persons supposedly for having resumed work. The victim was standing near a bus stop where he was dragged away. The assailants beat and kicked him mercilessly, leaving him unconscious. He died in a hospital four weeks later as a result of the injuries sustained. The report observes that the motive for this crime was 'rivalry over attending the work during strike period'. But the condition of the worker was such that the report also states: 'The deceased could not make any statement and hence no names or other particulars of the assailants could be known.'[34] Four active members of the MGKU were nevertheless arrested in connection with this crime but had to be released for lack of evidence. It seems slightly premature to attribute this murder case to the MGKU as the identity of the assailants remained unknown.

A second murder took place on 23 April when a worker of New Coorla Mills walked home after the second shift. He was assaulted with a dagger by a fellow worker who stabbed him four times before running away. The victim died the same day in hospital. The motive for this crime is given as: 'Previous enmity over union activities.' In this case the assailant was arrested and was still awaiting trial in 1987. Whether he belonged to the MGKU or not is not stated in the report, nor the nature of their quarrel about union activities.[35] Before a court ruling, this murder cannot be attributed to the MGKU.

A third case of murder was to follow on 5 May and involved once again a worker of Bombay Dyeing (Spring Mills) who used to attend work secretly for fear of detection by colleagues. While taking a walk in the afternoon he was assaulted by three men using knives. The victim succumbed to his injuries in hospital. The motive for the murder was simply stated as 'union rivalry'. In this case the police accused twelve persons (all active members of the MGKU), including P.N. (Dada) Samant.[36] The arrest of Dada Samant was based on a speech he had made in the office of the MGKU the day before the murder took place. Two workers testified that Dada Samant on that occasion instigated workers to throw soda water bottles on workers who resumed duty and to use knives 'freely'. A fortnight later Dada Samant would be released on bail as the judge concluded that Samant's exhortations, although utterly objectionable, could not be construed to mean a conspiracy to commit a particular crime. Samant's case was still pending in June 1987.

The fourth murder took place on 8 July at 10 a.m. and in front of Wakdi chawl in Parel. This time the victim was a member of the Hind Mazdoor Sabha while the four arrested assailants were all active members of the RMMS. The victim was stopped when he was cycling and stabbed with a dagger by persons who had arrived in a jeep and a lorry. The worker was brought to a hospital but died before he could be admitted. The motive for this murder was also given as 'union rivalry'. This case too was still pending trial in mid-1987.[37]

It appears that out of a total of four strike-related murders the first may have been committed by MGKU-members (although this is by no means certain). There is even less evidence in the second case. The third seems a clear case of murder by MGKU men but the fourth is equally clearly a murder by RMMS men. If one is ill-disposed towards Datta Samant one might attribute at most three murders to his union but possibly only one can stand the test of critical appraisal. In any case, accusations about 'many murders perpetrated by the MGKU' stand exposed as baseless as they are untenable in the light of the evidence supplied by the police. But the harm, of course, had already been done.[38]

Another important point to be observed is that the last murder which might be attributed to the MGKU took place in May 1982 (some three and a half months after the beginning of the strike) though the strike continued for another fifteen months. This is intriguing as even Samant's opponents are prepared to admit that for the first three months the strike was on the whole peaceful. Violence is supposed to have been resorted to at a later stage when workers started returning to the mills. On the face of it may seem, therefore, that the murders had little or no impact on the continuation of the strike. Such a conclusion, however, is unwarranted as at no point during the strike there was a clear view of which crimes could rightly be attributed to the MGKU and which not. Nevertheless, unsubstantiated reports of murders of textile workers kept figuring in the press. In the heated atmosphere of the time and in the absence of clarity about the antecedents and motives of the accused far too many murders were credited to the MGKU. It cannot be denied that the police and press together bear responsibility for this. The result has been that throughout the strike the MGKU would have to fight the image of being a bunch of cold-blooded killers. This impression was detrimental to the cause although helpful in prolonging the strike as will be seen shortly.

Before proceeding with other data, a word has to be said about the reliability of the information received from the police. The questions to be answered here are whether the police, as part of the law-enforcement machinery, could have a bias in reporting cases of violence and whether such a bias would lead to underreporting incidences of violence or overrating them. The answer to these questions involves the role played by the police during the strike. This role went far beyond the maintenance of law and order. A bias may therefore not be excluded. From the involvement of the police in strike-breaking activities it may be deduced that if any bias coloured the compilation of police statistics, it must have been a tendency to exaggerate the use of violence resorted to by Samant's MGKU and to minimize the use of violence by the Sangh (not to mention its own contribution).

But this does not solve all our problems. What is puzzling is that even though the police records do not attribute murders to the MGKU after May 1982, Dada Samant seems convinced that if any murders could be attributed to 'overzealous' workers of the MGKU these should have been committed after about a year when those who resumed work were given protection by the Sangh and the police: 'One or two INTUC people who organized workers to break the strike were murdered then' (interview, 15 April 1986). The period of a year corresponds to a stabbing which took the lives of Tukaram Wagde and B. Mishra at the end of December—killings which did not find a place in the police statistics (*TOI,* 29 December 1982).

The explanation for this irregularity might be that these statistics distinguish between homicide and premeditated murder but, unfortunately, this could not be ascertained. If this is really the explanation the figure for strike victims should be higher. Similarly, an incident costing the lives of two workers of Shree Ram Mills is missing in the police statistics. These workers were travelling by a company bus on 3 June 1982 when their vehicle was attacked by persons armed with acid bulbs and explosive inflammable material as a result of which two workers later died in hospital. Seven assailants were apprehended and according to newspaper reports sentenced to life imprisonment (cf. *IE,* 4 February 1984). In fact, this last incident could have been classified under 'violent acts' (category III) but in the month of June no such case was recorded (see Table 3.4).

Murders are not the only parameters for measuring the violent aspects of a strike or the extent to which force is resorted to by a union. Beatings too can effectively convey a message as do threats, and of these there have been hundreds. The 248 cases of violence registered by the police are largely cases of beatings (178) and intimidation (fifty-nine). It comes as a surprise that the police, when questioned about these two categories, maintained that all the registered cases refer to violence perpetrated by adherents of the MGKU. But at the same time the police readily admitted that in cases of inter-union rivalry it is customary for unions to retaliate when the violence continues for months on end. However, the information regarding the involvement of the MGKU in all these incidents could not be established as this would imply verification of all the files of the police stations in the city.

What has been found discussing the murder cases makes it unlikely that the Sangh refrained from violence with respect to the other categories and if the total figure of 248 registered cases has any bearing on reality then this number must include cases of Sangh violence as well. If not, we are faced with the intriguing question of why Sangh violence was not reported, or why it did not find its place in the statistics. Granting that all the registered cases have to be linked with the MGKU implies that the Sangh abstained from violence and this contradicts the earlier given point of view of the police. An obvious reason for not reporting RMMS violence would be that its victims had no faith in the law-enforcement machinery and therefore preferred to remain silent. Workers may have felt that the way the police maintained law and order was detrimental to their cause and they would not have to search long for evidence either. One can think of Section 144 prohibiting gatherings, lathi charges during morchas and jail bharo campaigns, protection of 'blacklegs', assistance for the removal of stocks from mill premises and so on. It could well be that the striking workers concluded at an early stage that the police did not just side with the government (as may have been expected) but also with the millowners and the Sangh, and that it would be wiser to take a beating instead of complaining about it. There is, in fact, ample evidence to bear this out.

On the whole the workers appeared to take a negative view of the police but in this they are not very different from large sections of Indian society. Over the years the Indian police have built up an unenviable reputation as far as reliability and moral rectitude is concerned. This has been due to a seemingly endless chain of incidents displaying questionable police behaviour, the causes of which fall outside the scope of this study. Accounts of beatings and torture at police stations found a fertile ground among the textile workers and added fuel to the battered image of the police. Press reports on such incidents were rare but the worker was not dependent on them as he had his own experience to go by and/or the evidence supplied by his fellow workers as was borne out by the interviews with the workers from the sample.

The role of the police as an instrument for repression surfaced in its attempts to break the strike as reported by the press and attested to by workers during the interviews. The 11 July 1982 issue of the *Sunday Observer* reported workers' complaints of being picked up at random from their chawls and being forced into waiting police vans with the purpose of transporting them forcibly to the mills. The 7 November issue of the same paper reported on activists who, after having gone underground, had to resurface when the police started harassing wives and relatives. In the same month the *IE* (30 November) carried the story of a worker who had been tortured at a police office.

The *Free Press Journal* (19 January 1983) some time later broke the news of a massive operation of vengeance by the police after workers had protested against maltreatment by them.[39] In the same report, workers of Madhusudan Mills were quoted as saying that at the police station in Worli one room had been reserved for this purpose when the strike began. An article analysing the strike-breaking activities of the Sangh, written a year after the beginning of the strike, stated bluntly that the RMMS had enlisted one of the most notorious gangs in Bombay to assist the Sangh 'where the police fail' (*Business Standard*, 19 January 1983). When Chief Minister Patil was confronted in the Legislative Assembly with reports of the misbehaviour of the police on many occasions during the strike he said that he agreed 'to some extent' that those who turned to the police for help were maltreated (*TOI*, 9 April 1983). In the same session he would not hesitate to compare Samant with Hitler.

As press reports on violence during the strike were of an incidental nature and insufficient to gauge the scope of its influence, this aspect was included in all the interviews. The workers were questioned on their experience with or knowledge of violent incidents in order to ascertain the extent to which they were subjected to or influenced by violence of any kind during the strike. In tabling the results there was no alternative but to take the victims' surmises regarding the background of the assailants for granted. This implies that such tricky cases as a union assaulting its own members with the assistance of anonymous persons in order to discredit its opponent have gone undetected. It is impossible to say whether this technique was resorted to by any of the unions. The results of the interviews are presented in Table 3.2.

TABLE 3.2
Violent Encounters and Threats During the Strike as Reported by Sample Workers

Offence	*Assailants*	*Mill A (n=75)*	*Mill B (n = 75)*
Beating by	Samant-walas	3	–
Stabbing by	"	–	1
Threats by	"	8	4
Beating by	Sangh-walas	1	–
Threats by	"	–	3
Beating by	Police	–	1
Threats by	"	2	4
Total:		14	13

The answers confirm the impression that all the elements mentioned earlier, that is, violence perpetrated by the MGKU, RMMS and the police, prevailed during the strike. Although the interviews were generally quite open it seems fair to assume that, if anything, the real incidence of violent encounters and threats was higher than appears from the Table. In any case, twenty-seven workers out of a total of 150 (that is, 18 per cent) were physically or verbally intimidated by any of the three agents, the MGKU, RMMS or the police. It also appears that according to the findings in this sample the use of forceful means was more readily resorted to by adherents of the MGKU than by those of the RMMS. However, if we include the encounters with the police (and the pressure they put on workers to resume work) on the Sangh side, then there appears to be more of a balance. The justification for doing so would be that if we want to map out the pressure to which workers were subjected it matters little whether it was the Sangh or the police telling a worker to resume work. Roughly speaking then, we would find sixteen acts of intimidation on the MGKU side as against eleven on the part of the Sangh.

There are various problems connected with the evaluation of these data. One is that the seriousness of all these incidents is difficult to compare. A threat may seem to be more innocent than a beating but if the threat comes from a group of persons wielding knives and swords and visiting the victim at home (as happened to a RMMS activist who thereupon left for his village), then it is certainly not less serious than the 'mild beating' reported by several workers who were stopped by 'MGKU-walas'.* Again, a threat of dismissal (as given by 'Sangh-walas') may have a greater impact on a worker whose endurance has been tried far too long than would a mild beating.

The tight corner in which many a worker found himself was aptly described by one of them: 'When I was on strike the Sangh-walas came to my place and told me that they would see me if I didn't return to the mills. Once I did, I was visited by Samant-walas who threatened to beat me up in case I would go.' The dynamics of inter-union retaliation were adequately illustrated by an MGKU activist who was caught in the process of threatening a worker who wanted to resume duty and who was subsequently beaten up by his opponents. Another stated that the RMMS had threatened to kill him but he added that he himself told other workers that he would hammer them if they considered returning to the mills. Under the circumstances, grave errors were probably unavoidable exemplified by the unfortunate worker who was stabbed by 'MGKU-walas' on the suspicion of wanting to resume work although he had no such intention.

Another problem is that a distortion of reality might have occurred in the sample as a result of contact with a worker who suffered from serious maltreatment by the police. This meeting was both shocking and revealing and would naturally lead me to ask the victim whether he knew of anybody else having undergone the same fate. In this fashion three more workers were contacted. As those who suffered from maltreatment by the police were known to each other, the result may well have been accumulation of relevant but possibly not very representative evidence. Even so, the accounts of the victims and the confirmation by other workers, in addition to the press reports, indicate such uniformity in the modus operandi of the police that there is no reason to believe that the extreme cases of harassment I chanced upon were restricted to the workers of the two mills under investigation.

* The Hindi and Marathi term 'wala' has a very flexible meaning and is used to denote persons employed with or concerned about something.

Contribution of the State: The role of the police in Bombay city had far greater impact on the development of the strike than in the rural hinterland where the police usually did not go beyond telling a worker to resume duty and warning him if he did not do so. In Bombay the confrontations were much more grim and may as a result have contributed to an escalation of violence. In certain quarters the police was stationed day and night, for the better part of the strike, to maintain law and order but also to bully activists. Warnings to resume duty were often given in threatening surroundings such as a police van or police station. If the worker appeared to be stubborn or an activist of the MGKU, policemen might go further and threaten his relatives as well. The display of force by the police would be such that workers preferred to stay at home rather than to go into the streets to avoid confrontations with them.[40] In September 1982 Samant publicly complained that police and security guards of the mills obliged scores of workers to resume duty at the risk of being locked up in their rooms if they refused (*Sunday Observer*, 19 September 1982). That this was no empty accusation is borne out by the account of Baluram, one of the sample workers, who was forbidden to contact his fellow workers and ordered to stay in his room (see case study no. 5).

The interference of the police could take gruesome forms too, as in the case of Damodar Narvekar, a worker from mill B, who was wanted by the Criminal Investigation Department (CID) and had gone underground. Damodar's wife still recalls with fear how she was confronted on 1 July 1982 by two policemen of the CID who wanted to know the whereabouts of her husband. When she said that she did not know where he was she was informed that her brother-in-law had died in an accident and that they wanted to convey this news to him. She was asked to enter a police van which was standing nearby. When she did so she found two brothers-in-law (including the one who was supposed to have died) waiting. The brothers were beaten in front of her and asked to reveal the whereabouts of her husband which they did not do. Then she herself too was threatened with a beating. They told her: 'If you don't tell us where your husband is, we will take you to the police station ... and then you will come to know what the police is like!' After a few more threats she was released and given a phone number which she was supposed to dial within eight days in order to give the required information. They also searched the hut for weapons but could find nothing.

Not waiting for the police to return she herself went to the police station in Masjid after eight days in the company of her sister to tell them that she had no idea where her husband was. She was taken to the jail where she saw her brothers-in-law who had been hung on an iron rod and were being beaten with fists and belts. She was told that she would undergo the same fate, if necessary upside down, but then her sister intervened and told the policemen that she would file a suit against the CID if they touched her sister as her condition was very fragile. After showing the police some papers, they were released. From that time onwards the police frequently dropped in at her place, sometimes at night.

Being an active supporter of Datta Samant, Damodar himself had been arrested several times before July 1982 but he had always been released after his wife paid bail for which she had to sell gold ornaments. On those occasions he was never beaten. After the murder in May he barely escaped retaliation by the Sangh and thought it wiser to go underground. When he was taking a walk in the neighbourhood the very day that the murder took place, he found himself being surrounded by a group of about twenty persons, many of whom he knew belonged to the RMMS. They carried knives and swords but in a split second, realizing his position and acting swiftly, he managed to escape. For a year he did not dare to return home and stayed with friends, ate in cheap hotels and spent a lot of money. Sometimes he had to jump into taxis when suddenly recognized. Friends conveyed news to his wife. In the end Damodar's wife was left in peace and he decided to return.

Another case illustrating the sort of action the police could take is that of Dasharath Wagh, a kingpin of the resistance in mill B against the RMMS. Dasharath was beaten up at a police station in Sewri at least five times, first in August 1982. A man in civil attire came to his room in the chawl and told him to follow him to a police van. Inside the van he was asked why he did not return to work, and when he retorted that it was up to him to go back or not he was beaten. They took him into custody and beat him again at the police station. The beating was done with hands and lathis and they took care that there were no eyewitnesses. He was held for three days and then released when the MGKU paid a bail of Rs 1500. A few days later, however, they came back, arrested him and started all over again. This time he was beaten by different persons for about five minutes every one or two hours. After two days he was released. Whenever he was arrested he was also released after two or three days, provided bail was paid. In his case too, the police came at odd times, twice at night.

Asked whether he filed a suit against his tormentors, Dasharath sighs: 'To whom should I go for that? To the police?!' His wife was also harassed although not by the police but by RMMS supporters. In his absence security guards from the mill came to his home and told his wife to vacate the room which she refused to do. In September 1982, when his morale was at a low ebb, Dasharath went to his mill where he was asked to sign a statement that henceforth he would refrain from action. When he refused to sign he was thrown out and on 24 September dismissed. Dasharath was one of the first and one of the comparatively few who would receive a formal order of dismissal. Most of his colleagues who were not reinstated after the strike were simply not taken back. One year later he would receive a registered letter ordering him to vacate the room in which he was staying as it was mill property.[41] Dasharath refused to budge and although he was threatened with dire consequences if he did not leave, the management of the company apparently thought it wiser to refrain from action for nothing happened afterwards. Dasharath did not stop his activities then and continued the struggle without means or income. In June 1987 he was still without a job but at least in the possession of his room.

These examples show that the police did more than merely maintain law and order. It has to be concluded that if the 248 registered cases refer to violence resorted to by adherents of the MGKU, as claimed by the police, then a few more cases are conspicuously absent in the statistics. It seems fair to assume that the registered criminal cases, apart from maintaining law and order, also served the purpose of undermining the morale of the striking workers. This impression is strengthened if we look at what happened to all these cases. Table 3.1 tells us that 53 per cent of all the cases were acquitted. Of all cases of violence, 17 per cent are pending trial and a mere 1 per cent resulted in conviction.

It is true that the figure for convictions may become higher once the cases that are sub judice now are tried. Similarly, if the 28 per cent cases classified as 'true but undetected' had resulted in arrests the percentage of convictions might also have been higher. But, even if we allow for a tenfold increase in the number of convictions, there is no denying the fact that the percentage of convictions will be far below what might be expected if these cases had been supported by strong evidence. This calls into question the sincerity of the police in registering complaints about violence by MGKU adherents and lends credibility to the accusation that registration of criminal cases was intended not only for maintenance of the law but also for harassment of the more determined workers.[42]

Hammer and Anvil: In spite of police protection and the fact that financial problems became more manageable after resuming work, life was not exactly easy for the workers who returned to the mills. Everyone who did so had to develop some tactic or other to camouflage the fact that he belonged to the (gradually growing) group of workers who saw no point in continuing the strike. To ease problems the Sangh suggested that workers should not resume duty at their own mill as this would facilitate recognition by workers on strike. Following this advice thousands of workers worked in other mills than their own, thereby greatly contributing to the confusion regarding the number of 'new recruits' employed in the course of the strike.

Workers kept an eye on each other and the resulting tension could be particularly strong in kholis* where both workers who supported and those who opposed the strike had to share a single room. Several interviewees explained that they were uncertain about the views of their roommates and therefore avoided discussions about the strike. This resulted in the highly curious and uneasy situation that the one subject that was taboo during the strike was the question of the continuation of the strike. In order not to appear too inquisitive, workers often tended to avoid direct questions and the answers given were usually sufficiently vague to ensure that living together in one room would not become impossible.

---

* Tenements.

From the interviews it appears that those who decided to resume felt more vulnerable and suffered from stronger feelings of insecurity than workers who continued the strike. Practically without exception the early resumers stated that they went straight home or to the mill and did not dare to go anywhere else for fear of molestation (see also case study no. 4). The very first workers who resumed work utilized the shelter provided by some mills and stayed on the premises for weeks together. One worker in the sample reported having spent about a month and a half months inside the mill without having ventured out even once. But this was only possible at a time when millowners wanted to prove to the outside world that the strike was collapsing and that workers were rejoining in ever-larger numbers.

Later the workers were no longer allowed to stay on the mill premises. They were left with no choice other than facing the ordeal of exposing themselves in the streets if they wanted to work. If they had to go out they preferred to move in groups as this would offer greater protection than venturing out alone. All sorts of excuses were made by workers to explain their absence in the room or the chawl. They told roommates for instance that they had gone to see relatives or that they were going out in search of work. The Sangh tried to make things easier for them by picking them up by lorry from several points in the city and in doing so an effort was made to hide these meeting places from workers on strike.

All this points to a widely prevalent fear psychosis in and outside the living quarters. However, there is a great difference to be observed in the reports of workers living inside the textile area and those who stayed far away from it. The reason for this is quite simply that acts of violence tended to be concentrated in those areas where many workers lived. Workers in such areas were more exposed to violent encounters than others. This is also borne out by the figures showing the distribution of cases of violence during the strike (Table 3.3). The Table shows that most violence occurred in the heart of the textile area: Dadar, Bhoiwada, Kalachowki (Lalbaug), Rafi Ahmed Kidwai Marg (Sewri). In Dadar, Lalbaug and Sewri alone nearly 50 per cent of all the registered cases of violence occurred. It stands to reason that the unreported cases (retaliation by the Sangh) were also concentrated in this area.[43]

TABLE 3.3
District-wise Distribution of Cases of Violence in the Strike Period

Police Station	*Categories**				
	I	*II*	*III*	*IV*	*V*
Dharavi	14	9			
R.A. Kidwai	26	15	1	2	2
Andheri	1	3			
Byculla	5	2	1	1	
Mahim	10	6			
Joshi Marg	5	5			
Worli	4	6			
Bhoiwada	13	1			
Matunga	5	2	1	1	1
Kurla	4	3	1		
Dadar	62	3			
Kalachowki	14	2			
Agripada	11	2			
Borivali	2				
D.N. Nagar	1				
Vikhroli	1				
TOTAL (= 248)	178	59	3	4	4

* See Table 3.1 for a description of the categories.

Source: Office of the Commissioner of Police, Bombay, May 1987.

If we look at the month-wise distribution of the cases of violence (Table 3.4) we find an erratic picture with a high incidence in the period February 1982 till December 1982. It appears that there was a considerable increase in October and November 1982, a sharp decline in the following month, a new peak in January 1983 (coinciding with the anniversary of the strike), a sudden drop in the following month and an increase in March 1983 after which the violence subsides (coinciding with the fizzling out of the strike) and comes to a total halt in July 1983.

TABLE 3.4

Month-wise Distribution of Cases of Violence in the Strike Period

Month	*Categories**					
	I	*II*	*III*	*IV*	*V*	*Total*
January 1982	4	1				5
February	14	4				18
March	17	3	1		1	22
April	12	4	1		1	18
May	13	1	1		1	16
June	9	5				14
July	5	7		1	1	14
August	6	5				11
September	12	3				15
October	18	7				25
November	15	9		2		26
December	10					10
January 1983	17	4		1		22
February	6					6
March	10	4				14
April	8	1				9
May	1					1
June	1	1				2
July						-
TOTAL	178	59	3	4	4	248

* See Table 3.1 for a description of the categories.

Source: Office of the Commissioner of Police, Bombay, May 1987

The fluctuations in the figures are not easily explained. On the face of it one might say that a rise in January 1983 could be expected as the anniversary of the strike required a show of strength and the same argument could be used with regard to November 1982 as the rejection of the second proposal (made by the state government on 30 October) ought to be supported by a display of renewed determination. But this does not explain why there should have been a sharp increase of reported cases of violence in October. This reasoning seems also contradicted by the remarkable decrease in violence in July and August 1982 when the first proposal (8 July) was rejected by the MGKU.

Of course, it is possible to argue that the determination of the workers at that stage was such that no extra help (beatings, threats) was needed to keep them away from the gates of the mills whereas the picture had changed drastically by October. To support this line of thinking one could point to the fact that the one murder attributed by the police to the RMMS took place in July 1982, suggesting the need for the Sangh to adopt strong measures to goad the workers back to the mills. The Sangh had meanwhile recovered from the initial shock and had begun to undermine the morale of the workers.

However, what militates against this is that the evidence of the interviews suggests that most workers were considering the possibility of resuming duty as early as mid-1982 but that it was the fear of violence that kept them away. This implies that just as in November 1982 the workers needed to be reminded of the necessity of continuing the strike in July and August and, therefore, these two months should have shown a higher rather than a lower rate of violence. This leaves us with the problem of explaining the drop in July and August 1982. Although the evidence does not permit us to say with certainty what caused the drop in reported violence in these months, there seem chiefly to be two factors which could explain this phenomenon.

The first was the still lingering psychological impact of the murders committed in the period prior to July, making lesser acts of violence superfluous. A second, and probably more important reason could be that although a majority of the workers may have wanted to resume duty at that time there were still many doubts in their minds. After all, they had supported the strike wholeheartedly and the fact that the government had finally made a proposal seemed to suggest that the government was ready to negotiate. Who could say for certain that more could not be gained by sticking it out a little longer? This type of reasoning was very common as exemplified in the case studies (chapter 5). It is quite likely that confusion and wavering in the minds of the workers then was much stronger than a few months later.

From the timing of the incidents reported by the workers in the sample, it seems that the Sangh activists became more assertive as the strike progressed. Backed by the police and the millowners, and noticing the unflinching support of the government, their morale was boosted at a time when that of the workers was sagging. From what has been said so far it is clear that (apart from the economic hardship the workers had to face) the pressure exercised by the MGKU, RMMS and the police had a great impact on the workers as was abundantly clear from the interviews. It is no surprise, then, that practically all workers who stayed in the mill areas during the strike reported that the atmosphere was tense, and this is corroborated by press reports on this subject.[44] A vivid description of the situation prevailing in the chawls of the textile area is provided by Baluram (case study no. 5) who was confined to his room during the hours that willing workers left for or returned from the mills.

Returning to the question of the influence of violence on the continuation of the strike, it has to be concluded that fear played a prominent role. Fear influenced the decision to resume duty in several ways. Intimidation from the side of the millowners (threat of dismissal), the Sangh and the police was intended to lure the workers back to the mills whereas threats and assaults by Samant's supporters served to keep them out. In this process, the ordinary worker was caught between the hammer and the anvil, and irrespective of his decision he would be on tenterhooks. What also has to be concluded is that the accusation that the strike lasted as long as it did due to the violent methods adopted by adherents of the MGKU suffers from deliberate blindness. The Sangh and the police resorted to means which were in essence no different from those used by the MGKU. What this means is that the opportunity for a worker to freely decide on the continuation of the strike was severely limited by the actual and the rumoured acts of violence.

MILLOWNERS AND THE GOVERNMENT

A Common Front

In order to cope with the strike, millowners employed several different strategies. Naturally, their tactics changed as the strike progressed. If it is true that many millowners were initially not averse to the strike as the demand for cloth was slack anyway and stocks were piling up, it is equally certain that, these advantages gradually disappeared as by then new (and to many millowners, attractive) prospects surfaced. One has to bear in mind that the tactics used by individual millowners to survive the crisis differed and depended on the specific position of their mill in the textile industry. For the same reason their policy might not be in tune with policies followed by their representative bodies such as the MOA and ICMF. The voice of the owner of an affluent mill carries more weight.[45]

Some millowners attempted to remove the stocks from the mill premises, others (or the same ones) explored the possibilities of maintaining production and sales by subcontracting. In order to break the strike (and Samant along with it), workers were requested and in the end simply ordered to resume duty. In many mills workers were at first lured to return by offers of hospitality, free meals and lodging and with promises of police protection. At a later stage millowners would start recruiting labourers from elsewhere. As the strike did not collapse, the millowners were offered the rare opportunity of carrying out rationalization and retrenchment and they liberally availed themselves of it. This policy was followed even as new recruits marched into the mills.

To be able to do all this the millowners needed harmonious relations with the powers that be, that is, the Congress government. The task to ensure this was entrusted to their representatives in the MOA and ICMF. It was also important to establish contact with the public in order to explain the millowners' views so that no aura of martyrdom would be attached to the striking workers. This task too fell to the MOA and the ICMF which sought to justify the millowners' stand with the aid of articles and advertisements in newspapers and by denouncing Datta Samant. But more important than image-building were close relations with the government at state as well as at national level. If required, the millowners would seek the help of the centre to overrule decisions taken at the state level and they were successful in this.

Prior to the strike they had to reckon with an unwilling state government. Whenever they sensed that the state government was likely to side with the workers on the wage issue they hastened to Delhi in an attempt to avert the danger. With the timely removal of Antulay and the arrival of Babasaheb Bhosale on the political scene even the state government fell in line with their approach to the strike. Unlike his predecessor, Bhosale had little sympathy for the cause of the workers. From that moment onwards the state and the central governments and employers pursued on the whole the same objectives. This mighty combine would prove to be more than a match for the striking workers.

The approach of the employers towards the strike was neatly summed up by Hareschandra Maganlal, chairman of the MOA, during the annual general meeting of the MOA in April 1983:

> The Bombay cotton mill industry, therefore, accepted the challenge of the striking leaders and weathered the storm with a view to inculcating in the minds of workmen not only a sense of responsibility but also a sense of appreciation, on their own, of the credibility of demands of their leadership in the context of the strength and weakness of the concerns to which they belong and not to be blindly swayed by false hopes of extravagant demands only to lose their precious earnings by being led into an illegal strike.[46]

The means adopted by the employers 'to inculcate a sense of responsibility into the workers' were diverse and the degree of success varied. Kid gloves and strong-arm tactics were used simultaneously and the more active workers were sure to see more of the latter. Throughout the strike the millowners resorted to warnings and threats of dismissal. No less than 30,000 millmen had received show-cause notices by May 1982.[47] The lead in this was taken by the prosperous Century Mills, the management of which believed in stern action and recruited a greater number of 'fresh hands' than all the other mills in order to break the strike. Other mills adopting a hard line were Hindoostan Modern Mills, Morarjee, Phoenix, Raghuvanshi and Svadeshi.

From a perusal of concerted action taken by the mills at the end of June 1982, the ICMF concluded that most mills had started some programme of new recruitment, that all except three took to cancellation of *badli* passes and that many but certainly not all took disciplinary action like enquiries, discharge from duty, show-cause notices or dismissals. The situation did not change drastically when compared with October although the number of dismissals rose sharply (see Table 3.5). As far as dismissals is concerned, it should be taken into account that many of those who were fired were later reinstated, thereby adding to the confusion regarding the number of workers who lost their jobs in the course of the strike. The problem of assessing the real number of strike victims and recruited 'fresh hands' will be discussed elsewhere.

TABLE 3.5
Disciplinary Action by Mills in June 1982 and October 1982

Category	*Number of cases*		*Number of mills*	
	June	*October*	*June*	*October*
Criminal prosecution	319	319	5	5
Enquiries in progress	2,094	2,231	18	19
Discharges	245	317	10	10
Show-cause notices	36,512	42,163	21	25
Dismissals	1,18	8,066	18	23
New recruitment			36	37
Cancellation of *badli* passes			44	45
Break in service			40	40
Deduction under Payment of Wages Act			36	37

Source: ICMF Files, 21 June and 14 October 1982

The employers did not always show an iron fist, they also tried to lure workers back by the more sophisticated means of letters from other workers persuading the strikers to resume duty. Sometimes such letters or telegrams, signed by a worker from the department in which the addressed worker was employed, were fake and contained the urgent message: '*Mill started. I have resumed. Come soon.*'[48] Other attempts to coax the workers into the mills took the shape of financial incentives like that in July 1982 when the government of Maharashtra announced that it would distribute free school books to the children of those workers who resumed before the end of the month (*TOI*, 16 July 1982). This was an unkind cut at a time when many striking workers were facing tremendous difficulties in making both ends meet and had to make great sacrifices to provide their children with the wherewithal to attend school. It is also an illustration of the way in which the policy pursued by the millowners was strengthened by the stand adopted by the government. In all 1,361 workers availed themselves of this opportunity.[49]

A much grimmer situation arose when the workers lost the benefits granted to them under the Employees State Insurance Scheme (ESIS). In January 1983, the corporation running this scheme announced that striking workers and their families had meanwhile lost their rights under the Employees State Insurance Act, 1948 (*TOI*, 6 January 1983). The object of the ESIS is to provide benefits in cases of sickness, maternity and 'employment injury' (injury caused by accident arising out of and in the course of employment). Occupational diseases like the dreaded byssinosis (if established) also amount to 'employment injury'. A remarkable feature of the Act is that the scheme applies to the dependants of the employee inclusive of the parents.[50]

A study carried out by the Ambekar Institute for Labour Studies in 1981 showed that the operation of the scheme was defective in several ways.[51] Although the working of the ESIS appeared to be faulty, being deprived of its benefits was a serious blow to those workers who heavily depended on it, as became clear from the interviews with some of the workers in the sample. The corporation pleaded with the government to exempt the workers from their compulsory contribution in order to relieve them of at least some of their worries but the government failed to respond to the suggestion. This also underlines a similarity in approach between the millowners and the government.

In the first few weeks of the strike, the state government may have acted of its own accord (as might be expected from a government confronted with large-scale labour problems), but whatever steps the state government took afterwards (which boiled down to appeals to resume duty and monotonous declarations that nothing could be done as long as the workers refused to do that), was in all probability orchestrated by the centre. The whole question of how the strike should be dealt with was transferred to Delhi with the government of Maharashtra merely acting as a service-hatch for decisions reached in Delhi and for communication between the central government, the millowners and the Sangh.

This view—based on CM Bhosale's visits to Delhi, the absence of any constructive steps taken by the state government and the arrival in Bombay of emissaries from Delhi sent to end the strike—is corroborated by the diligent communication between the representative bodies of the employers and the centre. There was a steady flow of letters and telexes from the millowners (most particularly from the ICMF) to the Union government. The most important issues covered were the strike (production figures and statistics relating to the number of workers who had resumed) and the desirability of a modernization fund. But also proposed changes in labour laws, such as amendments to the Industrial Disputes Act, 1947 pertaining to the selection of a representative union (verification of membership versus secret ballot), were discussed.

The ICMF secretary-general, C.V. Radhakrishnan, acknowledges that the millowners had excellent and direct access to the Union government. Similarly, the MOA was constantly in touch with the state government regarding developments in the strike, as was confirmed by the MOA secretary-general, Sanikop. Representing the oldest and possibly still most influential section of the Indian industry, the millowners approached the government also through the offices of Naval Tata, president of the Employers' Federation of India and a millowner himself, who wrote to PM Indira Gandhi on the right to close down non-viable units. An ever-recurring subject in the correspondence and meetings between the government and the millowners is the need for financial help to the mills in order to cope with the losses caused by the strike and the need to restore normalcy. These requests were substantiated by figures which were used by the government to explain its stand on the strike in Parliament. The ICMF and the MOA also supplied information to the office of the textile commissioner who could then forward this to the state government or to Delhi.

In order to obtain an overview of the situation, the government desperately needed information and the easiest way to collect data seemed to be to request the millowners of the private mills to send daily reports on the attendance in the mills. As the millowners needed the support of the government as much as the government needed their cooperation, they were willing to comply with this request. It has to be borne in mind that contrary to the situation in the nationalized mills, the conflict in the private mills did not directly involve the government.

Because of that there was no strong case for the government to send its own officials to the mills to gather the information it needed or to check the data it got. To this may be added that even had the government despatched its own people, these officials would probably still have depended on data supplied by the mills unless the government had ordered a twenty-four-hours watch of all the gates of all the mills in the city. Such a procedure was not feasible and neither was the government interested in such verification.

In fact, for all relevant data regarding the position of the private mills in the textile industry and with regard to the strike, both the state and the central governments were almost completely dependent on the cooperation of the millowners (the MOA and ICMF). This point has to be stressed, as for example recurring statements by the state government erroneously claiming the imminent end of the strike were based on this source of information.

The obvious disadvantage of this dependence on the millowners' information was that the presentation of an erroneous or distorted picture of the real situation would not be detected, or in any case not in time. One cannot exclude the possibility that the government might have adopted a different attitude had it known that the numerous predictions of a speedy end to the strike were built on thin air. It is unlikely that the millowners were at any time in a position to provide daily reports given the large number of mills in Bombay, their widely spread locations and the problems of commuting and communication (a faltering telephone system). It would be next to impossible to provide accurate data on a day-to-day basis and the requested daily reports were probably never written and must have been replaced by weekly reports at a very early stage. In the second year of the strike, at a time when ever more workers were resuming work, the reports would become even more irregular.[52]

The written communication with the centre would be complemented by personal meetings. In the first week of June, a series of discussions took place in Delhi between the central government and ICMF/MOA during which it became clear that the government was still fully in agreement with the employers' stand. The representatives of the millowners met Shivraj Patil, Union commerce minister, on 1 June and thereafter met the Union finance minister, P. Mukherjee and the Union planning minister. They also had meetings with A.K. Dutt

(Secretary, Textiles), Krishnaswamy Rao Sahib (Cabinet Secretary), P.C. Alexander (Principal Secretary to PM), V.S. Trivedi (Union Home Secretary) and B.G. Deshmukh (Labour Secretary).[53] These meetings were not reported by the press and went largely unnoticed.

In contrast to the many and fruitful discussions between the government and employers (at least from the employers' point of view), the attempts of the government to come into contact with labour representatives appear to be few and abortive (not to mention the purposeful isolation of Samant). One such attempt was at the end of July when Union Minister Shivraj Patil met labour officials and workers in order to try to break the stalemate (*TOI,* 25 July 1982). At the same time the centre was having a fresh round of talks with the millowners who met the ministers of finance, commerce and labour as well as the Secretaries of Textiles and Labour, but these discussions, as in the case of the earlier ones went largely unnoticed. The employers also met CM Bhosale and several state ministers at that time.[54] In March 1983 the Union government would display another burst of activity which would briefly raise the hopes of tens of thousands of striking workers but this would prove to be a mirage.

It is amazing to see how rapidly the representatives of the millowners (the ICMF in particular) developed warm and friendly relations with the Union government in the course of the strike. The government had not been exactly accommodating in the years preceding the strike (restricting expansion of machine capacity, limiting imports and raising excise duties), and the relation between the government and millowners then could not be termed cordial. But no sooner had the strike started than this changed. The fact that they fought a common foe (Datta Samant and militant trade unionism), shared a common friend (the 'responsible' RMMS) and had a common problem (finding a cure for the ailing textile industry) largely explains this fraternization.

Even so, the millowners were in for a rude shock when the government announced the takeover of thirteen private mills after the strike, although signals of such a decision had been given months before.[55] However, the feelings of hurt then must have been greatly assuaged by the textile policy of June 1985, giving the millowners practically everything they had asked for. The attitude of the government, which at first sight may seem to have been vacillating, becomes intelligible and even appears to be fairly consistent if one looks at the demands made on the government and the priorities it had. The attitude of the government was determined by the need for cooperation from the employers during the labour struggle (in order to break the strike), the need to placate the workers afterwards (takeover of mills) and, thirdly, the need to put the whole industry on a sound footing (which was thought to be possible with the New Textile Policy allowing for retrenchment, modernization and closing down of non-viable units).

The Executive and the Legislature

As said before, efforts by the government to settle the strike issues were few. Apart from the half-hearted attempt at mediation in July 1982 (discussions from which Samant was excluded), there was another effort at the time when the strike had practically collapsed (March 1983). There were also two offers: a. in July 1982, the centre announced that, pending the results of the Deshpande Committee, an interim wage increase of Rs 30 was to be paid and an advance of Rs 650. In October 1982 when the state government came with what was called 'a new formula' the same interim increase of Rs 30 was offered but this time with an advance of Rs 1500. Both the advances were to be paid back by the workers, giving them a dose of their own medicine. These were the only concrete offers by the government. Apart from that, the central govemment might be credited with the appointment of the Tripartite Committee, but the composition of this committee as well as its terms of reference were such that it could hardly contribute to the solution of the strike, and that may well have been the reason why the terms were not more specific.

The deliberate inertia displayed by the executive at the state and national levels is matched by the treatment the strike received in the legislature. Although it gradually dawned on everyone that India was witnessing its largest ever strike, no sustained efforts were made to come to terms with the problem and neither did the strike draw much attention in such parliamentary bodies as the Lok Sabha (House of the People), Rajya Sabha (Council of States), Vidhan Sabha (Legislative Assembly) and Vidhan Parishad (Legislative Council). To be sure, there is no dearth of casual references, brief skirmishes and questions about the textile strike in the course of the proceedings in 1982–83 but the number of debates devoted to the strike is very small and reflects a lack of serious concern about the plight of the workers. It is a rather unique phenomenon (one stressing the close links between trade unionism and politics in the Indian context) that several important actors in the strike drama, like A.T. (Bhai) Bhosale, Datta Samant, Haribhau Naik, Bhaurao Patil, were themselves members of one of the representative bodies. Yet this did not prevent the strike from being treated in a miserly way although it contributed to a lot of mud-slinging and strong abuses in the legislature which, of course, was not really helpful.

In the Legislative Assembly of Maharashtra there were three debates on the strike: 15 March, 20 September, and 17 December 1982. In the Legislative Council the only debate on the strike took place on 16 December 1982. The case of the Parliament in Delhi is somewhat different. In the Lok Sabha the strike was dealt with in two debates: 9 July 1982 and 25 February 1983. In the Rajya Sabha the textile stir was discussed on 14 October 1982, 1 and 2 March 1983. From these dates it appears that taking all the bodies of the legislature together, not more than nine debates were devoted to a strike lasting one and a half years and directly affecting the lives of a quarter of a million workers (or at least one million persons if one includes their dependents). It is also striking that nearly two months elapsed before the strike was for the first time seriously discussed in a legislative body.

Another noteworthy aspect is that only four of these debates were in Maharashtra and the remaining five took place in Delhi. This may come as a surprise as one would expect most action in Maharashtra, the state which was the scene of the labour struggle. Labour Minister Bhagwat Jha Azad seems to have felt the same, which may be deduced from his explanation of the position of the Union government in the Lok Sabha: 'Both the state government *which is the appropriate government to deal with the situation* [emphasis added], and the central government have made continuous efforts to end the strike.'[56] Stressing that the state government was the 'appropriate Government' to deal with the strike served the purpose of creating a smokescreen behind which the Union government could sit in idleness. What Azad's 'continuous efforts' encompassed could be summed up in a few lines and these do not portray the government as a beehive of activity in search of solutions to the strike.

On the whole, the debates in Maharashtra were considerably earlier (the last in December 1982) than those in Delhi which in itself is an indication that as the strike progressed it became increasingly clear that real action was only to be expected from the Union government, Azad notwithstanding. From that side, however, one should not expect too much as was aptly pointed out by Arvind Ganesh Kulkarni in a debate in the Rajya Sabha. Blaming the Union government for its inertia he told Commerce Minister Shivraj Patil: 'What you are doing is a backseat driving exercise. Mrs Indira Gandhi has got the power. Baba Saheb Bhosale has got the wheel without the brakes. What can that poor chap do?'[57]

The debates in the Maharashtrian Legislature were marked by evasive answers from the government side and lack of precision and persistence by the representatives in cross-questioning the government. The members also engaged in hurling unsubstantiated abuses at each other. At times emotions ran high, ending in chaos and at least on one occasion this led to a virtual pandemonium in the Assembly and the Legislative Council (*TOI*, 13 March 1982). On two other occasions representatives walked out of the House to show their dissatisfaction with the way the government was dealing with the strike. Frustrated over the refusal of the CM to disclose whether he had discussed the textile strike with the PM and Union ministers during his recent visit to Delhi, members of the Legislative Council staged a walkout (*TOI*, 9 September 1982). Another walk-out by the opposition in the Legislative Council followed in December when Labour Minister Gaekwad explained the position of the government. The members of the opposition left the hall on the plea that the government was merely repeating old platitudes instead of showing a dynamic approach to a solution (*IE*, 17 December 1982).

An all-time low in the discussions may have been reached when CM Patil accused Datta Samant of using violent means to continue the strike and of being a 'new Hitler' (*IE*, 9 April 1983). Instead of retracing his steps when he was severely rebuked, the CM offered to try to substantiate the claim. Samant did not clear the air by commenting: 'The time will come that every worker will turn out to be a Hitler to seek justice for himself.' His opponent, Bhai Bhosale, worsened matters by declaring that calling Samant a 'Hitler' was an insult to the latter ('that great hero') and preferred to compare him with Mussolini (*The Daily*, 21 April 1983).[58]

Leaving aside the accusations and qualifications, what transpires from both the proceedings in the Legislature and from the action taken is that the state government did not go much beyond reeling in the fish (the strike) to the shore and letting it wriggle. This is confirmed by former Labour Commissioner P.J. Ovid who had to handle the strike and who was fully informed about the government's point of view. He acknowledges that the government restricted itself to a policy of wait and see instead of diligently seeking ways to settle the strike: 'The responsibility for that was with the government. It was the strategy of the government to take care of law and order and to take no action. The other point was that the millowners were advised to be firm' (interview, 3 January 1987). Answering questions about the progress of the strike CM Bhosale stated baldly at an early stage: 'The strike is on and we are watching' (*The Daily*, 11 February 1982).

What is true for the state government is not very different for the Union government. But the centre, of course, was not going to acknowledge its failure to take constructive steps to end the strike and the suffering of lakhs of workers. In July 1982 Labour Minister Azad declared: 'Government has never stood on prestige in this issue and has repeatedly made it known to the workers that once normalcy is restored, expeditious steps should be taken to look into their genuine grievances and resolve them in a time bound programme'. The phrase 'once normalcy is restored' is a recurring theme and crucial as it required the workers to down their weapon (the strike) as a precondition to any consideration of their demands. In the same speech Azad announced the formation of the aforementioned Tripartite Committee which would deal, inter alia, with the textile stir.[59]

The terms of reference were impressive in scope and involved an analysis of the entire textile industry but a decision on the wage demands in Bombay would never be reached, not even a serious proposal for that matter. This development had been foreseen by many, including RMM leader Bhai Bhosale, who had stated in the Legislative Assembly a few months earlier that the RMMS had advised the government not to appoint a Tripartite Committee as it would be years before recommendations were forthcoming. Instead, he suggested the nomination of a small group (he probably meant another High Power Committee) to study the workers' demands.[60]

In the Lok Sabha too the idea of a Tripartite Committee met with suspicion and the very day the centre announced its intention to appoint such a committee one of the members of the House, Indrajit Gupta, pointed out its fundamental weakness:

> Millowners will be there. Unions will be there. Government will be there. In such a committee if it is not possible to come to an agreed decision, unanimous decision, as is very likely, then, what will happen? He [Labour Minister Azad] has not suggested anything. What will happen in such a case?[61]

The minister would fail to answer this question. Many more pertinent questions, usually raised by the opposition, would never elicit a clear answer. The discussions in Parliament were marked by evasiveness of the government whenever a pointed question was raised and by passing the buck. When members of the Rajya Sabha refused to accept that a strike wanted by so many so dearly could be termed 'illegal', Commerce Minister Shivraj Patil responded that it was not for him or anyone else to say whether the strike was illegal but for the High Court which had declared the strike illegal. Not satisfied with this, a Bombay-based member, Shanti G. Patel, hit the nail when he remarked. 'May I ask the minister a pointed question? Is a legal strike possible under the BIR Act?'

It was another of the questions which would be left unanswered. When the minister was pressed to explain why the government could not start direct negotiations with the striking workers he took refuge behind the Tripartite Committee: 'But here we have an independent authority created, where all are represented and we have given the responsibility for deciding as to what would be the wages to be given, to that independent authority.' Later he clarified that the centre did not want 'to make someone a leader who isn't one, and uproot the one who is a leader'.[62]

When several members of the House demanded that Patil declare whether the government would be prepared to give an interim relief of Rs 150 to the workers, the commerce minister answered that to take such a decision would be premature and illogical now that the committee was trying to sort out in a 'scientific manner' what the possibilities were. He told the members to try to convince the committee, not him. So, if the committee failed to produce results (the terms of reference and the composition of its members would take care of that), the government could not be blamed either and meanwhile nothing could be done.

The only tangible results in due time produced by the Tripartite Committee were a recommendation for the introduction of a House Rent Allowance (a side issue and in no way helpful in ending the strike) and a suggestion that there should be a different distribution of *badli*s in the mills. Even in the absence of all opposing unions it proved to be impossible to obtain unanimous support for this latter recommendation. As the existence and proceedings of the committee constituted the core of the government's responses throughout the strike, it is striking to note that the government did not even deem it fit to place the findings of this Committee before the Parliament, as was confirmed by its chairman, V.S. Deshpande (interview, 6 June 1987). The disappointing results of the work undertaken by the Deshpande Committee did not stop the government from appointing yet another committee to study the labour problems in the textile industry when the strike for all practical purposes was over. This time the exercise would be under the chairmanship of Union Labour Minister Veerendra Patil (*Indian Express*, 10 July 1983).

That the government adopted a policy of watch and wait was amply demonstrated again in March 1983 when the strike was in its fourteenth month. In a written reply to a question seeking a clarification of the steps the centre had taken so far to end the strike, the then Union commerce minister, Mrs Ramdulari Sinha, replied that the central government had done three things: (1) to set up a Tripartite Committee, (2) to grant an interim relief of Rs 30, (3) to announce an advance of Rs 1500 which had to be repaid by the workers.[63] Exactly the same points were made in the Lok Sabha by her predecessor, V.P. Singh, a month earlier in addition to which Singh had added that the government had on numerous occasions appealed to the workers to resume duty. It is not surprising that no one leapt to his feet to applaud the efforts.[64]

Singh must have sensed that something better was needed, declaring during the same session that the government would not stand on prestige and that he was ready to meet anyone, including Samant, in order to resolve the strike issue: 'I want to assure the House, whatever may be the inscriptions in the law book, but when it comes to the interest of the working class, comma, full stop, dash and even brackets will not hold us acting on their behalf.'[65] Singh's brave words were reported in the press and briefly raised hopes of many thousands of workers still on strike. Samant at once announced that he would go to Delhi to see Singh. Singh, however, saw the representatives of the INTUC and the RMMS before they met and made a stale offer which included the advance of Rs 1500 (granted already in October 1982) as being still payable to all workers who resumed, that the bonus over 1981 (decided upon in October 1981) was going to be paid and that no-one would be retrenched who wanted to resume duty (*TOI*, 6 March 1983).

On 6 March, Singh held discussions with Samant during which Samant stressed the need to scrap the BIR Act, wage revision and permanency of *badli*s as the most pressing issues. The meeting left Samant with the impression that even scrapping the BIR Act had become possible. Singh declared afterwards that ending the strike was no precondition for continuation of the discussions (*Business Standard*, 7 March 1983). Singh may have felt that he was overdoing things a bit, for a day later he hastened to declare that changing the BIR Act was not in his power. Instead, he promised to contact his colleagues to ask them to see to it that the most offensive clauses of the Act were changed (*TOI*, 8 March 1983). If this meant anything then it would have to mean that the clauses pertaining to the selection of a representative union, the greatest bone of contention, would be modified. Nothing of the kind, however, was to happen and the reason may well have been that Singh was severely criticized by CM Patil for taking a lenient view of the matter at a time when the strike had collapsed for all practical purposes (*The Telegraph*, 3 June 1983). From the aftermath of the strike it is clear that the employers had no wish to bring the labour force back to its strength before the strike and Singh's statements about taking everyone back were certainly out of tune with their priorities. He would not even succeed in making the NTC mills take back their workers.[66]

FIGHTING THE BIR ACT: A LEGAL NOOSE

Preparing for a War of Attrition

The greatest encumbrance in the representation of the textile workers by a union of their choice has been the Bombay Industrial Relations Act, 1946. This Act, already hotly disputed at the time of its birth, appeared to be a major obstacle over the years.[67] It protected the rights of the representative union to such an extent that it appeared to be virtually impossible to dislodge a union once it had gained the status of representative union. It is no surprise then that this Act, often dubbed a 'Black Act', came forcefully under attack during the textile strike and became the pivot of the agitation to many an activist. A clear distinction, however, should be made between the importance attached to repealing the BIR Act by strike leaders and by ordinary workers.

What leaders and workers agreed upon was the need to oust the Sangh but workers were, of course, not sufficiently familiar with the prevailing labour laws to know whether this necessitated an amendment or even the outright repeal of the Act. Following their leaders they raised the cry of scrapping the BIR Act although few had a clear perception of its complexities and significance. If in spite of that one wishes to argue that the workers were determined to do away with this piece of legislation, then it ought to be acknowledged that it was only by implication that workers had this desire. As they were bent on getting rid of the Sangh one might conclude that they must have been willing to support any move that could take them nearer to that goal but this is a matter of conjecture and usually poorly founded.

That the repeal of the BIR Act was not foremost in the minds of ordinary workers was amply borne out by the findings of the sample interviews from which it appears that financial gains (a wage hike in particular) were the most important to them. The removal of the Sangh came second in priority and was commonly understood to be a precondition for such gains, but few workers mentioned the BIR Act at all when they were asked what they were fighting for. Removal of the Sangh and/or abrogation of the BIR Act was mentioned by only 21 per cent of the workers in the sample when they were asked to state their personal strike priorities.

Whether the workers explicitly or implicitly wanted the BIR Act scrapped, there are no two opinions possible with regard to the question whether they wanted the RMMS to lose its privileged position of representative union. An impressive majority (63 per cent of the workers in the sample) stated that they had joined the MGKU before or during the strike with the hope of ousting the Sangh. The strike leadership was aware of that and concluded that it should aim at derecognition of the Sangh by establishing that the representative union had lost the support of 25 per cent of the entire labour force in the textile industry, the minimum required by the BIR Act.

Basically there were three ways open to achieve this goal. One was to clamour for the repeal of the BIR Act. If that did not work it might be possible to get the law amended in such a way that the Sangh could be toppled. In both cases it would be necessary to ensure that new legislation was introduced allowing for secret ballot. However, scrapping the BIR Act required a major political struggle which could only be won in the Legislative Assembly. The chances of achieving this were, to say the least, remote, given the hold of the Congress in the state. The possibility of amending the law were none too bright either but with the backing of the dramatic textile strike and skilful manoeuvring in order to win over dissidents within the Congress, this strategy might have paid off in the end. A third possibility, and seemingly the most promising one, would be a struggle for derecognition of the RMMS under the BIR Act. It was to this avenue that the strike leadership paid most attention in the course of the strike.*

It was not the first time an attempt had been made to oust the Sangh, the sole representative union in the cotton textile industry under the BIR Act.[68] Post-war history shows several instances of massive resistance against the RMMS and the attacks launched during the strike in the 1980s were but the latest (and unquestionably the most impressive) efforts to escape representation by the Sangh. It is symptomatic that this time too, the Sangh succeeded in surviving all assaults and this calls for a discussion of the procedure which the MGK followed to contest the right of the RMMS to represent the

* For the reconstruction of the legal struggle in the course of the strike, I was given full access to all the documents available at the office of the MGKU in Ghatkopar.

workers Such an analysis throws light not just on how the RMMS managed to ward off all attacks but also on the dubious nature of certain clauses of the BIR Act which has been hailed by employers and the government alike.

The battle to achieve cancellation of registration of the RMMS as the representative union was fought throughout the strike and lasted for years afterwards.[69] In the process an increasing number of workers realized that there was a connection between the existence of the Act and the unbroken presence for decades of the RMMS in the industry. Many workers also learned, rightly or wrongly, that reliance on the legal apparatus, the government or both, in order to find redress for their grievances would be misplaced. This awareness has been interpreted as an indication of an increase in political consciousness but before any such conclusion can be drawn, it is necessary to examine how this new consciousness expressed itself. A change in voting behaviour and a rise in participation in demonstrations or other political activities could under certain circumstances, provide indications of an enhanced political awareness. However, during the interviews with the workers little evidence was found pointing in that direction (see next chapter). The idea that the strike contributed to a conspicuous change in the political consciousness of the workers has yet to be proved. The battle-cry for scrapping the BIR Act is in itself insufficient to warrant such conclusions.

The long legal struggle started with a letter from the MGKU to the registrar of unions under the BIR Act (henceforth: registrar), in which cancellation of registration of the RMMS was demanded.[70] The MGKU supported this application by claiming that it had meanwhile about 90 per cent of all the textile workers in the cotton textile industry in Greater Bombay as its members and, secondly, that the RMMS did not have the membership required for eligibility to a continuance of registration. This first move on the legal front was readily answered by the assistant registrar who replied after a few weeks that the facts submitted by the MGKU were incorrect, that the membership of the Sangh did not fall below the minimum required by the Act and that there was therefore no case for cancellation.[71]

It was typical that the assistant registrar, Mrs Bhattacharjee in rejecting the plea by the MGKU, based her judgement solely on the figures supplied by the RMMS and the employers. This betrays a bias against contesting unions and the wish to accommodate the views of the representative unions. The verdict, of course, was not acceptable to the MGKU who thereupon appealed against it in the Bombay High Court. The MGKU requested the court to issue a writ of *mandamus* (an exceptional court order given when other legal ways are blocked) directing the registrar to cancel the registration of the Sangh. At the same time the MGKU requested the court to prohibit the MOA and the NTC from negotiating with the RMMS about the settlement of the strike or the COD framed by the MGKU. The union also wanted the court to pressurize the state government into starting negotiations with the MGKU in order to reach a settlement.

This request related to the refusal of CM Bhosale to have any talks with the MGKU on the plea that there was a representative union already. On behalf of the MGKU Datta Samant argued that this excuse was invalid and he referred to the strike in 1973–74 when the government held talks with Comrade Dange and again in 1979 which ended when the Fernandes–Pawar Award was concluded. Although the final agreements in both these cases were signed by the RMMS and not by Dange or another union, Samant had a point in referring to the more flexible stand adopted by the government then. Bhosale's point-blank refusal certainly called into question the sincerity of the state government in trying to find a way out of the ongoing strike. In December 1982 Justice S.C. Pratap of the Bombay High Court would indirectly support Samant's stand when he publicly chided the state government for not referring the case to the Industrial Court.

It did not take the High Court long to reach a conclusion. On 29 April 1982, the court decided that the order of the assistant registrar stood withdrawn and that the MGKU was free to amend their application to the registrar (made under Section 15 of the BIR Act) in order to comply with the requirements of that section. The time for amendment would end on 5 May, and the registrar would be required to give a verdict within two months thereafter. On the face of it, it seemed a hopeful sign that the registrar was given a time limit for reaching a conclusion. But if one takes into account that it would be impossible to give a verdict satisfying all the parties concerned, then the order could not be more than a halting place on a road which would take years to come to an end. The long-drawn-out proceedings would thus contribute to the prolongation of the strike and the suffering of lakhs of workers and their families. In the process the Sangh was given full opportunity to recover from the severe blows it had received at the hand of the MGKU and to revive its traditional but unwarranted monopoly in representing the workers' interests even if this was against their wishes.

However, nothing of this was evident in May 1982. Complying with the decision of the High Court, the MGKU submitted an amendment to the original application and claimed that it had a membership of 15,000 workers in the first week of November 1981, that the RMMS had been losing control over the workers from October 1981 onwards and that the Sangh in the end had completely lost the affiliation of the textile workers.[72] In addition, the union accused the Sangh of agreeing to massive retrenchment and unemployment during its tenure and observed that the Sangh in doing so had 'completely neglected the interests of the workers.[73]

This last point, if found to be true, would be a ground for cancellation of registration under Section 15, b (iv) of the BIR Act, but it would, of course, be very difficult to establish such neglect. To substantiate the accusation, the MGKU stated that the Sangh had supplied stocks for the so-called fair price shops in the mills and made a profit of lakhs of rupees in the process. Apart from that the Sangh was held responsible for supplying impure edible oil to a shop in Kohinoor mills, resulting in the serious illness of ninety workers, and of having done nothing to help the affected workers and their families.

More intriguing was the MGKU's submission in the same document that not one of approximately 90 per cent of the workers who had switched over to the union in November had approached the Sangh with a request to allow them to remain in arrears. The MGKU concluded that the figures presented by the Sangh were 'totally false, fabricated and incorrect'. The reference to the question of arrears was the most interesting part of the amended application and would prove to be the point on which the entire defence of the Sangh ultimately hinged.

Tightening the Noose

Having received the new application, the registrar now judged that the evidence supplied by the MGKU justified, on the face of it, the procedure for verification of membership. Subsequently, the registrar issued a show cause notice to the RMMS (21 May 1982), calling upon the Sangh to show-cause why the applicant union, that is, the MGKU, should not be registered in its place. This notice resulted in a number of letters from the RMMS and MGKU, and in a series of hearings in the first two weeks of June 1982 in the course of which the concerned parties (including the MOA) were heard.

The correspondence reveals that the case rapidly developed into a tournament for lawyers in which many aspects—at times highly irrelevant—were debated at length. These included the more important issues related to the nature of the provisions of the BIR Act, the powers of the registrar and the problem of the legality of the strike. With regard to this last point, the MGKU held the view that the legality or illegality of the strike had nothing to do with the proceedings under Section 15 (dealing with cancellation of registration) and Section 24 (dealing with removal of a union from the list of approved unions) of the BIR Act.[74]

By the cancellation of registration, but also by removal from the list of approved unions, the Sangh would lose its status as the representative union. Such removal is compulsory if the registration of a union under the Indian Trade Unions Act, 1926 is cancelled but also if such a union, after being included in the approved list, failed to observe the conditions laid down for such inclusion. These conditions are specified in Section 23 and state, inter alia, that the registrar shall not enter a union in the approved list if he is satisfied that it is not conducted bona fide in the interest of its members.[75]

The government, millowners and the RMMS stressed throughout the strike the importance of following the legal path so the peculiarities of this path need to be considered in greater detail. The letter from the RMMS sent to the registrar in reply to the show-cause notice is useful in surveying the various aspects of the legal struggle. The first line of defence of the RMMS, after the MGKU had amended its application, was to pretend that the notice was not valid as it was based on an application by a union not recognized under the BIR Act and therefore, not entitled to raise issues such as the cancellation of registration.

Secondly, the RMMS held that the questions touched upon by the show cause notice exceeded the authority of the registrar who had no right to demand information which would also come to the knowledge of the MGKU. The Sangh proceeded to claim that the MGKU had not produced 'a title of material' on the strength of which the union could claim any membership of workers in the textile industry and offered as its view that the MGKU, in fact, had no membership at all.[76] Not very logically, the Sangh holds in the same letter that the membership claimed by the MGKU relates to contributions paid for a year in advance and that this is in contravention of the law and cannot amount to membership. The Sangh rejected the view that membership of the MGKU necessarily implied that the concerned workers had ended their membership of the Sangh. Speaking about alleged arrears, the RMMS flatly denied that there were any such arrears. The clauses in the BIR Act pertaining to membership and arrears would provide the magic wand with the aid of which the RMMS would disentangle itself from an intricate and vulnerable position and seemingly certain defeat.

Some other points raised by the MGKU were summarily dealt with by the RMMS. As far as the delivery of impure edible oil was concerned, the Sangh denied any responsibility in the matter and stated that the shops were run by the mills. The Sangh added that it had done whatever it could to bring relief to the affected workers. Referring to the supposed lack of resistance shown by the Sangh in the case of automation, the Sangh retorted that this accusation was based on ignorance 'regarding the development of the industry which could never be resisted'.[77] Sensing probably that this defence was rather weak, the Sangh denied having sacrificed the interests of the workers and, instead, claimed to have achieved wage gains for the workers: 'The Sangh has from time to time taken stock of the prevailing circumstances of the earnings of the industry while entering into agreements of rationalization in the industry.'[78]

To shield itself from all damage following an eventual decision by the registrar to check the membership of the Sangh, the union concluded by stating that any type of verification of membership, be it an on the spot enquiry, sampling or an actual head count, would be impossible in the 'prevailing atmosphere of violence and fear psychosis created by the applicant'. It is worthwhile recalling the findings in which it was shown that violence did not play an important role at that stage. The RMMS president, Hoshing, acknowledged this after the strike while replying to a question relating to the participation of the workers in the strike and the scale on which violent incidents occurred. He admitted that the strike had been practically total and without violence in the first period of the struggle (interview d. 20 May 1986). Thus, going by the view of the man whose position was dramatically undermined by the strike, the need for the MGKU to keep the strike going by means of violence, was very limited at the time of the letter to the registrar. The argument, therefore, that no proper verification could take place under the circumstances rings false.

In the ensuing correspondence, the Sangh repeated most of these arguments, adding or changing details whenever it suited them. Every avenue of obstruction was tried, such as objecting to the amended application by the MGKU on the ground that the time given for the necessary adjustments ended on 5 May while the amended application had been submitted a day later. A similar technical objection was the Sangh's denial that Datta Samant was the president of the MGKU on the ground that he had not been formally elected as such. Because of this he was not entitled, according to the Sangh, to file an application as its president.[79]

This point had been raised by Hoshing who declared that after the MGKU registered as a trade union on 15 December 1981 new elections should have been held. As this had not happened, Samant was only president of the ad hoc organization and as such lacked the authority to represent his union.[80] It is curious to note that this objection came from the president of a union notorious for its irregularities in electing office bearers. Even the way Samant signed the application came in for criticism. According to the RMMS, the MGKU leader ought not to have signed the application adding his qualifications of medical doctor and Member of the Legislative Assembly (MLA), for in doing so he vitiated the document.[81]

The Sangh stated that the MGKU had first sought cancellation of the registration of the RMMS by referring to Section 16 of the BIR Act. This section allows an applicant union to request the registrar to be registered in place of the representative union on the ground of a larger membership but this possibility is not open to unions having instigated or conducted an illegal strike. The MGKU could not, therefore, avail itself of this section.[82]

It is important to note that the MGKU was not a registered union under the BIR Act but under the Indian Trade Unions Act, 1926. As a result the MGKU could not apply for registration under the BIR Act as the approved unions under this Act are bound to a code of conduct precluding strikes as long as all avenues for conciliation and arbitration provided for in the Act have not been explored.[83]

The elaborate system of conciliation and arbitration effectively nullifies the possibilities of a legal strike, the ultimate weapon of the working class. This was acknowledged by Additional Registrar Bhattacharjee after the strike:

> You see, the entire concept of the BIR Act is based on the idea of a constructive trade union movement...unions are not going on strike, they are going for conciliation etc. This means that all the teeth of the unions have been taken away. The provisions of law prevailing during the strike were very unfortunate but as a registrar I have to see that the law is maintained even though it has become outdated [interview, 5 February 1987].

As the MGKU could not use Section 16, it restricted itself to submitting an application for cancellation of registration of the RMMS as this would serve the same purpose. But the Sangh held that the problem of cancellation could only be dealt with by a Labour Court or an Industrial Court. The union vehemently opposed the interference of the registrar and even went to the extent of accusing that authority of harmful assistance to the MGKU to the detriment of the Sangh: 'The Sangh submits that if the registrar permits the MGKU to inspect documents as desired by them, the registrar will be acting without jurisdiction and will thereby be a party to allowing the MGKU to make a fishing enquiry to make out a case which it has failed to do so far and will cause irreparable harm and injury to the Sangh.'[84]

The MGKU responded to all these statements and accusations by upholding the right of the registrar to issue a show-cause notice and its own right to submit an application irrespective of the answer to the question whether the union represented the workers or not. The MGKU observed: 'If the contention of the Sangh is accepted, it will lead to patently absurd results and a union which is once registered as a representative union or as an approved union can never be dislodged from that position'.[85] The MGKU denied that the dispute pertaining to the status of the RMMS as the representative union could be considered an 'industrial dispute' or treated as an 'industrial matter' and held that for that reason the dispute did not fall within the jurisdiction of the Labour Court or the Industrial Court. The definitions given in Section 3 of the BIR Act (clauses 17 and 18) made it unlikely, however, that this position could be maintained and the MGKU therefore stressed that in any case the registrar was empowered to deal with the matter.

It is striking how the RMMS and MGKU waged war against each other regarding the powers and duties of the registrar. The reason for this may have been that both RMMS and MGKU felt that the Sangh stood a better chance in the Labour Court or the Industrial Court. The forceful attack launched by the RMMS against the registrar was matched by the tenacity of the MGKU in defending the powers of that authority. The MGKU stand is explained by its hope that a quick solution would be found to a burning problem and the fear of being dragged into a time-consuming procedure. That this was no chimera is amply borne out by the subsequent history of the legal struggle.

On 21 June 1982, the Additional Registrar gave an Interim Order acknowledging that the MGKU had a 'locus standi under the Act' and that the registrar was free to verify the membership of a representative union irrespective of an application to that extent submitted by a contesting union. The registrar observed that RMMS membership figures were available but that the MGKU had so far failed to produce the required counterfoils of subscriptions of membership for October 1981 and the period December 1981–April 1982 although the union had been asked to do so.[86] (Earlier, the MGKU had explained this omission by stating that it was not seeking registration and replacement of the representative union under the BIR Act.) The registrar observed that whatever figures were known pointed towards cases of double membership which posed a problem as the case law is not altogether clear on this subject.[87] The registrar rejected the plea of the Sangh that the MGKU had no right to make use of the BIR Act: 'As regards unfair labour practices, in which the applicant union is alleged to have indulged, such actions on the part of the applicant union do not bar it from taking recourse to the provisions of Sections 15 and/or 23.'[88]

In its rejoinder to the Interim Order, the Sangh reiterated all the arguments that had been used before, accused the MGKU of having malafide objectives in demanding verification of membership and submitted that verification by the MGKU held a risk as the records were 'liable to be tampered with'. The Sangh suggested that the purpose of the MGKU was to get to know the names of the workers in order to enhance its own membership and that the MGKU was not in a position to disclose its own membership at all.[89] How grim the situation was is clear from the fact that the office of the additional registrar, where the verification was done, was sealed daily to prevent malversation or the disappearance of documents. Clerks and assistants were under close scrutiny by the police for the same purpose.

The Importance of Arrears

If the MGKU could rely on the workers in the course of this struggle, the Sangh had even more powerful allies like the government and the millowners. The cordial relations between the RMMS and MOA, which might be termed 'touching' had they not been to the detriment of the workers, transpire from the support the millowners gave the Sangh in the course of the legal proceedings. Following the Interim Order the MOA sent a reply to the registrar harping on the injustice done when a union, breaching the provisions of the BIR Act, that is, the MGKU, is allowed to seek redress under the same law. The various references by the MGKU to the BIR Act were described as 'Satan quoting the Bible' and exemplify how the employers dreaded the possibility of Samant entering the textile industry.[90]

The millowners also raised the issue of the employment of *badli*s and stated that the difference between *badli*s and permanent workers, in the circumstances of a strike being declared illegal by the Labour Court, was irrelevant as far as the figure for daily employment was concerned. The employers referred to Rule 21 and Rule 23 of the Bombay Industrial Relations Rules, 1947 which stipulate that the employers must forward a statement to the registrar showing the number of employees on the first working day of the month.

The MOA opposed the idea of constituting a Tripartite Committee to look into the matter as it went beyond the scope of the BIR Act. At a later stage, however, the MOA would become a staunch supporter of such a committee and volunteered to abide by its recommendations. By that time the MOA had a much clearer perception of the opportunities offered by, and the outcome of, the strike. The association had meanwhile ascertained for itself the support of both the central and the state governments and could assess fairly well what the likely result of the proceedings of the committee would be. Samant's boycott of this committee gave the millowners the opportunity of keeping up an appearance of cooperation. It is worth recalling that in December 1982, the MOA effectively blocked the proceedings of the High-power Committee under Antulay on the pretext that Samant had refused to cooperate and failed to bring the demands of the MGKU to the knowledge of the millowners; a point which Datta Samant refuted.[91]

Meanwhile, the registrar was trying to sort out the claims and counterclaims. The verification of the membership took much longer than expected and for this the registrar was taken to task by Justice S.C. Pratap who directed the registrar to take a decision in the matter of derecognition before 3 September 1982 (*TOI*, 22 August 1982). In spite of an enlargement of the staff working daily on the verification of membership from twenty-five to fifty persons, the registrar did not succeed in complying. Bhattacharjee said:

> It was a stupendous task. The textile industry knows many different categories of workers like temporaries, *badlis*, permanent workers etc. You have to check a lot of things, not just the list of names but also the cash collections and who collected the fees. You have to check receipts, counterfoils, see whether these were signed and by whom. Many documents are required to establish the membership of one single person. I wanted my inquiries to be really sound so that it would not be necessary to do the job all over again (interview, 5 February 1987).

Finally, on 4 November 1982, and some four months later than the High Court intended, the registrar passed her order. She concluded that the returns given by the RMMS showed deficiencies but that the membership for the months under investigation definitely dropped below the minimum required by the BIR Act, that is, 25 per cent of the total number of employees employed in the textile industry. It must be pointed out here that the registrar made her calculations on the assumption that the total employment in the industry involved 2,25,000 places. The required membership ought, therefore, to have been 56,250 but the RMMS fell substantially short of that figure. If the registrar had started from the more likely figure of 247,000 the gaps would have been wider still.

For the month of December 1981, the RMMS had claimed a membership of 1,07,392 against 46,488 found by the registrar, for January 1982 the RMMS claimed 92,011 workers as members against 30,154 established by the registrar and for February 1982 the figures were 77,809 against a mere 1,135 found by the registrar.[92] The MOA had supplied figures relating to the employment in the months under investigation and submitted that 99,754 persons had worked in December 1981, 119,280 in January 1982 and 5,533 in February 1982. If the registrar had accepted these figures as the basis for her calculations then the RMMS could be said to have had sufficient members in these months, with the exception of February 1982. But the registrar rejected the MOA figures because they only reflected those actual working in the relevant months which was very different from the requirements relating to membership.

It being established that the RMMS fell short by a wide margin of the minimum membership required by law, the case seemed to be won at last. However, the registrar judged that even if the RMMS had failed to show sufficient membership there was still no case for cancellation of registration because the Sangh might not have been able to collect membership fees due to the ongoing strike. The judgement baffled all those who had believed that exposing the real and insufficient membership of the Sangh would automatically lead to derecognition of the union. No wonder then that the verdict struck many as being wholly unjustifiable. While doing the counting the registrar had carefully excluded all workers who had remained in arrears in the relevant months but once the counting was over, it appeared that being in arrears did not matter after all because the excluded workers could be included-again on the plea that they *might have been prevented from paying their contribution due to the prevailing circumstances*.

The benefit of the doubt clearly went to the RMMS. As will be seen shortly, members who had not paid their fees for the months under investigation did so purposely. In spite of that, the Sangh. was allowed to count them as members as long as it was not established that they had stopped paying because they had wanted to break away from the RMMS. Such was the law. The fact that the strike had completely paralysed the industry for at least six long months was not taken as clear proof that the workers had rejected the RMMS. The justification for the strange reasoning behind this decision was that the Sangh, as the representative union, was entitled to collect membership within the premises of the mills on pay day. Due to the strike it had become impossible to collect fees in this fashion and therefore, the Sangh was prevented from demonstrating that the union did have sufficient membership.

The very strike, resorted to by the workers to display inter alia dissatisfaction with the RMMS, now fully turned against them and became the most important instrument for the Sangh to remain in power. It seems that today even Bhattacharjee, the additional registrar who passed the order, questions the wisdom of a law that is so accommodating of the needs of the representative union (interview, 5 February 1987).

In the order the registrar disapproved of the resolution adopted by the RMMS in April 1982. In this document the Sangh, sensing danger, allowed its members to be in arrears.[93]

The MGKU had denounced this move and claimed that this resolution was without merit as the workers had not approved of it. The registrar could agree with this and judged that the RMMS should establish that the members who were in arrears either empowered the Sangh to adopt the said resolution or informed the union that they were not in a position to pay the fees. In the last case the Sangh should demonstrate that these members did pay their fees afterwards. The registrar noticed that nothing of that sort had come on record yet. Though she had requested the Sangh to supply information about the section of the membership that had actually paid and about the section that was in arrears, the Sangh failed to do so, claiming that this was irrelevant.[94] The sequel of the events would prove the union right but the registrar at that time felt differently: 'If the registered union wants to rely on the arrear component of the membership, it must be established beyond doubt that the member who has remained in arrears of membership fees has done so willingly.'[95] It was a great pity for the MGKU that this specific point afterwards never had to be established when the case wound its way through the corridors of the legal system.

At an early stage the registrar had informed the Sangh of the necessity of holding in camera inquiries to verify the membership. During such an inquiry a worker would have to testify before the registrar and in the presence of representatives of both the RMMS and MGKU to which union he really wished to belong. The RMMS objected to this procedure, saying that the employees under investigation may or may not give the correct reply. The registrar, however, held that this kind of fact finding fitted within the framework of the BIR Act and said that she could not understand why the representative union should be against it.[96] Although such inquiry was most opportune in the present case and although it did fall within the Act, the difficulty was that both the representative and the contestant union had to consent to this method and the Sangh, fearing defeat, was in no mood to accept in camera inquiries. The text of the order passed by the registrar clearly revealed the reluctance of the RMMS to comply with any kind of check on its membership. Taking a retrospective view of the whole verification procedure, Bhattacharjee observes: 'The in camera inquiries might have helped in establishing the real membership…but then the workers were staying in the villages. So the strike situation made this impossible too. As a result the whole thing remained guesswork only' (interview, 5 February 1987).

However, if the registrar had had the power to enforce such inquiries, it is practically certain that the RMMS would have been swept off its feet and the resistance against this procedure bears this out. Nearly all the workers in the sample who were asked whether they had wanted to pay Sangh membership fees during the strike but were prevented from doing so for whatever reason, answered in the negative. A mere 8 per cent declared that they had considered themselves to be Sangh members throughout the strike and indeed wanted to pay their membership fees but were unable to do so. The others stated that, on the contrary, they wanted to be considered as MGKU supporters during the strike although their financial difficulties and/or the distance (stay in the village) did not allow them to pay regular membership fees.

As in the case of the Sangh, the MGKU was well aware of the true feelings of the workers and it was natural that the latter had no objection at all to in camera inquiries. The MGKU offered to file affidavits of workers to support its claims and asked the registrar to interrogate workers but this proposal was rejected because scrutiny of the membership first had to be completed before interrogation of employees could be undertaken. Time, however, was clearly on the side of the Sangh because the workers' capacity to endure the effects of the prolonged strike weighed more heavily as weeks and months passed. With the passage of time the temptation to resume became irresistible, and even if this meant submission to the Sangh what choice did the worker have? More than any amount of legal quibbles, it was time that defeated the MGKU in the battle to oust the Sangh.

Juggling with the Badli *Component*

The division of the industrial workforce into *badli*s and permanent workers gradually gained importance in the course of the legal proceedings. The attempt by the MOA to exclude the *badli*s from the total workforce was thwarted by the Registrar and this decision was later on upheld by the Industrial Court as well as the High Court. A point, however, which has scarcely drawn attention is the substantial change within a short span of time in the numbers for *badli*s given by the MOA. This raises two questions: what was the real figure for *badli*s and why was the figure changed?

In the preceding chapter it has been demonstrated that the millowners had always been purposely vague with regard to the employment of *badli*s. But in a hearing before the registrar on 28 July 1982 the MOA stated explicitly that the number of *badli*s in the private mills prior to the strike was 40,000 to 45,000.[97] The total number of *badli*s in the Bombay textile industry is put by the MOA at 80,000 from which it must be concluded that the remaining *badlis* are to be found in the public sector but unless the entire labour force of this sector consists of *badli*s, this figure is patently wrong. The exact number of *badli*s in the NTC North, NTC South and the MSTC is unknown but the same is not true for the number of workers on the rolls prior to the strike. Going by the figures provided by the Kotwal Committee there were 43,205 workers on the rolls of the nationalized mills. This figure is roughly corroborated by figures obtained from the office of the commissioner of labour.[98]

If the percentage-wise division of *badli*s and permanent workers in the nationalized sector is comparable to that in the private sector, then approximately one-third of this total of 43,205 workers are *badli*s, that is, some 14,400. In fact, it is likely that the number of *badli*s in the public sector is less as it is government policy to give permanent employment to as many workers as possible. M.S. Divekar, director of the NTC South, confirms this and estimates that the *badli*s made up some 20 per cent of the total muster strength prior to the strike (interview, 9 April 1987). Going by this percentage the public sector did not employ more than. 8,000 *badli*s in January 1982. The puzzle to solve here is where the remaining 27,000 to 32,000 *badlis* have gone.

Why is the number of *badli*s employed in the private mills in the middle of 1982 given as 40,000 whereas this number clearly could not be made to fit in with the figure of 80,000 *badli*s for the whole industry? This last figure is mentioned time and again and was also given in a lengthy memorandum specifically dealing with the *badli* system in Bombay which was submitted to the Deshpande Committee a little later that year.[99] The only sensible answer to this question seems to be that the *badli* system had come seriously under attack. The MOA must have felt it wiser to reduce in advance the *badli* component of the labour force to the incredibly low figure of 40,000 to 45,000 as this would allow for large-scale retrenchment which would then not be noticeable in the statistics. By not questioning this number the RMMS came to the rescue of the millowners.

Again, why was the total muster strength prior to the strike stated as 2,25,000 before the registrar whereas it was put at 2,47,000 in the aforementioned memorandum? The lower figure came to be accepted throughout the legal proceedings and has not been questioned by employers or unions. This lower figure was obviously beneficial to the Sangh which sought to show that it had 25 per cent of the workers in the industry as members. Taking the lower figure as the point of departure this would mean the need to establish a membership of 56,250 workers against a minimum requirement of 62,500 in the case of the higher figure. Given the tremendous difficulties the Sangh had in establishing sufficient membership the union was greatly helped by the lower figure supplied by the MOA.

The mutual support of the RMMS and MOA had been visible on other occasions too. The correspondence between the MOA, RMMS and the registrar displays the close cooperation between the first two organizations. The MOA, like the RMMS, defended the view that the registrar had no business to question the figures supplied by the union.

The MOA had also pointed out that the registrar was going beyond the boundaries set by the order of the High Court of 29 April 1982 by starting an independent enquiry with the object of verifying the membership of the Sangh. But these objections, as those of the RMMS regarding the in camera inquiries, were rejected by the Registrar.[100]

The employers' organization had also tried to exclude all *badli*s from the total labour force. If this effort had met with success, it would have substantially reduced the minimum membership requirement of the Sangh and thus helped in securing the representative status of the Sangh. An attempt by the MOA to exclude workers whose services had been terminated in the course of the strike fared the same fate as that to exclude *badli*s and was rejected. The registrar pointed out that it was contrary to the law to consider as terminated the services of workers who were on strike and observed: 'Further, in cases of termination of services of employees, if any, the Association (MOA) has not given the relevant particulars such as number of employees whose services have been terminated, dates of termination of service. Besides, both the unions [that is, the MGKU and RMMS] have stated that such a termination is not acceptable to them.'[101]

Having found that the Sangh was wanting in membership, the registrar proceeded to list six possible reasons for this. The most important reasons are the continuation of the strike, the mental stress of the workers (both unions accusing each other of violence), the exodus to the villages and the financial difficulties faced by the workers due to the strike. The registrar emphasized that in a normal situation the Sangh 'could have been able to win over some employees who have chosen to remain neutral so far'. This understanding of difficulties faced by the RMMS sharply contrasts with that for the obstacles the MGKU had to overcome. The High Court would later on decide that the registrar was under no obligation to find out what caused the defaulting membership of the representative union. The registrar also judged that, broadly speaking, the performance of the RMMS was in accordance with the BIR Act and that it was impossible to maintain that the Sangh acted on behalf of the employers against the interests of the employees.

The MGKU, of course, had no choice but to appeal against the decision of the registrar in the Industrial Court, an authority constituted under the BIR Act (Section 10). Though the court gave its verdict within three to five months, precious time was lost. The endurance of the workers had been tried far too long already and with the assistance of the workers who returned to the mills the Sangh had started recouping its position. On the whole the Industrial Court upheld the arguments of the registrar except on the crucial issue of membership. The court ruled that the registrar's finding that the membership of the Sangh had fallen below the minimum was incorrect. Had it been otherwise then the refusal of the registrar to cancel registration on the ground that the employees were on strike, could not be sustained. This judgement was the severest blow the MGKU had received so far as it meant that the union was back to square one. The order of the Industrial Court was dated 17 February 1983 which meant that thirteen long months had passed since the beginning of the strike. Ever more workers resumed duty and the order of the Industrial Court seemed to seal the fate of a strike in which the financial demands had receded into the background and was now being fought more and more on principle.

Having come thus far, the MGKU felt obliged to file a petition against the order of the Industrial Court with the Bombay High Court and as a result the strike and the legal struggle would effectively become separated. For no apparent reason the time gap between filing this petition and the verdict of the High Court spanned more than fourteen months. One is reminded of the rebuke of the registrar by Justice Pratap of the High Court when she took too much time in completing the awesome task of verifying the membership of the RMMS. The High Court did not have to undertake such time-consuming activities and the importance of the question demanded a speedy trial. In the course of this long period the strike naturally collapsed totally. Predictably, the workers lost all interest in the legal proceedings in so far as they ever had any. Irrespective of the outcome of this last move, the Sangh would emerge victorious because, driven by the pangs of hunger, the workers would be forced to return. Most of them became members of the Sangh in order to get reinstated or to have some kind of protection inside the mills where the atmosphere had become grim, the workloads had increased and the management appeared determined not to brook resistance any longer.

The final order by the High Court meticulously spelt out the various positions taken by the registrar and the Industrial Court while upholding the views of the Industrial Court. The High Court too concluded that there was no evidence to show that the RMMS had not acted faithfully on behalf of the employees. The fact that the Sangh, just like the MOA, had argued in the course of the proceedings that the *badli*s need not be considered as employees did not prove that the Sangh acted against the interests of the workers.[102] This comes as a surprise for it must be hard for a *badli* to believe in the credibility of a union ready to denounce their very status as employees in the industry just in order to survive. *Badli*s had good reason to feel abused for apparently they were good enough to be made use of on certain occasions (catering to the needs of the industry) and to be discarded at others.

The High Court dealt at length with the problems of verification of membership and arrears, and demanded that the applicant union (that is, the MGKU) produce the counterfoils of the receipts of subscription for nine calendar months immediately preceding the month in which the application was made. It was obvious that the MGKU could in no way match this requirement and neither was it possible for the union to prove in a similar manner that it had at least 25 per cent of all the workers in the industry as members for the period of three calendar months preceding the month in which the application was made.

The High Court, like the Industrial Court before it, did not accept the way the registrar had calculated the membership of the Sangh and decided that it was wrong to exclude all the Sangh members who had been in arrears. The court ruled that only such a person ceases to be a member who has been in arrears for a period of more than three months 'during the spell of six months immediately preceding December 1981, and January and February 1982'.[103] The court decided to add the number of members who were in arrears to those who had paid their fees. The inspection team that checked the membership of the Sangh had found that 61,509 members had not paid in December 1981, 58,852 in January 1982 and 74,904 in February 1982. Correcting for these figures the court ruled that there was no question of the Sangh having insufficient membership to retain its position as the representative union.

The decision of the High Court, although a great disappointment to all who stood behind the MGKU, did not come as a total surprise any longer. The only step left now would be appealing against this decision in the Supreme Court but Dada Samant did not expect any better result there as the Supreme Court, in all likelihood, would conclude that the law had been applied correctly. Besides, there was little interest in another time-consuming process with predictable results. It appears that the protection enjoyed by the Sangh in this war of attrition has been threefold. The Sangh was shielded by the employers, by the law and by the government as the executer of the law. Before a fairer judgement could be expected, one that would do justice to the views of the textile workers, a minimum requirement would be the amendment or even replacement of the BIR Act.

Judging by the standards of the labour laws, the entire attempt to dislodge the Sangh had been premature and ill-conceived. To be successful a great deal more preparation ought to have been made than was possible under the circumstances that prevailed when hundreds of enraged workers besieged Samant's house demanding that he lead them in the strike. Merely saying that the law has been applied correctly, not only hurts the feelings of the participants in the strike but also fails to do justice to their demands. Even if the judiciary performed its task well, the same cannot be said of the government or the millowners. The juggling with facts and figures cannot but remain incomprehensible to the striking workers who had hoped for substantial material gains and to finish off the RMMS in one mighty blow.

Implications of the Strike

The example of the textile strike and the efforts of the MGKU to dislodge the representative union under the BIR Act show the deficiencies of the Act. The shortcomings basically relate to the selection of the representative union, the opportunities of replacing such a union and organizing a legal strike. The existence of several industrial laws having a bearing on the textile industry simultaneously does not contribute to greater clarity either.[104] Even if the textile strike failed in many respects, it did make clear that an overhaul of labour legislation was and is an urgent need. In the absence of substantial changes labour unrest is bound to surface again and again, and the executive will have to lean increasingly on suppression to keep up a semblance of industrial peace. However, it remains to be seen whether the government will draw any such lessons.[105]

Probably the most serious flaw in the BIR Act concerns its making it impossible to get rid of an unwanted, so-called representative union. A rival union aspiring to replace such a union is forbidden to take part in strikes for a long period preceding the application for replacement.[106] This makes it virtually impossible to unseat the representative union through a spontaneous mass movement, as in the present case. The law requires neat and long-drawn-out procedures in which there is no room for airing acute discontent. A restriction such as this would, perhaps, be acceptable if such an upsurge was merely to be coincidental, an outburst of anger or the result of the delusion of the day. But if such a movement is the expression of pent-up frustrations over the years, then the clauses protecting the representative union tend to become an instrument for repression and lose their justification.

In order to comply with the law and unseat the reigning union, workers should have a clear perception of the complexities of the law and, in addition, the willingness to support an aspirant union for a long time irrespective of its chances of surviving the confrontation with the representative union. Such willingness may not be demanded from workers as it exposes them to all sorts of pressure tactics which can be utilized by the representative union to defend its powerful position. A bone of contention is the privilege of the representative union to collect membership fees on pay day on the mill premises.[107] Next to the table where the wages are paid, the officials of the union are waiting for their share of the money. This system ensures that the less courageous workers (commonly the majority) can be bullied into paying fees as they fear the wrath of the union if they don't. This was abundantly clear from the interviews with workers, many of whom declared that they find it hard to resist the pressure exerted at that time. This pressure, of course, is not restricted to pay day but may extend to all working hours. Responding to the question why they became members of the Sangh after the strike although they had supported the MGKU during the struggle, workers, with rare exceptions, said they felt a strong need for protection inside the mills against harassment by supervisors or the Sangh. As the Sangh reigned supreme inside the mills, they felt that they were left no choice.

It would be naïve to believe that another union in the position of the Sangh would not avail itself of the opportunities of goading the workers into its fold. As the privilege to collect fees at pay day is given to all representative and, approved unions under the BIR Act, it would be better to do away with the clause pertaining to this right altogether. No other conclusion is possible if the law-giver really intended to guarantee free and unfettered choice of a union. To rely on the proviso that in this matter 'no coercion or force shall be used on any employee'—if made in good faith—shows remarkable unworldlyness. Stopping the collection of membership fees on mill premises will certainly not end all abuse of power inside the mills but neither will it unnecessarily add to the problems workers have already and it will release them of recurring tension on pay day.

A secret ballot is another hot issue in relation to improving industrial legislation. Non-INTUC unions have been clamouring for this for a long time. The grounds on which this has been rejected so far are none too clear. One argument heard often refers to the possibility that union leaders might easily entice workers to join their unions by promising them the earth at election time. One fails to see the merit of this argument unless it is meant to pave the way for a different political system in which elections too have no role to play. The argument is insulting to the thinking capacity of the worker. The present system of verification of membership in any case does not do justice to the democratic rights of the workers as their choice can be manipulated far better than would be possible with secret ballot.

State Labour Minister B.M. Gaekwad also touched on the issue of a secret ballot but rejected this possibility by using the customary argument:

> In the labour movement the situation is at present like this: supposing Naik's union gets an increase of Rs 60 for the workers in a certain industry, Patil's union will go there and say: come to us, we will get/you an increase of Rs 100. Workers will then go to that union, make a new agreement with the company and get Rs 100 increase. Then a third union will approach them and promise a Rs 300 increase. That means that there shall be problems of recognition every day. This is the main reason behind this. When Janata was ruling they could not agree on this either and for the same reason.[108]

Apart from displaying an utter lack of confidence in the workers' reasonableness, the argument is also invalid as it would be easy to stipulate that a union, once elected, will remain in power for a period of, for example, three years and that prior to new elections no crossing of floors would be permitted.

Faced with widespread criticism from the opposition Gaekwad had declared in the Legislative Assembly at an early stage during the strike that there was no need to have a strike in order to change a law. But if history was anything to go by then this statement did not apply to crucial aspects of the BIR Act. Datta Samant, therefore, countered that this had been tried several times before but to no avail.[109] However, in December Gaekwad followed this up by stating in the Legislative Council that the recent All-India Tripartite Conference in Delhi had decided that the BIR Act and other labour laws had become outdated: 'The old machinery for judging labour problems is too inefficient, so it should be changed. Therefore a new idea is being considered that would do more justice to the workers, the Industrial Relations Commission. This law will be nationwide so why should a new law be made for this state only?'[110]

The new idea Gaekwad referred to was less new than it seemed for already in August 1978 a new industrial law (Industrial Relations Bill, 1978) had been introduced in Parliament in which a National Industrial Relations Commission had been recommended. The preparation of this law ran parallel with the work of a Tripartite Committee consisting of employers, workers and state governments which drew attention to many lacunae in the prevailing legislation and made suggestions for improvement. However, with the fall of the Janata government and the return to power of Indira Gandhi nothing more was heard of this Bill.

Gaekwad's optimistic utterances had been preluded by reports on discussions taking place at the centre. The *Sunday Observer* (24 October 1982) reported that Union Minister Pranab Mukherjee, after discussions with his colleagues Shivraj Patil and Veerendra Patil, was prepared to suspend the most offensive parts of the BIR Act. This development had again been preceded by the National Labour Conference in September during which a committee had been appointed to prepare amendments to the Industrial Disputes Act, 1947 and the Trade Unions Act, 1926. These two Acts, together with the Industrial Employment (Standing Orders) Act, 1946, make up the body of central enactments regulating industrial relations in India. The committee, under the chairmanship of Sanat Mehta, minister of finance and labour in Gujarat, dealt with various issues including the problem how to select a collective bargaining agent (that is, a union representing the workers).[111] The multiplicity of trade unions had in the past often led to problems in identifying the negotiating agent. The absence of a central law created a chaotic situation, triggering off strikes with the purpose of ascertaining who had the right to represent the workers.

To solve this problem the Mehta Committee suggested the check-off system which provided for a written authorization by every employee to his employer in which he intimated to which union he wished to belong. This document would be valid for a period of three years and authorize the management to recover from the wages of a worker the union subscription and remit it to the union concerned.[112] The verification of membership would be entrusted to the Certificating Wing of the various Industrial Relations Commissions (IRCs) which had to be constituted at state and central level. These IRCs were the pivot of the new system and should be independent of the executive. Their main functions would be, (a) adjudication in industrial disputes, (b) conciliation and, (c) certification of representative unions.

The Certificating Wing would for its check-off rely on the relevant particulars available with the employers. Once a union gained the status of recognized union it alone should have the right to enter into collective agreements on wages and the right to call for a strike if all other avenues of settling the problem had been tried. Before resorting to a strike the Mehta Committee recommended that a strike ballot should be taken in which all the workers in the establishment should be allowed to participate. Only if 60 per cent of the workers voted for a strike could such action be undertaken.[113] The Mehta Committee refrained from fixing the percentage necessary to qualify as the sole bargaining agent and suggested that the IRCs might do that, taking into account the specific conditions of an industry.

The proposals of the Mehta Committee, although far from revolutionary, have some merit and were an improvement of the legislation in force. The best features are the selection of the bargaining agent and verification of membership. It would be no small matter if a recognized or representative union would periodically have to seek a fresh mandate from the workers. The same is true for the end of the system of payment of wages in the presence of union representatives. Before prolongation of the status of sole bargaining agent could be decided upon there would be a period of six months during which all contesting unions could do their canvassing.[114] Apart from INTUC-affiliated unions the proposal met with suspicion from most of the others. The unions in the Bombay textile industry were no exception to that. They were not overly enthusiastic about the check-off system as this did not preclude malversation by employers and/or representative unions. One can understand their hesitations given the labour history of the industry.

Expressing his doubts Dada Samant, for example, stated:

> How does it work? The workers have to say to which union they belong and give a statement to the management. Who collects these statements? Very often workers won't know what they are signing and it is easy to collect a number of fingerprints from illiterate workers. Who is going to control all chances of abuse? [interview, 29 May 1987].

It is true that the details of a check-off system should be worked out carefully to avoid the traps mentioned by Dada Samant and others but there is no reason why this could not be done if the non-INTUC unions are given a say in the matter. Besides, the possibility of the introduction of a secret ballot, the most mature manner for selecting a union and the method favoured by most non-INTUC unions, is remote. Accepting the check-off system might be the best under the circumstances provided the unions are allowed to and capable of working out a system minimizing the opportunity of abuse.

Unfortunately, there is evidence which seems to render the whole discussion about which method to adopt to select the collective bargaining agent, meaningless. Although the proposals of the Mehta Committee were submitted in 1984 nothing hopeful had come out of it by 1987. On the contrary, in that year the government discussed amendments to the Industrial Disputes Act, 1947 and the Trade Unions Act, 1926 which were a far cry from the improvements suggested by the Mehta Committee. The idea of an authorization of the employer by the worker to deduct the subscription from the wages had been maintained and so had the suggestion of a check-off system, albeit modified. Meanwhile, a few new proposals cropped up, ensuring the status quo in some situations and worsening the picture considerably in others.[115] This development, disconcerting as it may be, is in line with all preceding efforts to muzzle Indian trade unionism as exemplified by the Essential Service Maintenance Act (ESMA) and the National Security Act (NSA).

What are the new ideas being circulated in government circles? In some of them it is easy to recognize the peculiar way in which the government reacted to the textile strike and the challenge thrown by Datta Samant. A drastic proposal is the suggestion to fix a limit to the number of unions an outsider (someone who is not actually employed in that unit or in the industry to which the union caters) may handle. This proposal would certainly liquidate the Samant empire. But not only would Samant suffer, the entire trade union scene in India would be jeopardized as it is flooded by outsiders and few believe that it is possible to do without them.

The dominant position of outsiders in the trade union movement is considered to be necessary because too few capable workers come forward to take over the leadership of unions. In certain industries, particularly those in which predominantly highly skilled workers are employed, this requirement might not pose insurmountable problems but in others it will. In many cases trade union leaders would have to decide in which union (s) they want to be active. These leaders would then clear the field in other unions where workers with much less experience and stature would have to deal with employers and the government. For the textile industry in Bombay we may conclude that Bhai Bhosale would neatly fit the requirement of having worked in the industry but the leaders of powerful opposing unions would fall by the wayside.

Another noteworthy proposal is the one in which the government retires from the labour field. According to this, a trade union dispute should be resolved by arbitration or by Labour Court adjudication. Any party involved in such disputes may directly address itself to Labour Courts for adjudication 'and the government need not have the authority to refer such disputes'.[116] One is at once reminded of the refusal of the state government during the textile strike to refer the case to the Industrial Court. As soon as the right to do so has been removed (cf. Section 73 of the BIR Act), the government can claim that it can do nothing about it. It is a curious sort of generosity to give away rights that people want you to exercise.

The road to a legal strike is as complicated as ever, except that contrary to the requirement suggested by the Mehta Committee (60 per cent workers casting a vote in favour of a strike), the government felt it safer to propose that a strike call should not be given if less than three-fourths of the total membership of the Bargaining Council vote for the strike. This council is the platform for cooperation between registered unions in an industry where no union qualifies for the status of sole bargaining agent. Particularly in cases where there is more than one registered union and the rival unions are more or less of equal strength, it is highly unlikely that it will ever come to pass that 75 per cent of the members' of the Bargaining Council (note: not 75 per cent of the workers) will vote in favour of a strike. The road to a legal strike is thereby effectively sealed, that is, at the expense of the workers.

Probably the worst part of the various proposals concerns minimum membership required for registration as a trade union. So far a minimum of seven persons wishing to start a union and belonging to the same industrial enterprise have been permitted to do so under the Indian Trade Unions Act, 1926. In the new proposal this number is raised to 25 per cent of the workers. The presently registered unions would be given six months to comply with the new criterion. If this norm comes to be accepted, it will not only effectively stop multiplication of unions in future but also dramatically reduce the number of existing unions. In a great many cases unions would lose the ground they are standing on as it is a gigantic task to enlist 25 per cent of the workers in a unit or industry. All the more so, of course, if you have to do this within six months and are not allowed to draw attention to your union by means of agitation. The proposal will prove to be the death-blow for numerous unions, thereby arbitrarily shrinking the range of choice open to the workers.

Incredible as some of these suggestions may seem, they are still in concord with what the central government declared after the report of the Mehta Committee had been received. At that time Labour Minister Veerendra Patil praised in the Rajya Sabha the work of the committee but also stated that the measures suggested by the committee were only recommendations to the government. Patil warned that the wish for collective bargaining did not agree with multiplication of unions:

> We do not want multiplicity of unions. We want very few unions. We will be very happy if there is only one union in one establishment. Now, the question arises as to which union should be recognized. The problem is still there before us and we have not decided whether we should adopt the check off system or we should adopt the secret ballot system. The government has not taken any decision at all.[117]

Patil denied that the government wanted to increase its power and that the Tripartite Conference which preceded the Mehta Committee had suggested the reference of all powers of adjudication, arbitration and conciliation to an Industrial Relations Commission. While discussing this proposal with some trade union leaders he found to his surprise that they were 'deadly opposed' to the constitution of IRCs. Patil's statements were not taken for granted and vehemently criticized by Members of the House who wondered why the government was so keen on legislation like the ESMA and the NSA if the picture was as rosy as the minister made it out to be. To this Patil replied that these laws had been passed by both Houses of Parliament (not mentioning under what circumstances) and that they were going to be used sparingly, which was hotly desputed by several members of the House.[118] Wasudeo Dhabe said that over the past two years some 44,000 trade union leaders had been arrested under the NSA, inclusive of activists in the Bombay textile strike. Dhabe also pointed out that the National Labour Commission established by Jawaharlal Nehru in 1969 had concluded that the problem of recognition of trade unions was vital and required a speedy solution but that fourteen years had passed without any progress in the matter.

In this connection attention was drawn to the fact that India has still not ratified Convention 87 of the ILO (pertaining to freedom of association) and Convention 98 (stating the right to collective bargaining). Patil held that freedom of association in India was not hampered by this as it only played a role in sensitive areas like government services and defence.[119] The refusal to ratify the convention referring to collective bargaining he justified with the curious argument that most labourers are living in the countryside:

'So in the rural areas it is very difficult to organize them and have collective bargaining. Once we accept the convention, it is very difficult to implement that convention.'[120]

From the foregoing it may be concluded that whatever lessons the government drew from the past, they are not going to benefit the workers much. However, by placing ever greater restrictions on the free development of mature trade unionism in the country, the government runs the risk of evoking the spirit it seeks to subdue. If the government persists, it may find itself in a position in which it will have to rely ever more on repression in order to suppress the menace of rising discontent. In the end such a policy might prove to be self-defeating.

NOTES

1. The relevant part of the resolution reads:

   'The working and the service conditions of the textile workers are miserable and the disparity between the textile workers and their counterparts in other industries is very glaring. This situation warrants immediate rectification.

   The RMMS, the representative and the approved union under the BIR Act, which has lost the confidence of the textile workers, is solely responsible for this state of affairs. Hence, the RMMS be derecognized and the BIR Act be scrapped immediately. Trade union recognition be determined and decided by secret ballot.

   Taking into consideration about one lakh *badli* workers with six to thirteen years service, their meagre earnings of about Rs 150 to Rs 200 per month, inadequacy of permanent post as required according to the workload as well as the leave reserve, large number of *badli* workers should be made permanent and those continuing on *badli* status be paid attendance allowance equal to 50 per cent of the total wages' (Resolution adopted by Trade Unions' Joint Action Committee, d. 17 July 1982, Bombay.)

   The resolution was signed by the AITUC, CITU, UTUC, SSS, HMS, BMS and Datta Samant.
2. 1 quintal = 100 lb or 112 lb.
3. B.S. Dhume, *The Indefinite Strike of Millworkers and Their Problems* (Marathi), Bombay, 1982.
4. B.S. Dhume, 'Glorious Six Months of Bombay Textile Strike', *New Age*, 1 August 1982.

5. Apart from ideological differences there are personal differences between the leadership of the MGKU and the SSS. In discussions with Dada Samant great respect was expressed for the intellectual capacities of the SSS leaders, bordering on uneasiness. However, the 'distantness' Chavan speaks about is only to be found at the level of the top leadership. At a lower level the relations appeared to be very cordial, the leaders meeting daily, sitting behind each other's desks and sorting out the problems of the workers. Practically all court cases of textile workers are dealt with by the SSS.
6. '*Uphold Heroic Heritage of Textile Workers Faced with Unashamed Treachery*', Revolutionary Workers Coordinating Committee, 17 July 1982 (pamphlet).
7. That subduing RMMS activists was, indeed, a task of zonal committees is acknowledged by Gurbir Singh who, commenting on the organizational weaknesses of the strike, states: '... it can be safely said that the massive terrorization of RMMS functionaries kept the strike alive when it was threatening to break around November–December 1982' (G. Singh, 1987).
8. Bakshi describes the birth of the zone committees, an idea worked out by Budbadkar, one of Samant's trusted men: 'The establishment of the zone committees was coordinated by the Ghatkopar office. The activists of all mill committees were called there and twelve of the most active workers in each mill were selected for membership of the zone committee of their area' (Bakshi, 1987: 115). Bakshi mentions five zones: Kala Chowki, Delisle Road, Saat Rasta, Worli and Dadar. Gurbir Singh, who refers to zone committees, as 'the main contact point between activists and the mass of workers', puts the figure at six (Singh, 1983).
9. The Chembur committee is the best known and was probably the most active area committee in the city. It was divided into several sections and manned by a group of some thirty activists each addressing himself/herself to a specific task. Another active area committee with some ten leading activists was situated in Dharavi. The reputation enjoyed by a few of these committees cannot be compared to that of others and is an indication of the relative significance of the zone and area committees in general.
10. *Marxist Bulletin*, vol. 1, no. 7, 1982.
11. For all the importance Bakshi attaches to the various committees, she observes: 'The committees had some inherent limitations and could not prevent much of the rank and file from often feeling that they were floundering in the dark' (Bakshi, 1987: 126). She also noted: 'There were, of course, major differences of opinion on the handling of the

strike—within the mill and area committees. Those who disagreed with Samant, or some who even gently questioned his plans and actions, came away deeply embittered' (ibid).

12. It is with this aspect in mind that the ex-secretary-general of the RMMS, Bhai Bhosale, insisted that mill committees were no more than a means for other unions to enter the textile mills (quoted by Bakshi, 1987: 114).
13. Dada Samant explains his brother's modus operandi as follows: 'He is very independent and does not compromise. Not even for the active workers of the union he leaves scope to negotiate. You see, they are workers, poor and needy, and they can be purchased for a small sum' (interview d. 15 April 1986).
14. It was astonishing to note how many of the labour activists and correspondents the author spoke to mentioned the name of a very active unusual worker, Gulab Gajarmal, whose experiences and views have also been published in book form. Gulab Gajarmal and a few other worker activists like him were consulted time and again.
15. '*A Study of Textile Workers on Strike in Bombay*', L.K. Deshpande, Centre for the Study of Social Change, Bombay, 1983 (unpublished report, p. 2).
16. Gurbir Singh, 'Force and Counter-force: A Report from the Front', *The 10th Month*, Bombay, 1982.
17. 'The Bombay Textile Strike: An Historic Struggle', *Marxist Bulletin*, vol. 1, no. 7, 1982.
18. Hoshing explains that one-third of the workforce still has strong ties with the native place and these people in any case went home but that out of the remaining 66 per cent also 'many' left for the village (interview, 20 May 1986).
19. Cf. *Shramik Vichar*, 13 July 1982; *TOI*, 16 July 1982; *TOI*, 23 July 1982; *Shramik Vichar*, 23 November 1982. Four years after the strike Joshi, Samant and Fernandes would form a common front to oppose the Congress and to unite agricultural and industrial labourers (*TOI*, 16 January 1987). Whether this was more than a gimmick remains to be seen.
20. A very readable account of Samant's rural tour is given by Ashok Manohar in *Shramik Vichar*. He states that 10,000 persons attended a meeting in Bhor, 5,000 in Khandala Bawda, another 12,000 in Wai. In Satara not less than 30,000 persons are supposed to have gathered and in Uttur (Kolhapur district) about 7,000. In Nesri 25,000 persons are reported to have attended the meeting (6 March 1982).

    Kumar Ketkar observed in the *Economic Times*: 'Dr Samant's whirlwind tour has taken rural Maharashtra by storm. His meetings were attended by tens of thousands of poor farmers and agricultural workers in Pune, Kolhapur and Satara districts' (15 March 1982).

21. A small group very active in this phase of the struggle was Lok Adhikar Chalwal (Movement for People's Rights) which even ventured into areas from where no textile workers originated, attempts which did not meet with success.
22. There are stray reports about workers from companies like Hindustan Lever, Bombay Alloy, National Rayon or the BMTC giving money (*Shramik Vichar*, 24 April 1982). The union of the *Times of India* also decided to help the workers (*Shramik Vichar*, 1 August 1982).
23. *Nava Kal*, 14 November 1982; *Nava Kal*, 27 November 1982.
24. Cf. *Shramik Vichar*, 14 May 1982; *Shramik Vichar*, 13 September 1982; *Shramik Vichar*, 29 October 1982. See also para 2.2.5.
25. Workers of Premier Automibles distributed grain to workers of Swan Mills and Swadeshi Mills (*Shramik Vichar*, 2 April 1982). In Goregaon a committee established by the TUJAC collected and distributed cash and food (*Shramik Vichar*, 21 July 1982).
26. Letter to Indrajit Gupta, 30 March 1983.
27. The role of women in this strike has not received much attention although their attitude had a strong impact on the stand adopted by the striking workers as was borne out by the sample interviews. Women, apart from contributing to or even single-handedly providing the family income during the strike period, participated in morchas and gheraos (*Nava Kal*, 12 April 1982). They also took part in jail bharo campaigns, particularly in the rural areas (*Shramik Vichar*, 10 October 1982). One of the few articles focusing on the women of textile workers was written by Mukta Manohar (*Shramik Vichar*, 24 October 1982).
28. Cf. Kumar Ketkar, 'Who Is Afraid of Datta Samant?', *Economic Times*, 15 March 1982; *Shramik Vichar*, 11 July 1982.
29. Based on pamphlets and letters published by the Kamgar Mukti Sangarsh in 1983, 1984 and 1985.
30. It is possible that the rural tour opened the eyes of Datta Samant and made him aware of the significance of such an alliance, for during a press conference in Kolhapur he declared that agricultural labourers and industrial workers should become politically active. Asked whether he was thinking of founding a political party himself he replied: 'Until now all parties have failed these people so a kamgar party is needed' (*Shramik Vichar*, 6 March 1982). Before long Samant would launch his Kamgar Aghadi.
31. In a review of the strike Omvedt concludes: 'More than this, it can be said that the most advanced achievement of the struggle is the new

relation of workers with agricultural labourers and small peasants in the countryside' (1983).

32. MOA secretary-general Vijyanagar speaks of six murders (interview, 30 January 1986), RMMS president Haribhau Naik believes that there were eight murders (interview, 29 May 1986). Ex-secretary-general of the RMMS, Bhai Bhosale, talks about eleven murders (interview, 30 May 1987), whereas Y. Chavan, president of the SSS, speaks about 'some cases' at the end of the strike (interview, 18 March 1986). B.S. Dhume, vice-president of the AITUC, put the figure at ten.

33. An example of a grotesque distortion of reality is to be found in an editorial in the *FE* in which it was said that a reign of terror prevailed in the mill areas 'causing injury and even death to nearly 500 textile workers and supervisory personnel' (*FE*, 19 April 1982). For comparison it should be pointed out that during the miners' strike in England (1984/85) four workers died and during the miners' strike in South Africa (1987), lasting three weeks, at least eleven people died. See also footnote no. 2, para 2.1.2.

34. 'Note on cases of hurt/violence registered in Greater Bombay during the textile worker's strike from 18 January 1982 to 1 August 1983', Office of the Commissioner of Police, Bombay, May 1987.

35. Ibid.

36. Ibid.

37. Ibid.

38. Largely on the strength of these supposed murders, AITUC leader B.S. Dhume, for example, published a leaflet in which he condemns the recent use of violence and concludes: 'At the same time to defeat these tactics of terror by murders and the use of hired goondas, the unions must henceforward keep themselves in readiness to return such attacks in their own coin. This task has now become the most urgent task and its neglect any further is not only dangerous but unpardonable' (*This Is No Trade Unionism*, B.S. Dhume. MRTUC Publication, 1984/1985).

39. The article mentions false accusations, arrests and *razzias* as means of suppressing the workers: 'On December 24, 1982 ten truck-loads of police and SRP personnel surrounded the slum colony at Worli Koliwada. Dragging out the inmates of the huts, they beat them cruelly with lathis, chains and belts.' This was in retaliation to a demonstration by millworkers in the area who had protested against the government and police action against the textile workers which had taken place a few days earlier. 'Similar action was taken by the police at Hanuman Nagar and Gopal Nagar under Dadar police station two weeks later. Such terror was spread over there that for a few days after the incidents

had taken place, people were afraid even to answer calls of nature' (*Free Press Journal*, 19 January 1983).

40. See 'Millmen Angered by Police Terrorism', *Free Press Journal*, 23 February 1983.

41. The letter read: 'You ceased to be in the services of the Company from 24.9.82 and according to the terms of Leave & Licence, you were bound to surrender the vacant premises to us immediately thereupon. You have failed to do so.' Next he was ordered to vacate the room within a week failing which both criminal and civil proceedings would be instituted. The letter was signed by the manager of his mill and dated 9 August 1983.

42. In October 1982 three activists of the MGKU, who had been detained since March, were released by order of the Bombay High Court on the ground of errors in the indictment. On that occasion the court observed that 'detention orders were being issued in a most casual and cavalier manner' (*TOI*, 26 October 1982).

43. The police stations mentioned in the Table represent approximately one-third of all the police stations in the city. But, with the exception of a station in Wadala and one in Sewree, the other stations are not situated in areas with any significant number of textile workers. For the exclusion of Wadala and Sewree no explanation was given.

44. Cf. 'Textile Area Resembles Armed Camp', *Sunday Observer*, 11 July 1982.

45. R.D. Mohota, 1976: 197–200.

46. *Report for the Year 1982*, MOA, C.

47. *Indian Express*, 27 May 1982.

48. *Shramik Vichar*, 21 April 1982; *Truth*, November 1982.

49. *Kotwal Committee Report*, 1987, 9.

50. S.R. Samant, *Employer's Guide to Labour Laws*, Labour Law Agency, Bombay, 1986: 61. See also *Hand Book of Labour Laws* (The Employees State Insurance Act, 1948), Government of Maharashtra, Bombay, 1965).

51. In a survey covering 200 insured workers and fifty doctors (insurance medical practitioners) in Bombay in 1981, the common complaint of the workers was that they were harassed, rebuked, their ignorance exploited, by various authorities with whom they came into contact while availing of the benefits (*Research for Trade Unions: A Guide*, Ambekar Institute for Labour; Studies, Bombay, 1986). Other complaints regarded the non-availability of drugs at ESI chemists shops, the substandard quality of available drugs and insufficient number of hospitals. Doctors complained about the feigning of illnesses.

52. In a letter to the ICMF dated 18 July 1982 the ministry of commerce complains of not having received reports for several weeks. In a letter dated 4 October 1982 Jayalakshmi Jayaraman of the ministry of labour (Government of India) refers to the 'daily telex report' sent by the ICMF. From 6 November 1982 these reports were also sent to M.C. Shattna, director-general Industrial Contingency (ministry for industry). Source: ICMF files.
53. Information collected from personal files kindly made available by ICMF secretary-general, C.V. Radhakrishnan.
54. Ibid.
55. In a debate in the Legislative Assembly, the minister of state for labour, M. Kimmatkar, said that the government of Maharashtra studied the possibility of nationalizing fourteen sick mills. He added that the Centre was already discussing the subject with the Reserve Bank of India (*IE*, 22 July 1983).
56. Debates, Lok Sabha, 9 July 1982, GOI, 1982 a.
57. Rajya Sabha, Debates, 14 October 1982, GOI, 1982 b.
58. There seems to be an astonishing and disturbing lack of historical knowledge on the part of many Indian politicians about the Second World War. Home Minister Zail Singh (the later president of the nation) had sent a shock wave through the press a year earlier by praising Hitler in Parliament (*IE*, 27 March 1982). Union Industry Minister J. Vengal Rao launched an attack on the CM of Andhra Pradesh (N.T. Rama Rao) by comparing him to Hitler (*TOI*, 23 February 1987). It is also striking to note that Hitler is being evoked for conflicting reasons.
59. Point number 6 of the terms of reference of this committee stated: 'The demand of textile mill workmen of Bombay for grant of additional wages will be enquired into and reported on within a period of six months by the committee and steps will be taken to implement them expeditiously' (Debates, Lok Sabha, 9 July 1982), GOI, 1982 a.
60. Debates, Legislative Assembly, 15 March 1982, GOI, 1982a.
61. Debates, Lok Sabha, 9 July 1982a.
62. Debates, Rajya Sabha, 14 October 1982b.
63. *Idem*, 1 March 1983b.
64. Debates, Lok Sabha, 25 February 1983a.
65. Ibid.
66. In 1984, V.P. Singh assured a delegation of the RMMS that he would see to it that the NTC would formulate a time-bound plan to take back 40,000 workers who had remained unemployed after the strike (*TOI*, 29 April 1984).
67. On 7 November 1938, the textile workers in Bombay went on a one-day strike to protest the introduction of the Bombay Industrial Disputes

Act, 1938 which preceded the BIR Act, 1946 ('Ramifications of the BIR Act', *Economic Times*, 15 March 1982).

68. The BIR Act acknowledges three types of unions: the Representative Union having not less than 25 per cent of all the employees in any industry in any local area as its members, the Qualified Union having not less than 5 per cent of all the employees in an industry in any local area and the Primary Union. This last type can only exist in an industry in which there is no Representative or Qualified Union. In order to qualify as a Primary Union such a union should have not less than 15 per cent of all the employees in any industrial enterprise (Section 13, BIR Act, 1946). Unions complying with the legal requirements under Section 23 are entered by the registrar of unions in an approved list and are known as Approved Unions.

69. The Sangh is commonly referred to as the 'recognized union' which is incorrect as this term applies to unions registered under the Maharashtra Recognition of Trade Unions and Prevention of Unfair Labour Practices Act, 1971 (MRTU and PULP Act). The condition for being registered as the recognized union under this Act stipulates that 'a membership of not less than 30 per cent of the total number of employees employed in any undertaking' is required for qualifying as the recognized union (Section 11, MRTU and PULP Act, 1971).

70. Letter from the MGKU to registrar, 24 March 1982.

71. Letter from assistant registrar to the MGKU, 20 April 1982. It may be noted here that the registrar, the additional registrar and the assistant registrar hold the same powers under the BIR Act unless otherwise specified by the state government (Section 5, BIR Act, 1946).

72. Amendment Application to registrar of Unions, 6 May 1982.

73. Ibid.

74. Section 15 of the BIR Act, 1946 is vital to the present discussion as it deals with cancellation of registration. It reads as follows:

The registrar shall cancel the registration of a union:

> (a) if the Industrial Court directs that the registration of such union shall be cancelled;
>
> (b) if [after giving notice to such union to show cause why its registration should not be cancelled and] after holding such inquiry, if any, as he deems fit, he is satisfied:
>
> (i) that it was registered under mistake, misrepresentation or fraud; or
>
> (ii) that the membership of the union has for a continuous period of three [calendar] months fallen below the minimum required under Section 13 for its registration:

Provided that where a strike or a closure not being an illegal strike or closure under this Act in an industry involving more than a third of the employees in the industry in the area has extended to a period exceeding fourteen days in any calendar month, such month shall be excluded in computing the said period of three months:

Provided further that the registration of a union shall not be cancelled under the provisions of this subclause unless its membership [for the calendar month in which show-cause notice under this section was issued] was less than such minimum; or

(iii) that the registered union being a Primary Union has after registration failed to observe any of the conditions specified in Section 23; or

(iv) that the registered union is not being conducted bona fide in the interests of employees but in the interests of employers to the prejudice of the interest of employees; or

(v) that it has instigated, aided or assisted the commencement or continuation of a strike or a stoppage which has been held or declared to be illegal;

(c) if its registration under the Indian Trade Unions Act, 1926, is cancelled.

75. Vide Section 23 (viii), BIR Act, 1946.
76. Letter from the RMMS to the registrar, 28 May 1982.
77. Ibid.
78. Ibid.
79. Letter from the RMMS to the registrar, 18 June 1982.
80. Samant's brother, P.N. Samant, declared that elections had duly been held at that time and that Datta Samant was the elected president (interview, 23 December 1986).
81. Letter from the RMMS to the registrar, 18 June 1982.
82. Vide Section 14 (fifth provision), BIR Act, 1946.
83. The relevant section in the BIR Act pertaining to the conditions for being entered on the list of approved unions is Section 23. The rules of a union aspiring to become an approved union should, inter alia, provide that:

    (v) every individual dispute in which a settlement is not reached by conciliation shall be offered to be submitted to arbitration, and that arbitration under Chapter XI shall not be refused by it in any dispute;

    (vi) no strike shall be sanctioned [resorted to or supported by it] unless all the methods provided by or under this Act for the settlement of an industrial dispute have been exhausted [or unless the circumstances mentioned in the proviso to clause (h) of subsection (I) of section 97 obtain] and the majority of its members vote by ballot in favour of such strike;

(vii) no stoppage which is illegal under this Act shall be sanctioned [resorted to, or supported by it];

(viii) no 'go slow' shall be sanctioned, resorted to or supported by it:

84. Letter from the RMMS to the registrar, 18 June 1982.
85. Letter from the MGKU to the registrar, 14 June 1982.
86. Interim Order, 21 June 1982, p. 21.
87. While discussing this aspect Mrs Bhattacharjee mentioned a decision by the Industrial Court in the case of Bayer India according to which a worker can be member of more than one union. But there is another one by the Bombay High Court in 1982 contradicting this ruling (interview, 5 February 1987). The registrar stated as one of her problems that there is no commentary available on the BIR Act.
88. Ibid.
89. Letter from the RMMS to the registrar, 7 July 1982.
90. Letter from the MOA to the registrar, 6 July 1982.
91. Datta Samant declared in the Bombay High Court: 'I deny that the demands of the textile workers were not precise and that they were not placed before any specified authority. The Union had prepared a regular Charter of Demands on behalf of the textile workmen and sent the copies to the government and the Mill Owners' Association' (Affidavit in the Bombay High Court, 2 August 1982).
92. Order of the registrar, 4 November 1982, Annex. I, II and III.
93. Resolution adopted in the RMMS meeting, 10 April 1982.
94. Letter from the RMMS to the registrar, 7 July 1982.
95. Order of the registrar, 4 November 1982.
96. Clause 8 of Section 26 of the Bombay Industrial Relations Rules, 1947 reads:

    Where in respect of objections raised against the membership of a union, the number of witnesses to be examined is very large, the registrar may examine such number of witnesses as he may determine by adopting such sampling method as the registrar may deem fit. The registrar may, with the consent of the parties, examine the witnesses in camera.

97. Vide Order of the registrar, 4 November 1982, p. 27.
98. According to this source NTC and MSTC mills together had a muster strength of 33,151 prior to the strike (Note supplied by the office of commissioner of labour, May 1987). However, in this last figure the number of workers on the rolls of Western India Mills (2,740), New

Hind Textile Mills (3,131) and India United Mills No. 6 (2,381) were omitted. These figures are to be found in the Kotwal Committee Report (*Kotwal Committee Report*, 1987: 36–37). After correcting for this, the total muster strength in NTC and MSTC appears to have been 41,403, according to the office of the commissioner of labour. This still leaves a discrepancy of some 2,000 workers to be explained but accuracy in these matters seems to be an elusive dream.

99. See *Report for the Year 1982*, MOA: 187–88.
100. Order of the registrar, 11 November 1982.
101. Order of the registrar, 4 November 1982, pp. 24–25.
102. Order of High Court, 24 April 1984, pp. 16–17.

The Court gave the following explanation: 'It must be borne in mind that such a contention was urged by the Sangh before the authorities below with a view to maintain the registration as the representative Union and raising such pleas in the proceedings for defeating the application of the Union cannot be considered as acting prejudicial to the interest of the employees' (ibid.)

103. Order of the High Court, 24 April 1984, p. 28.
104. The MGKU had been registered under the Indian Trade Unions Act, 1926 which is a Central Act but not under the BIR Act, 1946. A second Central Act regulating industrial relations in Maharashtra is the Industrial Disputes Act, 1947. A different law applying to the same industries to which the BIR Act applies, thus inclusive of the textile industry, is the Maharashtra Recognition of Trade Unions and Prevention of Unfair Labour Practices Act, 1971 (MRTU and PULP Act). This last Act provides inter alia for recognition of trade unions, collective bargaining and declaring strikes illegal.
105. Veerendra Patil, minister of labour, declared in the Rajya Sabha in 1983 that there had been 'a definite improvement in the industrial relations situation in the country during 1982 compared to the years 1980 and 1981'. He substantiated this claim by pointing to a decline in the number of industrial disputes in those years and added: 'Number of man days lost in 1982 also compares favourably as against the previous years if the number of man days lost due to the textile strike in Bombay is isolated' (Debates Rajya Sabha, 2 March 1982). The day before Commerce Minister Ram Dulari Sinha had stated in the same House that slightly less than 50 million man days had been lost in the first twelve and a half months of the strike (Debates, Rajya Sabha, 1 March 1983). By Patil's reasoning one could argue that a disaster does not take place if we only decide to ignore it.
106. Cf. Section 14 (fifth proviso), Section 23 (vi).

107. Rule 29 of the Bombay Industrial Relations Rules, 1947 empowers leaders of approved unions or their delegates 'to collect sums payable by its members on the premises of an undertaking where wages are paid to them'. In the same Rule it is stipulated that such collections shall be made on the usual pay day during the hours of payment.
108. Debates, Legislative Council, 16 December 1982 b.
109. Legislative Assembly Debates, 15 March 1982 a.
110. Debates, Legislative Council, 16 December 1982.
111. The Mehta Committee, in fact, did the same as the committee that had been preparing the Industrial Relations Bill, 1978 before it. Both strove to remove inadequacies in prevailing labour legislation and inconsistencies between central and state enactments.
112. See *Report of the Committee Constituted to Examine Item 4 of the Agenda of the National Labour Conference* (undated). Kindly made available by the office of the commissioner of labour in Bombay, May 1987.
113. Ibid.
114. In cases where not one union could qualify for the position of the sole bargaining agent, the Mehta Committee recommended the constitution of 'a composite bargaining council with proportional representation subject to a minimum membership'.
115. The following discussion is based on an undated note circulated by the central government in the course of 1987 and captioned: *Proposed Amendments to the Industrial Disputes Act, 1947* and the *Trade Unions Act, 1926*.
116. Ibid.
117. Debates, Rajya Sabha, 2 March 1983b.
118. Ibid.
119. The minister declared that government personnel could avail themselves of the Joint Consultative Machinery in case of conflicts and that this was sufficient. He warned: '...if we allow the right to strike in the government departments or Ministries, then any trade union can hold to ransom the entire government at the centre or the governments in the states' (ibid.).
120. Ibid.

Chapter Four

AFTERMATH

THE MYSTERIOUS PRICE OF THE STRIKE

Dismissals and Rationalization

The effects of the unprecedentedly long textile strike were equally without precedent in terms of loss of employment and wages. The loss in production, man days and wages has been fixed and is not disputed but the loss in employment is still unknown. That is surprising as the loss of jobs to workers on strike and the reduction in the employment potential of the industry may be reckoned to be the gravest consequence of the strike. The takeover by the central government of thirteen mills in Bombay in October 1983 in order to sustain employment for the workers was an important step. These mills had a record of poor financial performance due to mismanagement and the takeover was a prelude to nationalization which was to follow in due course.[1] Although it ought to be fairly simple to arrive at an accurate picture of the employment prior to and after the strike, it proves to be a major problem.

Many individuals have tried to assess the consequences of the strike for employment in the textile industry. In these efforts various problems had to be tackled. The first problem is that although the strike was never formally called off by Datta Samant, production restarted gradually. This posed the problem of the point at which stock should be taken of the employment situation. It was abundantly clear that the workforce had shrunk immensely and that, as far as millowners and the government were concerned, employment would never again reach pre-strike levels. So somewhere a point had to be fixed, arbitrarily, indicating the end of the strike and thereby allowing for assessments and calculations. The government, millowners and the RMMS together decided that 2 August 1983 was the date marking the end of the strike. At that time the strike had lasted about eighteen and a half months.[2]

A more serious problem in estimating the damage done to the employment potential was that the mills made no effort to clarify the matter and, instead, tried to obscure the picture by supplying some and withholding other information. Apart from this, it had also been noted that an unknown number of workers (both employed and unemployed) were entitled to payments such as bonus and provident fund by the mills but that mills were unwilling to pay such amounts or sometimes blankly refused to do so. The extent to which mills resorted to these practices seemed enormous, albeit unknown, and wild guesses were made. This lack of clarity caused deep distrust among workers as well as unions, and in the end the government deemed it fit to appoint a committee to go into these matters.

This committee, under the chairmanship of Manohar Kotwal, hereafter referred to as the Kotwal Committee, was constituted in September 1986 and reported its findings in February 1987. It is no surprise that Datta Samant did not figure in the list of members of this committee but it is astonishing that Bhai Bhosale, the former RMMS chief, did although he had been ousted during the strike.[3] His presence on the committee cannot but imply some kind of rehabilitation. Given the composition of the committee, a negative view was bound to be taken of the strike but in spite of that the committee made some very critical remarks in respect of the millowners. It is typical that the committee had to observe in its introductory remarks that as yet it had been impossible to assess the number of strike-affected workers: 'The actual number of workers, who expired, retired, resigned and those who were not taken in employment and the amount of legal dues payable to each of them individually remained a mystery.'[4] As will be seen shortly, much would remain a mystery in spite of the report of the committee.

Against heavy odds, the committee completed its work within five months and the findings seemed to confirm the most gloomy expectations.[5] Although the *Kotwal Committee Report* suffers from serious drawbacks it is still the best (read: most complete) source of information available on the subject and it, therefore, has to be analysed in detail. Some of its major findings regarding the outcome of the strike were:

Number of workers dismissed/discharged		51,311	
Number of workers dismissed for violence		551	
Criminal cases under the BIR Act		390	
Recruitment in 28 mills		5,543	
Total man days lost		5.6	crores
Total loss of wages	Rs	90.1	crores
Total loss of production	Rs	985.5	crores

Source: Kotwal Committee Report (GOM 1987: 12–13).

As if this was not bad enough, the situation proved to be worse than it appears from these figures. The number of workers affected by the strike was, according to the committee, more than double the figure for those who had been simply dismissed. Tens of thousands of workers were not taken back, resigned (voluntarily or under pressure), retired and/or did not receive their legal dues. Similarly, the number of new recruits enlisted during the strike is far greater than the 5,543 mentioned above. As far as the position of *badli*s and permanent workers is concerned, the report displays a disturbing lack of information. This is not all the fault of the committee as the millowners resorted to a mind-boggling jugglery with figures, providing a thick smokescreen to conceal the real situation. In a separate note attached to the report, G.L. Reddy objected to the fact that the millowners did not supply a division of the workforce in *badli*s and permanent workers although they had been requested to do so. One wonders why a law-abiding employer should be so secretive about employment figures.[6]

The Kotwal Committee nevertheless found that in all 1,06,356 workers were affected by the strike (see Table 4.1) and that 46,575 workers had not been paid their dues (see Table 4.2). The first figure was pounced upon by the press and has often been reproduced uncritically and equated with the loss in job opportunities as a result of the strike but the data do not allow for such a simplification. The term 'affected workers' refers in the report to those who had lost their jobs, whether voluntarily or not (49 per cent), as well as to those who had meanwhile resigned (more than 40 per cent), retired (8 per cent) or expired (2.5 per cent).

TABLE 4.1

Final Picture of Strike-affected Workers Including Permanent and *Badli* Workers and Staff

	Number Mills	*Workers Retired*	*Workers Resigned*	*Workers Expired*	*Workers Displ.**	*Affected Workers*
Public Sector:						
NTC South	18	4460	11933	1054	18017	35464
NTC North	6	1315	3496	284	1215	6310
MSTC	1	244	641	46	-	931
Total	25	6019	16070	1384	19232	42705
Private Sector:						
Working mills	32	2910	26909	1250	23371	54440
Closed mills	3	-	-	-	9211	9211
Grand Total	60	8929	42979	2634	51814	106356

* Workers displaced for any reason (includes discharges, dismissals, medically unfit, those who did not report for duty and workers from closed mills).

Source: Kotwal Committee Report (GOM 1987: 22).

It should be borne in mind that the report was submitted some five years after the commencement of the strike, which implies that even without the strike retirement, resignation and expiry would have taken place. Given the stagnancy in demand in the textile industry and the craving for modern machinery, it was bound to happen that on superannuation vacancies would not be filled. Such a policy, while indeed reducing the number of job opportunities, was strike independent, although it is true that the millowners jumped at the opportunity offered by the strike to carry out large-scale retrenchment. Even so it is not permissible to credit the said policy to the strike as its causes reach far beyond that.

In a different Table, the committee presented the cases of all those whose dues had not been paid (see Table 4.2) and took care to distinguish the same categories here as had been used for figuring out the number of strike-affected workers. The amounts involved were also given. It appears that all in all not less than Rs 22.5 crores had been withheld by millowners and the government. The major part of this amount was payable by the government (Rs 13 crores) as against Rs 9.5 crores by the private mills. But in the latter case the dues payable by three mills (Bradbury, Mukesh and Shree Niwas) had not been calculated as these mills were closed and precise information was lacking. It should also be borne in mind that the figures for the public mills include the thirteen mills that were taken over by the government in October 1983 and placed under the aegis of the NTC South.[7]

The lion's share of the dues (82 per cent) was to be paid to workers who had been displaced or dismissed (Category 5). Another 11.6 per cent was to be paid to workers who had resigned.[8] The Kotwal Committee also checked the payment of provident fund and discovered that Rs 4.8 crores payable by twenty-nine mills had not been deposited with the provident fund commissioner. The thirteen mills that had been taken over had not paid Rs 1.2 crores, the remaining mills in the NTC failed to pay Rs 1.5 crores, and five private mills had to account for Rs 2.1 crores.[9] The committee observed that the concerned mills were guilty of 'committing breach of the provisions of the Employees Provident Fund Act' and recommended immediate action 'by penalizing them for this default'.[10]

It would have been useful if we could distinguish the cases of voluntary retirement and resignation from those that took place under pressure as the persons belonging to this last group would rightly have to be called strike victims. The categories of resigned and retired workers being sizeable, such a distinction would have been appropriate but the report does not make it. The text merely states that the balance number of workers (that is, the total of 'affected workers' from Table 4.1 minus the total of 'dues victims' from Table 4.2) 'though affected by the strike are supposed to have been paid their legal dues after their resignation, retirement, death, dismissal/discharge'. It follows that if this group of 59,781 (1,06,356–46,575) workers was not affected by non-payment of dues they were affected by something else.

However, the report fails to specify what this 'something' could be and restricts itself to placing strike-affected workers and dues-affected workers in four categories (columns 2 to 5 in Table 4.1 and Table 4.2). In the absence of any further specification we have to take it that the labels of these four categories (together making for the total of 'affected workers') provide a complete picture of the manner in which the workers were affected. However, the problem here is that this presupposes that all workers who, for example, resigned or retired did so against their will. Such an assumption is unwarranted as has been pointed out before.

TABLE 4.2
Number of Workers Whose Dues Have Not Been Paid

	Number Mills	*Workers Retired*	*Workers Resigned*	*Workers Expired*	*Workers Displ.**	*Affected Workers*
Public Sector:						
NTC South	18	2332	7579	576	11956	22443
NTC North	6	-	-	-	1215	1215
MSTC	1	-	-	-	-	-
Total	25	2332	7579	576	13171	23658
Private Sector:						
Working mills	32	205	1501	104	11896	13706
Closed mills	3	-	-	-	9211	9211
Grand Total	60	2537	9080	680	34278	46575

Source: *Kotwal Committee Report*, p. 23.

There is more to be said against this way of reasoning. Even while ignoring the evidence that a number of workers left the industry of their own accord and granting that all workers in the category 'displaced/dismissed' were removed involuntarily, we are still faced with a glaring anomaly. How does the category 'expired' relate to the strike? In so far as the relatives of expired workers were not paid their dues, one could argue that at least the workers (or rather their relatives) in these cases were affected by the strike. But Table 4.3 shows clearly that this is not so in 1,954 cases. Unless we know how many workers had to face compulsory superannuation, resignation under duress or whose death should be treated as strike-related expiry, it will not be possible to subscribe to the figure of 1,06,356 strike-affected workers given by the Kotwal Committee.

The report suffers from another drawback and that is its utter lack of accuracy with regard to calculations. In several instances the totals given do not correspond with the total of the added elements of the columns and the differences are often considerable. This is most disturbing in respect of the figures for what is called 'Total Separation'. In order to find out how many workers left the textile industry after the strike, the committee took down the muster strength prior to the strike and the number of old workmen on the muster-roll afterwards (that is, at 1 October 1986). The difference is called the 'Total Separation'. This separation is accounted for by four categories of workers: 1. retired, 2. resigned, 3. expired and 4. dismissed/discharged (including all other reasons). All figures are given mill-wise. The total of these four columns should therefore tally with 'Total Separation' but neither the mill-wise figures nor the grand totals match.

TABLE 4.3

Balance of Workers Affected, but Not by Non-Payment of Dues

Category	*Retired*	*Resigned*	*Expired*	*Displaced/ Dismissed*	*Affected Workers*
Strike-affected	8,929	42,979	2,634	51,814	1,06,356
Dues-affected	2,537	9,080	680	34,278	46,575
Balance	6,392	33,899	1,954	17,536	59,781

Source: Compiled from Tables 4.1 and 4.2.

Scrutinizing the Tables, it was found that the mill-wise total of the four categories corresponded with the mill-wise figure for 'Total Separation' in twenty-two out of fifty-seven cases (three mills did not provide information due to closure). In all other cases there were errors involving scores, hundreds and a few times even more than a thousand workers. The errors were made in two directions. Sometimes the figure for 'Total Separation' was found to be too high and at other times too low. More than 9,000 workers were involved in these cases.[11] It is an affront to the members of the committee to think that they were unaware of these miserable calculations but there is no hint of an explanation. The irregularities in the final text are not even pointed out.

In general, the way the committee renders an account of its findings is brief and insufficient, and the presentation of the results leaves plenty of room for confusion. The possibility may not be excluded that double counting further blurred the real picture. This sorry state of affairs cannot be wholly attributed to the members of the committee as they were largely dependent on cooperation from the mills, but the committee failed to account adequately for the numerous errors and lack of clarity in the data. Confusion prevailed also with regard to the interpretation of the data.

G.L. Reddy, one of the members, concluded in a note of dissent attached to the report, that the actual number of old workers who were not given their jobs back was 1,37,562. In this connection he discarded the statistics for displaced/dismissed workers as presenting a false picture. For his calculations, Reddy started from the muster strength prior to and after the strike. In doing so he too, made an arithmetical mistake involving 1,000 workers. He also tried to assess the damage done to the employment in a different manner and by utilizing this second approach he figured that the number of workers kept out of the mills should be put at 1,15,000. The best part of his note is probably that he draws attention to the fact that the workers of closed mills (Mukesh, Bradbury and Shree Niwas) should be included in the calculations, an aspect which was completely ignored by the committee.

If Reddy felt that the number of strike-affected workers was in reality much higher than stated by the report, another member, M.S. Divekar (director of the NTC South), felt that the figure should be much lower.[12] The employers in the private sector, too, denied that the workers were victimized on a large scale and maintained that in spite of their efforts to get the workers back on the job through the postal services as well as through volunteers, the response was very poor. The report gives as the view of the employers: 'It was only after failing in their effort to get the workers back that they took legal action of discharging/ dismissing the workers from service. As such the workers are not entitled to get any compensation for loss of job.'[13]

The NTC was in agreement with this line of thinking but, contrary to the millowners, was in favour of a golden handshake for the workers of closed mills which were not viable for reopening. The affected workers ought to be compensated in accordance with the Textile Workers' Rehabilitation Fund Scheme. It is somewhat bizarre to note how the employers, who throughout the strike heralded the collapse of the struggle, now stressed that all their efforts to get the workers back had failed. The text of their song had to be rewritten, of course, and it was now complained that the workers were simply not interested in coming back and stayed away. This served their intentions of retrenchment: 'When a very large number of workers had already abstained from work the question of displacing any workers on account of modernization or rationalization did not arise. Hence, no compensation on that account is payable.'[14] From this it appears that the greatest number of workers who did not receive their dues is likely to be found in the category of those who were discharged or dismissed. This is amply borne out by Table 4.2 from which it appears that 34,278 workers in this category did not receive their dues.

Although it is not possible to say with certainty how many workers were actually affected by the strike, this number may very well have exceeded the number of 51,814 persons in the category discharge/dismissal. In the course of the research programme-I encountered many workers who had been trying to get their job back but had not succeeded or did so only after three or four years. It seems fair to consider a worker who was without a job against his wishes for years together, as a strike victim, although he may have been taken back by the time the Kotwal Committee started its investigations.

Thousands of other workers reporting for duty were neither discharged nor dismissed; they were simply not taken back. As there is no hard evidence of their reporting for duty, the employers could conveniently place them in the group of those who 'abstained from work' and, as a result, were not entitled to any compensation. Similarly, many workers gradually concluded that they would not get their job back and stayed away or returned home. Statistically these persons may have been ranked in the category 'resigned' but they may as well have found a place in the category 'discharged'. The report does not explain this.

Going by the data it may seem that the 'dues-affected workers' are only to be found among those who for one reason or the other do not work any longer. To believe this, however, would be a fallacy. During the research programme it was found that a number of workers who did resume duty did not receive the payments they were entitled to. Such cases were not rare and received wide press coverage. The extent to which mills in general resorted to such practices seems to have differed greatly but in some mills sizeable groups seem to have suffered from the policy of the management not to pay dues. Some workers who refused to accept this treatment were threatened with loss of employment if they persisted. Others, who had been fired or who had been given to understand that they would not be taken back, did not dare to ask for their dues for fear of losing the housing facilities provided by the mill. Summing up, it must be concluded that the real number of strike victims is as obscure today as it was before and that the mystery the committee set out to unveil has remained unravelled.

Elasticity of Muster Strength

Even if the number of strike victims cannot be determined with certainty, some idea of the consequences of the strike for the employment potential may be had by comparing pre-strike and post-strike figures. This is not easy as the employers do little to make the picture transparent, which is aptly reflected by the contents of the *Kotwal Committee Report*. Essential data regarding the number of *badlis* and permanent workers are lacking and the mills are responsible for that. The few general figures that are available are presented in Table 4.4.

TABLE 4.4
Available Employment Statistics for the Bombay Textile Industry

Item	*Pre-strike*	*Post-strike*	*Difference*
Muster strength	2,33,000	1,55,938	77,062
Avg. Daily Empl.	1,69,000	1,20,037	48,963
Staff and W&W*	27,000	unknown	unknown
Permanent Workers	1,26,000	unknown	unknown
Badli force	80,000	unknown	unknown
Old workmen	100%	1,29,093	103,907
New recruits	-	25,589	25,589

* Figure taken from ICMF files.

Source: Kotwal Committee Report, passim

According to the *Kotwal Committee Report* there were 233,000 workers on the muster-roll in all mills of Bombay taken together (that is, private as well as public mills) on 1 October 1981. This figure included some 80,000 *badlis*, and if we correct the number of staff and watch and ward personnel we find that the number of permanent workers at that time was 126,000 workers. However, there are several flaws in these data but by adding up the relevant columns it is found that the figure should have been approximately 2.34 lakhs.

What is worse, is that the number of employees of three mills has been omitted which is explained away by saying that this information was not available. But in the absence of these data it cannot be maintained, of course, that the muster strength prior to the strike was in the magnitude of 2.32 lakhs. According to information obtained from the office of the labour commissioner, these three mills had 13,058 workers on their rolls prior to the strike which would bring the total muster strength to 247,189 employees.[15] This figure corresponds exactly with the total strength of the labour force mentioned in a statistical survey by the MOA undertaken in January 1983.[16] The figure also tallies with the data presented in the annual report of the MOA for the year 1982.[17]

Unfortunately, we do not possess the figure for the *badli* component in the labour force after the strike and neither do we know the number of permanent workers. The millowners will have their own reasons for not being specific about the size of the *badli* force but the absence of this information makes it very difficult to establish the damage done by the strike to the workers or to the employment potential of the industry. Yet, the available figures do allow for rough estimates. We found that the real muster strength before was 2,47,189. After the strike this strength came down to 155,938 (this figure needs not to be upgraded as the three mills remained closed and the workers concerned became unemployed), which means a difference of 91,251. We might conclude that this last figure indicates the number of workers who after the strike appeared to have left the textile industry.

This figure includes *badli*s as well as permanent workers and refers to voluntary as well as compulsory loss of employment. We also know the the number of old workmen employed (1,29,093) after the strike. It would be premature to conclude on the strength of these data that apparently some 1,20,000 job opportunities (2,47,000–1,29,093) were lost because of the labour struggle. One reason is that the muster strength also includes the names of thousands of *badli*s who used to get work for a few days a month only. The most accurate picture, therefore, would be obtained by converting all job opportunities before and after the strike into working hours and see how many hours have disappeared since 1981. Here, too, we would have to correct the figure for voluntary withdrawal by the workers from the employment market if we want to relate the outcome of this exercise to the strike. In the absence of precise information this cannot be done.

The employers prefer to look at the average daily employment before and after the strike and like to conclude that apparently less than 50,000 job opportunities were lost. But this procedure is not correct either as new recruits in the industry started taking over the jobs of old hands. If we want to arrive at the loss of job opportunities for those who participated in the strike then the average daily employment will at least have to be corrected for the presence of these new recruits. Here again, it might be necessary to distinguish between new recruits becoming *badli*s and those becoming permanent workers. Lacking specific information this cannot be done either. However, it seems that after the strike one of the most controversial elements of the *badli* system (that is, workers having to report for work daily but being given work for a few days a month only) was done away with and that today *badli*s are assured of at least fifteen days of work. If this is true then a distinction between *badli*s and permanent workers in terms of working hours seems less relevant.

It would in that case be justifiable to add the number of new recruits since the beginning of the strike (25,589) to the decrease in average daily employment (48,963) and conclude that in all 74,552 job opportunities were lost to old workmen (*badli*s as well as permanent workers) after the strike. This figure suggests an accuracy which is not real but it seems a better estimate than comparing the muster strength before the strike with the number of old hands afterwards or going by the average daily employment. In fact, the number of lost job opportunities to the striking workers might be higher still as this figure refers to full-timers and half-timers whereas the same amount of work was formerly done by more workers (the workload being less then and the number of workers with a few days' work per month being higher). Due to that one could say that, roughly speaking, one-third of the employment opportunities were lost to the strike participants.

The loss of job opportunities in the industry, however, is considerably lower than 74,552, as new recruits replaced old hands. Here, too, it is impossible to be very precise. It must be pointed out that the term 'new recruits' is vague and refers either to textile workers who started working in another mill during the strike or to workers coming from other industries or even other states. New recruits were popular with the management of certain mills as they were prepared to work for lower wages.[18] Referring to mill workers who started working in another mill than their own during the strike one could argue that these 'new recruits' ought not to be treated as a group taking away the employment of former textile workers. However, most representatives of the management I spoke to assured me that the old hands among the 'new recruits' returned to their own mill as soon as there was an opportunity for that and in doing so they left the group of 'new recruits'.[19] This means that the number for new recruits is only marginally inflated by old hands working in different mills. It may, therefore, be safely assumed that the figure for new recruits as found by the Kotwal Committee in 1987, refers to workers who entered the textile industry for the first time, both in the course of and after the strike.

If the number of *badli*s or permanent workers after the strike had been known it would have been fairly easy to see which of these two groups had suffered most. Representatives of the employers, like Secretary-General Vijayanagar of the MOA, maintain that *badli*s in particular suffered on account of the strike but this claim was not supported by any evidence. But with or without evidence it is likely that the *badli*s suffered more as they were the most vulnerable and least organized group in the industry. As even the RMMS seemed bent on curbing the number of *badli*s in the industry, this could very well have resulted in a far greater number of *badli*s being sacrificed than permanent workers but an estimate here would be too hazardous to be of any use.[20]

That *badli*s left the industry in greater numbers than permanent workers is confirmed by experiences gained during the fieldwork. It was striking to note that it was far easier to spot permanent workers than *badli*s, although the latter category was supposed to contain not less than 80,000 workers prior to the strike which means that roughly one out of every three textile workers then was a *badli*.[21] The reason for this difficulty may well have been that a great number of *badli*s left the textile industry during the strike and returned to the village. Working in the mills was only an additional source of employment for many *badli*s and being confronted with the problems of reinstatement they may have decided to concentrate on other avenues. This seems particularly true for those *badli*s who got only four or five days' work a month before the strike.[22]

A great number of workers in the sample stated that they had to report for duty many times before they were taken back by their mill and quite a number of them was never taken back at all. It is possible that the mill management hoped to discourage these workers and force them to seek employment elsewhere. If workers gave up coming to the mills, they could be treated as workers who had voluntarily retired and need not be given financial compensation. The Sangh's collusion with the millowners in this policy which, if successful, saved the employers a lot of money should not be discounted. If this point could be established, the Sangh would lose its right to represent the workers under Section 15 (b) (iv) of the BIR Act which stipulates that the union should be conducted bona fide in the interests of the employees. However, the possibility of that is infinitely small as such an understanding between the Sangh leadership and the millowners, if it really exists, will have been an oral undertaking only. Replying to the question of whether the RMMS entered into retrenchment[23] agreements with the management of mills in the course of the strike, Haribhau Naik, president of the Sangh, curtly remarked: 'No agreement. No understanding. The only understanding between the millowners and the RMMS was that workers who returned before the 31st of May 1983 should be taken back' (interview, 29 May 1986).

The MGKU has sought to prove that the Sangh did act against the workers' interests by signing retrenchment agreements during and after the strike. The union claimed that not less than 490 of such agreements had been signed between January 1982 and January 1987.[24] The MGKU, therefore, lodged a complaint with the registrar of trade unions against the RMMS on 17 March 1987, on the plea that the Sangh had indulged in anti-labour activities. All agreements between the employers and the Sangh have to be registered by the registrar under Section 44 of the BIR Act and from the data supplied by this authority it appears that the accusation made by the MGKU was not far from the truth. In all 426 accords (362 agreements and sixty-four settlements) were concluded between the Sangh and the millowners between January 1982 and May 1987. The year-wise break-up of these figures was not given but the majority of the agreements are likely to have been concluded after the strike.[25]

But more important than the number of accords is the number of posts involved in these agreements. It appears that in all 6,444 posts were formally abolished during and after the strike. Not only the private mills but also nationalized ones and those that were taken over in 1983 entered into agreements with the Sangh. However, it is unlikely that all these registered accords will be of much value to the MGKU. It is clear that they merely represent the tip of the iceberg but as such they will not suffice to prove conclusively that the Sangh acted to the prejudice of the workers. What the future has in store for the workers is bleak in any case. As late as May 1986, the RMMS president Haribhau Naik declared that 'with or without the strike, rationalization and modernization are the need of the hour for the textile industry' (interview, 28 May 1986).

Other Affected Industries and Activities

In the preceding paragraph the effect of the textile strike on the employment potential of the industry has been assessed and it was found that it was difficult to draw definite conclusions in the absence of sufficient and reliable data. The case for ancillary industries is even worse. No systematic data collection has been done and what remains are some scattered press reports in which the negative effects of the strike on ancillary industries are mentioned. From these reports it would seem that the manufacturers of textile machinery were particularly hard hit as many mill orders were postponed or even cancelled. To a lesser extent the same seemed to be true in the case of dyes and chemicals but useful figures are lacking.[26] The effects of the strike were nevertheless at once noticeable in the market. In the first month of the strike the price of chemicals like chlorine dropped from Rs 1,000 to Rs 300, and hydrochloric acid dropped from Rs 700 to Rs 75. This dramatic decline was due to the lack of storage space for these chemicals. Caustic soda dropped from Rs 4,500 to Rs 4,000 (*TOI,* 10 February 1982).

A specific problem for the ancillary industries has been that they were used by the mills as a buffer for passing on the financial difficulties they were facing as a result of the strike. The producers and traders of machinery and other equipment or materials used by the mills usually operate on a small scale and they are no match for the mills who dictate the terms of delivery. Whereas the producers of machinery have to pay in cash for raw material to the Steel Authority of India, their customers (the mills) demand a credit ranging between three and nine months after the goods have been delivered.[27] The secretary of the Association of Merchants and Manufacturers of Textile Stores and Machinery (India) acknowledges the problems caused by this credit but calls it 'a special feature of the business relation between the textile industry and its suppliers'.[28] The association is mild about the nature of the relationship with the mills and prefers to put the blame for the difficulties faced during the strike on the workers and the strike leaders rather than on the millowners. In the course of the strike the capacity utilization of the textile machinery and accessories industry was reduced to 20 per cent of its pre-strike level. The association estimated that the total loss as a result of the strike to the textile machinery and ancillary industries (including the textile auxiliary chemicals industry and dyestuffs industry) is about Rs 52 crores but a specification of this figure is not available.[29]

Apart from the problems caused by the credit extended to the mills, the ancillary industries had to face the consequences of the takeover of thirteen mills by the central government in October 1983. Due to this takeover 'the textile machinery and other ancillary industries could not take any legal steps for recovering the amounts due to them for the supplies of goods effected during the pre-strike period. The amount involved was Rs 20 crores'.[30] The reason for this is that although the government takes over the assets of a company, it is under no obligation to take over the financial liabilities incurred by the private management. The financial burden in such a case is simply transferred to the suppliers.

Another set of producers who seem to have suffered from the ongoing strike were the eating houses where workers take their meals or tea. M.V. Shetty, general-secretary of the Bombay City and Suburban Hotels Federation, declared in July 1982 that meanwhile 1,200 hotels, restaurants and eating houses in the mill area had to close down due to lack of customers and that another 1,300 were facing the same fate (*Indian Express,* 3 July 1982). This news was flatly denied the very next day by B.R. Murthy, secretary of the Hotel and Canteen Wing of the Bombay Labour Union (BLU) who claimed that not one hotel or restaurant had to close down. Accurate data are not available but it is likely that the income of many owners of restaurants and eating houses dwindled as a result of the exodus of the workers to the villages and the reduced income of those who remained in the city. In November the *Times of India* reported that most of the 2,500 establishments in the mill areas were facing grave difficulties and that there was little work to do for the 30,000 employees in this sector (*TOI,* 21 November 1982). Many eating houses were reported to open only in the morning and for an hour in the afternoon in order to benefit from breakfast time and tea time.

Eating houses not coming under the purview of the Hotel Federation or the Canteen Wing of the BLU are the *khanawli.** *A khanawl* is a room in which workers take their meals twice a day against a monthly contribution of Rs 180 to Rs 250. This food is prepared by women in their homes and it is certain that this group of food producers suffered from the exodus to the villages and the clients that remained in Bombay were without money.[31] Some years ago attempts were made to organize the women running *khanawli* to improve their working conditions (hours of work, leave facilities) and to make them independent of moneylenders for the purchase of rice, food grain and vegetables. Their cooperation during labour struggles may have been crucial because the worker still has to eat even though he may have no money to pay his monthly contribution. In the past (as during the forty-two-day textile strike in 1974) many of these women were prepared to give credit to workers on strike even if they had to mortgage their own jewellery to meet the expenses.[32]

An organization looking after their interests is the Annapurna Mahila Mandal to which presently some 6,000 women belong.[33] An annual report of this organization written after the strike observes:

* The Marathi word '*khanawl*' has as its plural '*khanawli*'.

'The Annapurnas were severely affected since a majority of their customers were textile workers who because of the strike returned to their villages.'[34] A second way in which they were affected was that many family members of these women were textile workers themselves who had lost their income on account of the strike. During the fieldwork, I came across two cases of textile workers setting up a *khanawal* with their wives as a source of employment and income during the strike. These instances seem to display a contrary development, but given the large-scale retrenchment in the industry after the strike there is no gainsaying that many women who formerly made a living by preparing food for workers lost this employment opportunity and were forced to seek alternative employment.

In the absence of more data it is impossible to say to what extent the strike affected employment opportunities in industrial undertakings allied to the textile industry or in any other economic activity based on the presence of a quarter million textile workers in the city. The available figures are sketchy and do not even allow for a rough estimate in terms of financial losses. The need for research in the field of economic activities related to the textile industry is sharply felt.

POSITION OF THE RMMS AND MGKU

Defeated but Not Converted

Enjoying the backing of the millowners, the Sangh was in an excellent position to reinforce its power base within the mills. The existence of a blacklist and the necessity of obtaining the approval of the Sangh before reinstatement in the mills was possible were naturally powerful means whereby the Sangh could cow the workers into obedience. The most notorious 'troublemakers' were dismissed or figured on the blacklist and could be kept out of the mills. Millowners and managers usually play down the importance of this. The representative union, too, tries to minimize the significance of these weapons apart from passing the buck to the employers as far as the policy of taking workers back is concerned.

Haribhau Naik, president of the Sangh, denies that workers needed the permission of the Sangh before they could resume work but he acknowledges the use of a blacklist, which he ascribes to the initiatives of the management (interview, 29 May 1986). It is reasonable to assume that management essentially relied on the Sangh for information pertaining to workers obstructing colleagues wanting to resume duty. By supplying that information the Sangh would undertake the orchestration for the victimization which was to follow.[35]

The management is not keen on acknowledging that the employers prepared a list of unwanted workers and it is usually suggested that only a few names figured on it. Just how many names has never been revealed. The reason for this is plainly that publishing the list would probably trigger off lawsuits against victimization. Secretary-General Vijayanagar of the MOA admits the existence of a blacklist while explaining the policy of reinstating workers:

> There was no pick and choose unless it was a goonda. We had given the names of such people to the police, saying that these are the people who in times like this are always acting. They exploit labour so we prevented that…but there were only a handful of these…not a big number. Maybe ten or fifteen persons in a factory of 2,000 workers. All the rest of the people were allowed inside [interview, 30 January 1986].

But even ten workers out of every 2,000 would still mean more than 1,000 workers for the entire industry, and with a number like that opposition within the mills could be effectively muzzled. Besides, there is no guarantee that the number of activists being victimized was not much larger—the enormous number of retrenched and/or dismissed workers after the strike certainly points in that direction.

Before being allowed to return to the mill the workers had to sign a statement in which they declared that they had participated in an illegal strike and that they would henceforth refrain from agitation. Secretary-general Vijayanagar explains:

> We were allowing anyone to come back unless we were sure of a particular workman with bad antecedents. But otherwise we said: all right you give an undertaking that you will work peacefully, that you will not give any trouble to the management and that you will carry on your work in normal operation and then we took them back [ibid].

In fact, several different undertakings were discussed by the millowners during the strike. One was meant for *badli*s whose passes had been cancelled, one for permanent workers and one for dismissed workers who had to humbly beg the management to reconsider the decision to fire them. Apart from some minor differences all these undertakings contained a statement by which the undersigned declared that he had participated in an illegal strike. What is worse, the text also stressed that the concerned worker had not joined the strike voluntarily although there is little prospect that anyone would be taken in by that.[36]

The *badli* text is, remarkable in that the undersigned requested the employer to enrol him as a *new badli* worker, thereby forsaking the advantages of all previous years of labour. There is a similarity here with permanent workers who were given the opportunity of starting work again but whose cards of permanency were stamped with the word 'Temporary', leaving them to find out whether they could henceforth be dispensed with by the management at any moment. Most Finlay workers in the sample could show such extraordinary cards. These workers appeared to be very uncertain about their present status. Except for the stamp, these yellow cards were the same as the ones they had had before the strike and they were not to be mistaken for the green *badli* cards.

According to the standing orders, there is no such thing as a 'temporary permanent worker' in the textile industry and the stamp must have been added with the purpose of creating uncertainty and confusion in the minds of workers. Should the management eventually decide to dismiss the worker, it is likely that he would be told that he was 'temporary' anyway, as his card showed. There is a similarity here with the position of certain clerks after the strike. Although clerks, supervisory staff and watch and ward personnel took no part in the strike, their position came under attack all the same due to large-scale retrenchment after the strike. A clerk of Bombay Dyeing (Textile Mills) reported that a number of colleagues who were permanent before the strike were now classified as 'surplus clerks'. These clerks were sometimes transferred to other departments but at other times kept at their old posts. All of them were given to understand that they were retained solely on humanitarian grounds. This new class of affected clerks is, according to this spokesman, excluded from periodic wage increases and profit-sharing which creates an ever-widening gulf between them and their former colleagues.

Dependence and Independence

As regards the power of the Sangh within the mills, it has to be stated that this power is real, albeit by no means unassailable. Nearly all the workers in the sample described the general atmosphere inside the mills as being much worse in comparison with the pre-strike situation. Workers are fined for the slightest mistakes, they are often abused and very easily charge-sheeted. The management succeeded in conveying the message that henceforth no resistance against its policy would be brooked. Under the circumstances workers did not want to add to their problems by alienating the Sangh.

Although nowadays its power inside the mills seems less than before, the Sangh is still much more capable of offering protection against arbitrariness than any other union. This capacity draws many workers to the RMMS. However, it is clear that the attraction of the Sangh is not based on sympathy for the union but merely on the fact that it is backed by the management and in consequence is capable of delivering basic benefits. Wages have increased substantially in recent years, thereby buttressing the position of the Sangh as did the policy of reinstatement of mill workers. Workers declaring that they had joined the Sangh for reasons of genuine affiliation were rare birds in the sample. This is true even though dozens of workers in the sample were contacted through the RMMS, which reduces the chances of bias due to the method of selection.

In spite of the outcome of the strike only a minority of the workers blame Samant for its disastrous results. A majority attributes the collapse to the stand adopted by the government and millowners. A surprisingly large number of workers (75 per cent of the sample) still felt sympathy for Samant although many of them realized that he would not be able to help them any further. Understanding this they stopped paying fees to the MGKU. About 22 per cent of the workers in the sample who were reinstated after the strike said they did not henceforth wish to belong to any union as they were disillusioned in the capacity of any union to change their lives for the better. Even though the MGKU is not emphatically present within the mills, the

Sangh is constantly aware of the strength of this opponent even there. A few examples may illustrate this.

The flag adopted by all Samant's unions is a fist popping out of a factory chimney. This symbol was to be found in every nook and corner of Bombay at the time of the strike and provides an indication of Samant's popularity. Just outside the gates of Finlay Mills workers put up a flag of the MGKU during the strike and saw to it that it remained there afterwards, which must have been a thorn in the flesh of the Sangh. To any outsider the flag suggests that the mill is in the hands of the MGKU, particularly as there is no flag of the Sangh in sight. Day after day all workers pass the flag when entering or leaving the mill and keep watch over it. Although the extreme weather conditions of Bombay have meanwhile reduced the once proud MGKU flag to a somewhat tattered piece of cloth, the Sangh has so far not dared to remove this permanent challenge to its authority.

It would be wishful thinking to declare that this flag symbolizes that the workers have not yet given up hope of ridding themselves of the Sangh. But the continued and unhampered presence of this flag in the absence of a similar Sangh symbol surely indicates that Samant could still count on a huge reservoir of goodwill among the textile workers. In this context it is worth noting that several workers insisted during the interviews that the strike was not over yet even though they themselves had resumed duty. Apparently they liked to think that the strike symbolized their whole struggle for emancipation and returning to the mills could not, in their perception, be construed to mean that the strike was over.

Another striking example is the visit I paid to Bombay Dyeing (Spring Mills) in April 1987 in the company of my assistant and Dasharath Wagh, a worker fired by Bombay Dyeing in September 1982 because of his stiff opposition to the Sangh and the management. Dasharath secured three passes (one valid and two invalid). The very evening we got the passes, we took our place in the queue among the workers going in for the night shift and when the gates were opened we passed the security guards waving our passes and marched into the mill. For a full hour we traversed the mill, visited all the major departments and chatted with workers. Before we left the mill, we were superficially searched by the guards and walked out. Dasharath exchanged some friendly words with them. It was obvious that he was known to them and it bespeaks the influence of the MGKU that a strike leader who has been dismissed, can enter the mill at will some four years after the strike and take a few companions along.

Also, from the contents of the interviews it is abundantly clear that the present numerical strength of the Sangh is not based on love but on fear. The return of thousands of workers to the Sangh's fold took place largely on pragmatic grounds. Samant's MGKU is simply not in a position to do or withhold favours in the way the Sangh can. Neither can the MGKU offer protection on the mill premises against demanding supervisors or management to the extent the Sangh can.[37] Workers have to face the Sangh day after day inside the mills and they feel that they have no alternative. The difficulties I had in finding sufficient Sangh supporters for the interviews also show that the workers are afraid to displease the Sangh. A few explicitly stated that the Sangh might not approve of discussions with outsiders. Many workers, most particularly those who stayed in chawls belonging to the mill, felt that talking about the strike might jeopardize their position inside as well as outside the mills and some needed a great deal of persuasion before they could be convinced that the Sangh would not be in a position to find out what they had said. No such reservations were found among workers who lived in areas where the Sangh could not control their movements.

Increases in Workload

The support of an unknown number of *badli*s could be bought by promoting them to the rank of permanent workers. Faithful permanent workers could not be rewarded in this way but in the prevalent tense atmosphere inside the mills they enjoyed relative protection by supervisors and the Sangh. This protection was valuable as practically all workers in the sample complained of increased workloads after the strike and harsh treatment by supervisors and management. The increases in workload are not denied by management and justified by pointing at the number of looms and spindles that had been lying idle earlier and the need for better performance in production to survive.

M.S. Divekar, director of the NTC South, observes:

> We would try to work the full capacity of a mill with the same number of workers by increasing their workload and

> compensating them for that. In that way the component of labour cost in the cost of production would go down and the mill would improve its performance. This was done only after a dialogue and in agreement with the RMMS [interview, 9 April 1987].

The increases in workloads have been widely criticized but it has to be realized that the extent to which these took place differed from mill to mill and depended largely on the technology employed. In a loomshed with automatic looms a weaver might be asked to attend to sixteen looms whereas a weaver in a department with obsolete powerlooms might need all the available time to keep four looms running. The quality of the raw material (yarn) is another important factor as it determines the number of breakages which again influences the output.

It is possible that the private mills, taking advantage of the failure of the strike, have been more demanding than the mills in the public sector. Divekar, for example, wanted to know why weavers in Morarjee Mill No. 2 could cope with eight looms and weavers in nationalized mills could not do the same. He found the Sangh willing to agree to an increase in workload, first to six and later to eight looms per weaver, but he refrained from a change in workload:

> I told them that we were not going to do the same because Morarjee had its looms reconditioned or had brought in new plain looms and they equipped them with certain additional gadgets, making them semi-automatic, and they worked only terry-cloth which is spun with filament yarn in which the breakage rate is very low. Due to the nature of the products we are making this would not be possible for us. I would only get a defective cloth and a low efficiency. I told them that I would be happy if the workers gave their stipulated 75 per cent efficiency and would keep the damage at 10 per cent [ibid.]

Without denying the possibility of workers in certain mills being required to work beyond their capacity, there is reason to doubt the general validity of the impression that workers are now subjected to inhuman workloads. Dasharath Wagh, a dismissed weaver from Spring Mills and prominent leader in the resistance against the Sangh, acknowledges without hesitation that workers prior to the strike did not work the full eight hours and that there was plenty of room for improved performance. But even if the workloads today do not demand a superhuman effort on the part of workers, there is no denying that the conditions of labour, a shared responsibility of millowners and the management, have to be improved practically everywhere. By demanding more from the workers, the employers have typically chosen the easiest and cheapest way of increasing production, but the simultaneous neglect of improvement in labour conditions inside the mills remains intolerable.

SUMMARY

Summarizing what has been said so far, a number of conclusions may be drawn. The outbreak of the textile strike was no mere accident or a simple case of inter-union rivalry but the result of accumulated frustrations among the textile workers built up over the years over wages, labour conditions and the performance of the Sangh. The choice of Datta Samant as the strike leader was no coincidence either as his brand of trade unionism promised high returns and attracted lakhs of workers. No one else at that time was as capable of firing the imagination of the workers as Datta Samant. The pent-up frustrations of the Bombay textile workers sought an outlet and the workers found a suitable leader in the daredevil Samant. His modus operandi adequately gave vent to their anger.

The various constituent elements of Samant's trade unionism (impressive wage demands, discarding balance sheets as a basis for settlement and refusal to be drawn into the time-consuming process of referring labour conflicts to courts) were not new. The same is true for the way he backed up this approach with massive militant action, long and exhausting struggles. The blending of these elements into an explosive and at times highly successful mix was, however, not done prior to his arrival on the Bombay labour scene. The question whether someone else with the passage of time might have been chosen by the workers to lead them in the struggle if Samant had not been there, cannot be answered with any degree of certainty and remains a matter of speculation. However, it is relevant to note that lakhs of textile workers at the end of 1981 apparently believed that Datta Samant was the man who could help them to improve their position. A great majority coupled this belief with the conviction that the Sangh had to go but there was much less unanimity regarding the question of whether the removal of the Sangh was the conditio sine qua non for realization of substantial material gains.

The importance of the workers' committees has been discussed and it was found that even though they emerged spontaneously from the ranks of the workers, they did not succeed in accurately reflecting the views and the mood of the workers. This was due to their inability to reach out to the entire labour force. Most workers in the sample appeared to have little or no knowledge of the work undertaken by these committees and of their significance—a great many were not even aware of their existence. It must be concluded that their influence on the behaviour of the striking workers has been overrated.

This leaves undecided the question of what influence these committees had on the strike leadership and thereby on the continuation of the strike. Given Samant's arbitrary style of operation (backed by his habit of seeking fresh mandates during huge rallies), one need not think that these committees on the whole were very influential. But whatever power they wielded, this power was not warranted by mandates, as in the case of Samant, but chiefly through self-assertiveness.

To be sure, the incapacity of these committees to remain in touch with the rank and file of the workers was not caused by any sort of narrow-minded promotion of group interests. One of the noteworthy aspects of this strike was the absence of overt groupism, be it based on caste, regional origin or terms of employment, a facet which will be dealt with in greater detail in Part II. The fact that the striking workers effortlessly crossed barriers of caste and avoided the traps of groupism, points at their overriding concern for the improvement of their working and living conditions. It may also be taken as an indication of the erosion of caste feelings in the context of metropolitan life.

The attitude of the red flag unions in the course of the strike and the parties to which they affiliate, was marked by a great deal of ambivalence. The sudden turn of the workers to Datta Samant took them by surprise. Noticing his popularity and the fervour of the mass of workers at that juncture, it was impossible to merely stand aside and watch the struggle. Yet, most unions from the outset doubted the chances of success. Their position was complicated by the realization that Samant's success in the textile industry might very well be followed by his unions entering other industries. By helping the success of the strike they were, in a way, digging their own graves elsewhere. On the other hand, withholding support from the strike would be regarded by the workers as a betrayal of their cause and also cost them dearly.

With the exception of the LNP-affiliated SSS, they decided on a policy of moderate support to the strike while trying to have a say in developments. They therefore stressed the need for negotiations between millowners, the government and the unions of the opposition. When this did not work out well they became convinced that the strike was bound to fail and opted out of the struggle. They did so as soon as they became aware of the fact that an ever-larger number of workers were becoming tired of the strike. This, of course, further weakened its chances of success.

From what has been said thus far it may be deduced that the strike, for all its unique aspects, cannot be dubbed a political struggle. The demands were predominantly economic, that is, if one includes in this term labour aspects like permanency of *badli*s, improvement of labour conditions and changes in workloads. Most important to the striking workers was a wage hike, the removal of the Sangh was basically seen as a step which might be necessary to achieve this goal. The struggle for the repeal of the BIR Act was of greater concern to the strike leadership and the activists than to the workers. The choice at the end of 1981 of Samant as the strike leader is further proof of the essentially economistic approach of the workers. There have been attempts at broadening the strike and converting it into a political struggle. With regard to this the efforts of the LNP/SSS to involve agricultural labourers in the strike have to be mentioned. The founding of the Kamgar Aghadi may also be seen in this light although the political objectives of its leader are unclear.

However, on the whole these attempts drew moderate response and the same may be said for the solidarity displayed by other sections of industrial workers. It has been indicated that the return of tens of thousands of workers to their villages was crucial in their efforts to cope with the strike. The villages offered opportunities for employment, shelter and food, aspects which will be elaborated on in Part II. Not much evidence, however, could be found to support the contention that the strike was unique in the sense that it created a new bond of unity between agricultural and industrial labourers. The collections of food in the rural hinterland, the participation in jail bharo campaigns and several long marches alone are insufficient indicators to maintain such a view.

Contrary to what is commonly believed, the great majority of the workers did not expect the strike to last long and neither did the millowners or the government anticipate its remarkable duration. Against the workers' firm conviction that the employers would have to give in soon, stood the employers' belief that the strike was bound to collapse before long. Both sides were proved wrong. The weapon of the indefinite strike proved to be a double-edged sword without a hilt; the risks for those who wished to use it appeared to be no less than for those against whom the weapon was used. As Samant himself was doubtful about the usefulness of such long-drawn-out struggles, it is to be expected that the phenomenon of indefinite strikes will disappear from the Bombay labour scene.

With regard to the incessant accusation made by the employers, that it was the use of violence that kept the strike going, it was found that this view can, indeed, be supported by facts. However, the full story of violence perpetrated during the strike, shows a picture quite different from what is suggested by the millowners. First, it has been established that the number of murders credited to the MGKU was wholly baseless. Secondly, it has been demonstrated that the support for the strike was nearly total in the first six months and that the importance of violence (as a means of keeping the workers out of the mills) grew only after that. Thirdly, it has been shown that violence was also resorted to by the Sangh and that the police colluded with the millowners in forcing the workers to resume work. It must, therefore, be concluded that if violence was resorted to by the MGKU to keep the workers out of the mills, counter-violence played an equally important role in chasing the workers back to the mills.

In the course of the strike positions did not remain static. Increasingly workers wanted to resume work as they had no alternative. But with the passage of time, the employers realized the advantages offered by the strike in effecting large-scale retrenchment and they availed themselves liberally of the opportunity. The government, as represented by the NTC, was not slow in adopting similar measures, be it by compensating the affected workers. It would not be wrong to say that the increased need of the workers to resume was met by a decreased wish to reinstate them.

In coping with the strike the employers were initially helped by the stocks that had been piling up and which could now be disposed of. But much more important than the stocks was the fact that the state government as well as the central government fully endorsed the employers' point of view. At a very early stage, the government and millowners decided that the strike should be Samant's undoing. Leaving aside minor digressions and some voices of dissent, employers and the government never swerved from this resolution.

This stand explains the otherwise inexplicable laxity on the side of the government in trying to find an imaginative answer to the problem at hand. Except for a few lame proposals, the government refrained from taking action and contented itself with monotonously repeating that the workers should resume work prior to any consideration of their demands. In doing so the government purposely overlooked the manifold frustrations underlying the strike and deliberately protected the position of the representative union. From the government's refusal to adopt a more flexible and imaginative approach, it may be deduced that the strike was used, inter alia, to curb militant trade unionism at the cost of the prolonged misery of lakhs of workers and their families.

It has been shown that the Sangh and the millowners took concerted action to face the menace of Samant entering the textile industry. This became very clear in the course of the legal struggle to achieve cancellation of registration of the Sangh as the representative union under the BIR Act. The proceedings in this case demonstrated a glaring deficiency of the Sangh in meeting the minimum requirement of law. Yet, the Sangh was given the benefit of the doubt and in this way the judiciary, after the executive and the legislature, also came to the rescue of the representative union. Abrogating the BIR Act, or at least amending crucial sections of it pertaining to the selection of a representative union, could help to avert the danger of a re-enactment of the textile drama in future. More particularly, the verification of membership and the clauses pertaining to arrears ought to be altered. It seems, however, that the government is moving in the opposite direction which implies that the RMMS bastion is today as impregnable as it was before. By acting in this way the causes of the strike have been ignored and the labour unrest is merely kept at bay.

Contrary to expectations, Samant did not meet his 'Waterloo' in the textile strike. No doubt, his influence suffered on account of its failure. The outcome of the struggle obliged him to even review some of his strategies, particularly his penchant for indefinite strikes. But he was still a force to reckon with and he could muster considerable strength. The very attitude which caused so much suffering to the workers, namely his refusal to call off the strike, helped him retain his image as an incorruptible leader. His popularity is visible today in the sympathy tens of thousands of textile workers feel for him in spite of the collapse of the strike.

A serious shortcoming of Samant's approach was that he seemed oblivious that ever-larger numbers of workers wanted the strike to end and that they were prepared to accept a temporary defeat in the face of starvation. The lack of a proper structure in his whole trade union movement (including the union for the textile workers) took its toll here. In addition to this, uncalled for feelings of prestige may have blinded him from gauging the real situation. By continuing the strike, even after a year, Samant prolonged the suffering of the workers against their wishes. Although he threw the challenge of a strike ballot at the RMMS and the millowners at the beginning of the strike, he himself refrained from putting this idea into practice as the strike progressed.

Had he done so, say, after about ten months, he would have found that a majority of the workers was tired of the strike and wanted it to be over. Following up such a vote with a decision to call off the strike, would have saved him from the accusation that he had given in to the management as he would only have given in to the wishes of a majority of the workers. His power base inside the mills would have remained intact as most of his adherents would have been employed again. Such a procedure would have had the twin advantages of acting democratically and of reducing the extent of demoralization among the workers, many of whom subsequently declared that they no longer saw any point in joining a union.

Finally, it was found that the exact number of strike victims remains mysterious, and this is something for which the employers are to be blamed. They hide behind a smokescreen of data, informing us about some aspects of the labour force and keeping us in the dark about others. It does not come as a great surprise that the government allows them to get away with this. In spite of all the uncertainty, it seems fair to assume that in all about 75,000 workmen on the rolls prior to the strike (both *badli*s and permanent workers), have lost their jobs. However, the loss of 'job opportunities' in the textile industry is of smaller magnitude as 'new recruits' have taken the place of old hands.

It has to be stressed that it would be unwise to believe that large-scale retrenchment, to which the millowners and the government resorted during and after the strike, could have been avoided if the strike had not occurred. The closure of several textile mills in recent years in Gujarat, where no comparable strike took place, is indicative of the many serious problems the industry is facing. But it can be said that the strike, in fact, accelerated the process of the much wanted modernization of the industry and helped the millowners, the affluent ones in particular, to do away with surplus labour and surplus capacity. In the cynical words of Manohar Kotwal, chairman of the Kotwal Committee: 'I feel that one day they [the textile tycoons] will raise a statue of Dr Samant for rescuing the textile industry.' (interview, 9 April 1986.)

NOTES

1. In a Bill replacing the original takeover ordinance the government observed: 'By reason of mismanagement of the affairs of these undertakings, their financial condition which became wholly unsatisfactory even before the commencement in January 1982 of the textile strike in Bombay further deteriorated thereafter' (Report MOA, 1984: 57). The government did not trust the millowners in the least as may be deduced from the following statement: 'Once the basic decision of nationalization was taken, a genuine apprehension arose in the government's mind that unless the management of the concerned undertakings was taken over on immediate basis, there might be large-scale frittering away of assets which would be detrimental to the public interest' (ibid).
2. The then labour commissioner, P.J. Ovid, explains the decision as follows: 'You can say that if 75 per cent of the workers resume work, a strike stops to be effective. In Maharashtra we follow this criterion

of 75 per cent but this is no hard and fast rule. Going by the average daily employment of 1.69 lakhs before the strike, the strike would be rendered ineffective if 1.26 lakhs workers would be employed daily. First we imagined that the employment may reach 1.40 lakhs one day but this never happened and finally we decided on August 2 although only 1.19 lakhs of workers had resumed at that time. You see, even today the figure of 1.26 lakhs has not been reached and yet it would be without meaning to claim that the strike is still going on' [interview, 1 February 1987].

3. Members of the committee were: 1. Manohar Kotwal (Congress leader of the Transport and Dock Workers Union), 2. A.T. (Bhai) Bhosale, 3. R.L. Vijayanagar (MOA), 4. Sushil Sain (chairman, NTC Maharashtra—South) who was later replaced by his successor M.S. Divekar, 5. G.L. Reddy (Mumbai Girni Kamgar Union), 6. R.S. Basakhetre (deputy commissioner of labour).
4. *The Bombay Textile Strike Affected and Unemployed Workers and Their Legal Dues Assessment Committee Report* (Bombay, February 1987), p. 1.
5. The work of the committee was hampered by material problems (no room, no staff, not even calculators) as well as by lack of cooperation from the millowners. Information supplied by the mills was not received in time and was erroneous in many cases. This would have its effect on the findings of the committee.
6. Reddy's experience was confirmed throughout the research programme. Time and again I noticed that the management tried to hide the real figures regarding the number of *badli*s and permanent workers before and after the strike. On several occasions I was provided with figures which seemed very unlikely and which were subsequently modified when I expressed disbelief. At other times I was told that the figures were confidential and ought not to be published.
7. On 18 October 1983 the President of India promulgated an ordinance allowing for the takeover of thirteen mills in Bombay: 1. Elphinstone Spinning and Weaving Mills, 2. Finlay Mills, Gold Mohur Mills, 4. Jam Manufacturing Mills, 5. Kohinoor Mills (No. 1), Kohinoor Mills (No. 2), 7. Kohinoor Mills (No. 3), 8. New City of Bombay Mills, 9. Podar Mills, 10. Podar Mills (Process House), 11. Shree Madhusudan Mills, 12. Shree Sitaram Mills, 13. Tata Mills.
8. Computed from the *Kotwal Committee Report*, p. 24.
9. Taken from the *Kotwal Committee Report*, pp. 48–51.
10. *Kotwal Committee Report*, p. 21.
11. In thirteen cases (involving 1,572 workers) the mill-wise figure for 'Total Separation' appeared to be too low and in twenty-two cases

(involving 7,799 workers) it appeared to be too high. This means that the committee has to explain differences involving 9,371 workers.

12. Divekar does not accept the figure of more than one lakh strike victims: 'There is a fallacy in that statement which was even discussed when the report was being prepared. At that time they looked at the muster strength which is always about 20 per cent higher than the average daily employment. The difference is made up by the *badli*s' (interview, 9 April 1987). This statement seems to suggest that the loss of employment for *badli*s ought not to be counted as loss of employment.
13. *Kotwal Committee Report*, p. 15.
14. *Kotwal Committee Report*, p. 16.
15. The three mills involved were: Bradbury (3,093), Mukesh Textile Mills (1,656) and Shree Niwas (8,309). 'Workers on Roll in Cotton Textile Mills Prior to Strike in Bombay'. Undated note kindly made available by the office of the commissioner of labour in May 1987.
16. The survey, dated 5 January 1983, is to be found at the office of the ICMF in Bombay.
17. Cf. *Report for the Year 1982*, MOA: 188.
18. This was confirmed by M.S. Divekar, director, NTC South, who stated that there was a selfish motive behind taking such workers: 'By doing so they [the millowners] could take workers with less service which means less liabilities. Their old workers have been legally dismissed or discharged and therefore they were not obliged to give them compensation' (interview, 9 April 1987).
19. At first the millowners and the RMMS denied that any 'new recruits' were taken by the mills (*TOI*, 31 May 1982). Labour Minister Gaekwad did the same in the Legislative Assembly where he stated that no workers from other states were recruited (Debates, Legislative Assembly, 17 December 1982). Against this there is the statement in September 1982 by the MOA secretary R.G. Shetye, in charge of labour statistics on behalf of the association, that by the end of October some 35,000 'new mill recruits' would have found a place in the industry (*Financial Express*, 30 September 1982). In an unknown number of cases these new recruits came from other mills in accordance with a directive of the RMMS. In the remaining cases they came from other industries or other states. Century Mills declared in September to have absorbed 3,000 'outsiders' (meaning workers from other closed units) and 1,200 'fresh hands' (newcomers to the industry) (*Indian Express*, 30 September 1982).
20. M.S. Divekar, director of the NTC South, stated that in the public sector 6,829 permanent workers were not absorbed after the strike as

against 12,000 *badli*s who had not been taken back (interview, 9 April 1987). It has to be pointed out that this figure does not agree with the per centage of *badli*s in the public sector (ibid.). This indicates the blurred state of employment statistics in the Bombay textile industry.

21. If this figure of 80,000, found in many documents, is correct then there must have been 140,000 permanent workers (247,000 minus 80,000 *badli*s and 27,000 staff) before the strike in which case *badli*s made up 32 per cent of the entire labour force or 36 per cent of the labour force minus staff.
22. In an article on the effects of the strike, H.V.V. Chellappa states that 60,000 mill workers left Bombay for good but, unfortunately as usual, any analysis or evidence is lacking. ('Bombay Mill Workers' Strike', *Economic Times*, 17 September 1985).
23. The term 'retrenchment' is not to be found in the BIR Act but is defined in the Industrial Disputes Act, 1947. The relevant part of Section 2 (o) (o) reads: 'retrenchment' means the termination by the employer of the service of a workman for any reason whatsoever, otherwise than as a punishment inflicted by way of disciplinary action, but does not include (a) voluntary retirement of the workman; etc.'
24. In a pamphlet circulated by the MGKU in February 1987, the union provided the following figures for retrenchment agreements between the RMMS and the millowners: twenty-six in 1982, forty-six in 1983, 206 in 1984, ninety-five in 1985 and 117 in 1986. The same figures were mentioned in a note supplied by Bhai Bhosale in May 1987.
25. Statement showing the number of posts abolished by cotton textile mills in Greater Bombay during the period from January, 1982 to May, 1987. Office of the registrar of trade unions, Bombay, undated.
26. Cf. 'Textile Mills Strike-Impact on Other Industries', *Economic Times*, 15 March 1982.
27. 'Struggle to Swim Against Tide', *Economic Times*, 26 July 1982.
28. Letter of secretary, K.G. Pillai, of the Association of Merchants and Manufacturers of Textile Stores and Machinery to the author, 5 December 1987).
29. Ibid.
30. Ibid.
31. The *khanawl* is generally organized on regional-cum-lingustic principles and has several advantages to offer the immigrant in Bombay who has left his family behind in the village. The system of *khanwalis* allows the worker to enjoy the food he is accustomed to in the presence of people who speak the same language and share a similar background. Often, though certainly not always, the clients of a *khanawl* follow the same occupation or (as in the case of textile

workers) work in the same mill. The system is widely prevalent in the textile area and provides food at affordable prices. By its nature the *khanawl* also serves the function of a meeting place for workers where labour news can be exchanged.

32. M. Savara, 'Organising the Annapurna', *IDS Bulletin*, vol. 12, no. 3, 1981.
33. Pamphlet published by the Annapurna Mahila Mandal, Bombay, 1985.
34. *Report of Activities Annapurna Mahila Mandal*, Bombay, 1984.
35. That the Sangh played a much more active role in the whole policy of taking workers back than is suggested by Naik is, inter alia, confirmed by former Labour Commissioner P.J. Ovid who declared: 'There was an understanding between the Sangh and the millowners that only those workers who were accepted by the Sangh, would be taken back' (interview, 31 May 1987).
36. The text meant for permanent workers reads as follows:
Dear Sir, I have decided not to participate hereinafter in the illegal strike which commenced in the mill from ——— shift on ———. I want to make it clear that I did not join it willingly. I now want to resume work forthwith. On resumption of work I am willing to perform my duties sincerely and diligently and continue to give normal output and observe normal discipline whilst on duty. I, therefore, request you kindly to permit me to resume work. Yours faithfully,
Name: T.No.: Dept:
Source: ICMF files.
37. While discussing the aftermath of the strike Dada Samant said: 'Today a lot of workers are with the RMMS again, you can't deny it. Maybe because of the fringe benefits or such things. It may not be out of love but they do pay fees to that union' (interview 29 April 1986).

PART II

Coping with the Strike

Chapter Five

FIVE CASE STUDIES

SURVIVING IN THE VILLAGE

Jairam

Jairam had been in the prime of life, not even twenty-three, when he first came to Bombay. In spite of his youth, however, Jairam was not brimming with plans for the years ahead nor joyously anticipating the adventures the metropolis had to offer. True, in going to Bombay he ended a depressing chapter in his life but would the future be any better? Would he be able to find work, a place to live in, to save money? Overawed by the strong impression Bombay made on him at the time of his arrival he felt quite out of place and had he not reached the point of no return he would have returned forthwith. As it was he decided to make the best of it and considered himself fortunate in having an uncle in Bombay who had offered shelter.

Before he left Ashta, his village, there had been a severe drought in the area. The crops failed miserably and subsequently the family had been reduced to the point of starvation. The mishap caused Jairam to leave the village in search of employment. Prior to this disaster, at the time of the partition of the land between his father and uncle, Jairam had already considered the possibility of having to leave the village for want of a job. The time to do so seemed to have come now. As the drought had left them completely without an income, Jairam decided to go to Bombay and, after proper consultation with his father, who had no objections whatsoever, Jairam reached Bombay in April 1973.

Fortunately, adjusting to the Bombay way of life proved less of a problem than it had seemed the day he arrived. His uncle was kind to him and provided lots of useful information. He told him where and how to go and what to do, and Jairam often wondered what he would have done without him. One of the things that struck him was that the quality of the food in the city was much poorer than in his own village in Sangli district. Being a farmer's son he couldn't help but notice that the vegetables of the bhaji-walas* often seemed to be the left-overs from the market. The food cooked in his khanawal too lacked freshness of taste but it was cheap and that was what mattered. Jairam was attracted by the many ways in which Bombay could entertain its inhabitants although he realized soon enough that the fun wasn't meant for him as you needed money for that. He was fascinated too by the various ways people seemed capable of making a fast buck but somehow such opportunities always eluded him. After a while he discovered that money was one of the things to which he gave a great deal of thought. Staying in the village he had never taken a strong interest in it but now it grew to become his central concern.

What did not change, however, were his religious feelings. Today as before, Jairam performs a puja† daily. He believes that religion has to do with the coming together of people and with spending a full life in harmony. Jairam is happy that his wife shares his views. He knows that his religious feelings are quite different from those of his father who doesn't give a damn. It was not the only thing his father didn't care about. Actually, the only thing that really mattered to him was the availability of *daru*‡ and so his father was frequently drunk, for which Jairam disliked him greatly.

Leaving the village had also meant saying goodbye to his young wife to whom he had been married two years earlier. His marriage had been a traditional one, his father taking the initiative and settling the affair without so much as consulting him. Naturally, Jairam had entertained some thoughts on how his wife should be. He had wanted her to be good-looking and to possess a soft nature. He agreed with his father though that she should be a Maratha like himself. As it was he saw his bride for the first time at the time of the marriage ceremony and fortunately, the experience proved a pleasant one. Although Jairam himself feels that he has nothing to complain about, he is positive that unlike his father he will leave his children free in the choice of their

* Vendor of vegetables.

† Religious worship.

‡ Alcoholic beverage of varying quality.

partner. The bride only has to be of the same jati;[*] but otherwise they can do as they like. He is prepared to make an exception to this rule if the bride happens to be of a higher caste. In no way, however, should she be of a lower one. A girl from another community is, of course, out of the question. If his son ever dares to turn up with a Muslim girl, Jairam is sure to throw him out of the house.

Having lived with his uncle for some time it became clear that he couldn't stay there forever, so Jairam started looking around for somewhere else to stay. He was lucky again and found a cheap kholi[†] shared by ten people, all from Sangli. At present everyone has to pay the 'owner' of the room (who is living in the same kholi) Rs 25 per month. The 'owner', in fact, is only the main tenant who rented the room a long time ago for Rs 9 per month from the mill to which the entire chawl[‡] belongs. The rent remained unaltered throughout these years whereas the contributions of the roommates increased periodically. Yet no one complains for the rent is comparatively low and everyone knows that in places of the same size often twenty workers or more are accommodated. Jairam's room has a surface of 12 square metres and there is a corner for washing. Jairam considered the possibility of renting a separate room in which he could live with his family but he discarded the idea. He is aware that he would have to pay much more for a similar room and he is not willing to do that. Even if he could pay the rent he would still prefer his wife and children to remain in the village to help his parents to cultivate the land.

Although Jairam is happy that all of his roommates speak the same language, living in the kholi is no pleasure trip. There are frequent quarrels, usually connected with someone being drunk but it rarely comes to blows. There are also frictions related to the very limited space available. There is just room enough to unroll your mat when it is time to sleep and often someone puts his legs on yours while

---

[*] Jati means subcaste.

[†] The term means chamber or room and is also used to denote rooms inhabited by a complete family or a group of workers.

[‡] Long narrow building, of several storeys inhabited—but not exclusively—by industrial workers. The chawl consists of scores or even hundreds of rooms all opening on long corridors. These corridors play an important role in the social life within the chawl.

sleeping which creates an awkward situation. There are also quarrels when someone claims more space than others, for example, by using more pegs for clothes than he is supposed to or when a roommate takes more space in the garret where everyone stores their luggage.

Another source of friction occurs when someone takes too much time washing his clothes which poses problems for the others, given the limited time that water is available. Usually the quarrels do not escalate and are resolved by the owner before they reach boiling point. In order to minimize frictions the owner has given timings to the workers for washing their clothes. Those who have the second or third shift wash their clothes in the morning, those having first shift do so in the evening. Although drinking daru is forbidden in some kholis, Jairam's kholi doesn't know such a rule but one should behave properly after coming home. That much is expected from everyone.

Another aspect of kholi life sometimes causing trouble is the sexual urge. Whenever workers feel like having sex there are not too many options open to them. Some frequent prostitutes (this can be cheap but is not without risk), others, like Jairam, take leave and go to their village (but this, of course, doesn't solve the immediate problem) and still others let it pass which appears to be the most common practice. The absence of a balanced sex life causes tension but Jairam feels that this is not the kind of thing one can talk about easily. It helps a lot, however, if you are able to make friends with some of your roommates.

Usually workers in the same shift are very close to each other. They go out together for a walk, they drink tea or go shopping together and they joke with each other. Jairam feels that without a friend there is not much comfort in the kholi. Jairam is separated from his wife and children who are staying in the village ten hours away by bus. Twice or at the most thrice a year he undertakes this journey for a period of a week or a month. At the time of the harvest he usually spends a month in Ashta but the other visits are limited to a week. Jairam misses his family a lot and the sight of a happy couple passing by sometimes pains him as he is reminded of the impossibility of seeing his wife and children. At such times it helps to write a letter to his wife although she can't read it. Today his son, who has learnt to read and write at school, is capable of reading these letters out to her and he can also convey her messages to him, but earlier she had to look around in the village for someone willing to read out his letters.

Jairam is fond of his village and enjoys going back and this is not just because he will see his family. He likes working in the fields no matter what type of work it may be—harvesting, ploughing or sowing. Jairam feels that he is respected in his village but he is not to be fooled. He knows that many, particularly those who go out of their way to please him, want something from him. But there are also those who genuinely appreciate him without hope of tangible gain.

Having stayed in Bombay for nearly fifteen years now Jairam feels that he would like to settle down in Ashta after retirement but that moment is still a long way off and it is not certain that the plan is feasible. Jairam's thoughts nevertheless go back time and again to his village where he had a lot of friends in his childhood with whom he used to spend leisurely evenings, chatting or cracking jokes. They used to talk about farming, studies and most of all about employment. As there was not much scope for employment in the village it was a source of constant worry. Jairam occasionally pondered on the necessity of having to go to Bombay one day but the thought never appealed to him as he liked farming and village life.

However, one day it was brought home to him that this lightly discarded possibility might well prove to be a necessity. This was at the time that the property was divided between his father and uncle. In the days of his grandfather the family possessed 36 acres of land but when his father and uncle separated each received 18 acres which greatly reduced the viability of farming the land. Jairam felt very bad about it but, of course, he had no say in the matter. His highest aim in life had always been to become a farmer, proper education ranking second. The partition shattered this dream as the remaining land was insufficient to support him and his brother, and he realized that he had to find new avenues of employment.

After having secured a job in Jupiter Mill with the help of a cousin who was working there, Jairam did whatever he could to help his folks back home. From his hard-earned money as an assistant sizer in the mill he saved Rs 300 a month which he sent home. Unfortunately, little of all that money could be used for improvement of the land as most was needed to meet the daily expenses and the costs of educating his three children. Whatever was left was spent on land improvement or on hiring agricultural labourers to work the land. He sometimes sent extra money for this purpose but it was never much and he didn't know how to earn more.

Then one day he heard his roommates talk about a militant labour leader, a man called Dr Samant, who appeared to be very successful. He had managed, or so it was believed, to secure at one stroke a wage increase of hundreds of rupees in Empire Dyeing! Empire Dyeing was a textile unit, that much he knew. It seemed that this doctor had done the same in other industries as well. Jairam found it difficult to believe. In the days to follow he compared this information with the achievements of the RMMS over the past ten years and concluded that a wage increase of that magnitude would outdo all that the pallbearers of the millowners had been able to accomplish within a time span of fifteen years or more. Even Comrade Dange in his time had settled for a few pitiable rupees. Jairam also thought of the ever-recurring humiliation of having to pay subscription to a union for which he felt no sympathy. Although he was a Sangh member, Jairam found that his complaints were not looked into seriously and whenever he had a problem it was difficult to get the Sangh representatives even interested in it. Jairam hated the treatment meted out to workers in the mill whenever they made a mistake and unless you were a staunch supporter of the Sangh not much support from that side was to be expected. Work in the mills was degrading.

So here there seemed to be an opportunity of gaining a fantastic wage increase and getting rid of the Sangh in the process. It sounded too good to be true. Imagine, if this were to be true for all textile mills then Jairam could save more money than before and eventually he might be able to buy a few acres more! He need not even work in the mills till the age of retirement! His heart started beating faster. However, it was also said that this Dr Samant demanded complete support from his workers and that many of his battles went on and on, and some had it that at times his strikes lasted for years. But that surely was an exaggeration.

Jairam now tried to keep track of what was going on. At the time of bonus at the end of 1981, tension built up rapidly in the mill area and suddenly the workers of a number of mills struck work but not so in his mill. A couple of days later all seemed to be over when many of the workers resumed work, having obtained some concession or the other. Only in a few mills did the strike seem to drag on. But all of a sudden the whole picture changed drastically and Jairam was never sure what had happened. He suddenly found himself in a huge mass meeting and for the first time he heard the famous Dr Samant addressing the textile workers. *Arré*, how the doctor had castigated the millowners! That was different mettle than the wishy-washy stuff usually coming from the mouth of Sangh-walas. The atmosphere was explosive. Workers demanded a strike but the doctor warned against it and told them to wait, making it clear that a strike could be a long-drawn-out affair.

As soon as the MGKU was founded Jairam became a member. He was not the only one. Thousands upon thousands in those days thronged the office of the union to enlist. After that Jairam went to a few more rallies, growing ever more convinced that here was the man who could do it. Then everything gained momentum and before long an indefinite strike was declared starting from 18 January 1982. Jairam realized that the doctor was right and that the strike would last very long indeed, six months easily. He decided that his presence in Bombay was not required, and as he had no means of earning a living in the city he might be able to do some useful work at home. He thereupon prepared for his journey to Ashta. A day before the commencement of the strike he left Bombay.

His stay in the village proved to be very strenuous, much more difficult than he had imagined. His presence in Ashta for many months at a stretch without any income strained his relations with his brother to breaking point. Ever more frequently they quarrelled. Minor things could trigger off a major fight, such as when his brother's wife scolded his children, which his wife would not brook and certainly not now that Jairam was around. The women would become so mad with each other that they would only stop short of fighting. Jairam was pained but helpless. He himself felt deeply hurt when his brother's son didn't pay him the respect he was entitled to. The show of disrespect escalated to quarrels so unnerving that in the end they decided to separate. When the partition became a fact he felt relieved but also very sad because of the inevitability of it all. His hopes of doing some farming later on were shattered once again and this time more thoroughly than before. Prior to the strike they had possessed 18 acres and now each was left with 9 acres only. In the course of less than twenty years the property of his grandfather had been slashed to pieces of 9 acres.

Meanwhile the strike was dragging on. There were many textile workers in his village and they used to meet to discuss the latest developments but Jairam was not so keen on that. He preferred to listen to the radio, to read the Marathi dailies and, occasionally, had a chat with a visitor coming from Bombay. The hopes for an early settlement faded out gradually and so did the expectation of a substantial wage increase. At the time of the first proposal of CM Bhosale (after six months), Jairam felt that it would be better to accept it although the CM merely offered a paltry Rs 30 increase and an advance which had to be paid back but then what would be gained by prolonging the struggle? Looking about him Jairam thought that most workers shared his view although few openly said so. Yet, the strike was not called off. He wondered how the decision to continue the strike was arrived at. Did the other workers not face starvation? Did they still believe in a miracle?

However, he was in no hurry to return to the mills as he first wanted to sort out the problems related to the partition which had thrown new tasks and responsibilities on his shoulders. Besides, there had been persistent reports about violence in Bombay, even murders. Going by the rumours one had to be particularly careful about threats coming from Samant-walas. So Jairam decided that it would be wiser to stick it out a little longer. Luckily, food was not a problem but he and his family, including his parents, had to economize on clothes and tea. Outings were not even thought of.

As time passed Jairam grew ever more disappointed with the government which apparently didn't care for the fate of the workers. So far the government had only supported the millowners in condemning the strike and insisting that the workers resume duty but no guarantee was given that the workers would get what they wanted. So why would the workers do that? There was also no sign that the blasted Sangh would disappear from the scene although everyone could see that it had no support worth the name. Jairam pulled on for another seven months after which financial problems became so acute that he decided to resume duty irrespective of the consequences. His morale was at its lowest ebb. Jairam had now come to the conclusion that strikes were useless as long as the Sangh was tied to the Congress. The Congress could only be toppled by elections and what were the chances of that? Surely not with the help of Samant's Kamgar Aghadi! There were far too few workers for that. Besides, workers adhered to different political parties so it would not be possible to unite the workers under one banner. Jairam decided that unions and parties were all useless. He would not belong to any of them in future.

On 23 February 1983, thirteen months after he had left Bombay, Jairam started working again in the mills after signing a statement, the contents of which he was never told.

FROM *BADLI* TO PERMANENT WORKER: THE FOLLOWER

Anil

Anil's coming to Bombay at the age of nineteen was largely determined by considerations of employment, just as it was in the case of most other workers from his village. He felt that there was no point in staying any longer in Velipale, his village in Sangli district, as his family land is rocky and not very fertile. Only during the monsoon are the crops (usually jowar* and wheat) sufficiently large to provide an income. Besides, there was his younger brother to look after. Anil felt that the boy should have a proper education. In due time he would be able to work on the 10 acres of land they possessed. Anil himself was not lacking in education. At one time he had wanted to become a civil engineer but he soon realized that the financial position of his parents was such that this was not feasible; at least not without great sacrifice.

Anil had passed his SSC and although his father (a former school teacher who became a farmer after he and his brother separated) had insisted that he should continue his studies, Anil successfully opposed the idea. Instead, he decided to go to Bombay and earn money as the responsibility for his younger brother's education (who was only four at the time) and for his sister's marriage was now on his shoulders, or so he felt. An elder sister had been married off already. His parents vehemently resisted his going to Bombay but in the end Anil's will prevailed.

---

* By far the most important cereal grown in Maharashtra in terms of area cultivated and out-turn in tonnes.

This is not to say that whatever young Anil wanted came to pass. In the matter of his marriage, for instance, which took place a couple of months after the start of the long textile strike, Anil had made it perfectly clear that he was not interested at all. He even opposed it but in vain. His father was in no mood to give in and arranged it all, saying that one could not wait for a strike to end in order to get married. Besides, Anil himself repeatedly said that the end of the strike was near. The best Anil could do under the circumstances was to tell his father that in any case his future wife had to be educated, a condition to which his father did not object. Anil took care to instruct his father that his bride should in no way be more educated than he himself was. Good looks or an agreeable temperament did not really matter to him. His father managed to find a Maratha girl who, like him, had passed her SSC and belonged to the same jati. After due consultation with the astrologer, the time of marriage was fixed and without further ado Anil got married.

Anil has one son now and reflecting on his own marriage he says that when the boy is grown up he should be free to choose his own partner, that is, within certain limitations: the bride has to belong to the same jati. However, in the unlikely event of his son falling in love with someone other than a Maratha or even belonging to a different community altogether, say a Christian girl, Anil feels that he might be forced to give in. There is not much one can really do. He realizes that his views in these matters and particularly those with regard to untouchability have undergone considerable change through his exposure to Bombay life. The groundwork for these changes, however, was laid by his father in the village. Anil remembers vividly that 'untouchables' in Vaipale were given water as they were not allowed to get it themselves and it was poured from a height. In Bombay such things were unthinkable. It just could not be so. Wherever you went, you were bound to come into physical contact with other people. In the market or in the always overcrowded 'locals'* your sweat mingled with that of others, squeezed as you were between your neighbours. But also in restaurants caste differences disappeared. You might be

* The 'local' is the word used by Bombayites to denote the railway system in the city. The term may be used to indicate a train, trains or the whole system of local train transport.

served by 'untouchable' waiters and the same was true for buses and the cinema.

Living in Bombay he was not really bothered about these things as his father had given him a good example of how to deal with such problems. Many years ago his father brought home a small boy whose father had died. The boy belonged to the Scheduled Castes* but his mother was in no position to look after him and so the boy remained with them till he was nineteen years old. He is married now and Anil claims to love him as a brother. Actually, Anil feels that even today his father is a more liberal-minded person than he himself is although he is by no means a bigot. As for religion, Anil doesn't consider himself a religious man. He is convinced that religions are made by people, not by gods. His wife, however, is definitely religious and upholds all Hindu beliefs, practises puja, undertakes fasts and celebrates all the major festivals. Anil cannot bring himself to join in all that but he doesn't object to it either. He thinks of himself as broad-minded and prides himself on having seen churches and mosques from the inside and even of having attended a Muslim marriage once.

Leaving the village was not at all difficult for Anil as there were many things he disliked. He particularly hated people who drank too much and those who used to fight. There was also a lot of political bickering going on in Vaipale. The major groups contesting for power were the Congress and the Janata. The Janata was clearly outnumbered but didn't eschew confrontation. Whenever they got a chance, adherents of one party would beat up those of the other, something which Anil thoroughly disliked. At times the fights threatened to escalate into riots. Anil felt that the only substantial contribution the political parties made in the village was to keep the people divided. There were other factors too that made migration to Bombay seem attractive. Living in the village was rather boring as there was little or no amusement and Anil had high hopes that

* The term 'Scheduled Castes' (SC) refers to castes which have been listed as such by the government. In the past, members of these castes have been given numerous names like outcastes, untouchables, panchamas or exterior castes. The term SC has been officially adopted since the Government of India Act 1935. It should be noted that the definition of SC allows for the inclusion of other than untouchable castes although this is rarely the case (Van Wersch, 184: 16–17).

Bombay might offer much more entertainment. Then, of course, Bombay was a magnet because of the employment opportunities it offered. Anil was convinced that a person with his qualifications would surely find a good job with a decent income. There were so many opportunities, Anil had thought, that one would get confused!

Anil reached Bombay early in 1978. He was instantly taken in by the bustle of metropolitan life. Everyone seemed so busy and everybody seemed to know where to go and what to do. He was surprised by the great distances one had to travel in Bombay. There was so much to see, to hear, to do! Anil was thrilled. Gradually, however, it dawned on him that Bombay not only has many faces to show but also different faces to different people. Some of these faces he would never get to know intimately. The southern part of the city, for example, with its wide avenues and parks, its huge hotels, offices and theatres was an area where he would venture not even once a year. His territory was predominantly Lalbaug with its many mills, the chawls, the overcrowded streets, the heaps of garbage.

There were other shadowy sides to living in Bombay. While in the village he had been told that he would be accommodated in a kholi belonging to the Satya Shodak Samaj Mandal. It had been impressed upon him that he was fortunate in this. The SSSM was an organization formed by workers from the same area who had got together for the purpose of purchasing a room in Bombay, hoping thereby to reduce living costs. Everyone staying in the kholi was asked to contribute Rs 20 per month to meet the costs of maintenance and to pay the bills for electricity and water. It had seemed a fair amount and Anil happily agreed. Upon arrival, however, Anil found the accommodation very depressing: fifteen and at times even twenty-five people staying in one small place, half of them sleeping in a garret. It was quite unlike the village. There was no room, no air. There were only two small windows, one facing the chawl opposite theirs and one through which the dark and dirty passage leading to the latrines could be seen. But there was no better alternative either and in that respect the information he had received proved to be correct. He had no choice but to adjust himself to kholi life, which he did.

Lack of space in the room appeared to be the major source of trouble in the kholi. Alcohol was fortunately not a problem as there was a rule that no one should enter the room after drinking. And if someone had had alcohol he took care not to disturb the roommates. Whenever there is a quarrel, which is fortunately not often, the others usually intervene and generally the problems are settled amicably. Once a month they have a meeting in which they discuss all the important matters regarding the kholi, including quarrels. There is genuine affection for each other and an atmosphere of camaraderie. When the workers gather they talk about many things but mostly about problems at work, their native places and politics. Whenever someone feels homesick, village life is sure to be the topic of the day. If there is a special occasion, for example, a marriage party, a puja or a funeral, the workers go together to attend the function. Anil has a friend in the kholi with whom he is very close. They always share the same shift and therefore sleep and eat at the same time. In fact, it was this friend who got Anil a job. One day he came home and informed Anil that Finlay Mills needed workers. He had seen it on the notice board. Anil acted swiftly and got the job. Anil likes to roam about with his friend on long walks.

Nowadays Anil feels at home in the kholi although he would prefer to stay in a separate room with his wife and son if that were not too expensive. If it were possible to get proper accommodation, say for Rs 100 or even Rs 150, he would do it, but he knows that it will be next to impossible to find something suitable for less than Rs 300. As Anil and his wife are both educated they can at least write letters to each other. That is a great consolation that most of the workers do not have. Most workers are as a result unaware of all that is going on in their village unless someone returns from a visit and informs them.

Ever since he started working in the mills Anil used to send home Rs 400 every month. This money was mainly utilized for improving the land, digging wells or hiring agricultural labour. For the future, however, Anil has other plans. He looks forward to returning to Vaipale to settle down. Another five or seven years of sweating in the mills will enable him to save enough money to open a grain shop in the village or otherwise he will go into the milk business. Anil is confident that he can manage this. His present preference for the village is chiefly the outcome of his experience with the working and living conditions in Bombay. When his fascination for Bombay life wore off Anil started appreciating village life again. He enjoys going back to Vaipale and he devotes considerable time and energy to maintaining all ties and links. The village folk treat him very respectfully as he is a man of the world now, one who lives and works in Bombay. Four or five times a year he visits his village for periods of one to three weeks. The distance makes more frequent visits impossible.

Anil was not taken by surprise when the textile strike started as he had seen it coming. The workers had been dissatisfied for as long as he could remember. There were good reasons for that too. The wages had been stagnant for a decade or more. The way the workers were treated inside the mills by supervisors and the Sangh was hard to digest. What disturbed him most was that workers were humiliated in front of others. They were scolded often and sometimes even beaten. When he himself was scolded once he felt like hammering the supervisor. Anil also disliked the long hours of continuous work, the heat and the deafening noise of the looms although he is less disturbed by that now than before. Having worked in the mills for nearly ten years now, Anil, who looks older than his age would suggest, knows that he will not allow his son to work in the mills—not even if he can't find work anywhere else.

Reading about Dr Samant in the newspapers had given Anil the feeling that here at last was a leader who was not corrupt, one who did not squander the demands of the workers for a few rupees. Prior to the strike Anil had been a member of the Sangh but this had not been a love marriage, rather one of convenience. It is not that the Sangh-walas did not look after his complaints but he disliked the way they acted. Anil also resented the harassment of workers who chose not to join the Sangh. Besides, the wage increases secured by the Sangh were poor, to say the least. He, therefore, had no difficulty in joining the strike. Anyway, given the overwhelming support for the strike it was obvious that the strike would last a few days only, a fortnight perhaps. After that the millowners would have to give in, pressurized by the government. True, the doctor had said that the strike could last even six months but that, of course, was to frighten the millowners. With such tremendous support it would be over soon, of that he was certain.

Immediately after the strike began he left for Vaipale as it was anyway time to go there. Reading *Sakal* every day and listening to the radio he found to his dismay that the strike, although a complete success, was not over even after one month which was puzzling. The best he could do, therefore, was to stay where he was. While remaining in the village he would occupy himself working in his own fields. He was lucky because he did have some work to do. How many workers, Anil wondered, would like to take his place? Those who had to remain in Bombay, what did they do? However, he soon found that he couldn't put his heart into cultivating the land, no matter how hard he tried. Removing weeds he thought a particularly tedious job and he had to do that often. His daily routine was quite simple: getting up early and drinking tea, going for work, returning home by 11 a.m., having lunch and afterwards working again till the evening.

When weeks became months Anil wondered what had gone wrong. At the beginning of the strike it had seemed so obvious that a fortnight would suffice. He knew perfectly well that Dr Samant had predicted a long-drawn-out battle, an 'indefinite strike' lasting six months at least. But then, how could the doctor say so when actually everyone had joined the strike! Anil couldn't think of one person who hadn't. Confronted with such unity of mind, such massive support, the government would step in and tell the millowners to come to terms. It just could not be otherwise. This hope kept Anil alive and afloat, and on the strength of this conviction the first 100 days were completed.

But when the duration of the strike had to be counted in three digits rather than in two, Anil was forced to review the chances of success. In July 1982, at the time of the first proposal of CM Bhosale, hope surged in his heart like that in those of countless others. Maybe now there was a chance for an honourable settlement. However, the terms offered by the CM were an insult. Even so the CM seemed bent on making the workers swallow it. Anil felt that they might as well accept nothing and go back to work, just like that! Rs 30 ... after all this struggle ... what could one do with that?! Anil's belief that endurance in the end would pay was shaken but not shattered. After all, the mills were incurring heavy losses every day, at least that was what the newspapers said. This could not go on. It just didn't make sense. All right, a demand of Rs 400 was not realistic but an offer of Rs 30 was a shame! Who could accept that?

But when Anil's indignation subsided he also felt that if the doctor had accepted the offer, Anil would have done the same. The work in the fields was boring and straining. In the evening he felt his muscles paining all over but most of all his back. Yet, the doctor had rejected the offer out of hand so there was nothing else to do as to pull on. In this fashion the second 100 days were completed and then the third drew to an end and still there was no solution in sight. In the beginning the textile workers in the village had gathered regularly in order to discuss the strike but these meetings became fewer as the strike dragged on. The zeal of those who had defended the strike vociferously in the beginning was clearly on the wane.

Then on 31 October 1982, the CM made a new proposal. However, as Anil rapidly came to understand, the second one was not different from the first, except that the advance offered to the workers was increased from Rs 650 to Rs 1500. This money the workers would have to pay back in instalments. The new proposal, like the earlier one, didn't talk about compensation for wages lost nor about a wage increase apart from the pittance which had been offered earlier. Sure enough, some committee was going to be appointed to look into the grievances of the workers but only a gullible person could put his faith in that. All this was humiliating! It was all too obvious now that the government was in league with the millowners in wanting to break the morale of the workers by hook or by crook. And what could the poor workers do against that? The seeds of doubt in Anil's mind, which had been lingering ever since the first proposal, started taking root more firmly now. Anil couldn't discard them as easily as before. What was in store for the striking workers ... what for him? Notices of dismissal had been appearing periodically in several newspapers. How much longer could they hold out? How realistic was it to expect that a third offer would be any better? If ten months had not been enough for the millowners to see reason, would twelve months make any difference? Had the time arrived for the workers to swallow their pride?

But there were other aspects to be considered. Rumours about violence perpetrated by workers and unions were persistent and kept growing. The newspapers reported stories of workers who had resumed and who were beaten up by Samant-walas. There had been stabbings, murders ... not just one but many. Some said that as many as ten workers had already been killed but figures of twenty and twenty-five could also be heard. Anil sincerely disliked violence. It gave him a nauseating feeling to think that workers like him had been killed only because they couldn't stick it out any longer. Were they really at fault, were they traitors? Could one honestly believe that these workers were blacklegs? Had not the duration of the strike surprised them as much as it had surprised him? Whatever the case, it seemed wiser to remain in the village for some more time … wait for the violence to subside. But how much more could he take? Too many workers had suffered far too long, and to hear from the leaders and a fast dwindling number of diehards that theirs was a 'heroic struggle' didn't make it any better. Where was the heroism? Surely not in the decision of so many workers like him to postpone the return to Bombay for fear of being beaten up or worse.

There should be an end to everything, Anil felt. He wondered how the decisions were taken in Bombay. Who took them and on what basis? He knew that the doctor used to consult the workers at mass meetings but was that all there was to it? Was it fair to expect workers to raise their voice against a prolongation of the strike when Dr Samant taunted them to carry on? Anil knew from experience how difficult it was not to raise your hand if you disagreed when surrounded by those who loudly proclaimed approval. Anil preferred to cast a vote in writing in matters of such great importance. He for one would have voted against continuation of the strike now. That is, if he had been asked but no one ever asked him.

Anil slowly veered round to the point where he felt that he must go back to Bombay, come what may. There was so much to lose and so little to gain by staying on in the village. Nearly one long dreadful year had passed now and the end of the struggle was as far off as ever. Anil felt that if the mill was prepared to take him back there was quite a chance that he could become permanent as he had never been a trouble-maker in the past. But every day longer he stayed in Vaipale, he figured, his chances of being taken back dwindled, not to mention the possibility of being promoted from *badli* to permanent worker. According to the newspapers and the radio, more and more workers were resuming duty. Several workers from his village had quietly left already.

Another two weeks and Anil undertook the journey to Bombay. He was taken back after signing a statement saying that he had taken part in an illegal strike and that he would not cause trouble in future. He was not given the time to read the statement, he had just to sign it. The supervisor who handed the text over to him refrained from explaining the contents and Anil in his turn wisely refrained from asking as he did not want to jeopardize his chances of getting work. Four more months and Anil became permanent. Another few months and Anil, who had warmly supported the MGKU during the strike, rejoined the RMMS, and for the same reasons. As before the Sangh seemed to be in full command and like before he became a member for fear of harassment. Those who refused to pay membership fees were given warnings, fined and charge sheeted by supervisors whenever they made a mistake. One simply *had* to become a member of the Sangh. Nothing had changed really. The separation of the representative union had been of short duration. The marriage was on again.

FROM PERMANENT WORKER TO *BADLI*: THE ACTIVIST

Shamrao

Going by the number of his children (four boys and three girls), Shamrao has to be considered a man of some consequence. His weight, however, can be judged more accurately from his hold over the workers. His far from impressive physical appearance, a flyweight and a height of merely five feet, is deceptive and once in his presence one forgets all that. With his sparkling eyes, clear voice, straightforward talk and vivid gestures Shamrao easily gains the confidence of those around him. It is not surprising then that the workers are usually willing to follow him as they have learned to trust his judgement.

Fifty-two years old, Shamrao was a boy of seventeen when he left Rashivade (Kolhapur District) to try his luck in Bombay. His father was a farmer with a few acres of land. It had been a practice of long standing in his family to send one of the family members to Bombay for a period of three years. This family tradition grew out of necessity as their income in Rashivade was marginal and the earnings from the family members in Bombay meant a substantial contribution to the family income. In this way his father had worked as a *begari** and one day it was Shamrao's turn.

---

* A casual labourer (for example, porter), often employed in construction work.

As a child Shamrao never had any clear idea as to what he would like to do. The only thing he knew was that he wanted a job and the job he finally found (as a weaver in a textile mill) was better than he had expected. Village folk feel that the job of a textile worker is one of some stature and Shamrao, oblivious of the part played by his pleasant manners, believes that this largely explains why he is always a welcome guest. In any case, his popularity didn't stem from his achievements in sports for the only thing he ever did in that field was swimming in the village well. His performance in the educational field was only slightly better although he belonged to the first batch of pupils when a school was opened in the village in 1943. When he was ten, however, his father decided that he had had enough schooling and Shamrao started working with him in the fields. For six, seven years he worked the land, after which the time had come for him to go to Bombay.

The thought of leaving Rashivade at once attracted and frightened him. There was nothing in the village he disliked. Shamrao was fond of the village folk, the good food and the fresh, clean air. He was apprehensive of Bombay and doubted that the city would be able to compensate for that. He regretted having to say goodbye to his friends and, more specifically, to his neighbour, a man who had always impressed him deeply. This neighbour was illiterate but a social worker in the true sense of the word. Once Shamrao overheard a quarrel between him and his wife. The problem had been that the neighbour had offered half the day's food to a worker who had just returned from the mills and wanted to settle down in the village. His wife rebuked him severely as they themselves had hardly anything to eat and their children were starving. Shamrao listened breathlessly to the quarrel, pressing his ears against the thin wall separating their houses. The neighbour stuck to his guns and Shamrao learned that day that sacrifice is the greatest service one individual can render to another. Then and there he decided that he would try to become like that man.

It was 1953 when Shamrao first entered Bombay. Although Bombay in those days looked quite different from what it is now Shamrao was taken aback by the splendour of it all: enormous buildings, factories, trains, trams and wide roads. He felt that he had entered a different world and he was so overwhelmed by the experience that for years together he didn't dare to venture beyond his direct neighbourhood for fear of losing his way. During the first five years' he only went from his home to the mill and back. Although he was overawed by the city, he saw no point in returning to Rashivade when his period in Bombay was over. Shamrao felt that he could do better by remaining in the city. He maintained, nevertheless, strong emotional bonds with his village although he couldn't go there often. The distance and his growing obligations in Bombay prevented that but he is certain that he will return to Rashivade after retirement.

Over the years Shamrao saw the quality of life rapidly deteriorating in the metropolis. The crowds kept on swelling, taxing the public transport system to breaking point, but to his great surprise the system never collapsed. Today there are far more beggars in the streets and near the stations than when he first came to Bombay. The scene changed irresistibly and tension increased. So did corruption. In fact, corruption reached a level he would not have been able to dream of while in the village. Gradually, Shamrao noticed that Bombay started eating into his guts. One day it occurred to him that whereas money had never really mattered to him before, it was now a primary aim. Not only that, he also found that while he had always been able to manage somehow in the village, he now never seemed to have enough although he earned far more than he had ever thought he would. He then realized that he had been absorbing the Bombay way of life. But could it be otherwise? Even today Shamrao is at a loss to explain where the money goes.

When he first came to the city Shamrao stayed with his uncle. Finding work was not much of a problem, within a month he started working as a *badli* in a mill. However, living with his uncle, who was a medical doctor and an activist for the Congress, was not so pleasant. Day after day Shamrao saw his uncle taking money from even very poor people, something which he thoroughly disliked. Later he felt that he was treading familiar ground when he discovered that within the mill the Sangh too took money from workers and it was not clear what they offered in return. The Sangh was also related to the Congress. As it happened, shortly after his arrival in the city he came in touch with dedicated social workers and trade unionists. Their ideas were new to him but he took an instant liking to them and rapidly developed views on the same lines. While working in the mills he observed what one particular union, the unrecognized Lal Bauta, had tried to do for the workers although their means were limited. This sharply contrasted with the attitude of the Sangh. It didn't take Shamrao much time to decide to join the Lal Bawta in which he remained active till the outbreak of the great strike.

Shamrao had only been in Bombay for a short while when his father and uncle decided that it was time for him to get married. They went about making enquiries. While Shamrao had a full-time job in adjusting himself to life in the metropolis and learning new skills in order to qualify as a weaver in the mill, his father found a suitable match. Without informing Shamrao, the parents of the girl and his father decided on the marriage. When Shamrao learned about it he was quite upset and refused to comply with his father's wishes. He felt that at twenty-one he was much too young and also that it would be better first to find a room in Bombay. The prospect of being married and having to keep your wife in the village didn't appeal to him at all. So when his father proposed the marriage Shamrao opposed.

But things took a different turn when Shamrao received word from his closest friend that he would be stupid to let the occasion pass as the girl was a gem. Not only was she from the same village and jati (Maratha) but she was also sweet-looking and very kind-hearted. Shamrao started thinking it over and with his father and uncle stressing his filial duties on one side and his friend spelling out the charms of the girl at the other, he was finally won over. Shamrao had warned his father and uncle that he didn't want an ambitious wife, nor should she have high expectations about economic prosperity either. About her education he wasn't bothered in the least as he himself had very little of that. Prema, as she was, fitted this profile to perfection. Why, she even surpassed his expectations manifold!

Although Shamrao himself found a happy companion in this way, both he and his wife feel that their own children should be free to choose their partners themselves but these future brides and bridegrooms have got to be Marathas. Shamrao knows that he will try his level best to see that at least that condition is fulfilled. With a helpless gesture he says: 'Of course, if my son falls in love with a girl from the Backward Classes and insists on marrying her ... what can we do?' With a twinkle in his eyes he adds that he would even accept a Dutchman as his son-in-law if it came to that.

Soon after the marriage they moved to Bombay where they stayed for many years in an utterly inadequate room which wasn't maintained at all and lacked all facilities. One day the roof collapsed. It proved to be a blessing in disguise as the Repair Board offered them the room in which they are staying now and for which they pay Rs 50 per month. It is a fairly big concrete room (15 square metres) in a housing block in the suburbs of Bombay. There are similar housing blocks in the same area and there is ample space in between. The distance Shamrao has to travel daily to the mill is a problem but otherwise they are happy with their present accommodation.

His wife keeps the place very clean. With a simple construction of wood and cloth they created a kitchen and a corner for washing. There is a shelf for crockery, a desk, a fan and even a bed. That is all the furniture there is. The walls are adorned with pictures of Hindu deities although Shamrao isn't exactly a religious-minded person. True, he daily observes puja and he enjoys the fun of festivals but there the matter ends. Shamrao is convinced that religion ought to be confined to temples and homes, and nowhere in between. Any sort of exhibition of religious feelings in the streets is no good as it easily provokes hurt feelings or envy. And that just doesn't serve any purpose. His wife takes a stronger interest in religious matters but shares his view that religion is something for the inward life, not for the outward.

At the time of the strike Shamrao was in the forefront. He had watched the rising star of Dr Samant and felt greatly attracted to him. It was wonderful to see how the doctor spoke for the workers and how he inspired confidence in them. The man was something of a magnet. For some time it seemed that the Lal Bawta was going to support the doctor but soon it appeared that their support was at best verbal. To his dismay he found that before long the Lal Bawta also stopped verbally supporting the doctor and a few months after that they even started criticizing him. This was more than Shamrao could stomach and he was greatly disappointed. Could they not see that Dr Samant was the right man at the right time? He bitterly remembered the good old days when Lal Bawta had stood with the workers. Why was the same not possible now? As soon as the MGKU was founded Shamrao shifted his loyalty from the Lal Bawta to Samant's union. If not with the Lal Bawta then without it!

His faith in the doctor hasn't wavered since. Not even during the strike. Yes, the strike brought hardship, tremendous suffering even, but at no point did he feel that the workers should give in. The fight should be to the finish. And so it was to be. Shamrao is fully aware that it would have been very difficult for him, if not impossible, to continue the strike without the full backing of his wife and children. The strike threatened to have a devastating effect on his family life. His daughter's marriage, for example, had to be postponed. Although Shamrao made a desperate effort to continue the education of his children, they failed to pass their exams as there was no money for the necessary books and other requirements. It was a boon, though, that his prospective son-in-law was a lance naik* in the army and he helped a lot by giving clothes, money and chappals† as he was greatly in sympathy with the struggle of the textile workers.

During the first three months of the strike Shamrao was very active. As vice president of the zone-committee in his zone he got up early and made a round of the mills. The mills in his zone comprised India United No. 1, Morarjee Mills No. 1, Finlay, Digvijay, Jam Mills and Western India. It took him a couple of hours to complete his round. He checked whether workers had resumed work or stocks had been removed from the premises of the mills. Having satisfied himself that the strike was still in full swing, he helped arranging meetings or attended meetings arranged by others. These first months appeared to be most revealing as the mills were completely paralysed by the strike although the MGKU didn't exercise any muscle power. It wasn't even necessary to have picket lines! Shamrao's committee looked after the distribution of money and foodgrains that were collected by others. He feels that the mill committees and zonal committees were crucial for the prolongation and the success of the strike. Asked why then so few workers were aware of the work of these committees he points to their stay in the villages, their lack of interest in union affairs and the need to search for other jobs.

Shamrao himself was forced to look for alternative employment as, quite unexpectedly, the strike was not over in the two months

---

* A non-commissioned officer (NCO) in command of a group of jawans (soldiers).

† Slippers.

he thought it would take. He knew, of course, that Dr Samant had predicted a long battle but looking at the enthusiasm of the workers he had believed that this could not be the case. When it was clear that his calculations were wrong, Shamrao started working as a *begari* in the construction of houses, earning thereby Rs 15 per day. He hated that type of work and gave it up after a month to start working on powerlooms in Madanpura in Bombay. Here he had to work for twelve hours a day earning the same amount of money. The thought that this work could be considered a strike-breaking act comes to him as a surprise. Shamrao is unable to see any link between the long and wearisome hours at the powerloom and work in the mills. He wishes to believe that even if the powerlooms produced cloth this could never have been much and, in any case, it couldn't have had a bearing on the outcome of the strike.

Shamrao talked often and for long hours to the workers during the strike and he is convinced that most of them wanted a settlement after about six months but even so the workers were not prepared to accept just anything. What to do? Casting a vote for the continuation of the struggle or ending the strike would perhaps be appropriate. It would surely reflect the mood of the workers in a better way, but how to do it? To start with, it would be next to impossible to reach the workers who had gone to the villages. Forget the workers in the villages, it might prove to be equally difficult and impossible to organize a vote in such a manner that at least the workers remaining in Bombay would all have a say in the matter. Who had the addresses? In what odd jobs were they all involved?

Shamrao believes that the doctor simply didn't get a chance to settle the matter even if he had wanted to. One of the reasons was that the government refused to oblige and didn't enter into talks with him. The second reason was connected with this. As a settlement had been made effectively impossible in this manner, Shamrao feels that the doctor was left with no alternative other than to call off the strike unconditionally but this would have meant the end of his hold over the workers. His grip on them, his reputation for militancy would have been shattered and he would have been just one more labour leader. This, of course, should not happen. Shamrao states that there were many workers who honestly didn't know what to make of the situation. Calling off the strike would mean that they could return to the mills, followed by a few dismissals, but it would also mean that all their suffering had been in vain. Also, there always seemed a chance of a settlement just around the corner, a settlement that would make up for all the losses they had incurred so far and one that might well be a monument for posterity. Again, the praise showered upon them by posterity was uncertain and far-off whereas the pangs of hunger were real and immediate.

When the strike showed no sign of coming to an end, Shamrao decided that he should try to get other work. With the help of a friend he got a job as salesman in a shop selling kitchen utensils. He started at a salary of Rs 300 per month but in the course of the next two and a half years this was increased to Rs 750 as the owner was happy with his work. Meanwhile his financial position worsened and his debts grew in spite of all attempts to live as simply as possible. There were quarrels at home because of the lack of money and when one of his sons fell ill, he had difficulty in getting him admitted to a hospital. But on the whole the family stood behind him.

While working in the shop Shamrao tried to follow the developments as best as he could. Right after its foundation, the MGKU had started legal proceedings to oust the Sangh and become the sole representative of the textile workers. It was said that if Samant's union had a larger membership than the Sangh for a period of six months, the MGKU would automatically become the recognized union. Shamrao had entertained high hopes of this as an overwhelming majority of the workers stood behind Samant. The first blow, however, had come in April 1982 when the registrar of unions rejected MGKU's plea to derecognize the Sangh. But the MGKU had successfully opposed this decision and the High Court had ordered a new investigation. Shamrao felt sure that this time it would not be difficult to prove who really represented the workers.

The registrar took so much time to figure out the membership of the unions that even a judge of the High Court was annoyed and Shamrao's confidence was boosted when he heard of it. But in November when Shamrao had nearly forgotten what was going on in the courtrooms, the registrar finally came to a decision. The verdict baffled him. The registrar had found that the Sangh was absolutely lacking in membership but, contrary to what one would expect, this didn't mean that derecognition of the Sangh was to follow. The registrar concluded that due to the strike the Sangh might not have been able to collect membership fees. Shamrao failed to understand what this was all about. He went to the union office and talked to leaders of the MGKU but they couldn't grasp it either. What nonsense! Had they gone nuts? How could the Sangh ever have collected membership fees now that they could not use pressure tactics! Was not the complete success of the strike the best proof that the workers despised the Sangh? He admitted that more and more workers started going back, forced as they were by starvation, but what did that have to do with it? Shamrao's confidence in the law, which had been weakened in the course of the years by the realization that workers gained precious little by going to court, was utterly shaken. It received a blow from which it was not to recover.

Shamrao now bitterly contemplated the possibility of the Sangh remaining in power within the mills for ever. He thought of the prevalent malpractices, the promotion of young workers (Sangh-walas) before senior workers, of the pressure put on the workers on pay day, of the abuse to which workers were subjected who refused to budge. He himself had been relatively free from harassment as he was known for his opposition to the Sangh and this position offered some protection. They knew he had considerable support among the workers who would rally behind him if need be. Shamrao had been often enraged by the treatment of workers inside the mills. Why should you humiliate a worker in front of others even if he had made a mistake? And who wouldn't make mistakes given the obsolete machinery they had to operate and the inferior quality of the yarn or the cloth they had to work with?

Way back Shamrao had decided that he would not allow his children to work in the mills. The working conditions are rotten. One gets used to that, of course, but it affects your health all the same: the terrible noise in the loomsheds, the suffocating heat in some departments, the air filled with fine cotton particles which you breathe day after day, year after year, filling your lungs till they collapse. Working in the mills was madness. Sitting on the sidewalk selling fruit or vegetables would be better even if it earned less. What is the use of earning more if your body is broken ... and your spirit along with it? Shamrao mused on such things while working in the shop. Financial problems kept nagging him and in March 1983, when it was clear that the workers could not win, he returned to the mill to resume work. He was sent away, however, with the message that there was no work for him. The reason became plain a couple of months later when the government took over the management of thirteen mills in Bombay. Gross mismanagement had brought the mill to the abyss and the government officials were appointed to put the mill back on the rails.

Shamrao was hopeful that he would get back his job now that the government had stepped in. But his trials had not come to an end yet. Although he went back several times it took another two years before Shamrao was allowed to enter the mill and when he did he learned that he had lost his permanency like hundreds of other workers. He had given all his life to the prosperity of the industry but now his status had been reduced to that of a *badli*, one who could be disposed of any time that seemed convenient. He received a card on which was stamped 'Temporary'. When he objected to this he was curtly informed that he could take it or leave it. Shamrao took it. He merely clings to the hope now that he reaches retirement before the axe falls.

THE STRIKE-BREAKER

Haricharan

Haricharan, forty-four years old, was one of those who opposed the strike. It is not that he was unable to see why his fellow workers wanted it but like many others who had long ago come from the north (Uttar Pradesh) in search of employment, he saw no point in putting a job at risk for the sake of a wage increase. Haricharan felt that the demands made by the textile workers were unreasonable and as he had spent a lifetime practising to be reasonable, he found it impossible to support the strike. Naturally, he was aware that his view wasn't shared by many but he didn't bother about that. Right is right and wrong is wrong, that is what he was taught and that is what he has been teaching his children. In upholding his beliefs Haricharan is not a little helped by his appearance. He certainly is a muscular man and that too, of a size that makes you think twice before attacking him. However, with his full-flowing beard and quiet eyes which betray acquiescence in what life has to offer, he doesn't radiate anything frightening. On the contrary, he is remarkably good-humoured and peace-loving and this, in addition to his exemplary hospitality, cannot but leave the impression of a friendly bear. He speaks softly but with great confidence and it is no surprise that he has a great many friends, people from UP as well as neighbours in the chawl he lives in.

Haricharan hails from Haldwani, a village in north UP. He was only fourteen when he got married. His marriage was an arranged one at the behest of his father who was a very strict man and expected to be obeyed. Immediately after the marriage ceremony his wife went back to her village, Mehnajpur, where she stayed for another three years. He himself left for Bombay for education but returned shortly afterwards without having accomplished that goal. At the appropriate time his young bride joined him and they spent an eventful six months together before Haricharan prepared to leave for Bombay again to earn money. The idea had been his own as he felt it his duty to shoulder the new responsibilities. His family approved of the idea. His wife thereupon returned to her mother's home. It was the last he saw of her for she died a couple of months later while he was in Bombay.

In contrast to his first stay in the metropolis, when he was under the obligation to study subjects he didn't care for, Haricharan had gone the second time at his own initiative. He liked the dynamics of city life. Everyone seemed so busy! He thoroughly enjoyed such wonders as electricity in the house and water from a tap. The food was good too, much better than he had seen in his village. And what a variety of fruit and vegetables! What he didn't like, however, were the frequent quarrels and fights in the neighbourhood and the numerous strikes, but then you can't have it all. With the help of one of his brothers, who had reached Bombay a couple of years before him, Haricharan got a job as an apprentice in Western India Mill. In 1964 he shifted to Bombay Dyeing where he worked as a *badli* till 1968 when he became permanent.

In 1966, at the age of twenty-two, he was to marry again and this time too, his father took the initiative and arranged it all. Haricharan saw his wife's face for the first time a year after the marriage ceremony, that is, when she came to stay with him. Being an orthodox Brahmin the marriage had been a traditional one and throughout the wedding ceremony his bride had been veiled. When asked what he had wanted his wife to be, Haricharan bursts out singing with a deep and melodious voice:

Oh Lord! Give me bhang* to eat,
Give me Ganga's water for a bath,
Give me a horse to ride on,
Give me a blanket to sleep on and
Give me a wife with eyes like a deer.

Haricharan has no doubt that the Lord gave him the wife he asked for but it hasn't changed his conviction that marriages ought not to be arranged. He will allow his children (they have four sons) to find their own partners and he is positive that he will not interfere. He doesn't mind if the children marry out of their caste nor will he object if they choose wives of a different religion. Smiling at his wife, Haricharan adds that she holds different views and in that sense there is still a problem to be solved.

Haricharan has four brothers and two sisters. His sisters died but all his brothers are alive. Two of them are mill workers in Bombay like himself. They had left the village for the same reason as he did, the lack of employment in Haldwani. Both the brothers are boiler attendants, one in India United and one in Century. The remaining two brothers are farming the land in the village. Immediately after coming to Bombay Haricharan stayed with one of his brothers but that didn't work out well and after a number of conflicts he asked friends to look for a separate room.

He considers himself lucky, for, with the assistance of one of them, he found the house he is staying in at present for which he paid Rs 2,000 then, and its value has appreciated ten or fifteen times. Haricharan's abode is a small room (9 square metres) in which only the bare essentials are to be found, such as some pots and pans and a stove. The only luxury (if it can be deemed such in the Bombay summer heat), is a fan which is kept on a stool. There is no table, no chair and there is only one bed. A bamboo ladder leads to a small room below the ceiling where the children sleep. A few clothes hang on pegs attached to the wall. The walls are of plastered stone and completely bare except for the weathered image of his guru displayed on a poster. The absence of any images of idols and deities is an unusual feature.

---

* A popular soft drug (derived from hemp) which is either smoked, drunk or eaten and gives a feeling of relaxation.

Sitting on his bed with crossed legs and carefully preparing bhang which he is going to offer after a plate of delicious mangoes, Haricharan speaks about religion. He gives as his view that all human beings are equal and that all differences between them are the result of karma.* Although all religions, in his perception, teach basically the oneness of mankind and the equality of all before God, it seems that today religion mainly succeeds in keeping men apart from each other. He is pained by that but refuses to give in to communal feelings. For him Hindus, Muslims, Christians and Sikhs are the same and he is happy that his wife agrees with him. In spite of his orthodox Brahmin upbringing, Haricharan doesn't adhere to any particular denomination although he feels greatly inspired by a Sikh guru, Nirankari Baba, a man who refuses to accept all that keeps people apart. For him as well as for Haricharan humanity is the only true religion. Living in Bombay hasn't altered his views. On the contrary. But Haricharan was overjoyed when he came into contact with Baba as he loved his teachings and had always wanted to serve saints.

There is one other person who strongly influenced his life and that is his father. Haricharan holds his father, who was leading the Congress in his village till his death, in high esteem and he thinks of him as an ideal man. His father took part in the freedom struggle and fought the British. His father's achievements were not just buried under the dust of the past, no, he showed a genuine interest in the problems of the poor throughout his life. Whenever he could, his father would help the people of the Backward Classes. What impressed Haricharan most in his father was not his outspokenness but his truthfulness. He resembled Gandhiji and Haricharan wanted to become just like him. He still remembers that painful day when he had approached his father to give him money to buy some underwear and the hurt he felt when his father refused, saying that there was no money for that. That very day Haricharan decided that he would go to Bombay to prove to his father that he was capable of looking after himself. He knew that his father had always been disappointed in him as he had failed to get properly educated.

---

* In the religious sense, karma means a person's fate as the consequence of his or her acts. The term transgresses the border of life and death.

Haricharan cherishes pleasant memories of his early life in Haldwani and he has made up his mind that one day he will return there to settle down. But this is a distant dream as there are still many years to go before he reaches the age of retirement. Whenever he goes to Haldwani he is treated with respect and the people there try to please him in many ways. He knows that part of this popularity is connected with his childhood and adolescence as he used to be good in sports. He was particularly fond of playing kabaddi* and wrestling in which he excelled. He never took part in competitions but after some time he had reached such proficiency that no one in the village wanted to wrestle with him any longer. Although he had many friends there weren't any with whom he was particularly close. His friends would talk about girls and quarrel a lot, both of which Haricharan disliked.

When he was a boy he had wanted to become a boiler fireman in a mill after he had read a book one of his brothers had left behind. The work of a fireman involves watching the pressure and controlling the water and fire in the boiler. Actually, he became a beam gater. It is his job to replace the beams on the looms and to see that the looms work properly. It is dangerous work as you constantly have to move between the looms with their fast-moving parts and flashing shuttles. Every now and then a shuttle shoots from the loom which poses great danger to the workers as a flying shuttle can easily pierce your head or cause loss of eyesight. Yet, the risks involved in his work are not his main worry. What troubles him more is the pressure put on the workers by superiors. They always seem in a hurry to get more work done. They abuse workers when a mistake is made but are quick to take the credit if something has been done well. It is for reasons such as this that Haricharan hopes that his boys will find suitable employment elsewhere. For the time being, however, his overriding concern is to see to it that they receive a proper education. A job will have to be found only after that.

One day a worker told him that a big strike was imminent. Haricharan had seen it coming for some time but he had kept himself aloof which was not too difficult for those whose mother tongue was

---

* Kabaddi is a very popular Indian game played by two groups of people, the members of each of which must try to touch the members of the other group without being touched themselves.

Hindi and not Marathi. He could see why the workers wanted it as their wages were lagging behind those of workers in other industries. But Haricharan felt that the case of textiles was different and that the millowners gave as much as they could afford. He sensed, however, that there was more to it and decided to wait and see. Next came the shocking news that his father had died and so he left with his family for Haldwani. While still in the village the radio brought the news that the rumours of the strike had become a reality and after reading the newspapers, Haricharan decided that it would be better for his family to remain in the village. Anyway, the strike would be over soon, in a month perhaps, after which they could join him again in Bombay. As it was, the month would stretch to two years.

In order to be able to resume duty at the earliest opportunity, Haricharan returned to Bombay where he found that all and sundry had joined the strike. It was contagious and Haricharan decided that he was in no hurry to report for work. After all, he too would benefit from the struggle if it succeeded and his membership of the Sangh, who had told the workers to resume, had only been for very practical reasons. When he first came to Bombay he hadn't known of the existence of other unions. It was only after several years that he discovered that there were other unions too. By that time he had already enlisted as a Sangh member because the RMMS was very visible within the mills and he thought it wise to have some protection in case of trouble. Coming from UP he felt that in his position it would be better to support the union that was in power instead of one that could only claim the support of a few activists. But now it seemed that the few had become many. A fever had spread throughout the mill area and Haricharan could sense it in the chawls too. He was glad that his family at least was safe in Haldwani. That was a great worry less.

After a few weeks Haricharan started thinking about ways of earning an income as the strike didn't show any sign of collapsing. Talking to workers he learned that the strike was as much for a wage increase as directed against the RMMS. Haricharan couldn't understand this as he couldn't think of the Sangh as a bad union. No doubt there had been malpractices. The top leadership of the Sangh in particular was no good; one might even say totally corrupt. But the workers themselves were largely to blame for that as they didn't dare to step forward to oppose the leaders. Apart from that, what was to be gained without the Sangh? Being affiliated to the INTUC, the Sangh was hand in glove with the Congress and Haricharan was deeply convinced that it was only the ruling party that could help the workers. He failed to see the logic of the strike and discussed his views with friends although the atmosphere was tense.

Meanwhile he had to survive. Watching a salesman selling ornaments, he made some enquiries regarding the possibilities of doing the same. It turned out that it was not too difficult to make these ornaments for they were simple things made of plastic, aluminium or iron. After he had made a sufficiently large quantity he started selling them in the streets but found to his dismay that there was hardly any market for them. Earning on an average a mere Rs 10 per day in this way he had to give it up as it was not profitable at all.

Next he decided to become a fruit vendor, selling bananas. This he did for two months, earning about Rs 20 per day but he had to stop when the monsoon started. He again looked for another job and became employed as a *begari* in the construction of buildings. His earnings now increased to some Rs 30 per day which was fairly good although less than he had earned at the mill. In fact, Haricharan considered the work of a salesman of ornaments and that of a *begari* below his dignity but as he was left with no alternative he took it in his stride. He was comforted by the knowledge that his wife and children were feeling quite at home in Haldwani. He missed them greatly but there was no point in having them around if he could not feed them. Even now he had to utilize his savings. By the time he resumed work he had spent not less than Rs 10,000 to meet the daily expenses of the households in Haldwani and Bombay and on loans. He is not much concerned about what he had to spend for his own family but what really troubles him is that the money he gave to fellow-workers (including those who wholeheartedly supported the strike) never came back.

In October 1982, nine months after the beginning of the strike, Haricharan felt that he had seen enough of it and decided to resume, come what may. He went to the mill and was taken back without difficulty as a permanent worker. He soon found that resuming work was less easy than it had seemed as he was often threatened by Samant's men. Particularly at the year's end Haricharan felt very insecure and expected to be beaten up any time. But on the whole he thinks that the police protection given to those who resumed early was adequate. He nevertheless developed the device of carrying two railway passes at a time. Whenever he was stopped by workers and asked where he was going, he would show the pass for Andheri (which is completely outside the mill area) and he would hide the one for Parel where he was actually heading. It may be due to his size but the threats made to him were never translated into action.

Haricharan thinks that the workers who undertook punitive action did so without the consent of Datta Samant whom he praises as a good and honest leader. He is convinced that the strike was forced on Samant by the workers and that the workers didn't realize that the mills were simply not in a position to pay. Haricharan, therefore, considers the strike a tragic accident for which nobody bears the responsibility, neither the workers not the millowners. But today he also believes that the Sangh would be swept off its feet if a different system was adopted to establish the representative union (for example, secret ballot). He doesn't dread the prospect of the MGKU marching in as he feels that this would be for the good of all but under the present circumstances the Sangh can't be dislodged and that is why he decided to join the Sangh again the day he re-entered the mill.

WORKING-CLASS HERO

Baluram

Baluram Shinde is no commonplace person and that is not because of his remarkable nose which, admittedly, would easily have aroused even Salim's envy. Nor is it because he strove hard to be different. It is simply because his studious nature and early interest in politics were bound to earn him a special place among his friends. Being earnestly interested in politics he did not have to make any special effort. It came quite naturally to him as his father, who had been a mill worker most of his life, used to take him to meetings of the Lal Bawta when he was still a child. His early exposure to red flag ideology made him dislike the Congress at an age when most others didn't even know who ruled the country. Baluram has never felt the need for another ideology since then. Whatever he read about the Congress afterwards and whatever he saw with his own eyes served to strengthen his conviction that workers couldn't expect much good from that side.

Some years after he had mastered the art of reading, but was still a child, he started reading out the newspapers to his father who was an illiterate. Although Baluram had a lot of friends and participated in games and sports like all others, his heart wasn't really in it. As a result he never excelled in these activities but he was liked and respected by his friends all the same as there was no one who could talk with so much ease and conviction about political matters. There is a smouldering fire in his otherwise warm and lively eyes whenever he touches on subjects like workers, unions and parties. It is this trait which puts him quite apart from the others. The fire in his heart and mind would occasionally demand a heavy price but at such times Baluram usually felt that he had no choice.

The person who, largely unwittingly, shaped his life most was a lady councillor from the CPM who happened to visit their home several times. Baluram liked her kind-heartedness and greatly admired her work as she was a selfless person, really working for the poor. He was so enthused by her that by the time he should have appeared for his SSC examinations, he skipped school just to help her with her election campaign. This meant quite a sacrifice for him as he had always wanted to pass the SSC. He felt, however, that with or without an SSC certificate he would have to become a mill worker as there were no other options for a person like him.

At the age of seventeen he started working in the same mill as his father. Six months later he quit the job as he felt insulted by a supervisor who had scolded him. Then he searched for three long years to find another job but didn't meet with success. Meanwhile he got married at the initiative of his uncle. In 1971 this uncle had met the uncle of his future bride and they had soon agreed to a tea party where the would-be bride and bridegroom could meet. Baluram had indicated to his uncle some time before that he wanted an obedient wife with simple manners and sympathetic appearance. At the party Baluram met his future wife, a Maratha like him, and as everything worked out nicely the marriage was settled and celebrated shortly afterwards.

The only thing Baluram regrets in connection with his marriage is that his father took a dowry from his wife's family for Baluram is opposed to such things. Having two daughters and two sons himself now Baluram can understand why his father insisted on it but he still rejects the idea. He feels that there is no way to end the dowry evil if you don't start yourself and so he has decided that he will not demand dowry from the families of the brides of his sons when their time comes. As for the girls, he just prays that he will not have to pay dowry for them. Another thing in which he differs from his father is that he will leave his children free to find their own partners and he will only come to their rescue if they can't find a suitable match by themselves. If they want to marry Marathas, well and good, but if they don't want to do that he has no objection either. The caste background of their partners is not his concern, Baluram feels. Apart from his ideas about marriage, Baluram respects his father greatly and they had a very cordial relationship.

Being married there was a pressing need to do something about employment. He tried everything but in vain. He was at his wit's end when he concluded that he would once more have to try his luck in the mills. However, when he applied for a job he was asked to bring his father. This proved to be a major obstacle as his father was dead set against his son working in the mills. Baluram pleaded for days on end and had to point out again and again that he was unable to find any other work before his father grudgingly gave in. His father had argued that Baluram's nature did not agree with the atmosphere inside the mills and that he would soon run into problems but in the end his father accompanied him to the mill and Baluram got the job.

Baluram, indeed, faced many problems, particularly in dealing with superiors and this largely explains why he remained a *badli* for eight long years even though he became a member of the Sangh a few years prior to the strike. This membership had been forced on him as he felt that his position was very insecure at the time and the Sangh-walas had threatened him with dire consequences if he didn't become a member. The promotion from *badli* to permanent worker should normally not take more than a few years. In his case, however, the appointment was postponed without explanation. When he finally became permanent he could not enjoy that status for more than a month as the strike broke out.

While working in the mill there were many things Baluram couldn't stomach. There were, for example, silly rules such as that of telling you to stand near the machinery you were normally working on even if there was no work whatsoever. One wasn't even allowed to sit down there! Another thing which he found hard to digest was the food served to the workers in the canteen. Granted, it was very cheap but it was of such poor quality and often so stale that it was hardly suitable for human consumption. Even though the workers were ready to pay more for better food, it was never forthcoming and this hurt all the more as they could see every day the food that was served to the staff. Baluram also objected strongly against the habit of supervisors to scold workers in front of others. At times workers were even beaten. Baluram could never get used to that and protested sharply whenever he was a witness to it. Such protests, however, didn't make him popular with supervisors or management although it gained him the trust of many workers.

His life in the mills has convinced him that his children need the best possible education as they should find employment anywhere but in the mills. His greatest anxiety at present is that, given the job scarcity in the city, his boys will in the end be forced to seek employment in the mills, just as he had to do many years ago. Baluram was born and bred in Bombay. His father had been living there for decades already, on the death of his grandfather. His father had been fourteen at the time and the burden of earning an income had fallen on his shoulders. He first found a job in the Railways but soon after he was employed as a weaver in the mill.

His father had maintained the relationship with Aundh village in Satara district as well as he could and during the first seven years of his life, Baluram visited their place of origin regularly but as it happened he fell ill every time he drank water there. Subsequently he wasn't allowed to go there for eleven years but when he went back as an adult the villagers proceeded to sacrifice a goat in order to relieve him of this mysterious sickness which always afflicted him in Aundh. Baluram did not approve of this but he didn't stop it either and, believe it or not, the illness disappeared, never to return. It is not that he is superstitious, Baluram affirms, he is not even religious, but this is exactly how it was!

Baluram explains that he has no need of religion. He prefers to look at the world as one in which predominantly two categories of people operate, the haves and the have-nots. Yet, the room in which he lives is full of religious symbols: pictures of Sai Baba of Shirdi,

Hanuman, Shiva. There is a beautifully carved wooden temple on a cupboard and there are some small sculptures too, one a bust of Shivaji. Baluram explains the presence of the temple and the other objects by pointing out that his father, for all his socialist views, was a very religious man. Baluram wants to maintain this inheritance out of respect for his father. As it is, he doesn't have to look after the religious paraphernalia of the past as his wife Meera is a devout Hindu who happily conducts puja every day, and to this Baluram doesn't object.

When the strike came Baluram and his family remained in Bombay as his links with Aundh had become weaker over the years. Besides, he wanted to be on the spot. He knew that this strike was different from others and that it would last longer. He tried to prepare for it mentally but what more could you do? He took ration on credit for Rs 200 but that was about all. Like so many others Baluram spent most of the time in the beginning talking to workers and attending meetings but as this didn't fetch him money and as the strike was sure to be of long duration, he tried hard to find some work. But however much he tried, they just wouldn't take him as he was not in the possession of an experience certificate. Such a certificate had to be given by your last employer (in his case the mill) and here there was a hitch. If he wanted the experience certificate then he would have to resign first and his participation in the strike had not been to lose his job!

There was another catch. For many years already Baluram and his father had been living in a room which his father had once rented from the mill and for which he had been paying a mere Rs 9 per month. This amount was deducted monthly by the mill from his dues. After his father retired Baluram had been allowed to take over this attractive and cheap arrangement and by resigning he would naturally jeopardize his chances of staying there. There was nothing to be gained in rendering his family shelterless. It was a comparatively good place too, right in the heart of the textile area. The chawl to which the room belongs is not in a very bad condition either. The rooms have solid stone walls and the floors are tiled. Each room has a surface of some 12 square metres, not counting the corner for washing and a small kitchen attached to it. There is tap water in each room, albeit for only twenty minutes a day.

Baluram, who knows what the living places of tens of thousands of other workers in the slums look like, realizes that it will be quite impossible to find another room even faintly resembling the present one for such a low rent. Resigning would necessarily mean having to vacate the room. Where would they all go? There were also three relatives staying with them. What would become of them? It was conceivable that even without his formal resignation they would be evicted from the room but he hoped that his father's long years of service would prevent such a calamity. In any case it seemed better not to draw attention to the matter, so getting a certificate was out of the question.

Baluram asked himself whether he should not start some business but concluded that he had better not do that as he lacked experience. Then what? He really didn't know but when the strike was six months old the financial problems had become so oppressive that Baluram decided that there was no alternative left but to sell their land and property in Aundh. He realized that in doing so he severed the last link with the village, but what else was one to do? Besides, the land was not very fertile and there was no one to attend to it. His father suffered poor health and wanted to spend the rest of his life in Bombay. He himself had no ambition either to cultivate the land so although selling was sad it was the most sensible thing to do.

Their financial problems had meanwhile reached such a pass that his mother, who was going to Aundh because of the sale, first had to mortgage a gold ring of one of the neighbours in order to get sufficient money to reach there. Baluram felt very depressed about all this but it didn't change his view that the strike ought to continue. It was July 1982 and the strike showed no signs of fizzling out so sacrificing the land on the anvil of the strike was the best he could do. He also thought that if he could manage to hold on for some more time, the strike would prove successful and then it would be possible to recover part of the losses.

However, as time dragged on nothing changed. Time and again his hopes soared only to stand exposed as wishful thinking when the strike continued. It proved to be the most trying time of their lives and sapped all their energy. They tried to economize on practically everything, clothes and food in particular. But how much can one do that? Baluram himself gave up the habit of drinking tea twice a day. Often they had to be satisfied with a meal of onion, curry and chillie powder. And worse was yet to come. Baluram took loans from relatives and in that way he pulled on but even the people who came to his rescue at that time could not be expected to go on furnishing money for what seemed an endless war, and one without victors. The days came when they had to eat the flour which Baluram carefully collected from the floor of a flour mill. Sometimes he didn't eat the whole day and just waited ... waited for someone to drop in who would give him money to buy food.

Problems increased when his father was struck by paralysis in August 1982. With great difficulty Baluram managed to get him admitted to the hospital. His father was given treatment under the Employees' State Insurance Scheme (ESIS) but later the doctor who treated his father refused to do so, saying that his father was not entitled to get treatment under the ESIS any longer. This was shortly after it had been announced that workers who continued the strike, stood to lose their rights to medical treatment under the prevailing insurance scheme. The doctor took away the papers and his father had to leave the hospital. The poor man would not live to see the end of the strike.

If Baluram and his wife suffered, so did his children. They never complained, however, for which Baluram feels very grateful. 'They are just like me,' he says with barely suppressed pride in his voice. One day Baluram came home and seeing his eldest son drinking water and preparing to sleep without having had anything to eat that day, he could take no more. It was as if something snapped inside him. Cursing and screaming, he rushed out of the house into the street and plunged into a jail bharo campaign which was in progress. He struggled to get arrested but didn't manage. In the end he just stood there and wept. Baluram falls silent when he recollects those moments.

Shortly after this incident he was confronted with the violent twist the strike was taking. He happened to be near the office of the Sarva Shramik Sangh, the union that had unflinchingly stood with the workers since the beginning of the strike, when a murderous attack was launched on the people of the office in broad daylight. Some four unknown hooligans had stormed the office and stabbed several people. When Baluram arrived on the scene there was utter chaos and blood all around. The next day he searched the newspapers in vain for a report on the attack. The bastards apparently only published what would discredit the doctor!

Life in the chawl became ever more difficult. In the first six months of the strike the chawls had offered a desolate appearance as most of the workers had left for their villages. It all looked so strange! The corridors, usually full of life and filled with the shouts of playing children, were remarkably quiet then. Security guards of the mill, who had actually no jurisdiction in the living quarters of the workers, behaved like policemen and dealt rudely with those who remained there. Workers who did not resume were ordered to vacate the rooms. Throughout the strike a posse of some thirty to forty security guards were always present near the chawl, day and night. When more and more workers started resuming, pressed by the need to survive, Baluram was ordered to stay inside his room during the hours that the workers were either to go to or to return from the mill. In this way they wanted to minimize the chances of contact between Baluram and the early resumers. In spite of these instructions Baluram often managed to slip away and collect membership fees for the MGKU from the workers who had returned to work.

In March 1983 there seemed to be a settlement in the offing when CM Vasantrao Patil met the then minister of commerce, V.P. Singh. Baluram believed that Singh was earnestly seeking a solution to the strike but once more he was disappointed. He feels now that Singh was influenced by Patil and Rajiv Gandhi not to give in as the strike at that time really showed signs of collapsing. After this new disillusionment Baluram too lost hope. He discussed the developments with other workers and friends, and they all shared a common desperation.

Baluram knows that most of the rapidly dwindling number of workers who were still on strike wanted a settlement, just like those who had already resumed, but the government did nothing to help them. The same empty words were repeated over and over again. Still he held on for another three months but in July 1983 he succumbed and reported at the mill to resume duty. The acceptance of defeat had come too late, however. The supervisor deciding on employment refused to take him back but he was not given an official letter of dismissal either. He was just told that he should try another time. Baluram is convinced that his name appeared on a blacklist; a list containing the names of those who had actively supported the strike.

He made a few more attempts but gradually he realized that never again would he be taken back and that he had better forget about it. Having been a *badli* for eight years, his life as a permanent worker had lasted a few weeks only.

Reflecting on the strike Baluram now feels that the decision-making process during the strike didn't work properly. A decision regarding the prolongation of a strike should not have been taken by acclamation or a show of hands but by a casting of votes. Only then would there have been a chance of accurately gauging the workers' mood. During the strike the zone committees conveyed the feelings of the workers to the strike leaders. Each committee had one representative informing Dr Samant about the frame of mind of the workers. The doctor thereupon decided on the course of action. But this was not a very accurate process. Apart from that there was a great need for more information. The workers in the villages were only vaguely aware of what was going on in Bombay and that too, Baluram feels, contributed to the failure of the strike. Strikes of such duration are demoralizing and should never occur again.

Having lost his job Baluram now set about trying to collect his dues. After considerable trouble and with great delay he succeeded in getting his provident fund and bonus but not gratuity. He was briefly informed that should he insist on gratuity he would be thrown out of the mill quarter he is presently occupying and so Baluram never dared to press the matter. With the money he did get he was able to partly pay off the debt which had meanwhile accumulated to some Rs 12,000.

A new long search for employment awaited him. In the course of 1985 (more than four years after the start of the strike) Baluram was appointed as an estate agent. In the first year, while still an apprentice, he earned not less than Rs 17,000 in the first six months as the salary consisted of a commission on sales. Since then, however, he hasn't earned a paisa. He now feels, albeit grudgingly, that in spite of everything mill work is better than his present job. It is more decent, it at least gives you a regular income and it doesn't necessitate shady deals. However, he is painfully aware that the chances of a mill job evaporated with the strike.

Chapter Six

MATERIAL CONDITIONS

GENERAL CHARACTERISTICS OF THE SAMPLE

The methods adopted to arrive at a representative sample have been outlined in the Introduction and in Appendix A. It may be useful to recall that in order to enhance the quality of the sample it had been planned to select a proportionate number of workers from various departments. This plan did not materialize because of difficulties in finding the required workers, the necessity of adjusting techniques in approaching workers and the lack of time which did not allow for a more extensive search for workers based on such a useful division. Much effort was however made to maintain a division of the sample in categories broadly reflecting the present composition of the labour force in terms of employment, that is, *badlis* versus permanent workers. Apart from that, it seemed important to include a significant number of workers who were left unemployed in the wake of the strike as little is known about them. The subdivision of the workers in the sample on the basis of these variables has been presented in Table I (see Introduction).

For the analysis of many aspects of the strike the division in the categories 'employed' and 'unemployed' is less important than that between *badli*s and permanent workers.* Because of that the variables 'employment' and 'terms of employment' are used interchangeably. Looking at the subdivision of the sample according to terms of employment, it is clear that the picture is different for Finlay (sixty permanent workers versus fifteen *badli*s) and Spring Mills (fifty-three permanent workers versus twenty-two *badli*s). From this it appears that the total number of *badli*s in the sample is thirty-seven, a quarter of the total number of the workers in the sample.

As the interviews progressed the need was felt to check certain findings with the aid of a smaller sample of 100 workers who were

* See Appendix C for a list of the topics discussed and the questions asked during the interviews with the workers.

selected at random and who did not belong to Finlay or Spring Mills. As the percentage of *badli*s in the large sample (25 per cent) was likely to be smaller than the proportionate share of the *badli*s in the Bombay textile industry, care was taken to ensure that they were represented in the small sample with about 40 per cent. The available time did not allow for a similar time-consuming process of contacting these workers with the assistance of the various unions (as was done in the case of the large sample). It was, therefore, decided to concentrate on rooms in which ten or more workers were staying. In this effort I was greatly assisted by the workers of the kholi where I had been staying during the first phase of fieldwork. As workers in such rooms are usually migrants it was inevitable that not less than 78 per cent of the workers in the small sample appeared to have stayed in the village of origin during the strike.

The procedures described in the Introduction yielded a very uneven department-wise distribution of workers and a glaring disparity between Finlay and Spring Mills (see Table 6.1). Weavers are, at 47 per cent, clear overrepresented in the sample. This should be borne in mind as it had bearing on the survival strategies of the workers during the strike. It is possible also that it affected the views and expectations of the workers and their attitude towards unions, the strike leadership, and so on. In his study of the organization of labour in the Bombay textile industry in the 1920s Kooiman observed, for example, that weavers were the first to get organized (Kooiman, 1978: 122). Murphy too, ascribes a very active role to the weavers in the organization of labour (Murphy, 1978: 299). However, during the interviews no evidence was found to show that weavers played an exceptionally active role during the struggle or that working in the weaving department had a strong bearing on strike-related views and attitudes.

As for the small sample of 100 workers, it should be said that although the workers belonged to twenty-nine mills, half the workers came from five mills only that is, Svadeshi (twelve), Swan (eleven), Crown (ten) Kamala (eight) and Bombay Dyeing Textile Mills (eight). The division of jobs among them appeared to be as uneven as in Finlay: fifty-six weavers, ten helpers, five doffer boys, five *begaris*, four fitters. The remaining twenty workers had such diverse occupations as siders, drawers, folders, winders, trimmers, among others. After the strike nine of these workers became unemployed.

TABLE 6.1
Occupation of Workers in January 1982

Occupation	*Finlay*		*Spring*		*Total*	*Percentage*
	Perm.	Badli	*Perm.*	Badli		*(n= 150)*
Begari	1	-	2	1	4	
Battery filler	-	-	1	2	3	
Back sizer	-	-	1	1	2	
Doffer boy	1	-	-	5	6	
Fitter	1	-	5	1	7	4.7
Folder	-	-	2	-	2	
Helper	6	-	5	3	14	9.3
Jobber (Spare)	6	-	5	-	11	7.3
Sider	-	-	2	1	3	
Tackler (Asst)	-	-	6	1	7	4.7
Trimmer	1	1	-	-	2	
Weaver	40	13	13	4	70	46.7
Winder	-	-	5	2	7	4.7
Other*	4	1	6	1	11	7.3
Total	60	15	53	22	150	

* Includes: Oiler, glass cleaner, bobbin carrier, beam gater, drawer, mixer, reliever.

It should be pointed out that those workers who called themselves helpers (the second-largest category in the sample) were either employed in the Maintenance Department or in the Weaving Department. There is also a fairly strong group of jobbers in the sample. In former days the jobbers could hardly have been included in the ranks of the workers but the distinctions have been watered down to such a degree that they scarcely rank above the workers. Most jobbers in the sample were actually spare jobbers, that is, persons who replace the jobber in his absence, and insisted on being classified as workers rather than supervisors—to which the other workers did not object.

Practically all the workers in the sample who were reinstated after the strike got their old job back. The only exception in the case of Spring workers concerned two *badli*s who were promoted—which may not necessarily be related to the strike if their permanency had been due. In Finlay, seven workers got a different job and, apart from two or three promotions among these workers, at least two demotions occurred.

Subdividing the twenty-five workers of Finlay classified in the sample as 'unemployed in the wake of the strike', it appeared that in the case of sixteen workers their former position of permanent worker was changed to what the mill called a 'temporary worker' with no assurance of employment. Another seven were reinstated as permanent workers in Finlay but not before more than two and a half years had passed since the beginning of the strike (in some cases even more than four and a half years), and the remaining two workers left the textile industry altogether. The case of the twenty-five unemployed Spring workers is quite different. None of them, to whom the two unemployed Finlay workers who left the textile industry may be added, was ever taken back. They were forced to seek employment elsewhere.

In the spring of 1987, more than five years after the commencement of the strike, only twelve of these twenty-seven workers had found alternative employment. A few workers (four) were able to find employment as *badli*s, in another mill but all the others had to quit the textile industry. Those who had some sort of work, apart from mill work, prior to the strike were in a better position to face the problem created by unemployment than those who were fully dependent on the textile industry. An indication of that is provided by the unemployed spring *badli*s in the sample. Realizing that they had lost their jobs, three of them intensified the other work they had hitherto been doing along with millwork. These *badli*s now concentrated fully on earlier work as cobblers, carpenters and vendors of *wada-pau* (a Maharastrian snack). The other four *badli*s were still looking for jobs. The new occupations of the remaining five workers who found alternative employment were: watchmen (two), shopkeeper, estate agent and packer of incense sticks.

It was surprising to note how many unemployed workers as late as March 1987 had still not given up all hope of being reinstated. To enhance their chances some of them had become members of the Sangh while others paid regular visits to the office of the Sangh in the hope of mollifying the Sangh leaders, convinced as they were that reinstatement was in the hands of the RMMS. Their tenacity was at times baffling (one worker declaring that he had visited the Sangh office daily for the past five years), and the best explanation for this persistence may well have been the absence of alternative employment or the comparatively poor earnings in other professions.

While comparing the level of education of the workers in the two mills, a noteworthy difference can be observed between the level of education of Finlay and Spring workers in the sample (see Table 6.2). While 80 per cent of the Finlay workers fitted in the first three categories not less than 87 per cent of the Spring workers had to be grouped in the last three categories. The number of Spring workers who obtained the SSC is impressive—nearly a quarter of the whole group.

Although the data pertaining to the educational level of the textile workers, as collected by Deshpande during the strike, are not wholly comparable, he also found a surprisingly large number of workers claiming education up to the SSC level, 36 per cent of the males (Deshpande, 1983: 5). By combining the percentages of the last two categories of Table 6.2 we arrive at a comparable figure.

TABLE 6.2
Level of Education

Category	*Finlay*	*Spring*	*Total*	*Percentage (n = 150)*
Illiterate	8	5	13	8.6
1–4th	20	5	25	16.6
5–8th	32	25	57	38.0
9–nth	10	22	32	21.3
SSC	5	18	23	15.3
Total	75	75	150	99.8

Meanwhile, the differences between Finlay and Spring workers are not easily explained. It may seem that Spring Mills picks out the best-educated among those that report for work at the gate. There is strong evidence that the level of education is an important criterion when it comes to recruiting new labour in the Bombay textile mills, but that does not explain why Finlay should adopt a criterion that differs from that of Spring Mills. Another explanation might be that the better-educated workers are more aware of the financial position (and thus paying capacity) of a mill and try to get a job in the most prosperous mill, in this case Spring Mills. There is also the possibility that the better-educated workers are more capable of pressurizing officials who decide on employment but this cannot be evaluated on the strength of the available data.

As far as marriage is concerned, it appeared that 140 out of 150 workers were married at the time of the strike and that most of the unmarried workers were *badli*s, which is to be expected as these workers are on the whole the youngest group. A career as a worker in the Bombay textile industry starts for everyone as a *badli.* Apart from the *badli*s (eight out of ten unmarried *badli*s worked in Spring mills), there was no noteworthy difference between Finlay and Spring workers as regards marriage. The same is not true, however, for the number of children of the various categories of workers.

Understandably, having or not having children had a strong bearing on the strike morale of the workers, particularly as most of these children were in school and college. Workers appeared to attach great value to the continuation of their childrens' education but despite this the schooling had to be interrupted for lack of resources in several cases. The same attitude was found by Chellappa in his study of the striking textile workers in Bombay (Chellappa, 1985). In consonance with age and marital status, the lowest average number of children was to be found among *badli*s. Taking the mills as a whole, there appeared to be a substantial difference, between Finlay workers (with an average of 3.3 children) and Spring workers (with an average of 2.7 children). This difference is partially explained by a larger number of unmarried *badli*s in Spring Mills.

Age seems to be another obvious factor influencing the number of children. In Table 6.3 the ages of the workers have been given. The largest group of the workers in the sample (44 per cent) consists of workers between thirty and forty years. This percentage, although higher than that found by Deshpande in his study of the Bombay textile workers, is corroborated by the age-wise division of the workers in the small sample which has been given in the last column.

TABLE 6.3
Age at Time of Interview

Age group	*Finlay*	*Spring*	*Total*	*Percentage*	*(Small Sample)*
21–30	13	21	34	22.6	23%
31–40	31	35	66	44.0	45%
41–50	25	17	42	28.0	24%
Above 50	6	2	8	5.3	8%
Total	75	75	150	100.0	100%

Deshpande calculated that 31 per cent of his sample belonged to this category, another 30 per cent to the age group of twenty-one to thirty and the remaining workers above forty (Deshpande, 1983: 4). What is more interesting, is that the Table shows that Spring workers are more strongly represented than those from Finlay in the youngest category while the reverse is true for the two highest categories. It seems therefore reasonable to assume that age, in addition to differences in the marital status of the workers, can explain the difference in the average number of children of the workers in the two mills.

Looking at the religion professed by the workers, it was found that 147 workers were Hindus and the remaining three (employed in Spring Mills) were Muslims. The caste-wise division of the 147 workers is given in Table 6.4. From this appears that no less than 75 per cent of the workers in the sample were Marathas. The dominant position of Marathas among textile workers has been frequently observed and explains why so many textile workers hold land in their village of origin. There is a fairly high incidence of the handloom weavers caste Padmashali in the case of Finlay, but this is largely explained by the high percentage of weavers in the sample from this mill. It is well known that handloom weavers from Andhra Pradesh and Uttar Pradesh are strongly represented in the mechanized textile industry (including powerlooms).

The Table also shows that there is a comparatively high incidence of workers belonging to either the Backward Classes or the Scheduled Castes in the case of Spring Mills against the near absence of such workers in Finlay. The reasons for this could not be traced but might well be coincidental. Whatever differences were found between the various categories of workers in the course of the research programme, only housing seemed to be an area in which caste origin may have played a role. Even here groupings on the lines of language and region seemed to be far more important than considerations of caste.

TABLE 6.4
Division of Hindu Workers by Castes

	Finlay	*Spring*	*Total*
Maratha	49	64	113
Padmashali	14	-	14
Vaishya	4	2	6
Backward Classes	1	4	5
Scheduled Castes	-	2	2
Rajbhar (UP)	2	-	2
Other*	5	-	5
Total	75	72	147

* Other: Koshti, Brahmin, Thakur, Rai, Reddi.

In fact, throughout the research, caste background never appeared to be a factor to which the workers paid much attention. At no point could any friction be discerned which might be attributed to caste differences and even less a clash of interests between persons belonging to different castes. This is not to say that caste awareness has completely disappeared among textile workers in the city but it plays no distinctive role in everyday life (see case studies). This finding corroborates Morris' impression that caste is of secondary importance in the organization of labour in the textile industry.

There have been labour conflicts in the past which seem to point at the significance of considerations of caste for the organization of labour in the mills as well as for the success of strikes (cf. Murphy, 1978: 308). The weaving department in particular has been named as a place where problems arose at the shop-floor level. Even there it was far from certain that caste and notions of ritual purity were behind these problems (cf. Morris, 1965: 201). At such times caste may well have served as an excuse to exclude newcomers from well-paying jobs. The absence of a narrow, caste-based solidarity during the strike in the 1980s is nicely illustrated by the choice of the strike leader. The striking workers, predominantly Marathas, had no difficulty in accepting the leadership of Samant, a Saraswat Brahmin.

REGIONAL TIES

The regional origin of the workers may be derived from Table 6.5. It appears that 14 per cent of the workers belong to places outside Maharashtra (UP and AP) and merely 10 per cent were born in Bombay district. This is indicative of the strong and persistent migratory character of labour in the Bombay textile industry and is corroborated by a study by Vaidya (Vaidya, 1984: 12). From the Table it appears that most of the sample workers originate from Ratnagiri district. Half the workers from this district came from the southernmost part (Sindhudurg).

TABLE 6.5
Place of Birth of Sample Workers

District	*Finlay*	*Spring*	*Total*	*Percentage*
Ratnagiri	23	15	38	25.3
Satara	7	21	28	18.6
Sangli	2	15	17	11.3
Andhra Pradesh	16	-	16	10.7
Bombay	3	12	15	10.0
Pune	9	5	14	9.3
Kolhapur	9	2	11	7.3
Uttar Pradesh	5	-	5	3.3
Kulaba	1	2	3	2.0
Other	-	3	3	2.0
Total	75	75	150	99.8

However, a difference may be noted if we compare these figures with the findings of a study undertaken by Gokhale in 1955. He found that 45 per cent of the textile workers came from Konkan (the narrow strip of land between the Arabian Sea and the Sahyadri mountain range), 30 per cent from the Deccan and 18 per cent from UP.[1] Tracing the origin of Bombay textile workers, Kooiman concluded that in the 1930s the percentage of workers belonging to Ratnagiri might well have been 40 per cent (Kooiman, 1978: 22). The present sample indicates a change in the origin of the Maharashtrian workers in favour of districts like Satara, Sangli and Kolhapur at the expense of the Konkan region (Ratnagiri).

The sample also points at changes in the regional origin of workers coming from places outside Maharashtra. Not less than 63 per cent of all workers were born in south Maharashtra, that is, in one of the districts of Satara, Sangli, Kolhapur or Ratnagiri. This implies that the distance between their villages of origin and Bombay might be anywhere between 250 and 500 kilometres. These distances show the necessity and difficulty of keeping in touch with the workers when they leave Bombay in the course of a strike. The rural tour made by Datta Samant during the strike was therefore far from superfluous. The tour, apart from being an attempt to enlist the support of those living in the rural hinterland, also served the purpose of communicating with numerous workers who tried to cope with the strike by returning to their places of origin.

Another indicator of the importance of the rural ties of the workers is provided by the remittance of money to the villages. Prior to the strike more than three-quarters of the workers (sixty from Finlay and fifty-five from Spring Mills) would send money to their village of origin. In all, thirty-five workers never sent any money as their ties with the village were weak or even non-existent. As a natural corollary, a large majority of this group remained in Bombay throughout the strike. Only five out of this group of thirty-five workers stayed in the village during the strike, twenty-six lived in Bombay and in the remaining cases a more or less equal amount of time was spent in both places. The percentage of *badli*s among those who never sent any money was twenty-three which is in proportion to the entire group of *badli*s in the sample (24.6 per cent). In Table 6.6 the amounts sent monthly by the 115 workers who habitually sent money to their village have been listed.

It appears that the monthly transfer of money is considerable. Separate columns for permanent workers and *badli*s have been omitted as the latter followed the general pattern of remittance established by the permanent workers in the respective mills. However, a noteworthy aspect is that Spring workers on the whole appear to send larger amounts than those from Finlay (forty-three Spring workers sending more than Rs 150 per month against twenty-three from Finlay). The most likely explanation for this is that the higher income of the Spring workers allows them to send more money. Having said this, it should be noted that the fact that Spring workers do send more money indicates that an increase in wages is not simply counterbalanced by a higher expenditure but does find its way (at least partially) to the family in the village. This observation undermines the merit (if any) of one of the arguments frequently used by employers, namely the necessity of freezing wages as wage increases will only widen the gap between agricultural and industrial labourers.

Although no large-scale data collection focused on the question of the purposes for which this money was utilized in the village, practically all workers who were asked this question said that it was used to meet the costs of living. Only one worker declared that part of the money was utilized both for land improvement and investment. This finding confirms the results of S. Vaidya's study of the use of money sent by workers to the village. From that study (based on repeated interviews with 500 workers) it appears that 71 per cent of the workers used to send money more or less regularly. From those who sent money, 84 per cent sent it to meet household expenses, 10 per cent intended it for special occasions (festivals, weddings) and only 3 per cent reported that the money was used for farming (Vaidya, 1984: 21–28). The money sent by the workers is badly needed in the village to cope with daily expenses. Any reduction in the earnings of the textile workers, therefore, directly affects the standard of living in their villages.

TABLE 6.6
Monthly Remittance of Money to Village

Rs	*Finlay*	*Spring*	*Total*	*Percentage (n = 115)*
50–150	37	12	49	42.6
151–250	11	16	27	23.5
251–350	5	10	15	13.0
351 or more	4	12	16	13.9
Irregularly	3	5	8	7.0
Total	60	55	115	100.0

The importance of the ties with the village may also be derived from the possession of property there. Not less than 137 workers (91 per cent) owned a house in the village and an equally impressive number of 116 workers (77 per cent) appeared to possess land. There was no difference in the possession of houses between Finlay and Spring workers. As for the property in land, there appeared to be eight more Finlay workers without land than Spring workers. One is tempted to believe that those without land were less equipped to continue the strike than the others. However, a glance at the average duration, of the strike for these thirty-four landless workers tells us that the average time they were on strike does not differ from the averages of the groups to which they belong. This means by implication that the factor of ownership of land offers an insufficient explanation for the duration of the strike. This, of course, is not a denial of the importance of possession of land for self-cultivation.

No effort was made to acquire details about the type of house in the village or its value as the answers would be rough estimates made by the owners. Besides, the collection and evaluation of such data would in itself require a minor research programme. Yet, it is reasonable to assume that these houses are in many cases barely more than huts or at best *pucca* structures. In practically all cases the house and/or the land was/were owned by the family and therefore, shared property. Although no details were collected about the type of land, its use or its fertility, the owners of some of the larger holdings volunteered to add that their land was rocky and infertile. Yet, the very fact that workers possessed land in the village, jointly or not, was of great significance to the success of the strike as it allowed them to leave Bombay and derive an income from self-cultivation.

Deshpande found a much lower figure for textile workers possessing land in the village. He reported that only 40 per cent of the workers in his survey possessed land and concluded that the ownership of land cannot be considered an important source of alternative income for the striking workers (Deshpande, 1983: 10). There appears to be a gap between the 40 per cent mentioned by Deshpande and the 77 per cent found here. One is led to believe that this striking difference can be explained by looking at the housing of the workers in Bombay, the assumption being that workers who left the village recently are to be found in chawls (whether provided by the mill or not) prior to moving into a privately owned house. In Deshpande's survey less than 4 per cent of the workers were provided accommodation by the mill whereas the overwhelming majority of the Spring workers in the present sample were housed in chawls belonging to the mill. Going by this reasoning, the high incidence of possession of land among Spring workers might be explained in terms of migration, their recent shift to the city. The technique of contacting workers in the chawls might in that case have caused a strong bias.

Yet, there is not much reason to believe that this is really the case, for the average duration of employment in Spring Mills does not indicate that the workers in the chawls moved recently to the city. They stayed in the rooms provided by the mill because the chances of finding better accommodation were distinctly low. It would even be difficult to find a mere hut in a *zopadpatti*.* What is more important, it appeared that the number of Finlay workers possessing land in the village was only slightly smaller than that of the Spring workers although the Finlay workers were much more city-based. Again, a study of the rural–urban economic ties of workers in the silk, textile-processing and hosiery industry by S. Vaidya confirms that a high percentage of textile workers possess land and other property in the village. She found that 60 per cent of the workers possessed land in the village and 85 per cent a house (Vaidya, 1984: 15). On the strength of the available data alone no satisfactory explanation can be given for the differences between this study and Deshpande's survey.

Maybe more revealing than the possession of land itself is the acreage of the land possessed by the workers. In order to obtain some idea of the size of these holdings it was decided to include this topic in the discussions. About one-third of the interviews had been completed by that time and excluding the thirty-four workers to whom the question did not apply, sixty-three workers remained to answer this question. Because of this small number the significance of the findings is limited but the answers do provide an indication of the size of the holdings. The findings are presented in Table 6.7.

* Marathi term for slum and shanty town.

TABLE 6.7
Size of Landholding of Sample Workers

Category	*Finlay*	*Spring*	*Total*	*Percentage (n = 63)*
1–4 acres	30	11	41	65.1
5–10 acres	4	10	14	22.2
11 or more	2	6	8	12.7
Total	36	27	63	100.0

As may be expected, the large majority of the holdings is very small. Still, there is a substantial minority possessing 5 to 10 acres. This time the differences with Deshpande's study are less dramatic although not negligible. Deshpande reported that of those who owned land in the village, 61 per cent possessed less than 2 acres and 25 per cent 3 to 5 acres (Deshpande, 1983: 10). It transpires from these figures that the income derived from the category with the smallest holdings must have been meagre as was the case for the majority of the workers. Even so there remains a substantial group who owned more than 3 acres and these workers might have greatly benefited from this. In fact, this is precisely what was reported by the workers in the course of the interviews, as will be shown later. What may come as a surprise is that the figures indicate a noteworthy difference between the holdings of Spring and Finlay workers. This finding corroborates the impression created already by the differences in educational level, that the Spring workers are a different category when compared with those from Finlay.

A further indication of differences between Finlay and Spring workers may be gained by taking a look at the occupation of the interviewees' fathers. It appeared that more than 45 per cent of the fathers of the interviewees were or are involved in agriculture. The textile industry proved to be the second most important source of employment. More than a quarter of the fathers of the textile workers in the sample had been (in a few cases still were) textile workers themselves. If we include handloom weavers then the percentage of those deriving an income from the textile industry rises further to about 35 per cent. It may be concluded that agriculture and the textile industry together account for 80 per cent of the employment of the fathers of textile workers in the sample. The remaining percentage includes occupations as diverse as postmen, peons, policemen, soldiers, vendors of fruit or vegetables, shop assistants, shopkeepers, cobblers, carpenters and medical practioners.

As in the case of education and age, a clear distinction is visible between Finlay and Spring workers. The number of farmers in the case of Spring Mills is nearly double Finlay's, and the number of persons who combined cultivation of their own plot of land with hiring themselves out as agricultural labourers is three times higher in the case of Finlay. Similarly, while there were no full-time agricultural labourers among the fathers of Spring workers, there appeared to be four agricultural labourers in the case of Finlay workers.

A corresponding picture of a higher social background for Spring workers emerges if we look at the employment in the textile mills. Combining the categories of actual and retired textile workers, we find that there are far more (75 per cent) fathers of Spring workers who themselves work or worked as mill workers than in the case of Finlay. As may be expected, the reverse is true with regard to the very poorly paid handloom weavers who are strongly represented in Finlay and not at all in Spring Mills. The conclusion is warranted that workers in Spring Mills come on the whole from a different and wealthier background in terms of landownership and/or the occupation of the father. This factor may also explain the higher level of education found in Spring Mills as compared with Finlay although it does not explain why Finlay would not absorb the better-educated and economically stronger workers. The finding calls into question the effectiveness of a system of strictly impartial recruitment of labour solely based on merit, as envisaged by the Decasualization Scheme.

LIVING AND WORKING CONDITIONS

Housing

In the preceding paragraph, the regional ties of the workers have been discussed as it was believed that these ties were vital for the survival of many workers during the strike period. There might be another important relation, namely between the ownership of a room in the city and strike participation. But before working out this connection, it is useful to study the living conditions of the workers in greater detail. Table 6.8 presents the terms of occupancy of the rooms or huts in which the workers in the sample were living at the time of the interview.

Three-quarters of the workers in the sample appeared to live in a rented room (shared with other workers or with their family) and about a fifth of the workers (nearly all from Finlay) owned the place in which they were living. A few workers lived with others in a room which was common property. On the face of it, it may seem that the Finlay workers are better off in this respect but there are several factors to reckon with. It has to be pointed out that the method of selecting workers may have created a strong bias as far as housing is concerned. Not all the workers of Spring mills are staying in chawls belonging to the mill but the available time did not allow for an extensive search for Spring workers living elsewhere. As a result there may have been a distortion in the proportion of workers renting the room they were living in.

TABLE 6.8

Present Living Place

Category	*Finlay*	*Spring*	*Total*	*Percentage*
Rented	43	68	111	74.0
Owned	26	3	29	19.3
Shared property	5	4	9	6.0
Not applicable	1	-	1	0.7
Total	75	75	150	100.0

More important than this, however, is the observation that the very fact of owning a room says little about some other vital aspects such as the quality of the living place and its surroundings. Similarly, the amount of rent payable by workers living in a rented room has to be taken into account and if that is done, the picture changes considerably. Many houses owned by Finlay workers are merely ramshackle huts in utterly depressing surroundings, such as overcrowded slum areas with few or no facilities. The rooms rented by Spring workers from the mill are no bungalows either but they are comparatively much better. The surroundings too are cleaner and more spacious. Besides, the rent is usually extremely low (Rs 9). So even if nine times as many Finlay workers own the place they are living in as compared with Spring workers in the sample, there is little doubt that a great many of the former would be glad to exchange their room for a place in one of the chawls belonging to Bombay Dyeing. The mere fact of owning a living place is, therefore, in this case a poor, if not utterly misleading, indicator of a worker's wealth.

There is another noteworthy phenomenon relating to terms of ownership. It appears that an unknown number of workers live in a place which they own together with other workers. In the course of the research, I found five rooms owned by a group of workers, usually coming from the same village or region. These workers had contributed money to purchase a room in Bombay and in two cases they even had a room constructed on their behalf. This enabled them to live at low cost in a fairly decent place. In one case they allowed other workers to share their room on a rental basis. The average number of people living in such jointly owned rooms was comparable to that of other kholis and could be anywhere between ten and thirty.

Table 6.9 provides information regarding the amount of rent workers pay for the rooms they are living in. This obligation did not apply to forty-one workers who either owned the place they were living in (be it common property or not) or stayed with relatives free of cost. It appears that more than 80 per cent of the rent-paying workers in the sample pay less than Rs 25 per month and a quarter of them (predominantly those who rent a room from Bombay Dyeing) pay even less than Rs 10 per month. This is a very low amount by any standard and although the price for paying so little rent is that workers have to share the same space with many others, the extremely low rent level is a strong incentive as possible alternatives are scarcely better.

TABLE 6.9
Amount of Rent Paid by Workers

Category (in rupees)	*Finlay*	*Spring*	*Total*	*Percentage (n = 109)*
10 or less	8	21	29	26.6
11–25	25	34	59	54.1
26–75	9	8	17	15.6
76 or more	3	1	4	3.6
Total	45	64	109	99.9

There is no conspicuous difference between Finlay and Spring workers as far as rent is concerned except that Spring workers are more strongly represented in the two lowest categories. The median for Finlay workers in the sample appears to be Rs 19.1 against Rs 15.5 for Spring workers. The reason for the lower rent paid by the latter is that the majority of them stay in rooms rented from the mill by a fellow worker who is commonly denoted as the 'owner'. Such a worker may have rented the room from the mill for Rs 9 per month. By subletting his room to other workers for amounts ranging from Rs 10 to 25, he manages to secure a handsome addition to his monthly income.

It goes without saying that these workers feel that this source of income (easily Rs 200 per month) should not be squandered. It appeared that the desire to resume work during the strike was very strong among them. They feared that the continuation of the struggle might first of all lead to the termination of their employment and subsequently to the need to vacate their room. Partly for genuine reasons and partly in order to put up a show of solidarity these 'room owners' would, after resuming work themselves, usually accept that the striking workers staying in their room would not pay rent for the period of the strike. In that way they were able to help fellow workers as well as themselves. By providing shelter to its workers, Spring Mills possesses a potent weapon for compelling workers to return. Although originally the rooms were not intended to become milch cows in the hands of some workers, the management of Spring Mills today probably sees no reason to interfere with this practice as it gives them a hold over the workers which may well be the envy of the management of other mills.

Having said that, the rooms in the chawls belonging to the mill are comparatively better than the dingy and dilapidated structures which are often the dwelling places of workers in the *zopadpatti*s, this should not be construed to mean that these rooms offer a lot of space to their occupants. In Table 6.10 the surface area of the rooms in which the workers stay has been indicated and these data should be read together with the information provided in Table 6.11 which gives the number of people with whom the workers have to share the space allotted to them.

TABLE 6.10

Surface of the Rooms Inhabited by the Workers

Category	*Finlay*	*Spring*	*Total*	*Percentage*
10 m2 or less	18	12	30	20.0
11–15 m2	28	44	72	48.0
16–20 m2	18	14	32	21.3
21 m2 or more	5	3	8	5.3
Unknown	6	2	8	5.3
Total	75	75	150	99.9

TABLE 6.11

Number of Persons Sharing the Room/Hut

Category	*Finlay*	*Spring*	*Total*	*Percentage*
5 or less	28	27	55	36.6
6–10	30	23	53	35.3
11–15	6	12	18	12.0
16–20	6	7	13	8.7
21–25	2	5	7	4.7
26 or more	3	1	4	2.7
Total	75	75	150	100.0

It appears that practically all workers (90 per cent) live with or without families in rooms with a surface area of less than 20 m^2. It has been pointed out before that, space-wise, the situation for those without families is usually worse as they live in rooms that may be bigger but are shared by many more people per square metre. A shockingly large number of workers live in rooms with a surface area of even less than 10 m^2. The figures graphically illustrate dismal living conditions of Bombay textile workers. Out of the 150 rooms and huts visited, 122 did have a tap and a corner for washing, in eighteen cases the existence of such a facility could not be determined, and in the remaining ten cases there was no such facility in the hut or room. Having a tap, of course, did not necessarily mean the unlimited availability of water. In fact, such unrestricted availability was found to be non-existent. In most cases the tap produced water only twice a day, during a certain hour in the morning and another in the evening, obliging the workers and their families to regulate their activities accordingly.

Just how many persons have to share the cramped space available to them is illustrated by Table 6.11. It appears that there is hardly any difference between Spring and Finlay workers as regards the number of persons who have to share the rented or owned space. The two lowest categories are predominantly populated by workers who stay with their family in a room (be it rented or owned). However, a very substantial number of workers cannot afford to bring their families to Bombay or do not want to do so. They stay in overcrowded kholis. They are to be found in the four highest categories of the Table, that is, the most densely populated rooms.

Although the number of people living in such rooms varies considerably there is not much difference in the space available to each, usually being restricted to a suitcase or box for personal belongings, a peg to hang clothes on and, at night, the two square metres needed to unroll a mat when it is time to sleep. The upper limit of the last category is unknown but can be stretched enormously. Although most kholis are virtually cramped dormitories, some have not less than sixty inhabitants.

Whether his family is living with him in a room or not, the responsibility of the textile worker is usually not restricted to his own family. More often than not he has to support other people and relatives as well. Table 6.12 shows the number of dependents (family and others) allowing for an assessment of the number of people who partly or fully depend on the textile workers and their income.

TABLE 6.12

Number of Dependents of Textile Workers

Category	*Finlay*	*Spring*	*Total*	*Percentage*
1–3	14	10	24	16.0
4–6	34	37	71	47.3
7–10	17	19	36	24.0
11 or more	10	9	19	12.7
Total	75	75	150	100.0

The Table shows that with regard to the number of dependents, there is hardly any difference between Finlay and Spring workers. Figures found by Vaidya in her study of workers in the silk, textile processing and hosiery industries closely correspond with the percentages given above.[2] It may, therefore, be safely assumed that the findings are also true for other mills in the textile industry. It can be seen that only a minority has not more than three dependents (in most cases wife and children). Nearly half the workers have four to six dependents. An impressive 37 per cent bear responsibility for the welfare of seven or more dependents. This largely explains why so many workers whose families are left behind in the villages are sent money, and illustrates the financial significance of the rural–urban nexus.

Fortunately, not all dependents are wholly dependent on the income of the textile workers. The larger the group of dependents, the greater the number of people who contribute to the group income. Even so, it was found that in 54 per cent of the cases the wages of the mill worker were the only source of income for the dependents. In another 27 per cent there is only one more breadwinner. In the remaining cases (19 per cent) two or more members of the family were said to contribute to the family income apart from the worker. This is particularly true for families who remained behind in the village to cultivate the land, which explains why a difference was found between Finlay and Spring workers.

To sum up, it has been shown that Finlay workers differ from Spring workers in the sample not just in terms of age or the number of children but, more importantly, in terms of parental occupation, wealth (landed property) and education. These general differences should be borne in mind as they have a bearing on survival strategies and possibly even on the views of the workers regarding the strike.

Employment and Wages

The readiness to go on strike may have to be related to many factors such as wage level, permanency, treatment of complaints and so on. All these factors gain in weight the longer a worker has worked in a particular mill. Table 6.13 shows how many years the workers had worked in the textile industry on the day the strike began. From the interviews it appeared that most of the workers had worked in a single mill from the day they were absorbed in its labour force.

Finlay workers worked on the whole longer in the mills than those from Spring Mills. The difference is particularly clear in the group of those who had worked seventeen years or more in the mills prior to the strike. This finding is in tune with Table 6.13 in which the age-wise division of workers is given. Differences in ages may also explain why the Finlay workers on an average had more children than their fellow workers from Spring Mills. *Badli*s, of course, appear to be concentrated in the two categories with the lowest number of working years. However, a conspicuous difference is to be noted between Finlay and Spring Mills in the second category from which it transpires that ten *badli*s in Spring Mills had put in five to eight years of service without graduating to the rank of a permanent worker.

TABLE 6.13

Number of Years Worked Prior to the Strike

Number	*Finlay*		*Spring*		*Total*	*Percentage*
	Perm.	Badli	*Perm.*	Badli		
4 or less	–	11	3	7	21	14.0
5–8	6	-	11	10	27	18.0
9–12	17	2	17	3	39	26.0
13–16	12	2	8	1	23	15.3
More	25	–	14	1	40	26.7
Total	60	15	53	22	150	100.0

Even in the three highest categories of the two mills (nine or more years of service) there are nine *badli*s to be found. Before condemning the mill management for exploitation of workers, it should be realized that this alone does not necessarily mean that all these workers were interested in becoming permanent. It is possible that some of them preferred irregular mill work as it might have been only one of their sources of income. It could well be that other activities provided them with sufficient income and induced them to keep permanency at bay.

Although this reasoning may explain some of the cases in which workers remained *badli* for a very long time, the interviews strongly suggest that this does not apply to the majority of them.

*Badli*s employed in Spring Mills in particular, complained about the inordinately long time they had to wait before being promoted to the rank of the permanent workers. About 37 per cent of this group of twenty-two explicitly mentioned achieving permanency as one of their strike objectives. In this group there were five *badli*s who had already served five to eight years, and two who had served over nine years. The Table clearly shows that more than half of all the *badli*s (in the case of Spring Mills even more than 68 per cent) were still working as *badli*s more than four years after recruitment. It is apparent that for a great number of *badli*s undue postponement of permanency was a serious complaint and a reason to go on strike.

The dissatisfaction among Spring *badli*s is clearly related to the period they have to wait before being promoted and this discontent is fanned by the fact that the wages in Spring Mills are higher than in other mills. The greater the difference the stronger the frustration about not being regularly employed. In Table 6.14 the wages of the workers in Finlay and Spring Mills before and after the strike (as stated by them) have been given.

TABLE 6.14
Monthly Wages Before and After the Strike

Rs	*Finlay*		*Spring*	
	Before	*After*	*Before*	*After*
650 or less	6	3	8	1
651–800	30	4	15	1
801–950	15	11	14	1
951–1100	20	17	16	8
1101–1250	3	24	12	14
1251–1400	1	12	5	9
1401–1550	-	-	4	6
1551–1700	-	2	1	8
More	-	-	-	4
Total	75	73*	75	52*

* The total is less than 75 because of workers who left the textile industry altogether.

By comparing the wages of Finlay and Spring workers it can be seen that the wages in Spring Mills were definitely higher than those in Finlay, both before and after the strike. While practically all Finlay workers, numbering seventy-one earned less than Rs 1100 before the strike, nearly one-third of the Spring workers, numbering twenty-two earned more than that. Similarly, 19 per cent of the Finlay workers claimed to earn more than Rs 1250 after the strike; the corresponding figure is 52 per cent for Spring workers. *Badli*s are to be found in the lowest wage categories in both mills. In fact, fifty-nine workers in the sample (about 40 per cent of the whole sample) were earning less than Rs 800 prior to the strike which largely explains why better wages figured prominently on their list of demands. In his study of the labour market structure in the Bombay textile mills, Bhattacherjee too, noticed a substantial wage increase after the strike. After dividing the mills in two sectors, he found that the mean pay in the economically strongest sector (Rs 1035) was Rs 175 above the mean for the weakest sector (Bhattacherjee, 1988b). He also noted that the average monthly pay of the permanent workers was double that of the *badli*s, which he ascribes to differences in the number of days worked in the mills and the absence of fringe benefits for *badli*s.

The great improvement in wages after the strike, as revealed in Table 6.14, is corroborated by the median for each column. It appears that the median of wages for Finlay workers was Rs 816 before the strike and Rs 1,110 afterwards (an increase of 36 per cent). In the case of Spring Mills, the median appeared to be Rs 956 before and Rs 1,268 afterwards (an increase of 33 per cent). In order to obtain a more accurate view of the changes that took place, the difference in wages before and after the strike was calculated for each worker and these differences were then grouped in several categories (Table 6.15). This procedure could for obvious reasons not be applied to workers who had meanwhile left the textile industry. However, Table 6.15 includes the cases of twenty-three Finlay workers who have been defined earlier as 'unemployed in the wake of the strike' but who were taken back as 'temporary' workers years after the collapse of the strike. The figures also include two Spring workers who found employment in another mill. The results are presented in Table 6.15.

TABLE 6.15

Differences in Wages Before and After the Strike

Category	*Finlay*	*Spring*	*Total*	*Percentage (n = 125)*
Same or less	10*	4	14	11.2
0–15%	8	11	19	15.2
16–30%	22	20	42	33.6
31–45%	17	8	25	20.0
46–60%	8	5	13	10.4
61 or more	8	4	12	9.6
Total	73	52	125	100.0

* Four workers in this group reported that their wages had decreased. This decrease averaged 26 per cent.

It appears that there was not much change in the wages of a quarter of the workers after the strike, which means that there was a change in those of 75 per cent. These changes may even be called dramatic, for no less than 20 per cent of the workers saw a wage hike of 46 per cent or more. When I expressed disbelief in the scope of this virtual wage jump the workers insisted that the increase was a fact but added that the real increase was much lower because of the rise in prices and corresponding inflation. Although this certainly explains part of the wage hike, it cannot explain why the price compensation did not reach everyone and why not everyone in the same proportion.

Going by the workers' information about their take-home pay after the strike, one is obliged to conclude that Samant's wage demands, usually discarded as fantastic and unreal, were accepted after all. Even an increase of 20 per cent on a wage of Rs 800 is Rs 160 but most of the wages as well as the increases were higher than that. It seems that other factors in addition to price compensation have to explain the irregular changes. It is likely that the millowners wanted to help the Sangh to regain its position by giving a substantial wage hike when the time for a new settlement came. In that case the credit would go to the Sangh and Samant would be exposed as a powerless outsider. If there is any truth in this then the millowners' calculations were only partly right for even though the workers rejoined the Sangh after the strike they were well aware that nothing would have changed without the strike.

DURATION OF STRIKE AND EMPLOYMENT AVENUES

Differences Between Categories

Before attempting to describe in detail the various means employed by the workers to survive this unprecedentedly long strike, we need to know for what period the workers remained on strike. A problem here is that the strike was never called off and as a result the workers started resuming gradually. If this study solely intended to focus on the survival strategies of the workers in times of crisis, it would have been justifiable to fix an arbitrary criterion on the duration of the strike for each individual worker, for example, selecting workers who had been on strike for a period of at least nine or twelve months. But as the purpose of this study is to throw light also on the attitudes of the workers (for example, towards trade unions, leaders and strike events) such a criterion would cut out all the less-motivated workers and would thereby distort reality. The advantage offered by a time limit had to be weighed against a likely bias in the sample as far as the views and attitudes of the workers were concerned.

I decided against a time limit in the expectation of finding an answer to the question of survival strategies. In any case, hardly anyone resumed work within three months because of the tremendous support of the workers for the strike. Besides, ninety days seemed to be a long enough period to be able to say something meaningful about the means adopted by the workers to tide over this period. When the interviews were over, it transpired that without any time limit, a mere seven workers in the sample had resumed work within the first three months of the strike.

In Table 6.16 the averages of the duration of the strike for permanent workers and *badli*s in the two mills have been given separately. In calculating the average strike duration, the fifty workers in the sample who were rendered unemployed in the wake of the strike have been excluded. This includes the twenty-three 'unemployed' Finlay workers who were labelled as such because of the extremely long time that elapsed between the commencement of the strike and their reinstatement or because of the terms of employment (permanent workers taken back as 'temporary' workers). The justification for this is illustrated by the fact that these twenty-three workers on an average had to wait for over thirty-six months before they were allowed to enter the mill premises. In the case of the unemployed Spring workers it is impossible to say when the strike ended for them as they never got back their jobs.

TABLE 6.16
Average Duration of the Strike in Months
(100 Re-employed Workers)

Category	*Finlay**		*Spring**		*Average**	
Permanent	18.9	(35)	9.5	(35)	14.2	(70)
Badli	11.3	(15)	8.5	(15)	9.9	(30)
Total		(50)		(50)		(100)

* Number of workers in brackets.

The weighted arithmetic average for the thirty employed *badli*s and the seventy employed permanent workers in the large sample works out to 12.9 months. This average compares well with the average strike duration of the 100 workers in the small sample which appeared to be 12.6 months. In view of the large number of mills involved in the small sample no comparison could be made between them. The s.d. for permanent Finlay workers is 8.9 against an s.d. of 5.0 for Spring Mills. The s.d. for *badli*s in Finlay is 6.8 against 3.9 for Spring Mills.

In the Table above the first thing to be noted is that there is a conspicuous difference between Finlay and Spring workers regarding the time that passed between the beginning of the indefinite strike and resumption of work. Finlay workers in both categories remained on strike much longer. There are several factors which may explain this. One is that the Spring workers were more exposed to pressure from the mills than Finlay workers. It should be recalled that the majority of all Spring workers were living in rooms and chawls belonging to the mill, the implications of which have been discussed above.

Secondly, pressure from the Sangh and the police to end the strike was most noticeable in the mill areas (the surroundings of the chawls belonging to Bombay Dyeing were described by several workers as resembling an armed camp). The Finlay workers were much more dispersed in the city and in consequence they were not confronted daily with the concentrated effort of millowners, the Sangh and police to break the strike. A third important factor is that Spring Mills opened its gates long before Finlay did. This too, contributed to undermining the morale of the striking workers for as long as the gates were closed there was no strong incentive to report for work.

A fourth factor, the possibility that Spring workers on the whole had fewer opportunities of finding alternative employment and were forced as a result to resume earlier, may be ruled out as will be shown shortly. Both groups had comparable, though different opportunities of tiding over the difficulties. In fact, it is possible to argue that the opportunities for Spring workers were, if anything, better as more Spring workers than Finlay workers owned land and their level of education and income was higher. It may be concluded that essentially a combination of three factors can explain, by and large, why such a striking difference is to be found between the average duration of the strike in the case of Finlay and Spring workers. These factors relate to exposure of Spring workers to concentrated pressure by the mill, police and the Sangh, to the fact that Spring Mills reopened at an early stage and to strong dependence on the mill in terms of housing.

Another noteworthy aspect of the figures in Table 6.16 is that *badli*s appeared to resume duty much sooner than permanent workers. In the case of Spring Mills the difference is not so great as both categories returned to the mill at a comparatively early stage but in the case of Finlay the difference is striking. By computing the total average for *badli*s in the sample and comparing this with the average for permanent workers, the differences are reduced but by no means wiped out. This calls for an explanation. The finding is important as it seems to belie the often heard opinion that *badli*s were the most determined participants in the strike and its most zealous propagandists. If there is any truth in that view then it could only have been so at the beginning of the strike for as time progressed *badli*s apparently gave in sooner.

Instead of going by the impressions of persons who were no textile workers themselves, it seemed more sensible to ask the workers themselves which group, if any, was in the forefront of the struggle. Subsequently this question was put to fifty-four workers, forty-three permanent workers and eleven *badli*s. The answers were revealing because only five workers positively believed that *badli*s were the most eager to start and continue the struggle. Against this, twenty-three workers declared that permanent workers were most interested in doing so. The remaining twenty-six workers stated that there was really no difference in this regard between these two categories of workers. What is perhaps most revealing is that none of the eleven *badli*s who were asked this question thought that *badli*s were most active in the strike.

It may be concluded that if there was any difference at all between *badli*s and permanent workers in terms of strike involvement, there is no reason to believe that the former were the most determined strike participants. Any statement to the contrary is usually based on impression influenced by what may seem to be most logical (a higher stake for the *badli*s in the strike) but nevertheless ill-founded. The undeniable fact that they gave in sooner may have to be related to their means of continuing the struggle, the assumption being that these were fewer and/or of inferior quality compared to those of the permanent workers.

It has been asserted in the foregoing that the workers' ties with the villages of origin were of vital importance to their chances of surviving a prolonged period without an income. For this reason, the average duration of the strike is a fact that has to be related to the stay of the workers during the strike if we want to judge the importance of the rural connections for the workers. It has been shown in chapter 3 that nobody knows for certain just how many workers left for their villages. But what could not be established for the entire labour force was fairly easy to find for the workers in the sample. To be able to assess the significance of the rural ties for the workers in the sample, the workers have been classified according to where they lived during the strike (Table 6.17).

It was found that a large majority of the workers spent time in the village as well as in the city during the strike period. This finding obscured the fact that in most cases workers stayed predominantly in one place. To be able to say where the worker spent most of his time it appeared necessary to introduce a new criterion. If a worker spent 70 per cent or more of his time in the city then he was put in the category 'Bombay' and similarly for the village. The remaining percentages have been clubbed together in the category 'Other' (see Table 6.17).

TABLE 6.17
Stay of Workers During Strike

	Finlay	*Spring*	*Total*	*Percentage*
Bombay	45	35	80	53.3
Village	26	35	61	40.7
Other	4	5	9	6.0
Total	75	75	150	100.0

It appears that more than half the workers remained in Bombay during the strike, but given the method of selection it would be too hazardous to generalize this finding and conclude that the same might be true for the rest of the textile workers. What the figures do suggest is that any statement that a substantial majority of the workers left Bombay ought to be treated with caution.

Avenues of Alternative Employment

Importance of Agriculture: Having described the socio-economic background of the workers, their living conditions and the average time they were on strike, it is time to see how they survived the strike period. It became clear that only few workers remained completely without work during the period they were on strike. In the majority of cases they kept themselves occupied (for example, cultivating their own land) or were alternatively employed at least for some time. When discussing the various avenues open to the worker, it should be borne in mind that a large group of workers practised more than one trade in the course of the strike which is why the grand total of the figures presented in Table 6.18 does not add up to 150.

Looking at the Table it is obvious that cultivation of land, be it as an agricultural labourer or as owner, was the most important source of alternative employment for the striking workers. Not less than thirty-five workers in the sample (23 per cent) wholly occupied themselves in the cultivation of their own plot of land and/or herding their own cattle. In the case of the eleven workers this did not suffice and they had to combine cultivation of their own land with agricultural wage labour. Finlay workers are particularly strongly represented in this category.

TABLE 6.18

Alternative Employment During the Strike

Category	*Finlay*			*Spring*			*Grand Total*
	Perm.	*Badli*	*Total*	*Perm.*	*Badli*	*Total*	
I: Farming	9	1	10	19	6	25	35
II: Agr. Labourer	5	1	6	6	9	9	15
Combining I + II	8	1	9	1	1	2	11
Powerloom weaver	14	5	19	1	-	1	20
Textile worker*	5	-	5	1	-	1	6
Handloom weaver	2	-	2	-	-	-	2
Begari	14	1	15	4	1	5	20
Mazdoor	6	1	7	2	-	2	9
Factory work	3	2	5	1	1	2	7
Helper**	6	3	9	5	-	5	14
Selling on road	2	-	2	-	-	-	2
Vendor fruit/ vegetables	9	1	10	2	2	4	14
Other***	1	1	6	5	6	11	17
Unemployed	3	2	5	8	3	11	16

* Refers to workers who started working during the strike in another mill than their own.

** Helper in odd jobs, usually casual labour (for example, watchman, *hamal*, bidi-making, painting).

*** Includes: shop assistant, shopkeeper, postman, peon, policeman, soldier, cobbler, carpenter, working at home.

A third group consists of those workers who possessed no land worth the name and who had to hire themselves out as agricultural labourers. The jobs were diverse. Apart from tilling the land they were employed in herding cattle, digging wells, constructing water tanks or employed in seasonal labour. A few of them were employed under the Employment Guarantee Scheme (EGS) which seeks to provide employment to the poor in the rural areas.[3] Benefiting from this scheme they were employed in levelling land, constructing roads, percolation tanks and so on. By including these workers in the group who tried to survive in the village we find that in all sixty-one workers (40 per cent) were thus engaged in agriculture or related activities during the strike. This corresponds with the number of sample workers staying in the village. It should be recalled that 53 per cent of the workers in the sample remained in Bombay but even this cannot undermine the predominance of agriculture in all sources of alternative employment.

There are conspicuously more Spring workers to be found in the category 'farming' than those of Finlay, and this is in consonance with occupational differences between the fathers of the workers, as pointed out earlier. On the other hand, the group of workers who had to combine cultivation of their own plot with agricultural wage labour (the third category) shows a higher incidence of Finlay workers. This too corresponds with the occupations of the fathers. Combining the first three categories it becomes clear that Finlay workers have sought recourse to agriculture to a much lesser degree than their counterparts from Spring Mills.

The picture is reversed if we look at two other remarkable sources of employment, namely working as a weaver in the powerloom sector and working in other mills than the one to which the worker actually belonged. It appears that in all twenty-four Finlay workers availed themselves of these opportunities against only two from Spring. As the employers sought the assistance of the powerloom sector to keep up production, it is justifiable to categorize work in the powerlooms as a strike-breaking activity although hardly any worker saw it as such. The large majority of the workers simply failed to see the connection between working in the mills and in the powerlooms. Of course, those who started working in other mills were well aware that their behaviour jeopardized the success of the strike, although even in their case working in another mill was considered more as a survival strategy than as a strike-breaking act. The fact that many more Finlay than Spring workers sought employment in the powerlooms will have to be related to the overrepresentation of weavers in the Finlay sample. As working in the powerlooms was only open to weavers, Finlay workers were bound to be more numerous among those seeking employment in the powerlooms than those from Spring (see Table 6.1).

It is surprising, however, that merely 10 per cent of the workers in the sample declared that they remained unemployed throughout the strike period despite attempts to find alternative employment. Contrary to what one might expect, this group is not dominated by those who returned to the mills within the first few months of the strike. In fact, six of them lost their jobs altogether and the average strike period for the remaining ten workers appeared to be nearly eight months.

Working as a *begari* appeared to be another important avenue for alternative employment. The work of a *begari* eludes precise definition as the term is applied to various sorts of skilled labour inclusive of carpentry, masonry, digging wells and so on. It appears that far more Finlay than Spring workers found a job as a *begari* for which the fact that the Finlay workers were more strongly city-based may well be responsible. The two cases of selling on the roadside refer to the sale of toys and ornaments. It should be noted that in all five workers said they had worked under the Employment Guarantee Scheme. Another eight workers (two from Finlay and six from Spring Mills) did not seek alternative employment, usually because they intended to resume work at the mills at an early stage, that is, within two months.

Time Worked During Strike: The various jobs found by workers during the strike helped them to tide over the strike period but the importance of these activities cannot be assessed adequately without knowing how much time they were engaged in such alternative employment. An obvious difficulty here was that many workers took various jobs in the course of the strike and in many cases it appeared to be difficult to estimate the time they were employed or self-employed. In consequence, the percentages are only estimates but they provide an insight into the importance of alternative employment. In order to arrive at a percentage in the case of workers who were rendered unemployed, it was necessary to fix a deadline. In their case the strike period was considered to have ended the day they were informed about their dismissal or the day they concluded that they had lost their jobs.

With the aid of the figures in Table 6.19 it is possible to draw some conclusions. It appears that only a tiny fraction of the striking workers could hardly find any alternative employment during the period when they were on strike. If we combine this fraction with the group that worked little (that is, less than half the time), we find that twenty-four workers (seven plus seventeen) of the workers on strike worked less than 50 per cent of the time. If we include the category 'Unknown' in this group (twenty-six workers), it appears that no more than fifty workers (33 per cent of the sample) were incapable of finding employment for the better part of the duration of the strike. Actually, the real number of those who did not have alternative employment is smaller for this figure of 33 per cent includes all those who never intended to go on strike and wanted to resume at the earliest opportunity. This group comprises eighteen workers (see Table 7.12: the categories 0 and 1). But even so, the Table shows clearly that in any case half the workers worked practically throughout the strike period and two-thirds of the workers were employed for more than half the time.

TABLE 6.19
Time Worked During the Strike

Category	*Finlay*			*Spring*			*Grand Total*
	Perm.	Badli	*Total*	*Perm.*	Badli	*Total*	
25 per cent or less	2	1	3	3	1	4	7
26 per cent–50 per cent	5	-	5	9	3	12	17
51 per cent–75 per cent	16	6	22	4	2	6	28
76 per cent or more	32	5	37	23	12	35	72
Unknown*	5	3	8	14	4	18	26
Total	60	15	75	53	22	75	150

* Usually workers who did various jobs of short duration, were unable to indicate for how much time. The category also includes early resumers.

Being alternatively employed does not mean, of course, that the earnings of the workers were comparable to those in the mills. In practically all cases these earnings were less and often even very poor. This is borne out by the fact that a large majority mentioned financial worries as their greatest problem during the strike. But there is no denying that textile workers were apparently very successful in finding alternative employment. Although the earnings were (very) poor in many cases, the workers' success in finding new avenues of employment largely explains why the strike did not collapse through sheer exhaustion of the workers and lasted as long as it did.

The case of the badlis: It has been observed in the preceding paragraph that there was a notable difference in the average strike duration for *badli*s as compared with permanent workers. A possible explanation for this difference could be that *badli*s had fewer chances of finding alternative employment than permanent workers. Table 6.20 regroups the data provided in Table 6.18, with the emphasis on the variable '*badli*' versus 'permanent'.

TABLE 6.20

Alternative Employment According to Status

Category	*Permanent*	Badli	*Total*
I : Agricultural labourer	11	4	15
II : Farming	28	7	35
III : Combining I + II	9	2	11
Powerloom weaver	15	5	20
Textile worker	6	-	6
Handloom weaver	2	-	2
Begari	18	2	20
Factory work	4	3	7
Helper	11	3	14
Mazdoor	8	1	9
Selling on roads	2	–	2
Vendor fruits/vegetables	11	3	14
Other	10	7	17
Unemployed	11	5	16

It appears that there are indeed some differences in the work undertaken by *badli*s and permanent workers during the strike but given the variety of jobs done by the workers, it would have been surprising if such differences had not existed. On the whole, however, the pattern of alternative employment is not very different. It transpires that the most important avenues of employment are alike. Against forty-eight permanent workers employed in agriculture (the first three categories of Table 6.20) there are thirteen *badli*s. This means that from a total of sixty-one sample workers engaged in agriculture, 21 per cent are *badli*s which corresponds well with their proportionate share in the sample (24.7 per cent). In the case of work in the powerlooms the share of the *badli*s is exactly 25 per cent. By clubbing together the employment opportunities grouped in the somewhat vague categories of '*begari*' and 'Other' we find that permanent workers had a share of 76 per cent of the opportunities coming under these categories against 24 per cent for *badli*s.

Some differences remain. It is worth noting, for instance, that the *badli*s in the sample did not take recourse to working in other mills (the category 'textile worker') although this might have been expected given the fact that *badli*s resumed work earlier. In the category of those who could not find a job they seem slightly overrepresented (31 per cent). Again, in the category 'mazdoor' they seem underrepresented. Broadly speaking it may be said that the opportunities for alternative employment were open to both permanent workers and *badli*s in the same measure. It follows that lack of employment opportunities as compared with those for permanent workers cannot be considered a strong incentive for *badli*s to return to the mills before the permanent workers did so. The contention, therefore, that *badli*s had fewer chances than permanent workers to find alternative employment has to be rejected.

This still leaves us with the possibility of attributing the early return to work of *badli*s to their incapacity to secure alternative employment for an equally long period. By relating the findings of Table 6.20 to the terms of employment we can decide this question. This has been done in Table 6.21.

After dividing *badli*s and permanent workers according to the amount of time spent working during the strike, we find that there is not much difference to be noted. Broadly speaking, *badli*s are represented in a percentage of approximately 25 per cent in each category, corresponding to their number in the large sample. Therefore, neither the sort of work *badli*s undertook during the strike nor the duration of their alternative employment can adequately explain why they resumed earlier.

TABLE 6.21
Time Worked During Strike for *Badli*s and Permanent Workers Separately

Category	*Perm.*	Badli	*Total*
25% or less	5	2	7
26%–50%	14	3	17
51%–75%	20	8	28
76% or more	55	17	72
Unknown	19	7	26
Total	113	37	150

A different explanation is therefore necessary. Although no questions were asked to verify this possibility, it is likely that job uncertainty among *badli*s was stronger than among permanent workers. It was to be expected that if the employers started dismissing workers and resorted to retrenchment, *badli*s would be their first victims as there was no obligation to provide them with work since there was no labour contract. The announcement by the millowners of the cancellation of *badli* passes at an early stage may have had a stronger impact on them than the threat of dismissal on permanent workers.

A less honourable possibility is that *badli*s hoped to secure permanency by replacing permanent workers in the mills. Such promotions seemed more likely by adopting a servile/cooperative attitude towards the management as the strike dragged on. However, this last possibility ascribes motives to *badli*s for which there is no evidence. If this factor really played a significant role then there should have been friction between *badli*s and permanent workers as the latter would certainly have been aware of the objectives of the former. To my surprise I could scarcely find a trace of this. Only two workers from the whole sample confirmed tensions between *badli*s and permanent workers and explained this by pointing to the tendency of *badli*s to resume earlier. One of them said that *badli*s were sometimes beaten up for that by permanent workers but he hastened to add that this happened very rarely. Even here it is far from certain that the beating up of these unfortunate workers is attributable to their *badli* status. It is only reasonable to assume that permanent workers in their case would have received the same treatment.

What was found (or rather, not found) among the 150 workers was confirmed by the replies of 100 workers from the random sample. No less than ninety-seven of the 100 workers from that sample affirmed that there had been no frictions between *badli*s and permanent workers and that the cooperation between them during the strike was good. In the remaining three cases the question was accidentally overlooked. It is evident from this that the hope of replacing a permanent worker played at best a minor role in the decision of the *badli*s to resume work.

Apart from job uncertainty and the fairly remote possibility of considerations like benefiting from the continuation of the strike by permanent workers if they resumed early, there is a third factor which might provide an explanation. As pointed out earlier, *badli*s are the youngest workers in the textile industry. It is a common experience in the world of trade unionism that younger workers in particular strongly press for a strike if there is a labour conflict. Because of their age they usually have fewer responsibilities with regard to maintaining a family, and this also applies to the workers in the sample (eight out of ten unmarried workers, for example, were *badli*s). It is likely that the zeal demonstrated by them in the beginning turned quickly into frustration as the strike progressed. It is certainly imagineable that this had a stronger impact on their decision to resume work than in the case of the more experienced permanent workers who were less easily frustrated. One could term this the endurance factor.

To sum up, the factor of unequal opportunities for alternative employment cannot explain the differences between *badlis* and permanent workers. Differences in the average duration of alternative employment appeared to be equally untenable. We may conclude that three other factors, that is, job uncertainty, replacing permanent workers and differences in endurance or any combination of these explain better why *badli*s on the whole tended to resume earlier. The available data, however, do not allow for a positive identification of these considerations among the *badli*s, although they seem to offer the best explanation.

Flexibility of the Labour Market: That most workers did find alternative employment during the strike indicates that the labour market, within as well as outside the city, is very flexible. Yet, one would expect that the flooding of this market by tens of thousands of jobless textile workers would not go unnoticed. One imagines that the arrival of so many newcomers on the scene would be resented by regular workers in the trades concerned, and cause ill will. Following this line of thinking it would be imaginable that this uneasiness among those who were suddenly confronted with the entry of numerous competitors for employment and income would even, at times, result in outright aggression.

In order to check the validity of these thoughts the workers were asked to indicate what sort of problems they faced when entering the employment territory of others. This question was not asked to those who remained unemployed throughout the strike. The unemployed workers seem to have met with other problems. Several of them declared that the reason why they remained unemployed during the strike was not that they could find no job but that employers tried to exploit the situation by offering them work for wages far below those they were paying their own workers for the same type of work. Such offers could be as low as 30 per cent of the regular wage. Generally speaking, textile workers were also hampered by another problem, namely the stigma attached to them. Employers often refused to give them work fearing that employing a textile worker might herald the entry of trade unions in their factory or shop.

Leaving aside the group of workers who remained unemployed, the question of what sorts of problems the workers encountered in their attempts to enter new fields was not applicable to all those who, for whatever reason, did not seek alternative employment. Neither did it apply to those who cultivated their own land. In all, the question was put to eighty-nine workers, eighty-two of whom declared that they had not faced any problem. The remaining seven did have problems but of an unexpected kind. Their complaint was not that persons employed in the fields they desired to enter prevented or hindered them from doing so but that they were troubled by others, particularly the police and representatives of the municipality. Officials of these organizations insisted on bribes (*hafta*)* to allow newcomers to practise a trade.

---

* Literally 'weekly'. A weekly extortion in compensation for turning a blind eye to a violation of law.

The workers explained this by saying that those who tried to make a living by selling articles, fruits or vegetables on the roadside did not have a licence and could be fined for this. To avoid such harassment it was necessary to bribe the representative of the municipality and/or the police. The amounts differred and seemed to depend on the sort of activity and the supposed earnings. A worker selling vegetables said that he paid a *hafta* of Rs 20 per month to people from the municipality. A worker with a flourishing business of selling snacks, however, said that he had to pay Rs 600 per month to officials of the police and the municipality. A licence would cost him Rs 12,000, he declared, and so he preferred to pay. He soon learned the lesson that the price for not paying is high. Once, when he refused to pay, his carriage was confiscated. Another worker too, saw his goods (vegetables) being confiscated on one occasion. Harassment could also take the shape of articles or vegetables being taken without payment.

Compared to such fairly frequent trouble caused by officials, only one worker (who sold vegetables) complained of opposition from other vendors. He circumvented this problem by regularly shifting his place of work. Another worker said that he found it difficult to sell vegetables as no one would buy from him because he was a newcomer but here the problem was evidently not created by other vendors but by the public. His problems ended, however, the day he decided to sell coconuts instead.

It may be concluded that what is usually and imperfectly designated 'the informal sector' appeared to be very flexible, the striking workers could enter and leave this sector at will. If the workers faced any serious problems at all they are attributable to employers trying to exploit the situation, officials or the police. They did not, however, meet with any resistance worth the name from those already employed in this sector. It may be concluded that the elasticity of this sector is a boon to workers in distress although the employment opportunities it has to offer are hardly an alternative to mill work which guarantees the textile worker not only a regular but also a better income.

PROBLEMS DURING THE STRIKE

Time but No Money

Although it is true that nearly all workers found some sort of alternative employment during the strike, Table 6.22 also indicates that twenty-four workers (16 per cent) worked for less than half the strike period. Besides, many disliked the work they were obliged to do. How to spend the time during this seemingly endless strike was a great problem for many. After a few weeks many workers began to realize that they had been overoptimistic in expecting an early end to the struggle. Certainly after a couple of months the workers understood that the strike was going to be the long-drawn affair Datta Samant had predicted. As time dragged on, the need to seek alternative employment or, at least, to find some activity to kill time became more pressing.

Whenever workers did not have work they were obliged to spend a lot of time sitting at home, roaming about, talking to friends, visiting relatives, and relaxing (*aram*). It is no surprise then that such ways of passing time (ways which one could club together as 'leisure activities') rank second to work. Apart from those who found alternative employment, providing them with work throughout the strike, most workers combined work with an unusual amount of such activities. Only a small number of workers (about 10 per cent of the sample) mentioned looking for a job as their major occupation during the strike, which corroborates the earlier finding that practically all workers were employed in the course of the strike even if this work did not occupy them the full day.

A few of those who did not seek alternative employment or who could not find it, made themselves useful at home by doing the shopping, fetching children from school or helping their wife with various household tasks. Not more than seven workers said they had made themselves useful in this way. Some others contributed to community life by organizing sports and games, bhajans* or by undertaking construction work on behalf of the village.

---

* 'Bhajan' means devotional song but the term is also used to denote sessions of devotional singing in which many people may take part.

Finally, a small number of workers (two from Finlay and eight from Spring) mentioned altogether different activities during the strike. These workers were often active in the union and devoted a lot of time to helping to organize meetings, keeping a watch over the mill gates and collecting or distributing food and money. These activities tended to be concentrated in the first few months of the strike after which they gradually petered off. Not all of these workers could, after this period of agitation, concentrate on alternative employment because their exposure had made them vulnerable. Several of them were hounded by the police and, rightly or wrongly, implicated in murder cases, obliging them to be constantly on the move.

Staying at home, be it in the village or in the city, may have been a welcome change from the dullness of daily routine in the first few days or even weeks of the strike but before long problems would come, and rarely one at a time. Table 6.22 presents the principal categories of difficulties experienced by the workers. While studying this Table it should be borne in mind that a majority of the workers mentioned more than one problem when they were asked to state what problems they had to face during the strike. Understandably, financial problems were the most pressing and the overwhelming majority of the workers (87 per cent) suffered from them. This implies that even workers who permitted themselves a lifestyle similar to that they had assumed prior to the strike were not altogether free from financial worries.

TABLE 6.22

Major Problems Experienced During the Strike

Category	*Finlay*	*Spring*	*Total*	*Percentage (n = 150)*
Finance	67	64	131	87.3
Boredom	40	41	81	54.0
Tensions at home	33	27	60	40.0
Unaccustomed hard work	12	16	28	18.7
No problems	3	7	10	6.7
Other	5	6	11	7.3

The Table has another important implication, namely that the income derived from alternative employment was usually not enough to make both ends meet. Only for a small group (about 7 per cent of the sample) did the prolongation of the strike seem to have posed no problems whatsoever. These workers are, of course, included in the much larger group of 37 per cent of the sample (see Table 6.23) declaring that they did not (have to) economize during the strike and that they could afford to live as they were used to before the commencement of the struggle.

TABLE 6.23
Items to Economize

Category	*Finlay*	*Spring*	*Total*	*Percentage (n = 150)*
Lived as before	20	36	56	37.3
Meals	34	23	57	38.0
Clothes	24	16	40	26.7
Bidi	14	7	21	14.0
Outings	10	14	24	16.0
Tea	11	7	18	12.0
Daru*	8	4	12	8.0
Everything	8	6	14	9.3

* Hard liquor

Money was not the only problem troubling the striking workers. Another problem, which is easily overlooked, was boredom. As the strike dragged on, more and more workers had to cope with it. More than half the workers (54 per cent) complained of serious boredom accompanying the unending struggle. Often they had no work to do and just sat at home. Even if they had work, it was often only temporary and frequently they intensely disliked the type of work they had to do. Those workers who had nothing or little to do were, of course, most troubled by boredom but working too (particularly in the fields) was boring to a great many others.

To be sure, not all workers disliked the sort of work they had to do. Particularly among those who could work in the fields, there were many who greatly enjoyed cultivating the land and working in the fresh air. Twelve workers expressly stated that they liked working in the fields but against these there are twenty-eight who disliked or even hated the type of work they had to do. They longed to go back to the mills as they realized (or discovered) that working in the fields meant hard labour for long hours under a scorching sun. Besides, the yield and/or earnings were very poor. Even the twelve workers who liked cultivating the land were unanimously of the view that they had no choice but to return to the mills as their work in the fields did not pay. These findings show that the millowners' claim, that tens of thousands of workers never showed up at the gates after the strike because they had meanwhile discovered the joys of village life, are patently false and are intended to disguise the fact that these workers were not taken back.

Being at home for many days and for many hours of the day was a novel experience for the workers but not always a happy one. The conditions created by the strike (job uncertainty, financial problems, boredom) were such that enjoyment of family life was clearly more an exception than the rule. Not surprisingly, 40 per cent of the workers said that marital tensions and/or frictions with family members and other relatives poisoned the atmosphere. The combination of lack of resources and boredom was a source of trouble not easily overcome. The first element (lack of money) reinforced the other and not less than forty-one out of the sixty workers who mentioned tensions at home, ascribed their problems to them.

Finally, it must be noted that Table 6.22 shows that there is hardly any difference in the problems experienced by workers from Finlay and Spring. This strongly suggests that the findings are applicable to workers from other mills as well. The conclusion that boredom played a significant role in the strike is therefore, warranted, as is the conclusion that boredom in combination with lack of resources is an important source of tension influencing the morale of striking workers. Its obvious implication is that the leaders of a long strike can ill afford to neglect the impact of these factors on strike morale as they have a strong bearing on the success of a struggle. In the course of the strike under study, several campaigns were launched in the rural hinterland which, inter alia, served the purpose of boosting the sagging morale of the workers. However, these campaigns were restricted to certain periods only and could do little to help the workers cope with day-to-day problems.

Surviving with Debts and Sales

The earnings of the workers during the strike were in many cases far below those they had been used to. This necessitated a drastic change in the pattern of expenditure but the income of a worker is such that it is very difficult to economize. Whatever frills existed in their lives had to be cut down but there was hardly any scope for reducing expenses with the result that a majority of the workers started cutting into essential commodities such as food and clothes. Having exhausted the limited possibilities offered by reducing the consumption of drinks, tea and *paan*,* they tried to save on vegetables, food grains and pulses.

Table 6.23 bears out that the workers could only economize on a few items. The first thing to note is that an amazingly large group of fifty-six workers declared that they lived more or less as they had before the strike (the reasons for this will be discussed in the next paragraph). It is no surprise that food and clothes were mentioned most often as items on which the workers tried to save money. Bidis,† a poor man's luxury, was also an item of economy. Tea, an item which can scarcely be called a luxury and which was already taken with a very low frequency (workers in the chawls did not take it more than twice a day), was economized on. In some cases this meant that workers gave up drinking tea altogether.

As there were not many ways of living cheaper (for those in the city even less than for those who could move to the village), workers had to take recourse to selling property or contracting debts. It is logical that the overwhelming majority of the workers resorted to such devices. In all, 125 workers said that they had to sell or mortgage property and/or to take loans in the course of the strike. Given that Spring workers had, by and large, a wealthier background, it is no surprise that Finlay workers, with sixty-seven cases, are slightly stronger represented than Spring workers, with fifty-eight cases. The difference in the average strike duration for the workers of these mills contributed to the differences in taking loans

---

* Betel leaf.

† Bidis are a cheap alternative for cigarettes in India A bidi consists of a rolled leaf of *tembhurni* containing a small amount of tobacco. The rolled leaf is tied at one end with cotton thread.

(cf. Table 6.16). There is a similarity here with the *badlis* for 50 per cent of the few workers who did not have to sell property or take loans during the strike were *badlis,* which may be related to their shorter strike participation.

Table 6.24 shows the means the workers adopted to obtain money. Only a few workers mentioned that they spent their savings and a reason for that may have been that they hardly had any. In general, the savings of textile workers are meagre. Deshpande provides some figures. Merely 31 per cent of the workers had savings in cash or deposits prior to the strike. Three-quarters out of that group of workers had savings of less than Rs 2,000, a fifth even below Rs 500. It is clear that this money was not going to take them far. The number of workers who had savings after eight months on strike (the time when Deshpande conducted his survey) had come down to 3 per cent (Deshpande 1983: 9–13). Going by official figures, the strike was not even halfway then. In the course of this research no questions were included in the interviews pertaining to savings and hence a comparison with the data supplied by Deshpande is not possible.

TABLE 6.24

Sale of Property and Taking of Loans

Category	*Finlay*	*Spring*	*Total*	*Percentage (n = 150)*
Property sale*	4	3	7	4.7
Loans	31	38	69	46.0
Property sale + Loans	32	17	49	32.7
Nothing	8	17	25	16.7
Total	75	75	150	100.1

* Includes two cases of workers who only spent their savings.

The largest group by far is that of those who managed solely on loans. Another substantial group (forty-nine workers) were forced to sell property, besides taking loans or vice versa. Very few workers mentioned that they utilized their savings to tide over the difficulties, which suggests that these savings were small anyway for it seems unlikely that workers would resort to interest-bearing loans or selling property before using up their savings. Needless to say, these figures do not allow any judgement to be passed regarding the category of workers who came off worst.

In the course of the strike the newspapers published several stories about how moneylenders took advantage of the distressed workers by demanding exorbitant interest or by paying miserly rates for jewellery offered for sale by the workers. Just how many workers sought the help of moneylenders is unknown. Some idea of the persons to whom the workers addressed themselves when they needed money may be gained from Table 6.25. As relevant questions allowing for a comprehensive view were asked when the interviews schedule had already been in progress for some time, only 103 workers were questioned about this aspect, who provided in all 110 answers. The remaining forty-seven cases include twenty-five workers to whom the question did not apply.

TABLE 6.25
Source of Loans to Workers

Category	*Finlay*	*Spring*	*Total*	*Percentage (n = 110)*
Friends	25	23	48	43.6
Relatives/Family	10	16	26	23.6
Moneylender	11	3	14	12.7
Bank	3	10	13	11.8
Credit Society	5	4	9	8.2
Total	54	56	110	99.9

These 103 workers mentioned basically five sources from which they drew money. As some workers had to take recourse to several sources the total does not equal 103. It appears that two-thirds of the loans involved money borrowed from friends and relatives.[4] Many workers insisted that this should not be construed to mean that these friends and relatives were in sympathy with the strike but their bonds were such that they had to oblige. As time passed, however, it became increasingly difficult to ask for more money.

Looking at the Table it is at once clear that the moneylender played a minor role in the supply of money to the workers. Concluding that the role of the moneylender as a supplier of funds was fairly limited is not the same as denying that they could play havoc in the lives of individual workers. The interest workers had to pay was at times stunning. Only three workers in this group of fourteen workers said that they had to pay an interest of 2 per cent per month which comes to 24 per cent on a yearly basis. This percentage was comparatively moderate for three others were obliged to accept an interest of 5 per cent per month (60 per cent on an annual basis), another 7.5 per cent interest per month and a third 10 per cent per month.

These incredible percentages help explain why one worker in the sample could state that he had a debt of not less than Rs 45,000 to a moneylender which implies perpetual bondage. This particular worker was forced to take recourse to a moneylender because of a couple of marriages in his family. Fortunately, this was an exceptional case. Excluding this one worker, the average debt with the moneylender for the remaining thirteen workers was Rs 6,300 which is not very different from the debt incurred by other workers during the strike and indicates that workers try to avoid taking loans or mortgaging property with moneylenders.

Banks could do a great deal to relieve the workers from the burden of borrowing money against unjustifiable interest. For workers the banks are, however, not a common source of finance. There is a remarkable difference between Finlay and Spring workers as far as their recourse to banks and moneylender is concerned. The difference shows a mirror picture, for if more Finlay workers than Spring workers approached moneylenders, we see that Spring workers had less difficulty in finding their way to the bank. If we add to this that apparently more Spring workers could borrow money from relatives than their counterparts from Finlay, then this finding corroborates what has been observed in the earlier part of this chapter, namely that Spring workers are as a whole a wealthier and better-educated group. Even so, it has to be pointed out that getting a loan from the bank was by no means easy for an ordinary worker and several of them had to invent stories to obtain money. Some said that they needed the money for the repair of a roof, others declared that they wanted it for land improvement (for example, to buy a pump for irrigation) and still others convinced the bank that they wanted to set up a business.

Ornaments and jewellery were items most often sold by the workers when they were in need of money. Not less than 57 per cent of those who sold property appeared to have sold jewellery. The sale of (a portion of the) land owned, a room or even a house came second and occurred with a much lower but still considerable frequency (20 per cent). Kitchen utensils make up another 13 per cent of the sales. The remaining 10 per cent is accounted for by the sale of trees, animals (goats, buffaloes), equipment (for example, sewing machines), radios and so on.

Just staying alive was difficult enough for a number of workers but the situation could worsen drastically on special occasions or times of crisis. In all sixty-five workers reported cases of birth (eleven), sickness (eighteen), marriage (twenty-three) and death (twenty-two) occurring in the course of the strike. Some had to cope not just with one but with several problems during the period. The cases of birth and sickness were predominantly related to their own (nuclear) family, but marriages, apart from the marriages of their own children, might involve sisters or the children of other relatives. Death referred mostly to expenses at the funeral of one of the parents but also to the death of other relatives. In 63 per cent of the cases the expenses involved were met through loans, in 28 per cent the problems were resolved differently, usually by the family stepping in to meet the expenses. In the remaining 9 per cent of the cases workers took recourse to mortgaging or selling property.

It has been said before that workers were forced to take loans and/or sell property in order to survive the strike period. The extent to which this happened depended, inter alia, on the duration of the strike for each individual worker, on the availability of alternative employment, on the existence or otherwise of other breadwinners and on the need to remain in the city. The figures relating to the number of people who had to take loans and sell property need to be complemented with data on how much debt the workers had incurred when they returned to the mills. These figures are presented in Table 6.26.

Surprisingly, a quarter of all the workers managed to tide over the strike period without incurring debts. Another quarter appears to have incurred considerable debts (Rs 7,001 and above). However, in this last case debts were rarely caused solely by the ongoing strike. In most cases, events like marriages, purchase of a house or land, chronic illness or the death of a relative required extraordinary expenditure which—even without the strike—would have necessitated loans or the sale of property.

TABLE 6.26
Debts at the End of the Strike

Rupees	*Finlay*	*Spring*	*Total*	*Percentage*
No debt	16	22	38	25.3
500–1,500	3	12	15	10.0
1,501–3,500	7	9	16	10.7
3,501–7,000	25	17	42	28.0
7,001–11,000	13	9	22	14.7
More	11	6	17	11.3
Total	75	75	150	100.0

This is not to say that the strike made no difference, for the absence of a regular income greatly increased the financial burden. The Table shows that most workers had incurred a debt ranging between Rs 3,501 and Rs 7,000, an amount which proved to be a heavy burden as late as 1987. Deshpande's survey corroborates these findings. He found that the average debt after nine months of the strike was nearly Rs 3,000 (Deshpande, 1983: 15). Another important conclusion may be drawn. If we are prepared to consider a debt of Rs 1,500 or below as relatively moderate then it is clear that in spite of the strike not less than 35 per cent of the workers remained free of debt or incurred little debt.

Loans were needed to meet the daily expenses, including food. During the strike practically all workers, whether they were city- or village-based, took their meals at home (with their family or with relatives). However, there was a small group of workers whose families stayed in the village but they themselves did not go there. They remained in the city because they believed that there were better chances for employment in Bombay or because they wanted to return to the mills as soon as the situation allowed that. These workers were accustomed to having meals in a khanawali and were faced with the problem of how to secure food if the women running the khanawali refused to give them credit. It appears, however, that this food problem applied to only a very few workers and they (not more than three in the sample) reported that they were given credit for a period of several months. The fact that only three workers were confronted with this problem suggests that all those who stayed in rooms shared with other workers (under normal circumstances the clientele of the khanawali) left for the village after the commencement of the strike. This suggests that the women running the khanawali must have suffered greatly as a result of the strike.

The village-based workers could overcome the food problem by shifting from the city to the village, but was the same true for payment of rent? It seemed unlikely that the room owners would accept an endless postponement in payment. Those workers who owned the place they were living in had, of course, an advantage over the others. In all thirty-three workers (twenty-four from Finlay and nine from Spring) owned the place they were living in (sometimes they shared its ownership with others). They did not face the problem of paying rent although they may have faced other costs like municipal taxes and costs of maintenance, but these appear to be of a minor magnitude. In Table 6.27 the payment of rent by the remaining 117 workers to whom the problem of rent applied has been categorized.

TABLE 6.27

Payment of Rent During the Strike

Category	*Finlay*	*Spring*	*Total*	*Percentage* (n = 117)
Did pay	14	8	23	18.8
Credit	23	35	58	49.6
Others paid	4	7	11	9.4
Did not pay	5	9	14	12.0
Stopped	5	7	12	10.2
Total	51	66	117	100.0

Less than 19 per cent of the workers appear to have paid rent during the strike period. All the others could not pay, did not pay or did not have to pay. The largest group, no doubt, is of workers who got credit throughout the strike period and made up for it afterwards or is still in the process of doing so (almost 50 per cent). Nearly a quarter of this group consists of workers who were living in chawls belonging to Bombay Dyeing. Their dues were substracted from their wages the moment they resumed duty. To the group that did not pay rent during the strike belong fourteen workers (12 per cent) whose rent was remitted by the owner of the room or by the one who let the room out to them. These benevolent landlords were usually workers who rented a room from the mill and sublet it to other workers. Some workers (9 per cent) had relatives who paid the rent for them. More than 10 per cent stopped paying rent altogether when the strike began and they have not resumed paying rent since. In this group there are also workers who had stopped paying rent even prior to the strike.

There is a remarkable difference between the Finlay and Spring workers in the sample as far as credit is concerned. It appears that many more Spring workers got credit than those of Finlay. However, the picture is the reverse if we look at the number of workers who did not have to pay rent as they (sometimes jointly) own the place they are living in. This comparatively convenient position applied to twenty-four Finlay workers as against only nine Spring workers.

No Change in Lifestyle

Apparently an impressive fifty-six workers (see Table 6.23) did not change their pattern of consumption during the strike. This accounts for more than 37 per cent of the entire sample and calls for an analysis.[5] There is also a noteworthy difference to be observed between Spring and Finlay in the group reporting that they lived during the strike as they did before the struggle began. In order to find an explanation for these curious phenomena a number of questions have to be answered.

One rather obvious explanation would be that the greater number of Spring workers who did not change their lifestyle, is related to the fact that these workers, on the whole, resumed work much earlier which would allow them to carry on their customary pattern of consumption till they resumed. However, it was found that of the thirty-six Spring workers in this group, merely seven resumed work within a period of 3 months and, therefore, this factor alone cannot explain the difference. Even if one extends this period to five months the number increases only to eleven, which means that for the remaining twenty-five Spring workers (70 per cent of this category) another explanation has to be found. What is more, in the case of

Finlay, only one worker out of the group of twenty workers under review resumed within five months. Here, early resumption of work fails completely in explaining why so many workers, henceforth called no-changers, did not have to change their lifestyle.

The remarkable phenomenon of 37 per cent no-changers might also be explained by looking at the debts these workers had at the end of the strike. The reason for this would be that another way of allowing for the same level of expenditure, albeit a treacherous one, is to sell property or to take loans, a strategy resorted to by a majority of the workers. If we do so we find that 75 per cent of the Finlay no-changers and nearly 70 per cent of the corresponding Spring workers took recourse to this strategy. However, in this these workers do not substantially differ from their less fortunate colleagues, for more than 80 per cent of the entire sample took loans and/or sold property. Where a difference is to be noted is regarding the extent of debts incurred by the workers in the course of the strike (see Table 6.28).

TABLE 6.28
Debts at End of the Strike of 56 Workers

Amount in Rs	*Finlay*	*Spring*	*Total*	*Percentage*
No debt	7	16	23	41.0
500–1,500	2	6	8	14.3
1501–3500	1	2	3	5.4
3,501–7,000	1	8	9	16.1
7,001–11,000	4	2	6	10.7
More	5	2	7	12.5
Total	20	36	56	100.0

It appears that 41 per cent had no debt at all and that thirty-one of fifty-six workers (55 per cent) had a debt of less than Rs 1,500 when they resumed work. In fact, the picture is even better than that if one takes into consideration that most of the workers in the two highest categories did not attribute the high debt to the strike but to special events like marriages and the purchase of a house or land. If we correct for that we find that approximately forty out of fifty-six workers (71 per cent) had little or no strike-related debt, which means that the percentage of debts in this group is the reverse of that for the sample as a whole. It follows that taking loans and incurring debts was not the way of sustaining expenditure at the customary level.

Looking at the residence of these fifty-six workers during the strike might offer a better explanation, the assumption being that living in the village offers more scope for continuation of the usual pattern of expenditure than living in the costly city (see Table 6.29). It appears that in the case of Finlay workers the majority spent their time in Bombay whereas the reverse is true for those from Spring. If we combine the figures we find that actually the group that did not change its pattern of consumption is divided equally between those who stayed in Bombay and those who left for the village. By looking at the mill-wise division of the no-changers it is found that (excluding the category 'other'), 60 per cent of the Finlay no-changers remained in Bombay whereas 55 per cent of the Spring no-changers stayed in the village. It has to be concluded that the factor of residence cannot explain why so many workers lived more or less as before.

TABLE 6.29

Stay of 56 Workers During the Strike

Residence	*Finlay*	*Spring*	*Total*
Bombay	12	14	26
Village	5	20	25
Other	3	2	5
Total	20	36	56

This leaves us to explain the circumstances that may have enabled the fairly easy survival of 37 per cent of the workers as well as why there should be such a striking difference between workers from Finlay and Spring. The comparatively easy survival of so many workers appears to be independent of the environment, be it city or village. It would seem that the sort of work and, maybe more importantly, the amount of time spent working during the strike matter more than the environment. The division of the group of fifty-six workers, the easy survivors, according to the approximate time they worked during the strike is given in Table 6.30.

It appears that nearly 68 per cent of the workers who did not have to change their pattern of expenditure belonged to the group who worked more than half the time, which is almost 20 per cent above the average for the entire sample. The difference with other workers is in fact greater as the average for the sample as a whole includes the substantial group of no-changers. Excluding them would cause a drop in the average time worked for the rest of the sample, by several percentage points. It may be concluded that if the working and living environment (that is, the village or city) does not determine how well one survives, the amount of time worked does play a significant role. This finding may have to be related to the sort of work done.

TABLE 6.30
Average Time Worked for 56 Workers

Time worked	*Finlay*	*Spring*	*Total*	*Percentage (n = 56)*
25 per cent or less	1	1	2	3.6
26 per cent–50 per cent	-	6	6	10.7
51 per cent–75 per cent	7	3	10	17.8
76 per cent or more	9	19	28	50.0
Unknown*	3	7	10	17.8
Total	20	36	56	99.9

* Includes the workers who resumed early (that is, within three months) and did not search for a job.

Table 6.31 shows what sort of work was done by the group of fifty-six easy survivors, For the sake of simplicity all work relating to cultivation of land (including agricultural labour) has been clubbed together. No distinction has been made either between working in the powerlooms, working as a handloom weaver and working in a mill other than the one to which the striking worker belonged. These activities have all been grouped under textile work. It has also to be noted that some of the workers did various jobs, in which case the most important one in terms of time and money was selected.

To summarize, early resumption of work, taking loans (incurring debt) and selling property appeared to be wholly insufficient in explaining why such a large percentage of workers had no difficulty in surviving. Even the place where they stayed (village or city) seemed to make no difference. But the fact that a majority of the

Finlay workers in the sample were weavers was important as this made it possible for them to seek employment in the powerlooms, an avenue of employment closed to other categories of mill workers. Not less than 50 per cent of the Finlay workers in this group found employment in either the textile industry or in other factories. On the other hand, Spring workers in this category availed themselves largely of the opportunities offered by agriculture; possibilities utilized by more than half of them. It may be concluded that if fifty-six workers could claim that they lived during the strike more or less in the same way as they were used to doing prior to this event, this is largely because most of them were fortunate enough to have alternative employment for the better part of the strike.

TABLE 6.31
Employment of 56 Workers During the Strike

Category	*Finlay*	*Spring*	*Total*
Textile work	7	1	8
Factory work	3	2	5
Cultivation	3	19	22
Other work	4	7	11
Not searching	1	2	3
Unemployed	2	5	7
Total	20	36	56

Communication with the Hinterland

It has been shown that the connections with the rural hinterland were of vital importance for the striking workers but this raises the question of how the workers were informed about developments in Bombay. As may be expected, the main sources of information appeared to be newspapers and the radio, discussions with fellow workers, letters, visits to the union office but also visits to Bombay by those who stayed in the village when no news was forthcoming (see Table 6.32).

The totals of the various columns do not add up to 150 because, naturally, most workers mentioned more than one source of information. For the sake of convenience, discussions with workers who resided in the same village or with those who happened to pay a visit and correspondence between workers (conveying news regarding strike developments) have been included in the category 'friends'. Some workers staying in the village were fortunate in having relatives in the city who kept them informed about the strike. 'Union' refers to visits paid by the worker to the union office to hear the latest news. It also includes the attendance of meetings and going to the gates of the mills to see what was going on, avenues which were not open to the workers who remained in the village. It may be noted that Sangh supporters, very much like the MGKU supporters, used to visit the union office to get information or receive instructions regarding the strike.

TABLE 6.32
Sources of Information Related to Stay

Residence	*Newspapers*	*Friends*	*Union*	*Radio*
Bombay	56	35	36	17
Village	47	32	-	33
Other	5	4	4	2
Total	108	71	40	52

Newspapers were the most important source of information for all workers, whether or not they stayed in the village. Discussions with friends and letters from other workers or relatives ranked second. The significance of this source for the village-based workers was greater than for city-based workers. Unlike the worker in the city, the village-based worker could not avail himself of the opportunities grouped under 'union' and the significance of the other sources of information rose correspondingly.

To get some idea of the relative importance of specific newspapers for the textile workers, thirty-eight workers (twenty-one from Finlay and seventeen from Spring) were asked to state which newspaper they read. Several of them said that they read more than one newspaper. It was found that twenty-nine workers (76 per cent) said they read *Nava Kal,* five workers mentioned *Lok Satta,* three *Mumbai Sakal* and six mentioned other newspapers. Although the group of thirty-eight workers is much too small to make any definite statement about the popularity of various newspapers among the workers, it seems that *Nava Kal* is the most widely read paper among Bombay textile workers which is why it was selected for further study. This impression is corroborated by the fact that there was a proportionate number of *Nava Kal* readers among workers from both mills, namely sixteen from Finlay and thirteen from Spring.

The radio was another source of information. A conspicuous difference is to be noted here between the city-based and the village-based workers. Nearly twice as many workers who lived in the village during the strike mentioned this medium as a source of information. The difference is still greater if one realizes that the number of workers in the sample who stayed in the village was much smaller than the number of those remaining in Bombay (see Table 6.17). It may be concluded that the radio and the newspapers were the most important sources of information for the workers in the village. Most of the information conveyed by friends was also largely based on these sources.

In order to get an idea of the traffic up and down the country during the strike, the workers were asked to indicate how often they visited the village while staying in Bombay or vice versa. Such visits were usually restricted to a couple of weeks (in case of a visit to the village) or a couple of days (in case of a visit to the city). The purpose of visiting Bombay was largely to get acquainted with the latest developments and/or to try to resume duty. Those who were refused work by their own mill would, after a few attempts, return to the village to await better times.

It appears that half the workers who stayed in the village paid no visits to Bombay at all, that a quarter came only once to the city and that the remaining quarter came twice or more often. These findings clearly illustrate the need for workers in the rural hinterland to be informed in detail about what was going on in Bombay. Some 16 per cent of the workers in the village went more or less regularly to the city for the dual purposes of hearing the latest news and finding out about the possibilities of resuming work. Naturally, getting to know these things was far easier for the workers who remained in Bombay. If they left the city it was usually to see relatives in the village and to spend some time there, rarely to seek employment. Many of these city-based workers played an important role in conveying information to workers in the villages who for one reason or the other could not or would not go to Bombay during the strike.

NOTES

1. Quoted in, *Report of the Badli Labour Inquiry Committee Cotton Textile Industry—1967* (GOM, 1968: 6).
2. Vaidya found that 11.5 per cent of the workers had one to three dependents, 45 per cent had four to six dependents, 31 per cent seven to ten dependents and 12 per cent had eleven or more dependents (Vaidya, 1984: 17).
3. The EGS was launched in May 1972 and, according to information supplied by the Directorate General of Information and Public Relations, about 1,18,000 works had been completed by March 1986 (Advertisement in EPW, vol. X111, 1987, no. 18). Apart from the construction of water tanks, the EGS provides for projects like soil conservation, bunding, terracing and afforestation. A critical assessment of the results produced by the scheme is given by S. Bagchee (Bagchee, 1984).
4. Deshpande found that 10 per cent of the workers borrowed from moneylenders, 52 per cent from friends and relatives, 7 per cent from the provident fund and 31 per cent from cooperatives and banks (Deshpande, 1983: 10).
5. H.V.V. Chellappa too, noticed that 'there was no substantive difference in the expenditure pattern of households' during the strike but does not go beyond suggesting that alternative employment, loans and sales of assets were means of supplementing income ('Bombay Mill Workers' Strike: Effect on Households', *Economic Times*, 17 September 1985).

Chapter Seven

CHANGING VIEWS

SUPPORT AND PRESSURE

Support by the Union

In the first part of this book an assessment has been made of the scope of the food and money distribution during the strike. It was found that hard evidence allowing for an accurate assessment is lacking and that the figures provided by strike leaders, although by no means impossible, could not be taken at face value. On the face of it, this caution is confirmed by the replies workers in the sample gave to the question whether they personally received any help from any union and if so of what sort.* This question was put to all the 150 workers and only fifty-nine said that they had received help. The *badlis* were with 19 per cent somewhat underrepresented in this group. There was no noteworthy difference between the workers from the two mills, either in terms of food or financial support.

As many as ninety-one workers (60 per cent) declared that they had not received any help. A reason for this could be that they had stayed in the village during the strike and the answers had to be compared with that variable. Dividing the workers who did not receive help according to their stay during the strike showed that a large section could not have benefited from the support as they had stayed in the village. Of the group of ninety-one workers, 63 per cent stayed in the village, 27 per cent in Bombay and the remainder elsewhere. Even so, a figure of 27 per cent for workers in Bombay seemed fairly high but it should be noted that some workers refrained from seeking help because they found another job and did not want to add to the burden of less fortunate colleagues by demanding a share of the meagre resources. Others explained that the distance to the nearest centre of distribution was such that they preferred not to go. Apart from this, there were also workers who reported that the stock of food and food grain was exhausted by the time their turn came.

The assistance of the MGKU, which was concentrated in the early phase of the struggle, was basically restricted to supplying food grain and money, and that too in limited quantities. Of the fifty-two workers who received food help during the strike, forty-two got a total quantity of five to fifteen kgs of food grain, eight received sixteen to thirty kgs and only two received more. A similar picture emerged when they stated how much money they had received. Of the thirty-one who did receive financial help, seventeen received an amount of Rs 50 or less in all, ten workers got between Rs 51 and Rs 100, two received more but 1 do not remember how much he had received. From this it appears that 87 per cent of the few workers in the sample who received any financial help at all did not get more

* See Appendix C for a list of the topics discussed and the questions asked during the interviews with the workers.

than Rs 100. As in the case of the distribution of food, here too, one has to account for stay in the village and voluntarily refraining from seeking financial support. Yet, the figures provide sufficient evidence to conclude that material support for those workers who did receive support was far from substantial and meant only a minor contribution to their means of surviving this trying period.

Support was extended by the union but the union (that is, the MGKU) had no resources and was dependent on the sympathy of the people in the rural hinterland and on workers in the city. Bombay saw numerous collections of money on behalf of the textile workers during the strike but knowledge of these contributions seems to have bypassed many textile workers. Not less than sixty-one workers (more than 40 per cent of the sample) appeared to be unaware of this support (see Table 7.1).

TABLE 7.1

Views of Support Related to Stay During the Strike

Category	*Village*	*p.c.*	*Bombay*	*p.c.*	*Other*	*Total*
1 There was no support	18	(29.5)	19	(23.8)	2	39
2 No knowledge of support	12	(19.7)	9	(11.3)	1	22
3 Support was insufficient	9	(14.8)	23	(28.8)	2	34
4 There was enough support	19	(31.1)	24	(30.0)	3	46
5 Other	3	(4.9)	5	(6.3)	1	9
Total	61	(100.0)	80	(100.2)	9	150

These workers were either convinced that there was no such support (thirty-nine workers: 26 per cent) or declared that they knew nothing about it (twenty-two workers: 15 per cent). As compared with these figures, 54 per cent stated that they knew of actions of solidarity by other industrial workers. This group can be divided into 31 per cent who said that this support was sufficient and 23 per cent who felt that it was not. The remaining 6 per cent expressed different views. The percentage of workers who were unaware of the support extended by other workers and citizens is high and it is reasonable to expect that the whereabouts of the workers during the strike (village or city) can largely explain why they had no knowledge of it. Table 7.1 relates the answers to the stay of the worker during the strike.

It appears that the percentage of workers who felt that the support had been adequate was equal in the village and in the city. The proportion of workers who had no knowledge of the support (the first two categories) was, however, in the village much larger than in Bombay. Nearly half the workers in the village were unaware of support against 35 per cent for the city-based workers. There is also a considerable difference in the appreciation of the support. The figures for workers who felt that the support had been insufficient is in the city double that of the village. This indicates that workers in the rural areas had fewer problems in making both ends meet than workers in Bombay. This finding supports the contention that the factor 'stay during the strike' partially explains why so many workers in the sample had such a low opinion of or remained ignorant of the solidarity displayed by other workers during the struggle. On the strength of these data alone it is not possible to say whether (the impression of) lack of solidarity contributed to the collapse of the strike, for even if workers were disappointed in the support they may have anticipated, this response and in that event the (supposed) response would not have greatly influenced their decision to continue the struggle.

Attitude of the Family

A much stronger influence on the strike morale of the workers may have come from the attitude of the family and friends towards the struggle. In particular, the influence of the immediate family was bound to have a strong impact as many striking workers had to face their wives and children every day. If it can be said that the workers, by and large, favoured the strike then it must be noted that the support for the strike from their families was considerably weaker, as is shown by Table 7.2.

Going by the workers' statements, 28 per cent of their families (which might include other relatives apart from wife and children) were against the strike right from the outset. This may be broadly attributed to the issues at stake being more remote to them than to the workers (this certainly holds true for the families living in the villages). More vital than the removal of the Sangh or even a wage hike seemed the danger of risking a job. The families in the villages felt the pinch of the sudden interruption of the monthly remittances. On top of that they often had to feed a striking worker.

TABLE 7.2
Views of the Family Regarding the Strike

Category	*Finlay*	*Spring*	*Total*	*Percentage*
Resisted throughout	12	18	30	20.0
For demands but not for strike	7	5	12	8.0
Indifferent	1	2	3	2.0
Supported initially*	35	23	58	38.7
Supported fully**	18	25	43	28.7
Unknown	2	2	4	2.6
Total	75	75	150	100.0

* Less than twelve months
** More than twelve months

The support of family and friends was more direct and more important than that of the union, both in the material as well as in the moral sense. The scope of the financial help extended by relatives and friends has been discussed elsewhere but an impression of the frequency of such support may be gained from the fact that 48.6 per cent of the entire sample claimed not to have received any support from relatives or friends. This seemed to be a high percentage bulk was not always possible to ascertain whether the workers excluded the provision of loans when they answered the question referring to material help during the strike (cf. Table 6.25). Questioned about the absence of support, the customary explanation given was that as their friends were mill workers themselves and had to face the same problems they were not in a position to help.

As for relatives, many other workers emphasized that although they did receive material help from them, no moral support was forthcoming as relatives on the whole tended to disapprove of the strike and increasingly so. This disapproval was less connected with the objectives of the strike than the acutely felt need for money. A much smaller group of workers declared that their family and friends simply lacked all means of material support which is why they could extend no more than moral support to the cause of the striking workers. The workers who received both material and moral support from relatives and friends form the smallest group.

Although the families in the city had to face the same hardships as those in the villages, there may have been a psychological difference between the two. In the city everyone had seen the strike coming and most families of workers lived in close proximity which was advantageous as far as mutual support was concerned. This also allowed for easy (or uneasy) social control. On the other hand, many families in the village were taken by surprise by the strike and to cap the difficulties caused by the sudden halt to the steady flow of money from Bombay, they were abruptly confronted with the problem of feeding an additional mouth. In contrast to the families in the city they may have felt more isolated as well. Although the strike and its prolongation had very real and direct consequences for everyone, it is likely that the families in the villages were less prepared to cope with them.

Fear and Threats

Unwillingness to support the strike resulted in pressure by the family, either openly or covertly but this is not the only pressure the workers had to cope with during the strike. Only a tiny minority of the workers would be able to decide whether to join and/or continue the strike without pressure from one side or the other. All the rest had to face one form of pressure or the other and many had to cope with pressure from several sides. The push and pull factors at work were very diverse and included threats from the management of the mill, the Sangh or fellow workers, lack of money, pressure of wife and children to resume, letters inviting the workers to return to the mills and blandishments of a better position. By the time a worker had made up his mind, he still had to overcome fear which appeared to be an effective deterrent to resuming work.

In Table 7.3 the various pressures to which the workers were subjected have been grouped in a few categories. The efforts of the management of the mills and the Sangh to get the workers back, referred to earlier, were cited most often as a source of pressure.

TABLE 7.3

Pressure Influencing Decision to Resume Work by Agent

Category	*Finlay*	*Spring*	*Total*
Mill/RMMS	35	38	73
Fear of violence	34	25	59
Family	21	12	33
Other*	1	4	5
No pressure	14	8	32

* For example, pressure by the *patil*, police, *sarpanch*.

On the face of it, the efforts of the mills to get the workers back and the refusal to re-employ those who reported for work are irreconcilable. The most plausible explanation for this paradox is that the objectives of the policy of the mills in taking workers back were multifarious apart from differing from mill to mill. From the management point of view there is not necessarily a contradiction in aiming at the restoration of production and availing themselves simultaneously of the opportunity of retrenching workers and getting rid of the most troublesome elements among them in the process. Besides, the mills might need evidence to prove that they had attempted to move the workers to return. Letters seeking their return would serve that purpose.

Contrary to what one might believe, the pressure exercised by families wanting their relatives to return to the mills was not restricted to those who had been opposed to the strike from the outset. Of the thirty-three families pressurizing the workers to resume, only eight families were against the strike, twenty-two supported it initially but gradually changed their position and three belonged to the category of those who could rightly be called staunch supporters, that is, in favour of the strike for over a year. It is a clear illustration of the change in views in the course of the strike that so many families who first stood behind the workers later tried to convince them that they should start working again. In most cases the changes in the views of families merely reflected changes in the views of the striking workers themselves.

Fear of violence ranks second as an agent influencing the workers' decision to resume work. Predictably, the effect of this fear was that workers tended to suppress the wish to resume. This fear was in the minds both of the workers and their families. To what extent this fear was realistic has been discussed in Chapter 3. However, for an answer to the question of what place should be assigned to fear in the decision to return to the mills, the problem of whether this fear was baseless or not is, of course, irrelevant. Fear itself was very real in its consequences and led invariably to a postponement of the return to the mills. In Table 7.4 the fifty-nine workers who reported that fear played a role in their decision to resume have been related to their strike attitude.

TABLE 7.4

Fear Related to Strike Attitude

1 Against the strike	14
2 Against the strike but for demands	5
3 Supported initially	35
4 Supported fully	4
5 Indifferent	1
Total	59

It appears that it was not only those who were against the strike who were influenced by fear but also, and even to a larger extent, those workers who initially supported the strike. Even some of the workers who had supported the strike for more than a year were affected by fear when they finally reached the stage of wanting to return. No less than thirty-nine workers (26 per cent of the entire sample and nearly a third of all who favoured the strike) stated that they would have resumed earlier had they not feared physical harm. The data establish without doubt that fear played a significant role in the continuation of the strike. This finding helps, not only in bridging the time gap between the actual duration of the strike and the point at which workers had wanted to resume but also explains the disparity between strike objectives and the behaviour of the workers discussed in the next paragraph.

WORKERS' PERCEPTION OF THE STRIKE

Causes of the Strike

In order to understand the attitude of the workers it is necessary to learn from them what the main issues at stake were. The answers need not be in consonance with the strike objectives of the strike leaders. The replies appeared to centre around a few main themes and could be grouped into five categories (see Table 7.5). As might have been expected, a wage hike towered above all other replies almost to the exclusion of several other categories. Naturally, a great number of workers mentioned more than one cause which explains why the grand total in the Table exceeds 150 and why the total of other columns does not correspond with the number of workers in those categories.

By comparing the two mills we find that the figures display a fairly regular and similar pattern which suggests that the findings have much wider applicability than merely the two mills under scrutiny. With the exception of those who were against the strike and may have thought that there was no reason for it, practically all workers mentioned the financial condition of the workers as a reason for the strike.

TABLE 7.5

Causes of the Strike as Mentioned by Workers

Category	*Finlay*			*Spring*			*Grand Total*
	Perm.	Badli	*Total*	*Perm.*	Badli	*Total*	
1	57	15	72	45	20	65	137
2	10	2	12	19	7	26	38
3	19	6	25	8	3	11	36
4	2	-	2	3	1	4	6
5	1	-	1	1	1	2	3

1 = Poor financial condition of workers/wage hike
2 = Disappointing performance of the RMMS
3 = To improve leave facilities/paid leave/HRA/TA
4 = Wish to topple RMMS/repeal of the BIR Act
5 = Other (includes permanency of *badli*s/lay-off compensation)

This position is, of course, linked with the achievements of the RMMS over the years and it was to be expected that disillusionment with the RMMS would figure as a second important source of discontent. The lack of proper leave facilities (the workers wanting more leave and paid leave) and House Rent and Travel Allowances were a third and equally often mentioned source of dissatisfaction. HRA has meanwhile been granted and was one of the very few tangible results of the Deshpande Committee.

Very few workers mentioned the desire to get out of the clutches of the Sangh and/or the clauses of the BIR Act as one of the causes of the strike but it would be premature to conclude from this that it did not matter to them (the contents of the interviews do not permit such a view) but it seems likely that this aim, very dear to many workers, came later. It would not be wrong to say that strong anti-Sangh sentiments are implicitly present in the second and third categories. This is corroborated by the fact that when workers were asked to state specifically which strike objective mattered most to them, many of them would mention the removal of the Sangh. Nevertheless, there is no reason to believe that it triggered off the strike or even that it was one of the root causes. Indeed, it is likely that the strike would not have occurred at all if the Sangh had been able (or willing) to secure greater material benefits for the workers. Whether this was a realistic expectation has been discussed in Chapter 2.

The combination of financial distress and the need to improve leave facilities and various allowances was cited most often by those who mentioned several causes for the strike. This was followed by the combination of financial distress and the poor performance of the RMMS. There is a difference to be noted here between workers from Finlay and Spring. Whereas Finlay workers appeared to be more interested in leave facilities, Spring workers stressed the disappointing performance of the Sangh. It is striking that the latter, who resumed much earlier than the former, bore a stronger grudge against the Sangh. This points to different circumstances for Finlay and Spring workers, compelling the latter to give in sooner. After subdividing the replies presented in Table 7.5 according to terms of employment (that is, *badli* versus permanent worker) it was found that there was no difference at all between the two categories. *Badli*s are represented with a neat 25 per cent (corresponding to the percentage of this group in the sample) in the three most important (numerically speaking) categories. The same is true if we look at the workers who mentioned more than one cause for the strike.

Citing the cause of a strike is one thing but this does not necessarily mean that an individual who mentions the cause attaches much value to it himself. In order to find out in what way the causes of the strike mentioned by the workers differed from their personal stake in the strike, they were asked which demand mattered most to them. The answers are presented in Table 7.6 which largely confirms the findings of the earlier Table. The total exceeds 150 replies because some workers kept repeating several demands despite persistent attempts to elicit the demand that mattered most. However, these instances were few and of little consequence to the general picture. Their answers have been listed in several categories but this does not distort reality.

It must also be pointed out that in reply to the question of the most important demand, many workers said: 'The poor financial condition of the workers.' As their condition can hardly be called a demand and as this reply is indicative of their frustration about their wages, such answers have been converted into wage demands. It appears that the overwhelming concern of the workers here, as in the case of the Table on strike causes, is with their wage package. This is true for *badli*s as well as for permanent workers.

Both Tables prove beyond doubt that the foremost concern of the workers was with their financial position and not with more ideologically inspired demands such as the abrogation of the BIR Act and the removal of the Sangh. This conclusion does not in any way diminish the right or even the duty of the strike leadership to put up demands which it holds to be crucial for the achievement of the goals set by the workers. It gives a poor impression of the capabilities of union leaders if they are not a few steps ahead of those whose interests they seek to serve. The poor performance of the Sangh over the years has to be treated as a strike cause even though few workers translated their frustration and anger about this performance into demands to remove the Sangh and to repeal the BIR Act. These issues were initially stressed by the strike leadership but before long workers readily acknowledged their validity and stood behind them.

By comparing the two Tables we find that the number of workers mentioning the Sangh's (disappointing) achievements as a reason for the strike (thirty-eight in Table 7.5) and the number of those who clamoured for the ousting of the Sangh (thirty-two in Table 7.6) is comparable. The smaller sample among 100 workers broadly confirms what has been shown so far. It appears from the replies that 72 per cent was most interested in a wage hike as a means of improving their financial position. Another 20 per cent mentioned the removal of the Sangh and a few workers among them cited the scrapping of the BIR Act. The remaining 8 per cent said that they were most interested in leave and travel facilities. Most findings presented in the two Tables are comparable, which might be expected. The overwhelming majority of the workers took their own strike priorities as representing those of the other workers and in doing so the distinction between strike causes and strike demands became blurred.

TABLE 7.6

Demands According to Priority

Category	*Finlay*	*Spring*	*Total*	*Perm.*	Badli	*Total*
Wage hike	62	54	116	89	27	116
Removal of the RMMS/BIR Act	10	22	32	27	5	32
Leave facil./ allowances	5	11	16	14	2	16
Permanency or comp. *badlis*[*]	1	8	9	-	9	9
Other	1	1	2	1	1	2

[*] (Partial) compensation in case of lay-offs.

There is, however, a difference with regard to specific *badli* problems such as permanency and compensation for those *badli*s who could not be employed (lay-offs). From the Tables it may be deduced that permanency figured more prominently as a demand than as a strike cause. Apparently, and understandably, this demand was of little or no concern to the permanent workers. This is borne out by the smaller sample in which only two workers mentioned permanency and compensation for lay-off as important demands. On the other hand, scores of workers (including *badli*s) in both samples volunteered to say that the demand for permanency was not very important as permanency anyway depended on seniority. The situation in Finlay and Spring Mills is not, however, the same. That the demand for permanency was mentioned much more frequently by Spring workers than by Finlay workers is noteworthy. This is another strong indication that the situation for *badli*s in these two mills is quite distinct and that those in Spring Mills had more to complain about than their Finlay counterparts (cf. Table 6.13).

This finding seems to point to a divergence of interests between *badli*s and permanent workers. In fact, a clash of interests between these two categories of workers had been postulated in the research, the assumption being that the *badli*s' demand for permanency might threaten the employment of permanent workers, and that at a time when the industry was striving to reduce its labour force. To check this, the workers were asked to say whether the strike objectives of *badli*s and permanent workers corresponded. When one worker after another confirmed this, it was felt that the framing of the question might be responsible for the unanimity of the answers received. The question was thereupon modified in such a way that the interviewee might be tempted to acknowledge differences in objectives. The result, however, was exactly the same.

The replies did not change even when it was suggested ever more strongly that *badli*s and permanent workers were actually two different groups with, at best, partially congruent interests. Practically all workers—and in this there was no difference between *badlis* and permanent workers—insisted that there was no contradiction in objectives and even less a conflict of interests. Even the *badli*s' demand for permanency was no cause for friction because permanency dependend on seniority and could not be wrested from the millowners by means of a strike. It is interesting to note that *badli*s on the whole subscribed to this reading of their demands. The finding was confirmed by the reply to the question relating to cooperation between *badli*s and permanent workers. Not less than 146 out of 150 workers felt that this cooperation had been good, only three workers declaring that they did not know and only one mentioned frictions. As before, the smaller sample reinforces the findings of the large sample: all 100 workers declared that *badli*s and permanent workers had been fighting for the same cause.

Why Samant?

The tremendous wave of support from the textile workers which carried Datta Samant to the front pages of the national newspapers is unmistakable evidence of the faith the workers had in their leader.

The workers in the sample were no exception. Practically all workers (136 out of 150) believed that Samant was the right man to lead the struggle, eleven said he was not and only three were uncertain. In order to understand what made Samant tick, the workers were asked to indicate why they thought that Samant was the right man. The answers are presented in Table 7.7. The total of the answers exceeds 150 as many workers gave more than one reason for their appreciation of Datta Samant.

Although the answers have been grouped in several categories, the first three categories are obviously interlinked, particularly the first and the third. Most frequently there were combinations of the first and the second, and the second and the third categories. From the Table it appears that there is no noteworthy difference in the views of Finlay and Spring workers. The same is true if the answers are grouped according to the terms of employment (*badlis* and permanent workers).

TABLE 7.7

Reasons for Choice or Rejection of Samant

Category	*Finlay*	*Spring*	*Total*
1 Successful/powerful	48	43	91
2 Honest/not corrupt	24	27	51
3 Militancy	8	12	20
4 Untrustworthy	-	2	2
5 Unreasonable	5	2	7
6 Strike timed badly	3	-	3
7 Different position	2	3	5

More than 60 per cent of all the workers mentioned Samant's success as a trade unionist as a reason why they were attracted by him. They felt that he was very powerful (see case studies). This is no surprise, but what is astonishing is that more than a third of the answers refer to Samant's reputation for incorruptibility and sincerity. Workers not only felt that he understood their problems better than anyone else but also that he would really fight for them and would not compromise their cause for a few paltry rupees. This high incidence of workers who were attracted by the doctor's assumed honesty is in itself an indictment of the other unions, above all the RMMS. Those who were opposed to the strike gave reasons like the poor timing of the strike or Samant's stubbornness and refusal to come to terms. Only two workers (who were against the strike) felt that Samant could not be trusted, which is eloquent testimony to his reputation for honesty.

Samant apparently appealed to the workers because of his supposed success and his honesty, elements providing at least a partial answer to the question why other (red) unions could not do the same. Whether the workers were right or wrong in crediting Samant with sincerity and a high success ratio is immaterial, the important point being that they did.

During the interviews it transpired that workers had great confidence in Samant's leadership (Question 34 A). Nearly as many workers that believed Samant was the right leader, 127 out of 150, felt that no other union could have led them in the struggle. Only three workers believed that an alternative union could have done the same, fifteen others were uncertain about that possibility. In five cases the question was not asked, the interviewees being staunch Sangh-walas. The reasons why the workers believed that other unions could not help them with their problems are listed in Table 7.8.

TABLE 7.8

Reasons for By-passing Alternative Unions

Category	*Finlay*	*Spring*	*Total*
1 Powerless/no support	51	48	99
2 Betrayed workers' cause/corrupt	10	10	20
3 They lacked interest	5	4	9
4 Other	5	2	7
5 Doesn't know/uncertain	7	8	15
6 Not asked	2	3	5

In a few cases workers gave more than one reason which is why the total of the answers slightly exceeds 150. It appears that two-thirds of the workers were convinced that no other union was in a position to help them simply because they lacked the power to do so.

The second-largest group consists of workers who felt that alternative unions had cheated them in the past by settling for a pittance. The size of this group is comparable to that of the workers who wanted Samant because of his reputation for honesty. In all, nine workers declared that no other union took a real interest in their problems which is why they had to seek assistance elsewhere. In all 135 answers (referring to nearly as many workers) indicate that the workers had no faith in any other union (including the red flag unions) at the time of the strike. This finding is a sad comment on the position of all trade unions active in the textile industry.

Rightly or wrongly, the workers believed that Samant could deliver the goods. This suggests that workers had high expectations about the outcome of the strike. It is worth examining whether these expectations were moderated by an awareness of the conditions prevailing in the textile industry and a sense of the political context in which the struggle was to be fought. Table 7.9 provides a rough indication of how much the workers thought they could gain through a strike.

TABLE 7.9
Expectation of Acceptance of Demands

Category	*Finlay*			*Spring*			*Grand Total*
	Perm.	Badli	*Total*	*Perm.*	Badli	*Total*	
All demands	22	11	33	15	6	21	54
Most demands	3	1	4	7	1	8	12
Some demands	28	3	31	29	13	42	73
None	5	-	5	2	1	3	8
Other	2	-	2	-	1	1	3
Total	60	15	75	53	22	75	150

The first thing to be noted is that almost half the workers felt that they had hoped to gain at least something through the strike although not necessarily everything. This proves that right from the outset, half the workers did not have inflexible expectations. Although this should not be taken to mean that these workers could be purchased for a handful of rupees, it is clear that they were ready to accept less than what was demanded. If Samant had been aware of this, he might have shown a greater flexibility in the negotiations. But one may not exclude the possibility that Samant, confronted with such an attitude, would have declined the honour of leading the workers.

What is striking is that more than one-third of the workers had such great confidence in Samant's powers that they believed that all the demands would be conceded. If we add to this the group that believed that most of the demands (that is, the most important demands) would be accepted by the millowners then we find that this section is not much smaller than the one showing greater realism by declaring that at least some of the demands would have to be conceded.

If we look at the first category then there is a clear difference between the expectations of Finlay and Spring workers. The former clearly expected more from the strike than the latter. The findings indicate that the Spring workers were more realistic than those of Finlay. This is corroborated by looking at the group of workers who hoped to gain something from the strike. Here the picture is more or less the reverse, a much larger group of Spring workers than those of Finlay expecting some results.

The differences between the expectations of Finlay and Spring workers are continued if we look at the division between *badli*s and permanent workers. Here we find that almost 60 per cent of the Spring *badli*s would have been satisfied if at least some demands had been conceded while 73 per cent of the Finlay *badli*s entertained higher hopes of realizing all the demands. The explanation for the differences between the workers of the two mills under investigation remains a matter of speculation but it is possible that the earlier observed superior educational level and socio-economic background of the Spring workers is responsible. It may be that these workers were better equipped to assess the realistic possibilities and the complexity of the situation.

The expectations of the workers are interlinked with their ideas about how the employers viewed the strike ahead. It is to be expected that Spring workers would show a more cautious attitude while replying to the question of whether they felt at that time that the millowners wanted the strike. The answers to this question have been given in Table 7.10. A large majority of the workers was of the view (at least at the beginning of the strike) that the millowners did not want the strike. Even so, a substantial number (20 per cent) felt that the millowners actually welcomed the strike and in this group the Spring workers are conspicuous. After subdividing for terms of employment it was found that there was no noteworthy difference between *badli*s and permanent workers with regard to the question of whether or not the millowners wanted the strike.

TABLE 7.10
View of Millowners' Position

Category	*Finlay*	*Spring*	*Total*
1 Welcomed strike	12	20	32
2 Opposed strike	56	46	102
3 Uncertain	7	8	15
4 Other	-	1	1
Total	75	75	150

If we look at the reasons why the workers felt that the millowners either welcomed or regretted the strike, we find a greater diversity among Spring than Finlay workers (see Table 7.11). The total number of replies does not equal 150 as several workers gave more than one reason for their assessment of the position of the millowners.

TABLE 7.11
Reasons for View of Millowners' Position

Category	*Finlay*	*Spring*	*Total*
1 Piling up of stocks	4	5	9
2 Wish to retrench workers	7	10	17
3 Wish for modernization	–	9	9
4 Feared losses	36	29	65
5 Feared Samant/MGKU	3	6	9
6 Resented paying more	4	3	7
7 Other reason	2	7	9
8 Doesn't know	20	14	34

There is not too much difference between the second and the third category as modernization in the Indian textile industry is usually accompanied by a reduction of labour. Similarly, the desire to retrench workers is not only linked to shedding surplus labour but is as often connected with an intended programme of modernization. Many workers appeared to be well aware that modernization frequently implied retrenchment and vice versa. If we combine the second and third categories we find that twenty-six answers refer to the aspects of modernization and retrenchment. As far as the Spring workers are concerned nineteen answers (73 per cent) out of the total of twenty-six answers may be related to the fact that Spring Mills is considered to be one of the most modern in the city. Working there may have given the workers first-hand experience.

A substantial number of workers appeared incapable of explaining why they felt that the millowners were averse to the strike. For these workers it was usually enough to know that employers in general don't like strikes. In any case, this view is not very different from the undifferentiated notion that strikes mean losses to the employer, a view to which the great majority of the workers subscribed. Here, as in the earlier question, no striking differences are to be noted in the position between *badli*s and permanent workers.

As noted before, thirty-two workers were under the impression that the millowners welcomed the strike while 102 did not think so (Table 7.10). Practically all workers who believed that the employers were 'hoping' for the strike appeared to think so for one of the reasons falling under the first three categories of Table 7.11. After subdividing the 102 workers who did not share this view with the aid of the categories in the Table we find that two-thirds referred to the losses, 18 per cent could not explain their view while the other views are evenly divided between fear of Samant's entry into the textile industry and annoyance at the prospect of having to pay higher wages.

OBJECTIVES AND REALITY

Elasticity of Demands

Views about the strike were bound to change as the struggle progressed. In order to trace the changes in the views of the workers many aspects have to be considered. What, for example, were the workers' expectations when they started the strike? How did they view the position of the millowners? How much did they hope to gain by their action and how long did they think that the strike would have to last to achieve their goals? Would they only be satisfied with the full pound of flesh?

To start with the last question, it seems that the average strike duration is a fairly good indicator of the willingness of workers to suffer for the achievements of their goals. Table 6.16 shows how much time elapsed between the beginning of the strike and actual resumption of duty. It is tempting to equate this time-span with the time the workers wanted to be on strike but such an equation is not permissible. Although no systematic information could be collected allowing for an accurate assessment of the difference between the desire to resume work and actual resumption, whatever evidence is available points to a considerable time gap between these two points. A group of approximately forty workers was questioned on this subtle but significant difference and about half of them said that they would have resumed earlier had there been an opportunity of doing so. There were basically two reasons why they started working later than they had intended. In most cases they had stayed away from work for fear of violence and in other cases they were sent back when they reported for work.

The discrepancy between the desire to resume and actual resumption of work is great. Apart from a few cases in which the gap was not more than a couple of months, in a majority of cases it was as much as six to twenty months. There was even a case of a worker who started working three years after he had wanted to rejoin (that is, after six months). This is, however, scarcely more telling than the situation of the worker who resumed after ten months although he had wanted to rejoin the mill after a month. Even though it was not possible to pinpoint the disparity between actual resumption of work and the wish to do so for each worker, the examples suffice to show that it could be utterly misleading to equate the duration of the strike with the determination of the workers to remain on strike.

Another way of gaining an insight into this discrepancy was to ask workers how long they had been in favour of the strike. The answers help in tracing the gradual shift in views in the course of the strike. By comparing the figures of Table 6.16 (showing the strike duration) with those of Table 7.12 (recording strike attitudes) we can visualize the gap.

The Table shows that only a quarter of the workers in the sample favoured the strike for more than a year which is far less than is suggested by the average strike duration of fourteen months for permanent workers and ten months for *badli*s (see Table 6.16). Furthermore, we can see that the group of determined strikers was composed of 62 per cent Spring workers against 38 per cent of Finlay. What all this evidence strongly suggests is that the difference in the duration of strike participation between Finlay and Spring workers cannot be taken to indicate a difference in determination. If Finlay workers resumed work later than their counterparts from Spring Mills, this should not be attributed to a more heroic bent of mind of the first but to different circumstances.

Table 7.12 is interesting for other reasons too. It appears that only a tiny minority of eighteen workers (12 per cent) was against the strike from the beginning. Actually, nearly half these workers were not against the strike demands but had various reasons for not wanting a strike at that time. A group of eight workers (three *badli*s among them) were indifferent to the strike and whether it succeeded or not made no difference to them. It is worth noting that if the Finlay workers are strongly represented in the small group of opponents of the strike then the Spring workers are prominent among those who did not care about the outcome of the strike. It is also clear that only a very few workers had no opinion at all or could not make up their mind about this. This suggests that the strike and its objectives struck a deep emotional chord in the hearts of the workers and hardly anyone was left untouched by it.

The various categories of the answers allow for some rough calculations. In order to see how many workers really favoured the strike at the outset it is justifiable to club together the last four categories 4–7). If we do so we find that more than 81 per cent stood behind the strike, which refutes any claim that the strike was unwelcome to the workers and/or forced on them. Against this percentage there are 12 per cent workers who for various reasons opposed the strike and 7 per cent who were indifferent or ambivaalent to it. It can also be deduced that if we juxtapose the first four categories and the last four for each mill, that there is hardly any difference between workers from Finlay and Spring Mills. In both cases approximately 80 per cent of the workers supported the strike. Repeating this procedure for *badli*s we find that a total of twenty-eight *badli*s (thirteen from Finlay and fifteen from Spring) favoured the strike which is 75 per cent of the *badli*s in the sample. It therefore appears that in the beginning there was no difference in strike support between the two mills or between *badlis* and permanent workers.

TABLE 7.12
Views Regarding the Strike

Category	*Finlay*			*Spring*			*Grand*
	Perm.	Badli	*Total*	*Perm.*	Badli	*Total*	*Total*
0	8	-	8	0	2	2	10
1	5	1	6	2	-	2	8
2	-	1	1	3	4	7	8
3	-	-	-	1	1	2	2
4	5	5	10	9	2	11	21
5	14	4	18	8	5	13	31
6	14	4	18	13	2	15	33
7	14	-	14	17	6	23	37
Total	60	15	75	53	22	75	150

0 = Against the strike and against the demands
1 = Against the strike (for example, because of poor timing, need of money, wrong method) but not against the demands
2 = Indifferent
3 = Ambivalent/ uncertain
4 = In favour of strike for three months or less
5 = In favour of strike for three to six months
6 = In favour of strike for six to twelve months
7 = In favour of strike throughout (that is, more than twelve months)

If there was no difference in strike support between various categories of workers and between workers from different mills, there was also no difference in the reasons why workers wanted to resume work. In reply to the question of the reasons for their decision to resume work, a large majority of the workers (71 per cent) said that they were forced to do so largely for financial reasons (see Table 7.13). This finding aligns with that showing financial worries to be the greatest problem the workers had to face. It should be noted, however, that a number of workers mentioned more than one reason but with few exceptions it did not take them long to indicate what mattered most to them when they decided to return to the mills.

TABLE 7.13

Reasons for Resuming Work

Category	*Finlay*	*Spring*	*Total*	*Percentage*
Financial	55	52	107	71.3
Fear of dismissal	6	13	19	12.7
Against strike	8	1	9	6.0
Other	6	9	15	10.0
Total	75	75	150	100.0

In the Table only the most compulsive reason to resume work has been tabulated. Fear of dismissal figured as a second important category. Those who were dead set against the strike from the beginning (6 per cent) naturally needed no particular reason to rejoin as they had always wanted to resume at the earliest possible time. In the last category various reasons have been clubbed together, including cases in which a worker found it impossible to attach greater weight to any specific reason.

The reasons to resume work cannot be separated from the expectations the workers had at the beginning of the strike. An important expectation influencing the workers' attitudes is how long they believed it would take for the strike to be successful. This is very relevant in understanding why the strike call received such a tremendous response. Table 7.14 gives a clear insight into the time the workers thought that the strike would last.

TABLE 7.14

Expectation of Strike Duration

Number of months	*Finlay*			*Spring*			*Grand*
	Perm.	Badli	*Total*	*Perm.*	Badli	*Total*	*Total*
0–1	21	8	29	10	8	18	47
2–3	33	5	38	23	12	35	73
More	5	-	5	18	2	20	25
Other	1	2	3	2	-	2	5
Total	60	15	75	53	22	75	150

It was most unexpected that 80 per cent of the workers in the sample (the first two categories) believed that the struggle would be over within three months. They believed this despite the fact that Datta Samant had told them time and again that the struggle ahead would be a long one and that they would have to prepare themselves for an indefinite strike lasting six months at least. Even more astonishing is the fact that about one-third of the workers were convinced that the fight would be over within a couple of weeks. Some even thought that it would not take more than a few days.

These findings were startling and in order to check whether the workers were perhaps wrongly informed about what was in store for them I asked scores of workers whether they knew that Datta Samant had said that the strike would probably last for six months. Without exception they all declared that they knew Samant had said so. Lack of information and/or warnings, therefore, cannot explain the workers' expectations. It appears that they were aware of Samant's warnings but chose to ignore the predictive value of his words. Asked why they could be so optimistic about the success of the strike, the answer was invariably that they thought that it had to be so, given the overwhelming support of the workers to the strike. They felt that the government would be forced to step in and work out a settlement with Samant and the millowners.

The finding brings to mind an event at the very beginning of the fieldwork, when I was still trying to find as many openings to the workers as possible. At that stage I enlisted the help of Datta Samant's brother, Dada Samant, who during a memorable but unplanned meeting with three workers, volunteered to act as my research assistant. While discussing their expectations of the strike duration prior to the strike the workers stated that they believed it would not take more than two months. Dada Samant was annoyed with the answer and told them that his brother had always said six months, but despite Dada's annoyance and severe rebukes the workers stuck to their earlier statements. It is amazing that merely 16 per cent of the workers expected the strike to take more than three months, a smaller percentage still counted on six months or more. Not more than five workers (grouped together under 'Other') declared that they had no idea at all how long the strike was going to last.

These facts pose the problem of what to do if you want to prepare a large group for a planned struggle of long duration. Apparently it is not enough to warn workers by means of speeches and/or pamphlets of the likely duration. In this case, for example, the message simply failed to reach them and wishful thinking took over where reason should have prevailed. One is at a loss to suggest what more the strike leadership could have done to get the message across. This finding, meanwhile, raises the poignant but unanswerable question of what would have become of the strike if the strike leaders had really succeeded in convincing the workers of its likely duration.

Given the optimistic, albeit unwarranted, belief regarding the duration and outcome of the strike it is no surprise that hardly anyone bothered to prepare himself for the coming event although it must be admitted that the possibilities of doing so were very limited. Financially speaking, a worker cannot go much beyond trying to get some cash by way of taking loans or cutting into his savings. The mental preparation usually consists of talking to other workers and joining meetings and morchas during which long-standing grievances are forcefully aired.

Participation

As has been pointed out before, a lot has been made of the significance of the various workers' committees for the continuation of the strike. It was, therefore, expected that many workers would have joined or at least heard of such committees. While questioning the workers on their participation in strike-related activities, it soon became clear that a large number of them were groping in the dark when they tried to understand what a mill committee, an area committee or a zone committee was about. Many different descriptions were used to make clear what sort of work the committees did but even so a large majority insisted that they knew nothing of the existence of such committees. In the end their answer had to be accepted, although this lack of knowledge meant a death blow to the often ventured view that the various committees were the backbone of the strike without which it would have collapsed much sooner.

Nearly 63 per cent of the workers in the sample (ninety-four out of 150) appeared not to have even heard of any such committees. Of the fifty-one workers who knew of the existence of workers' committees, a quarter appeared to have themselves participated in the work of such committees. In the remaining five cases the question was not asked. There was no conspicuous difference between *badli*s and permanent workers but a higher number of Finlay workers had no knowledge of strike committees than Spring workers although the overall participation in the work of these committees was comparable.

One might like to attribute the amazing (and to some, disturbing) fact that two-thirds of the workers did not even know about the existence of mill committees to the residence of the workers during the strike. The assumption then would be that all those workers who stayed in the village had fewer opportunities of contact with workers' committees and, therefore, remained unaware of their existence and significance. If that were true then it would be reasonable to expect a higher incidence of workers with knowledge of workers' committees among those who stayed in Bombay. However, this is belied by the fact that more Finlay than Spring workers were unaware of the committees even though a larger number of Finlay than Spring workers remained in the city.

In order to be in a position to pass a verdict on this possibility, the ninety-four workers who knew nothing of the committees should be related to their place of stay during the strike. This has been done in Table 7.15. It appears that a majority of those who had no knowledge of workers' committees stayed in the city. It is, therefore, abundantly clear that the factor 'stay in the village' cannot explain why so many workers were unaware of the activities of the workers' committees. It is hard to find an explanation for this remarkable phenomenon except that the importance of the workers' committees has always been

TABLE 7.15

Residence of Workers Who Were Unaware of Committees

Residence	*Finlay*	*Spring*	*Total*
Bombay	32	16	48
Village	20	21	41
Other	2	3	5
Total	54	40	94

overestimated. The figures suggest convincingly that the workers manning the committees did not really reach out to the less active workers but confined themselves to the much smaller circle of other active workers.

Having found that knowledge about workers' committees was distressingly poor, it does not come as a surprise that the participation of the workers in various strike-related activities is not particularly impressive either. Attending meetings and joining a few demonstrations appeared to be the most common form of action, as is borne out by Table 7.16. The Table shows that about half the workers (category 4) did not go beyond being on strike. For various reasons they were not inclined to attend meetings or join morchas, the most important strike-related activity of the other workers. If participation in such activities were the sole criterion for assessing the involvement of the workers, then this Table would prove that many workers were not really concerned with the outcome of the strike but this is unwarranted. The interviews established beyond doubt that the mass of the workers was definitely involved in the progress of the strike but they did not always see the need to publicly demonstrate this concern on every occasion. For those who stayed in the village, the distance was an obvious barrier to expressing their feelings about the strike and the others apparently believed that merely continuing the strike was sufficient.

TABLE 7.16

Participation in Strike-related Action

Category	*Finlay*			*Spring*			*Grand*
	Perm.	Badli	*Total*	*Perm.*	Badli	*Total*	*Total*
1–Morchas*	32	8	40	24	5	29	69
2–Jail bharo	16	4	20	12	1	13	33
3–Other**	5	-	5	5	1	6	11
4–Nothing	23	7	30	25	17	42	72
5–Not asked	3	-	-	-	-	-	3

* Includes: demonstrations, rallies, gate meetings.

** Includes: collection and distribution of food and money, picketing, bullying of strike-breakers, gherao.

On the face of it, Finlay workers seem to have been more involved in strike-related action than Spring workers but this finding should be related to the peculiar situation of Finlay and the fact that this mill opened much later than Spring Mills. Finlay workers were in consequence not in a position to resume early even if they had wanted to and this gave them more time to take part in campaigns. Not too much value should, therefore, be attached to the differences between the two mills. The same is true for the differences between *badli*s from Finlay and Spring.

Participation in *morcha*s and related action appears to be something in which 46 per cent of the sample workers took part. This was done very irregularly and many workers stated that after an initial period in which they attended meetings and rallies, they gave up joining demonstrations and similar action. The participation in jail bharo campaigns seems fairly high. More than a fifth of all the workers took part in it at one time or the other but very few workers took part in more than one campaign. This low frequency shows the limited scope of this strike-related action for it should be realized that the participation refers to the entire strike period. In most cases, taking part in a jail bharo did not result in imprisonment as the police dispersed the crowds or released the workers the same day. Particularly among those who were arrested and had to spend some time in jail, the urge to participate in another jail bharo campaign dwindled. A similar phenomenon was evident at the time of the Indian struggle for independence when several massive civil disobedience campaigns were launched. The desire to be jailed dwindled considerably after the first experience.

REFLECTIONS ON THE STRIKE

Retrenchment and Negotiability of Demands

Having seen the disastrous results of the strike in terms of loss of employment and income, it would have been understandable if workers had become embittered and blamed Datta Samant and the MGKU for all the evil befalling them. It might have been expected that as a result many of them are now convinced that modernization and retrenchment could have been avoided if the strike had not occurred. Although half the workers now feel that the slaughter in terms of employment which followed the strike could have been avoided, they are not prepared to blame Samant. In the course of the interviews several questions were asked which were far from easy, and often a worker failed to answer a particular question. With regard to the problem of retrenchment and the question of responsibility for the outcome of the strike, however, all workers did have to offer a view. At times they showed a remarkable understanding of the complexity of the situation.

Half the workers are deeply convinced that modernization and retrenchment could have been avoided if the strike had not occurred (see Table 7.17). Even when I expressed disbelief the workers would hold to that position. What is less surprising is that many more Finlay workers (nearly two and a half times as many) held such a view than Spring workers. The reverse is true for the category of workers who felt that retrenchment was unavoidable but that the disastrous effects could have been limited without the strike. They believed that in such cases the affected workers would have been (partially) compensated for their premature loss of employment. More than a third of the workers believed that the flood of dismissals following the strike could at least have been partially averted. By adding to this figure the 50 per cent of the last category it appears that an impressive 85 per cent of the workers in the sample felt that retrenchment could have been prevented (partially or fully) if the strike had not occurred.

TABLE 7.17

Expectation of Retrenchment in the Absence of the Strike

Category	*Finlay*			*Spring*			*Grand*	*Percentage*
	Perm.	Badli	*Total*	*Perm.*	Badli	*Total*	*Total*	
1	5	-	5	12	6	18	23	15.3
2	17	-	17	26	9	35	52	34.7
3	38	15	53	15	7	22	75	50.0
Total	60	15	75	53	22	75	150	100.0

1 = Large-scale retrenchment could not have been avoided anyway.
2 = Retrenchment would have occurred but to a limited extent and with (full) compensation.
3 = Retrenchment could have been wholly prevented.

If we combine this finding with the continuing sympathy of a large majority of the workers for Datta Samant (as will be shown later), then it is abundantly clear that the workers at large do not hold him responsible for the outcome of the strike. Among the workers who do not blame Samant for retrenchment are the 15 per cent who felt that even without the strike the millowners would have resorted to large-scale retrenchment. Looking at the views offered by the *badli*s it transpires that those from Spring Mills appear to be much more realistic than their colleagues from Finlay. In that they follow the pattern set by the permanent workers.

In the course of the strike there were a few apparently serious attempts at conciliation. It is important to know what the workers felt at that time but also what they feel in retrospect about the possibilities of ending the strike. They were asked both these questions and also asked to indicate when, if at all, their views started to change. It was, of course, impossible to pinpoint a specific day but the two proposals by the government (after five and ten months) appeared to be mental landmarks which enabled them to indicate at what stage their earlier opinions started crumbling. The answers to the question of whether the strike should have been called off before it fizzled out are listed in Table 7.18. The Table throws light on the crucial question of whether the strike leader was in touch with the real feelings of the workers and whether he should have adopted a different approach in order to end the strike.

It appeared that even in retrospect 10 per cent of the workers maintained that continuation of the strike was the right thing to do. If we include the workers of the second category, who appeared to have no regrets about the prolonged struggle, then we may conclude that over 15 per cent of the workers in the sample were convinced of the necessity of continuing the struggle at all costs. There is no difference in this regard between Finlay and Spring workers. Neither is there a difference if we combine categories 3 and 4, although the Spring workers proved to be more in favour of gaining at least something from their struggle whereas the spirit of the Finlay workers seems to have been broken more completely. It is no coincidence that the expectations among Finlay workers were higher too.

TABLE 7.18

Attitudes to Settlement

Category	*Finlay*			*Spring*			*Grand*	*Percentage*
	Perm.	Badli	*Total*	*Perm.*	Badli	*Total*	*Total*	
1	8	-	8	5	2	7	15	10.0
2	3	-	3	5	-	5	8	5.3
3	18	6	24	23	11	34	58	38.7
4	29	9	38	18	9	27	65	43.3
5	2	-	2	1	-	1	3	2.0
6	-	-	-	1	-	1	1	0.7
Total	60	15	75	53	22	75	150	100.0

1 = Continuation of the strike was the correct thing to do.
2 = No settlement could have been reached before most, or at least substantial demands (wage hike, repeal of the BIR Act, removal of the Sangh) were conceded.
3 = Settlement should have been reached after some demands had been conceded.
4 = Strike should have ended with acceptance of a token concession/even without any demand being met.
5 = There should have been no strike at all.
6 = Different position.

It may be said that the strength of conviction of the workers during the strike is better reflected by this Table than by the one showing the average duration of the strike because many incalculable factors influenced the actual date of resumption of work. As has been shown before, merely going by the averages of strike duration creates the wrong impression that Finlay workers were the better motivated strikers. Taking a clue from the findings presented in several Tables, it seems more than likely that there was no such difference but if there was a difference then it might well be that after all, Spring workers were better motivated. The fact that they resumed earlier could then be explained in terms of a better understanding of the unfavourable context of the strike and a more acute awareness of the hopelessness of the struggle.

It is likely that the findings of Table 7.18 still give a distorted picture of reality as there might be a discrepancy between what the workers felt at the time of the strike and what they felt afterwards.

In order to check this the workers were requested to indicate at what time they started doubting the usefulness of the strike. As the workers grouped under the first two categories felt that the strike should not have ended without substantial concessions from the employers and/or the government, it may be concluded that changes in their view can only have been marginal. A better purpose is served by focusing on the third and fourth categories involving 123 workers (80 per cent of the sample). Table 7.19 relates these categories to the approximate time at which the workers involved became convinced of their views regarding the need for a settlement.

The figures show that besides the three workers in category 5 of Table 7.18, another fifteen workers felt right from the start that a token concession or even less than that was acceptable. This means that eighteen workers had from the outset serious misgivings about the need and/or the success of the strike, a figure which corresponds exactly with the total of the first two categories of Table 7.12 (that is, workers who for one reason or the other were opposed to the strike). In due course other workers would come to share their point of view. After about six months, half of the workers in the sample who had started with high expectations had developed serious misgivings about the prolongation of the strike. This period coincides with the first proposal of the state government, an offer that was generally held by the workers to be too poor, even insulting, but which may have succeeded in fanning lingering doubts about the chances of success.

TABLE 7.19
Continuation of the Strike and Changes in Views

Time	*Category 3*	*Category 4*	*Total*	*Percentage (n = 150)*
No change	4	11	15	10.0
1–3 months	6	19	25	16.7
4–6 months	28	24	52	34.7
7–10 months	8	5	13	8.7
11–14 months	6	3	9	6.0
In retrospect	4	3	7	4.7
Unknown	2	-	2	1.3
Total	58	65	123	

The important implication of this finding is that a strike ballot after six months might well have established that a majority of the workers was not keen on continuing the struggle. This change either escaped the attention of Datta Samant and the MGKU or was simply ignored by them. Just as other trade union leaders did, Samant would call a meeting during which vital decisions, such as the prolongation of the strike, were taken. Sounding out the feelings of the workers was done by observing their response to the speeches and/or by asking them to raise their hands in favour of a certain proposition. It need not be elaborated that such a procedure may totally distort the general feelings of the workers.

The Table also shows that nearly 11 per cent of the sample workers needed eleven months or more before they concluded that the strike was bound to fail and that they should accept less than was asked for when the struggle began. If we add to this group the 15 per cent of Table 7.18 (categories 1 and 2) who at no point were prepared to give in then we must conclude that a large minority of the workers (26 per cent) maintained a high strike morale for the better part of the strike. If this section was very vocal during meetings and morchas then it becomes understandable that the strike leadership remained unaware of significant changes in the views of the workers for far too long. The findings clearly suggest the need for a more or less regular check on the views of the workers in the course of a prolonged struggle.

Lessons from the Strike

The strike was for many workers a harrowing experience; some seem to have had little or no difficulty in surviving it but all the workers have had ample time to reflect on the struggle. As strikes intensify, the confrontation with the political context in which they occur may accelerate political awareness. In other words, strikes may act as a catalyst for political thinking. The best way to trace this is discussing with workers their views before and after the strike but such a longitudinal approach was impossible under the circumstances. The second best is to ask them to indicate what they learned from the strike. Naturally, many workers found this question difficult to answer, and this is indicated by the fact that some 8 per cent of the workers appeared to be incapable of replying to it. Some others who had reflected on the strike knew what they felt but it proved to be an arduous task for them to enunciate it.

In Table 7.20 an attempt has been made to present the various answers category-wise. A great many workers, of course, had learned more than one lesson which is why the totals of the columns exceed the seventy-five workers per mill or the 150 workers for the entire sample. The most frequent combination of answers appeared to be 1 and 5. Not less than thirty-four workers mentioned these two points when they were asked to state what they had learned from the strike. Second in importance was the combination of 2 and 5 which was mentioned nine times. The remaining combinations were incidental in nature. There was no conspicuous difference in the views of *badlis* and permanent workers, which is why this subdivision has been omitted.

TABLE 7.20

Lessons from the Strike

Category	*Finlay*			*Spring*			*Grand Total*
	Employed	*Unempl.*	*Total*	*Employed*	*Unempl.*	*Total*	
1	30	10	40	23	8	31	73
2	15	12	27	22	9	31	58
3	1	4	5	2	1	3	8
4	3	-	3	7	2	9	12
5	28	6	34	10	5	15	49
6	2	2	4	3	5	8	12

1 = (Illegal) Strikes are useless
2 = Strikes should be for a limited period only
3 = Strikes remain necessary/ indispensable
4 = No strike is possible without the backing of the government/no strike is possible without the support of the Congress Party
5 = Will never/hardly ever strike again
6 = Don't know/other

It is no surprise that more than 38 per cent of the workers felt that if strikes were to occur at all they should not be of an indefinite duration as this implies untold misery (category 2). In fact, one might have expected a much higher percentage of workers to draw such a conclusion and by taking a closer look at the several categories it becomes clear that this is indeed the case. That strikes should not be indefinite is a view shared by practically all workers, as is evident if we combine categories 1, 2 and 5. This procedure is justifiable as it stands to reason that those who feel that strikes are useless and those who (usually because of this view) said that they would not like to participate in any strike in the future, would certainly object to indefinite strikes. A combination of these categories is, therefore, warranted and presents a picture closer to reality than taking into account only those workers who explicitly stated that they learned that strikes should be of limited duration.

The balance sheet of the strike is depressing if the views of the workers after the strike are a criterion for judging the impact of the struggle on their strike attitude or their fighting spirit. Almost half the workers have come to the conclusion that strikes in general are useless. This high percentage is corroborated by the figure for workers who declared that they would in any case not want to go on strike again (category 5). When pressed, a few workers modified this statement and declared that under exceptional circumstances they would consider striking for a day or two. The heavy blow to the workers' capacity to resist employers and the Sangh is also evident from the very limited number of workers who insisted that, whatever the outcome of the strike, strikes can't be done away with (category 3). By comparing this figure (5 per cent) with the percentage of workers favouring the strike when the struggle began (80 per cent), we find that their number has dwindled dramatically.

The differences between the two mills are limited, which strongly suggests that the findings have a much wider application. The only exception here are the permanent workers of Finlay who in much greater numbers than their colleagues from Spring declared that they would never go on strike again (category 5). Nearly thrice as many permanent workers from Finlay said so as compared to those from Spring. This may partly be the result of the difference in average strike duration between Finlay and Spring workers.

The fact that only ten permanent Spring workers indicated that they would not or never strike again suggests that the strike morale among workers from that mill was stronger. This impression can be further substantiated with the aid of categories 1 and 2 from which it appears that fewer Spring workers than of Finlay felt that strikes were useless whereas the opposite is true for workers who attach value to a limitation of the strike period. The Table effectively settles the question whether the strike attitude of Spring workers is weaker than to that of Finlay workers. There appears to be no reason to believe that Spring workers are less motivated strike participants. The findings also bear out that no purpose is served by organizing indefinite strikes and crushing the workers' spirit.

On the whole there is not too much difference between the views of employed and unemployed workers although one would expect those who became unemployed to pass a more severe judgement on the usefulness of strikes. As far as the role of the government or of the party in power is concerned (category 4), it appears that many more Spring than Finlay workers concluded that any strike which is not approved of by the government or at least by the party supporting the government is bound to fail. In fact, the replies in this category may be added to the first category as it is inconceivable that the Congress government will approve of strikes as long as it is in power. If we combine these categories then we find that the differences between the two mills are minimal with the exception of category 5. This again suggests that the findings might be applicable to the mill sector as a whole.

Discussing the outcome of the strike there appeared to be great unanimity among the workers regarding the question of responsibility for the failure of the strike (see Table 7.21). In this no noteworthy difference was found in the views expressed by *badli*s and permanent workers. It appears that the overwhelming majority of the workers (79 per cent) holds the government responsible for the outcome of the strike. The workers did not care to distinguish here between the state and central governments.

Contrary to what one might expect, only 15 per cent of the workers put (part of) the blame on the millowners, while a quarter of the workers accused the Sangh. The combination mentioned most often was that of the government and the Sangh (thirty times), the second place being taken by a combination of the government and millowners (seventeen times). Only a few workers stated that all three of them (that is, government, Sangh and millowners) bear responsibility for the failure of the strike. A somewhat puzzling combination was that of attributing the responsibility to both the government and the workers, a combination found seven times. Probing this reply, it transpired that what these workers intended to say was that the government was responsible for not intervening and bringing about an honourable solution but that the workers were responsible too because they started returning to the mills which caused the strike to collapse.

TABLE 7.21

Responsibility for the Outcome of the Strike

Category	*Finlay*			*Spring*			*Grand*
	Employed	*Unempl.*	*Total*	*Employed*	*Unempl.*	*Total*	*Total*
Government	38	20	58	40	20	61	119
RMMS	13	5	18	13	6	19	37
Millowners	6	4	10	7	6	13	23
Workers	8	3	11	9	2	11	22
Datta Samant	4	2	6	1	1	2	8
Don't know	2	1	3	4	1	5	8

Be that as it may, it must be noted that in all these combinations the government was one of the agents held responsible for the outcome of the struggle. It is a striking phenomenon that the responsibility for the strike, first a confrontation between workers and employers in the private sector, should be laid at the doorstep of the government. A mere 5 per cent of the workers held Datta Samant responsible for the failure of the strike. These two findings combined prove that the government failed completely in convincing the textile workers that Datta Samant was an irresponsible trade unionist who ought to be avoided. Apparently this policy backfired and left the government naked in the eyes of the striking workers. The same may not be true, of course, for the public at large.

Another important finding is that there is no noteworthy difference between the views of employed workers and those who became unemployed. Broadly speaking, the unemployed are represented with their proportionate share (one-third of the sample) in every category. Maybe more important is the finding that not only is there no difference between employed and unemployed workers but also not between workers from Finlay and Spring mills which strongly suggests that the findings may be generally applicable to the Bombay textile industry.

Even if the government failed in discrediting Datta Samant, it did succeed to a large extent in impressing on the workers that nothing can be achieved so long as the government is opposed to a strike. This is borne out by the replies to the question whether political changes are necessary in order to improve the situation for the workers. In this again, there appeared to be no difference between the two mills or between the various categories of workers.

Given the fact that a great majority of the workers holds the government responsible, it was to be expected that most of them would feel the need for political change. This happened to be so in the case of 53 per cent of the workers but only very few workers had any idea of how such changes could be brought about. The second largest group, a substantial minority of (35 per cent), seems to feel that there is no point in changing the political power structure if a new government has the same attitude towards labour as its predecessor. In their view, what is required is not so much a change in government as a change in the attitude of the party in power. Less than 10 per cent of the workers did not know what to make of this question and the remaining workers felt that there was no need for political change.

It transpired in the course of the interviews that although a majority of the workers expressed a need for changes, this did not necessarily imply that they considered Samant's Kamgar Aghadi to be a real alternative. In order to obtain information allowing for a rough indication of the scope of the support for the Kamgar Aghadi, a relevant question was included in the interviews. About 40 per cent of the eighty workers who were asked whether a workers' party would be of any use, declared that such a party, be it Samant's Kamgar Aghadi or any other, would be of no use as it would be incapable of changing the plight of the workers. The number of Spring workers who saw no point in a workers' party was double the number of Finlay workers. The hesitations of the workers are connected with their scepticism about the objectives of political parties in general. Datta Samant capitalized on these doubts by repeating time and again that political parties subordinated the interests of the workers to their own political objectives. Many workers may have remembered that warning when Samant started his own Kamgar Aghadi. There is no strong evidence that Samant's workers' party will in due time be able to dispel the doubts these workers have about mixing politics and trade unionism.

The question of the desirability of mixing politics with trade unionism allows for division of the labour force into several sections but there is near unanimity about the need to be able to select the representative union in the textile industry through secret ballot. This question too was introduced at a late stage of the research and put to only fifty-five workers (thirty-three from Finlay and twenty-two from Spring) from the large sample. No less than fifty-one workers declared that they wanted secret ballot to decide which union should become the representative union. The remaining four workers, all RMMS supporters, were against a secret ballot. This finding is fully confirmed by the workers in the smaller sample. All the seventy workers from that sample who were asked whether support for a union should be decided on the strength of its membership (checked by means of verification) or through a secret ballot, replied that it should always be through a secret ballot. Combining the two findings it may be concluded that 121 out of the 125 workers who were asked this question appeared to be in favour of a secret ballot and this supports the contention that the Sangh is only in power because it is shielded by the power that is.

The possibility of a secret ballot is closely interlinked with the existing labour laws, the BIR Act in particular. This Act not only lays down the procedure for verification of membership but also provides the rules for solving labour and wage problems by way of conciliation and adjudication in court. The workers were, therefore, asked their opinion on the usefulness of the legal apparatus designed to solve wage and labour problems (see Table 7.22). This question appeared to be very difficult for them to answer. Some had never paid much attention to this problem and did not venture a view (category 4), others even failed to grasp its meaning (category 5). In consequence, twenty-five sample workers did not answer the question.

A division of the replies to this question in terms of employment (*badli*s vs permanent workers) was not revealing. Neither was this the case when the workers from the two mills were juxtaposed. It is clear from the Table that the confidence workers have in the legal apparatus is none too great. In all, 28 per cent stated that they feel that courts are useful even if it takes a long time for a decision to be reached. Some of them added that the time factor is not so important as the workers will be compensated for the time that elapses between referral to a court and the verdict. A much larger group, however, doubted the usefulness of the courts and put up conditions. The condition heard most often was that there should be a time limit (usually fixed by them at six months) for a case to be in court. By exceeding this limit a case would rapidly lose its significance for the workers involved. This limit is rarely, if ever, reached by courts when the stakes are high. This means by implication that these workers seriously question the usefulness of the legal system for solving their problems.

TABLE 7.22

Usefulness of Referring Wage and Labour Problems to Courts

Category	*Finlay*	*Spring*	*Total*	*Percentage (n = 125)*
1 Not useful	20	23	43	34.4
2 Conditionally useful	29	18	47	37.6
3 Useful	20	15	35	28.0
4 Doesn't know	6	7	13	
5 Not understood	-	12	12	
Total	75	75	150	100.0

Another condition put up by some workers was that the verdict should be in favour of the workers, a condition which, apart from displaying a lack of understanding of the modus operandi of labour courts, also indicates a lack of confidence in the results. Almost as sizeable as the group who questioned the usefulness of the courts and put up certain conditions, was the group who saw no advantage whatsoever in the possibility of referring wage and labour problems to courts. It has been suggested that the outcome of the legal struggle (the attempts at derecognition of the RMMS) dealt a severe blow to the already shaky confidence of the workers in the legal apparatus. In order to be more specific one needs data indicating the views of the workers prior to the strike. However, even in the absence of such data it cannot be denied that the lengthy ordeal in the courtroom did nothing to improve the situation. Leaving aside the dubiousness of the verdict favouring the Sangh, one can only agree with the workers' preference for speedy results.

The most important differences found so far between workers from Finlay and Spring related to factors like education and income/wealth. Several other distinctions appeared to be vaguely connected with these two variables or strongly dependent on them. Given these differences one might expect that the views of the workers of these two mills would differ on the system of wage negotiations. In the present system the RMMS negotiates with the representatives of the employers and, after taking the differences in the textile mills into account, concludes an agreement which applies to the Bombay textile industry as a whole. Wage disparities between the mills in consequence are less than would otherwise have been the case.

One could imagine that the workers in the more profitable mills would regret such industry-wise negotiations as these go against great wage disparity and oblige them to accept wages at a lower level than would have been the case with mill-wise negotiations. In order to test this contention a relevant question was included in the interviews. The workers were asked whether wage negotiations with the millowners should be on a mill-wise or an industry-wise basis. In this case the assumption was that workers of Spring Mills (the prosperous mill) would be more inclined to mill-wise negotiations than workers from Finlay, the backward mill. If no differences existed between the views of the workers of these two mills regarding the system of wage negotiations, then it could be argued that considerations of solidarity are more important to the the textile workers than the possibility of higher wages.

It turned out that this particular question posed more problems than any other question in the interview schedule. In spite of careful explanation, workers very often thought that they were being asked whether there should be one union in the textile industry or not (see Table 7.23). Due to this incurable misunderstanding quite a number of replies are of no use in studying the question of mill-based versus industry-based negotiations. It should also be noted that the views of those who defended a particular position were often not firmly rooted. This became clear as these views could be changed into their opposite after a brief discussion. In those cases in which the workers' view appeared to be uncertain or shallow, the answers have been grouped in the category 'Don't know', a sizeable one.

TABLE 7.23
Preference for Type of Negotiations

Category	*Finlay*	*Spring*	*Total*	*Percentage (n = 126)*
1 Mill-wise	15	36	51	40.5
2 Industry-wise	21	21	42	33.3
3 Other position	1	1	2	1.6
4 Doesn't know	19	12	31	24.6
5 Only by one union: MGKU	15	4	19	
6 Only by one union: RMMS	4	1	5	
Total	75	75	150	100.0

Even though the answers of the workers in category 4 did not show firm conviction, it is clear that they do throw some light on the question of mill-based group interests. One can argue that the fact that these workers did not devote much time to this problem is in itself a strong indication that considerations of the relative prosperity of a mill are not important to a substantial group of workers when deciding whether to have mill-wise negotiations or not. Those workers who, even after careful explanation, simply failed to understand the question and continued to give their preference for a particular union should in any case be excluded (categories 5 and 6). This implies that, at best, only the answers grouped in the first four categories, involving 126 workers, have a bearing on the problem.

It appears that the largest group of workers (40.5 per cent) is in favour of mill-wise negotiations and also that many more Spring workers prefer such negotiations (allowing for differentiation in wages but also speedy results) than Finlay workers. This seems to confirm the impression that workers will base their preference to a large extent on their understanding of the financial position of the mill. In this respect it is noteworthy that several of the Finlay workers who declared that they preferred mill-wise to industry-wise negotiations insisted that their mill belongs to the group of prosperous mills in the city. The finding seems indicative of a shift in the direction of plant-based trade unionism but before any such conclusion can be drawn more study, particularly with a longitudinal approach, is required.

It is noteworthy that there is an equally strong group in both mills (together accounting for one-third of the sample answers) maintaining that only industry-wise negotiations are the proper way of negotiating with the millowners. They stuck to that view even after I appealed to their self-interest by pointing out to them that mill-wise negotiations would imply wage differentiation. Because Spring workers might be held to benefit more from mill-wise negotiations than their counterparts from Finlay, this check on the reliability of the answers was always done in their case. Frequently, these workers would retort that wage differentiation was the very reason why mill-wise negotiations were wrong. Starting from the assumption that (narrow) group interests prevail as soon as it comes to money, it is remarkable that such a sizeable group did not succumb to the temptation.

MOVEMENTS IN UNION MEMBERSHIP

Popularity and Resentment

It has been shown that the workers rallied en masse behind Dr Samant when the strike began. No worker at that time knew the ordeal that was ahead of him and it was inevitable that workers increasingly grew tired of the strike as time dragged on. However, no settlement was reached. It would have been natural for the feelings towards Dr Samant to turn sour in the process. Such a development might have been expected in the case of the workers who (finally) resumed work but even more so in the case of those who lost their jobs as a result of the strike. In order to check whether Samant's popularity suffered a tremendous setback because of the failure of the strike, the workers were asked to say what they felt about him. It should be remembered that the interviews took place some five years after the commencement of the strike which means that meanwhile the workers had plenty of time to draw conclusions. While tabulating the answers no noteworthy difference could be noted between the views of permanent workers and *badli*s. The pattern of sympathy for Samant among them follows closely the pattern established by permanent workers. However, a distinction in terms of the categories 'employed' and 'unemployed' proved to be revealing (see Table 7.24).

TABLE 7.24
Popularity of the Strike Leader Five Years Afterwards

Category	*Finlay*		*Spring*		*Total*
	Employed	*Unempl.*	*Employed*	*Unempl.*	
Samant-wala	24	15	16	17	72
Samant cannot help	13	4	20	3	40
Indifferent	3	1	-	2	6
Samant beguiled workers	9	3	12	3	27
Different position	1	2	2	-	5
Total	50	25	50	25	150

First of all, it appears that 50 per cent of the workers are still with Samant in spite of everything although they may not be paying members of his union. These workers have been dubbed 'Samant-walas'. The percentage is actually higher still because the second category contains all those workers who concluded that Samant could not help them but who are still in sympathy with him. They do not blame him for his powerlessness. In most cases these workers feel that the government is responsible for the outcome of the struggle. The first and the second category together make up nearly 75 per cent of the workers who are still positively inclined towards the strike leader. By combining these two categories we see that there is no difference at all to be noted between Finlay and Spring workers for in each group there are exactly fifty-six workers. It is true, the incidence of workers who realized that Samant was not in a position to help them is higher in case of the Spring workers but this does not alter the feelings of sympathy of these workers for him. Given the similarity and unanimity of these results, there is no reason to assume that Samant's popularity among the workers of other mills is different. It was to be expected that the number of workers who felt betrayed by Samant grew as a result of the fruitless struggle. However, this group appeared to be limited to a few per cent. They are to be found in category 4 which also includes those who had always been against the strike.

The most surprising aspect of the Table is that unemployed workers appear to be such staunch supporters of Datta Samant although they suffered most in the wake of the strike. In the case of Finlay 76 per cent of this category feel positive about Samant and in the case of Spring Mills even 80 per cent. How should this phenomenon be explained? The method of selecting workers (seeking the help of the MGKU and the SSS) may have introduced some bias regarding Finlay workers. Many cases of these workers were being fought in court and for this they sought and received help from these two unions. It is possible to argue that they may have felt obliged to Samant in consequence. This does not, however, explain the sympathy for Samant among workers in Spring mills. These workers were predominantly selected at random in the chawls and in spite of that they were more numerous among the Samant supporters. Contrary to the unemployed Finlay workers, who were finally reinstated on dubious terms after years of unemployment, practically all unemployed Spring workers had to leave the textile industry altogether. In spite of that, they are even more numerous among the Samant-walas than their more fortunate brethren from Finlay who were taken back.

The reasons that may explain the support for Samant among the unemployed workers in the sample are basically two. First, there is the hope that Samant will still be able to do something for them (it being clear that nothing may be expected any longer from the Sangh). Secondly, there is a strong possibility that those who were fired were often the most outspoken opponents of the Sangh. These two factors, separately and in combination, may explain why workers, who lost so much in the course of the struggle, are still not inimical to the strike leader.

It may safely be concluded that if the sympathy for Samant in two divergent mills is the same for those who lost their job and for those who retained if and if it is the same for *badli*s and permanent workers, that Samant's popularity among the textile workers hardly suffered on account of the outcome of the strike. This, of course, does not mean that the 75 per cent of the workers who do not blame Dr Samant are ready to follow him in a new struggle because even those who are with him do not believe that he can successfully lead them if the government is determined to break the strike.

The facts presented above were confirmed by the replies to the question whether Dr Samant pursued his own objectives or restricted himself to doing what the workers wanted him to do. More than two-thirds of the workers (108) were of the opinion that Samant acted according to the workers' wishes. Another twenty-eight qualified this statement by adding that this was so only in the beginning but that he ignored the workers' views at a later stage. A group of nine workers took a different stand and a mere five workers felt that Samant acted contrary to the wishes of the workers. This low figure confirms that even among those who, for one reason or the other, were opposed to the strike (eighteen workers), the view prevailed that the strike was wanted by the workers.

Membership Before and After the Strike

To conclude that Samant can still count on a huge reservoir of goodwill is not the same as saying that his union wields much power in the textile industry. Although it would be saying too much to claim that the MGKU has become defunct, there is no denying that the popularity of the union has been on the wane ever since the formal end of the strike. Sympathy for the union is of a passive nature now and surfaces sporadically in a morcha, or a week of action, as in June 1987. But the attendance at such occasions is meagre and incomparable to the masses thronging the streets and squares in Bombay in the heyday of the Maharashtra Girni Kamgar Union. From what has been said so far it may be deduced that the popularity of a union may not be equated with its strength and neither may the membership be equated with its popularity. The shifts in union membership are a sure indication of that. Table 7.25 shows these shifts.

The total of the columns does not match exactly the number of workers from each mill because several workers declared that they were members of more than one union. Such cases were rare before the strike and occurred even less during the strike. In cases of double membership, workers were nearly always members of the Sangh (because they felt that they were left with no alternative), but adhered to another union simultaneously. There appeared to be no noteworthy difference between *badli*s and permanent workers.

As may be expected, the Table shows a dramatic shift from the RMMS to the MGKU shortly before and in the course of the strike. The group of those who did not belong to a union rose from 12.6 per cent prior to the strike to 29 per cent during the struggle. It has been explained that one of the central arguments not to withhold the status of representative union from the RMMS (in spite of defaulting membership) has been that the Sangh members might have been wanting to pay membership fees but were prevented from doing so in the context of the strike. In order to be able to judge the merit of this argument the workers were asked to say whether they had wanted to pay the Sangh during the strike period or not. Merely seven workers out of the multitude that left the ranks of the RMMS stated that they, indeed, had wished to pay but did not know how to do this. The smaller sample largely confirms this picture for, of the fifty-seven workers who were asked the question whether they—for any reason—had wanted to pay the Sangh during the strike, only one admitted that he had wished to do so. The argument as put forward by the court to uphold the Sangh's status of representative union, therefore, stands exposed as baseless.

TABLE 7.25

Union Membership Before and During the Strike

Union	*Finlay*		*Spring*		*Total*	
	Before	*During*	*Before*	*During*	*Before*	*During*
RMMS	61	10	59	2	120	12*
MGKU	-	47	-	48	-	95
BGKU	7	-	1	-	8	-
Shiv Sena	5	-	1	-	6	-
Other	1	1	1	-	2	1
None	5	17	14	26	19	43
Total	79	75	76	76	155	151

* This figure is inflated. Seven workers in this category declared that, in fact, they were not Sangh members during the strike but that they would have liked to pay membership.

The general picture emerging from the large sample is corroborated by the small sample (covering 100 persons). In all ninety-four workers in the small sample stated that they paid Sangh membership prior to the strike, five said that they were members of no union and one claimed membership of the Mumbai Girni Kamgar Union. As in the case of the larger sample, the picture changed drastically shortly before and during the strike for sixty-two workers went over to Samant, thirty-seven reported not to have belonged to any union at that time while the member of the Mumbai Girni Kamgar Union stuck to his union. The figure of 37 per cent workers not adhering to any union during the strike is 8 per cent higher than in the case of the large sample but this might be explained by the fact that many more workers from the small sample stayed in the villages.

Differences between Finlay and Spring appeared to be minimal as far as Sangh membership before the strike is concerned. As for the high incidence of this membership prior to the strike, it should be remembered that the figures present a distorted picture of reality as the payment of membership was for many a worker an irregular affair. If these workers could avoid having to pay on pay day they would try do so but from time to time they felt that payment was unavoidable. As a result of these irregular payments they would figure on the lists of the Sangh as members.

With regard to Sangh membership, the picture is more or less the same in both the mills but where other unions are involved the differences are very clear. Prior to the strike, Spring workers in the sample were either Sangh members or members of no union at all which suggests that Spring workers are less concerned with principles than with the possibilities of effectively influencing the situation. In the case of Finlay, 17 per cent of the workers belonged to other unions. However, if we look at the strike situation, we find that those Finlay workers who adhered to another union before the strike dropped this allegiance with ease and joined the MGKU or refrained from all membership. There is no difference in the total number of workers from both these mills shifting their loyalty to Datta Samant.

What has been said about the value of the figures relating to Sangh membership is to a lesser extent also true for the MGKU, with the important distinction, however, that workers were under no pressure to become members of the latter. The similarity consists in the fact that the data pertaining to MGKU membership have also to be treated with caution. Collection of membership fees by the MGKU during the strike watered down rapidly and was—for understandable reasons—haphazardly done. The loose way in which membership fees were collected is confirmed by the figure for workers who said that they did not belong to any union during the strike. This figure tripled as compared with the pre-strike situation. More often than not these workers were in sympathy with the MGKU but they had no opportunity or wish to pay membership fees due to distance, lack of money or both. The findings have to be compared with the membership figures after the strike (see Table 7.26).

TABLE 7.26
Membership of Unions in 1981

Mill	*Union*	*Perm.*	Badli	*Unempl.*	*Total*
Finlay	RMMS	28	14	5	47
	MGKU	13	3	19	35
	Other	1	1	-	2
	No union	1	-	1	2
Spring	RMMS	22	14	2	38
	MGKU	4	2	4	10
	Other	-	-	-	-
	No union	11	1	19	31

The totals of the columns do not correspond with the number of workers in the sample due to cases of double membership. The Table shows that some five years after the beginning of the strike, the RMMS had largely recouped its power within the mills. In all, eighty-five sample workers appeared to be paying membership to it. Alongside, the MGKU was significantly reduced in size with merely forty-five workers adhering to it. Payment of membership to the latter was irregular and often symbolic. As explained before, these membership figures do not indicate the true feelings of the workers but they do reflect the workers' assessment of the balance of power within the mills. It was clear to them that the strike was lost and that henceforth they would have to depend on the Sangh for protection.

Excluding those who were not members of a union after the strike (thirty-three workers), we find 132 cases of membership referring to 117 (namely 150–33) sample workers being employed in the textile industry. This implies fifteen cases of double membership. The position of the MGKU in Finlay seems better than that in Spring Mills but it should be recalled that practically all unemployed Spring workers left the textile industry but nearly all so-called unemployed Finlay workers were re-employed (see Introduction for an explanation). That there were union members at all among the unemployed Spring workers, is surprising. A more realistic assessment of the situation can be gained by excluding the category 'unemployed' from the discussion. It then appears that the difference between Finlay and Spring is not particularly striking. Finlay appears to have more RMMS members but also more MGKU members than Spring Mills. Wholly in line with earlier findings, Spring Mills appears to have more workers who claimed that they no longer belonged to any union.

Motives for Membership

Knowing the motives for joining a union throws light on the workers' expectations from unions as also on the reasons for double or even triple membership. All the workers who claimed membership of either the RMMS (eighty-five) or the MGKU (forty-five) after the strike or who were no longer members of any union (thirty-three) were asked to explain their reasons. The answers reveal once again that the Sangh might be the legal spokesman of the workers but certainly not the real one (see Table 7.27). From the Table it is abundantly clear that the overwhelming majority of workers rejoined the RMMS for pragmatic reasons. These include the conviction that the RMMS is the one union wielding power within the mills, the belief that there is no alternative, fear of repercussions and the need of giving in to pressure exercised by the Sangh on pay day. Membership of the MGKU, on the contrary, is predominantly based on sympathy with its objectives. The workers who are no longer members of any union are in essence those who were never re-employed in the textile industry. A substantial number among them were of the view that unions are useless, an opinion that will have been greatly influenced by the outcome of the strike.

It is not possible to distinguish clearly between fear and pragmatic reasons because more often than not these two elements were combined. The role played by pressure and fear in the choice of a union is borne out by the answers to the question whether there was any compulsion to become member of the union. Not less than forty-one workers mentioned pressure at pay day against sixty-seven who said that there was no such pressure. Another fifteen workers (seven *badli*s among them) declared that they were threatened with dire consequences if they did not become members of the Sangh. In the case of the *badli*s the threat was usually that they would never become permanent if they remained outside the fold of the Sangh. Permanent workers were commonly threatened with harassment by supervisors (often Sangh supporters), demotion or sometimes dismissal.

TABLE 7.27

Motives for Joining or Not Joining a Union

Category	*RMMS*	*MGKU*	*No member*
Pragmatic reasons	75	5	-
Sympathy	9	36	-
Uncertain	1	4	-
Being unemployed	-	-	19
Unions are useless	-	-	8
Other	-	-	6
Total	85	45	33

Fear of uncertain consequences was one of the reasons for joining a union, especially in the case of the Sangh. This fear could also be exploited to extort money or services from the workers. If the Sangh favours a worker in return for money received from them, we cross the none too clear border between exploitation and corruption. The reputation of the Sangh in this is not enviable, for even employers and government officials acknowledge malpractices by the representative union. An attempt was made to receive first-hand information on such practices from the sample workers but due to the nature of the problem this proved to be a very difficult task.

Workers do not want to discuss the payment of bribes (*dasturi*) with outsiders, certainly not in the presence of others. If a worker did pay *dasturi* in order to get a job or promotion he would not like to acknowledge this. The question was so sensitive that all those workers who seemed to be staunch Sangh-walas were left out as detailed knowledge about several aspects of the interviews might jeopardize the progress of the research programme. In all, 142 workers answered the question whether they, at any time, had paid *dasturi* to members of the Sangh. Only fourteen workers (six from Finlay and eight from Spring Mills) declared that they did have to pay money for 'privileges' like being admitted to the mill, receiving a *badli* pass, becoming permanent or for promotion. These fourteen workers represent merely 10 per cent of the sample. Of the 100 workers in the small sample only three workers admitted to having paid money for Sangh favours.

Even though the findings should be treated with caution and although the real incidence of *dasturi* is likely to be higher than it appears to be from this figure, there is reason to believe that malpractices like the bribing of Sangh-walas or supervisors is less prevalent than commonly suggested. One of the reasons is that most of the workers who admitted to having paid money said that this happened at the stage when they entered the mills as *badli*s. It should be remembered that the question referred to the entire period of employment in the mills. In most cases these workers did not acknowledge payments afterwards. Furthermore, it is striking to note that although the method of contacting workers for interviews varied considerably from mill to mill, the same number of workers from both mills admitted to having paid money on one or several occasions.

In the foregoing paragraphs, we discussed the motives of the workers in joining a union but the conditions during the strike were different from those prevailing afterwards. While the war was waged on the MGKU the Sangh resorted to techniques designed to break the morale of the workers who resumed. Workers who reported for duty at the gates of the mill were requested to sign a bond of good conduct in which they declared that they participated in an illegal strike and undertook to abstain from any sort of trouble in future at the risk of immediate dismissal. Several kinds of undertakings for various categories of workers circulated in the textile industry but the legal value of these documents, which were diligently collected by the mills, is limited. First of all, because workers signed under duress and, secondly, because many workers did not know what they were signing. After a while the practice of asking workers to sign a statement was given up.

From the 125 sample workers who were afterwards employed in the textile industry, more than a quarter never had to sign a statement promising to refrain from creating trouble. More than 42 per cent from these 125 workers knew what they signed, 28 per cent did not. To be sure, not all the workers who knew the contents of the bond of good conduct were properly informed about it. Many workers had been informed by colleagues before they went to the mill and, therefore, they knew what they had to sign. But just like the workers who were never told what it was about, they refrained from asking questions that might be termed impertinent. At that stage the workers were ready to accept even more humiliation to avoid being rejected by the mill.

It is likely that the purpose of asking the workers to declare that they would henceforth refrain from action was not so much the legal value of such an undertaking but to give them a feeling of insecurity, to impress on them that they were taken back through the benevolence of the management and that they could be dismissed at will.

Workload and Atmosphere

One of the complaints often heard from the workers after the strike is that the workload increased and the atmosphere became poisoned. There is indeed great unanimity among workers about this. Of all the workers in the sample to whom this question applied (that is, all those who were employed in the textile industry after the strike), 76 per cent said that their workload had increased. In this there was no difference between workers from Finlay and Spring Mills. What is more, many workers of the 24 per cent declaring that there had been no change in workload explained that this was because the department they were working in was for varying reasons not affected by retrenchment and modernization like the other department. In this group of 24 per cent there were three jobbers who said that the post-strike situation affects the ordinary worker much more than jobbers or supervisors.

Saying that the workload increased should not be equated with saying that such increases cannot be justified. The fact, for example, that one of the strike leaders in Spring Mills was of the view that there was ample scope for rationalization of labour inside the mill, suggests that such an increase was called for. But this former leader had meanwhile become unemployed and it is possible that the demands made on the workers today go beyond a reasonable and necessary increase of workload. In order to check this, the 100 workers in the sample who were reinstated after the strike were asked to say whether they were prepared to work more in return for higher wages. The replies to this question give a fairly reliable indication of the burden the workers have to shoulder every day.

An overwhelming majority of 80 per cent said that they would not like to work harder for more money against a minority of 15 per cent with a contrary view The remaining 5 per cent had so many caveats that they might sooner be reckoned among those who were squarely against such ideas than among those who favoured the suggestion. There appeared to be no noteworthy difference between Finlay and Spring Mills although a difference could be noted between *badli*s and permanent workers. Half the workers who had no objection to working harder were *badli*s who may not have been given sufficient and regular employment which could explain why in their view there was scope for an increase in workload. It is also important to note that thirty-eight of the eighty workers who were opposed to an increase of work for more money stressed that even if they had wanted to earn more, working harder was simply impossible. They emphasized that the work was already beyond their capacity.

The views of the Finlay and Spring workers are shared by the 100 workers from the random sample, 75 per cent of whom reported a substantial increase in the workload. Another 15 per cent reported no changes whereas the question did not apply in the remaining 10 per cent cases as these workers had become unemployed. Here, too, a few workers who reported no change in workload explained that they were aware of the increases but that these did not affect them because of their position as jobbers or weaver-masters.

Workload and working atmosphere are closely interlinked and it may be expected that the appreciation of the latter corresponds with the judgement of the former. This appears to be true. The most common complaint with regard to the worsening of atmosphere referred to the increase in production which causes a lot of tension. In all, fifty workers of the 125 who had started working again in the mills after the strike, mentioned the workload as the most important source of friction. Another thirty-nine workers stressed the ease with which they were fined, warned or charge sheeted and twenty-four workers emphasized the treatment meted out to them, the scoldings they received and the humiliation they had to undergo. These findings were confirmed by the 100 workers of the random sample. Seventy-four per cent of these workers (sixty-seven of the ninety workers to whom the question applied) reported that the atmosphere had turned sour and/or that the treatment of the workers after the strike had worsened. A vivid description of the grim atmosphere inside the mills has been given by several workers selected for case studies.

Although there was no remarkable difference between Spring Mills and Finlay with regard to complaints about the workload, a striking difference emerged when discussing the atmosphere inside the mills. Whereas the ratio between those who reported a worsening of the atmosphere after the strike and those who said that nothing much changed was 4:3 in Finlay, this ratio was 4:1 in Spring Mills. The finding is clear evidence that the situation in Spring Mills after the strike became much more grim than in Finlay. This points at the possibility of a different attitude towards the workers in private mills as compared with mills that had been taken over or nationalized by the government. It is no remote possibility that the management of mills in this last group took a more lenient view. But before any such conclusion can be drawn more research is required. An explanation for this could be that the management of the mills run by the government, unlike the management of the private mills, may have attached some value to convincing the workers of the good intentions of the government. It did not fit the image of the government as a benevolent employer to be too harsh on the workers. After all, the government was not unaware of the resentment felt by the workers although the extent of their anger and frustration may have been greatly underrated.

SUMMARY OF PART II

Summarizing the findings of the 150 interviews presented in the last two chapters, it may be concluded that the workers of Finlay and Spring Mills represent different groups in terms of education, income and wealth. It has also been shown that Finlay workers are more strongly city-based and that the average strike duration for the workers of these mills differed considerably. However, external circumstances (the fact that Finlay opened its gates much later than Spring Mills, dependence of the Spring workers on cheap accommodation provided by the mill and carefully directed pressure by the management) can adequately explain the differences in the average strike duration.

It has been shown that it is fair to assume that the observed differences had some effect on the survival strategies adopted by the workers and that they contributed to slight differences in strike-related expectations. But there appeared to be no reason to believe that the views of the workers of these mills with regard to crucial aspects of the strike (for example, demands, leadership, choice of a representative union, responsibility for the failure of the strike and so on) differed materially. On the contrary, there appeared to be a great unanimity in all important matters suggesting that the findings have a much wider applicability than for the two mills under investigation.

What has been said about a division of the workers according to mills, was also true of division according to terms of employment. Although one of the assumptions underlying the research programme was that *badli*s and permanent workers were divergent groups with at least potentially conflicting interests, no trace of a clash of interests between these categories could be found even though *badli*s appeared to have resumed work earlier than permanent workers. The reasons for this early resumption could not be determined with certainty but seem to be related to a combination of age, job uncertainty and hope to be promoted as permanent worker. As far as avenues for alternative employment, strike expectations, views and appreciation of the strike leader is concerned, *badli*s and permanent workers proved to be a homogeneous group. A noteworthy finding is that although it has been said time and again that *badli*s were the most determined strike participants, no evidence could be found to support this contention.

As far as survival strategies are concerned, it turned out that the possibilities offered by agriculture were the most important avenue for alternative employment. This emphasizes the importance of the rural connections the workers have. These ties became visible by looking at the places of origin, the monthly remittances and the great number of workers possessing a house and/or land in the village. Because of these strong connections not less than 40 per cent of the workers could take recourse to cultivating their own land, working as agricultural labourers or combining the two. After agriculture, work in the textile industry was the second important avenue of employment. This alternative was particularly attractive for weavers (as in the powerlooms) but working in other mills was also resorted to. Working as a *begari* or selling fruits and vegetables appeared to offer equally important avenues of employment to tide over the strike period.

The workers were very inventive in creating or searching for alternative employment. But all this would not have taken them far if they had been alternatively employed for a short period only. However, the percentage of workers who remained unemployed throughout the strike was small (10 per cent). Although workers had to change jobs more than once (apart from those who could cultivate a sufficiently large plot of their own), at least two-thirds of the workers appeared to have worked for the better part of the strike period. This explains more than anything else why the workers could remain on strike as long as they did. They were greatly helped in this by the flexibility of the labour market in the city. The average duration of this alternative employment may also largely explain why an amazing one-third of the workers declared that they did not (have to) change their lifestyle in spite of the strike.

Even though the overwhelming majority of the workers stood behind the strike when the struggle began, this majority shrunk to a minority as time passed. The available evidence suggests that a majority of the workers may have lost heart, possibly after six months but certainly after ten months of the strike, a fact which either remained hidden from the strike leadership or was ignored by it. One of the surprising findings in this context was that a perplexing 80 per cent of the workers had believed that the strike would be over within two or three months even though the strike leader had warned that it would take six months at least. Equally amazing was the utter lack of knowledge regarding the existence and work of the various sorts of workers' committees, which seriously undermines the importance with which these committees have often been credited.

It appears that the workers showed a much greater willingness to arrive at a settlement than was displayed by the strike leadership. But even so it should also be noted that although the strike ended in large-scale retrenchment and unemployment for tens of thousands of workers, the victims do not blame Dr Samant for this disastrous result. Even later, as before, he could count on the sympathy of the workers although the number of those that were ready to follow his leadership dwindled substantially. Near unanimity prevails among the workers as far as the question of the responsibility for the failure of the strike is concerned. A resounding 80 per cent of the workers hold the government responsible for the failure. But instead of concluding that only a change in the political balance of power holds a promise for their future, the workers seem to have decided that a strike which is not approved of by the government stands no chance of success. The unavoidable conclusion is that their morale has been greatly sapped by the past struggle.

As far as the membership of unions is concerned, it has been shown that even though the Sangh had lost practically all its membership at the beginning of the strike, it has meanwhile regained its position of power by utilizing all the pressure tactics at its disposal—the collection of fees on pay day in particular. Workers felt obliged to become members in order to gain some degree of protection inside the mills. It has been established, that the formal membership of the Sangh, as indicated by payment of fees (and verification of this), is not a reliable measure to gauge the real support enjoyed by the union. The adoption of a secret ballot as a means of selecting the representative union would be a much sounder index of the true feelings of the workers and is, therefore, sought by all workers, barring a few diehard Sangh supporters.

Chapter Eight

THE TEXTILE STRIKE

AN OVERVIEW

SURVIVAL STRATEGIES

The Concept of the Informal Sector

This study has sought to throw light on the various strategies resorted to by workers to tide over the strike period. In the case of the textile strike this meant a study of the ways in which the workers succeeded in surviving such a long period without a regular income. Due attention needed to be given to the ways in which different categories of workers (workers in prosperous and in backward mills, *badli*s and permanent workers) were affected by the strike, bringing to light the employment opportunities offered by what is known as the informal sector. This question seemed all the more important as the textile workers, unlike their counterparts in the West did not have strike funds at their disposal. True, the scope of these funds varies greatly from country to country and so does the amount workers receive during the struggle. A striking worker may be able to count on as much as 80 per cent of his normal income, as in West Germany, or the strike pay may barely exceed 10 per cent of his usual earnings, as in the UK (Crouch 1982: 89–92), but even 10 per cent is not a bad starting point if the family of striking workers can count on support from social security funds.

The Bombay textile workers neither had regular strike pay nor a system of social security, and their savings (another important source of sustenance in times of crisis) too are not comparable to those of workers in the West. Every man had to look after himself and his family. Those who had strong ties with their native village could choose between trying to make both ends meet in the city or leaving for the village. Workers without such ties did not have this option and were forced to remain in Bombay. The environment (village or city) largely determined what means the worker had at his disposal.

If the rural connection proved to be important for workers who returned to the village, then the study also indicates that this connection had little or no significance for all those who remained in the city during the strike. Unfortunately, the magnitude of this last category could not be established with any degree of certainty. It might have been smaller, of the same size or larger than the category residing in villages. Whatever its scope, there is no denying that tens of thousands of workers remained in Bombay and succeeded in finding employment in the city. Moreover, these workers were able to find alternative employment for the better part of the strike period. This is a remarkable aspect of the strike which did not surface with comparable force during earlier struggles and merits detailed discussion. It touches on the significance of what is alternately called the informal or the unorganized sector.

The concept of the 'informal sector', which is counterpoised by the term 'formal sector', is diffuse and has remained so in spite of a long and ongoing debate. The concept was probably first used by Keith Hart (Hart, 1973). Gradually the term came to replace earlier concepts like the traditional versus the modern sector, the small-scale versus the large-scale sector or the unorganized versus the organized sector. But even today reference is made not only to the informal sector but also to earlier concepts. Banerjee, for example, who wrote in 1981 on the complex relationship of the formal and informal sector, treats the concepts 'informal sector' and 'unorganized sector' as interchangeable and seems now to prefer the latter term (cf. Banerjee 1981, 1985). In this work no distinction is made between the unorganized and the informal sector.

The names of the sectors may have differed but what the dichotomies had in common was the attempt to lay bare certain characteristics of the structure of the urban economy and urban labour market. In the spectrum of the urban economy we find the large, unionized enterprises with a comparatively high level of wages and technology employed at one end and countless small, unorganized industrial and commercial activities (usually associated with self-employment), in which the mass of the urban workers are employed, at the other. As a corollary to the lack of organization and as a result of its untransparent mode of production, the wages in the informal sector are much lower although the entry to it is supposed to be much easier.

However, the clarity of the dichotomy, so visible at the extreme ends of the spectrum, becomes diffused as soon as one tries to become more specific. Structuring the urban labour market or the mode of production with the aid of these dichotomies proved to be increasingly difficult. In the debate on the usefulness and the applicability of the dichotomies, no unanimity emerged although most authors agree that a division of the urban economy into two sectors is beset with problems which defy any easy solution (cf. Gerry, 1974; Bromley and Gerry, 1979; Davies, 1979; McGee, 1979; Breman, 1976, 1980; Moser and Young, 1981; Papola, 1981).

There has also been a lot of confusion regarding the field to which the term should apply. Some argued that the informal sector concept should be used to denote specific forms and conditions of industrial activity in the urban economy. Others tended to focus on the labour and employment aspects of this sector. The Joshis, for instance, speaking about the distinctions between the organized and unorganized sector, stressed the importance of the technology employed, the market structure and the relationship with the government (H. Joshi and

V. Joshi, 1976: 44–46). Papola used the same criteria to demarcate the formal and informal sector but emphasized unionization, legislation and formal recruitment as elements characterizing the formal sector (Papola, 1981). In doing so Papola stressed the labour aspects of the division of the urban economy.

Attempts to untangle the knot binding the formal and informal sector elicited a long debate and so did the nature of the relationship between these sectors. Some consider the existence and expansion of the unorganized sector in Third World economies as an inevitable phase in the development process. They stress its importance as a buffer zone, a source of employment for the urban masses but also one that is subservient to the needs of the formal sector which alone can perform the task of raising the standard of living of the population as a whole. Others (including the World Bank) prefer to point to the very real contribution of the informal sector to the economy (one may think of the ever-expanding system of subcontracting) and emphasize the need to protect it because it promises high returns while providing employment to the masses. Those who subscribe to the latter view defend programmes for the development of the informal sector.

Papola has argued that upgrading the informal sector is not without risks and would ultimately lead to the integration of this sector in the formal sector (Papola, 1981). This would imply the loss of the advantages the informal sector offers today. Much depends, of course, on the extent to which upgrading will occur. However, given the complex structure of the urban industrial society it seems better not to reckon with one development but with several (maybe even conflicting) developments simultaneously. From the employers' point of view the advantages of production in the informal sector centre on low wages, freedom from unions and labour legislation, and the concomitant opportunity of adjusting production to market demand. However, these advantages apply only to some sections of the unorganized sector, not to all. Work in the informal sector is extremely diverse and by no means confined to work that might also be done in the formal sector if the advantages of the informal sector diminish or even disappear. From the workers' point of view, the greatest advantage of the informal sector is the opportunity of employment this sector provides as the barriers against entry are much lower here than in the formal sector.

Given the elasticity of the informal sector some authors have argued that the existence of this sector poses a threat to the position of the workers in the organized sector because a whole gamut of activities, today carried out in the organized sector, might be transferred to the unorganized sector under certain circumstances. The subcontracting resorted to by buoyant textile companies like Reliance is a case in point. It is this insight which causes Banerjee to conclude that, in the long run, the security of formal sector workers rests on the wage differential between the two sectors narrowing: 'Rational self-interest as well as humanitarian consideration appear to point in the same direction—towards greater organization of all workers' (Banerjee, 1981).

It cannot be taken for granted, however, that rationality will dictate the terms for industrial development and the labour movement any more than will humanitarian aspects. Besides, the type of rationality which people might like to apply is not the same for everyone and may vary according to the situation. It is certainly imaginable, for example, that trade unions in the organized sector conclude wage and retrenchment agreements with the management of companies on the understanding that part of the production will be transferred to the unorganized sector. Also, the possibilities of trade union organization in the informal sector seem today as remote as ever. It is a moot question whether the rational need for workers of both sectors to come together, as postulated by Banerjee, will really result in any such development.

In fact, from a later study by Banerjee, focusing on female workers in the informal sector in Calcutta, one may deduce that she too realizes that the chances for that are slim. It transpires from this study that not only do workers in the unorganized sector pose a threat to those employed in the organized sector but that there is ample scope for conflict also within the boundaries of the informal sector. Men, for example, are increasingly facing pressure from women because women tend to accept lower wages and worse labour conditions than they (Banerjee, 1985). This can only result in a further deterioration of the position of workers in the unorganized sector. After observing that the capacity of endurance of employers is superior to that of workers, Banerjee concludes that the female workers' capacity for adjustment is turning against them as the informal sector promotes organizations which survive primarily by increasingly shifting the burden of adjustment to risks involved on the workers (ibid). A development of this kind has to be seen as an unlikely starting point for closer cooperation, not to mention a coming together, of the workers in both sectors.

The Case of Bombay

The diversity of activities in the informal sector is borne out by a study by the Joshis who supplied a wealth of data with regard to the economy of the unorganized sector in Bombay. They grouped the work in this sector into several main divisions, the most important of which were 'Services', counting for 30 per cent of the activities, 'Manufacturing' and 'Trade and Commerce' counting for 26 per cent each, and 'Transport and Communications' with 11 per cent (H. Joshi and V. Joshi, 1976: 54–55). The data on which they based their study may have become obsolete by now as they pertained to the situation in the 1960s but the tendency which they noticed has not diminished since. They found that the number of workers seeking employment outside the organized sector increased rapidly both in absolute numbers as well as in proportion to the labour force as a whole (H. Joshi and V. Joshi, 1976:57). Seeking employment in the informal sector evidently offers prospects other than those in the organized sector, a world which is hard to penetrate.

Breman cautions against overoptimistic expectations regarding the capacity of the informal sector to expand. He considers the idea that 'newcomers can set themselves up as self-employed with almost no money or without too much trouble' a dangerous and misplaced romanticization of the hard-fought existence at the bottom of the urban economy (Breman, 1980: 19). He believes that the social and communal connections of the workers largely determine their chances of finding employment in the informal sector. However, if socio-economic background is as important as Breman wants us to believe, and if financial resources are necessary to buy entry into the informal sector, then one would expect serious problems to arise if suddenly thousands upon thousands of persons flood the urban labour market. That is exactly what happened during the textile strike when an unknown number of textile workers (to be counted in tens of thousands rather than in thousands) sought and found regular and irregular employment in this sector. However, of all the workers who were questioned about their problems in trying to find employment in the city in the course of the strike, only one said that he had met with opposition from those already employed in the field he wanted to enter. The only problems others had faced had been encounters with officialdom, that is, the municipality and/or the police.

It is difficult to explain this phenomenon. If the view that access to the informal sector is impeded or hindered by financial, social and communal barriers holds any merit, then we must look for explanations like the excellent connections the textile workers had with people employed in the informal sector or their sound financial position which would allow them to enter it. This last possibility may be ruled out, however, as money was the one thing workers greatly lacked. Besides, if we exclude the encounters with officials, not one of them ever mentioned that he had to buy the right to work or to sell in the informal sector. Neither did I find evidence pointing to a particularly strong relationship between workers and persons already employed in that sector. The most important relationships for textile workers are usually with other workers employed in the same industry and/or with those from the same region. If neither money nor social connections can adequately explain the smooth entry of these workers into the informal sector then this strongly suggests that the boundaries of and within this sector are less rigid and far more flexible than Breman would have us believe.

However, two more explanations may be mentioned. One refers to the point(s) at which the striking workers entered the labour market. This may offer a clue to understanding why these workers did not face any serious problems or opposition from those already employed in the informal sector. It could be that the workers chose to operate in fields with less rigid rules of entry. In this context it is important to recall that (not counting those who found employment in agriculture) the only discernable homogeneous groups alternatively employed in the informal sector consisted of workers who worked in the powerlooms, who started selling vegetables or fruits or who worked as *begaris*. The remaining activities constituted a motley collection of jobs defying convenient classification.

The second explanation relates to the superior position of the textile workers in comparison with workers in the informal sector.

On the whole they are materially better off, they have had more education, they come from a higher caste and, as a corollary, they enjoy greater respectability. These advantages may have helped them in finding alternative employment. If that is true then it would point to a sort of one-way traffic, allowing an already privileged section of the labour force to utilize the opportunities offered by the informal sector in times of crisis but not vice versa. However, before it can be concluded that either the type of jobs sought by the striking workers explains why they did not encounter any difficulty in entering the informal sector or that it was because of their superior position, much more research is required. What may be said is that the existence of an informal sector was crucial for the survival of the textile workers during the strike.

Significance of Rural Connections

The multiple connections between the city and the rural hinterland, particularly the significance of the regional origin of the workers, have been discussed at length (see chapters 3 and 6). It appeared that practically all those workers who prior to the strike lived alone in Bombay (that is, without family) returned to their villages of origin after the struggle began. If their plot of land in the village was large enough they cultivated it and if it was not they combined cultivation with agricultural wage labour. Those who did not own land were usually left with no other option than to work as agricultural labourers.

These facts underline the undiminished importance of the rural connections of the textile workers in times of crisis. One is tempted to believe that without these connections the strike might have collapsed much sooner. However, in the course of this study it was found that workers remaining in Bombay managed equally well to tide over the strike period. There is no way of knowing to what extent the exodus to the villages eased the problems of finding alternative employment for those who stayed on in the city. In any case it may be concluded that the workers who returned to their places of origin did not have to search long for alternative work even though their earnings were in most cases distressingly meagre. This sharp reduction in income proved to be the propelling force behind their desire to return to the mills when the struggle showed no signs of achieving success.

The significance of the rural roots of the workers became visible also in actions like the rural collections of food and money, and participation in jail bharo andolans. It is natural that textile workers in the course of a strike avail themselves of the advantages offered by their rural background when in normal circumstances the reverse is true. Then it is the family in the village which benefits from the presence of a worker in the city. The importance of this connection surfaces most clearly in the regular remittance of money from the city to the village. It is also reflected in the opportunities for workers, already established in Bombay, to take care of those who have just arrived from the village and in textile workers returning to the village to help with the harvest. The latter contributes both to the financial income in the village and to a high incidence of absenteeism in the mills (circulatory migration).

Apart from the jail bharo agitation, all these aspects of the rural connection have received attention over the years and they have existed throughout the labour history of the textile industry (cf. Thakker, 1962; K. Patel, 1963; Morris, 1965; Kooiman, 1983; Vaidya, 1984). However, there seems to be a new element too. The adjustment of workers with a rural background to city life has meanwhile reached such a stage that a sizeable section of the workers who stayed in villages during the strike said that they preferred mill work to working in the fields. This was not or not only because of the much higher earnings in the textile industry and/or because the families of the workers needed the income derived from mill work. These workers had given up working in the fields because they found it tedious and hard labour. This aversion was present not only amongst agricultural labourers but also among those who owned land themselves, although the feeling of aversion may have been stronger in the former.

THE ELUSIVE 'WORKING CLASS'

Labour Aristocracy

A discussion of the importance of the informal sector cannot be separated from the debate regarding the existence of a 'labour aristocracy' in India. This concept, too, has relevance for the strike because the textile workers belong to the strongest and best organized section of the industrial labour force. Although it might be impossible to draw clear-cut boundaries between workers in the formal and informal sectors or between various groups of workers within both these sectors, it seems far easier to prove the existence of a labour aristocracy. The term itself, however, is almost as vague as the concept of the informal sector but, contrary to the latter, the term has a long history behind it. Marx and Engels had already used it in the mid-nineteenth century to distinguish the mass of revolutionary workers living in proletarian conditions, from those who were better off and reformist in ideology (Bottomore, 1985: 265). The labour aristocracy was even then considered a privileged stratum of the labour force and credited with conservative ideology.

Basically, these distinctions remain the same today. The term 'labour aristocracy' is normally used to denote a group of workers who by the sheer strength of their position (in terms of job security and income), lifestyle and world view (awareness of privileged position and lack of interest in extending solidarity beyond the borders of their group) can be set apart from other workers. Most authors feel that to this description it should be added that these workers not merely show an indifference towards the plight of less fortunate workers but even try to fence off their position in an attempt to preclude other workers from intruding. If it can be established that workers in modern large-scale enterprises do have a strong tendency to focus on the problems and prospects within their own company or industry without caring (much) for what is happening outside, then this may render the hope of working class solidarity, let alone working class unity, a chimera. Recent developments in India, like the increase in plant-based unionism, seem to point in the direction of a strengthening of such attitudes. Symptoms of it can be found within the textile industry.

The case of a privileged section of the working class taking shelter behind nearly impregnable walls has been argued forcefully by Mark Holmström who used the metaphor of a citadel (Holmström, 1976). A problem related to the supposed existence of such a labour aristocracy was the question whether the privileged position of these workers was at the expense of other workers (both in the city and the countryside) or not. There seems to be fairly wide agreement that the backwardness of one section of the labour force cannot be attributed to the privileged position of another. There is no direct causal relation as such.

Yet, with regard to the wider notions of the formal and informal sector (exclusive of its meaning for the division of the labour force), it is more difficult to make a similar statement. It then becomes possible to argue that the linkages between the two sectors are such (one need only think of subcontracting) that a formal sector, with all its concomitant characteristics, could not exist or prosper in the absence of an informal sector (cf. Davies, 1979; Gerry, 1979). In this context Armstrong and McGee speak of cities as theatres of accumulation of capital in which a privileged few (the upper echelons in society) appropriate the surplus value produced by the subordinated many (Armstrong and McGee, 1985).

As for the division of the labour force, it soon became clear that a simple dichotomy of the working class into a labour aristocracy versus other workers was as untenable as a rigid division of the complex industrial world into two sectors, a formal sector and a more backward sector in which earnings and security are notoriously less. One of the first to attack the rather crude concept of a dual economy and a dualistic labour system as neither correct nor fruitful was Breman (1976). Breman sought to refine the analytical tools for the study of the labour force by introducing a division of this force into four broad social classes: labour elite, petit bourgeoisie, subproletariat and 'lumpen proletariat' (Breman, 1980). In this approach the labour elite roughly corresponds to what others formerly called or still call the 'labour aristocracy'. They are the best off in terms of wages, labour conditions and job security. At the other end of the scale Breman places an uprooted 'lumpen proletariat' with little or no cohesion and without property, ready to do anything to stay alive. They are the worst off. In between he situates the petit bourgeoisie and the subproletariat.

The petit bourgeoisie refers to a rather undifferentiated group of people working in a variety of jobs (usually, though not necessarily, self-employed) and sharing a strong attachment to autonomy. Breman characterizes them also as penny capitalists having 'a great urge towards self-achievement, confident in the openness of the system, appreciative of the value of education' (Breman, 1980: 25). Workers in the subproletariat, however, constitute the biggest chunk of the urban labour market, including not only ambulant craftsmen and the casual and unskilled labourers but also those employed by small-scale workshops and the labour reserve of large enterprises.

Breman cautions several times that the boundaries between the various categories are by no means absolute, that there is a gradual transition and that it is far easier to define the extreme ends of the scale than the parts in between. He agrees with Gerry that the distinction between the subproletariat and petit bourgeoisie is of limited importance and he follows him in the assertion that the difference between these two categories on the one side and permanently employed workers on the other is of greater importance (Gerry, 1974). Breman is even prepared to admit that the difference between the lumpen proletariat and subproletariat should not be overstressed but insists that a classification of workers on the basis of their participation in the production process and on concomitant lifestyles should be possible (Breman, 1980: 27).

In view of the limitations of his own fourfold division, it seems justified to ask whether any such attempt is not bound to fail. It could well be argued that the close and multiple links between various sectors and groups and the fact that members of one household frequently operate in different industrial settings and at various levels, defy description in conveniently arranged categories and sectors. It appears that ultimately the most clearly definable social class in Breman's approach is the labour elite and in this his analysis resembles Holmström's earlier approach more than he may have intended.

Holmström himself soon realized that the complex reality did not permit oversimplification and taking his cue from Breman's criticism, he ventured to present a new image of industrial reality. Subsequently, he changed his metaphor from a citadel to a steep slope. Picturing Indian society as a mountain with the very rich at the top, he proceeds to describe various layers, plateaus and the connections between them: 'There are well-defined paths up and down these slopes, which are easiest for certain kinds of people' (Holmström, 1985: 319). Although he acknowledges the existence of an enormous gap between the best factories and the worst, Holmström continues to give prominence to workers in the organized sector. Now, as before, he assigns the first place to the permanent workers in the organized sector (inclusive of government employees). It appears that the labour aristocracy, or labour elite if you will, is still very much alive. He proceeds to state that this group 'shades into workers with fairly regular employment unprotected by law'. Boundaries, one must conclude, have here been replaced by shades. These distinctions become even less clear when he moves to the third group which he does not define any longer but simply describes with the words: 'A sharper line separates both kinds of regular workers from unskilled casual labourers' (Holmström, 1985: 280).

This distinction between permanent and non-permanent workers (that is, casual, temporary, contract workers) proves to be of paramount significance for the third category. This group of workers transgresses the boundaries set between the earlier two and is characterized by terms of employment rather than by employment itself. It is a highly ambiguous group which, hierarchically speaking, does not necessarily rank under the first two categories. For example, what is one to make of those casual labourers (Holmström's third category) who may live in realistic anticipation of a permanent job in a modern company? Such workers may well be considered to be on the same horizontal plane as workers in his second category. Depending on the prospects they have, they may at times be on the same plane even as permanent workers in poorly performing companies in the organized sector.

Holmström ends by defining a fourth group: '... the self-employed, ranging from those depending on one or a few customers who can dictate terms, to independent craftsmen like carpenters who have a real market for their work' (ibid). One recognizes much of Breman's fourfold division in Holmström's new industrial image except for the pivotal role of the concept of permanency as a delicate tool in the classification of industrial society.

By looking at the structure and composition of the Bombay textile industry, it is possible to see how soon an attempt to classify industries and workers with the aid of a few categories runs into problems. Within the boundaries of the mill sector it is possible to discern vast differences between prosperous and backward mills in terms of technology applied, assortment of goods produced, markets and job security. These differences have important consequences for the labour employed and require a subtle classification. Again, within the mills there is a clear-cut distinction between permanent workers and *badli*s. Going by the uncertain terms of employment, *badli*s ought to be ranked under Breman's subproletariat but going by their job prospects they might be ranked as worker elite. In any case they do come under the umbrella of the organized sector.

One might solve this problem by *labelling* them according to their actual employment situation at a given time. It would then, however, not appear that there is tremendous scope for self-improvement and labour mobility between the subproletariat and the elite (at least in the case of the *badli*s), which greatly undermines the usefulness of these categories. If the number of workers involved was small, one might decide to overlook these objections to the various classifications but in reality they represent a substantial segment of the labour market in and outside Bombay.

Overviewing the situation in the textile industry, Papola observed that the formal sector availed itself (liberally, one might add) of the services rendered by casual workers which led him to suggest distinguishing between an 'informal sector labour market' and an 'informal labour market' in urban economies (Papola, 1981). In the last category Papola would like to include casual, contract and irregular workers in the formal sector but it is difficult to see how this distinction contributes to greater clarity in understanding the complexity of the urban labour market.

Class Consciousness and Measurement

Acknowledging the complexity of the factual situation, Holmström discusses the concept of 'working class' which he refers to as a group of people having common interests, sharing consciousness of these interests and living in a comparable economic situation. He notes that the industrial workforce includes people in large and small firms, permanent and casual labourers, contract workers, high and low castes, skilled and unskilled, educated and uneducated, those who possess land and those who don't. He proceeds to raise the fundamental question: 'When all these people are called or call themselves "workers" or "working class" is this mere rhetoric, or does it mean they share and know they share important common interests?' (Holmström, 1985: 287). After observing that there is no dual economy as he had postulated before and that the well-paid are not privileged at the expense of the others, he concludes that organized and unorganized sector workers 'do not think of themselves and act as separate classes with conflicting interests, and the reason is that they are not separate classes. There is no clear boundary between the two social worlds' (Holmström, 1985: 322).

It is one thing to note that certain groups do not consider themselves as separate classes but it is quite another to say that they share a common class feeling. Holmström raises the question of class consciousness several times without, however, providing a clear answer. From the unmistakable and crucial differences he noted between various categories of workers in several industrial settings and from the unconcern of these workers (frequently noted at first-hand by him) to the fate of workers in other industries, one would expect him to believe that no such uniform class consciousness prevails. Yet, at the end of his book Holmström says that the answer to the question of the existence of one working class with common interests and a common fate will probably be positive (Holmström, 1985: 315). This comes as a surprise as his findings do not point in that direction. At best he might have postulated the existence of a Marxian class-in-itself. Having done so he could have avoided blurring the distinctions he took so much pains to establish throughout his book.

Breman proved to be more consistent in discussing the concept of class. Speaking about the labour elite, a group showing much more internal cohesion and uniformity than other groups so conveniently taking shelter under the umbrella 'working class', he observed that even in their case it is easier to demonstrate that they constitute a *Klasse an sich* (class-in-itself) rather than a *Klasse für sich* (class-for-itself). Discussing the case for the other social categories distinguished by him, Breman concluded: 'In view of the heterogeneous make-up of the subproletariat, there is probably no question of class consciousness, even when it is narrowed down by segregating the paupers and the petit bourgeoisie' (Breman, 1980: 28). Although he refrained from making predictions about the future course of development, Breman asserted that the urban subproletariat at the present stage lacked the level of consciousness required to form one class capable of taking action to further its interests.

The debate regarding the presence or absence of class consciousness in a particular group is fairly abstract and this will not change if the contents of this concept are not made more specific. What is needed are criteria with the aid of which class consciousness can be measured for if this cannot be done to any appreciable degree, the exercise will remain theoretical. Unfortunately, no such clear-cut criteria exist and we are left with a number of indicators of varying usefulness. For example, it can be argued that the existence of class consciousness may be derived from strike objectives and ought to express itself in actions of solidarity and in strike participation. A mere quantitative analysis of the incidence of strikes, however, does not take us far if it is not related to the historic and socio-economic context in which all these strikes took place and to the expectations and views of the persons involved. Van Kooten, who recently undertook an extensive statistical analysis of post-war strikes in the Netherlands, was forced to conclude the same. He found that in the absence of any qualitative analysis it was not possible to make meaningful statements (Van Kooten, 1988: 144–49).

The difficulties involved in trying to nail down the existence or absence of class consciousness are probably the reasons why not much research is done in this field. However, some insight may be gained from a comprehensive research project conducted by Lieten *et al.* in the course of which workers in multinational corporations in India were questioned about their class attitudes. He informs us that these workers consider themselves an integral part of the working class and believe that workers all over the country have common interests (Lieten, 1987). These findings cannot, however, be taken at face value.

First, the acknowledgement of 'common interests' is too vague a statement to be of any use. It may be taken for granted that all workers share an interest in rising wages, social security, education, protection at the shop floor and so on. In this they are no different from other citizens. Secondly, there is reason to question his methodology. For example, Lieten says that due to his method of sampling there was a high incidence of activists in the various samples. He also states that he selected workers not only with the assistance of unions but also with that of the management, and that the interviews were often conducted in union offices. Thirdly, he admits that his findings did not apply to very profitable companies, and this is corroborated by Gooskens in her study of workers in a Philips factory in Pune. She observed that class solidarity stopped abruptly at the gates of the factory (Gooskens, 1984: 120–22). The same negative attitude towards cooperation with other workers was encountered by me in the course of research in a modern factory in Thane. In this there was hardly any difference to be noted between trade union leaders and workers (Van Wersch, 1983).

However, the state of class consciousness among workers may be gauged not only from what workers say about common interests but also from causes and objectives of strikes (as stated by them) and from the motives for joining a union. As for the causes of the strike, there is the obvious difficulty that the immediate cause triggering off a strike may have little to do with the real source of dissatisfaction. This problem, although not wholly absent, seems less important in the case of strike objectives. The motives for joining a union are yet another criterion for assessing the workers' aims and attitudes. A combination of these criteria will, of course, provide the best insight but, as has been said before, data are scanty.

Lieten's earlier mentioned study also attempts to shed light on the objectives of workers in joining unions. He questioned the workers, inter alia, about their motives for union membership. He noted that the attainment of 'economic benefits' inspired 25 per cent of the workers to become members of a union. Forty per cent considered it to be a necessary step 'for strengthening the position of the workers against the management'. Another 30 per cent wanted a union to protect themselves against 'victimization' (Lieten, 1987). Although Lieten refrained from explaining these categories (apparently taking them to be self-evident), it should be noted that the second and the third category are not necessarily opposed to the first category. Indeed, one may wonder why workers feel such a need to strengthen their position and ward off the risks of victimization if not to launch struggles to wrest economic gains from employers.

In the course of this study it has been established that economic demands and not political objectives were foremost in the mind of the workers. Ousting the Sangh was largely considered a precondition for realizing the demands. In reply to the question of the desirability of mill-wise negotiations as a substitute for industry-wise negotiations, it appeared that a majority preferred mill-wise negotiations as these seemed to promise higher returns. This suggests that it would be wrong to expect too much from class solidarity or class consciousness. In the absence of a proper system of collective bargaining in the industry (that is, providing for direct negotiations between the employers and the real representatives of the workers without the interference of a third party) all textile workers rallied behind Datta Samant but at the back of their minds was the hope that the government might come to their rescue if Samant's intervention resulted in a deadlock.

As regards the reasons for joining a union, it was found that fear played a prominent role in the decision to become a union member (most particularly in the case of the Sangh). This fear related to the union itself (which could punish workers for not joining the RMMS) and to the supervisors and management in the mill. For very pragmatic reasons (protection inside the mills), textile workers appeared to remain with the Sangh although their sympathy was with another union (the MGKU). But even with regard to this sympathy, it has to be said that this was at first largely based on high expectations of a substantial wage hike with the assistance of the MGKU. At a later stage, when the strike had failed, they could still feel sympathy for that union because the leadership had not betrayed their cause. But for all the unanimity and solidarity which surfaced in the course of the struggle, it ought to be realized that this was confined to the textile industry.

Relevance of Statistics

To assess the scope of class consciousness it is also possible to look at statistics pertaining to strike objectives. A source of information in India is provided by official statistics referring to labour disputes but, unfortunately, these do not provide a deep insight. For the past twenty years statistics pertaining to labour unrest have been classified in six categories: wages, bonus, personnel, leave and hours of work, violence and indiscipline, and 'others'. The attempt to classify labour unrest on the basis of these broad categories is bound to distort reality and denies the complexity of the factors underlying any outbreak of labour unrest. More often than not the root of the discontent is to be found in a combination of some of these factors. Neither do the categories reveal the importance of inter-union rivalry as a source of labour unrest. A rival union wanting to establish itself as an alternative to the union in power might seize upon any of these categories to launch a struggle. The size of the category 'others', which ought to be a 'rest' category of a few per cent, is usually of such magnitude that it tends to invalidate the contents of the remaining categories.

To give an example, Karnik presents figures for causes of industrial disputes in India for the period 1921–50, that is, at a time when the strike causes were grouped in five categories only, namely, exclusive of 'violence and indiscipline'. The only thing one learns from it is that 'wages' count for 43 per cent, bonus for 7 per cent, 'personnel' for 19 per cent, 'leave' for 6 per cent and 'others' for 25 per cent (Karnik, 1967: 402). E.A. and U. Ramaswamy, too, tried to analyse industrial disputes with the aid of official statistics and addressed themselves to the period 1951–75. They conclude that causes of strikes have shown a remarkable consistency over the years with 'wages' accounting for a third of the disputes, 'personnel' for another quarter to a third of the problems, 'bonus' for 7 to 10 per cent, 'violence' (a category introduced in 1968) gradually growing from 3 to 9 per cent and 'other' accounting for 20 to 30 per cent throughout the period (E.A. and U. Ramaswamy, 1981: 218–21). On the strength of these data they assert in their otherwise lucid exposition of industrial disputes, that the common view that the majority of industrial disputes takes place over the question of economic issues is a myth. To prove their point they reshuffle the categories and divide them into 'economic causes' (including wages and bonus) and 'non-economic causes' (the remaining categories). Next they find that economic issues have led to substantially fewer disputes than non-economic ones (E.A. and U. Ramaswamy, 1981: 222).

This procedure, however, is unwarranted. First of all, there is no justification for adding the complete category of 'other causes' to the group of non-economic causes. E.A. and U. Ramaswamy acknowledge that this very substantial category has a diverse character and refers to problems about the quantity and quality of food, availability of drinking water, toilet and canteen facilities, disputes over allotment of machines, workload and so on. In the absence of detailed knowledge regarding the numerical strength of these causes, the proper thing to do therefore would have been to exclude this category for their division. If they had done so the picture would have changed completely. Secondly, many of the strikes coming under 'others' do have clear economic overtones and might have found a place in the group 'economic causes'.

The most important shortcoming perhaps is the fact that the causes of the strike are not related to the strike duration and to the number of strike participants. In consequence we do not know what significance to attach to a strike for economic reasons. It is perfectly possible that strikes for wage hikes and similar objectives drew a much wider response and showed much more tenacity than strikes for the purpose of forcing the management to reinstate a dismissed worker or to improve leave facilities. A real comparison, therefore, cannot be made merely in terms of the frequency of causes of strikes like 'economic' versus 'personnel' but has to relate these causes to participation in strikes and their duration. The foregoing illustrates the dangers implicit in juggling with official statistics when trying to uncover the root causes of labour unrest.

Statistics with regard to the strike history in the Bombay textile industry suffer from the same infirmities. Thakker, for instance, collected data for the period 1928 to 1960 and, although he does relate the frequency of strikes to the number of workers involved and to the number of working days lost, he does not relate the various strikes to their causes. In separate Tables he presents the reasons, the duration and the frequency of strikes (Thakker, 1962: 136–39). More recently Bhattacherjee attempted to track down data on causes of strikes, while restricting himself to the Bombay textile industry over the period 1947–76. In this effort he was helped by annual reviews of the labour situation compiled by the MOA. The author grouped the causes in three broad categories (that is, 'Wages and bonus', 'Personnel and retrenchment' and 'Workload, hours, leave and holidays'). Apart from the fact that the categories he provides are too vague, Bhattacherjee, in his turn, omits to relate these causes to duration and participation (Bhattacherjee, 1987). The results, naturally, do not allow for any far-reaching conclusion to be drawn.

That labels and categories hide more than they reveal is also clear from the strike under investigation which provides an excellent example of the dangers of forcing the complexity of reality into a single category. It is possible to argue that this strike could fit in practically any of the categories customarily utilized in labour statistics. The strike started on a bonus issue in seven mills and may be labelled a strike for bonus. Very soon the workers raised wage demands which would make it a strike for better wages. However, workers were greatly perturbed about the treatment meted out to them by union officials and supervisors which would allow the strike to be categorized under the heading personnel. But the event immediately preceding the strike was a violent clash in Kohinoor Mills where Sangh representatives attempted to collect membership fees and called in the police. This immensely angered the workers and caused them to demand an immediate start to the strike. This could justify labelling the strike as having been caused by violence or inter-union rivalry. If one chooses to concentrate on the persistent legal efforts to dislodge the Sangh and to repeal the BIR Act, one might term the strike a political struggle. Complaints of long standing regarding labour conditions, leave facilities, workload and so on. would make it possible to place the strike in the category 'other'. What this small exercise shows is that reducing the manifold causes of a struggle to a single category will only result in obscuring the close interrelationship of all these causes.

No Class, No Communalism and No Groupism

The importance textile workers attach to mill-wise negotiations makes it clear that it would be wrong to conclude to a strong class consciousness on the strength of the outstanding unity demonstrated by them during the first six to ten months of the strike. It is certainly possible that if the present system of industry-wise negotiations (with compulsory arbitration in case of disagreement) were to be replaced by one in which workers sat face to face with the management of their own mill (collective bargaining at mill level), this would mean the end of the conspicuous solidarity shown during the strike. In the absence of such a system the workers stuck together as it was the only way to make progress but it would be premature to take this phenomenon as evidence of class consciousness.

The solidarity of the workers was inspired by common frustrations and equal interests but hardly transgressed the borders of their own group. Their mobilization was possible because of a rational choice (which does not preclude emotional tinges) and it was an example of what Hirschmann might term a 'hybrid of the two mechanisms exit and voice' (Hirschmann, 1970). It should be noted that the shift from the RMMS to the MGKU prior to and during the strike was perfectly logical and the same is true for their return to the Sangh. Leaving the Sangh represented an 'exit' from the organization which did not serve their interests well. It was also a 'voice' in the sense that there was no legal viable alternative to the RMMS, which forced the workers to return to the Sangh when the exit option failed.

It should be emphasized that within the boundaries of this group solidarity no discord could be found referring to communal, religious or regional attachments. This is of great significance as it points to a gradual erosion of the importance of communal feelings in an urban industrial setting. In this the findings of this study differ from other studies on textile strikes which exposed strong communal overtones. Murphy, for example, in his study of the strike in 1920 in the Madras Labour Union, concluded that strike-breakers chiefly belonged to a group of 'untouchables' (adi-Dravidas). He also observed, however, that the presence of caste and community loyalties need not block the road to the development of class consciousness and that the significance of these loyalties varied according to region (Murphy 1978).

Lieten, in his study of the textile strike in 1928 in Bombay, observed that caste played a prominent role in breaking the strike. Here too 'untouchables' broke the strike although other lines of communal division could be drawn as well, such as Brahmin versus non-Brahmin and Hindu versus Muslim (Lieten, 1982). The behaviour of 'untouchables' at the time was understandable and even pardonable as no labour organization had hitherto cared to look after their welfare. They were not even permitted to work in the Weaving Department on account of untouchability, as pointed out by Keer (Keer, 1981: 119–21).

In this study, not only was there no trace of communal fissures in the strike but there were also no differences to be noted in attitude to the strike between workers of various factories or between various groups of workers (permanent workers vs. *badli*s) in the course of six long months. Thereafter the ranks of the workers started breaking, but not along communal lines. The reasons for the collapse of the strike were many. A common factor, of course, was the exposure to financial exhaustion which ultimately forced even the most determined strikers to return to the mills. Those who struggled against all odds and persisted in their refusal to budge were in the end left with no option other than to quit the textile industry.

There is a clear difference here to be noted between the participants in the British miners' strike of the 1980s and the striking textile workers. Miners working in comparatively strong pits with high productivity and relatively secure employment, were unwilling to support the cause of those working in less productive mines and suffering from the constant threat of retrenchment (cf. *News Line*, 1985; Ottey, 1985; Reed and Adamson, 1985). No such internal dissension surfaced in the course of the textile strike. The miners' strike led to a virtual split in the ranks of the workers and the foundation of a new union but such a phenomenon was wholly absent in the Bombay strike. The textile workers perceived no conflict of interests among themselves and fought unitedly.

True, the strike duration was not the same for everyone. The averages differed from mill to mill and from one category of workers to another, but the differences could largely be attributed to factors like dependence on the mill for housing, pressure by the management (threats of dismissal) and the disparity in the time that the mill gates remained closed. Some mills opened within weeks of the commencement of the strike while others remained closed for a year and still others never opened their gates again. In the case of workers of certain mills, the decision to resume was taken under strong pressure exerted by the mill and the police. Such pressure was by no means the same for the workers of all the mills. Some mills excelled in taking punitive measures, others resorted to much milder action. The risk of losing accommodation provided by the mill appeared to be a strong motive to resume work for those textile workers who were housed by the mill. All these factors greatly influenced the average strike duration. To this must be added the factor of fear which proved to be very significant both in the decision to resume as well as in the decision to stay away.

Perhaps more striking than the absence of communal friction was the fact that there were no clashes between workers who were permanently employed and those who were casual labourers even though *badli*s tended to resume work earlier. The resumers were usually motivated by job uncertainty, a difference in the capacity of endurance or a combination of the two. But even though *badli*s went back sooner this did not lead to a confrontation between them and permanent workers. It seems hardly justifiable to label *badli*s (or anyone else, for that matter, who stayed away from the mills for more than ten months) as strike-breakers because both categories showed an astounding ability to continue the struggle. When workers finally started going back no one blamed the *badli*s in particular. Workers had suffered beyond capacity and mortgaged their future by taking loans. What more could anyone expect? It is very impressive, indeed, that the striking workers, in spite of all the differences between them, managed to put up a common front for such a long period. At no time was there so much as friction between the group of permanent workers and those who strove for that coveted position.

Workers themselves explained this phenomenon by pointing out that it was not possible for *badli*s to be appointed in the place of permanent workers, but given the determination of the millowners to break the strike and their capacity to legally dismiss workers, everything was in a flux and no one could rely on customary rights. Nevertheless in spite of the opportunity for *badli*s to try to take advantage of the strike situation, there appeared to be great unanimity among the workers as far as strike objectives were concerned. Quite naturally, permanency was of more importance to *badli*s than to permanent workers but the overriding concern of both groups was with improving material conditions (wages in particular). Added to this was the common disgust for the Sangh and these forces were so impelling that they wiped out the otherwise crucial distinction in terms of employment.

The second question of the study, which related to the differences between the various categories of textile workers, has meanwhile been answered. The problem here was whether differences could be observed in the effect of the strike on *badli*s and permanent workers and/or between workers from prosperous and backward mills. Apart from a tendency of *badli*s to resume earlier than permanent workers, no such differences could be found. The second question also sought to answer whether the various categories of workers had the same means at their disposal to tide over the strike period. It was found that, by and large, the workers had the same or comparable opportunities to find alternative employment and also that there was not much difference in the average time they were employed during the strike.

From what has been said so far about class and class solidarity some conclusions may be drawn. It may be recalled that this strike, in spite of the impressive solidarity displayed by the striking workers in the first phase, remained essentially an isolated, albeit heroic, struggle. In the beginning the strike seemed to offer evidence of a growing class awareness and of class solidarity. There was, however, far too little evidence of solidarity coming from other quarters of the labour field to allow for optimistic expectations regarding future class solidarity and joined struggle. What remains is the determination displayed by a group of angry workers with a common purpose.

Even within the limited category of textile workers, therefore, a fairly strong element of self-interest could be noted from the preference of mill-wise to industry-wise negotiations. One cannot but conclude that the mere existence of a group of workers, be it of the size of the striking textile workers, sharing a common interest in wage hikes and the removal of the Sangh (as a precondition to that), is insufficient to conclude to an existence of class consciousness transgressing the borders of simple group interests. This strike does not warrant the contention that class feeling or class awareness pervades the various sections of the working class, wiping out the manifold distinctions of several interest groups and forging them into an entity capable of opposing employers. Besides, if one excludes the foundation of the Kamgar Aghadi there is no convincing evidence either of the formation of a new class organization behind which the workers could or would rally.

POLITICAL IMPLICATIONS

Politics and Trade Unionism: The two sides of a coin

It has been observed that the founding of the Kamgar Aghadi by Datta Samant, an outgrowth of the textile strike, is at first sight a somewhat illogical step for a man who created a furore in harping on the theme of the harmful effects of a connection between trade unions and politics. This is not to say that the step itself is incomprehensible. It may, in fact, be considered a logical decision, underlining the important relation between trade unionism and politics. That it was taken by someone who until then professed not to believe in the usefulness of such a connection, serves to stress that there is a natural link between politics and trade unionism and that a separation of these two spheres is artificial. The popularity of the Kamgar Aghadi with many textile workers is proof that linking politics and trade unionism does not pose a major problem for workers.

The former rejection of this connection by Samant (and still by the government) centred on the complaint that trade unions were merely vehicles for political parties to further their political aims. Samant believed that they were not interested in the fate of the workers. The reverse he claimed to be true for his Kamgar Aghadi in which politics are supposed to be subservient to trade union goals (broadly formulated as promoting the interests of the working class). However, it is impossible to maintain such a distinction because political and trade union aims are most of the time blended. Any substantial change in the position of the 'working class', even (some might say, particularly) if this concerns merely bread-and-butter issues, is bound to have strong political implications and any major shift in politics will not leave the 'working class' untouched. In such a situation it is unavoidable that political parties and trade unions develop a symbiotic relationship and the Kamgar Aghadi is no exception to that rule.

The founding of the Kamgar Aghadi establishes once again that unions have no option but to enter the political arena if they have long-term perspectives. It is only plant-based unions, with very short-term perspectives and concentrating on highly economic issues, that eschew politics. For all other trade unions, furthering the interests of the workers necessarily involves political action apart from industrial action. A non-political trade union movement might well be termed a contradiction in terms and differences between trade unions as far as political involvement is concerned are only of degree. This is also exemplified by the RMMS, the darling of the INTUC and the Congress, which displays its strong political commitment by the actions it takes, or rather, does not take. The easy switch from politics to trade unionism and vice versa by many prominent RMMS leaders (Patil, Naik, Bhosale) proves this beyond doubt.

That many splits in the Indian political parties were accompanied by corresponding splits in the trade union movement has, according to some authors, considerably weakened the unity of the working class. It may also be argued, however, that the resulting fragmentation has merely exposed the real divergent interests of many groups of workers which had been clubbed together all too easily in the concept 'working class'. In any case, it is pointless to discredit the concerned trade unions as being politicized. In so far as these fissures were unavoidable it may be more constructive to see in them an attempt of the unions to preserve as much effective influence as possible under the circumstances. It should be realized that a trade union might not just be forced to follow the lead given by the political grouping to which it adheres but has also sound reasons to do so. One may then agree with the Ramaswamys who observed that trade unions stay fragmented because the industrial and political environment in which they have to operate makes it possible and profitable for them to do so (E.A. and T U. Ramaswamy, 1981: 121). If trade unions seem to serve the interests of political parties, then the reverse is equally true. No party can afford to neglect the vote of the labour force and all are bound to make an effort to win the workers over.

But acknowledging the inseparable ties between parties and unions is not the same as denying that each has its own duties, its own tasks to perform. Ramaswamy put it as follows:

> The fundamental purpose of a party is to govern, while that of a union is to protest. All parties hope to wield the reins of power and run the government. That is the explicit purpose for which they are created. In contrast, a union is an instrument of protest, not of government. It can govern neither an industry nor a nation. Its aim is to protest against and redress inequities in any form of government, whether of the enterprise or of the nation. Because of the fundamental opposition in their character, a union cannot become a party, and vice versa. [Ramaswamy, 1981: 122–23.]

It would be going too far to say that the trade union sets the goals and that the affiliated party strives to find the ways to achieve them as this would give undue weight to the unions. Besides, it suggests more of a one way traffic than is real or intended. Reality is more complex than that and it is more realistic to say that the determination of goals, objectives and means occurs in a process in which the participants constantly influence each other.

Coming back to the situation prevailing during the Bombay textile strike, it may be concluded that the strike cannot be quoted as a strong case in support of the contention that workers were fed up with the dominant role that politics play in these parties. Workers naturally wanted their problems to receive top priority and the founding of the Kamgar Aghadi seemed to promise just that which is why they rallied under its banner. It is to be expected that before long it will follow the others (no matter what their persuasion is) in furthering political aims with the assistance of the trade union wing and vice versa. There is no problem in that as long as communication is more than one-way traffic and provided the workers are completely free to choose their union.

In fact, one might argue that the Indian situation has the advantage over the situation in many Western countries in that the relationship between the union and the party is much more explicit. This is not to say that membership of a union should automatically lead to membership of the associated political party or the other way round but striving for a complete separation of the two (so persistently done in numerous discussions on the role of trade unions) seems to be as fruitless as meaningless. Political parties and trade unions with a similar world view share a large common ground and there is no harm in acknowledging that. However, real problems in the connection between politics and trade unionism are bound to manifest themselves if the free choice of a union is fettered by rules which make it possible for a union to represent the workers without their consent or, still worse, against their will.

If the Bombay textile workers want to break away from the hold of political parties, then this is not so much because they fear that politics and trade unionism get mixed up but because they feel that the parties who hitherto were supposed to cater to their needs have got the wrong priorities and/or because those parties are not in a position to bring the workers' goals any nearer. The views of the textile workers might be applicable to a much larger group of industrial workers. The recent rise of plant-based trade unionism which has been observed by many is a case in point. Some emphasized the emancipatory aspects of this process and were inclined to see it as the manifestation of a working class throwing off the yoke of party-dominated trade unionism (Kadam, 1982; Omvedt, 1983; Patankar, 1982 and 1983). Others (for example, Pendse, 1981; Kurian and Chhachhi, 1982) have pointed to the dangers of a militant working class asserting its rights at the plant level and thereby endangering working class solidarity.

Those who consider the textile strike an example of new political processes, from which the working class emerges (or will emerge) as an independent contender for power, usually stress the importance of action starting at the base. In a wider context such developments have been discussed in the debate focusing on the non-party political formations, processes marked by the fact that the base takes the initiative and that those who lead the action are reluctant to cooperate with political parties (Sethi, 1983; Pendse 1983; Kothari, 1984).

If the strike under investigation is anything to go by then the prospects for this self-assertive type of trade unionism at shop-floor level are not promising. The influence of the various committees of workers on the strike leader was very limited, their ability to stay in touch with the rank and file of the workers appeared to be doubtful and subsequent dismissals of the most militant workers after the strike will have further reduced their power. It remains to be seen whether the spontaneous assertion of workers at shop-floor level can survive outside the framework of regular trade unionism or can do without the protection offered by a union federation and its political connections. If it cannot, the very problems which are characteristic of the present state of Indian trade unionism (a bureaucratic and dogmatic modus operandi, often with little regard for democracy) will soon surface.

But even if the process of a burgeoning shop-floor level activism comes to stay within Indian industry, allowing for more direct democracy, there is still the problem of a threatening disintegration of the labour class movement, a compartmentalization which will not be halted by brave appeals to working class solidarity. The phenomenon of expanding plant-based unionism, for example in Greater Bombay and Pune, has strong economic overtones. If one is prepared to abandon the cherished idea of working class unity, one can accept such developments as reflecting the real interests of the workers. If not, it will prove an uphill task to broaden the 'base of workers' solidarity once specific categories of workers or workers in particular branches of the industry are able to secure benefits which are out of the reach of others. Although a development on these lines is not intended by the advocates of direct militant action by workers, it may well be its most likely outcome.

Today the industrial field resembles a mosaic with stones of varying colour, shape and size with little or no pattern. A rise in plant-based unionism is bound to increase the complexity of the situation and it is equally certain to be matched by a corresponding decrease in the possibilities of working class solidarity.

Role of the Government

It was found that the textile workers, by and large, identified the government as the chief culprit for the failure of the strike but the number of workers who concluded from this that the government should therefore be opposed tooth and nail is small. Samant's (limited) success in launching the Kamgar Aghadi, which draws its support principally from the textile workers, is no guarantee that the workers who voted for the party will not shift their allegiance if Samant proves incapable of improving their situation. It is not without meaning that many workers in the sample felt that a change of government did not really matter to them so long as the workers' plight remained the same. Others seemed prepared to wait for a Gandhian 'change of heart' rather than to throw in their lot with the opposition even if the chances for such a change are remote. The tough stance of the millowners did not come as a surprise (although many workers expected them to give in sooner), and apart from some internal frictions they put up a convincing show of unity which they were able to sustain throughout the strike.

The real miscalculation of the workers lay in an evaluation of the position of the government. If an overwhelming majority of the workers condemn the government for the outcome of the strike, then that is because they feel that the government ought to have intervened and settled the strike honourably. On many occasions in the past the government stepped in and there seemed to be no reason why the same could not happen now. It has been explained why the government (both at the state and at the national level) refrained from intervention and, instead, preferred a policy of watch and wait. This, however, places the government in a dubious position, as watching the agony of fish on the sand ill agrees with a proclaimed love of animals, that is, the avowed concern for the position of workers in general.

But the attitude adopted by the government did not come as a surprise and is in line with its refusal to ratify conventions No. 87 (freedom of association) and No. 98 (right to collective bargaining) of the ILO which imply the right to strike although this right is not explicitly stated. The approach of the Indian government towards labour is permeated by the Gandhian principles of harmony and cooperation between labour and capital, a philosophy that worked nicely in the case of the Textile Labour Association in Ahmedabad (cf. Pinches and Lakha, 1987). But what worked at a specific time in a specific place under specific circumstances cannot be made to work in the whole nation.

By upholding the BIR Act and granting the status of sole bargaining agent for the Bombay textile workers to the RMMS, the government acknowledged to a certain extent the right to strike. A union ultimately has no other weapon to back up its demands than the (threat of a) strike. If labour is only entitled to agree with decisions reached by the employers then there is obviously no purpose in bargaining. It is widely accepted, although not by the Indian government, that apart from a revolutionary overthrow of society, the sole power that labour ultimately can wield in its negotiations with capital is the strike or—even more importantly—the threat of a strike. Any infringement on this power places labour at a great disadvantage vis-à-vis capital.

It is true that the BIR Act, which governs industrial relations in the most important industrial undertakings in Bombay, does not forbid strikes de jure but the conditions which have to be fulfilled before a lawful strike can take place amount to a virtual ban on strikes. The cumulative effect of the whole structure of conciliation, adjudication and arbitration amounts to a de facto ban on strikes. Having created a body which effectively blocks the road to legal strikes, the government can sit back and treat any strike as a law and order problem. The judiciary, often viewed by labour as an accomplice of the government, is helpless in the matter and duty-bound to see that the law is applied. For the workers it matters little that an individual judge may sympathize with their plight. The fact remains that in their perception they have to struggle with the executive and the judiciary in addition to capital.

Not satisfied with the existing unfriendly labour laws the government recently embarked upon new industrial legislation which will further circumscribe the opportunities of workers to back up their demands with (threats of) strikes. The Indian government seems bent on curbing the freedom to strike as far as possible, and if it persists in this it will in the end be guilty of preventing the exercise of a fundamental right by its citizens and place itself outside the tradition of the democratic countries of the world.

The government's fear of any liberalization of the right to strike is based on political as well as economic considerations. Usually the economic considerations (loss of production, lack of parity in wages, weakening of the opportunities for competition and the danger to employment) are emphasized but given the strong connection between politics and trade unionism in the Indian context, it is obvious that the government dreads the effect of a liberal strike policy on its hold over the masses. The government fears that the strike might be used as a political weapon and holds that there is no need for such an armour because workers, just as other citizens, can avail themselves of customary civil rights such as of voting, protesting and petitioning if they have any political grievances.

Here again, we run into the vain attempt to separate politics from economics. Because of the increasing state intervention in the economy (one need only think of the nationalization of textile mills), this stand is increasingly untenable. Is it possible to attach the correct label (that is, 'political' or 'economic') to a strike organized to enforce or oppose nationalization, to enforce or oppose a central wage and price policy? Or, to give one more example, how should a strike be called which is designed to oppose the introduction of labour saving techniques? Or does the answer to these questions depend on whether the government has given its blessings to such changes? It goes without saying that a strike, any strike for that matter, might be resorted to by politicians for ulterior (political) purposes but the remedy cannot be to cut the Siamese twin in twain.

With a government so deeply involved in trying to run the economy through policies with far-reaching consequences for the labour force, it is pointless to demand a separation of economic and political issues when dealing with labour problems. It is clear that it will practically always be possible to dub a strike 'political' if it suits a ruling party. Yet, the solution is not to simply outlaw strikes with political implications on the plea that workers have a chance to cast their votes at the proper time and for a party of their choice. Brushing aside all these questions and referring them to the periodicity of the elections and the ballot box is ignoring the fact that these problems ought to be sorted out in a different context, in which the workers have a much greater say in matters that influence their day-to-day lives.

Outsiders: a Necessary Evil?

Choosing Datta Samant, an outsider, as the strike leader has once again turned the spotlight on the role and significance of the outsider in the Indian trade union movement. Practically all important trade unions have, over the years, been launched and led by outsiders. There are historical and very pragmatic reasons for this but the result is that a very limited number of people wield great influence over the labour force. In an attempt to curb this development the government seems bent on restricting the number of unions that may be under the leadership of a single individual. It may be expected that the workers will be the worst sufferers from the attempt to liberate them from the influence of outside leadership.

The reasons commonly advanced to explain the significant place of outsiders in the trade unions are many. They include the ability of such persons to hold discussions with the management on equal terms (having had a comparable education and often a similar caste background they speak the same language), their knowledge of labour laws and of English, their understanding of technical matters such as book-keeping and, in consequence, their negotiating skills. To this must be added the advantage that outsiders, unlike workers, cannot be victimized which gives them a free hand in talking to managements. The trade union leaders I spoke to (nearly all of them outsiders) subscribed almost without exception to the view that outsiders are a necessity, at best a boon to unions and, at worst, a necessary evil. But not everyone is prepared to assign such a pivotal role to outsiders in the trade union movement.

E.A. and U. Ramaswamy have questioned the need to have outsiders managing trade unions, stating that the earlier rationale may have applied to a situation in the past but is no longer valid. They are convinced that the new worker is fully capable of perceiving what lies in his best interests, and effectively puts across his point of view to the employer: 'He can discuss workloads, wages, bonus, manning arrangements, machine speeds and a host of other questions' (E.A. and U. Ramaswamy, 1981: 107). Indeed, we are informed that in contrast to the situation prevailing earlier many employers nowadays prefer to deal with outsiders rather than with their own men who drive a harder bargain and are more difficult to bribe. In short, the key to the problem is not so much the workers' ability, status, education or background but self-confidence. The workers are very well able to look after themselves and the outsider is only required to sign a contract (E.A. and U. Ramaswamy, 1981: 108).

The contention that the workers can take care of their own problems has great charm as it seems to do justice to their capacities and throws up images of a truly democratic trade union movement. The observation that workers increasingly tend to bypass existing channels of communication in order to confront management directly with their grievances seems to corroborate this view. However, the answer is not that simple. There is no denying the fact that leaders rising from the ranks of the workers have become more experienced but in spite of that, unions are by and large still in the hands of outside leaders. E.A. and U. Ramaswamy explain this by pointing to the Industrial Disputes Act, 1947 which empowers the government to interfere with any industrial dispute either of its own accord or at the request of one or more of the parties concerned. In a system of collective bargaining the workers' capacities might be sufficient to conclude an agreement with management but the intervention by the government, implies the end of collective bargaining and puts the problem on a different footing altogether.

As a result, the role of the government has become crucial on many occasions and unlike the worker, the outsider (often a politician) is an expert in dealing with bureaucracy and exerting pressure on other politicians. In the words of Ramaswamy: 'The outside leader, especially the politician, is relied upon to secure a satisfactory outcome to industrial disputes by interceding with ministers, Members of Parliament and the state assembly, party leaders and officials on behalf of the workers' (E.A. and U. Ramaswamy, 1981: 110). Many seasoned union leaders are of the view that in a situation in which full-time leadership of unions holds few incentives (financial compensation is usually poor), workers do not opt for a union career. They also lack contacts in the political field. Ramaswamy concludes that no changes may be expected in the dependence of workers on outsiders as long as the legal system discounts collective bargaining and encourages conciliation and adjudication (E.A. and U. Ramaswamy, 1981: 112).

In what way does the textile strike confirm this picture? First of all, there is the obvious fact that workers bypassed the representative union, in the process displaying their militancy. However, the choice of Datta Samant does not fit exactly in the image of the knowledgeable outsider. Samant knew next to nothing about either the textile industry or accountancy but this problem was easily resolved by Samant by adhering to his practice of disregarding balance sheets. By profession he was a medical doctor and not a lawyer with an intricate knowledge of labour laws but he shared with other trade union leaders the educational level and middle class background. Although some of the qualities usually attributed to outsiders did not apply to him, he had proved his worth in a number of confrontations with management in other industries which gave him the reputation of being a skilful negotiator. He was a politician (first an MLA and later an MP) but his political clout did not stem from a party but from his tremendous hold over labour in the Bombay–Thane belt, his trade union empire.

It is difficult, of course, to compare the complex situation prevailing in the textile industry with that in a single firm or even a group of companies in the same branch. One reason is that in the textile industry private companies and nationalized mills coexist. Secondly, because it is a huge and unwieldy industry with great diversity in terms of technology, production and paying capacity. It is no wonder then that the textile workers did not trust themselves to negotiate with management or the representatives of the millowners. Does this prove their lack of ability or their lack of self-confidence? Probably both simultaneously and it is questionable whether this situation would be altered materially if they only had to concentrate on collective bargaining in their own mill.

There is certainly truth in the observation of trade union leaders in the textile industry that workers, at best, may have detailed knowledge of their own mill but not a comprehensive view of the wider context in which their mill operates. This objection does not only apply to the textile industry but to all industries. True, union leaders in modern companies (for example, multinationals), coming from the ranks of the workers, are often better qualified for the job than their colleagues in more backward industries but they too, often seek expert help from outside. This might even be termed wisdom for, after all, employers too enlist the assistance of lawyers, accountants or experts in particular fields. The important point is whether the power to decide on proposals remains in the hands of the union leaders and the rank and file or not. Indeed, with the growing complexity of industrial relations, it seems unlikely that any union can afford to do without expert knowledge, and this is likely to lead to ever greater professionalization.

Ramaswamy has suggested that the absence of collective bargaining is largely responsible for the continuing dependence of unions on outsiders. He has also acknowledged that there are few incentives for workers to take over the outsider's job. This is amply borne out, for example, by the average age of the leadership of the several unions in the Bombay textile industry, which is close to sixty. In the light of the foregoing it seems improbable that a proper system of collective bargaining will end the influence of the outsider, but what might not be achieved by collective bargaining may come about by the ageing of the union leaders.

This was pointed out by Vasant Gupte, secretary-general of the MMS and director of the research institute of the MMS/HMS which conducted a survey to find out the age of trade union leaders:

> We collected the annual returns of about 3,000 unions in Maharashtra and we found that the general age of the secretary-general was about fifty-two years some five years ago and has increased to fifty-six now. The average age of the presidents is going up too. Where will this lead to in a few years from now? The presence of outsiders in the unions is bound to go down. [Interview, 15 March 1986.]

But whether the influence of outsiders diminishes because of age or because of some other mechanism, the development is likely to create a vacuum. This gap might be filled by alert politicians, but to safeguard the workers against abuse by opportunists a minimum requirement would be to strengthen the democratic structure of trade unions, to enforce regular elections of the leadership and to introduce a secret ballot as the means of selecting the representative union, that is, the bargaining agent.

New Chapter in Trade Unionism?

This study aimed at providing an answer to the question whether the workers' shift in loyalty from established trade unions in the Bombay textile industry to a complete outsider (Datta Samant), indicated the end of the confidence workers have in improving their condition within a legal framework and with the aid of existing (politically oriented) unions. In fact, this question consists of two elements, one referring to faith in the legal system and one to the behaviour and success of the existing trade unions.

Inspired by the example of the Bombay textile strike many authors heralded the beginning of a new era in Indian trade unionism (cf. Kadam, 1982; Patankar, 1982, 1983; Bhattacherjee, 1987). They feel that if it can be established that the workers have lost confidence in the ways of and prospects offered by the traditional unions and have thrown overboard the wish to follow legal procedures, then such a development might rightly be called the beginning of a new chapter in the history of Indian trade unionism.

As regards the question of the end of the workers' faith in the conventional methods adopted by traditional trade unions, it must be concluded that the textile strike does not offer convincing evidence to support it. True, the choice of Datta Samant as the strike leader was certainly inspired to a large extent by the disappointing experiences of textile workers over the years with the trade unions traditionally operating within the Bombay textile industry. But even though the workers expected a great deal more from Samant's leadership, this by itself does not mean that choosing him as their leader necessarily implied that they had given up all hope of improving their position by utilizing one or several of the existing unions.

The only thing that may be said is that their confidence in these unions was at a very low ebb and this prepared the ground for a drastic change, a shift in loyalty. But given the chronic discontent among textile workers there is good reason to believe that in the absence of Datta Samant somebody else might have triggered off a historic strike though this could have meant a postponement of the struggle for several years. This is not to say that Samant's role was merely instrumental and that just anybody else could have taken his place, but conditions within the industry were such that little was needed to provoke a dramatic confrontation between labour and capital, and between the textile workers and their official representative, the RMMS. Samant's presence on the industrial scene accelerated the process. He acted as a catalyser for the discontent which had been accumulating over the years and culminated in the strike.

That the workers prior to the strike had en masse lost their faith in the redress offered by the law and had reached the conclusion that there was no alternative but to take the law into their own hands is another contention for which the strike offers insufficient evidence. 'The law' is a fairly abstract concept to most workers and, probably, their faith in it and commitment to it has been at no time particularly strong. This situation worsened, if that is the right term, in the course of the strike. The process of deterioration of the workers' faith in the law received an impetus because of it. One may even say that the battle for derecognition of the Sangh as the representative union opened the eyes of many a worker who had hitherto believed that the law was just and impartial. It is undeniable that the outcome of the legal struggle has shaken the confidence of those workers who dared to rely on the justice rendered by the legal apparatus, but of what magnitude was this group? The proceedings in the courtroom with regard to the derecognition of the Sangh are sure to have influenced the activists and the strike leaders more than their followers who mostly had only vague notions of what the BIR Act was about.

The fact that the Sangh remained in power in spite of insufficient membership (taking advantage of a favourable interpretation of the question of arrears) seemed incomprehensible to many, and not just to workers. But rather than concluding from this that nothing will be gained by abiding by the law, workers seem convinced that bypassing the law will not lead to success as long as the government does not endorse such action. But even admitting that (an unknown number of) workers may have entertained high expectations from the proceedings under the law, it still doesn't follow that a general collapse of faith in the legal system was one of the propelling forces behind the strike. Bypassing the law was not the expression of deep distrust in the inscrutable ways of the judiciary (a remote entity) but of pent-up frustrations caused by their day-to-day experiences.

The various post-war strikes in the textile industry preceding the one in the 1980s were similar expressions of dissatisfaction and anger, yet no one has claimed that these strikes and work stoppages (as illegal under the law as the one under investigation) ought to be considered to be a break with the legal system. Strikes in the Bombay textile industry have always meant ignoring the law and the one in the 1980s simply fits in that scheme. In this there is nothing new.

The legality of a strike is generally of little or no concern to workers and India is no exception. For instance, the British Royal Commission on Trade Unions and Employers' Associations noted in its Report at the end of the 1960s that 95 per cent of all strikes in the UK are unofficial (McCarthy 1972: 372). The government's attitude to the conflict is of greater importance, and in the case of the textile strike the workers were in for a bad surprise. Contrary to the expectations of most workers, the government preferred not to interfere, worse, seemed determined to break the strike at all costs. If the strike taught them anything then it is that the government backed the Sangh and the millowners, and that nothing much will change as long as this situation does not change.

If it cannot be said that choosing Datta Samant demonstrated the end of the workers' faith in the legal system, it may still be possible to maintain that the strike signified that the workers had lost confidence in the traditional trade unions and their political preoccupation and opted for a new apolitical approach. There is no denying that the workers' faith in the traditional unions had become feeble before the strike but this is less connected with the specific ideology or political party affiliations of these unions than with their proven incapacity to deliver the goods (for which their party affiliation might partly be responsible). Again and again, workers pointed out that the unions in the textile industry (whether coming under a red banner or not) were powerless. In this they showed a realistic assessment of the prevailing balance of power.

Apparently, what is most important to the textile worker is the strength a person or union can muster and not the particular analysis of society to which that person or union adheres. This strength, is measured first of all by the ability to procure financial gains. The ideological banner under which this is achieved is of secondary importance. Similarly, if the workers' resentment against the RMMS is strong then this is not to be related to its ideology but to its impotence or unwillingness to deliver the desired goods and to its many shortcomings in operating the union (corruption, pressure tactics, lack of militancy).

To put it bluntly, Samant's political views were of little or no consequence to his popularity among the workers. This popularity rested basically on his reputation (rightly or wrongly) for gaining impressive wage hikes and on a seemingly effective way of realizing these objectives, that is, his militancy, expressed by his long-drawn battles and his rejection of balance sheets. To this must be added his reputation for honesty. None of these characteristics, however, betray a particular world view going beyond bread-and-butter ideology. His political party, the Kamgar Aghadi, claims to focus on workers' issues, and even though its programme shows conspicuous lacunae and is vague with regard to many problems, it is obvious that Datta Samant does not aim at overthrowing a bourgeois society. But even if he had had any such intentions, this would hardly have affected his popularity provided he was capable of achieving the desired goals. That is the criterion on the basis of which the average worker will ultimately decide the person, union or party to which he wishes to belong.

In this context it is important to recall the findings showing the great shifts in union membership. Prior to the strike it could be observed that the frustrated textile workers had no qualms in obeying en masse a strike call of the Shiv Sena. When they found it did not follow up the successful strike with further action they changed their allegiance. Leaving the despised RMMS during the strike posed no problem to the workers but returning to it when the strike was over seemed to pose no insurmountable problem either. It has been demonstrated that these rapid changes are not indicative of similar fluctuations in sympathy. There appeared to be far more consistency in sympathy for the MGKU than the return to the RMMS would lead one to believe. However, the workers had nearly as compelling reasons to return to the Sangh's fold as they had when they decided to quit it. This means that loyalty to the union is subject to other (one may say, more coercive) considerations, job security in particular. Instead of clinging, against their better judgement, to a particular person or union, workers on the whole thought it wiser to accept defeat and to hope for the best while grudgingly becoming Sangh members again.

The third question centred on changes in the trade union field, the assumption being that workers in increasing numbers start shunning assistance offered by politically oriented trade unions. The question also sought to explore whether the textile strike might be considered a significant example of a new type of trade unionism, marked by direct action and bypassing the law. It was found that although there is good reason to expect an expansion of plant-based unionism in India, this development should not be confused with evidence for an aversion to mixing politics and unionism. In fact, the dislike is chiefly a matter of expediency. If blending of politics and trade unionism promises or appears to be successful (one could think of the Kamgar Aghadi), the objections will disappear. It has also been shown that in ignoring the legal procedures laid down for the settlement of disputes, the textile workers acted in accordance with past behaviour and the contention that the strike heralded a new phase in trade unionism has, therefore, to be rejected as an exaggeration.

Lastly, it may be observed that the consequences of the strike were disastrous. Not only did the strike result in colossal losses in terms of employment and wages but the fighting spirit of the workers has been largely extinguished. A substantial majority of the workers sank back into apathy and acquiescence. If a strike, in Lenin's terms, is 'a school of war', then this one seems to have been particularly successful in producing drop-outs and if its performance is to improve, a rewriting of the curriculum seems to be decisive for its success.

ACKNOWLEDGEMENTS

The reprint of this study of the dramatic and in many ways unique Bombay Textile Strike in the eighties shows that this struggle has been a landmark in the history of trade unionism in India. The strike represented an unequalled collision of labour and capital and displayed serious shortcomings in the legal provisions designed to solve such disputes. Workers paid an extremely high price for this struggle. The strike heralded the end of an era. For all these reasons the strike has not been forgotten and should not be forgotten.

In all fairness I acknowledge my gratitude to the then Government of India which permitted me to undertake research in this sensitive area. This generosity demonstrates that democracy in India is more than an empty shell, it is the foundation on which a future can be built. Without the help of many Government officials at that time and the cooperation of the Indian Cotton Mills Federation and the Bombay Mill Owners' Association this study would not have had the width and depth that it may have acquired.

For all practical purposes this edition is the same as the original manuscript. In a few places passages that appeared to be ambiguous have been clarified. In order to understand the wider political context in which the strike took place the terms and concepts that were prevalent at the time of the strike (e.g. the USSR and the EEC) have been maintained.

Countless are the people and organizations that in one phase or the other supported this research. The Netherlands Foundation for the Advancement of Tropical Research (WOTRO) supplied the necessary funding. I am grateful for the help I got from the Indian trade unions and even more so from the workers who spent so much time in helping me to understand what sorrows and hardships they had to face during this seemingly endless struggle.

APPENDIX A

METHODOLOGICAL DIFFICULTIES

The problem of finding sufficient workers matching certain criteria and willing to give an interview proved to be a major obstacle in conducting fieldwork. Making a justifiable division of the sample was comparatively easy but the opposite was true in finding and persuading workers to cooperate with the research. A multipronged approach seemed to promise the best results. Because of that I requested the help of trade unions active in the Bombay textile industry and combined this with a direct approach to the workers. As Datta Samant's Maharashtra Girni Kamgar union (MGKU) could still count on widely prevalent sympathy among the workers, I sought its assistance, which was readily offered by Samant's brother P.N. Samant, one of the leaders of the MGKU. At a later stage I contacted the Rashtriya Mill Mazdoor Sangh (RMMS), the opponent of the MGKU in the textile industry. Here too, I received help but it may be said that in both cases this assistance was inadequate.

Explaining to the union leaders that it would not serve the purpose of the research to take just any 150 workers employed in the textile industry complicated the matter. They also did not like the idea of the interviews being conducted outside the sphere of the union office. To them it seemed that the office was a natural point of convergence for the workers, and would enhance the chances of finding the required workers and speed up the process of interviewing them. But it may be said to the credit of the leadership of the MGKU that as soon as it was realized how specific the requirements for the interviews were, I was referred to leaders of the Sarva Shramik Sangh (SSS) who proved to be better equipped to deal with these problems. The SSS too can count on a lot of sympathy among textile workers as it stood by them throughout the strike. With the assistance of leaders and activists of the SSS I succeeded in getting in touch with some workers matching the criteria. Adopting the stepping-stone method and plodding along I gradually enlarged my field of contacts.

Initially I had decided to select workers from two mills, that is, Apollo Textile (one of the nationalized mills) and Spring Mills (one of the two mills of Bombay Dyeing). Workers of both Bombay Dyeing units were concentrated in chawls belonging to the mill. This had a great advantage as proximity made it fairly easy to contact them. But I soon discovered that many (if not most) workers in the Bombay Dyeing chawls were scared to talk as they feared that discussing the strike might jeopardize their relations with the supervisors and management in the mill. Some workers needed a great deal of persuasion before they were ready to give an interview. The reason for trying to convince them was as compelling as their reluctance to be included in the sample. A group of that magnitude could ill be excluded from the sample if the findings were to be representative of the Spring workers.

If I had problems in finding sufficient Spring workers, it soon proved to be equally difficult to make headway with workers employed in Apollo Textile Mills, persistent efforts notwithstanding. At that juncture I had already enlisted the cooperation of the SSS. A helpful leader suggested that I should take workers from Finlay Mills instead. This was a mill which had been taken over by the government in October 1983 and corresponded to the condition that one of the the mills should belong to the backward section of the industry.

All problems were far from solved after I decided to concentrate on Finlay workers but now, at least, it became possible to make a beginning by tracking down seventy-five workers matching certain sample criteria and ready to be interviewed. Unlike the Spring workers, the Finlay workers were not living in close proximity in chawls belonging to the mill. Their living places appeared to be widely scattered over the city. This had an important bearing on the findings as has been shown elsewhere. Given the problems in finding enough workers who were prepared to talk, the idea of a stratified sample based on a neat division in proportion to the number of workers employed in the various departments had, of course, become irrelevant.

The Case of the Unemployed

From the outset it had been the idea to subdivide the seventy-five workers per mill into various categories reflecting not only the painful results of the strike (that is, employed versus unemployed) but also mirroring the terms of employment (that is, permanent worker versus *badli*). The figure for *badli*s employed in the industry was commonly put at 80,000, one-third of the labour force as a whole, which implied that *badli*s should constitute one-third of the sample. Under ideal circumstances the sample would therefore have to include 100 permanent workers against fifty *badli*s. But at the same time the aftermath of the strike would have to be taken into account. It was highly desirable to allocate a proportionate share of the sample to workers who had lost their jobs. However, the number of dismissals as well as the scale of retrenchment in the wake of the strike were unknown when I started my fieldwork. Because little was known about the fate of the strike victims I decided to include fifty unemployed workers in the sample. If this scheme could have been put into practice I would have interviewed 100 employed workers (subdivided into seventy permanent workers and thirty *badli*s) and fifty workers who lost employment as a result of the strike (subdivided into thirty-three permanent workers and seventeen *badli*s). This division would provide for a ratio 2:1 both in terms of employment (that is, permanent versus *badli*) and in terms of the outcome of the strike (that is, employed versus unemployed).

But this was not to be. It proved to be very difficult to locate unemployed workers and even more so to find unemployed *badli*s. The reason for the ostensible disappearance of unemployed *badli*s from the Bombay labour scene is probably that they either left Bombay and returned to their native villages or found employment in the unorganized sector. In both cases the difficulties in finding them were enormous. To cap it, unemployed *badli*s from Spring mills, contrary to their permanently employed colleagues, did not usually stay in the mill chawls but scattered over a wide area.

There were also problems with the definition of the term 'unemployed' in the case of the Finlay workers. On the face of it there seemed to be a clear distinction between those who resumed work after the strike and those who didn't. But after some time I discovered that many workers who were permanent before the strike had been taken back as 'temporary' workers which made their employment very insecure (see also Chapter 4). It would be indefensible to treat these workers as permanent workers as the loss of permanency cuts at the root of their economic existence. There were also Finlay workers who were taken back by their mill three or even four years after the commencement of the strike. Throughout that period they had lived in uncertainty about their employment and many had quite naturally given up all hope by the time they were informed that they could come back. Besides, it proved to be extremely difficult to find Finlay workers who had been simply and irrevocably dismissed. This explains why some of those who had not been taken back still entertained hopes at the time of the interview that they might be taken back one day.

There seemed to be no point in stretching the criterion for deciding who became unemployed in the wake of the strike to such an extent that even those workers who managed to get back after four or five years could be treated as regular permanent workers whose employment had not suffered on account of the strike. Besides, the basis for their re-employment had been altered drastically. It was, therefore, necessary to develop a criterion that would take these aspects into account. I thereupon decided to introduce a time limit to enable us to decide which Finlay workers ought to be considered 'unemployed in the wake of the strike'.

There was another complicating factor, however. The government, millowners and the RMMS agreed on 2 August 1983 as the day marking the end of the strike. Fixing a date had become necessary as the strike was never called off and there was no point in pretending that it was still going on. Because of that all workers who had not been taken back by the mills by August 1983 could rightly be treated as 'unemployed in the wake of the strike'. This date worked fine for Spring Mills as it had either taken workers back prior to that date or dismissed them. Unfortunately, this deadline could not be applied in the case of Finlay because it was taken over by the government in October 1983 and prior to that date not more than a few hundred workers had been taken back. Recruiting seventy-five workers from these few hundreds would pose incalculable problems, require close cooperation of the RMMS and create a strong bias in favour of those who resumed early.

If the government had kept the mill open after the takeover it would have been permissible to adopt the August 1983 deadline. However, as soon as the government moved in, the gates of the mill were closed only to reopen in March 1984. Only after that month did the workers start streaming in. A time limit in the case of Finlay had to reckon with these specific circumstances. Extending the time limit in the case of Finlay seemed unavoidable even though this would impair a neat comparison of the situation of unemployed Spring workers with that of unemployed Finlay workers. Finally, I decided to fix the time limit for Finlay workers on 2 August 1984, some five months after the mill started working again and exactly one year after the deadline for Spring Mills.

As a result I had to work with different criteria for the two mills under investigation. But even this did not solve all problems for I stumbled upon Finlay workers who were permanent before the strike and resumed before 2 August 1984, but this time as *badli*s. Going by the time limit alone these workers would have to be classified as normally employed workers. However, this seemed unjustifiable as the loss of permanency for the vagaries of a *badli*'s fate after the strike ought to weigh more heavily than the fact that a worker resumed work prior to an arbitrary deadline. In the end I was forced to develop a second different criterion for Finlay workers, which also took the terms of employment into account. I decided to consider the loss of permanency as loss of employment. With the aid of this, all the permanent workers who resumed before or after 2 August 1984 either as *badli* or as 'temporary' worker could be treated as 'unemployed workers in the wake of the strike'. With this set of criteria the problems became manageable and a division of the 150 workers into the required categories became possible at last (see Table I in the Introduction).

Approximately 50 per cent of the sample workers were ultimately selected by approaching them directly without the intervention of a union. This technique proved to be particularly rewarding in the chawls of Bombay Dyeing where the Spring workers resided. In other cases I had to resort to contacting workers at the gates of the mill when their shift was over but here again I would not have been very successful without the help of a worker who commanded the trust and loyalty of his colleagues and whose assistance in taking down appointments for interviews was indispensable. About 15 per cent of the sample workers were found with the Sangh's assistance. The remaining 35 per cent were found with the assistance of either the SSS or the MGKU.

Selecting 100 workers for the smaller sample posed far fewer problems as these workers did not have to match the criteria for those in the larger sample. The only criterion here was that they did not belong to Spring Mills or Finlay Mills. An effort was made to see to it that the percentage share of badlis in the smaller sample was larger than in the bigger sample. It may be noted that just as in the case of the bigger sample it proved to be far easier to find enough permanent workers than *badli*s. Mostly these workers were approached directly. For the sake of convenience it was decided to concentrate this time on rooms in which the interviewees were staying with other workers and their families were away in the village.

Contents and Context of the Interviews

In the course of the interviews the workers were questioned about their background, their present financial position and their activities during the strike period. Apart from that they were asked to state their views and expectations regarding the struggle, the unions and Samant's leadership (see Appendix C). As the research was in progress, questions were sometimes added to the already unwieldy list because it seemed worthwhile to gain an insight in matters which otherwise might have remained obscure. Sometimes questions had to be skipped because of their sensitivity. There was reason to believe that the RMMS would have withdrawn its cooperation altogether had these Sangh-walas been confronted with questions pertaining, for example, to abuse of power or corruption perpetrated by their union. This is why such questions were then omitted. Fortunately, this happened only sporadically and in cases of the interviewee being a staunch Sangh-wala.

Many workers initially feared repercussions from the management and/or the Sangh, but after they had convinced themselves that the interviews were confidential and that the contents would only serve purposes of research, they were able to overcome their initial hesitations. A notable exception to this generally prevalent fear were active workers who were known for their unveiled rejection of the Sangh. They spoke candidly even in the presence of others. It is likely that their admirable frankness offers them some protection against bullying by the Sangh because putting pressure on such workers is bound to create disturbances. On the whole, the Finlay workers were found to be more communicative than those from Spring but it should not be forgotten that the latter stayed in rooms belonging to the mill while the former lived in rooms and huts scattered over the city.

The interviews of workers in the larger sample lasted on an average one and a half to two hours. Except for a few interviews taken in a nearby restaurant, all these interviews were conducted at the residence of the interviewee which involved a great deal of travelling in the city. If the opportunity presented itself the interviews were conducted without the presence of others. However, very often the circumstances did not allow that and in such cases the discussion was followed eagerly by roommates or family members. On the whole, as the interview progressed, the bystanders refrained from interfering. Generally speaking, one may say that interference occurred more at the beginning of an interview than at a later stage when it was realized that many questions were not easy to answer. As the topics for discussion were rather complex and my mastery of the local language (Marathi) was inadequate, I sought and found the help of an excellent interpreter who happened to be proficient in three languages, and this greatly facilitated the interviews. A large majority of the interviewees spoke Marathi but a substantial minority (particularly those from Uttar Pradesh and Andhra Pradesh) did not know this language and in such cases the interpreter spoke Hindi. Utilizing a standard list of mostly open questions we conducted all the interviews of the large sample together.

APPENDIX B

CHRONOLOGY OF EVENTS

1981

20 October	The MOA announces an agreement with the RMMS regarding the payment of bonus in mill sector. Bonus is dependent on the paying capacity of a mill. Of the privately owned mills, nine are to pay 17.33 per cent bonus, four to pay 15 per cent, three mills 14.5 per cent, one mill 14 per cent and the remaining mills are to pay anything between 8.33 per cent (the minimum required by law) and 12.5 per cent.
21 October	Workers of fifteen mills object to the agreement by staging a sit-down strike.
22 October	Workers of eight mills remain on strike. These mills are: Standard Mills, Prakash Cotton Mills, Shree Niwas Cotton Mills, Madhusudan Mills and four mills of Hindustan. Workers of Standard Mills march to the residence of Datta Samant to demand that he lead the strike. They are later joined by workers from other mills. In the end Samant accepts leadership.
30 October	Samant announces the formation of a new union for textile workers, the Maharashtra Girni Kamgar Union. He also threatens a strike if no new agreement is forthcoming.
11 November	Chief Minister Antulay announces the appointment of a High Powered Committee (HPC) to study

	the problems of the textile workers. Massive gate meetings at the mills meanwhile prove the overwhelming support for Samant who postpones the start of a general strike to await the results of the HPC. The strike in the eight mills, however, continues.
6 December	Samant seeks the intervention of PM Indira Gandhi but in vain.
8 December	Samant tells the workers to prepare for an indefinite strike.
9 December	The RMMS criticizes Samant for adventurism and warns that the millowners welcome the strike.
24 December	The MOA announces its withdrawal from the proceedings of the HPC on the grounds of the inability of the state government to end the ongoing strike in eight mills. Samant promises a token strike on 6 January 1983.

1982

3 January	Union Commerce Minister Pranab Mukherjee announces discussions with employers, the RMMS and state government.
6 January	Total strike paralyses the Bombay textile industry in spite of the RMMS' call not to participate.
13 January	CM Antulay resigns after charges of corruption are levelled against him.
18 January	Start of the indefinite textile strike in all the mills in Bombay. The strike is total and peaceful.
19 January	PM Gandhi appoints Bhosale as the new CM in Maharashtra.
23 January	CM Bhosale invites Samant for talks on the strike.
28 January	MOA secretary-general Vijayanagar visits CM Bhosale to inform him that the strike demands are wholly unacceptable.
1 February	The RMMS expects the strike to be Samant's 'Waterloo'.
5 February	Union Labour Minister Bhagwat Jha Azad expresses the centre's support of the state government's stand.

7 February	CM Bhosale declares the strike to be illegal. He reiterates that the RMMS is the sole representative of workers and that talks with Samant are out of the question.
9 February	Labour Minister Gaekwad declares that the state government will reconstitute the HPC to consider the demands provided these are made by the official spokesman of the workers, that is, the RMMS. A deputation of the employers (representatives of the MOA and the ICMF) meets the PM to discuss the strike.
12 February	Parrying CM Bhosale's call to the workers to resume duty, Samant declares that he is not against it provided a majority of the workers want this. He suggests a secret ballot.
20 February	Union Labour Minister Bhagwat Jha Azad declares in Parliament that the formal procedure for arbitration should be followed.
21 February	CM Bhosale claims that the strike is petering out.
March	Datta Samant's rural tour.
11 March	Mammoth rally of striking workers in Bombay. Dissatisfaction within the Congress about the party attitude towards the strike grows.
13 March	Turbulent scenes in the state assembly. Discussions suspended. Deputy Labour Minister Y. Sherekar informs the House that the proceedings of the HPC had to be stopped.
16 March	Gaekwad announces that the centre will set up a tripartite panel.
20 March	Gaekwad declares that workers in twenty-nine mills have resumed work.
14 April	Mayor P.S. Pai of Bombay holds the state government responsible for the continuation of the strike.
17 April	The MOA heralds the collapse of the strike.
19 April	Partial bandh in Bombay following a call by non-INTUC unions.
20 April	The Registrar of unions rejects the plea by the

	MGKU for cancellation of the status of the RMMS as the representative union.
23 April	Registration of Samant as an independent candidate for the Kamgar Aghadi in the Thane constituency.
29 April	The registrar of unions withdraws her earlier verdict. New inquiry into the membership of the RMMS is to follow.
5 May	Former CM of Maharashtra, Vasantrao Patil, makes it known that he will attempt to end the stalemate.
7 May	Y.B. Chavan, former deputy PM, declares that he will cooperate with Patil.
21 May	Samant loses elections in Thane.
31 May	CM Bhosale announces that the strike will end within a fortnight. He denies that workers from outside are being brought into the mills.
10 June	After a visit to the PM in Delhi, CM Bhosale reiterates that there can be no negotiations until the strike is called off.
3 July	Mukesh Mills requests the government's permission to close down.
4 July	The Soviet Union declares that the strike cannot be regarded as an excuse for failure to deliver the cloth ordered.
9 July	The Union labour minister notifies Parliament of the appointment of a National Tripartite Committee under the chairmanship of Justice V.S. Deshpande to look into the problems of the textile industry. He further announces a new offer: an interim wage increase of Rs 30 per month, an advance of Rs 650 and an assurance that no worker will be victimized.
15 July	Janata Party leader S.M. Joshi apprises the PM in Delhi of the situation in Bombay.
16 July	The state government announces free distribution of textbooks to children of non-striking textile workers.
19 July	Huge rally held at Nardulla Tank. Samant states that most demands are negotiable but the RMMS and BIR Act have to go.

28 July	S.M. Joshi's suggestion that workers be given an interim wage rise of Rs 100 is rejected by the government.
15 August	The police commissioner of Bombay issues a ban order, prohibiting the assembly of more than five people in mill areas.
16 August	Thousands court arrest during the jail bharo agitation, including the cadres of CITU, AITUC and HMS. Workers refrain from violence.
18 August	Rebellious policemen hold the city to ransom. Many civilians, including striking workers, join in violent riots. Houses of RMMS boss Hoshing and RMMS secretary-general A.T. Bhosale are looted. The government calls in the army, the Border Security Force, Central Reserve Police and State Reserve Police to restore order.
28 August	Newspapers announce that CM Bhosale will be replaced soon.
6 September	The RMMS demands that the government put an end to the strike.
11 September	The government is blamed in the Legislative Assembly for inertia.
16 September	Mammoth rally near Hutatma Chowk. Massive march to Vidhan Bhavan. Samant announces a new jail bharo campaign which results in 5,000–10,000 arrests in the weeks to follow.
20 September	The MOA claims that 47,000 persons have resumed work.
2 October	Huge rally at Shivaji Park.
12 October	Riots in Bombay as a result of the new jail bharo campaign. Samant arrested along with 5,300 workers. Police resort to lathi charges to disperse the crowds that offer themselves for arrest. Samant sentenced to fifteen days' imprisonment. Start of three-day bandh which was partially successful.
15 October	MPs in the Rajya Sabha flay the government for its passive stand.

21 October	Anniversary of the beginning of the textile strike in eight mills.
23 October	Ministers of the centre fly to Bombay to find a solution to the strike. This move is denounced by the RMMS as 'unwise and hasty' and attributed to undue pressure by the Congress Party.
25 October	Samant released from jail. Welcomes the initiative taken by the centre and declares that scrapping the BIR Act is most important.
28 October	Leaders of the Lok Dal (George Fernandes), Shiv Sena (Bal Thackeray) and Congress (S) (Sharad Pawar) threaten action if the strike is not resolved within a week. Contact between millowners, the state government, and the centre intensifies.
31 October	The government of Maharashtra proposes 'new formula': interim relief of Rs 30, payment of bonus for 1981 and an advance of Rs 1,500. CM Bhosale explains that he does not want to increase the interim payment pending the decision of the Tripartite Committee under the chairmanship of Deshpande.
1 November	Samant rejects proposals as they do not deal with the demands for wage increase and the repeal of the BIR Act.
5 November	The registrar of unions states in her verdict that derecognition of the Sangh is impossible in spite of insufficient membership.
6 December	Morcha by the RMMS to demand implementation of the 'new formula'.
8 December	Pressure on CM Bhosale to resign increases.
21 December	The government refuses to refer the dispute to the Industrial Court now that the Deshpande Committee has started its work.
24 December	Justice S.C. Pratap of the Bombay High Court decries the stand taken by the government as a 'breach of a statutory duty'.

1983

16 January	Production has started in most mills although the quantity of cloth produced is not more than 40 per cent of normal production.
18 January	Anniversary of the strike in all mills.
20 January	PM Gandhi suggests that a change in the leadership of the RMMS might be necessary to restore the workers' confidence.
22 January	N.K. Bhat, president of the INTUC, appointed as president of the RMMS.
1 February	Vasant Rao Patil appointed new CM of Maharashtra.
4 February	The MOA claims that attendance in mills has reached 1,04,000 persons.
12 February	Samant meets CM Patil to discuss the strike.
22 February	Haribhau Naik appointed as president of the RMMS and Manohar Phalke as the secretary-general.
6 March	Union Minister V.P. Singh starts a fresh round of talks and promises greater flexibility in the government stand.
7 March	Samant meets V.P. Singh and reports progress in discussions. A new formula would include the abrogation of the BIR Act.
22 March	Union minister of Labour, V. Patil, declares in Delhi that the strike has fizzled out. Attendance now put at 1,06,872.
29 March	Following a unanimous recommendation by the Deshpande Committee, V.P. Singh announces a House Rent Allowance for the textile workers. The report submitted by the committee contains also a recommendation regarding the position of *badli*s.
9 April	CM Patil accuses Samant in public of being 'a new type of Hitler' and claims to possess a list with names of persons used by Samant to foment violence.
15 April	Samant and 1,000 trade unionists arrested during a morcha.
3 May	Beginning of campaign by Samant and the MGKU to persuade workers who have resumed work to rejoin the strike.

July	Failure of the struggle now widely acknowledged although the strike is never formally called off. The minister of state for labour, Kimmatkar, declares that the attendance in the mills has reached a figure of 1,18,276 persons and that 51,000 permanent workers have been dismissed.
1 August	Huge morcha of lakhs of workers in Bombay in support of Datta Samant and the textile workers.

Source: Based on numerous newspaper articles, official documents and a chronological account covering the first ten months by Javed Anand in *The 10th Month* (see Bibliography).

APPENDIX C

TOPICS FOR DISCUSSION AND STANDARDIZED QUESTIONNAIRE FOR INTERVIEWS WITH WORKERS

Personal data

1. Mill;
2. Former job + status;
3. Present job + status;
4. Education;
5. Marriage status;
6. Children;
7. Religion/Caste;
8. Place of birth;
9. Age;
10. Living place;
    Rented/owned;
    Surface;
    Number of occupants;
    Impression interior;
11. Possession of house in village;
12. Possession of land in village;
13. Profession of father;

14. Number of dependents;
15. Other breadwinners.

Work

16. When did he start working in the mills?
17. A: To whom did he turn in case of complaints?
    B: How were complaints dealt with?
18. Wages (take home basis) before and after strike?
19. A: Did the workload change after the strike?
    B: Was there a change in atmosphere?
    C: Would he like to work more for higher wages?
20. A: When and why did he resume work?
    B: When and how did he learn that he had lost his job?
    C: When and why did he decide to quit his job?

Socio-economic aspects of the strike

21. Did he send money remittances to his village prior to the strike? How much?
22. A: Did he (mainly) stay in Bombay or in the village? When?
    B: Did he visit Bombay/village during the strike? How often?
    C: How did he keep himself informed about developments in the strike situation?
23. A: Did he search for alternative employment during the strike?
    B: How did he find it and for what period(s)?
    C: What income did he derive from it?
    D: Did he face problems encroaching upon the territory of others?
24. A: How did he spend the day during the strike?
    B: What were the major problems? Was there any tension at home?
    C: Did he suffer from boredom?
25. A: Did he *personally* receive help from any union? What help (money/food grain/other)?
    B: Was there help from friends/comrades?
    C: What was the support from workers of other industries? Did he expect this?
    D: How did his own people (family/relatives) view the strike?
    E: Was there any pressure to resume work (mill, family, union)?

26. Did he have: to sell property or take loans during the stride?
27. On what did he economize during the struggle?
28. Have there been important events in his family during the strike, such as sickness, birth, death, marriage?
29. If so, how did he cope with this financially?
30. Did he (have to) pay rent? Could he get credit?
31. How much strike-related debt did he incur in the course of the strike?

Views and strategies

32. A: Was he in favour of the strike? Throughout?
    B: Before the strike, how long did he expect the strike to last?
    C: Did he make any preparations?
33. A: Why did the strike occur? Who was responsible for it?
    B: What demands were most important to him?
    C: Were *badlis* and permanent workers fighting for different things?
    D: How was the cooperation between *badli*s and permanent workers?

34 A: Did he feel that Dr Samant was the right man to lead the strike? Why/why not?
    B: Could not other (for example, red flag) unions have done the same?
    C: Did he expect all the demands to be conceded?

35. A: Did he feel when the strike began that the millowners welcomed it? Why/why not?
    B: Does he now feel that retrenchment and modernization could have been avoided if the strike had not taken place?
    C: Should the strike have been called off before it fizzled out? Even without all or at least some demands being met?
    D: Did he feel the same during the strike? Since when?
36. A: Did he join meetings (refers to entire strike period)?
    B: Did he express his views during meetings and did he have the feeling that he was listened to?
    C: Was Dr Samant doing what the workers wanted him to do?
    D: Did he join mill or area committees during the strike?
    E: Did he participate in any agitation (for example, jail bharo, picketing, morchas, gherao andolan)?

F: What does he feel about Dr Samant now?

37. A: Was he ever threatened or did he himself experience any violence in the course of the strike (for example, from other workers, unions, mills, police)?

    B: How was the atmosphere in his immediate surroundings (chawl/slum)?

38. A: Was he a union member before or during the strike? Which union?

    B: Is he a member of any union now? Which union? Why/why not?

    C: Was there any compulsion to become a member?

    D: Did he ever have to pay money *(dasturi)* to get work in the mills?

    E: Did he know what statement he signed before resuming work?

39. A: What did he learn from the strike?

    B: Who is responsible for the failure of the strike?

    C: Would he follow a strike call now (for example for a day or a week)?

    D: The BIR Act offers the option of referring wage and labour problems to courts. Is this useful for the workers?

    E: Are changes in the political field required to improve the plight of the (textile) workers? Could a workers' party be useful for that?

    F: Should (wage) negotiations with millowners be mill-wise or not?

    G: How should a representative union be selected? By counting the membership, as of now, or by means of a secret ballot?

APPENDIX D

FINANCIAL POSITION OF PRIVATELY OWNED MILLS IN BOMBAY PRIOR TO STRIKE

I

Balance of Profits after Bonus, Gratuity and Depreciation

	(Lakhs of Rupees)				
Mill	*1977–78*	*1978–79*	*1979–80*	*1980–81*	*1981–82*
Bombay Dyeing	95.0	217.8	278.7	18.6	n.a.
Bradbury Mills	-213.9	-41.3	-149.3	-187.9	n.a.
Century	-178.8	143.6	352.7	352.5	-73.2
Dawn	24.8	16.9	62.6	74.3	54.5
Elphinstone	-125.6	-55.1	53.0	-23.2	-229.8
Finlay Mills	-172.2	-113.0	-1.2	1.4	-8.3
Gold Mohur	-159.8	-173.4	-10.9	9.5	-26.2
Hindoostan	-277.0	98.6	120.0	22.7	n.a.
Jam	-26.3	17.9	-38.7	-42.9	n.a.
Kamala	-25.4	23.4	6.0	-29.0	-172.7
Khatau Makanji	69.2	149.0	167.7	140.8	228.0
Kohinoor	n.a.	n.a.	n.a.	349.0	n.a.
Mafatlal	49.2	105.2	95.1	-109.8	-598.1
Matulya (Rajesh)	n.a.	29.7	-26.1	-23.6	-39.0
Modern	-10.9	-20.4	43.6	-87.6	n.a.
Morarjee Goculdas*	60.8	118.4	245.5	154.5	132.7
Mor. Goculdas (Sayaji)*	-158.7	-69.3	-111.1	-100.2	-179.9
Mukesh Textile	n.a.	-54.0	-55.4	-42.9	-82.3
New City of Bombay	-4.0	n.a.	38.3	94.7	-234.7
New Great Eastern	1.9	-14.9	-14.6	-28.3	n.a.
Phoenix	-36.4	-159.9	-114.8	-20.4	n.a.
Piramal	10.8	37.1	58.9	51.1	1.0

	(Lakhs of Rupees)				
Mill	*1977–78*	*1978–79*	*1979–80*	*1980–81*	*1981–82*
Podar	-55.7	7.3	-32.2	-131.3	n.a.
Prakash Cotton	n.a.	n.a.	-91.1	-81.1	n.a.
Raghuvanshi	14.3	50.3	25.0	6.5	-119.9
Ruby	48.6	52.0	49.4	8.8	-74.1
Shree Madhusudan	-268.8	-198.1	-61.1	-44.9	-89.1
Shree Niwas Cotton	-118.6	-7.4	9.9	-50.1	-232.2
Shree Ram	-152.4	-85.3	67.0	35.9	-226.0
Shree Sitaram	-90.8	-108.8	-94.0	-168.5	n.a.
Simplex	21.4	8.4	59.3	58.2	-3.0
Standard	199.9	189.7	160.3	-1.3	-969.1
Swadeshi	29.8	68.3	57.7	52.5	-150.2
Swan	66.8	37.4	98.1	23.4	59.6
Swan (Coorla)**	18.2	-	-	-	-
Tata	-133.2	11.6	-7.1	-272.2	-470.9
Victoria	53.6	80.0	117.5	114.6	101.0

* Morarjee Goculdas amalgamated with Sayaji Mills in the course of 1981–82. The latter is known as Morarjee Goculdas Unit No.2.
** Coorla Mills amalgamated with Swan Mills in 1978–79.

Source: Report for the Year 1982, MOA 1983b, 269.

II

Percentage of Gross Profits to Capital Employed

Mill	*1977–78*	*1978–79*	*1979–80*	*1980–81*	*1981–82*
Bombay Dyeing	19.8	22.2	24.9	16.4	n.a.
Bradbury Mills	N.N.*	N.N.	N.N.	N.N.	n.a.
Century	0.4	5.2	7.3	7.2	2.8
Dawn	22.3	15.2	26.0	25.9	19.4
Elphinstone	N.N.	N.N.	62.8	18.3	N.N.
Finlay	N.N.	N.N.	30.8	12.6	9.6
Gold Mohur	N.N.	N.N.	7.5	11.4	4.6
Hindoostan	N.N.	20.4	20.8	15.5	N.N.
Jam	25.8	34.2	8.5	12.0	n.a.

Mill	*1977–78*	*1978–79*	*1979–80*	*1980–81*	*1981–82*
Kamala	10.4	24.4	18.1	11.1	N.N.
Khatau Makanji	22.6	31.5	34.8	28.4	30.4
Kohinoor	N.N.	N.N.	N.N.	N.N.	n.a.
Mafatlal	10.0	13.0	12.7	8.6	N.N.
Matulya (Rajesh)	7.9	8.3	10.4	11.9	6.6
Modern	10.3	7.7	16.4	N.N.	N.N.
Morarjee Goculdas**	22.5	32.9	41.6	25.0	11.6
Mukesh Textile***	-	-	-	-	-
New City of Bombay	25.0	40.2	32.0	N.N.	N.N.
New Great Eastern	19.6	14.0	16.3	15.8	n.a.
Phoenix	6.6	N.N.	N.N.	16.6	n.a.
Piramal	12.0	16.5	21.7	19.4	13.0
Podar	N.N.	8.9	3.2	N.N.	N.N.
Prakash Cotton***	-	-	-	-	-
Raghuvanshi	18.8	29.5	22.0	16.5	N.N.
Ruby	24.8	26.3	24.0	16.6	2.3
Shree Madhusudan	N.N.	N.N.	2.5	9.3	N.N.
Shree Niwas Cotton	N.N.	14.7	20.4	13.5	N.N.
Shree Ram	N.N.	N.N.	22.0	19.2	N.N.
Shree Sitaram	N.N.	N.N.	N.N.	N.N.	n.a.
Simplex	9.5	8.4	23.9	26.4	14.0
Standard	13.8	12.9	12.2	9.8	N.N.
Swadeshi	12.3	15.9	16.9	15.5	2.9
Swan****	11.5	15.6	18.8	16.0	11.6
Tata	N.N.	17.3	13.4	N.N.	N.N.
Victoria	22.2	31.3	38.3	34.0	31.7

* Numerator Negative

** Figures include those for Sayaji Mills which was amalgamated with Morarjee Goculdas in 1981–82.

*** Information for Mukesh Textile Mills and Prakash Cotton Mills is not available.

**** In 1978–79 Coorla Mills was amalgamated with Swan Mills.

Source: Report for the Year 1982, MOA 1983b, 353.

III

Ratio of Total Debt to Net Worth

Mill	*1977–78*	*1978–79*	*1979–80*	*1980–81*	*1981–82*
Bombay Dyeing	2.2:1	2.1:1	1.9:1	1.9:1	n.a.
Bradbury Mills	N.N.*	N.N.	N.N.	N.N.	n.a.
Century Mills	0.5:1	0.4:1	0.3:1	0.5:1	0.5:1
Dawn Mills	1.7:1	1.7:1	1.6:1	1.6:1	1.6:1
Elphinstone Mills	N.N.	N.N.	N.N.	N.N.	N.N.
Finlay Mills	7:1	7:1	5:1	4:1	4:1
Gold Mohur	25:1	25:1	20:1	11:1	14:1
Hindoostan	4:1	3:1	2.7:1	2.5:1	4.8:1
Jam	N.N.	N.N.	N.N.	N.N.	n.a.
Kamala Mills	13:1	7:1	3.6:1	4.6:1	28.5:1
Khatau Makanji	1.5:1	1.4:1	1.6:1	1.6:1	1.7:1
Kohinoor	N.N.	N.N.	N.N.	N.N.	n.a.
Mafatlal	1.7:1	1.9:1	2.2:1	2.5:1	4:1
Matulya (Rajesh)	18:1	13:1	8.6:1	14:1	6.6:1
Modem Mills	5:1	6:1	4:1	4:1	n.a.
Morarjee Goculdas**	1.6:1	1.5:1	1.6:1	1.9:1	3:1
Mukesh Textile***	-	-	-	-	-
New City of Bombay	2.9:1	2.9:1	2.6:1	2.2:1	4.2:1
New Great Eastern	3.8:1	3:1	2.6:1	3:1	11:1
Phoenix	N.N.	N.N.	N.N.	N.N.	n.a.
Piramal	3:1	3.4:1	2.5:1	2.9:1	3:1
Podar	2.9:1	2:1	1.7:1	2.4:1	N.N.
Prakash Cotton***	-	-	-	-	-
Raghuvanshi	2.5:1	2.8:1	2.9:1	3:1	5.9:1
Ruby Mills	2.3:1	2.3:1	2:1	2.2:1	2.9:1
Shree Madhusudan	N.N.	N.N.	N.N.	N.N.	N.N.
Shree Niwas Cotton	8:1	8:1	6:1	6:1	N.N.
Shree Ram	N.N.	N.N.	N.N.	N.N.	N.N.
Shree Sitaram	N.N.	N.N.	N.N.	n.a.	n.a.
Simplex	2.2:1	2.4:1	1.9:1	1.6:1	2.3:1
Standard	1.5:1	1.2:1	1.3:1	1.4:1	1.8:1
Swadeshi	2.4:1	2.3:1	2.1:1	2.3:1	2.4:1

Mill	*1977–78*	*1978–79*	*1979–80*	*1980–81*	*1981–82*
Swan****	2.1:1	1.9:1	2.2:1	2.5:1	3.4:1
Tata	48:1	17:1	12:1	N.N.	N.N.
Victoria	1.3:1	1:1	0.9:1	1:1	0.9:1

* Numerator Negative

** Includes information for Sayaji Mills which was taken over by Morarjee Goculdas.

*** Information in respect of Mukesh Textile and Prakash Cotton is not available.

**** This includes information for Coorla Mills which amalgamated with Swan Mills.

Source: Report for the Year 1982, MOA 1983b, 350.

IV

Percentage of Net Worth to Capital Employed

Mill	*1977–78*	*1978–79*	*1979–80*	*1980–81*	*1981–82*
Bombay Dyeing	51.2	54.1	57.3	50.8	n.a.
Bradbury	N.N.*	N.N.	N.N.	N.N.	n.a.
Century	91.8	90.1	90.3	90.6	91.1
Dawn Mills	52.9	45.1	53.1	52.0	50.2
Elphinstone	N.N.	N.N.	N.N.	N.N.	N.N.
Finlay	28.2	28.2	66.9	30.1	29.0
Gold Mohur	7.3	7.5	7.5	13.3	11.0
Hindoostan	29.9	40.0	42.1	42.2	27.8
Jam	N.N.	N.N.	N.N.	N.N.	n.a.
Kamala	16.6	26.9	42.6	35.1	9.5
Khatau Makanji	56.0	61.5	61.9	52.0	52.1
Kohinoor	N.N.	N.N.	N.N.	N.N.	n.a.
Mafatlal	48.1	49.0	44.9	39.6	31.1
Matulya (Rajesh)	11.1	13.8	25.7	15.4	19.2
Modern Mills	21.8	20.9	27.7	23.6	n.a.
Morarjee Goculdas**	53.6	63.1	60.2	51.2	30.9
Mukesh Textile***	-	-	-	-	-
New City of Bombay	57.0	57.0	55.2	53.5	33.1
New Great Eastern	53.8	47.8	54.0	50.5	17.8
Phoenix	N.N.	N.N.	N.N.	N.N.	n.a.

Mill	*1977–78*	*1978–79*	*1979–80*	*1980–81*	*1981–82*
Piramal	31.7	30.7	36.6	33.9	30.7
Podar	41.8	50.1	51.1	41.4	N.N.
Prakash Cotton***	-	-	-	-	-
Raghuvanshi	38.8	39.2	39.9	37.1	23.2
Ruby Mills	41.7	42.9	43.6	42.1	35.0
Shree Madhusudan	N.N.	N.N.	N.N.	N.N.	N.N.
Shree Niwas Cotton	20.3	21.9	28.5	27.8	N.N.
Shree Ram	N.N.	N.N.	N.N.	N.N.	N.N.
Shree Sitaram	N.N.	N.N.	N.N.	n.a.	n.a.
Simplex	40.6	41.0	48.9	54.4	46.4
Standard	58.4	62.6	59.0	55.6	46.6
Swadeshi	39.9	42.4	43.4	44.1	42.8
Swan****	44.6	44.5	41.9	43.3	35.1
Tata	3.4	9.8	12.9	N.N.	N.N.
Victoria	55.6	60.1	68.7	67.0	73.2

* Numerator Negative

** Includes figures for Sayaji Mills which amalgamated in 1981–82 with Morarjee Goculdas.

*** There are no figures available for Mukesh Textile and Prakash Cotton.

**** Includes figures for Coorla Mills which amalgamated with Swan in 1978–79.

Source: Report for the Year 1982, MOA 1983b, 351.

Note: The figures presented in the Tables of this Appendix should not be taken at face value (see pages 138-40).
The figures are nevertheless the only ones available.

BIBLIOGRAPHY

GOVERNMENT OF INDIA

1964 *Report of the Powerloom Enquiry Committee* (A. Mehta Committee Report), Ministry of Industry.

1971 *Census of India 1971, Series 11:* Maharashtra.

1981 *India: A Reference Annual*, Publications Division, Ministry of Information and Broadcasting.

1982 a. *Parliamentary Reports: Lok Sabha Debates.*
b. *Parliamentary Reports: Rajya Sabha Debates.*

1983 a. *Parliamentary Reports: Lok Sabha Debates.*
b. *Parliamentary Reports: Rajya Sabha Debates.*
c. *Report of the Tripartite Committee on Cotton Textile Industry*.

1985 Statement on Textile Policy.

1986 *Mass Media in India, 1985,* Publications Division, Ministry of Information and Broadcasting.

GOVERNMENT OF MAHARASHTRA

1963 *Handbook of Labour Laws* (The Indian Trade Unions Act, 1926).

1965 *Handbook of Labour Laws* (The Employees State Insurance Act, 1948).

1967 *Maharashtra State Gazetteers, History, Part I: Ancient Period* (P. Setu Madhava Rao, ed.).

1968 *Report of the Badli Labour Inquiry Committee, Cotton Textile Industry, 1967.*

1972 *Maharashtra State Gazetteers: History Part II: Mediaeval Period* (B.G. Kunte).

1973 *Handbook for Labour Laws in Maharashtra State* (Minimum Wages Act, 1948).

1975 a. *Handbook of Labour Laws* (Payment of Wages Act, 1936).

b. *Maharashtra: Land and its People* (I. Karve).
c. *Statistical Abstract of Maharashtra State for the Year 1974–75.*
1981 *Handbook of Basic Statistics of Maharashtra State, 1980.*
1982 a. *Maharashtra Legislative Assembly Debates.*
b. *Maharashtra Legislative Council Debates.*
c. *Statistical Abstract of Maharashtra State for the Year 1977–78.*
1983 a. *Maharashtra Legislative Assembly Debates.*
b. *Maharashtra Legislative Council Debates.*
1984 a. Maharashtra Act No. 1 of 1972, The Maharashtra Recognition of Trade Unions and Prevention of Unfair Labour Practices Act, 1971.
b. Bombay Act No. XI of 1947, The Bombay Industrial Relations Act, 1946.
c. The Bombay Industrial Relations Rules, 1947.
1987 *The Bombay Textile Strike Affected and Unemployed Workers and their Legal Dues Assessment Committee Report* (Kotwal Committee Report).

PUBLICATIONS BY MILLOWNERS' ORGANIZATIONS

(Published by the Indian Cotton Mills' Federation, Bombay, unless otherwise stated)

1981 *Report for the Year 1980–81.*
1982 *Report for the Year 1981–82.*
1983 *Report for the Year 1982–83.*
1984 a. *Report for the Year 1983–84.*
b. *Handbook of Statistics on Cotton Textile Industry.*
1985 a. *Report for the Year 1984–85.*
b. *ICMF Submissions to the Expert Committee on Textile Industry.*
1986 *Handbook of Statistics on Cotton Textile Industry.*
1988 a. *Handbook of Statistics on Cotton Textile Industry.*
b. *Draft Annual Report, 1987–1988* (cyclostyled).
n.d. Files at the ICMF offices.

(Published by the Millowners' Association, Bombay, unless otherwise stated)

1975 *Hundred Years of Dedicated Service 1875–1975*, Centenary Souvenir.
1979 *Mill Statement for the Year 1979.*
1980 *Handbook of Service Conditions of Operatives and Clerks in the Bombay Cotton Textile Industry.*

1981 'Textile Strike: Let the Public Know the Facts', in *Times of India*, 24 December.

1983 a. *Mill Statement for the Year 1983.*

b. *Report for the Year 1982.*

1984 *Report for the Year 1983.*

OTHER LITERATURE CONSULTED

Abraham, A. 1978. 'Conditions of Bombay's Textile Workers', *Economic and Political Weekly,* 13 (42), 1761–62.

Acharji, N. 1980. *Trade Union Leadership Profile* (New Delhi: Ambika Publications).

Adarkar, Neera. 2006. The Lost Century of Workers. In D. D'Monte (Ed.), *Mills for Sale: The way Ahead* (pp. 94–107). Mumbai: Marg Publications.

Adarkar, Neera, Menon, Meena, & Chandavarkar, Rajnarayan. 2004. *One hundred years, one hundred voices: the millworkers of Girangaon: An oral history*. Calcutta: Seagull Books.

AILS (Ambekar Institute for Labour Studies). 1977. '*Absenteeism: A Case Study in Textile Industry*' (Bombay: AILS).

———. 1978. *Report on an Inquiry into Indebtedness Among the Textile Workers in Greater Bombay* (Bombay: AILS).

———. 1979. *Education of Workers' Children: Report on an Enquiry into the Problems Experienced by Textile Workers in Bombay* (Bombay: AILS).

———. 1986. *Research For Trade Unions: A Guide; AILS Experience, 1976–85* (Bombay: AILS).

Ambedkar, B.R. 2005. Girni Malak Va Kaamgar, Editorial, Bahiskrit Bharat, 29 March 1929. In P. Gaikwad (Ed.), *Kaamgar Chalval: Dr. Babasaheb Ambedkaranchi Nivadak Bhashana Va Lekh* (pp. 17–19). Nagpur: Kshitij Publications.

———. 2014a. *Dr Babasaheb Ambedkar: Writings and Speeches, Vol. 2*. New Delhi: Dr Ambedkar Foundation, Ministry of Social Justice & Empowerment, Govt. of India.

———. 2014b. On the Industrial Dispute Bill, Bombay Legislative Assembly Debates, Vol. 4, pp. 1330–59, dated 15th September 1938. In V. Moon & H. Narke (Eds.), *Dr Babasaheb Ambedkar: Writings and Speeches Vol. 2* (pp. 201–232). New Delhi: Dr Ambedkar Foundation.

Anand, Javed. 1983. 'The Tenth Month: A Chronology of Events', in *The 10th Month: Bombay's Historic Textile Strike* (Bombay: CED).

Armstrong, W. and T.G. McGee. 1985. *Theatres of Accumulation: Studies in Asian and Latin American Urbanization* (London: Methuen).

ATIRA (Ahmedabad Textile Industry's Research Association). 1985. a. *Inter-Firm Comparison of Financial Statements for 1983* (Ahmedabad: ATIRA).

———. 1985. b. 'Sectoral Costs of Production', in *Rehabilitation of the Textile Industry* (Ahmedabad: ATIRA).

Azhar, Ahmad. (Forthcoming). *Revolution in Reform: Trade-Unionism in Late-Colonial Lahore*. New Delhi: Orient Blackswan.

Bagchee, S. 1984. 'Employment Guarantee Scheme in Maharashtra', *Economic and Political Weekly,* 17 (37), 1633–38.

Bakshi, Rajni. 1986. *The Long Haul*. Bombay: BUILD Documentation Centre.

———. 1987. *The Long Haul* (Bombay: BUILD Documentation Centre).

Banerjee, N. 1981. 'The Weakest Link', *IDS Bulletin,* 12 (3).

———. 1985. *Women Workers in the Unorganized Sector* (Hyderabad: Sangam Books).

Barve, V.R. 1967. *Complete Textile Encyclopaedia* (Bombay: Taraporevala Sons and Co.).

Basu, Subho. 2004. *Does class matter?: Colonial capital and workers' resistance in Bengal (1890–1937)*. Delhi; Oxford: Oxford University Press.

Baud, I.S.A. 1984. *Women's Labour in the South Indian Textile Industry* (Tilburg: Tilburg University, IVO).

———. 1985. 'Industrial Subcontracting: The Effects of Putting-out Systems on Poor Working Women in India'. Paper contributed to the conference on Women and the Household, Indian Statistical Institute, New Delhi.

Belin, L. 'Byssinosis in Card-room Workers in Swedish Cotton Mills', in *British Journal of Industrial Medicine,* no. 22: 101–08.

Ben-Israel, R. 1988. *International Labour Standards: The Case of Freedom to Strike* (Deventer: Kluwer Law Taxation Publishers).

Berry, G. *e.a.* 1974. 'Relationships Between Dust Level and Byssinosis and Bronchitis in Lancashire Cotton Mills', in *British Journal of Industrial Medicine,* no. 31: 18–27.

Betten, Lammy. 1985. *The Right to Strike in Community Law* (North-Holland: Elsevier Science Publishers).

Bhattacherjee, D. 1987. 'Union-type Effects on Bargaining Outcomes in Indian Manufacturing', *British Journal of Industrial Relations* 15 (July), 247–66.

———. 1988. a. 'Unions, State, and Capital in Western India: Structural Determinants of the 1982 Bombay Textile Strike', in Roger Southall, ed., *Labour and Unions in Africa and Asia: Contemporary Issues.*

———. 1988. b. 'The Evolution of Unionism and Labor Market Structure: The Case of the Bombay Textile Mills', 1947–1985, paper.

Bhiwandi Powerloom Weavers' Federation. 1985. Memorandum submitted by the Bhiwandi Powerloom Weavers' Federation to PM Rajiv Gandhi, 14 October 1985.

Bidwai, Praful. 1983. 'Hard Times: The Imperatives of Modernisation', in *The 10th Month. Bombay's Historic Textile Strike* (Bombay: CED).

———. 1984. 'From Riches To Rags', in *Times of India,* 19, 20, 22 March.

Bienefeld, M. 1981. 'The Informal Sector and Women's Oppression', in *IDS Bulletin,* vol. 12, no. 3 (July).

Bohnsack, A. 1981. *Spinnen und Weben: Entwicklung von Technik und Arbeit im Textilgewerbe* (Hamburg: Rowohlt Taschenbuch Verlag GmbH).

Bombay Union of Journalists. 1983. *Bombay's Textile Strike* (Bombay: Arun Vinayak).

Bottomore, T., ed. 1985. *A Dictionary of Marxist Thought* (Oxford: Blackwell).

Breman, Jan. 1976. 'A Dualistic Labour System? A Critique of the "Informal Sector" Concept'. I: The Informal Sector', *EPW,* 11 (48): 1870–75; 'II: A Fragmented Labour Market', *EPW* 11 (49): 1905–08; 'III: Labour Force and Class Formation', *EPW* 11 (50): 1939–44.

———. 1980. 'The Informal Sector' in *Research: Theory and Practice* (Rotterdam: Comparative Asian Studies Programme).

———. 1985. *Of Peasants, Migrants and Paupers – Rural Labour Circulation and Capitalist Production in West India* (Delhi: Oxford University Press).

———. 2004. *The making and unmaking of an industrial working class: Sliding down to the bottom of the labour hierarchy in Ahmedabad, India*. New Delhi: Oxford University Press.

Bromley, R. and C. Gerry. 1979. *Casual Work and Poverty in Third World Cities* (Chichester: John Wiley and Sons).

BTRA (Bombay Textile Research Association). 1987. *Overall Employment in Textile Industry: Trends in the Last Decade* (Coimbatore: SITRA).

Cashman, R.I. 1968. The Politics of Mass Recruitment: Attempts to Organize Popular Movements in Mahar, 1891–1908, PhD Thesis, Duke University, Ann Arbor.

Cashman, Richard I. 1975. *The myth of the Lokamanya: Tilak and mass politics in Maharashtra*. Berkeley: University of California Press.

Chakravarti, A. 1982. 'Size and Protection: Synthetic Fibres and Yarns Industry in India', *EPW,* 17 (35): M-85-M-89.

Chandavarkar, R. 1981. 'Workers' Politics and the Mill Districts in Bombay Between the Wars', *Modern Asian Studies* 15 (3): 603–47.

Chandavarkar, Rajnarayan. 1994. *The origins of industrial capitalism in India: Business strategies and the working classes in Bombay, 1900–1940*. Cambridge: Cambridge University Press.

———. 1998. *Imperial power and popular politics: class, resistance and the state in India, c.1850–1950*. Cambridge: Cambridge University Press.

———. 1999. Questions of class: The general strikes in Bombay, 1928–29. *Contributions to Indian Sociology, 33*(1–2), 205–237.

———. 2009. *History, Culture and the Indian City: Essays by Rajnarayan Chandavarkar*. Cambridge, UK; New York: Cambridge University Press.

Chandrasekhar, C.P. 1979. *Growth and Technical Change in a Stagnant Industry: The Case of Textiles*. Paper Contributed to Long-term Project on the Indian Economy, Institute of Development Studies, Madras.

———. 1981. 'Growth and Technical Change in Indian Cotton Mill Industry', PhD Thesis, Jawaharlal Nehru University.

———. 1982. 'Textile Industry: I. Growth of Decentralised Sector', 'Textile Industry: II. Handloom Development Programme', *Economic Times,* 9 and 10 August.

———. 1984. 'Growth and Technical Change in Indian Cotton-Mill Industry', *EPW,* 19 (4).

Chatterji, B. 1983. 'The Political Economy of "Discriminating Protection": The Case of Textiles in the 1920s', *The Indian Economic and Social History Review*, 20 (3), 239–77.

Chatterji, R. 1980. *Unions, Politics and the State: A Study of Indian Labour Politics* (New Delhi: South Asian Publishers).

Chaudhuri, K. 1983. 'Changing Concept of "Industry" under Industrial Disputes Act', *EPW,* 18 (22): *M-67,* M-85.

Chellappa, H.V.V. 1985. 'Bombay Mill Workers' Strike: Effect on Households', *Economic Times,* 17 September. 'Textile Strike: The Future', *Economic Times,* 18 September.

———. 1986. 'Bombay's Textile Strike, 1982–83: How the Workers Coped', *Business India,* 7–20 April.

Chitta Ranjan, C.N. 1983. 'Bombay Textile Strike', *Mainstream,* 26 February.

Chugh, R.L. and J.S. Uppal. 1986. *Black Economy in India* (New Delhi: Tata McGraw-Hill).

Clarke, T. and L., Clements, eds. 1977. *Trade Unions under Capitalism* (Glasgow: Fontana/Colling).

Crouch, Collin. 1982. *Trade Unions: The Logic of Collective Action* (Glasgow: Fontana).

Dahrendorf, R. 1969. 'On the Origin of Inequality Among Men', in Andre Beteille, ed., *Social Inequality* (Harmondsworth: Penguin Books).

———. 'Changes in the Class Structure of Industrial Societies', in André Beteille, ed., *Social Inequality* (Harmondsworth: Penguin Books).

Dange, S.A. 1932. *Statement in the Court of the Additional Sessions Judge, Meerut Conspiracy Case, Meerut*. Accessed on 1 December 2018 from https://dspace.gipe.ac.in/xmlui/.

Datar, B.N. 1978. *Constitution, Labour Legislation and International Conventions* (Bombay: Tata Institute of Social Sciences).

Davies, R. 1979. 'Informal Sector or Subordinate Mode of Production? A Model', in Bromley and Gerry, eds., *Casual Work and Poverty in Third World Cities.*

D'Cunha, J. 1983. 'The Evolution of the Textile Industry', in *The 10th Month: Bombay's Historic Textile Strike* (Bombay: CED).

Desai, A.V. 1983. 'Technology and Market Structure under Government Regulation: A Case Study of Indian Textile Industry', *EPW,* 18 (5): 150–60.

Desai, K.G. 1966. 'Absenteeism in Industry', *The Indian Journal of Social Work,* no. 1.

Desai, M. 1971. 'Demand for Cotton Textiles in Nineteenth Century India', in *IESHR,* vol. 8: 337–61.

Desai, Rajaram. 1982. *Ani jwalamukhicha udrek zala* (Marathi) (Bombay: Samashti Prakashan).

Deshpande, L.K. 1983. *A Study of Textile Workers on Strike in Bombay*, Paper, Centre for the Study of Social Change, Bombay.

Dhingra, L.C. 1983. 'The Concept, Evolution and Nature of Bonus', in *Indian Labour Journal,* 24 (3).

Dhume, B.S. n.d. *This Is No Trade Unionism,* Brochure (MRTUC Publication).

Digest of Decisions. 1984. Digest Of Decisions under Bombay Industrial Relations Act, 1946 (Industrial Courts, High Courts and Supreme Court), cyclostyled, Auro Consultants, Pune.

Dijkmeijer, E. 1944. *Textiel: Deel I: Grondstoffen; Deel II: Spinnen en Weven* (Amsterdam: Uitgeverij Lieverlee).

Divekar, V.D. 1982. 'The Emergence of An Indigenous Business Class in Maharashtra in the Eighteenth Century', *Modern Asian Studies,* 16 (3): 427–43.

Doornink and Leutscher. 1947. *Textiel Vademecum* (Enschede: Enschedese Hogere Textielschool Vereniging).

Doraiswamy, I. and B.V. Iyer. 1985. 'Inter-Sectoral Production Capacity', in *Rehabilitation of the Textile Industry.* (Ahmedabad: ATIRA).

Duff, Grant James. 1986. (1863) *History of the Mahrattas,* vols. I, II, III (Jaipur: Aavishkar Publishers, Distributors).

Eapen, Mridul. 1977. 'Emerging Trends in Cotton Textile Consumption', in *Social Scientist,* 54–55, January–February.

———. 1984. 'And Now Legislation for Handloom Protection', *EPW,* 19 (14): 583–84.

———. 1985. 'The New Textile Policy', *EPW,* 20 (25 and 26): 1072–73.

Eapen, M. and R. Nagaraj. 1983. 'Textiles and Industrial Growth', *EPW,* 18 (12): 425–26.

Engels, F. 1977. 'Labour Movements', reprinted in T. Clarke and L. Clements, eds., *Trade Unions under Capitalism.*

Enthoven, R.E. 1975. (1922) *The Tribes and Castes of Bombay,* vols. I and III (Delhi: Cosmo Publications).

Evers, H.D. 1982. 'Politische Ökologie der Südasiatischen Stadt: Neuere theoretische Ansätze zur Urbanisieringsproblematik', in H. Kulke, ed., *Städte in Südasien* (Wiesbaden: Franz Steiner Verlag).

Fernandes, Leela. 1997. *Producing workers: The politics of gender, class, and culture in the Calcutta jute mills*. Philadelphia, Pa.: University of Pennsylvania Press.

———. 2006. *India's new middle class: Democratic politics in an era of economic reform*. Minneapolis: University of Minnesota Press.

Financial Express. 1982. 'Fact Series: Textile strike in seven mills for higher bonus and threatened general strike for higher wages and fringe benefits: Is there any justification?', in *Financial Express*, 15 January.

Flanders, A. 1972. 'What Are Trade Unions for?' Reprinted in W. McCarthy, ed., *Trade Unions.*

Gajarmal, Gulab. 1982. *Girni Kamgar: Vedana ani Vidroka* (Marathi) (Bombay: ISRE (Narendra Panjwani)).

Gangal, Ravi. 1986. *Understanding Financial Statements: A Guide for Trade Unions* (Bombay: Popular Prakashan).

Ganneri, Namrata R. 2014. The Hindu Mahasabha in Bombay (1923–1947). *Proceedings of the Indian History Congress, 75*, 771–782.

GATT (General Agreement on Tariffs and Trade). 1985. *International Trade 1984/85* (Geneva: GATT).

Gerry, Chris. 1974. *Petty Producers and the Urban Economy: A Case Study of Dakar* (Geneva: ILO, Working Paper No. 8).

———. 1979. 'Small-scale Manufacturing and Repairs in Dakar: A Survey of Market Relations Within the Urban Economy', in Bromley and Gerry, eds., *Casual Work and Poverty in Third World Cities.*

Gibbon, Peter. 1988. 'Analysing the British Miners' Strike of 1984–85', in *Economy and Society,* 17 (2): 139–94.

Gokhale, R.G. 1957. *The Bombay cotton mill worker*. Bombay: Millowners' Association.

Goldthorpe, J. 1977. 'Industrial Relations in Great Britain: A Critique of Reformism', in T. Clarke and L. Clements, eds., *Trade Unions under Capitalism*.

Gooptu, Nandini. 2007. Economic Liberalisation, Work and Democracy: Industrial Decline and Urban Politics in Kolkata. *Economic and Political Weekly, 42*(21), 1922–1933.

Gooskens, Pit. 1984. *Tussen Ekonomisme en Klassestrijd*, M.A. Thesis, Universiteit van Amsterdam, Amsterdam.

Gore, M.S. 1970. *Inmigrants and Neighbourhoods: Two Aspects of Life in a Metropolitan City* (Bombay: Tata Institute of Social Sciences).

Goswami, O. 1985. 'Indian Textile Industry, 1970–1984: An Analysis of Demand and Supply', *EPW,* 20 (38): 1603–14.

Gould, J. and W. Kolb, eds. Dictionary of the Social Sciences. 1964 (New York: Free Press of Glencoe).

Groenou, W.B. van. 1971. Worldviews of Textile Workers in India, PhD Thesis, University of Illinois, Urbana, Champaign.

Hansen, Thomas Blom. 200). *Wages of violence: Naming and identity in postcolonial Bombay*. Princeton, N.J.; Oxford: Princeton University Press.

Hart, Keith. 1973. 'Informal Income Opportunities and Urban Employment in Ghana', in *Journal of Modern African Studies,* 11 (March): 61–89.

Hirschman, A.O. 1970. *Exit, Voice, and Loyalty* (London: Oxford University Press).

HMS (Hind Mazdoor Sabha). 1983. *Labour in Free India* (Bombay: Hind Mazdoor Sabha [Kamalakar Potdar].

Holmström, M. 1972. 'Caste and Status in an Indian City', *EPW*, 7 (April): 769–74.

———. 1976. *South Indian Factory Workers: Their Life and Their World* (Cambridge: Cambridge University Press).

———. 1985. *Industry and Inequality: The Social Anthropology of Indian Labour* (Bombay: Orient Longman).

Hutt, W.H. 1975. *The Theory of Collective Bargaining, 1930–1975* (London: The Institute of Economic Affairs).

Hyman, R. 1977. 'Marxism and the Sociology of Trade Unionism', reprinted in T. Clarke and L. Clements, eds., *Trade Unions under Capitalism.*

ILO (International Labour Organization). 1952. *Textile Wages: An International Study* (Geneva: International Labour Office).

Indian Chamber of Commerce. 1974. *Industrial Wages in India* (Calcutta: Eastern Law House).

Indian Labour Journal. 1982. *Indian Labour Journal,* vols. 23 (1982), 24 (1983), 25 (1984).

Indian Textile Bulletin. 1981. *Indian Textile Bulletin,* vols. XXVII (1981), XXVIII (1982), XXIX (1983).

Industrial Disputes Act. 1987. *Industrial Disputes Act, 1947* (Bombay: Labour Law Agency).

Ingleson, John. 1986. *In Search of Justice: Workers and Unions in Colonial Java, 1908–1926* (Oxford: Oxford University Press).

INTWF (Indian National Textile Workers' Federation). 1983. Memorandum submitted by the Indian National Textile Workers' Federation to the Tripartite Committee, INTWF, Bombay, 13 January.

Iswalkar, Datta. 2009. *Punha Sangharsh*. Mumbai: Mill Mazdoor Welfare Trust.

Iyer, B.V. and T. Narasimham. 1985. 'Domestic Consumption of Textiles in India', in *Rehabilitation of the Textile Industry* (Ahmedabad: ATIRA).

Iyer, R. 1980. 'The Datta Samant Factor', *Business Standard,* 15 September.

———. 1981. 'Samant's Textile Trap', *Business Standard,* 30 December.

———. 1982. 'Where Small is Not Beautiful', *Business Standard,* 31 August.

Jain, L.C. 1983. 'Handlooms Face Liquidation', *EPW,* 18 (35): 1517–26.

———. 1984. 'The Phenomenon, Scale and Process of Displacement of Women in Traditional Industries: Some Instances and Issues', Paper, Madras Institute of Development Studies, Madras.

———. 1985a. '1985 Textile Policy: End of Handloom Industry', *EPW,* 20 (27): 1121–23.

———. 1985b. 'Textile Policy, 1985: Anti-poor to the Core', *Economic Times,* 26 September.

Jain, S.C. 1971. *Indian Manager: His Social Origin and Career* (Bombay: Somaiya Publications).

James, R. 1958. 'Trade-union Democracy: Indian Textiles' in *The Western Political Quarterly,* no. 11: 563–73.

Jawaid, S. 1982. *Trade Union Movement in India* (Delhi: Sundeep Prakashan).

Jayaraman, J. 1984. 'Trends in Manday Losses Due to Industrial Disputes: A Decadal Analysis', in *Indian Labour Journal* 25 (i): 3–17.

Jellinek, L., C. Manning, and G. Jones. 1978. 'The Life of the Poor in Indonesian Cities', Paper, Monash University, Clayton Victoria.

Jha, S.C. 1970. *The Indian Trade Union Movement* (Calcutta: K.L. Mukhopadhyay).

Johri, C.K. 1967. *Unionism in a Developing Economy: A Study of Interaction Between Trade Unionism and Government Policy in India* (Bombay: Asia Publishing House).

Joint Report. 1983. 'Storming the Citadel: The Bombay Industrial Relations Act', in *The 10th Month: Bombay's Historic Textile Strike* (Bombay: CED).

Joseph, Cherian. 1978. 'Workers' Participation in Industry: A Comparative Study and Critique', in E.A. Ramaswamy, ed., *Industrial Relations in India* (Delhi: The Macmillan Company of India Ltd).

Joshi, C. 1981. 'Kanpur Textile Labour: Some Structural Features of Formative Years', *EPW,* 16 (44, 45, 46).

Joshi, Chitra. 2002. On De-industrialization and the Crisis of Male Identities. *International Review of Social History, 47*(Supplement S10), 159-175.

Joshi, H. and V. Joshi. 1976. *Surplus Labour and the City: A Study of Bombay* (Delhi: Oxford University Press).

Joshi, P. 1985. *International Labour Organization and Its Impact on India* (Delhi: B.R. Pub. Corp.).

Kadam, M. 1982. 'The Textile Strike and Datta Samant', in *Frontier,* 15 (14).

Kahn-Freund, O. and B. Hepple. 1972. *Laws Against Strikes* (London: Fabian Research Series).

Kapoor, H. 1983. 'The Bombay Textile Workers Strike: An Enquiry', Paper.

Kapoor, M.C. and S.K. Jain. 1982. 'Changing Patterns of World Production and Trade in Cotton Textiles', *EPW,* 17 (9).

Karat, P. 1984. 'Action Groups/Voluntary Organisations: A Factor in Imperialist Strategy', in *The Marxist,* 2 (April–June): 19–54.

Karkal, M. 1983. 'Population Growth in Greater Bombay: Some Emerging Patterns', *EPW,* 18 (4).

Karnik, V.B. 1966. *Indian Trade Unions* (Bombay: Manaktalas).

———. 1967. *Strikes in India* (Bombay: Manaktalas).

———. 1974. *Indian Labour: Problems and Prospects* (Calcutta: Minerva Associates).

Karve, I. 1975. *Maharashtra: Land and Its People* (Bombay: Directorate of Government Printing, Stationery and Publications, Maharashtra State).

Keer, Dhananjay. 1981. *Dr. Ambedkar: Life and Mission* (Bombay: Popular Prakashan).

Keesings Historisch Archief. 1987. *Keesings Historisch Archief,* vol. 56, 3 September: 439–43; (9 July), 561–63.

Khogali, M. 1976. 'Byssinosis: A Follow-up Study of Cotton Ginnery Workers in the Sudan', in *British Journal of Industrial Medicine,* no. 33: 166–74.

Kimothi, O.D. and A.R. Garde. 1977. *Modernisation and Renovation in Textile Industry* (Ahmedabad: ATIRA Report).

Klein, Ira. 1986. Urban Development and Death: Bombay City, 1870–1914. *Modern Asian Studies, 20*(4), 725–754.

Koningsveld, H. and J. Mertens. 1986. *Communicatief en strategisch handelen: Inleiding tot de handelingstheorie van Habermas* (Muiderbcrg: Coutinho).

Kooiman, D. 1977. 'Jobbers and the Emergence of Trade Unions in Bombay City', in *International Review of Social History*, 22 (3): 313–28.

———. 1978. *Koppelbazen, Kommunisten en ekonomische krisis; arbeidersorganisatie in de textielindustrie van Bombay 1917–1937* (Amsterdam: Rodopi).

———. 1980. 'Bombay Communists and the 1924 Textile Strike, *EPW*, 15 (29): 1223–36.

———. 1981. 'Labour Legislation and Working Class Movement: Case of Bombay Labour Office, 1934–1937', *EPW,* 16 (44, 45, 46).

———. 1983. 'Rural Labour in the Bombay Textile Industry and the Articulation of Modes of Organization', in Peter Robb, ed., *Rural South Asia, Linkages Change and Development* (London: Curzon Press).

Kooten, G. van. 1988. *Stakingen en stakers* (Delft: Eburon).

Kosambi, M. 1985. 'Commerce, Conquest and the Colonial City: Role of Vocational Factors in Rise of Bombay', *EPW*, 20 (I): 32–37.

Kothari, R. 1984. 'The Non-Party Political Process', *EPW,* 19 (5).

Kruijt, D. and M. Vellinga. 1975. *Arbeidsrelaties en Multinationale Onderneming* (Utrecht: Sociologisch Instituut).

Kulkarni, V.B. 1979. *History of the Indian Cotton Textile Industry* (Bombay: Millowners' Association).

Kulke, Eckehard. 1978. *The Parsees in India: A Minority as Agent of Social Change* (New Delhi: Vikas Publishing House).

Kumar, Radha. 1983. 'Family and Factory: Women in the Bombay Cotton Textile Industry, 1919–1939', in *IESHR,* 20 (I): 80–110.

Kumar, S. 1978. 'Health Hazards in Textile Industry: The Horror of Heat and Humidity', in *Science Today*, February.

Kurian, P. and A. Chhachhi. 1982. 'New Phase in Textile Unionism?', *EPW*, 17 (8).

Lakdawala, D.T. *e.a.* 1963. *Work, Wages and Well-being in an Indian Metropolis: Economic Survey of Bombay City* (Bombay: University of Bombay).

Lakha, Salim. 1987. 'Ideology and Class Relations in Early Twentieth Century India: The Case of Ahmedabad', in M. Pinches and S. Lakha, eds., *Wage Labour and Social Change: The Proletariat in Asia and the Pacific* (Monash Paper on Southeast Asia, No. 16. (Clayton, Victoria: Monash University).

———. 1988. 'Organized Labor and Militant Unionism: The Bombay Textile Workers' Strike of 1982', in *Bulletin of Concerned Asian Scholars,* 20 (2): 42–53.

Lambert, R.D. 1963. *Workers, Factories and Social Change in India* (Princeton: Princeton University Press).

Lenin, V.I. 1977a. 'On Strikes', reprinted in T. Clarke and L. Clements, eds., *Trade Unions under Capitalism,* pp. 57–63.

———. 1977b. 'What Is to be Done?' reprinted in T. Clarke and L. Clements, eds., *Trade Unions under Capitalism,* pp. 64–76.

Lieten, Georges Kristoffel. 1982. Strikers and Strike-Breakers-Bombay Textile Mills Strike, 1929. *Economic and Political Weekly, 17*(14-15-16).

Lieten, G.K. 1982. 'Strikers and Strike-Breakers: Bombay Textile Mills Strike, 1929', *EPW*, 17: 14, 15, 16.

———. 1984. *Colonialism, Class and Nation: The Confrontation in Bombay Presidency, 1928–1932* (Calcutta: K.P. Bagchi and Company).

———. 1987a. 'Indian Workers in Multinational Companies', *EPW, 22* (18): 810–22.

———. 1987b. 'Fallacies of Workers' Ownership', *EPW*, 22 (36, 37): 1563–6.

Lipset, S.M. *e.a.* 1956. *Union Democracy* (Glencoe: The Free Press).

Mamkoottam, K. 1978. 'Industrial Relations in a Steel Plant', in E.A. Ramaswamy, ed., *Industrial Relations in India* (Delhi: Macmillan, India).

Maniben Kara Institute. 1985. *Minimum Wages Series: Maharashtra State* (New Delhi: Research and Training Programme, HMS).

Markovits, C. 1981. 'Indian Business and the Congress Provincial Governments 1937–39', in *Modern Asian Studies* 15 (3): 487–526.

Marxist Bulletin. 1982. 'The Bombay Textile Strike: An Historic Struggle', *Marxist Bulletin* I (7).

Masselos, J. 1982. 'Jobs and Jobbery: The Sweeper in Bombay under the Raj', in *IESHR,* 19 (2).

McCarthy, W. 1972. *Trade Unions* (Harmondsworth: Penguin Books).

McGee, T.G. 1979. 'The Poverty Syndrome: Making Out in the Southeast Asian City', in Bromley and Gerry, eds., *Casual Work and Poverty in Third World Cities.*

McGee, T.G. and Y.M. Yeung. 1977. *Hawkers in Southeast Asian Cities: Planning for the Bazaar Economy* (Ottawa: International Development Research Centre).

Mehta, Makrand. 1982. *The Ahmedabad Cotton Textile Industry: Genesis and Growth* (Ahmedabad: New Order Book Co).

Mehta, Pramod. 1985. 'The Sweatshops of Surat', in *Business Standard,* 6 March.

Mehta, S.D. 1953. *The Indian Cotton Textile Industry: An Economic Analysis* (Bombay: Textile Association).

———. 1954. *The Cotton Mills of India, 1854–1954* (Bombay: Textile Association).

Ménez, C. 1983. 'Essay on the Indian Workers', in *Indian Resurrection,* no. 4.

MGKU files. n.d. Files spanning the years 1980–85 available at the Ghatkopar office of the Maharashtra General Kamgar Union.

Mhaskar, Sumeet. 2012. *The Unmaking of the Worker-Self in Post-Industrial Mumbai: A Study of Ex-Millworkers' Responses to the Closure of Textile Mills in Girangaon.* (D.Phil Thesis), University of Oxford, Oxford.

———. 2013. Encountering 'Inclusion' and Exclusion in Postindustrial Mumbai: A Study of Muslim Ex-millworkers' Occupational Choices. In U. Skoda, K. B. Nielsen & M. Q. Fibiger (Eds.), *Navigating Social Exclusion and Inclusion in Contemporary India and Beyond: Structures, Agents, Practices* (pp. 149–166). London; New York: Anthem Press.

———. 2014. Locating Caste in a Globalising Indian City: A Study of Dalit Ex-millworkers' Occupational Choices in Post-Industrial Mumbai. In C. Still (Ed.), *Dalits in Neo-Liberal India: Mobility or Marginalization?* . New Delhi: Routledge.

———. 2016. The Roots of the Maratha Unrest Lie in Mumbai's Changing Political Economy, *The Wire,* pp. 5 December, Last accessed 20 August 2018 https://thewire.in/politics/maratha-unrest-linkages-mumbai-political-economy.

———. 2018. Ghettoisation of Economic Choices in a Global City: A Case Study of Mumbai. *Economic and Political Weekly, 53*(29), 29–37.

Michael, V.P. 1979. *Industrial Relations in India and Workers' Involvement in Management* (Bombay: Himalaya Publishing House).

Mohota, R.D. 1976. *Textile Industry and Modernisation* (Bombay: Current Book House).

Momin, A.R. 1974. 'Tensions in an Industrial Slum', *EPW*, 9 (5): 177–81.

Moore, Barrington. 1978. *Injustice: The Social Bases of Obedience and Revolt* (New York: M.E. Sharpe).

Moore, W.E. 1965. *Industrialization and Labour* (New York: Russell and Russell).

Moore, W.E. and A. Feldman, eds. 1960. *Labour Commitment and Social Change in Developing Areas* (New York: Social Science Research Council).

More, Satyendra. 2003. *Dalit wa Communist Chalvalicha Sashakta Duva: Comrade R.B. More*. Mumbai Paryay Prakashan.

Morris, Morris David. 1955. 'Labor discipline, trade-unions, and the state in India', in *The Journal of Political Economy*, vol. 63: 293–308.

———. 1960a. 'The Recruitment of an Industrial Labor Force in India, with British and American Comparisons', in *Comparative Studies in Society and History,* 2: 305–28.

———. 1960b. 'The Labor Market in India', in W.E. Moore and S. Feldman, eds., *Labour Commitment and Social Change in Developing Areas.*

———. 1965. *The Emergence of an Industrial Labour Force in India: A Study of the Bombay Cotton Mills, 1854–1947* (Berkeley: University of California Press).

Moser, C. 1981. 'Surviving in the Suburbios', in *IDS Bulletin*, vol. 12 (3).

Moser, C. and K. Young. 1981. 'Women of the Working Poor', in *IDS Bulletin,* vol. 12 (3).

Moses, B.C. 1982. 'Textile Bonus Issue', *EPW,* 17 (46–47): 1849–52.

Mukhopadhya, A. 1982. 'Trade Unionism in India: Some Observations', in *Frontier,* 14 (42).

Murphy, E.D. 1978. 'Class and Community in India: The Madras Labour Union, 1918–21', in *IESHR,* 15 (3): 291–321.

Murphy, William S., ed. n.d. *The Textile Industries: A Practical Guide to Fibres, Tarns and Fabrics in Every Branch of Textile Manufacture,* vols. I–VIII (London: The Gresham Publishing Company).

Nagaraj, R. 1984. 'Sub-contracting in Indian Manufacturing Industries: Analysis, Evidence and Issues', *EPW,* 19 (31, 32 and 33): 1435–53.

Narayan, Ramesh. 2004, 27 April. Lower Parel to Upper Worli, *The Hindu Business Line,* http://www.thehindubusinessline.in/bline/blbby/stories/2004042700230900.htm.

Nehru, Jawaharlal. 1980. (1962) *An Autobiography* (Delhi: Oxford University Press).

Newman, R. 1981. *Workers and Unions in Bombay, 1918–1929: A Study of Organisation in the Cotton Mills* (Canberra: Australian National University).

News Line. 1985. *The Miners' Strike 1984–85 in Pictures* (London: New Park Publications).

Nijhuis, H.D. 1950. *De Structurele Ontwikkeling van de Nederlandse Katoen-, Rayon- en Linnenindustrie* (Arnhem: S. Gouda Quint/ D. Brouwer and Zoon).

Nissel, H. 1982. 'Jüngste Tendenzen der Zuwanderung nach Bombay', in H. Kulke, ed., *Städte in Südasien* (Wiesbaden: Franz Steiner Verlag).

Olle, W. and W. Schoellcr. 1984. 'World Market Competition and Restrictions upon International Trade-Union Policies', in P. Waterman, ed., *For A New Labour Internationalism* (The Hague: ILERI), 39–58.

Olson, Mancur. 1977. *The Logic of Collective Action: Public Goods and the Theory of Groups* (Cambridge: Harvard University Press).

Omvedt, Gail. 1976. *Cultural revolt in a colonial society: The non-Brahman movement in western India, 1873 to 1930* (1st ed.). Bombay: Scientific Socialist Education Trust.

Omvedt, G. 1981. 'Capitalist Agriculture and Rural Classes in India', *EPW*, 16 (52).

———. 1983a. 'Textile Strike Turns Political', *EPW*, 18 (35): 1509–11.

———. 1983b. 'Bombay 1982: The World's Biggest Strike?' in *Newsletter of International Labour Studies*, no. 17.

Ottey, Roy. 1985. *The Strike: An Insider's Story* (London: Sidgwick and Jackson).

Pagadi, S.M. 1974. *Chhatrapati Shivaji* (Poona: Continental Prakashan).

Panjwani, N. 1984. 'Living with Capitalism: Class, Caste and Paternalism among Industrial Workers in Bombay', in *Contributions to Indian Sociology,* 18 (2): 267–92.

Pant, S.C. 1970. *Indian Labour Problems* (Allahabad: Chaitanya Publishing House).

Papola, T.S. 1981a. 'Dissecting the Informal Sector', *EPW,* 16 (31).

———. 1981b. *Urban Informal Sector in a Developing Economy* (New Delhi: Vikas Publishing House).

Patankar, B. 1981. 'Textile Workers and Datta Samant', *EPW,* 16 (49).

———. 1982. 'Old and New Trends in the Trade Union Movement', *Frontier,* 15 (10–12).

———. 1983a. Peasantry and the Trade Unions, Paper.

———. 1983b. 'Invincible Textile Workers', *Frontier,* 15 (46).

———. 1984. Beyond the Textile Strike, *Frontier,* 16 (17 March).

———. 1988. 'The Bombay Textile Workers' Strike of 1982: The Lessons of History', in *Bulletin of Concerned Asian Scholars,* 20 (2): 54–56.

Patel, Kunj. 1963. *Rural Labour in Industrial Bombay* (Bombay: Popular Prakashan).

Patel, S. 1984. 'Class Conflict and Workers' Movement in Ahmedabad Textile Industry, 1918–23', *EPW,* 19 (20, 21): 853–64.

———. 1985. 'Nationalisation, TLA and Textile Workers', *EPW,* 20 (49): 2154–55.

Pendse, S. 1981. 'Labour: The Datta Samant Phenomenon', *EPW,* 16 (16): 695–99; *EPW,* 16 (17): 745–49.

———. 1982. *Politics, Parties and Political Processes in a Metropolitan Slum,* Background Papers, No. 10 (Bombay: BUILD Documentation Centre).

———. 1984. 'Politics and Organisations of Urban Workers', *EPW,* 19 (8).

Philips, C.H., ed. 1963. *Handbook of Oriental History* (London: Offices of the Royal Historical Society).

Pol, Prabodhan. 2015. *From the Margins to Mainstream: Dalit Journalistic Writings in Maharashtra, 1920–56.* (PhD Thesis), Jawaharlal Nehru University, New Delhi.

Potter, Beatrice. 1889. *Life and Labour of the People,* vol. I (London: Charles Booth).

Punekar, S.D. *e.a.* 1981. *Labour Welfare, Trade Unionism and Industrial Relations* (Bombay: Himalaya Publishing House).

Puroshothama, S. 1978. 'Health Hazards in Textile Industry: The Noise Nuisance', in *Science Today*, February.

Radhakrishnan, C.V. 1985. 'New Textile Policy: I, Through a Looking Glass', and 'New Textile Policy: II, Bold and Welcome Departure', *Financial Express,* 22 and 23 July.

Rajagopalan, C. 1962. *The Greater Bombay: A Study in Suburban Ecology* (Bombay: Popular Book Depot).

Ramachandran, P. 1972. *Pavement Dwellers in Bombay City* (Bombay: Tata Institute of Social Sciences).

Ramaswamy, E.A. 1976. 'Trade Unionism and Caste in South-India', *Modern Asian Studies*, 10: 361–73.

———. 1977. *The Worker and his Union* (Delhi: Allied Publishers).

———. 1978. 'The Meaning of the Strike', in E.A. Ramaswamy, ed., *Industrial Relations in India* (Delhi: Macmillan, India).

———. 1985. 'Trade Unions, Rule Making and Industrial Relations', *EPW,* 20 (12): 517–24.

———. 1986. Indian Trade Unionism: The Crisis of Leadership, Paper contributed to the Ninth European Conference on Modern South Asian Studies, Heidelberg.

Ramaswamy, E.A. and U. 1981. *Industry and Labour: An Introduction* (Delhi: Oxford University Press).

Ramaswamy, U. 1979. 'Tradition and Change Among Industrial Workers', *EPW,* 14 (7 and 8): 367–76.

Ramu, G.N. 1977. *Family and Caste in Urban India* (New Delhi: Vikas Publishing House).

Ranade, M.G. 1974. (1900) *Rise of the Maratha Power* (Delhi: Publications Division, Government of India).

Ray, R.K. 1982. 'Pedhis and Mills: The Historical Integration of the Formal and Informal Sectors in the Economy of Ahmedabad', in *IESHR,* 19 (3 and 4).

Red Flag. 1983. 'Bombay Textile Workers' Strike: Learn from the Workers and Lead Them', in *The Red Flag*, March.

Reed, David and Olivia Adamson. 1985. *Miners Strike 1984–1985; People Versus State* (London: Larkin Publications).

Revolutionary Workers Coordinating Committee. 1982. *Uphold Heroic Heritage of Textile Workers Faced with Unashamed Treachery*, Pamphlet, (Bombay: RWWC).

RMMS (Rashtriya Mill Mazdoor Sangh). 1982. *Strike in the Bombay Textile Mills: The Position of the RMMS,* Brochure (Bombay: B.B. Arolkar).

———. 1983. Statement of the Rashtriya Mill Mazdoor Sangh, in Memorandum submitted by the INTWF to the Tripartite Committee, 13 January.

Roemer, J. 1985. 'Rational Choice Maxism: Some Issues of Method and Substance', *EPW,* 20 (34): 1439–42.

Romatet, E. 1983. 'Calcutta's Informal Sector: Theory and Reality', *EPW,* 18 (50): 2115–28.

Royal Commission on Trade Unions and Employers' Associations, 1965–68. 1972. 'Limitations in the Use of the Law to Prevent Unofficial, Unconstitutional Strikes', in McCarthy, ed., *Trade Unions.*

Russell, R.V. 1969. *The Tribes and Castes of the Central Provinces of India,* vols. I–IV. Photomechanic reprint of the edition of 1916, Anthropological Publications (Oosterhout (N.B.): The Netherlands).

Rylander, R. and M. Snella. 1976. 'Acute Inhalation Toxicity of Cotton Plant Dusts', in *British Journal of Industrial Medicine,* no. 33: 175–80.

Saha, S.K. 1982. 'Trends in the Textile Industry and the Dilemma in Indian Cotton Textile Policy', *EPW,* 17 (9), M-23.

Sakhalkar, S.B. 1985. 'Growth and Structures of Industries in Maharashtra', *EPW*, 20 (34).

Samant, S.R. 1986. *Employer's Guide to Labour Laws* (Bombay: S.L. Dwivedi, Labour Law Agency).

Samanta, D.K. 1979. 'Tradition and Migrant Group: A Case from Maharashtra', in *The Eastern Anthropologist,* 32 (1): 25–37.

Sardesai. G.S. 1949. *The Main Currents of Maratha History* (Bombay: Phoenix Publications).

———. 1957. *New History of the Marathas,* vol. I (Bombay: Phoenix Publications).

Sarkar, Jadunath. 1973. (1919) *Shivaji and His Times* (New Delhi: Orient Longman).

Savara, M. 1981. 'Organising the Annapurna', in *IDS Bulletin,* 12 (3).

Saxena, R.C. and S.R. 1984. *Labour Relations in India* (Lucknow. Prakashan Kendra).

Sen, Surendranath. 1928. *Military System of the Marathas* (Calcutta: The Book Company).

Sethi, H. 1984. 'Groups in a New Politics of Transformation', *EPW,* 19 (7): 305–16.

———. 1985. 'The Immoral "Other": Debate between Party and Non-Party Groups', *EPW,* 20 (8): 378–80.

Shaikh, Juned. 2011. Translating Marx: Mavali, Dalit and the Making of Mumbai's Working Class, 1928–1935. *Economic and Political Weekly, 46*(31), 65–73.

Sharma, B.R. 1970. 'The Industrial Worker, Some Myths and Realities', *EPW,* 5: 875–78.

Shenai, V.A. 1978. 'Health Hazards in Textile Industry: I, The Scourge of the Cotton Dust; II: Chemical Hazards in Textile Mills', in *Science Today,* February.

Shenfield, A. 1986. *What Right to Strike?* (London: The Institute of Economic Affairs).

Sheth, N.R. 1968. *The Social Framework of an Indian Factory* (Manchester: Manchester University Press).

———. 1972. 'Management of Organizational Status: A Case Study of the Supervisor in a Textile Mill', in *Indian Journal of Industrial Relations,* 8 (July): 97–119.

———. 1977. 'Sociological Studies of Indian Industrial Workers', in *Sociological Bulletin,* 26 (March).

———. 1978. 'Trade Union in Social Reality', in E.A. Ramaswamy, ed., *Industrial Relations in India* (Delhi: Macmillan, India).

Sills, David, ed., 1968. David Sills, ed., *International Encyclopedia of the Social Sciences,* vol. 15 (New York: Macmillan Company and the Free Press).

Silver, Beverly J. 2003. *Forces of labor: Workers' movements and globalization since 1870*. Cambridge: Cambridge University Press.

Singh, Gurbir. 1982. 'Textile Strike: The Last Phase', *Frontier,* 15 (13).

———. 1983. 'Force and Counter-force: A Report from the Front', in *The 10th Month: Bombay's Historic Textile Strike* (Bombay: CED).

———. 1987. 'Blood, Sweat and Struggle', *EPW,* 22 (24): 931–34.

———. 1987. Labour Displaced Textile Workers Kotwal Report. *Economic and Political Weekly, 22*(13).

Singh, Harwant. 1978. 'Health Hazards in Textile Industry: Byssinosis', in *Science Today,* February.

Sinha, A.P. 1983. 'Innovation in Indian Firms: Myths and Reality', *EPW,* 18 (35): M-111, M-115.

Sovani, N.V. 1966. *Urbanization and Urban India* (London: Asia Publishing House).

Srinivasan, K. 1984. 'How To Kill a Mill and Make a Profit', in *Sunday Observer,* 4 March.

Subramanian, K.N. 1967. *Labour-Management Relations in India* (London: Asia Publishing House).

———. 1977. *Wages in India* (New Delhi: Tata McGraw-Hill).

Teulings, A. 1974. *Nieuwe vormen van industriële aktie: arbeidersstrijd en vakbeweging in Nederland en Engeland* (Nijmegen: Socialistische Uitgeverij).

———. 1976. *Philips: geschiedenis en praktijk van een wereldconcem* (Amsterdam: Van Gennep).

Thakker, G.K. 1962. *Labour Problems of Textile Industry: A Study of the Labour Problems of the Cotton Mill Industry in Bombay* (Bombay: Vora and Co.).

Times of India. 1982. *Directory and Yearbook 1982* (Bombay: The Times of India Press).

Tindall, G. 1982. *City of Gold: The Biography of Bombay* (London: Temple Smith).

Trotsky, L. 1977. Marxism and Trade Unionism', reprint in T. Clarke and L. Clements, eds., *Trade Unions under Capitalism* (Glasgow: Fontana/ Collins).

Truth. 1982. 'Without Militancy Labour Cannot Go Forward', in *Truth* (July).

———. 1983. 'Where Do We Go From Here?' in *Truth* (March).

Tulpule, B. 1982a. 'Bombay Textile Workers' Strike: A Different View', *EPW,* 17 (17 and 18).

———. 1982b. 'More Labour Legislation: More Amendments', *EPW,* 17 (25).

———. 1984. Workers' Participation in Central Public Sector: A Fresh Hoax?' *EPW,* 19 (12): 493–94.

Union Research Group. 1983. The Wages of Wrath: The Need for a New Union Policy', in *The 10th Month: Bombay's Historic Textile Strike* (Bombay: CED).

Vaidya, S.A. 1978. *Industrial Worker in Bombay: A Socio-Economic Profile* (Bombay: Mill Mazdoor Sabha).

———. 1981. *Power-Loom Workers in Maharashtra: A Study of Unorganised Textile Labour* (Bombay: Mill Mazdoor Sabha).

———. 1984. Rural-Urban Economic Ties: Flow of Industrial Workers' Earnings to Rural Areas, paper (Maniben Kara Institute, Bombay).

———. 1985. *Trade Union Organisations in Maharashtra* (Bombay: Research and Training Programme (HMS) and Maniben Kara Institute).

Vanguard. 1983. 'The Historic Battle of the Bombay Textile Workers', in *Vanguard,* 1 (4).

Varerkar, Bhargavarama Vitthala. 1972 [1933]. *Dhavata Dhota*. Mumbai: Abhinav Prakashan.

Vijayanagar, R. 1978. *Diversion of Funds: Myth or Reality?* (Bombay: P.P.S.I.).

Washbrook, D.A. 1981. Law, State and Agrarian Society in Colonial India. *Modern Asian Studies, 15*(3), 649–721.

Waterman, Peter. 1975. 'The "Labour Aristocracy" in Africa: Introduction to a Debate', in *Development and Change,* 6 (3).

———. 1976. 'Third World Strikes: An Invitation to Discussion', in *Development and Change,* 7 (3).

———. 1983. 'Seeing the Straws; Riding the Whirlwind: Reflections on Unions and Popular Movements in India', in *Journal of Contemporary Asia,* 12 (4): 464–83.

———. 1984. *For a New Labour Internationalism,* a set of reprints and working papers. Peter Waterman, ed. (The Hague: International Labour Education, Research and information Foundation).

Webb, Sidney and Beatrice. 1902. *Industrial Democracy* (London: Longmans, Green and Co.).

Werner International (Management Consultants). 1984. *Spinning and Weaving: Labour Cost Comparisons* (Brussels: WI).

———. 1985. *Spinning and Weaving: Labour Cost Comparisons* (Brussels: WI).

———. 1987. *Spinning and Weaving: Labour Cost Comparisons* (Brussels: WI).

Wersch, Hub van. 1983. *Sociologische aspecten van de positie van arbeiders bij een multinationaal bedrijf*, Research Report, Amsterdam.

———. 1984. *Preferential Treatment for SC in Maharashtra: Some Negative Aspects of 'Positive Discrimination'*, MA Thesis, Amsterdam.

Wolcott, Susan. 2008. Strikes in Colonial India, 1921–1938. *Industrial and Labor Relations Review, 61*(4), 460–484.

Zachariah, K.C. 1968. *Migrants in Greater Bombay* (London: Asia Publishing House).

Anonymous. 1983. 'Fiddling With Figures: An Honest Accountant's Nightmare', in *The 10th Month: Bombay's Historic Textile Strike* (Bombay: CED).

Dailies scrutinized for the period October 1981–August 1983

Indian Express (English)
Nava Kal (Marathi)
Times of India (English)
Shramik Vichar (Marathi)

Other newspapers and periodicals quoted

Business
Commerce
Daily
Economic Scene
Economic Times
Evening News
Far Eastern Economic Review
Flashes from Trade Unions
Free Press Journal
Garjana
Indian Management
Indian Textile Monitor
India Today
Industrial Times
Kesari
Loksatta
Maharashtra Herald
Mid-day
Mumbai Sakal
Nabbharat Timesl
New Age
Patriot
Statesman
Sunday
Textile India
Telegraph
Update